Oracle SQL & PL/SQL

Annotated Archives

ABOUT THE AUTHORS ...

Kevin Loney, a veteran ORACLE developer and DBA, is the author of the best-selling *Oracle DBA Handbook,* and coauthor of *Advanced Oracle Tuning and Administration* and *Oracle: The Complete Reference*. He frequently makes presentations at ORACLE conferences and contributes to ORACLE Magazine.

Rachel Carmichael has been an Oracle DBA for over eight years. She currently chairs the DBA Special Interest Group for the NY Oracle Users Group and has presented at both international and regional conferences.

Oracle SQL & PL/SQL

Annotated Archives

Kevin Loney and Rachel Carmichael

Osborne/**McGraw-Hill**

Berkeley   New York   St. Louis   San Francisco   Auckland   Bogotá
Hamburg   London   Madrid   Mexico City   Milan   Montreal   New Delhi
Panama City   Paris   São Paulo   Singapore   Sydney   Tokyo   Toronto

Osborne/**McGraw-Hill**
2600 Tenth Street
Berkeley, California 94710
U.S.A.

For information on translations or book distributors outside the U.S.A., or to arrange
bulk purchase discounts for sales promotions, premiums, or fund-raisers, please
contact Osborne/**McGraw-Hill** at the above address.

Oracle SQL & PL/SQL Annotated Archives

1234567890 AGM AGM 901987654321099

ISBN 0-07-882536-9

Publisher
Brandon A. Nordin

Editor-in-Chief
Scott Rogers

Acquisitions Editor
Scott Rogers

Project Editor
Madhu Prasher

Editorial Assistant
Marlene Vasilieff

Copy Editor
Claire Splan

Proofreader
Paul Tyler

Indexer
Valerie Robbins

Computer Designers
Jani Beckwith
Ann Sellers

Illustrator
Brian Wells

Series Design
Peter Hancik
Roberta Steele

Cover Design
Regan Honda

To Peter, you were right. I can.
— R.C.
For Sue, Emily, and Rachel,
— K.L.

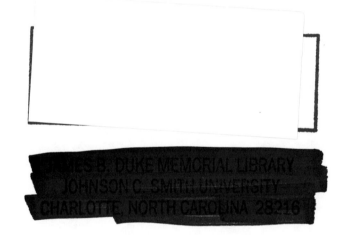

Contents at a Glance

Contents

ACKNOWLEDGMENTS

Writing this book was the second hardest thing I have ever done in my life. And like all things in life, I could not have done it without the help and support of others.

The ORACLE user community is an extraordinary mix of people willing to share their efforts with others. Much of the knowledge in this book was gathered from talking with and listening to other users at conferences and user group meetings. The tips, tricks, and wish lists they have shared have contributed in large measure to the scripts here.

To the wonderful people at Osborne/McGraw-Hill: Scott Rogers, Marlene Vasilieff, Claire Splan, and Madhu Prasher—thank you. You made an otherwise overwhelming task easy with your encouragement and help.

My thanks especially to Kevin Loney, whose willingness to answer a seemingly endless barrage of e-mail from this strange lady, inevitably led us to this point. You always have the answer I need. Thank you for your confidence in me.

Next, to my dear friend Marlene Theriault, the other "DBA goddess," thank you for your belief that I could do this and your insistence that I try. You have inspired and encouraged me throughout my time as a DBA. Special thanks to Ian Fickling, scriptwriter *extraordinaire*. Your willingness to write scripts on request helped to make this book as useful as it is.

Thank you to my parents for their constant, unfailing support through some of the worst and best times of my life. I love you both.

To Wendy, Ali, and Chris, who keep me sane (and sometimes insane). You remind me constantly of what is truly important.

Finally, to my guardian angel Peter, whose love taught me joy and whose death taught me courage. You will live in my heart forever.

—Rachel Carmichael

I am deeply indebted to my family, friends, and co-workers who shape and share and profoundly influence my life. My happiness and achievements and successes are theirs as well. Thank you all.

The technical content of this book was made possible by many people separately and collectively focusing on the needs of users. At this book's core is a set of scripts developed by ORACLE Support personnel to make the lives of their customers easier. The altruism of those authors helped bring this book to fruition. Many of the other scripts in this book were written by Rachel Carmichael and Ian Fickling, and they have contributed greatly to the book's utility.

Beyond those contributors, I would like to recognize the people who have repeatedly demonstrated an altruistic approach to the sharing of technical knowledge dealing with ORACLE. Among them are the frequent presenters and authors for the ORACLE user group conferences and publications: Eyal Aronoff, Noorali Sonawalla, Tony Jambu, Rich Niemiec, Marlene Theriault, Michael Abbey, Mike Corey, Steve Feuerstein, Mark Gurry, Peter Corrigan, Bradley Brown, Joe Trezzo, Paul Dorsey, Mark Ramacher, Rama Velpuri, David Kreines, Matt Reagan, John Beresniewicz, Reem Adranly, and Nuno Suoto. I'm sure there are others I've forgotten at the moment; thanks to all of the user group chairmen, meeting coordinators, staff workers, and bookstore workers (Hi, Buffie & Warren!).

Thanks to the daily sanity staff—my family and co-workers. All play a part in enabling me to participate in this enterprise. Thanks to the readers who, by their questions, actively direct the topics covered and improve the books.

Over at the publishing side of the house, thanks to Julie Gibbs and Marsha Bazley of ORACLE and the crew at Osborne/McGraw-Hill: Scott Rogers, Marlene Vasilieff, and my editors, Madhu Prasher and Claire Splan.

Very special thanks to Rachel Carmichael and Ian Fickling for their invaluable contributions to this book.

As always, to Sue, Emily, and Rachel.

—Kevin Loney

INTRODUCTION

util•i•ty *n*

1: fitness for some purpose or worth to some end

2: something useful or designed for use

—*Webster's New Collegiate Dictionary* tenth edition

Although SQL and PL/SQL scripts are useful, you will not attain much utility from a canned script that is undocumented, or whose output you cannot properly interpret. When reviewing a library of scripts, you will receive the greatest utility from the scripts that are well-documented and which illustrate proper interpretation of sample results provided. The better the library of scripts is documented, the greater the utility of those scripts.

In this book, you will see a comprehensive collection of SQL and PL/SQL scripts, organized into chapters by function. Within each chapter, you will see scripts you can use to manage your data or the database structures affected by your data. Each script is fully documented, and sample results are shown. After reviewing a sample script, you should be able to:

1. Understand how the script works.

2. Customize the script with confidence.

3. Act properly on the script's results.

The second point is important: The documentation for a script should provide the information you need to make the script work well for your specific needs. If a script does not provide exactly the information you need, then you should be confident enough in your understanding of the script to customize it properly. You can use the annotations provided with each script to navigate through the script and confidently modify it to meet your needs.

The scripts in this book come from a variety of sources: some originated within ORACLE Support, some came from the authors' personal scripts archives, and many were written specifically for this book. Because of the detailed annotations provided for each script, this book is more than just a manual accompanying a library of scripts on a CD; it is a set of examples of coding styles and data retrieval that have wide-ranging application within your ORACLE systems. Thus, the utility of the scripts is twofold: in their content and in their style.

In the first chapter, you will see scripts written specifically to deal with objects introduced in ORACLE8 (including abstract datatypes and partitions). In the following chapters, you will see scripts dealing in greater detail with issues common to all versions of ORACLE: managing performance, identifying deadlocks, forcing **commit**s during **delete**s, identifying missing indexes, estimating space needs, and generating **create table** commands—among many others. If you are new to PL/SQL, you should also read Appendix A for descriptions of PL/SQL, stored procedures, and dynamic PL/SQL.

You should use the annotations to understand the scripts in this archive. The better you understand the scripts, their structure, and their output, the more useful they will be for you—and utility scripts will actually provide utility.

ORACLE8-
Specific Scripts

hile you can use the scripts in the rest of this book for both ORACLE7 and
ORACLE8, in this chapter you will see several scripts that specifically
address the management needs for database objects introduced in
ORACLE8. The scripts either provide diagnostic information (such as data
distribution statistics for partitions) or generate SQL scripts (such as **create type**
commands). For each script, you will see sample results followed by an annotated
walk-through of the script. You can use the annotations that are provided with each
script to understand its workings and modify it to best meet your needs. The major
scripts covered in this chapter are:

gen_type.sql	Generates the code necessary to re-create existing abstract datatypes.
desc_adt.sql	Shows the full column description of tables that use abstract datatypes.
pwd_warn.sql	Generates warning messages for impending password expirations.
alterpwd.sql	Generates a stored procedure to facilitate password changes.
part_dis.sql	Shows the distribution of values across a table's partitions.
part_idi.sql	Shows the distribution of values across an index's partitions.

There are more than six scripts in this chapter. Throughout this book, the major
scripts are listed at the beginning of the chapter; the annotations of those scripts
yield new scripts, variations, and coding techniques.

All the scripts in this chapter should be run from an account with DBA privileges
or which has been granted select on all the DBA_ views.

Generating create type Commands

gen_type.sql
As of ORACLE8, you can create *abstract datatypes* and use them as if they were
ORACLE-provided datatypes such as NUMBER and VARCHAR2. By using abstract
datatypes, you can standardize the representation of complex data (such as address
information). Because they are abstract datatypes, you can create methods for the
datatypes you create. *Methods* are user-defined functions that you can use to act on
and access data stored using your abstract datatypes. In this section, you will see
how to regenerate the commands used to create abstract datatypes and their
methods. All types of abstract datatypes, including nested tables, varying arrays,
and incomplete types, are covered by this script.

The gen_type.sql script regenerates **create type** commands. For example, consider
a simple abstract datatype. The script in the following listing creates an abstract
datatype named ANIMAL_TY.

```
create or replace type ANIMAL_TY as object
(Breed        VARCHAR2(25),
 Name         VARCHAR2(25),
 BirthDate   DATE,
member function AGE (BirthDate IN DATE) return NUMBER,
PRAGMA RESTRICT_REFERENCES(AGE, WNDS));
```

In this example, the ANIMAL_TY datatype has three attributes: Breed, Name, and BirthDate. You can use the ANIMAL_TY datatype as a datatype in your tables:

```
create table ZOO_INVENTORY
(Section      VARCHAR2(25),
 Animal       ANIMAL_TY);
```

Since the Animal column of the ZOO_INVENTORY table is defined via the ANIMAL_TY datatype, you can specify Breed, Name, and Birthdate for the Animal column's values. You can use any methods defined on the ANIMAL_TY datatype on the data in the ZOO_INVENTORY table's Animal column. A full explanation of the usage of abstract datatypes is beyond the scope of this book; see *ORACLE8: The Complete Reference* by George Koch and Kevin Loney (Osborne/McGraw-Hill, 1998) for detailed examples of the creation and usage of abstract datatypes and methods.

The ANIMAL_TY datatype's **create type** command includes a specification for a method called AGE:

```
member function AGE (BirthDate IN DATE) return NUMBER,
PRAGMA RESTRICT_REFERENCES(AGE, WNDS));
```

You must use the **create type body** command to create the AGE method:

```
create or replace type body ANIMAL_TY as
member function Age (BirthDate DATE) return NUMBER is
begin
  RETURN ROUND(SysDate - BirthDate);
end;
end;
/
```

The AGE method, when provided with the animal's birthdate, will return the current age of the animal. Because the ANIMAL_TY method is dependent on the ANIMAL_TY datatype, you must create the datatype before you create the method.

You can also create a nested table using ANIMAL_TY. The command in the following listing creates a nested table called ANIMAL_NT.

```
create type ANIMAL_NT as table of ANIMAL_TY;
```

Once the ANIMAL_NT datatype has been created, you can use it as a datatype in tables, the same way ANIMAL_TY was used in the previous example. Since ANIMAL_NT is a nested table, a single record in a table can contain multiple sets of values in a column defined via ANIMAL_NT.

To limit the number of possible entries in a nested table, you should use a varying array in place of the nested table. You can use a varying array as a datatype in tables. A single record in a table can contain multiple values for the varying array column, up to the limit defined for the varying array. Varying arrays are created via the **create type** command, as shown in the following example.

```
create type ANIMAL_VA as varying array (10) of ANIMAL_TY;
```

In this example, the **create type** command creates a varying array named ANIMAL_VA, using the ANIMAL_TY datatype as its base structure. You can use the ANIMAL_VA datatype as the datatype for a column in a table. The ANIMAL_VA varying array has a limit of 10 entries per record.

If two types depend on each other, then you must have a way to create one of the two types first. For example, if the ANIMAL_TY datatype used the MAMMAL_TY datatype for one of its attributes, and MAMMAL_TY used ANIMAL_TY for one of its datatypes, then you need to be able to create one of those two types first. You can use the **create type** command to create *incomplete types*, which resolves the interdependency problem. As shown in the following listing, an incomplete type does not have attributes. After creating the incomplete type, you can create additional types that use the incomplete type; you can later use the **create or replace type** command to specify the attributes for the incomplete type.

```
create or replace type incomp_type as object;
```

When you create an incomplete type, you will receive an error:

```
Warning: Type created with compilation errors.
```

Despite the error message, the incomplete type will be created.

Since there are four different types of abstract datatypes (abstract datatypes, nested tables, varying arrays, and incomplete types), the script that re-creates abstract datatypes must re-create each type correctly. The script must also re-create the type bodies containing the code for methods associated with abstract datatypes. The gen_type.sql script, shown in the following listing, will create a SQL script that contains the **create type** commands needed to re-create all existing types. The output will be written to a file called cre_type.sql. Sample input is shown following the code. An annotated walk-through of the gen_type.sql script follows the sample output.

```
set echo off verify off feedback off pagesize 0
set term on
select 'Creating abstract datatype build script...' from DUAL;

accept datatype_name prompt "Enter the name of the datatype: "
accept datatype_owner prompt "Enter datatype owner: "
set term off

drop   table TYPE_TEMP
/

create table TYPE_TEMP (
       Lineno NUMBER,
       Id_Owner VARCHAR2(30),
       Id_Name VARCHAR2(30),
       Text VARCHAR2(2000))
/

declare
   cursor TYPE_CURSOR is
       select Owner,
              Name,
              Type,
              Line,
              Text
         from DBA_SOURCE
        where Type in ('TYPE','TYPE BODY')
          and Owner = UPPER('&&datatype_owner')
          and Name like UPPER('&&datatype_name')
        order by Owner, Name, Type, Line;

   Lv_Owner            DBA_SOURCE.Owner%TYPE;
   Lv_Name             DBA_SOURCE.Name%TYPE;
   Lv_Type             DBA_SOURCE.Type%TYPE;
   Lv_Text             DBA_SOURCE.Text%TYPE;
   Lv_Line             DBA_SOURCE.Line%TYPE;
   Lv_String           VARCHAR2(2100);
   Lv_String2          VARCHAR2(2100);
   Lv_Lineno           NUMBER := 0;

   procedure WRITE_OUT(P_Line INTEGER, P_Owner VARCHAR2, P_Name VARCHAR2,
                  P_String VARCHAR2) is
   begin
     insert into TYPE_TEMP (Lineno, Id_Owner, Id_Name, Text)
```

```
                    values (P_Line,P_Owner,P_Name,P_String);
    end;

begin
   open TYPE_CURSOR;
   Lv_Lineno  := 1;
   loop
      fetch TYPE_CURSOR into Lv_Owner,
                             Lv_Name,
                             Lv_Type,
                             Lv_Line,
                             Lv_Text;
      exit when TYPE_CURSOR%NOTFOUND;

      if (Lv_Line = 1)
      then
          WRITE_OUT(Lv_Lineno, Lv_Owner, Lv_Name, '/');
          Lv_String  := 'CREATE OR REPLACE ' || UPPER(Lv_Type)  || ' ';
          WRITE_OUT(Lv_Lineno, Lv_Owner, Lv_Name, Lv_String);
          Lv_Lineno  := Lv_Lineno + 1;

          Lv_String  := SUBSTR(Lv_Text,LENGTH(Lv_Type)+1,
                          (LENGTH(Lv_Text) - LENGTH(Lv_Type)));
          Lv_String  := Lv_Owner || '.' || LTRIM(Lv_String);
          WRITE_OUT(Lv_Lineno, Lv_Owner, Lv_Name, Lv_String);
          Lv_Lineno  := Lv_Lineno + 1;
      else
          WRITE_OUT(Lv_Lineno, Lv_Owner, Lv_Name, Lv_Text);
          Lv_Lineno := Lv_Lineno + 1;
      end if;
   end loop;

   WRITE_OUT(Lv_Lineno, Lv_Owner, Lv_Name, '/');
   close TYPE_CURSOR;
   delete from TYPE_TEMP where Lineno=1 and Text='/';
end;
/
spool cre_type.sql
select Text
  from TYPE_TEMP
 order by Id_Owner, Id_Name, Lineno
/
spool off
```

Sample results for the gen_type.sql script are shown in the following listing.

```
CREATE OR REPLACE TYPE
DORA.ANIMAL_NT as table of ANIMAL_TY;
/
CREATE OR REPLACE TYPE
DORA.ANIMAL_TY as object
(Breed        VARCHAR2(25),
 Name         VARCHAR2(25),
 BirthDate    DATE,
member function AGE (BirthDate IN DATE) return NUMBER,
PRAGMA RESTRICT_REFERENCES(AGE, WNDS));
/
CREATE OR REPLACE TYPE BODY
DORA.ANIMAL_TY as
member function Age (BirthDate DATE) return NUMBER is
begin
   RETURN ROUND(SysDate - BirthDate);
end;
end;
/
CREATE OR REPLACE TYPE
DORA.ANIMAL_VA as varying array (10) of ANIMAL_TY;
/
CREATE OR REPLACE TYPE
DORA.INCOMP_TYPE as object
/
```

PROGRAMMER'S NOTE *The **create type** commands generated by gen_type.sql may not be in the proper order. The datatypes are listed in alphabetical order.*

As shown by this output, you may need to edit the cre_type.sql file prior to running it. In this example, the first type creates the ANIMAL_NT datatype:

```
CREATE OR REPLACE TYPE
DORA.ANIMAL_NT as table of ANIMAL_TY;
/
```

However, the ANIMAL_TY datatype is not created until the next step in the script, so attempting to create ANIMAL_NT before ANIMAL_TY will fail.

ANNOTATIONS

As noted in the previous section, the output of the gen_type.sql script attempts to create datatypes in alphabetical order. Although the script may be modified to account for some dependencies, other dependencies cannot be accounted for. For example, if you create an incomplete type and later modify the type to create its attributes, the data dictionary no longer records the earlier (incomplete) structure of the type. Suppose you create an incomplete type called INCOMP_TYPE:

```
create type INCOMP_TYPE as object;
```

You can then create another datatype that uses INCOMP_TYPE as a datatype. You may then modify the INCOMP_TYPE datatype:

```
create or replace type INCOMP_TYPE
(Some_Attribute  VARCHAR2(30));
```

When you issue the **create or replace type** command, the earlier definition of the INCOMP_TYPE datatype is overwritten. If INCOMP_TYPE and the second type you created are both dependent on each other, then gen_type.sql will not generate the proper **create type** commands because the information it needs about the incomplete type is no longer in the data dictionary. To create the proper sequence of commands, you will need to manually edit the cre_type.sql file generated.

The code needed to re-create datatypes is stored in the DBA_SOURCE data dictionary view. Because each line of code for a datatype is stored as a separate row in DBA_SOURCE, the gen_type.sql script uses a cursor both to extract the datatype information and to allow you to enter a wildcard value for the datatype name (%*datatype_name*%) or to modify the script to select all datatypes for an owner or all datatypes in the database. The gen_type.sql script generates a script (called cre_type.sql) to re-create the requested datatype. The gen_type.sql script uses a temporary table to hold individual lines of the **create type** and **create type body** commands, writing to the table rather than using the DBMS_OUTPUT.PUT_LINE procedure. By writing the data to a temporary table, you can extract the information for an individual datatype from the table. Using the DBMS_OUTPUT procedure would force you to save and edit the output file for the datatype you want.

PROGRAMMER'S NOTE   *Abstract datatypes have owners. If you create an abstract datatype via the **create type** command, you can **grant** other users EXECUTE privilege on the datatype. See Chapter 5 for a script to recreate **grant** commands.*

The first section of the gen_type.sql script, shown in the following listing, does the initial setup, prompting for the datatype name and datatype owner for later use via the **accept** command. Using the **accept** command allows you to define your own prompt for the variable. You can enter a value for the datatype name with '%' to generate a script for all datatypes with a similar name.

The SQL*Plus **set** command turns off headers (**pagesize 0**), row counts (**feedback off**), and displays of old and new values for the *datatype_name* and *datatype_owner* variables (**verify off**).

```
set echo off verify off feedback off pagesize 0
set term on
select 'Creating abstract datatype build script...' from DUAL;
```

```
accept datatype_name prompt "Enter the name of the datatype: "
accept datatype_owner prompt "Enter datatype owner: "
set term off
```

The next section of the script creates a temporary table to hold each **create type** and associated **create type body** command and owner. The Lineno column orders the lines of the **create type** and **create type body** commands.

```
drop    table TYPE_TEMP
/

create table TYPE_TEMP (
        Lineno NUMBER,
        Id_Owner VARCHAR2(30),
        Id_Name VARCHAR2(30),
        Text VARCHAR2(2000))
/
```

The next section of the script, shown in the following listing, creates the TYPE_CURSOR cursor. The TYPE_CURSOR cursor selects the information from DBA_SOURCE where the datatype name matches the input variable *datatype_name* and the datatype owner matches the input variable *datatype_owner*. Using **like** in the **where** clause instead of = allows for wildcards. Selecting for **Type in ('TYPE', 'TYPE BODY')** selects all the lines for both the datatype specification and the datatype body. The **order by** clause orders by Type before Line, so all lines of the datatype specification will be returned before any line of the type body.

```
    declare
        cursor TYPE_CURSOR is
            select Owner,
                    Name,
                    Type,
                    Line,
                    Text
               from DBA_SOURCE
              where Type in ('TYPE','TYPE BODY')
                and Owner = UPPER('&&datatype_owner')
                and Name like UPPER('&&datatype_name')
              order by Owner, Name, Type, Line;
```

The procedure variables for the cursor are declared as TABLE_NAME.Column_ Name%TYPE. Anchoring the variable declarations to columns via the **%TYPE** operator takes the column definition from within the database itself. If the column definition changes in a different version of ORACLE, the procedure will still work because the definition of the column has not been hard-coded. The variable *Lv_Lineno* orders the lines of the **create type** statement and is initialized to 0.

```
Lv_Owner                   DBA_SOURCE.Owner%TYPE;
Lv_Name                    DBA_SOURCE.Name%TYPE;
Lv_Type                    DBA_SOURCE.Type%TYPE;
Lv_Text                    DBA_SOURCE.Text%TYPE;
Lv_Line                    DBA_SOURCE.Line%TYPE;
Lv_String                  VARCHAR2(2100);
Lv_String2                 VARCHAR2(2100);
Lv_Lineno                  NUMBER := 0;
```

The next section of the script creates WRITE_OUT, an internal procedure to
perform the **insert**s into the temporary table.

```
procedure WRITE_OUT(P_Line INTEGER, P_Owner VARCHAR2, P_Name VARCHAR2,
                    P_String VARCHAR2) is
begin
    insert into TYPE_TEMP (Lineno, Id_Owner, Id_Name, Text)
          values (P_Line,P_Owner,P_Name,P_String);
end;
```

The lines of a datatype specification or type body are stored as separate lines in
the data dictionary. The cursor TYPE_CURSOR extracts all the lines of both the
datatype specification and the type body. *Lv_Lineno*, in conjunction with the
datatype name, orders the rows in the temporary table TYPE_TEMP so you can
extract the **create type** command for a single datatype at the end of the procedure. In
the next section of the gen_type.sql script, shown in the following listing, the
TYPE_CURSOR cursor is opened and a value is fetched into the script variables. See
Appendix A for details regarding the management of cursors in PL/SQL and
dynamic SQL.

```
begin
   open TYPE_CURSOR;
   Lv_Lineno   := 1;
   loop
      fetch TYPE_CURSOR into Lv_Owner,
                             Lv_Name,
                             Lv_Type,
                             Lv_Line,
                             Lv_Text;
      exit when TYPE_CURSOR%NOTFOUND;
```

The **order by** clause of the cursor ensures that all the lines of a datatype
specification are returned before the lines of the type body. ORACLE does not store
the final '/' used to execute each **create type** or **create type body** command. Because
the script is creating multiple SQL statements, a '/' is inserted into the temporary
table before each command is generated. The next section of the script, shown in the
following listing, inserts the '/' line and then generates the **create or replace**

command. The **or replace** clause prevents the loss of **grant**s you would experience if you dropped and re-created the datatype.

```
if (Lv_Line = 1)
then
    WRITE_OUT(Lv_Lineno, Lv_Owner, Lv_Name, '/');
    Lv_String  := 'CREATE OR REPLACE ' || UPPER(Lv_Type)  || ' ';
    WRITE_OUT(Lv_Lineno, Lv_Owner, Lv_Name, Lv_String);
    Lv_Lineno  := Lv_Lineno + 1;
```

ORACLE stores the first line of each part of a datatype as **TYPE [BODY]** *datatype_name*. Because the script concatenates the owner's name to the name of the datatype in the generated script, the next section of the gen_type.sql script has to remove the word **TYPE** or **TYPE BODY** from the first line of the stored source code. The **SUBSTR** function, along with the variable *Lv_Type*, extracts the rest of the line and places it in the string variable *Lv_String* to be written to the temporary table. The **LTRIM** function removes extra blanks from the beginning of the string.

```
Lv_String  := SUBSTR(Lv_Text,LENGTH(Lv_Type)+1,
                   (LENGTH(Lv_Text) - LENGTH(Lv_Type)));
Lv_String  := Lv_Owner || '.' || LTRIM(Lv_String);
WRITE_OUT(Lv_Lineno, Lv_Owner, Lv_Name, Lv_String);
Lv_Lineno  := Lv_Lineno + 1;
```

If this is not the first line of the datatype or type body in DBA_SOURCE, the text as read from the database is inserted into the temporary table. The cursor loop ends and the procedure will loop back through the TYPE_CURSOR until all datatypes have been generated. The cursor then closes and the procedure exits. Once the **create** statements for all the types and type bodies have been generated, they are spooled to a file for later execution. A final **delete** command deletes the extra '/' generated prior to the first **create** command in the output file.

```
    else
        WRITE_OUT(Lv_Lineno, Lv_Owner, Lv_Name, Lv_Text);
        Lv_Lineno := Lv_Lineno + 1;
    end if;
end loop;

WRITE_OUT(Lv_Lineno, Lv_Owner, Lv_Name, '/');
close TYPE_CURSOR;
delete from TYPE_TEMP where Lineno=1 and Text='/';
end;
/
spool cre_type.sql
select Text
  from TYPE_TEMP
```

```
 order by Id_Owner, Id_Name, Lineno
/
spool off
```

Sample contents of the cre_type.sql script are shown in the following listing. Note that the types are listed in alphabetical order, and all of the types are created before their associated type bodies. The sample listing shows that the gen_type.sql script generates the source code for abstract datatypes, nested tables, varying arrays, and incomplete types.

```
CREATE OR REPLACE TYPE
DORA.ANIMAL_NT as table of ANIMAL_TY;
/
CREATE OR REPLACE TYPE
DORA.ANIMAL_TY as object
(Breed        VARCHAR2(25),
 Name         VARCHAR2(25),
 BirthDate    DATE,
member function AGE (BirthDate IN DATE) return NUMBER,
PRAGMA RESTRICT_REFERENCES(AGE, WNDS));
/
CREATE OR REPLACE TYPE BODY
DORA.ANIMAL_TY as
member function Age (BirthDate DATE) return NUMBER is
begin
  RETURN ROUND(SysDate - BirthDate);
end;
end;
/
CREATE OR REPLACE TYPE
DORA.ANIMAL_VA as varying array (10) of ANIMAL_TY;
/
CREATE OR REPLACE TYPE
DORA.INCOMP_TYPE as object
/
```

If you want to use this script to document all the datatypes for a particular owner, remove the **accept** *datatype_name* statement at the beginning of the script and change the **where** clause for the TYPE_CURSOR cursor to:

```
where Owner  = UPPER('&&datatype_owner')
```

If you want to document all datatypes in your database that are not owned by SYS, remove the two **accept** statements from the beginning of the script and change the **where** clause for the TYPE_CURSOR cursor to:

```
where Owner != 'SYS'
```

You can determine which of your datatypes are nested tables or varying arrays by querying the DBA_COLL_TYPES data dictionary view (USER_COLL_TYPES is also available). The Coll_Type column of DBA_COLL_TYPES will have a value of 'TABLE' for nested tables and 'VARYING ARRAY' for varying arrays. For varying arrays, the Upper_Bound column of DBA_COLL_TYPES shows the maximum number of entries in the array. As shown in the following listing, the Elem_Type_Name column of USER_COLL_TYPES lists the datatype on which the nested table or varying array is based.

```
select * from USER_COLL_TYPES;
```

TYPE_NAME	COLL_TYPE	UPPER_BOUND
ELEM_TY ELEM_TYPE_OWNER	ELEM_TYPE_NAME	LENGTH
PRECISION SCALE CHARACTER_SET_NAME		
ANIMAL_NT	TABLE	
DORA	ANIMAL_TY	
ANIMAL_VA	VARYING ARRAY	10
DORA	ANIMAL_TY	

You can use this information to further customize the gen_type.sql script. To retrieve only nested tables and varying arrays, modify the TYPE_CURSOR cursor's query to only retrieve types listed in DBA_COLL_TYPES.

```
    cursor TYPE_CURSOR is
        select Owner,
               Name,
               Type,
               Line,
               Text
          from DBA_SOURCE
         where Type in ('TYPE','TYPE BODY')
           and Owner = UPPER('&&datatype_owner')
           and Name like UPPER('&&datatype_name')
           and exists
               (select 'x' from DBA_COLL_TYPES
                  where DBA_COLL_TYPES.Owner=DBA_SOURCE.Owner
                    and DBA_COLL_TYPES.Type_Name=DBA_SOURCE.Name)
         order by Owner, Name, Type, Line;
```

The condition that was added,

```
and exists
    (select 'x' from DBA_COLL_TYPES
    where DBA_COLL_TYPES.Owner=DBA_SOURCE.Owner
    and DBA_COLL_TYPES.Type_Name=DBA_SOURCE.Name)
```

performs an existence check; if the type is listed in both DBA_SOURCE and DBA_COLL_TYPES, then it is either a nested table or a varying array. You could also query the DBA_TYPES data dictionary view; if the TypeCode column of DBA_TYPES has a value of 'COLLECTION,' then the datatype is either a nested table or a varying array.

To determine which datatypes are incomplete, you can query the DBA_TYPES data dictionary view. If a type is incomplete, then the Incomplete column of DBA_TYPES will be set to a value of 'YES.' If the type is complete, then the Incomplete column of DBA_TYPES will have a value of 'NO.'

See Chapter 5 for scripts you can use to generate the DDL for other database objects such as tables, indexes, and database links.

desc_adt.sql

Describe Tables That Use Abstract Datatypes

The more you use abstract datatypes, the more complicated your **describe** commands become. If you create abstract datatypes that rely on other abstract datatypes, then your ability to see the full description of a table will be adversely affected unless you write utility scripts to retrieve the full hierarchy of the abstract datatypes. In this section, you will see a script, desc_adt.sql, that describes tables with one or more abstract datatypes. In order to illustrate the problem that the script solves, the initial portion of this section creates a sample table based on multiple datatypes.

For the examples in this section, a new datatype will be created: AUTHOR_TY. The AUTHOR_TY has two attributes about an author: Name and Date_of_Birth. The command in the following listing creates the AUTHOR_TY datatype.

```
create or replace type AUTHOR_TY as object
(Name            VARCHAR2(50),
 Date_of_Birth  DATE);
```

Next, a second datatype, ARTICLE_TY, is created. The ARTICLE_TY datatype relies on the AUTHOR_TY datatype. Each article has an Author (as defined by the AUTHOR_TY datatype), a Title, a Year_Published, and a Publication. The SQL command shown in the following listing creates the ARTICLE_TY datatype.

```
create or replace type ARTICLE_TY as object
(Author          AUTHOR_TY,
 Title           VARCHAR2(100),
```

```
Year_Published    NUMBER(4),
Publication       VARCHAR2(100));
```

The following listing uses the ARTICLE_TY datatype to create a table named COMPILATION_ARTICLES. The COMPILATION_ARTICLES table will have one record for each article published as part of a special compilation.

```
create table COMPILATION_ARTICLES
(Sequence_Number    NUMBER(4),
 Article            ARTICLE_TY);
```

What columns can you select from the COMPILATION_ARTICLES table? Since the Article column uses the ARTICLE_TY datatype, you can select the following columns:

◆ Sequence_Number

◆ Article

◆ Article.Author

◆ Article.Title

◆ Article.Year_Published

◆ Article.Publication

Since Article.Author uses the AUTHOR_TY datatype, you can also select

◆ Article.Author.Name

◆ Article.Author.Date_of_Birth

Thus, there are eight different columns you can select from the COMPILATION_ARTICLES table. However, the **describe** command does not show these columns:

```
describe COMPILATION_ARTICLES
```

```
Name                              Null?    Type
--------------------------------- -------- ----
SEQUENCE_NUMBER                            NUMBER
ARTICLE                                    ARTICLE_TY
```

The **describe** command shows only the first two columns—the attributes of the Article column (and the attributes of the datatypes nested within it) are not shown.

PROGRAMMER'S NOTE   *In ORACLE8.0.3, the **describe** command does not show the actual datatype; it shows a value of "NAMED TYPE" instead. To see the real datatype in ORACLE8.0.3, you need to query USER_TAB_COLUMNS.*

The following script, desc_adt.sql, creates a view called DBA_DESCRIBE. You can query the DBA_DESCRIBE view to see a listing of all columns that you can select from a table using abstract datatypes. The desc_adt.sql script will show the full details for any table whose datatypes use no more than two levels of nesting; the annotations show how to expand this script to support even greater levels of nesting.

```
create or replace view SYS.DBA_DESCRIBE
      (Owner, Table_Name,
       Column_Name, Data_Type, Data_Type_Mod,
       Data_Type_Owner, Data_Length, Data_Precision,
       Data_Scale, Column_Id, Character_Set_Name )
   as
select Owner, Table_Name,
       Column_Name, Data_Type, Data_Type_Mod,
       Data_Type_Owner, Data_Length, Data_Precision,
       Data_Scale, Column_Id, Character_Set_Name
  from DBA_TAB_COLUMNS
 union all
select B.Owner, B.Table_Name,
       '  '||B.Column_Name||'.'||A.Attr_Name, A.Attr_Type_Name,
       A.Attr_Type_Mod, A.Attr_Type_Owner, A.Length,
       A.Precision, A.Scale, B.Column_ID,
       A.Character_Set_Name
  from DBA_TYPE_ATTRS A, DBA_TAB_COLUMNS B
 where B.Data_Type = A.Type_Name
   and B.Data_Type_Owner = A.Owner
 union all
select C.Owner, C.Table_Name,
       '   '||C.Column_Name||'.'||B.Attr_Name||'.'||A.Attr_Name,
       A.Attr_Type_Name, A.Attr_Type_Mod,
       A.Attr_Type_Owner, A.Length, A.Precision,
       A.Scale, C.Column_ID, A.Character_Set_Name
  from DBA_TYPE_ATTRS A, DBA_TYPE_ATTRS B, DBA_TAB_COLUMNS C
 where C.Data_Type = B.Type_Name
   and C.Data_Type_Owner = B.Owner
   and A.Type_Name = B.Attr_Type_Name
   and A.Owner = B.Attr_Type_Owner;
```

Sample output from the DBA_DESCRIBE view is shown in the following listing.

```
column Column_Name format A40

select Column_Name, Data_Type
  from DBA_DESCRIBE
 where Table_Name = 'COMPILATION_ARTICLES';
```

```
COLUMN_NAME                              DATA_TYPE
----------------------------------       --------------------------------
SEQUENCE_NUMBER                          NUMBER
ARTICLE                                  ARTICLE_TY
   ARTICLE.AUTHOR                        AUTHOR_TY
   ARTICLE.TITLE                         VARCHAR2
   ARTICLE.YEAR_PUBLISHED                NUMBER
   ARTICLE.PUBLICATION                   VARCHAR2
      ARTICLE.AUTHOR.NAME                VARCHAR2
      ARTICLE.AUTHOR.DATE_OF_BIRTH       DATE

8 rows selected.
```

The DBA_DESCRIBE output shows the eight possible columns you can select from the COMPILATION_ARTICLES table. Attributes of abstract datatypes are preceded by sets of blanks to indicate that they are datatype attributes.

ANNOTATIONS

You can expand the desc_adt.sql script to handle a third level of datatype nesting by adding an additional query to the **union** query that provides the basis for the DBA_DESCRIBE view. The following query will retrieve the attribute data for a datatype that is nested three levels deep (for instance, if AUTHOR_TY relied on an abstract datatype).

```
select D.Owner, D.Table_Name, '      '||
       D.Column_Name||'.'||C.Attr_Name||'.'||B.Attr_Name||'.'||A.ATTR_NAME,
       A.Attr_Type_Name, A.Attr_Type_Mod,
       A.Attr_Type_Owner, A.Length, A.Precision, A.Scale, D.Column_ID,
       A.Character_Set_Name
  from DBA_TYPE_ATTRS A, DBA_TYPE_ATTRS B, DBA_TYPE_ATTRS C, DBA_TAB_COLUMNS D
 where D.Data_Type = C.Type_Name
   and D.Data_Type_Owner = C.Owner
   and A.Type_Name = B.Attr_Type_Name
   and A.Owner = B.Attr_Type_Owner
   and B.Type_Name = C.Attr_Type_Name
   and B.Owner = C.Attr_Type_Owner;
```

In the combined version of the desc_adt.sql script, this new query is **union**ed to the rest of the view definition script, as shown in the following listing:

```
create or replace view SYS.DBA_DESCRIBE
      (Owner, Table_Name,
       Column_Name, Data_Type, Data_Type_Mod,
       Data_Type_Owner, Data_Length, Data_Precision,
```

```
Data_Scale, Column_Id, Character_Set_Name )
    as
select Owner, Table_Name,
       Column_Name, Data_Type, Data_Type_Mod,
       Data_Type_Owner, Data_Length, Data_Precision,
       Data_Scale, Column_Id, Character_Set_Name
  from DBA_TAB_COLUMNS
 union all
select B.Owner, B.Table_Name,
       '  '||B.Column_Name||'.'||A.Attr_Name, A.Attr_Type_Name,
       A.Attr_Type_Mod, A.Attr_Type_Owner, A.Length,
       A.Precision, A.Scale, B.Column_ID,
       A.Character_Set_Name
  from DBA_TYPE_ATTRS A, DBA_TAB_COLUMNS B
 where B.Data_Type = A.Type_Name
   and B.Data_Type_Owner = A.Owner
 union all
select C.Owner, C.Table_Name,
       '     '||C.Column_Name||'.'||B.Attr_Name||'.'||A.Attr_Name,
       A.Attr_Type_Name, A.Attr_Type_Mod,
       A.Attr_Type_Owner, A.Length, A.Precision,
       A.Scale, C.Column_ID, A.Character_Set_Name
  from DBA_TYPE_ATTRS A, DBA_TYPE_ATTRS B, DBA_TAB_COLUMNS C
 where C.Data_Type = B.Type_Name
   and C.Data_Type_Owner = B.Owner
   and A.Type_Name = B.Attr_Type_Name
   and A.Owner = B.Attr_Type_Owner
 union all
select D.Owner, D.Table_Name,    '        '||
       D.Column_Name||'.'||C.Attr_Name||'.'||B.Attr_Name||'.'||A.ATTR_NAME,
       A.Attr_Type_Name, A.Attr_Type_Mod,
       A.Attr_Type_Owner, A.Length, A.Precision, A.Scale, D.Column_ID,
       A.Character_Set_Name
  from DBA_TYPE_ATTRS A, DBA_TYPE_ATTRS B, DBA_TYPE_ATTRS C, DBA_TAB_COLUMNS D
 where D.Data_Type = C.Type_Name
   and D.Data_Type_Owner = C.Owner
   and A.Type_Name = B.Attr_Type_Name
   and A.Owner = B.Attr_Type_Owner
   and B.Type_Name = C.Attr_Type_Name
   and B.Owner = C.Attr_Type_Owner;
```

The first portion of the desc_adt.sql script, shown in the following listing, defines the columns for the DBA_DESCRIBE view.

```
create or replace view SYS.DBA_DESCRIBE
    (Owner, Table_Name,
     Column_Name, Data_Type, Data_Type_Mod,
     Data_Type_Owner, Data_Length, Data_Precision,
     Data_Scale, Column_Id, Character_Set_Name )
  as
```

The next portion of the DBA_DESCRIBE view is the base query for the view. The first portion of the **union**ed query, shown in the following listing, retrieves the names of the table's columns from the DBA_TAB_COLUMNS data dictionary view.

```
select Owner, Table_Name,
       Column_Name, Data_Type, Data_Type_Mod,
       Data_Type_Owner, Data_Length, Data_Precision,
       Data_Scale, Column_Id, Character_Set_Name
  from DBA_TAB_COLUMNS
 union all
```

The second part of the **union**ed query for the view retrieves the data for the table's abstract datatypes. The query joins the DBA_TAB_COLUMNS data dictionary view to the DBA_TYPE_ATTRS view.

```
select B.Owner, B.Table_Name,
       '  '||B.Column_Name||'.'||A.Attr_Name, A.Attr_Type_Name,
       A.Attr_Type_Mod, A.Attr_Type_Owner, A.Length,
       A.Precision, A.Scale, B.Column_ID,
       A.Character_Set_Name
  from DBA_TYPE_ATTRS A, DBA_TAB_COLUMNS B
 where B.Data_Type = A.Type_Name
   and B.Data_Type_Owner = A.Owner
 union all
```

The third part of the **union**ed query, shown in the next listing, generates the data for the next level of abstraction (when abstract datatypes rely on other abstract datatypes). In this query, the DBA_TAB_COLUMNS view joins to the DBA_TYPE_ATTRS view, and DBA_TYPE_ATTRS joins to itself.

Within DBA_TYPE_ATTRS, ORACLE tracks the relationships between different abstract datatypes. Thus, DBA_TYPE_ATTRS has a Type_Name column and a Attr_Type_Name column. Consider the example of the COMPILATION_ARTICLES table and its use of the ARTICLE_TY datatype. In the preceding part of the **union**ed query, the first join between DBA_TAB_COLUMNS and DBA_TYPE_ATTRS returns the name of the column, Article.Author, with a datatype of AUTHOR_TY. In that instance, AUTHOR_TY is the value in the Attr_Type_Name column. To go one step further down the hierarchy of datatypes, you need to select from a second instance of DBA_TYPE_ATTRS—this time, where the Type_Name column is equal to AUTHOR_TY, the Attr_Type_Name value returned from the first join.

The next query accomplishes this join. DBA_TAB_COLUMNS, given the alias
"C," joins to DBA_TYPE_ATTRS ("B") and DBA_TYPE_ATTRS ("B") then joins to
DBA_TYPE_ATTRS ("A") to retrieve the second-level data for the attributes. In the
select, the second line references three columns, which are, in order, C, B, and A.
When expanding the desc_adt.sql script, you will need to maintain the order of
values selected.

```
select C.Owner, C.Table_Name,
       '     '||C.Column_Name||'.'||B.Attr_Name||'.'||A.Attr_Name,
       A.Attr_Type_Name, A.Attr_Type_Mod,
       A.Attr_Type_Owner, A.Length, A.Precision,
       A.Scale, C.Column_ID, A.Character_Set_Name
  from DBA_TYPE_ATTRS A, DBA_TYPE_ATTRS B, DBA_TAB_COLUMNS C
 where C.Data_Type = B.Type_Name
   and C.Data_Type_Owner = B.Owner
   and A.Type_Name = B.Attr_Type_Name
   and A.Owner = B.Attr_Type_Owner
union all
```

The next part of the **union**ed query is not part of the standard desc_adt.sql script,
but is provided to demonstrate the way in which the script can be easily extended.
In this query, a third instance of DBA_TYPE_ATTRS is added to the **from** clause.
DBA_TAB_COLUMNS is given the alias of "D" and the three instances of
DBA_TYPE_ATTRS are given the aliases "A," "B," and "C."

PROGRAMMER'S NOTE   *The more complicated you make the base query for the DBA_DESCRIBE view, the
greater the impact you will have on its performance. The underlying data dictionary tables are not
optimized for this query.*

```
select D.Owner, D.Table_Name,   '        '||
       D.Column_Name||'.'||C.Attr_Name||'.'||B.Attr_Name||'.'||A.Attr_Name,
       A.Attr_Type_Name, A.Attr_Type_Mod,
       A.Attr_Type_Owner, A.Length, A.Precision, A.Scale, D.Column_ID,
       A.Character_Set_Name
  from DBA_TYPE_ATTRS A, DBA_TYPE_ATTRS B, DBA_TYPE_ATTRS C, DBA_TAB_COLUMNS D
 where D.Data_Type = C.Type_Name
   and D.Data_Type_Owner = C.Owner
   and B.Type_Name = C.Attr_Type_Name
   and B.Owner = C.Attr_Type_Owner
   and A.Type_Name = B.Attr_Type_Name
   and A.Owner = B.Attr_Type_Owner
;
```

The modifications to this script were

1. Adding another call to DBA_TYPE_ATTRS in the **from** clause.

2. Modifying the table aliases so that DBA_TAB_COLUMNS is D and DBA_TYPE_ATTRS is now A, B, and C.

3. In the first line of the query, selecting the columns from D (DBA_TAB_COLUMNS).

4. In the second line of the query, changing the string being selected. The first value should be from DBA_TAB_COLUMNS, and the rest should be from the three instances of DBA_TYPE_ATTRS, in order from D to C to B to A.

5. In the fifth line of the query, selecting the Column_ID value from D (DBA_TAB_COLUMNS).

6. In the **where** clause, joining D to C, C to B, and B to A.

Based on these steps, you can generate the query needed to select a fourth level of hierarchy of datatypes from the data dictionary. However, each new part of the **union**ed query affects the performance of the DBA_DESCRIBE view. Even if you do not have any datatypes nested three levels deep, you incur the performance penalty of that part of the **union**ed query each time you **select** from DBA_DESCRIBE.

Unfortunately, you can't use **connect by** to simplify the query. You cannot use **connect by** in conjunction with joins, so you can't select data about columns (from the underlying COL$ table) and attributes (from the ATTR$ table) while using **connect by**.

Generate Password Expiration Warnings

pwd_warn.sql

As of ORACLE8, you can force users' passwords to expire. A DBA can manually force a user's password to expire via the **password expire** clause of the **alter user** command:

```
alter user DORA password expire;
```

A user's password may also expire based on the parameters set in the user's profile. As of ORACLE8, profiles can contain settings for the number of days a password can be used before it expires (its "lifetime"). You can also specify the length of the grace period a user has to change his or her password after the password has expired.

PROGRAMMER'S NOTE   *The script in this section covers only the password expiration parameters of the **create** profile command. See Chapter 7 for a full description of the password management options.*

When the user's password expires, the user will need to change his or her ORACLE password. The potential problem with this implementation is that there is no proactive warning given to the user. The user is only notified of the password expiration *after* the password expiration date has been reached. Although this accomplishes the system's needs—forcing user password changes—it may not meet the user's needs. Rather than tell the users to change their password after it expires, you can warn the users before their passwords expire via the pwd_warn.sql script provided in this section.

You can set the maximum duration of a password via the PASSWORD_LIFE_TIME parameter of the **create profile** and **alter profile** commands. A second parameter, PASSWORD_GRACE_TIME, limits the *grace period*—the duration of time after the first post-expiration login that the user can continue to use the same password. For example, the following **create profile** command creates a profile named LIMITED_DURATION. Users of this profile will have to change their passwords every 60 days. After their first login following password expiration, users will have 10 days to change their passwords.

```
create profile LIMITED_DURATION
limit
PASSWORD_LIFE_TIME  60,
PASSWORD_GRACE_TIME 10;
```

You can associate users with the LIMITED_DURATION profile via the **alter user** command, as shown in the following listing.

```
alter user DORA profile LIMITED_DURATION;
```

Once a user has a profile assigned, you can use the pwd_warn.sql script, shown in the following listing, to generate warning messages.

```
set pagesize 0
column Warn_Msg format A80 word_wrapped

select Username,
    'Your database password is about to expire. You must change it by '
        ||Expiry_Date||'. '
  from DBA_USERS
 where Account_Status = 'OPEN'
   and Expiry_Date is not null
   and Sysdate-Expiry_Date <10
 union
select Username,
    'Your database password expired on '||Expiry_Date||
        '. You must change it during your next login. '
  from DBA_USERS
where Account_Status = 'EXPIRED'
union
```

```
select DBA_USERS.Username,
       'Your grace period for changing your expired database
       password will end on '||Expiry_Date+TO_NUMBER(Limit)||
       '.  You must change your database password before then. '
 from DBA_USERS, DBA_PROFILES
where DBA_USERS.Account_Status = 'EXPIRED(GRACE)'
  and DBA_USERS.Profile = DBA_PROFILES.Profile
  and DBA_PROFILES.Resource_Name = 'PASSWORD_GRACE_TIME'
  and DBA_PROFILES.Limit not in ('UNLIMITED', 'DEFAULT')
order by 1;
```

By default, the pwd_warn.sql script generates output which you can spool to a file. You may wish to run the three **union**ed queries that constitute pwd_warn.sql separately if that simplifies your user notification process. Sample output is shown in the following listing:

```
DORA
Your database password is about to expire.  You must change it by 01-SEP-98.

MARCIA
Your database password expired on 31-AUG-98.  You must change it during your
next login.
```

You can process the output of the pwd_warn.sql script via command scripts at the operating system level. Since mail scripts are operating system-specific and mail program-specific, they are beyond the scope of this book. For example, you could call external C programs to process the file via the external library capabilities introduced in ORACLE8. Since such programs usually involve C and OCI calls, they are beyond the scope of this book; see the demo files provided under the /plsql/demo subdirectory under the ORACLE software home directory. The demo files are named extproc.sql and extproc.c.

ANNOTATIONS

The pwd_warn.sql script is driven by the possible values of the Account_Status column in the DBA_USERS data dictionary view. The status for each user will be one of the following values:

OPEN	The current password has not expired.
EXPIRED	The password has expired, but the user has not since logged in.
EXPIRED(GRACE)	The password has expired and the user has since logged in. The user has not yet exceeded the grace period for expired passwords.

If your password has not expired, or if you do not have a profile that enforces password expiration, then your account status is 'OPEN.' If the Account_Status value is 'OPEN,' then the first part of the pwd_warn.sql script checks for a value in the Expiry_Date column of DBA_USERS. The Expiry_Date column records the expiration date of a user's current password; if no password expiration is set, then Expiry_Date will be NULL. The first part of pwd_warn.sql, shown in the following listing, generates a warning if a user's Expiry_Date is within ten days of the current system date.

```
select Username,
      'Your database password is about to expire. You must change it by '
        ||Expiry_Date||'. '
  from DBA_USERS
 where Account_Status = 'OPEN'
   and Expiry_Date is not null
   and Sysdate-Expiry_Date <10
```

If your account has expired, then your account status can be either 'EXPIRED' or 'EXPIRED(GRACE).' If your password has expired but you have not logged in since the password expired, you will have an account status of 'EXPIRED.' The grace period, if defined, does not start until the first time you log in after the password expiration. The second part of the **union**ed pwd_warn.sql query, shown in the following listing, creates a warning message for users with an Account_Status value of 'EXPIRED.'

```
select Username,      'Your database password expired on '||Expiry_Date||
        '. You must change it during your next login. '
 from DBA_USERS
where Account_Status = 'EXPIRED'
```

If you have logged in since your password expired, but did not change your password, then you are using the grace period defined for your profile. The PASSWORD_GRACE_TIME setting for the profile sets the number of days during which you can continue to log in after your first post-expiration login.

The third part of the pwd_warn.sql script, shown in the following listing, generates a warning message for users who are using the grace period. If the PASSWORD_GRACE_TIME value has been set, then its value is added to the Expiry_Date to determine the end date of the grace time. If the user did not log in on the password expiration date, then the calculated date may differ from the actual expiration date of the password.

```
select DBA_USERS.Username,
        'Your grace period for changing your expired database
        password will end on '||Expiry_Date+TO_NUMBER(Limit)||
        '. You must change your database password before then. '
  from DBA_USERS, DBA_PROFILES
 where DBA_USERS.Account_Status = 'EXPIRED(GRACE)'
   and DBA_USERS.Profile = DBA_PROFILES.Profile
```

```
and DBA_PROFILES.Resource_Name = 'PASSWORD_GRACE_TIME'
and DBA_PROFILES.Limit not in ('UNLIMITED', 'DEFAULT')
```

There are three different possible values for the PASSWORD_GRACE_TIME parameter: a value (such as 10), 'UNLIMITED,' and 'DEFAULT.' It is not helpful to set a PASSWORD_LIFE_TIME value while leaving the PASSWORD_GRACE_TIME setting at 'UNLIMITED,' since the user would never be required to change his or her password. If you set PASSWORD_LIFE_TIME, you should also set PASSWORD_GRACE_TIME.

PROGRAMMER'S NOTE *Once your account status has changed to 'EXPIRED' or 'EXPIRED(GRACE),' changing the profile's parameters does not affect your status—you will still need to change your password.*

alterpwd.sql

Facilitate Password Changes

If you use the password expiration facilities introduced with ORACLE8, then you need to give users a simple way to alter their passwords. Most users are not familiar with the syntax of the **alter user** command, nor should they be expected to be. In ORACLE8, ORACLE introduced a new SQL*Plus command, **password**, that mimics the password-changing interface used by operating systems such as UNIX. However, your end users may never log into SQL*Plus, thus removing the **password** command from the list of viable solutions for your users. If your users only use client-server applications, how can they easily change their passwords?

The script in this section solves that problem by creating a stored procedure called CHANGE_MY_PASSWORD. The only parameter for the procedure is the new password for the user. You can execute this stored procedure from within your application the same way you execute other stored procedures for your application. Thus, your users do not have to know the syntax for the **alter user** or **password** commands; they only need to provide the new password. For example, you may create a front-end form for a client-server application to prompt the user for a new password and then automatically execute the CHANGE_MY_PASSWORD procedure.

The CHANGE_MY_PASSWORD procedure executes the **alter user** command, which is a DDL command. In order to execute a DDL command via PL/SQL, you need to use dynamic SQL.

PROGRAMMER'S NOTE *See Appendix A for a discussion of the structures and options for dynamic SQL.*

The CHANGE_MY_PASSWORD procedure will only change the password for the current user; the User pseudocolumn provides the username value to the procedure. The alterpwd.sql script that creates the CHANGE_MY_PASSWORD procedure is shown in the following listing.

```
create or replace procedure CHANGE_MY_PASSWORD(NewPass IN VARCHAR2) AS
    Cursor_Name INTEGER;
    String VARCHAR2(100);
    cursor USERNAME_CURSOR is
       select User from DUAL;
    UserNm VARCHAR2(32);
BEGIN
   open USERNAME_CURSOR;
   fetch USERNAME_CURSOR into UserNm;
   close USERNAME_CURSOR;
   String:= 'alter user '||UserNm||' identified by '||NewPass ;
   Cursor_Name := DBMS_SQL.OPEN_CURSOR;
   DBMS_SQL.PARSE(Cursor_Name, String, dbms_sql.Native);
   DBMS_SQL.CLOSE_CURSOR(Cursor_Name);
END;
/
```

When you execute the CHANGE_MY_PASSWORD procedure, you pass the new password value as shown in the following example execution.

```
execute CHANGE_MY_PASSWORD('myn3wp');
```

If your password passes the password management criteria defined by the profile established for your account, ORACLE will respond to that command with the following message:

```
PL/SQL procedure successfully completed.
```

ANNOTATIONS

The alterpwd.sql script creates a stored procedure called CHANGE_MY_PASSWORD. See Appendix A for coverage of the syntax and privileges used to create stored procedures. In this procedure, there is only one parameter—the new password, defined via the VARCHAR2 datatype.

```
create or replace procedure CHANGE_MY_PASSWORD(NewPass IN VARCHAR2) AS
```

The next section of the procedure declares the variables used by the procedure. The first two variables, *Cursor_Name* and *String*, are used by the dynamic SQL portion of the procedure. The USERNAME_CURSOR cursor and the *UserNm* variable provide the information needed to properly construct the **alter user** command that the dynamic SQL will execute.

```
    Cursor_Name INTEGER;
    String VARCHAR2(100);
    cursor USERNAME_CURSOR is
```

```
   select User from DUAL;
 UserNm VARCHAR2(32);
```

The next section of the procedure, shown in the following listing, is the Executable Commands section of the script. The first set of commands opens the USERNAME_CURSOR cursor and selects the current username into the *UserNm* variable.

```
BEGIN
  open USERNAME_CURSOR;
  fetch USERNAME_CURSOR into UserNm;
  close USERNAME_CURSOR;
```

The next set of commands builds and executes the **alter user** command. In the first line, the SQL *UserNm* and *NewPass* variables are concatenated with character strings to form the **alter user** command. In the second line, a cursor is opened. The third line, the PARSE command, parses the **alter user** command. Since the **alter user** command is a DDL command, ORACLE automatically executes the command when it parses it.

```
  String:= 'alter user '||UserNm||' identified by '||NewPass ;
  Cursor_Name := DBMS_SQL.OPEN_CURSOR;
  DBMS_SQL.PARSE(Cursor_Name, String, dbms_sql.Native);
  DBMS_SQL.CLOSE_CURSOR(Cursor_Name);
END;
/
```

If the command was a DML command (such as an **insert**) instead of a DDL command, then you would have needed to execute the cursor immediately after parsing it. In the Declarations section, you would need to declare a variable to hold the number of records processed by the cursor:

```
Ret  INTEGER;
```

In the Executable Commands section, you would need to add the following command after the PARSE step to execute the cursor:

```
Ret := DBMS_SQL.EXECUTE(Cursor_Name);
```

When you execute the **alter user** command, ORACLE attempts to change the user's password to the new password. You can use the password management features introduced with ORACLE8 to enforce your security standards on users' passwords. For example, you can set a minimum length for passwords, and you can prevent users from reusing the same password within a given time period. If you use the password management features and the user's new password fails the criteria you have established, then the execution of the CHANGE_MY_PASSWORD procedure will fail with an error. See Chapter 7 for details and scripts related to password complexity management.

The CHANGE_MY_PASSWORD procedure is loosely based on the ANYSTRING procedure. The ANYSTRING procedure, shown in Appendix A and in the following listing, takes any DML or DDL command as its input. The ANYSTRING procedure uses the procedures provided with the DBMS_SQL package to execute dynamic SQL statements.

```
create or replace procedure ANYSTRING(String IN VARCHAR2) AS
    Cursor_Name INTEGER;
    Ret INTEGER;
BEGIN
    Cursor_Name := DBMS_SQL.OPEN_CURSOR;
    DBMS_SQL.PARSE(Cursor_Name, String, dbms_sql.Native);
    Ret := DBMS_SQL.EXECUTE(Cursor_Name);
    DBMS_SQL.CLOSE_CURSOR(Cursor_Name);
END;
/
```

Since you can execute any SQL command by executing the ANYSTRING procedure, you can pass a complete **alter user** command to ANYSTRING in order to change a user's password. For a full description of the use of the DBMS_SQL package, see Appendix A.

part_dis.sql

Display Data Distribution Across Table Partitions

As of ORACLE8, you can use *partitions* to create physically separate sections of data within a table or index. When you create a *partitioned table*, you specify the maximum value for a *partition key* for each partition. When you store a row in the partitioned table, ORACLE compares the partition key column's value to the ranges specified for the partitions. The row will be stored in one of the table's partitions, as determined by the value ranges defined for the partition key. By storing the data in partitions, you may simplify your database administration since the partitions will be smaller than a single table containing all of the partitions' data.

For example, if you have partitioned your table on time-based criteria, then you may store all of the records for 1999 in one partition and all of the records for 2000 in a separate partition. Since the data is stored in two separate segments, you may find those segments easier to manage than if the data had been stored in a single segment. If you use partitions, you can also take advantage of the ability to perform DDL operations such as **truncate** and **alter index rebuild** on the partitions.

You must select your partition range values with care. You should monitor the distribution of data values across your table's partitions. If the table's data distribution does not match your expectations, then you should consider altering the partition key ranges for the partitions. If the data values in your partitions are unevenly distributed, then you may achieve only limited performance and administrative improvements from the use of partitions.

For this section, consider a table named WORKER. The **create table** command for the WORKER table is shown in the following listing.

```
create table WORKER (
Name            VARCHAR2(25),
Age             NUMBER,
Lodging         VARCHAR2(15),
constraint      WORKER_PK PRIMARY KEY(Name)
)
partition by range (Name)
 (partition PART1    values less than ('F'),
  partition PART2    values less than ('N'),
  partition PART3    values less than ('T'),
  partition PART4    values less than (MAXVALUE));
```

The WORKER table is partitioned based on the Name column. Names that begin with the letters "A" through "E" are stored in the partition called "PART1," names beginning "F" through "M" are stored in partition "PART2," names beginning "N" through "S" are stored in partition "PART3," and the rest of the names are stored in partition "PART4." The Name column is the partition key, so its value determines where each row is physically stored.

For this example, sample records were inserted into each table. The WORKER table was then **analyze**d:

```
analyze table WORKER compute statistics;
```

PROGRAMMER'S NOTE   *You can* **analyze** *individual partitions. By default, all partitions of a table will be analyzed when you analyze a partitioned table.*

The part_dis.sql script, shown in the following listing, graphically displays the distribution of rows across partitions.

```
column Percent_of_Total format A60
column Partition_Name format A10
column High_Value format A8

select Partition_Name,
       High_Value,
       LPAD('o',100*DTP.Num_Rows/DBA_TABLES.Num_Rows-1,'o')
         Percent_of_Total
  from DBA_TAB_PARTITIONS DTP, DBA_TABLES
```

```
where DBA_TABLES.Table_Name = '&table_name'
  and DBA_TABLES.Owner = '&owner'
  and DBA_TABLES.Table_Name = DTP.Table_Name
  and DBA_TABLES.Owner = DTP.Table_Owner
order by Partition_Position;
```

Sample output for the WORKER table is shown in the following listing.

```
PARTITION_  HIGH_VAL PERCENT_OF_TOTAL
----------  -------- -------------------------------------------------
PART1       'F'      ooooooooooooooooooooooooooooooooooooooooooooooooooo
PART2       'N'      oooooooooo
PART3       'T'      ooooooooooooooooooooooooooooooo
PART4       MAXVALUE oooo
```

The output graphically shows the distribution of rows across the partitions of the WORKER table. The PART1 partition, with a high value of 'F,' contains the most rows, followed by PART3. The actual percentage values are not shown in this display, since the part_dis.sql script is intended to provide a quick visual report of the data distribution. In the Annotations section you will see additional ways to display the data.

Since the sample data is distributed unevenly, you may wish to alter the partitioning rules used to create the table. You can use the partition-related clauses of the **alter table** command to modify partition ranges and add new partitions.

ANNOTATIONS

The part_dis.sql script uses the **LPAD** function to create a string of 'o' characters. In the part_dis.sql script, a partition's percentage of the total number of rows determines the number of 'o' characters displayed. If a partition accounts for 50 percent of the rows in a table, then its record will contain 50 'o' characters.

The expression that generates the 'o' characters is:

```
LPAD('o',100*DTP.Num_Rows/DBA_TABLES.Num_Rows-1,'o')
    Percent_of_Total
```

The number of rows in the partition (DTP.Num_Rows) divided by the number of rows in the table (DBA_TABLES.Num_Rows) is multiplied by 100 to determine the number of 'o' characters to print. Since one additional 'o' is always printed at the end, 1 is subtracted from the calculated percentage. If you add additional columns to the query, then you will need to shorten the graphical part of the output. For example, you could cut the space required for the graphics in half by changing 100 to 50:

```
     LPAD('o',50*DTP.Num_Rows/DBA_TABLES.Num_Rows-1,'o')
          Percent_of_Total
```

although doing so will result in a graph that does not accurately show differences across partitions whose row volumes are very similar.

In addition to showing the row percentages graphically, you can select them by querying the Num_Rows values directly from the DBA_TAB_PARTITIONS data dictionary view. You can display the partitions across the page instead of down the page by creating a cross-tab report, as shown in the following listing. The cross-tab method requires you to know the names of the partitions; for this example the partition names for the WORKER table are used.

```
select SUM(DECODE(Partition_Name, 'PART1', Num_Rows, 0)) Part1,
       SUM(DECODE(Partition_Name, 'PART2', Num_Rows, 0)) Part2,
       SUM(DECODE(Partition_Name, 'PART3', Num_Rows, 0)) Part3,
       SUM(DECODE(Partition_Name, 'PART4', Num_Rows, 0)) Part4
  from DBA_TAB_PARTITIONS
 where Table_Name = '&table_name'
   and Table_Owner = '&table_owner';
```

Sample output is shown in the following listing.

```
PART1      PART2      PART3      PART4
---------- ---------- ---------- ----------
      9216       2048       5120       1024
```

In the query, the Num_Rows values in DBA_TAB_PARTITIONS are summed. For the PART1 column of the query, any DBA_TAB_PARTITIONS row with a Partition_Name other than 'PART1' has its Num_Rows value replaced by 0:

```
select SUM(DECODE(Partition_Name, 'PART1', Num_Rows, 0)) Part1,
```

The same operation is performed on each partition name, resulting in the cross-tab report.

part_idi.sql

Display Data Distribution Across Index Partitions

ORACLE supports two types of indexes on partitioned tables. A *local* index has a one-to-one relationship to a partition. For the example WORKER table, a local index would have four partitions, each matching one of the table's partitions. The data distribution among the local indexes would match the data distribution among the table partitions.

A *global* index spans the entire partitioned table. For example, an index on the Lodging column of the WORKER table could contain values from all four partitions. To complicate matters further, you can partition a global index. You can create the index on the Lodging column with multiple index partitions, in which case the distribution of data values in the index's partitions would not match the distribution of values in the table's partitions.

For example, the following command creates an index on the Lodging column of the WORKER table created in the previous section. The index has two partitions: one for values less than 'N' and a second for all other values.

```
create index WORKER_LODGING
    on WORKER(Lodging)
global partition by range (Lodging)
(partition IPART1 values less than ('N'),
 partition IPART2 values less than (MAXVALUE));
```

The following query selects the index partitioning data from DBA_IND_PARTITIONS and statistical data from DBA_INDEXES. Like the query of the table partition ranges, this query generates a graphical display of the distribution of values across your index partitions.

PROGRAMMER'S NOTE   *Prior to running this script, you must **analyze** the global index to populate the statistics columns queried by the script.*

```
column Percent_of_Total format A60
column Partition_Name format A10
column High_Value format A8

select Partition_Name,
       High_Value,
       LPAD('o',50*DIP.Num_Rows/DBA_INDEXES.Num_Rows-1,'o')
         Percent_of_Total
  from DBA_IND_PARTITIONS DIP, DBA_INDEXES
 where DBA_INDEXES.Index_Name = '&index_name'
   and DBA_INDEXES.Owner = '&owner'
   and DBA_INDEXES.Index_Name = DIP.Index_Name
   and DBA_INDEXES.Owner = DIP.Index_Owner
 order by Partition_Position;
```

Sample output is shown in the following listing.

```
PARTITION_ HIGH_VAL PERCENT_OF_TOTAL
---------- -------- ------------------------------------------------------------

IPART1     'N'
IPART2     MAXVALUE ooooooooooooooooooooooooooooooooooooooooooooooooooooooooooooo
```

As this output shows, the IPART2 partition contains all of the Lodging values. Given this distribution, partitioning the index has not helped you from either a performance or administrative standpoint.

ANNOTATIONS

Since partition ranges are set when tables and indexes are created, the ranges are based on estimates of the data distribution. You should therefore periodically evaluate the actual distribution of values to make sure the estimates used at creation time accurately reflect the actual data distribution.

Like the part_dis.sql script in the previous section, the part_idi.sql script relies on the statistics generated by executing the **analyze** command. You may **analyze** an index without analyzing the table it indexes. If the index is partitioned, then you can **analyze** all partitions or only specific partitions of the index. You can create a partitioned global index on a nonpartitioned table.

The part_idi.sql script, shown in the following listing, retrieves statistics about the index partition from DBA_IND_PARTITIONS and compares them to statistics from DBA_INDEXES.

```
column Percent_of_Total format A60
column Partition_Name format A10
column High_Value format A8

select Partition_Name,
       High_Value,
       LPAD('o',50*DIP.Num_Rows/DBA_INDEXES.Num_Rows-1,'o')
         Percent_of_Total
  from DBA_IND_PARTITIONS DIP, DBA_INDEXES
 where DBA_INDEXES.Index_Name = '&index_name'
   and DBA_INDEXES.Owner = '&owner'
   and DBA_INDEXES.Index_Name = DIP.Index_Name
   and DBA_INDEXES.Owner = DIP.Index_Owner
 order by Partition_Position;
```

The LPAD expression, shown in the following listing, generates the line of 'o' characters representing the percentage of the index's rows found in the index partition.

```
       LPAD('o',50*DIP.Num_Rows/DBA_INDEXES.Num_Rows-1,'o')
         Percent_of_Total
```

In this example, a multiplier of 50 is used instead of 100 in order to reduce the space requirements of the output; every 2 percent is represented by one 'o' character in the output.

You can use the output of the part_dis.sql and part_idi.sql scripts to determine if your actual space usage and data distribution mirror your expected values. In Chapter 6, you will see additional scripts related to the evaluation of current space usage and future space needs.

Scripts for Managing Performance

T o tune an application, you need to first understand how the application's environment works. For example, is the application making the best use of the available shared memory areas in the System Global Area (SGA)? Is the shared SQL area large enough? How much of the SGA is going unused? Once you verify that the environment is functioning properly for a well-performing system, you can then focus on tuning individual queries that are experiencing performance problems.

In this chapter, you will see scripts that allow you to verify the performance of the application. Many of the queries focus on the usage of specific shared memory areas, allowing you to pinpoint potential environmental causes of performance problems. At the end of this chapter, you will see how to generate explain plans to help evaluate the performance of specific queries.

The major scripts presented in this chapter are:

sgasize.sql	Overall SGA size
hitr.sql	Data block buffer hit ratio
hitr_thr.sql	Data block buffer hit ratio, with threshold
hitr_usr.sql	Data block buffer hit ratio, by user
buff_usg.sql	Buffer usage within the SGA
hitrpool.sql	Shared SQL area hit ratio
pool_str.sql	Shared SQL area structures
poolstat.sql	Shared SQL area user statistics
obj_spac.sql	Estimate space usage by shared SQL objects
log_bufs.sql	Log buffers size
multblck.sql	Multiblock read count setting
enq_res.sql	Enqueue resources setting
fts_larg.sql	Full table scans of large tables
disksort.sql	In-memory vs disk sorts
pqo_stat.sql	Check parallel query server processes status
redocopy.sql	Check for contention on redo copy latches
mts_stat.sql	Multithreaded server statistics
dbwrstat.sql	Database writer/wait statistics
fileio.sql	Datafile I/O distribution
params.sql	Show parameter setttings
gen_stat.sql	General statistics
explain.sql	Show explain plan for a query

When tuning an application, you should be aware of the growth rates for the objects used by the application. If the application's tables grow quickly—or if some of its tables grow far more quickly than the rest of its tables—then you will need to schedule regular performance tuning checks, using the diagnostic and utility scripts provided in this chapter.

In evaluating the performance of the database environment, the scripts in this chapter examine:

◆ The SGA—including the data block buffers, the shared SQL area, the redo log buffers, and latches

◆ The use of large table scans and temporary segments

◆ The use of the multithreaded server (MTS)

◆ The parallel query server process usage

◆ The distribution of I/O among datafiles

Once you have evaluated your environment with the scripts provided in this chapter, you will be able to test the impact of any environmental changes you make. For example, if you change the size of the sort area, you could check to see whether the percentage of sorts performed in memory has increased following the change. The impact of all environmental changes on the database and on the server and operating system should be monitored.

PROGRAMMER'S NOTE   *Except where noted, the scripts can be run from any user account with DBA privileges.*

sgasize.sql

LOOKING INSIDE THE SGA

The database structure with the greatest performance impact is the SGA. The SGA allows multiple users to share data within memory, avoiding the need to physically access data from disks repeatedly. As the Oracle RDBMS products and options grow in complexity, the types of objects shared via the SGA increase in number. For example, the SGA may share data blocks, rollback segment blocks, SQL statements, and multithreaded server information. If the SGA is well tuned for your application, the database's memory usage may be eliminated as a cause of potential performance problems.

You can query V$SGA to see the size of the SGA, as shown in the following listing.

```
REM    SGA Size
REM
select *
 from V$SGA;
```

Sample output from V$SGA is shown in the following listing. The output shows the size of the different areas within the SGA.

NAME	VALUE
Fixed Size	38904

```
Variable Size              10313056
Database Buffers           10240000
Redo Buffers                  16384
```

As shown in the V$SGA query output, the database has 10,240,000 bytes dedicated to its database block buffer cache (the "Database Buffers" line). The redo log buffer cache (the "Redo Buffers" line) is 16,384 bytes in size. The shared SQL area is the chief component of the "Variable Size" of the SGA, which accounts for 10,313,056 bytes in the example.

The SGA sizing information is also available from within Server Manager. In the following example, the **svrmgrl** command is used to access the line mode interface of Server Manager. The **show sga** command retrieves data from V$SGA, and adds a "Total" line to show the total memory area required by the SGA.

```
svrmgrl
SVRMGR> connect internal
SVRMGR> show sga
Total System Global Area    20608344 bytes
Fixed Size                     38904 bytes
Variable Size               10313056 bytes
Database Buffers            10240000 bytes
Redo Buffers                   16384 bytes
```

In general, increasing the size of the SGA will improve the performance of your database environment. The size of the SGA is usually 2 percent of the size of the total allocated datafile space for the database. The hit ratio calculations shown in the next section will allow you to measure the performance impact as you increase the size of the SGA. However, the SGA should not be so large that it causes swapping and paging to occur at the operating system level. The queries of the shared SQL area shown later in this chapter will help you to identify whether there is unused space within the SGA that can be made available to the operating system.

The Hit Ratio

hitr.sql
hitr_thr.sql

The data block buffer cache of the SGA stores blocks of data as users issue requests. The blocks of data stay in memory so that future requests for the same data by any user can be resolved without requiring the datafile containing the data to be accessed. The data block buffer cache is limited in size, so a least recently used (LRU) algorithm is used to manage the contents of the cache. When more space is needed within the data block buffer cache, the least recently used blocks are removed from the cache and replaced with the new blocks. If the data block buffer cache is too small, then requests for data blocks will result in a low *hit ratio—the percentage of time a data block request is satisfied by data already in the data block buffer cache. A low hit ratio indicates that your database is not using the data block buffer cache effectively, and performance will suffer.*

If you know the hit ratio for the data block buffer cache, you can estimate the adequacy of the data block buffer cache's size for the application. The threshold values indicating acceptable performance vary by type of application:

◆ For OLTP (online transaction processing) applications, in which many users execute small transactions, the hit ratio should be at least 98 percent. The target hit ratio is artificially high because it is inflated by the database activity associated with index-based accesses common to OLTP applications.

◆ For batch applications, in which few users execute large transactions, the hit ratio should be at least 89 percent.

If the hit ratio is below your target values, then you should examine the database environment to determine if the size of the data block buffer cache should be increased. After changing the size of the database block buffer cache, you should test the impact of the change on the hit ratio.

The following queries allow you to measure the hit ratio for the data block buffer cache, either alone or against a threshold value. The queries reference the V$SYSSTAT dynamic performance statistics table. Since the statistics in V$SYSSTAT are cumulative, the results will show the cumulative hit ratio since the database was last started. Since the data block buffer cache is initially empty at database startup, the first queries will require physical data accesses, thereby initially lowering the cache's hit ratio. Although system startup will have an effect on the data block buffer cache hit ratio, the effect is usually negligible over time.

```
REM   Data Block Buffer Cache Hit Ratio
REM
REM   target minimum: 89%.   (98% for OLTP applications.)
REM
select
   SUM(DECODE(Name, 'consistent gets',Value,0)) Consistent,
   SUM(DECODE(Name, 'db block gets',Value,0)) Dbblockgets,
   SUM(DECODE(Name, 'physical reads',Value,0)) Physrds,
   ROUND(((SUM(DECODE(Name, 'consistent gets', Value, 0))+
    SUM(DECODE(Name, 'db block gets', Value, 0)) -
    SUM(DECODE(Name, 'physical reads', Value, 0)) )/
   (SUM(DECODE(Name, 'consistent gets',Value,0))+
    SUM(DECODE(Name, 'db block gets', Value, 0)))) *100,2)
      HitRatio
 from V$SYSSTAT;
```

The query in the preceding listing determines the data block buffer cache hit ratio by selecting three values from V$SYSSTAT. The statistics for consistent gets and db block gets, added together, give the total number of logical reads (requests for rows or blocks) for the database. The physical reads statistic reflects the number of times the database had to perform a physical read of a datafile in order to satisfy the logical read request. If the data is already in the data block buffer cache, then no physical read is required.

The first three columns selected by the query are the consistent gets, db block gets, and physical reads statistics from V$SYSSTAT:

```
select
    SUM(DECODE(Name, 'consistent gets',Value,0)) Consistent,
    SUM(DECODE(Name, 'db block gets',Value,0)) Dbblockgets,
    SUM(DECODE(Name, 'physical reads',Value,0)) Physrds,
```

The hit ratio is determined by subtracting the number of physical reads from the number of logical reads, and dividing the difference by the number of logical reads. To determine the hit ratio, the statistics for the consistent gets and db block gets are added together, and are compared to the physical reads statistic. The result is rounded to two decimal places via the **ROUND** function.

```
ROUND(((SUM(DECODE(Name, 'consistent gets', Value, 0))+
SUM(DECODE(Name, 'db block gets', Value, 0)) -
SUM(DECODE(Name, 'physical reads', Value, 0)) )/
(SUM(DECODE(Name, 'consistent gets',Value,0))+
    SUM(DECODE(Name, 'db block gets', Value, 0)))) *100,2)
        HitRatio
```

The higher the hit ratio, the greater the number of logical reads resolved by data already in memory. The following listing shows sample output from the hit ratio query, for an OLTP application.

```
CONSISTENT DBBLOCKGETS    PHYSRDS   HITRATIO
---------- -----------  ---------- ----------
   1208863        1179        8826      99.27
```

As shown in the output listing, the database has performed over 1.2 million logical reads. The logical reads required only 8,826 physical reads in order to be satisfied. Since this is a cumulative hit ratio, it reflects the physical reads needed since the database was first started. The hit ratio, 99.27, is above the target hit ratio of 98 percent used for OLTP applications, so it is not necessary to increase the size of the data block buffer cache.

You can use the number of logical reads to compare the relative activity level of the database at different times. For example, you could monitor changes in the number of logical reads after increasing the number of users or adding a new module to an application.

There are two primary causes of data block buffer cache hit ratios below your target value: either the cache is too small or the application's queries do not take advantage of indexes. You can increase the size of the data block buffer cache by increasing the value of the DB_BLOCK_BUFFERS parameter in the database's init.ora file and performing an instance shutdown/restart. The DB_BLOCK_BUFFERS parameter is expressed in term of database blocks, so if you change the database block size (the DB_BLOCK_SIZE parameter) during a database rebuild, then you will need to change the DB_BLOCK_BUFFERS parameter. For example, if you increase the DB_BLOCK_SIZE from 2,048 to 4,096, your data block buffer cache will double in size unless you halve the DB_BLOCK_BUFFERS parameter.

If your data block buffer cache hit ratio is below your target value, you should first try to increase the size of the cache. If increasing the size of the data block buffer cache has no impact on the hit ratio, then you should examine the longest-running queries to determine whether they have been properly optimized.

The data block buffer cache hit ratio query can be modified to only return a record if the hit ratio is below a specified threshold. In the following listing, a variable (*&threshold*) is used; the user will be prompted to enter a value for the threshold. If the hit ratio is below the threshold, a record will be returned. If the hit ratio is above the threshold, no record will be returned.

```
REM  Data Block Buffer Cache Hit Ratio, with Threshold
REM
select
   SUM(DECODE(Name, 'consistent gets',Value,0)) Consistent,
   SUM(DECODE(Name, 'db block gets',Value,0)) Dbblockgets,
   SUM(DECODE(Name, 'physical reads',Value,0)) Physrds,
   ROUND(((SUM(DECODE(Name, 'consistent gets', Value, 0))+
    SUM(DECODE(Name, 'db block gets', Value, 0)) -
    SUM(DECODE(Name, 'physical reads', Value, 0)) )/
    (SUM(DECODE(Name, 'consistent gets',Value,0))+
    SUM(DECODE(Name, 'db block gets', Value, 0)))) *100,2)
      HitRatio
  from V$SYSSTAT
having ROUND(((SUM(DECODE(Name, 'consistent gets', Value, 0))+
   SUM(DECODE(Name, 'db block gets', Value, 0)) -
   SUM(DECODE(Name, 'physical reads', Value, 0)) )/
    (SUM(DECODE(Name, 'consistent gets',Value,0))+
    SUM(DECODE(Name, 'db block gets', Value, 0)))) *100,2)
     < &threshold;
```

In order to add the threshold check to the hit ratio query, the following clause was added to the query:

```
having ROUND(((SUM(DECODE(Name, 'consistent gets', Value, 0))+
   SUM(DECODE(Name, 'db block gets', Value, 0)) -
   SUM(DECODE(Name, 'physical reads', Value, 0)) )/
```

```
(SUM(DECODE(Name, 'consistent gets',Value,0))+
 SUM(DECODE(Name, 'db block gets', Value, 0)))) *100,2)
  < &threshold;
```

The **having** clause in the preceding query calculates the hit ratio via the same calculation used in the query, and compares that result to the user-specified value (*&threshold*).

When evaluating a below-threshold hit ratio, it is often useful to determine the hit ratio for each current user's data requests. In the next section, you will see how to calculate the hit ratio for users who are currently logged into the database.

Hit Ratio by User

htr_usr.sql

In order to identify which users are having the greatest negative or positive impact on the overall hit ratio, you can query V$SESS_IO. The query output will show the hit ratio per user as well as the number of logical and physical reads per user. The number of logical reads per user allows you to quickly judge which users are the most active users in the database. If the overall hit ratio is below your target value, you should look for very active users who have hit ratios below your target value.

PROGRAMMER'S NOTE

The following query will only show hit ratio information for users who are currently logged into the database. If a user is no longer logged into the database, the user's session will have no entry in V$SESS_IO, and therefore will not be reported via this query.

```
REM  Hit Ratio by User
REM
column HitRatio format 999.99
select Username,
       Consistent_Gets,
       Block_Gets,
       Physical_Reads,
       100*(Consistent_Gets+Block_Gets-Physical_Reads)/
           (Consistent_Gets+Block_Gets) HitRatio
  from V$SESSION, V$SESS_IO
 where V$SESSION.SID = V$SESS_IO.SID
   and (Consistent_Gets+Block_Gets)>0
   and Username is not null;
```

The preceding query selects data from V$SESSION and V$SESS_IO. V$SESS_IO contains columns named Consistent_Gets, Block_Gets, and Physical_Reads, making this query of hit ratio information simpler than the query in the previous section.

The user's hit ratio is calculated in the same manner as the overall hit ratio was calculated. The number of physical reads is subtracted from the number of logical reads (Consistent_Gets+Block_Gets) and the difference is divided by the number of logical reads:

```
100*(Consistent_Gets+Block_Gets-Physical_Reads)/
        (Consistent_Gets+Block_Gets) HitRatio
```

Two limiting conditions are placed on records returned by the query. The first condition eliminates from the result set all users who have not performed any logical reads. This limiting condition prevents the result set from containing many entries for users who are not contributing to the overall database hit ratio.

```
and (Consistent_Gets+Block_Gets)>0
```

The second limiting condition eliminates from the result set any user who has a Null value for Username. This limiting condition prevents the ORACLE server background processes from being listed in the query's result set.

```
and Username is not null;
```

The following listing shows sample output from the query for an OLTP application.

USERNAME	CONSISTENT_GETS	BLOCK_GETS	PHYSICAL_READS	HITRATIO
SYSTEM	214	8	9	95.95
APPL_MAINT	1232681	66	4669	99.62
OPS$APPL_1	28	8	0	100.00
APPL1_MAINT2	5687	4	53	99.07
APPL1_MAINT2	29677	20	49	99.84

The results shown in the preceding listing are consistent with the overall system hit ratio calculated in the previous section. Every user—except for SYSTEM—has a hit ratio that exceeds the target 98 percent hit ratio. The user with the highest number of physical reads also has the highest number of logical reads, and a high hit ratio.

If your users can perform ad hoc queries against your application, then you may see hit ratio by user output that resembles the following listing.

USERNAME	CONSISTENT_GETS	BLOCK_GETS	PHYSICAL_READS	HITRATIO
SYSTEM	214	8	9	95.95
APPL_MAINT	1232681	66	4669	99.62
OPS$APPL_1	28	8	0	100.00
APPL1_MAINT2	5687	4	53	99.07
APPL1_MAINT2	29677	20	49	99.84
USER_ADHOC	200000	50	100000	50.01

In the revised listing, the user named USER_ADHOC has a hit ratio well below the target hit ratio for the database. The high number of physical reads used by this user will adversely affect the overall data block buffer cache hit ratio. This query output allows you to determine which users are causing the greatest negative impact on your data block buffer cache hit ratio. In this example, you should work with the USER_ADHOC user to determine which queries are causing the observed system usage. It is very likely that the user is not using indexes during the query, either because of the query syntax or because of the lack of an available index. Having isolated the problem, you can then begin to address it specifically, while the rest of the database environment is left unchanged.

You could use a threshold value to limit the query set to only those sessions whose hit ratios fall below your target value, but that may not give you an accurate picture of your database. If you eliminate sessions based on their hit ratio, you may not see sessions which account for the majority of the logical and physical reads in the database (and therefore have the greatest impact on the overall hit ratio).

buff_usg.sql

Buffer Usage Within the SGA

The data block buffer cache is used to share different types of blocks. For example, when a table is read by a user, the table's blocks are stored in the data block buffer cache. If the table is accessed via an index, then the relevant index blocks are also read into the data block buffer cache. If the table's records are changed, then the rollback segment's blocks are stored in the data block buffer cache as well, so that other queries using the data can reconstruct the data as it existed prior to the start of the transaction.

At any time, the data block buffer cache contains several different types of blocks. If you know the number of each type of block currently stored in the data block buffer cache, then you can measure the impact of increasing the size of the cache. You can also use this information to measure the impact of large transactions (with their associated rollback segment blocks) on the data block buffer cache.

The following query lists each type of buffer stored in the data block buffer cache, based on data in the SYS.X$BH table. The query should be run while logged into the database as the SYS user or in Server Manager, connect internal. Only four classes of blocks—Data, Sort, Header, and Rollback—are reported via this query.

```
REM   Number of each type of buffer in the SGA
REM
column Class format A10
select DECODE(GREATEST(Class,10),10,
         DECODE(Class,1,'Data',2,'Sort',4,'Header',
         TO_CHAR(Class)),'Rollback') Class,
         SUM(DECODE(BITAND(Flag,1),1,0,1)) NotDirty,
         SUM(DECODE(BITAND(Flag,1),1,1,0)) Dirty,
```

```
            SUM(Dirty_Queue) OnDirtyQ, count(*) Total
  from X$BH
 where Class in (1,2,4,10)
 group by DECODE(GREATEST(Class,10),10,
       DECODE(Class,1,'Data',2,'Sort',4,'Header',
       TO_CHAR(Class)),'Rollback')
/
```

The following listing shows the query output for a small database. Of the four classes checked by the query, there are three present in the data block buffer cache. There are no Sort blocks (associated with sorting operations) in the data block buffer cache in the example database. There are 54 header blocks (such as table header blocks and rollback segment header blocks) and 10 rollback segment data blocks.

CLASS	NOTDIRTY	DIRTY	ONDIRTYQ	TOTAL
Data	1209	6	0	1215
Header	54	0	0	54
Rollback	10	0	0	10

In the preceding listing, there are references to blocks that are "not dirty," "dirty," and "on the dirty queue." A *dirty block* is one that has changed since being read into memory. Thus, of the 1215 data blocks in memory, 6 of them are dirty. The *dirty queue* is a list of dirty blocks to be written to the datafiles. If there are not enough DBWR (database writer process) I/O slave processes in use in your database, then you will see non-zero values for the dirty queue count throughout the application's usage. You can then increase the number of DBWR I/O slave processes by setting or changing the DB_WRITERS (ORACLE7) or DBWR_IO_SLAVES (ORACLE8) init.ora parameter and stopping and restarting your database.

hitrpool.sql

Shared SQL Area Hit Ratio

The shared SQL area stores several different caches in memory. The shared structures include the library cache (which caches information about database objects such as stored procedures and views) and the cursor cache that caches SQL statements. In a multithreaded server (MTS) configuration, the shared SQL area is used to store session-specific information such as the context area and the sort area. You need to verify that the shared SQL area is being accessed in an effective manner, with a high hit ratio for accesses to its entries.

The shared SQL area can consume a large amount of memory. In applications that make use of stored procedures or the MTS, the shared SQL area may be larger than the data block buffer cache. The demand on the shared SQL area is directly dependent on the breadth of your application. OLTP applications require more shared memory than batch-oriented applications, because there are more users executing more distinct transactions. Aggravating the memory requirements for shared SQL area is the implementation of stored procedures, packages, triggers, and even views in the shared memory.

In this section and the sections that follow, you will see scripts that help you determine whether your shared SQL area is being used effectively. You can use the scripts in these sections to determine the size of the memory area used by individual objects as well as the proper sizing of the shared SQL area.

In the following script, the shared SQL area hit ratio is calculated; like the database block buffer cache, the shared SQL area is fixed in size and is managed by an LRU algorithm. The shared SQL area hit ratio reflects the number of times a statement is parsed and stored in memory (*pinned*), compared to the number of times the statement has been aged out of memory and must be re-parsed (*reloaded*). If the shared SQL area is not large enough, then previously parsed statements will have to be continually reloaded. If the shared SQL area is large enough, then the shared SQL area hit ratio, as calculated by the following script, will continually be over 99 percent. The script also calculates the *miss ratio*, which is the percentage of time a statement had to be reloaded into the shared SQL area.

```
REM   Shared SQL Area Hit Ratio
REM   Target:  Hit Ratio > 99 percent.
REM
column Miss_Ratio format 999.99
column Hit_Ratio format 999.99
select
    SUM(Pins) Execs,
    SUM(Reloads) Cache_Misses,
    DECODE(SUM(Pins),0,0,(SUM(Reloads)/SUM(Pins))*100)
      Miss_Ratio,
    DECODE(SUM(Pins),0,0,((SUM(Pins)-SUM(Reloads))/SUM(Pins))*100)
      Hit_Ratio
from V$LIBRARYCACHE;
```

Sample output from the shared SQL area hit ratio query is shown in the following listing. The Execs column shows the number of times a SQL statement was executed. The Cache_Misses column shows the number of times a needed statement was no longer in the shared SQL area.

```
    EXECS CACHE_MISSES MISS_RATIO HIT_RATIO
--------- ------------ ---------- ---------
     8436           10        .12     99.88
```

The Execs column value is based on the Pins column value in the V$LIBRARYCACHE dynamic performance view. The Cache_Misses value is taken from the Reloads column of V$LIBRARYCACHE. The Pins and Reloads columns are used to generate the shared SQL area hit ratio:

```
DECODE(SUM(Pins),0,0,((SUM(Pins)-SUM(Reloads))/SUM(Pins))*100)
    Hit_Ratio
```

To calculate the hit ratio, the number of Pins is first checked. If there have been 0 pins, then the shared SQL area hit ratio is 0. Next, the number of Reloads is subtracted from the number of Pins, and the difference is divided by the number of Pins. The result is the hit ratio for the shared SQL area.

In the sample data shown in the prior listing, the shared SQL area hit ratio was 99.88. If the shared SQL area hit ratio is below 99 percent (or the Miss_Ratio value exceeds 1.0), then you should increase the size of the shared SQL area. The size of the shared SQL area is controlled via the SHARED_POOL_SIZE parameter in the init.ora file. Changes to the SHARED_POOL_SIZE value (expressed in bytes) in the init.ora file take effect when the database is shut down and restarted. After changing the shared SQL area size, check the new hit ratio. When increasing SHARED_POOL_SIZE, make sure the increase in SGA size does not cause swapping or paging to occur at the operating system level.

PROGRAMMER'S NOTE   *The shared SQL area uses the LRU algorithm to manage the statements within the library cache. The most recently used statements are placed at the bottom of the LRU list and are kept the longest within the shared SQL area. To improve the performance of the shared SQL area, you can pin frequently used packages in the library cache. A pinned package is immediately placed at the bottom of the LRU list, thus staying longer within the shared SQL area.*

pool_str.sql

Shared Pool Structures

Just as you can query the database for information about the internals of the SGA, you can query it for information about the structures within the shared SQL area. The script in this section will show information on the total allocated and used space within the shared SQL area, as well as the number of statements currently stored in the library cache.

In this example, a different programming style is introduced. The data needed by the script is stored in many different tables and views. In order to present the data in a unified fashion, data is read via multiple queries. As data is retrieved from a query, the value returned is stored in a variable via the **new_value** option of the SQL*Plus **column** command. Once all of the variables have had values assigned to them, a final query is executed to present the results in a unified fashion.

Following the script, you will see a sample data listing, followed by an annotated walk-through of the script.

```
REM   Shared Pool Structures
REM
set pagesize 60 heading off termout off echo off verify off
ttitle off
REM
REM  The results from each query are assigned to
REM    variables via the new_value column option.
REM
col val1 new_val x_sp_size noprint
select Value val1
  from V$PARAMETER
 where Name='shared_pool_size'
/

col val2 new_val x_sp_used noprint
select SUM(Sharable_Mem+Persistent_Mem+Runtime_Mem) val2
  from V$SQLAREA
/

col val3 new_val x_sp_used_shr noprint
col val4 new_val x_sp_used_per noprint
col val5 new_val x_sp_used_run noprint
col val6 new_val x_sp_no_stmts noprint
select SUM(Sharable_Mem) val3,
       SUM(Persistent_Mem) val4,
       SUM(Runtime_Mem) val5,
       COUNT(*) val6
  from V$SQLAREA
/

col val7 new_val x_sp_no_obj noprint
select COUNT(*) val7
  from V$DB_OBJECT_CACHE
/

col val8 new_val x_sp_avail noprint
select &x_sp_size-&x_sp_used val8
  from DUAL
/

col val9 new_val x_sp_no_pins noprint
select COUNT(*) val9
  from V$SESSION A, V$SQLTEXT B
```

```
where A.SQL_Address||A.SQL_Hash_Value = B.Address||B.Hash_Value
/

col val10 new_val x_sp_sz_pins noprint
select SUM(Sharable_Mem+Persistent_Mem+Runtime_Mem) val10
  from V$SESSION A,
       V$SQLTEXT B,
       V$SQLAREA C
 where A.SQL_Address||A.SQL_Hash_Value =
         B.Address||B.Hash_Value
   and B.Address||B.Hash_Value = C.Address||C.Hash_Value
/

set termout on
ttitle -
  center   'Shared Pool Library Cache Information' skip 2

select  'Size                                              : '
  ||&x_sp_size sp_size,
        'Used (total)                                      : '
  ||&x_sp_used,
        '         sharable                                 : '
  ||&x_sp_used_shr sp_used_shr,
        '         persistent                               : '
  ||&x_sp_used_per sp_used_per,
        '         runtime                                  : '
  ||&x_sp_used_run sp_used_run,
        'Available                                         : '
  ||&x_sp_avail sp_avail,
        'Number of SQL statements                          : '
  ||&x_sp_no_stmts sp_no_stmts,
        'Number of programmatic constructs                 : '
  ||&x_sp_no_obj sp_no_obj,
        'Pinned statements                                 : '
  ||&x_sp_no_pins sp_no_pins,
        'Pinned statements size                            : '
  ||&x_sp_sz_pins sp_sz_pins
  from DUAL
/
```

Sample output from the script is shown in the following listing, followed by output interpretation and an annotated walk-through of the script.

```
                    Shared Pool Library Cache Information


Size                                       : 8000000
Used (total)                               : 6022354
     sharable                              : 4465514
     persistent                            : 221624
     runtime                               : 1335216
Available                                  : 1977646
Number of SQL statements                   : 253
Number of programmatic constructs           : 211
Pinned statements                          : 9
Pinned statements size                     : 400628
```

The script output shows that for the example database, the shared SQL area is 8,000,000 bytes in size (as set via the SHARED_POOL_SIZE parameter in the init.ora file). Of that area, 1,977,646 bytes are available and the rest is used. Of the 253 SQL statements that have been parsed into the shared SQL area, 9 statements have been pinned.

ANNOTATIONS

The shared SQL area structures script uses a unique method of assigning variables and generating a unified presentation of the disconnected data. Because of its structure, the script is easy to customize and enhance.

The first section of the script establishes the system settings needed by the script. The **set verify off** command is critical, since it suppresses the writing of "before" and "after" value information each time a variable is assigned a value. The **set termout off echo off** will suppress the display of the intermediate queries which generate the variable values. You should also turn **ttitle off** at this point, or else the report title will be displayed for each query that is executed.

```
REM   Shared Pool Structures
REM
set pagesize 60 heading off termout off echo off verify off
ttitle off
REM
```

In the next section, the first query is executed, and its variable is assigned. In the first query, the V$PARAMETER view is queried for the Value setting for the SHARED_POOL_SIZE init.ora parameter. In the query, the Value column is given an alias of Val1. Because of the **column** command that precedes the query, the value of Val1 is assigned to the variable named *X_SP_SIZE*. The *X_SP_SIZE* variable will be used in the final query of the script.

```
REM
REM   The results from each query are assigned to
REM    variables via the new_value column option.
REM
col val1 new_val x_sp_size noprint
select Value val1
  from V$PARAMETER
 where Name='shared_pool_size'
/
```

In the next part of the script, the same technique is used to store data from the V$SQLAREA view in the *X_SP_USED* variable.

```
col val2 new_val x_sp_used noprint
select SUM(Sharable_Mem+Persistent_Mem+Runtime_Mem) val2
  from V$SQLAREA
/
```

The next part of the script, shown in the following listing, provides greater detail about the memory usage in the shared SQL area. Four variables are assigned, for use in the final query.

```
col val3 new_val x_sp_used_shr noprint
col val4 new_val x_sp_used_per noprint
col val5 new_val x_sp_used_run noprint
col val6 new_val x_sp_no_stmts noprint
select SUM(Sharable_Mem) val3,
       SUM(Persistent_Mem) val4,
       SUM(Runtime_Mem) val5,
       COUNT(*) val6
  from V$SQLAREA
/
```

In the next listing, the number of objects in the shared SQL area is queried from V$DB_OBJECT_CACHE. As with the previous queries, the result is stored in a variable for future use. The variable columns are marked as **noprint** via the **column** command so that no results from intermediate queries will be displayed to the user; only the final query's results will be displayed to the user.

```
col val7 new_val x_sp_no_obj noprint
select COUNT(*) val7
  from V$DB_OBJECT_CACHE
/
```

In the next section, a variable is assigned based on the difference between two previously defined variable values. The SYS.DUAL table (a one-row, one-column table) is used to generate the output. The difference between the two variables will be calculated, and the result will be assigned to a new variable, *X_SP_AVAIL*.

```
col val8 new_val x_sp_avail noprint
select &x_sp_size-&x_sp_used val8
  from DUAL
/
```

In the next section, the number of pinned objects is determined by querying V$SESSION, V$SQLTEXT, and V$SQLAREA.

```
col val9 new_val x_sp_no_pins noprint
select COUNT(*) val9
  from V$SESSION A, V$SQLTEXT B
 where A.SQL_Address||A.SQL_Hash_Value = B.Address||B.Hash_Value
/

col val10 new_val x_sp_sz_pins noprint
select SUM(Sharable_Mem+Persistent_Mem+Runtime_Mem) val12
  from V$SESSION A,
       V$SQLTEXT B,
       V$SQLAREA C
 where A.SQL_Address||A.SQL_Hash_Value =
         B.Address||B.Hash_Value
   and B.Address||B.Hash_Value = C.Address||C.Hash_Value
/
```

At this point in the script processing, all of the variables have had values assigned to them. The final query selects text strings from DUAL, followed by the variables. In the output, the values of the variables will be shown, as seen in the sample output listing repeated following the final query.

Before the final query is executed, the **set termout on** and **ttitle** commands are executed so that data will be displayed and the report will be properly titled.

```
set termout on
ttitle -
  center  'Shared Pool Library Cache Information' skip 2

select  'Size                                     : '
  ||&x_sp_size sp_size,
        'Used (total)                             : '
  ||&x_sp_used,
        '          sharable                       : '
  ||&x_sp_used_shr sp_used_shr,
        '          persistent                     : '
  ||&x_sp_used_per sp_used_per,
        '          runtime                        : '
  ||&x_sp_used_run sp_used_run,
        'Available                                : '
```

```
   ||&x_sp_avail sp_avail,
         'Number of SQL statements                    : '
   ||&x_sp_no_stmts sp_no_stmts,
         'Number of programmatic constructs           : '
   ||&x_sp_no_obj sp_no_obj,
         'Pinned statements                           : '
   ||&x_sp_no_pins sp_no_pins,
         'Pinned statements size                      : '
   ||&x_sp_sz_pins sp_sz_pins
   from DUAL
/
```

The sample output does not show the result of any of the interim queries. It shows a single, unified set of data generated by queries of many different views and tables. Because it involves so many queries, it may take longer for this script to complete than a script containing only one query.

```
       Shared Pool Library Cache Information


Size                                : 8000000
Used (total)                        : 6022354
      sharable                      : 4465514
      persistent                    : 221624
      runtime                       : 1335216
Available                           : 1977646
Number of SQL statements            : 253
Number of programmatic constructs    : 211
Pinned statements                   : 9
Pinned statements size              : 400628
```

If the Available value is small, or shrinks over time, increase the SHARED_POOL_SIZE init.ora parameter and stop and restart the database.

poolstat.sql

Shared SQL Area User Statistics

In the previous sections, you have seen how to measure how well the shared SQL area is being used (via its hit ratio) and how many statements are stored in the shared SQL area. In addition to that information, you can also determine the number of times statements have been executed, and the number of users per statement. This additional information may be useful in measuring the impact of changes to the size of your shared SQL area. For example, you can monitor changes in the number of users per statement as the shared SQL area increases, showing measurable benefit from the increase in the available area.

The output of the following script contains three main sections: the data block buffer cache hit ratio, the shared SQL area hit ratio, and the user information for the shared SQL area. Although the hit ratios were shown in previous sections, they are repeated here to provide context to the user statistics.

The script is a set of queries, using the variable assignment technique described in the "Shared Pool Structures" section. The script will be shown in its entirety, followed by sample output and an annotated walk-through.

```
REM  Shared SQL area user statistics
REM
clear columns
set pagesize 60 heading off termout off echo off verify off
ttitle off
REM
col val1 new_val lib noprint
select 100*(1-(SUM(Reloads)/SUM(Pins))) val1
  from V$LIBRARYCACHE
/

col val2 new_val dict noprint
select 100*(1-(SUM(Getmisses)/SUM(Gets))) val2
  from V$ROWCACHE
/

col val3 new_val phys_reads noprint
select Value val3
  from V$SYSSTAT
 where Name = 'physical reads'
/

col val4 new_val log1_reads noprint
select Value val4
  from V$SYSSTAT
 where Name = 'db block gets'
/

col val5 new_val log2_reads noprint
select Value val5
  from V$SYSSTAT
 where Name = 'consistent gets'
/

col val6 new_val chr noprint
```

```
select 100*(1-(&phys_reads / (&log1_reads + &log2_reads))) val6
  from DUAL
/

col val7 new_val avg_users_cursor noprint
col val8 new_val avg_stmts_exe    noprint
select SUM(Users_Opening)/COUNT(*) val7,
       SUM(Executions)/COUNT(*)    val8
  from V$SQLAREA
/

set termout on
set heading off
ttitle -
  center  'SGA Cache Hit Ratios' skip 2

select  'Data Block Buffer Hit Ratio : '||&chr db_hit_ratio,
        '   Shared SQL Pool                        ',
        '   Dictionary Hit Ratio      : '||&dict dict_hit,
        '   Shared SQL Buffers (Library Cache)          ',
        '     Cache Hit Ratio          : '||&lib lib_hit,
        '     Avg. Users/Stmt        : '||
            &avg_users_cursor||'          ',
        '     Avg. Executes/Stmt     : '||
            &avg_stmts_exe||'          '
  from DUAL
/
```

Sample output from the script is shown in the following listing.

```
                        SGA Cache Hit Ratios

Data Block Buffer Hit Ratio : 99.6101479
  Shared SQL Pool
  Dictionary Hit Ratio      : 98.5751095
  Shared SQL Buffers (Library Cache)
    Cache Hit Ratio          : 99.906068
    Avg. Users/Stmt        : .010791367
    Avg. Executes/Stmt     : 10.7230216
```

The sample output shows the data block buffer cache hit ratio, followed by the hit ratios for the dictionary cache and library cache portions of the shared SQL area.

The average number of users per statement shows that an average user executes 100 statements. Each statement is executed an average of 10.7 times.

The *dictionary cache* stores information about the objects used by queries. For example, a query of a table requires the data dictionary information for the table, its indexes, its columns, and any relevant table-level or column-level privileges. The data dictionary information required by the query is stored in the dictionary cache portion of the shared SQL area. You cannot size the dictionary cache; it is automatically created as part of the shared SQL area. If the dictionary cache hit ratio is below 98 percent, you should check the library cache hit ratio to determine if you need to increase the size of the shared SQL area. In the example database, the library cache hit ratio is very high (99.9 percent), so you do not need to increase the size of the shared SQL area.

ANNOTATIONS

The shared SQL area user statistics script uses the variable assignment technique described in the "Shared Pool Structures" section. In the header of the script, the script's settings are established. The **set verify off** command is used to suppress information displays each time a variable has a value assigned to it. The **set termout off echo off** command suppresses the display of the interim queries.

```
REM   Shared SQL area user statistics
REM
clear columns
set pagesize 60 heading off termout off echo off verify off
ttitle off
REM
```

In the next section of the report, a series of queries is executed. As the queries are executed, the **new_value** option of the **column** command is used to assign the retrieved value to a variable. The **noprint** option of the **column** command prevents the data from being displayed to the user at this point; no data is displayed until the final report is generated.

The first two queries generate the library cache hit ratio and the dictionary cache hit ratio.

```
col val1 new_val lib noprint
select 100*(1-(SUM(Reloads)/SUM(Pins))) val1
   from V$LIBRARYCACHE
/

col val2 new_val dict noprint
select 100*(1-(SUM(Getmisses)/SUM(Gets))) val2
   from V$ROWCACHE
/
```

The next series of queries is used to determine the data block buffer cache hit ratio. The logical reads statistics (consistent gets and db block gets) and physical reads statistics are used to calculate the overall data block buffer cache hit ratio. This series of queries is an alternative to the single-query method shown in "The Hit Ratio" at the beginning of this chapter.

```
col val3 new_val phys_reads noprint
select Value val3
  from V$SYSSTAT
 where Name = 'physical reads'
/


col val4 new_val log1_reads noprint
select Value val4
  from V$SYSSTAT
 where Name = 'db block gets'
/


col val5 new_val log2_reads noprint
select Value val5
  from V$SYSSTAT
 where Name = 'consistent gets'
/


col val6 new_val chr noprint
select 100*(1-(&phys_reads / (&log1_reads + &log2_reads))) val6
  from DUAL
/
```

The final series of queries compares the number of users and executions to the number of statements in the V$SQLAREA view. The result will show the average number of users per statement and executions per statement.

```
col val7 new_val avg_users_cursor noprint
col val8 new_val avg_stmts_exe    noprint
select SUM(Users_Opening)/COUNT(*) val7,
       SUM(Executions)/COUNT(*)     val8
  from V$SQLAREA
/
```

Once all of the variables have had values assigned to them via the queries, the final query of the script selects the variables' values and formats them into a unified output.

```
set termout on
set heading off
ttitle -
```

```
 center   'SGA Cache Hit Ratios' skip 2

select   'Data Block Buffer Hit Ratio : '||&chr db_hit_ratio,
         '  Shared SQL Pool                        ',
         '  Dictionary Hit Ratio        : '||&dict dict_hit,
         '  Shared SQL Buffers (Library Cache)                  ',
         '    Cache Hit Ratio           : '||&lib lib_hit,
         '    Avg. Users/Stmt           : '||
               &avg_users_cursor||'              ',
         '    Avg. Executes/Stmt        : '||
               &avg_stmts_exe||'              '
   from DUAL
/
```

The output from the script is shown in the following listing. You can customize the report by adding or removing queries. For each new query, assign its output a unique column name, and use the **new_value** option of the **column** command to assign the result to a variable. Once the value has been assigned to a variable, you can use the variable in the unified report.

```
                      SGA Cache Hit Ratios

Data Block Buffer Hit Ratio : 99.6101479
  Shared SQL Pool
  Dictionary Hit Ratio        : 98.5751095
  Shared SQL Buffers (Library Cache)
    Cache Hit Ratio           : 99.906068
    Avg. Users/Stmt           : .010791367
    Avg. Executes/Stmt        : 10.7230216
```

obj_spac.sql

Estimate Space Usage by Shared SQL Objects

In addition to determining the hit ratios of the SGA's caches, you can measure how much of the shared pool is currently in use. The following script measures the amount of space used by objects within the shared SQL area and estimates the space required by the multithreaded server processes.

The script gathers data from many different views via a set of queries. In previous examples, the query results were read into SQL*Plus variables and later reported via unified queries. In this script, PL/SQL is used to manage the variables. The queries are executed within a PL/SQL block and the query results are stored in PL/SQL variables. At the end of the script, the values are displayed via the DBMS_OUTPUT package.

The script is shown in the following listing, followed by sample output and an annotated walk-through of the script.

```
REM  Space Usage for shared SQL objects
REM If running MTS uncomment the mts calculation and output
REM commands.
REM
set echo off
set termout on
set serveroutput on;

declare
        object_mem number;
        shared_sql number;
        cursor_mem number;
        mts_mem number;
        used_pool_size number;
        free_mem number;
        pool_size varchar2(512);
begin

-- Stored objects (packages, views)
select SUM(Sharable_Mem) into object_mem
  from V$DB_OBJECT_CACHE;

-- Shared SQL -- need to have additional memory if dynamic SQL used
select SUM(Sharable_Mem) into shared_sql
  from V$SQLAREA;

-- User Cursor Usage -- run this during peak usage.
--   assumes 250 bytes per open cursor, for each concurrent user.
select SUM(250*Users_Opening) into cursor_mem
  from V$SQLAREA;

-- For a test system -- get usage for one user, multiply by # users
-- select (250 * Value) bytes_per_user
-- from V$SESSTAT S, V$STATNAME N
-- where S.Statistic# = N.Statistic#
-- and N.Name = 'opened cursors current'
-- and S.SID = 25;   -- where 25 is the sid of the process

-- MTS memory needed to hold session information for shared server users
-- This query computes a total for all currently logged on users
-- (run during peak period). Alternatively calculate for a single
```

```
--  user and multiply by # users.
select SUM(Value) into mts_mem
  from V$SESSTAT S, V$STATNAME N
 where S.Statistic#=N.Statistic#
   and N.Name='session uga memory max';

-- Free (unused) memory in the SGA: gives an indication of how much
-- memory is being wasted out of the total allocated.
select Bytes into free_mem
  from V$SGASTAT
 where Name = 'free memory';

-- For non-MTS add up object, shared sql, cursors and 20% overhead.
used_pool_size := ROUND(1.2*(object_mem+shared_sql+cursor_mem));

-- For MTS mts contribution needs to be included (comment out
-- previous line)
-- used_pool_size  :=
-- ROUND(1.2*(object_mem+shared_sql+cursor_mem+mts_mem));
select Value into pool_size
  from V$PARAMETER
 where Name='shared_pool_size';

-- Display results
DBMS_OUTPUT.PUT_LINE ('Object mem:      '||TO_CHAR (object_mem) || ' bytes');
DBMS_OUTPUT.PUT_LINE ('Shared SQL:      '||TO_CHAR (shared_sql) || ' bytes');
DBMS_OUTPUT.PUT_LINE ('Cursors:         '||TO_CHAR (cursor_mem) || ' bytes');
-- DBMS_OUTPUT.PUT_LINE ('MTS session:     '||TO_CHAR (mts_mem) || ' bytes');
DBMS_OUTPUT.PUT_LINE ('Free memory:     '||TO_CHAR (free_mem) || ' bytes ' ||
'('    || TO_CHAR(ROUND(free_mem/1024/1024,2)) || 'MB)');
DBMS_OUTPUT.PUT_LINE ('Shared pool utilization (total):  '||
TO_CHAR(used_pool_size) || ' bytes ' || '(' ||
TO_CHAR(round(used_pool_size/1024/1024,2)) || 'MB)');
DBMS_OUTPUT.PUT_LINE ('Shared pool allocation (actual):  '|| pool_size
```

```
||' bytes ' || '(' || TO_CHAR(ROUND(pool_size/1024/1024,2)) ||'MB)');
DBMS_OUTPUT.PUT_LINE ('Percentage Utilized:  '||to_char
(ROUND(used_pool_size/pool_size*100)) || '%');
end;
/
```

Sample output from the query (with the MTS data displayed) is shown in the following listing. If you do not enable the MTS query output (see the "Annotations" section), the "MTS session" line will not be displayed in the output.

```
Object mem:     610546 bytes
Shared SQL:     2951830 bytes
Cursors:        1250 bytes
MTS session:    611376 bytes
Free memory:    1209000 bytes (1.15MB)
Shared pool utilization (total):  5010002 bytes (4.78MB)
Shared pool allocation (actual):  8000000 bytes (7.63MB)
Percentage Utilized:  63%

PL/SQL procedure successfully completed.
```

The query output shows that for this database, only 63% of the shared SQL area is utilized. The MTS session information is second in size to only the library cache (the "Shared SQL" value). In systems that make extensive use of the MTS, the memory area required by the MTS session information may exceed the size of the library cache.

ANNOTATIONS

By default, several sections of the script are not executed. You should customize the script to reflect your database's structure and usage, as described in the following comments. To see the most relevant output, the script should be run during a time of peak usage in the database; the views it queries are sensitive to the number of active users in the database at the time the script is executed.

In the first section of the script, the variables used to hold the query results are defined. The variables will be referenced twice more in the script: when they are populated via queries and when their values are displayed at the end of the script.

```
declare
        object_mem number;
        shared_sql number;
        cursor_mem number;
```

```
mts_mem number;
used_pool_size number;
free_mem number;
pool_size varchar2(512);
```

In the next section of the script, the PL/SQL block starts and the first query is executed.

```
begin

-- Stored objects (packages, views)
select SUM(Sharable_Mem) into object_mem
   from V$DB_OBJECT_CACHE;
```

The result of the preceding query is assigned to the *object_mem* variable via the query's **into** clause. The *object_mem* variable stores the amount of memory used by objects in the shared SQL area's library cache. In the next query, the memory required by shared SQL is calculated. If dynamic SQL—available as of ORACLE7.1—is used in your application, the amount of space used by shared SQL may increase dramatically.

```
-- Shared SQL -- need to have additional memory if dynamic SQL used
select SUM(Sharable_Mem) into shared_sql
   from V$SQLAREA;
```

The next section of the script attempts to estimate the memory area used by cursors. The query assumes that an average cursor requires 250 bytes. If you run the query during peak usage of the application, then you will be able to see the maximum amount of space required by the cursors.

The commented-out query in this section allows you to estimate the cursor usage more accurately, but the query should not be run as part of this script. The query determines the number of cursors opened by a particular user, and uses that to estimate the space usage, in bytes, of the cursors used by that user. You can then estimate the total cursor memory used for all of your users. Run this query on a test system, using the V$SESSTAT.SID for a typical user process.

```
-- User Cursor Usage -- run this during peak usage.
--   assumes 250 bytes per open cursor, for each concurrent user.
select SUM(250*Users_Opening) into cursor_mem
   from V$SQLAREA;

-- For a test system -- get usage for one user, multiply by # users
-- select (250 * Value) bytes_per_user
-- from V$SESSTAT S, V$STATNAME N
-- where S.Statistic# = N.Statistic#
```

```
-- and N.Name = 'opened cursors current'
-- and S.SID = 25;   -- where 25 is the sid of the process
```

In the next section of the script, the MTS memory statistics are queried to determine the amount of memory used to hold MTS user session information.

```
-- MTS memory needed to hold session information for shared server users
-- This query computes a total for all currently logged on users
-- (run during peak period). Alternatively calculate for a single user
-- and multiply by # users.
select SUM(Value) into mts_mem
  from V$SESSTAT S, V$STATNAME N
 where S.Statistic#=N.Statistic#
   and N.Name='session uga memory max';
```

In the next query in the script, the V$SGASTAT view is queried to determine the amount of unused memory within the SGA. Since the SGA is allocated when the database is started, unused ("free") memory is wasted—no other applications can use that memory, and the database is not using it. If you persistently have large portions of your SGA marked as free memory, then you should examine whether the memory can be better used for your application. For example, you may wish to reclaim space from the shared SQL area and make that memory available to the data block buffer cache or log buffer cache. Alternatively, you may decide to reduce the size of your SGA, allowing user processes to access more memory directly. If you manipulate the size of your SGA, you should run this script periodically to verify the used and unused space measures for the database.

```
-- Free (unused) memory in the SGA: gives an indication of how much
-- memory is being wasted out of the total allocated.
select Bytes into free_mem
  from V$SGASTAT
 where Name = 'free memory';
```

The next section of the script needs to be modified, depending on whether or not you are using MTS. If you are using MTS, then the first assignment of a value to the *used_pool_size* variable should be commented out by adding two dashes (--) to the front of the line, and the comment marks should be removed from the second assignment of the variable.

For databases using MTS, this section of the script should read:

```
-- For non-MTS add up object, shared sql, cursors and 20% overhead.
-- used_pool_size := ROUND(1.2*(object_mem+shared_sql+cursor_mem));
```

```
-- For MTS mts contribution needs to be included (comment out
-- previous line)
used_pool_size :=
-- ROUND(1.2*(object_mem+shared_sql+cursor_mem+mts_mem));
select Value into pool_size
  from V$PARAMETER
 where Name='shared_pool_size';
```

For databases that are not using MTS, this section of the script should be modified, as shown in the following listing. For both the MTS and non-MTS calculation, 20 percent overhead is added to the memory requirements estimates. The 20 percent overhead estimate may be high for systems with a small number of users, and may result in report output showing that you are using more memory than you have allocated.

```
-- For non-MTS add up object, shared sql, cursors and 20% overhead.
used_pool_size := ROUND(1.2*(object_mem+shared_sql+cursor_mem));

-- For MTS mts contribution needs to be included (comment out
-- previous line)
-- used_pool_size :=
-- ROUND(1.2*(object_mem+shared_sql+cursor_mem+mts_mem));
select Value into pool_size from V$PARAMETER
 where Name='shared_pool_size';
```

Now that all of the variable assignments are complete, the report output is generated via the DBMS_OUTPUT package. Each line is created via the PUT_LINE procedure of the DBMS_OUTPUT package, and the PL/SQL block is ended.

One of the output lines is commented out. If you are using MTS, then you should remove the comment marks that precede the output showing the 'MTS session' output.

```
-- Display results
DBMS_OUTPUT.PUT_LINE ('Object mem:    '||TO_CHAR (object_mem) || ' bytes');
DBMS_OUTPUT.PUT_LINE ('Shared SQL:    '||TO_CHAR (shared_sql) || ' bytes');
DBMS_OUTPUT.PUT_LINE ('Cursors:       '||TO_CHAR (cursor_mem) || ' bytes');
-- DBMS_OUTPUT.PUT_LINE ('MTS session:   '||TO_CHAR (mts_mem) || ' bytes');
DBMS_OUTPUT.PUT_LINE ('Free memory:   '||TO_CHAR (free_mem) || ' bytes ' ||
 '('  || TO_CHAR(ROUND(free_mem/1024/1024,2)) || 'MB)');
DBMS_OUTPUT.PUT_LINE ('Shared pool utilization (total):  '||
TO_CHAR(used_pool_size) || ' bytes ' || '(' ||
```

```
TO_CHAR(ROUND(used_pool_size/1024/1024,2)) || 'MB)');
DBMS_OUTPUT.PUT_LINE ('Shared pool allocation (actual): '|| pool_size
|| ' bytes ' || '(' || TO_CHAR(ROUND(pool_size/1024/1024,2)) || 'MB)');
DBMS_OUTPUT.PUT_LINE ('Percentage Utilized: '||TO_CHAR
(ROUND(used_pool_size/pool_size*100)) || '%');
end;
/
```

If you modify the size of your SGA, you should use this script to determine if the amount of free space within the SGA changes. If your 'Percentage Utilized' value reaches 100 percent, you should check the data block buffer cache hit ratio and the library cache hit ratio to determine which could benefit the most from increased available memory.

log_bufs.sql

Log Buffer Cache Size

The *log buffer cache* is the portion of the SGA used to store records of transactions before the transaction information is written to the online redo log files. The size of the log buffer cache is set (in bytes) via the LOG_BUFFER parameter in the database's init.ora file.

Records are written from the log buffer cache to the online redo log files on a timed basis. Every few seconds, the log writer (LGWR) background process reads the data from the log buffer cache and writes the data to the online redo log files. If the log buffer is not large enough to hold the data from the ongoing transactions, the transactions will be delayed by the wait for space in the log buffer cache. Because the log buffer cache entries provide a chronological history of the transactions in the database, an LRU algorithm cannot be used to manage the cache. If the log buffer cache is full, incoming transactions must wait.

You can determine the number of waits for log buffer cache space by querying V$SYSSTAT. You should compare the number of waits to the size of the log buffer cache, as shown in the following example.

```
REM  Log Buffer Size - check for redo log space requests
REM
column log_buffer_size format A20
select A.Value  Log_Buffer_Size,
       B.Value  Log_Buffer_Space_Waits
  from V$PARAMETER A, V$SYSSTAT B
 where A.Name = 'log_buffer'
   and B.Name = 'redo log space requests';
```

Sample output from the preceding query is shown in the following listing.

```
LOG_BUFFER_SIZE        LOG_BUFFER_SPACE_WAITS
--------------------   ----------------------
327680                                     33
```

The output shows that for the sample database, the log buffer is 327,680 bytes in size. There were 33 waits for space in the log buffer cache. It is difficult to completely eliminate log buffer space waits; you should monitor your database activity to establish a threshold value for log buffer cache space waits.

The following version of the script adds a threshold value check to the query. When the script is executed, the user will be prompted for a threshold value for the redo log space requests. A record will only be returned if the number of redo log space requests exceeds the threshold value.

```
REM   Log Buffer Size - with threshold
REM
column log_buffer_size format A20
select A.Value   Log_Buffer_Size,
       B.Value   Log_Buffer_Space_Waits
  from V$PARAMETER A, V$SYSSTAT B
 where A.Name = 'log_buffer'
   and B.Name = 'redo log space requests'
   and B.Value > &threshold;
```

multblck.sql

Multiblock Read Setting

When a table is scanned via a TABLE ACCESS FULL operation, multiple blocks are read during each read from the table. The number of blocks read at a time is determined by the setting of the DB_FILE_MULTIBLOCK_READ_COUNT parameter in the database's init.ora file. Multiblock reads only affect full table scans; table accesses by RowID and index accesses are not affected.

When they are read into the data block buffer cache, the blocks read via a full table scan are automatically marked as the least recently used blocks in the cache (unless the table is marked as a "cache" table, or if the table is five or fewer blocks in size). Thus, as the table is scanned, the blocks read via the full table scan occupy very little space within the SGA. The space occupied by the full table scan blocks is equal to the product of the database block size and the multiblock read count setting.

For example, if the database block size is 4KB, and DB_FILE_MULTIBLOCK_READ_COUNT is set to eight, then 32KB (eight 4KB blocks) is read during each database read, and 32KB within the data block buffer cache is used by the scan. When data from the second read arrives at the data block buffer cache, the blocks read via the first read are removed from the cache and replaced with the blocks from the second read. Thus, although you may be performing a large full table scan, the majority of your data block buffer cache is unaffected; only 32KB of the data block buffer cache is used. The rest of the data block buffer cache will not be overwritten by the data read via the full table scan, and the ability to share commonly used data among users via the data block buffer cache will not be impacted.

Setting your DB_FILE_MULTIBLOCK_READ_COUNT parameter to a higher value will improve the performance of the full table scan, since more data will be read during each read of the table. However, increasing the multiblock read count parameter will increase the impact of full table scans on the data block buffer cache—the temporary holding area for the table scan blocks will grow in size. Thus, setting the DB_FILE_MULTIBLOCK_READ_COUNT parameter involves balancing the performance of the full table scans against the use of the rest of the data block buffer cache.

If your application is an OLTP application, with many users executing small transactions, you should try to minimize the impact of full table scans on the database. If your application is a batch application, with few users executing large transactions, then you may increase the multiblock read count to improve the table scan performance without negatively impacting the application as a whole.

In general, you should set the multiblock read count parameter so that a single physical read takes advantage of the buffer used by the operating system during a physical read. For example, if the operating system's read buffer is 64KB in size, then you should start with a multiblock read count that enables 64KB to be buffered per read. That is, if your database block size is 4KB, then your DB_FILE_MULTIBLOCK_READ_COUNT parameter should be set to 16.

The query in the following listing queries V$PARAMETER to determine the current settings for the database block size and the multiblock read count value. The two parameter values are multiplied to determine the amount of data read during each multiblock read. You should compare the output of this query to the size of your operating system's read buffer and the overall space available in the data block buffer cache to determine the adequacy of the setting.

```
REM Multiblock Read Count check
REM
select to_number(v1.Value)*to_number(v2.Value)
    Batch_Read_Size
  from V$PARAMETER V1, V$PARAMETER V2
 where V1.Name = 'db_block_size'
   and V2.Name = 'db_file_multiblock_read_count'
/
```

Sample output from the preceding query is shown in the following listing.

```
BATCH_READ_SIZE
---------------
          65536
```

The batch read size in the listing is expressed in bytes. 65536 bytes is 64KB, which is the size of the operating system's read buffer in the test system.

enq_res.sql

Enqueue Resources

An enqueue resource is needed for every table that is locked by the database lock manager. You need to have enough enqueue resources—as set via the ENQUEUE_RESOURCES parameter in your database's init.ora file—to support the locking requirements of your application. The number of locks on a table is irrelevant; the number of tables locked determines the number of enqueue resources required.

If your application is an OLTP application with many small tables, you will need to increase the default ENQUEUE_RESOURCES setting in order to avoid waiting for resources to become available. Enqueue waits are reported via the V$SYSSTAT dynamic performance view. In the query in the following listing, the ENQUEUE_RESOURCES setting (from V$PARAMETER) is compared to the number of enqueue waits (from V$SYSSTAT).

```
REM   Enqueue_resources - check against enqueue waits
REM
column Enqueue_Resources format A20
select A.Value Enqueue_Resources,
       B.Value Enqueue_Waits
  from V$PARAMETER A, V$SYSSTAT B
 where A.Name = 'enqueue_resources'
   and B.Name = 'enqueue waits';
```

Sample output from the query is shown in the following listing.

```
ENQUEUE_RESOURCES     ENQUEUE_WAITS
--------------------  -------------
520                               0
```

For the test application, 520 enqueue resources were established, with no subsequent enqueue waits. You may therefore choose to decrease the number of enqueue resources allocated to the database. If you decrease the number of available enqueue resources, you should monitor the database for an associated rise in the number of enqueue waits.

ANNOTATIONS

You may wish to add to the query a threshold value as a limiting condition for the number of enqueue waits. Enqueue waits are common, and you can monitor your applications to determine a typical number of waits for your application. If the number of waits exceeds this threshold, then the following query will return a record; if the number of waits is below the threshold, no rows will be returned by the query.

```
REM  Enqueue_resources - with threshold
REM
column Enqueue_Resources format A20
select A.Value Enqueue_Resources,
       B.Value Enqueue_Waits
  from V$PARAMETER A, V$SYSSTAT B
 where A.Name = 'enqueue_resources'
   and B.Name = 'enqueue waits'
   and B.Value > &threshold;
```

Full Table Scans of Large Tables

fts_larg.sql

Full table scans usually indicate that either no indexes are available for the table being queried or the query is written in a manner that prevents the use of indexes. Full table scans of small tables may be efficient data access methods, since the database may be able to read the full table into memory quickly. Full table scans of large tables typically perform worse than comparable index-based accesses of large tables.

PROGRAMMER'S NOTE

In ORACLE7, the Parallel Query Option (PQO) cannot parallelize index scans; therefore, you may have written queries deliberately using full table scans in order to exploit the PQO. If you use the PQO extensively in ORACLE7, you will have a high percentage of full table scans of large tables. As of ORACLE8, the PQO can parallelize index scans. If you have previously modified your queries to use full table scans in order to parallelize them, you should investigate the use of parallelized index scans instead.

The following query determines the percentage of full table scans that are performed on large tables. A "large" table is one that is larger than five database blocks in size. If you have many table scans of large tables, you should evaluate the queries being executed within your application.

```
REM  Full table scans of large tables
REM
select A.Value  Large_Table_Scans,
       B.Value  Small_Table_Scans,
```

```
     ROUND(100*A.Value/
     DECODE((A.Value+B.Value),0,1,(A.Value+B.Value)),2)
         Pct_Large_Scans
 from V$SYSSTAT A, V$SYSSTAT B
where A.Name = 'table scans (long tables)'
  and B.Name = 'table scans (short tables)';
```

Sample output from the query is shown in the following listing.

```
LARGE_TABLE_SCANS SMALL_TABLE_SCANS PCT_LARGE_SCANS
----------------- ----------------- ---------------
              292              5067            5.45
```

The sample output shows that scans of large tables make up over 5 percent of all table scans. Table scans of small tables appear to be very frequently used (over 5,000 times) in the test application.

ANNOTATIONS

You should monitor your databases to determine the acceptable percentage of large full table scans for your applications. If large tables account for over 20 percent of your full table scans, you will typically have a data block buffer cache hit ratio that falls below your target hit ratio. If large tables account for over 10 percent of your full table scans, you should closely examine the queries and processes within your application to determine if queries need to be rewritten or indexes need to be added.

The following query will prompt you for a threshold value for the percentage of full table scans caused by large tables. If the percentage of full table scans that is caused by large tables exceeds the threshold, a record will be returned by the query. If the percentage of table scans caused by large tables is below the threshold, no record will be returned from the query.

```
REM  Full table scans of large tables - with threshold
REM
REM  Can use a threshold value (e.g., 10 for 10 percent)
REM
select A.Value Large_Table_Scans,
       B.Value Small_Table_Scans,
       ROUND(100*A.Value/
       DECODE((A.Value+B.Value),0,1,(A.Value+B.Value)),2)
         Pct_Large_Scans
  from V$SYSSTAT A, V$SYSSTAT B
 where A.Name = 'table scans (long tables)'
   and B.Name = 'table scans (short tables)'
```

```
and ROUND(100*A.Value/
    DECODE((A.Value+B.Value),0,1,(A.Value+B.Value)),2)
        > &threshold;
```

If you use the Parallel Query Option extensively, the threshold-based version of this query will not be as useful for you, since you may be forcing full table scans of large tables to occur.

disksort.sql

Sort Area

Sorting operations—such as index creations or **order by** clauses within queries—require temporary work areas within the database. If possible, the sorting is performed entirely within memory. If not enough memory is available to support the sort's space requirements, a temporary segment is allocated and the sort uses disk space.

Managing the sort area requires balancing two competing objectives. First, you should minimize the amount of sort data written to disk, since writing and reading from disk is much slower than writing and reading from memory. The more sort data you write to disk (via temporary segments), the worse the query may perform. Second, available physical memory is limited, so you don't want to use all of the available memory for sort space. Your objective should be to allocate enough sort area in memory so that most sorts initiated by OLTP users complete within memory, while sorts initiated by long-running batch users employ temporary segments.

The available sort area in memory is set via the SORT_AREA_SIZE parameter in your database's init.ora file. The SORT_AREA_RETAINED_SIZE should be set to a value at or below that of SORT_AREA_SIZE; a low retained size lets users release memory from the sort area after the sort completes.

In the query shown in the following listing, the number of sorts performed in memory is compared to the number of sorts performed via temporary segments. Both statistics are retrieved from V$SYSSTAT, a dynamic performance view that maintains cumulative totals for these statistics.

```
REM   In-memory vs disk sorts
REM
select A.Value Disk_Sorts,
       B.Value Memory_Sorts,
       ROUND(100*A.Value/
       DECODE((A.Value+B.Value),0,1,(A.Value+B.Value)),2)
           Pct_Disk_Sorts
  from V$SYSSTAT A, V$SYSSTAT B
 where A.Name = 'sorts (disk)'
   and B.Name = 'sorts (memory)';
```

Sample output from the query is shown in the following listing.

```
DISK_SORTS MEMORY_SORTS PCT_DISK_SORTS
---------- ------------- --------------
        91         81771            .11
```

The output in the preceding listing shows that disk sorts have almost never been used since the database was last started. The very low percentage of disk sorts is typical for OLTP applications with a high value for SORT_AREA_SIZE. Since the percentage of sorts performed on disk is so low, you may consider reducing SORT_AREA_SIZE and dedicating the saved memory area to the shared SQL area or the data block buffer cache.

ANNOTATIONS

You can establish a threshold percentage of disk sorts to serve as a limiting condition for the query. If the percentage of sorts performed on disk exceeds the threshold, a record will be returned; if it is below the threshold, no record will be returned. The threshold version of the disk sort percentage query is shown in the following listing.

```
REM   In-memory vs disk sorts - with threshold
REM
REM   Specify a threshold percentage, such as 10 for
REM   10 percent disk sorts.
REM
select A.Value Disk_Sorts,
       B.Value Memory_Sorts,
       ROUND(100*A.Value/
       DECODE((A.Value+B.Value),0,1,(A.Value+B.Value)),2)
         Pct_Disk_Sorts
  from V$SYSSTAT A, V$SYSSTAT B
 where A.Name = 'sorts (disk)'
   and B.Name = 'sorts (memory)'
   and ROUND(100*A.Value/
     DECODE((A.Value+B.Value),0,1,(A.Value+B.Value)),2)
          > &threshold;
```

If you are performing more than 10 percent of your sorts on disk, then you should either increase the SORT_AREA_SIZE or evaluate your processes to see if you can eliminate unnecessary sorts. For example, you may be able to replace a **union** operator (which performs a SORT UNIQUE after merging rows from two queries) with a **union all** operator (which does not eliminate duplicates prior to merging the queries' output). The **union** and **union all** operators return different sets of records (**union** eliminates duplicates, **union all** does not), so they are not always interchangeable; however, this is one example of the kind of change that can help reduce sorting requirements.

A high number of sorting operations may indicate a high number of joins performed via the MERGE JOIN operation (which first executes a SORT JOIN on each table in the join). A MERGE JOIN may be used if indexes cannot be used for the join conditions of the query. If indexes can be used, a NESTED LOOPS join may be used instead—eliminating the need for sort area either in memory or on disk.

pqo_stat.sql

Check Parallel Query Server Processes

In order to effectively use the Parallel Query Option (PQO), you need to manage the pool of parallel query server processes available to the database. The number of parallel query server processes started when the database is started is determined by the setting of the PARALLEL_MIN_SERVERS parameter in the database's init.ora file. If you set the minimum number of parallel query server processes too high, you will waste system resources. If you set the minimum number of parallel query server processes too low, you will force the database to continually start new parallel query server processes in order to support the processing requirements.

The maximum number of parallel query server processes that can run simultaneously in your database is determined by the setting of the PARALLEL_MAX_SERVERS parameter in the database's init.ora file. If you set the maximum number of parallel query server processes too high, you will be wasting system resources. If you set the maximum number of parallel query server processes too low for your application, you will reduce the degree to which the application's queries can be parallelized.

Activity involving the parallel query server processes can be seen via queries of V$PQ_SYSSTAT. The queries in this section compare the number of parallel query server processes in use (from V$PQ_SYSSTAT) with the PARALLEL_MIN_SERVERS and PARALLEL_MAX_SERVERS settings.

The first query, shown in the following listing, checks if PARALLEL_MIN_ SERVERS is set too high. The query of V$PQ_SYSSTAT requires you to perform an **RTRIM** function on the Statistic description column; although it is a VARCHAR2 column, it is right-padded with blanks to be 30 characters wide.

```
REM   Are parallel query server processes unused?
REM
column Parallel_Min_Servers format 999999999
select TO_NUMBER(A.Value) Parallel_Min_Servers,
       B.Value Servers_Busy
  from V$PARAMETER A, V$PQ_SYSSTAT B
 where A.Name = 'parallel_min_servers'
   and RTRIM(B.Statistic) = 'Servers Busy';
```

Sample output for the first query is shown in the following listing. According to the output, the minimum number of parallel query server processes started for the database is 20. Of those 20, only 16 are currently in use. If the current usage is typical of the application, then the PARALLEL_MIN_SERVERS parameter may be lowered to 16 without causing the database to dynamically start new parallel query server processes.

```
PARALLEL_MIN_SERVERS SERVERS_BUSY
-------------------- ------------
                  20           16
```

In general, you should set PARALLEL_MIN_SERVERS to a low value, and bear the performance penalty of starting and stopping parallel query server processes. If the minimum number of parallel query server processes is high, then unused processes will remain on your server—and may not release the memory they acquired during their processing. As a result, the server may become flooded with unused processes holding memory that no other users can address.

The second query of the set checks to see whether any parallel query server processes have been started since the database was started and the initial parallel query server processes were created. The 'Servers Started' statistic in V$PQ_SYSSTAT is cumulative, and thus reflects activity that occurred before the current users logged in to the database.

```
REM     Have any servers have been started?
REM
select Statistic, Value Servers_Started
  from V$PQ_SYSSTAT
 where RTRIM(Statistic) = 'Servers Started';
```

Sample output from the second query of the set is shown in the following listing. The query output shows that 472 parallel query server processes have been started since the database was started. Thus, although the current number of busy parallel query server processes is below the initial number of parallel query server processes created (from the first query's output), there have been previous times during which the number of parallel query server processes required exceeded the PARALLEL_MIN_SERVERS setting. When more than the minimum number of parallel query server processes was required by the database, more servers were started—and the 'Servers Started' statistic was incremented, as reflected in the following listing.

```
STATISTIC                       SERVERS_STARTED
------------------------------- ---------------
Servers Started                             472
```

The third query of the set, shown in the following listing, compares the highest number of busy parallel query server processes to the PARALLEL_MAX_SERVERS setting in your database's init.ora file. If the highest number of parallel query server processes ever in use is within 10 percent of the maximum number of parallel query server processes, you may need to consider increasing the PARALLEL_MAX_SERVERS setting. This query refers to the 'Servers Highwater' statistic in V$PQ_SYSSTAT.

```
REM Is Parallel_Max_Servers high enough for current usage?
REM
column Parallel_Max_Servers format 999999999
select TO_NUMBER(A.Value) Parallel_Max_Servers,
       B.Value Servers_HW
  from V$PARAMETER A, V$PQ_SYSSTAT B
 where A.Name = 'parallel_max_servers'
   and RTRIM(B.Statistic) = 'Servers Highwater';
```

Sample output from the third parallel query server process query is shown in the following listing.

```
PARALLEL_MAX_SERVERS    SERVERS_HW
--------------------    ------------
                 160           120
```

As shown in the query output, the highest number of busy parallel query server processes since the database started is 120. The maximum number of parallel query server processes is set to 160. If the current usage of the test database is typical of the application's database activity, then you may be able to decrease the PARALLEL_MAX_SERVERS setting without adversely affecting the application's performance. Decreasing PARALLEL_MAX_SERVERS reduces the potential parallelism of database activities during heavy application usage.

redocopy.sql

Contention for Redo Copy Latches

The *redo allocation latch* serializes the writing of entries to the log buffer cache of the SGA. The redo allocation latch allocates space in the log buffer cache for each transaction's entry. If transactions are small, or if there is only one CPU on the server, then the redo allocation latch also copies the transaction data into the log buffer cache.

If multiple CPUs are available, you can create multiple *redo copy latches*. The redo copy latches will copy transaction data into the log buffer cache, freeing the redo allocation latch from performing this task. You can create multiple redo copy latches (usually up to two times the number of available CPUs). The number of redo copy latches created is set via the LOG_SIMULTANEOUS_COPIES parameter in your database's init.ora file.

If LOG_SIMULTANEOUS_COPIES is set to a non-zero value, the redo allocation latch will check the size of the transaction entry and compare it against other init.ora settings. If the size of the transaction entry is smaller than the value of the LOG_SMALL_ENTRY_MAX_SIZE init.ora parameter, then the copy of the transaction entry into the log buffer cache is performed by the redo allocation latch. If the size of the transaction entry exceeds LOG_SMALL_ENTRY_MAX_SIZE, then the transaction entry is copied into the log buffer cache by a redo copy latch.

The following query determines the miss ratio and the "immediate" miss ratio for redo copy latches. If either miss ratio is greater than 1 percent, you should increase the number of redo copy latches (set LOG_SIMULTANEOUS_COPIES > 0) and decrease the value of the LOG_SMALL_ENTRY_MAX_SIZE parameter.

```
REM   Latch contention check
REM
select SUBSTR(V$LATCH.Name,1,30)  Name,
       (Misses/(Gets+.001))*100 Miss_Ratio,
       (Immediate_Misses/(Immediate_Gets+.001))*100
           Immediate_Miss_Ratio
 from V$LATCH, V$LATCHNAME
where V$LATCH.Latch# = V$LATCHNAME.Latch#
  and V$LATCH.Name = 'redo copy';
```

Sample output from the preceding query is shown in the following listing.

```
NAME                          MISS_RATIO IMMEDIATE_MISS_RATIO
----------------------------- ---------- --------------------
redo copy                     49.9750125          .001483911
```

The query output shows that the redo copy latch has a miss ratio of almost 50 percent. The performance of transactions within the database could be improved (if multiple CPUs are available) by increasing the number of redo copy latches enabled within the database.

mts_stat.sql

Multithreaded Server Statistics

The MTS allows multiple users to share common dispatcher (user process manager) and server (database request manager) processes, thereby reducing the memory requirements per user process. At instance startup, init.ora parameters are used to determine the number of dispatchers and servers started. If more dispatchers or servers are needed by the user processes, the database will start more, up to the maximum number specified via init.ora parameters. If the maximum number of dispatchers or servers is too low, user requests will be forced to wait and the perceived performance of the application will suffer.

The MTS_SERVERS parameter in the database's init.ora file specifies the number of server processes to start when the database starts. As more servers are needed, they are added until the number of servers reaches the setting of the MTS_MAX_SERVERS init.ora parameter.

The query shown in the following listing will show the average wait, in hundredths of seconds, in the request queue. If the average wait is greater than one second, then you should increase the MTS_MAX_SERVERS setting, thereby increasing the number of available servers.

```
REM    Is MTS_MAX_SERVERS high enough?
REM
select DECODE( Totalq, 0, 'No Requests',
       ROUND(Wait/Totalq,2) || ' hundredths of seconds')
        Avg_Wait_Per_Request_Queue
  from V$QUEUE
 where Type = 'COMMON';
```

Sample output for the preceding query is shown in the following listing.

```
AVG_WAIT_PER_REQUEST_QUEUE
------------------------------------------------------------
.25 hundredths of seconds
```

Since the average wait in the request queue is less than one second, there is no need to increase the MTS_MAX_SERVERS setting in the test database.

The MTS_DISPATCHERS parameter in the database's init.ora file specifies the number of dispatcher processes to start when the database starts. As more dispatchers are needed, they are added until the number of dispatchers reaches the setting of the MTS_MAX_DISPATCHERS init.ora parameter.

The query shown in the following listing will show the average wait, in hundredths of seconds, in the response queue. If the average wait is greater than one second, then you should increase the MTS_MAX_DISPATCHERS setting, thereby increasing the number of available dispatchers.

```
REM  Average wait per response queue
REM
select DECODE(SUM(Totalq), 0, 'No Responses',
       ROUND(SUM(Wait)/SUM(Totalq),2) || ' hundredths of seconds')
             Avg_Wait_Per_Response_Queue
  from V$QUEUE Q, V$DISPATCHER D
 where Q.Type = 'DISPATCHER'
   and Q.Paddr = D.Paddr;
```

Sample output for the preceding query is shown in the following listing.

```
AVG_WAIT_PER_RESPONSE_QUEUE
------------------------------------------------------------
.04 hundredths of seconds
```

Since the average wait in the response queue is less than one second, there is no need to increase MTS_MAX_DISPATCHERS in the test database.

dbwrstat.sql

Compare DBWR vs. Data Block Waits

The DBWR process writes changed blocks from the data block buffer cache to the datafiles. If the database has a heavy transaction load, then the DBWR process may not always be able to keep up with the pace of changes in the data block buffer cache. When the DBWR process fails to write the changed data promptly, a *data block wait* is recorded. The cumulative number of data block waits that have occurred since the database was started is recorded in the V$WAITSTAT dynamic performance view.

The following query will show the number of DBWR processes in the database as defined by the DB_WRITERS (for ORACLE7) or DBWR_IO_SLAVES (ORACLE8) parameter in the database's init.ora file and the cumulative number of data block waits. The script looks for both parameters—only one of them will be found in V$PARAMETER, so the query will work in both ORACLE7 and ORACLE8. You will very rarely have a value of 0 for data block waits.

```
REM Check for data block waits
REM
column DB_Writers format A20
select A.Value    DB_Writers,
       B.Count    Data_Block_Waits
  from V$PARAMETER A, V$WAITSTAT B
 where (A.Name = 'db_writers' or A.Name = 'dbwr_io_slaves')
   and B.Class = 'data block';
```

You should monitor your applications to determine the typical acceptable value for data block waits in your databases. You can then establish a threshold—for example, 10,000 data block waits for an OLTP application—and increase the number of DBWR processes or I/O slaves when the number of data block waits exceeds the threshold. Since the number of data block waits is cumulative, you should be sure to measure the number of waits at a set point in time following database startup.

Sample output for the data block wait query is shown in the following listing.

```
DB_WRITERS              DATA_BLOCK_WAITS
--------------------    ----------------
2                                  98414
```

The query output shows that there are two DBWR processes active for the test database (the default is for only one DBWR process to be used). To interpret the data block waits statistic, you need to be familiar with the application and the timing of the query. Applications that have many users executing many concurrent transactions will by their nature have a higher number of data block waits. Also, since the data block waits statistic is cumulative, you need to know how long it has been since the database was last started.

ANNOTATIONS

You should monitor the data block waits in your database over time, and determine the typical pattern of DBWR processing for your application. You can then select a threshold to use when evaluating the data block waits statistic.

You can add a threshold to the query by adding the following limiting condition:

```
and B.Count > &threshold
```

When the revised query is executed, a record will only be returned if the number of data block waits exceeds the threshold value you specify.

In some performance guides, the number of DBWR processes to create is tied to the number of available disks in the database. Instead of using the disk-based method for setting the number of DBWR processes, monitor the data block waits as described in this section.

BEYOND THE SGA

The SGA is directly involved in almost every effort to tune queries and applications. Once your SGA is properly tuned, you can look beyond the SGA to other aspects of the database that affect performance. In this section, you will see:

◆ how to analyze the I/O against datafiles

◆ how to query overall system usage statistics

◆ how to view current parameter settings, along with undocumented parameters

◆ how to generate explain plans

◆ how to use the utlbstat/utlestat scripts to supplement the scripts in this chapter

fileio.sql

Datafile I/O Distribution

You may encounter performance problems with your application if the I/O performed by the application is not properly distributed across files, disks, and hardware controllers. The queries in this section will help you to determine which files are the most actively accessed within your database. Once you know which files are the most frequently accessed, you can tune the accesses to those files.

Tuning accesses to files may involve the following:

◆ *Moving objects into separate tablespaces.* For example, you may wish to move very frequently used tables into their own tablespaces, apart from smaller static tables. Isolating very active tables in this manner makes it easier to move them onto less actively used hardware devices.

◆ *Striping extents across files.* You can structure a table's space allocation to force it to create extents in different files, thereby distributing the table's I/O load across multiple files.

◆ *Striping files across disks.* You can use the operating system to spread a single file across multiple disks (using mirroring or RAID technology). By involving multiple disks in the resolution of the I/O request, the burden on any single disk is reduced, and a potential I/O bottleneck is avoided.

When tuning I/O, you need to be aware of the most frequently accessed files, and the manner in which the database is using them. In the query in the following listing, the V$FILESTAT view is joined to the V$DATAFILE view; the result will show the total I/O by datafile. The I/O is expressed in terms of database blocks read and written.

```
REM   Datafile I/O distribution, across all datafiles
REM
column File_Name format A39
select DF.Name File_Name,
       FS.Phyblkrd Blocks_Read,
       FS.Phyblkwrt Blocks_Written,
       FS.Phyblkrd+FS.Phyblkwrt Total_IOs
  from V$FILESTAT FS, V$DATAFILE DF
 where DF.File#=FS.File#
 order by FS.Phyblkrd+FS.Phyblkwrt desc;
```

Sample output for the datafile I/O distribution query is shown in the following listing.

FILE_NAME	BLOCKS_READ	BLOCKS_WRITTEN	TOTAL_IOS
/db01/oracle/APP1/sys01.dbf	70601	83	70684
/db10/oracle/APP1/apptab01.dbf	35642	70	35712
/db10/oracle/APP1/apptab02.dbf	8481	4	8485
/db07/oracle/APP1/users01.dbf	7640	0	7640
/db13/oracle/APP1/tools01.dbf	7052	0	7052
/db07/oracle/APP1/temp01.dbf	0	418	418
/db10/oracle/APP1/rbs01.dbf	55	89	144

```
/db01/oracle/APP1/users02.dbf                    132          0      132
/db01/oracle/APP1/appindx02.dbf                   83          0       83
/db06/oracle/APP1/apptest.dbf                     64          0       64
/db01/oracle/APP1/users03.dbf                     60          0       60
/db01/oracle/APP1/appindx04.dbf                   22          1       23
/db01/oracle/APP1/appindx03.dbf                   17          0       17
/db01/oracle/APP1/appindx01.dbf                   14          1       15
```

14 rows selected.

In the preceding listing, the datafiles are listed in descending order of total I/O activity. The "read" and "write" I/Os are shown as well, so you can identify the type of activity prevalent in each file's access pattern. In the preceding example, the datafile for the SYSTEM tablespace accounts for most of the I/O activity, followed by the data tablespace for the application (the "apptab" datafiles). The application is read-intensive, with many more reads than writes. Although it is read-intensive, there have been very few accesses to the index tablespace for the application (the "appindx" datafiles). Based on this information, you should check the hit ratio for the database to determine if you need to investigate the queries used and index structures available. You may also wish to separate the datafiles for the APPTAB tablespace onto separate devices (both are presently on /db10, as is the rollback segment tablespace's datafile).

ANNOTATIONS

You can modify the full datafile I/O distribution query to show only those datafiles that account for more than a given percentage of the total I/O performed in the database. You can select a threshold percentage—for example, 10 percent—and only the datafiles that account for at least that percentage of the database I/O will be shown.

In the following listing, the datafile I/O distribution query is shown with a threshold variable. When the query is executed, you will be prompted for the percentage to use as the threshold (such as 10 for 10 percent).

```
REM   Datafile I/O distribution - with threshold.
REM
REM   You will be prompted for a threshold percentage,
REM   such as 10 to check for any file that accounts for
REM   at least 10 percent of the I/O in the database.
REM
set verify off
column File_Name format A39
select DF.Name File_Name,
       FS.Phyblkrd Blocks_Read,
       FS.Phyblkwrt Blocks_Written,
```

```
        FS.Phyblkrd+FS.Phyblkwrt Total_Ios
  from V$FILESTAT FS, V$DATAFILE DF
 where DF.File#=FS.File#
   and (FS.Phyblkrd+FS.Phyblkwrt)>
       (select (&threshold/100)*sum (FS.Phyblkrd+FS.Phyblkwrt)
          from V$FILESTAT FS, V$DATAFILE DF
         where DF.File#=FS.File#)
 order by FS.Phyblkrd+FS.Phyblkwrt desc;
```

Sample output for the datafile I/O distribution query with a threshold is shown in the following listing.

```
Enter value for threshold: 10


FILE_NAME                               BLOCKS_READ BLOCKS_WRITTEN  TOTAL_IOS
--------------------------------------- ----------- -------------- ----------
/db01/oracle/APP1/sys01.dbf                   70601             83      70684
/db10/oracle/APP1/apptab01.dbf                35642             70      35712
```

The threshold-based datafile I/O query output shown in the preceding listing allows you to quickly identify the most frequently accessed files. Because it does not show all of the files, it does not show any other files on those devices. For example, in the test database, only one of the APPTAB tablespace's datafiles is listed in the output of the threshold-based query; there is no indication that a second datafile for the same tablespace is stored on the same device. Therefore, you should use the threshold-based report to identify candidates for I/O bottlenecks, and the full report to see the distribution of datafile I/O across all datafiles and disks.

params.sql

Parameter Settings

The database initialization parameters may be stored in several different operating system files and, as of ORACLE7.3, may be altered after the database has been started. Certain parameters can be changed either at the session level (via the **alter session** command) or at the database level (via the **alter system** command). If you change parameter settings at the session level, the settings remain in effect for the duration of your session. If you change parameter settings at the database level, the new settings stay in effect even after you shut down and restart the database—the new settings override the init.ora parameter settings! You should therefore check the database settings against the init.ora settings on a regular basis and update the init.ora settings as needed.

Because parameters can dynamically change, you cannot always rely on the database's init.ora file to show the most recent settings for the instance parameters. Instead, you should query the V$PARAMETER dynamic performance view directly, as shown in the following listing.

```
REM   Current parameter settings, from V$PARAMETER
REM
column Name format A50
column Value format A28
select Name,
       Value
  from V$PARAMETER;
```

ANNOTATIONS

The V$PARAMETER view contains columns you can use to determine which parameters can be dynamically modified at the session and database levels. If a parameter can be altered at the session level, then the IsSes_Modifiable column in V$PARAMETER will have a value of TRUE. If a parameter can be altered at the database level, then the IsSys_Modifiable column in V$PARAMETER will have a value of IMMEDIATE.

The query in the following listing will list the parameters that you can dynamically change at session or database level.

```
REM   Dynamic parameter settings, from V$PARAMETER
REM
column Name format A50
column IsSes_Modifiable format A5
column IsSys_Modifiable format A10
select Name,
       IsSes_Modifiable,
       IsSys_Modifiable
  from V$PARAMETER
 where IsSes_Modifiable = 'TRUE'
    or IsSys_Modifiable = 'IMMEDIATE';
```

Sample output showing dynamically changeable parameters (in an ORACLE Release 7.3.2.3 database) is shown in the following listing.

```
NAME                                                ISSES ISSYS_MODI
--------------------------------------------------- ----- ----------
timed_statistics                                    TRUE  IMMEDIATE
log_checkpoint_interval                             FALSE IMMEDIATE
log_checkpoint_timeout                              FALSE IMMEDIATE
log_small_entry_max_size                            FALSE IMMEDIATE
db_file_multiblock_read_count                       TRUE  IMMEDIATE
partition_view_enabled                              TRUE  FALSE
v733_plans_enabled                                  TRUE  FALSE
b_tree_bitmap_plans                                 TRUE  FALSE
```

```
text_enable                                    TRUE   FALSE
optimizer_percent_parallel                     TRUE   FALSE
parallel_min_percent                           TRUE   FALSE
hash_join_enabled                              TRUE   FALSE
hash_area_size                                 TRUE   FALSE
hash_multiblock_io_count                       TRUE   IMMEDIATE
user_dump_dest                                 FALSE  IMMEDIATE
max_dump_file_size                             TRUE   FALSE

16 rows selected.
```

PROGRAMMER'S NOTE   *The parameters that can be dynamically modified at the session and database level may change between database versions. For example, ORACLE Release 7.3.3.3 added eight new parameters.*

While V$PARAMETER shows the parameter settings for the documented parameters, there are additional parameters you can set. Usually, these parameters are either left over from previous versions of the RDBMS or will be documented as supported parameters in later versions of the RDBMS. In almost all cases, the first letter of the parameters is an underscore (_). The parameters can have their values specified via your database's init.ora file. For example, ORACLE Financials users should use the

```
_optimizer_undo_changes = TRUE
```

parameter setting in their init.ora file to dynamically undo changes to the way the ORACLE optimizer interprets correlated subqueries in RDBMS versions after ORACLE Release 6.0.31.

The query shown in the following listing must be run as the SYS user. The query will list all of the parameters starting with an underscore that are recognized by the database.

PROGRAMMER'S NOTE

The undocumented parameters are subject to change without notice as database versions change.

```
REM   Undocumented parameters - subject to change!
REM
col Ksppinm format a28 head 'Parameter' justify c trunc
col Ksppdesc format a40 head 'Description' justify c trunc
  select Ksppinm,
         Ksppdesc
   from X$KSPPI
  where Ksppinm like '\_%' escape '\'
  order by Ksppinm;
```

The **where** clause of the query in the preceding listing searches for strings beginning with an underscore (_). In ORACLE, the underscore is a single-character wildcard. If your **where** clause had read

```
where Ksppinm like '_%'
```

then every row whose Ksppinm value contained at least one character would have passed that **where** clause criteria. Instead, you can use the **escape** clause of the **like** operator. The **escape** clause tells the database that the character that follows it (in this example, a backslash) is a special character. In the **like** clause, the character following the backslash (the underscore) will be interpreted literally, as an underscore instead of a wildcard. Thus, the **where** clause

```
where Ksppinm like '\_%' escape '\'
```

is interpreted by the database as limiting the output to those records whose Ksppinm values begin with an underscore.

PROGRAMMER'S NOTE

Before modifying one of the undocumented parameters, check with ORACLE Support to find out alternatives to the modification you are making, and whether the change is supported.

gen_stat.sql

General Statistics

You can query V$SYSSTAT and V$SGASTAT to see general statistics regarding the database's activity. The queries earlier in this chapter referred to specific rows in V$SYSSTAT and V$SGASTAT. The queries in the following listing will show all statistics available via those dynamic performance views.

```
REM   Query of general statistics
REM
select *
  from V$SYSSTAT;


select *
  from V$SGASTAT;
```

In the section dealing with the management of the pool of available parallel query server processes earlier in this chapter, specific rows of the V$PQ_SYSSTAT dynamic performance view were queried. You can see all of the statistics concerning the Parallel Query Option by executing the query shown in the following listing.

```
REM   General statistics concerning parallelism
REM
select *
  from V$PQ_SYSSTAT;
```

The statistics available via V$PQ_SYSSTAT are shown in the following listing.

```
select Statistic
  from V$PQ_SYSSTAT;


STATISTIC
------------------------------
Servers Busy
Servers Idle
Servers Highwater
Server Sessions
Servers Started
Servers Shutdown
Servers Cleaned Up
Queries Initiated
DFO Trees
Local Msgs Sent
Distr Msgs Sent
Local Msgs Recv'd
Distr Msgs Recv'd
```

The length of each Statistic value is 30 characters. Although the column is a VARCHAR2 column, each value is padded with spaces. To query V$PQ_SYSSTAT for a particular Statistic value, you should use the **RTRIM** function to strip the trailing blanks, as shown in the following listing.

```
select Statistic,
       Value
  from V$PQ_SYSSTAT
 where RTRIM(Statistic) = 'Servers Busy';
```

explain.sql

Generating Explain Plans

You can determine the path that ORACLE will choose for a query's execution (known as the *execution path* or the *explain plan*) without running the query. To determine the execution path, you must use the **explain plan** command in ORACLE. This command will evaluate the steps in the execution path for a query, and will place one row for each step into a table named PLAN_TABLE. The records in PLAN_TABLE will describe the operations used at each step of the query execution, and the relationships between the execution path steps. If you are using the cost-based optimizer (CBO), the explain plan will show the relative "cost" of each step in the execution path.

To use **explain plan**, you first need to create a PLAN_TABLE table in the schema that you will be using (usually, the schema that owns the tables used by the query). ORACLE provides a script to create the PLAN_TABLE; named utlxplan.sql, it is usually stored in the /rdbms/admin subdirectory under the ORACLE software home directory. Run the utlxplan.sql script from within SQL*Plus, as shown in the following example of a UNIX user creating PLAN_TABLE.

```
@$ORACLE_HOME/rdbms/admin/utlxplan

Table created.
```

If the utlxplan.sql script fails to create the table, you lack one of the following:

◆   the CREATE TABLE privilege

◆   adequate free space within your default tablespace

◆   any more space within your space quota for your default tablespace

PROGRAMMER'S NOTE   *The utlxplan.sql script may change between ORACLE versions and sometimes between minor releases. You should drop PLAN_TABLE and run this script every time you upgrade your ORACLE version to guarantee you will see all available execution path information.*

Once PLAN_TABLE has been created in your schema, you can begin to determine the execution paths of selected queries. To determine the execution path of a query, prefix the query with the SQL shown in the following listing.

```
explain plan
set Statement_ID = 'TEST'
for
```

To make the tuning process simpler, always use the same Statement_ID value, and delete the records for each execution path before using the **explain plan** command a second time.

An example of execution of the **explain plan** command is shown in the following listing. The query shown in the listing will not be run during the command; only its execution path steps will be generated, and they will be inserted as records in PLAN_TABLE.

```
explain plan
set Statement_ID = 'TEST'
for
select Name, Lodging, BirthDate
  from WORKER
 where Lodging = 'ROSE HILL'
   and Name like 'J%';

Explained.
```

The records have now been inserted into PLAN_TABLE. You can query the
PLAN_TABLE using the following query. The results of this query will show the
operations performed at each step, and the parent-child relationships between the
execution path steps.

```
REM   Standard query of PLAN_TABLE
REM
select LPAD(' ',2*Level)||Operation||' '||Options
               ||' '||Object_Name    Q_Plan
  from PLAN_TABLE
 where Statement_ID = 'TEST'
connect by prior ID = Parent_ID and Statement_ID = 'TEST'
   start with ID=1;
```

The query shown in the preceding listing uses the **connect by** operator to
evaluate the hierarchy of steps in the query's execution path. The query in the listing
assumes the Statement_ID field has been set to 'TEST.' The execution path steps will
be displayed in the column given the Q_Plan alias.

If the WORKER table in the prior example had two single-column, nonunique
indexes on its Lodging and Name columns, then the Q_Plan value—the execution
path—may resemble the output shown in the following listing.

PROGRAMMER'S NOTE

*The actual execution path chosen by the optimizer will vary depending on the distribution of values
within the table and the selectivity of the indexes.*

```
Q_PLAN
---------------------------------------------------------------
TABLE ACCESS WORKER BY ROWID
  AND-EQUAL
     INDEX RANGE SCAN WORKER$NAME
     INDEX RANGE SCAN WORKER$LODGING
```

The AND-EQUAL operation combines the results of the two index scans (on the
WORKER$NAME and WORKER$LODGING indexes).

If you are using the cost-based optimizer, you can query PLAN_TABLE to
determine the relative cost of the query. The relative cost of the query is stored in
the Position column of PLAN_TABLE, in the row that has an ID value of 0. The
query shown in the following listing will show the cost of the query whose explain
plan has just been generated.

```
REM   Show relative cost of a query's execution path
REM
select Position   Cost
  from PLAN_TABLE
 where ID = 0
   and Statement_ID = 'TEST';
```

The relative cost of a query cannot be compared to the cost of any other query; it is only useful when estimating the performance impact of modifications to the query.

ANNOTATIONS

As of ORACLE7.3, you can have the explain plan automatically generated for every transaction you execute within SQL*Plus. The **set autotrace on** command will cause each query, after being executed, to display both its execution path and high-level trace information about the processing involved in resolving the query. The explain plan generated via **set autotrace on** will show the cost associated with each step of the query, the number of rows returned from each step of the query, and any parallelism used during the query's execution.

PROGRAMMER'S NOTE *In order to use the **set autotrace on** command, you must have first created the PLAN_TABLE table within your account, and you must have access to the dynamic performance views. If you do not have DBA authority, you can access the dynamic performance views if you have been granted the PLUSTRACE role. The PLUSTRACE role is not created in the database by default; a script provided by ORACLE (usually called plustrce.sql) to create the role is typically located in the /sqlplus/admin subdirectory under the ORACLE software home directory. Once the script has been run by a DBA, you can be granted the PLUSTRACE role and you will then be able to use the **set autotrace on** command.*

When using the **set autotrace on** command, you do not set a Statement_ID, and you do not have to manage the records within the PLAN_TABLE. To disable the autotrace feature, use the **set autotrace off** command.

To use the autotrace capability, turn it on for your SQL*Plus session, execute your queries, and then turn it off, as shown in the following listing.

```
set autotrace on

select... from ...
<records displayed>
<explain plan displayed>
<parallelism displayed>
<statistics for the query displayed>

set autotrace off
```

If you use the **set autotrace on** command, you will not see the explain plan for your queries until after the queries complete. The **explain plan** command, on the other hand, shows the execution paths without running the queries first. Therefore, if the performance of a query is unknown, use the **explain plan** command to analyze the query before running it. If you are fairly certain that the performance of a query is acceptable, use **set autotrace on** to verify its execution path.

Using utlbstat/utlestat

Two scripts—utlbstat.sql and utlestat.sql—are the current versions of two original ORACLE tuning scripts called bstat.sql and estat.sql, which were included with ORACLE Version 5. The utlbstat.sql and utlestat.sql scripts allow you to determine the differences in statistics between two points in time. When you run the utlbstat.sql script, a number of tables are created and the tables are populated with the initial (beginning) Statistics values. When you run the utlestat.sql script at a later point in time, a second set of tables is populated, and a report is generated showing the changes in the statistics for the period tested.

The output report generated by utlestat.sql script gives you an overview of the database performance, but does not focus on specific problems to the degree that the scripts in this chapter do. The chief benefit of the utlbstat/utlestat scripts is that they reflect the statistics during a set period of time and do not reflect statistical changes due to database startup. The utlbstat/utlestat scripts also let you determine the differences in the database usage by the OLTP and batch portions of your application. For example, if your application is used by OLTP users during the day and batch users at night, you could run utlbstat/utlestat to measure the statistics twice—once to reflect the OLTP usage, and a second time to reflect the batch usage.

Most systems do not have an equal mix of OLTP and batch usage. Therefore, you can bypass using utlbstat/utlestat and use the scripts provided in this chapter in their place. Since many of ORACLE's statistics are cumulative, the database startup activity will contribute to the overall statistics and may suppress performance-related statistics such as the hit ratio. For OLTP applications in particular, the impact of database startup on performance-related statistics is a small concern. The nature of index-intensive queries leads to a high hit ratio even if the data block buffer cache is initially empty.

You can minimize the impact of database startup on the hit ratio for the shared SQL area by pinning commonly used packages in the shared SQL area when the database is started. The process of pinning packages in the SGA is described in Chapter 5.

Because you can minimize the impact database startup activities have on the overall cumulative statistics, you should use the scripts provided in this chapter to evaluate your database environment. For best results, run the scripts during a time of high activity, at least one day of normal usage following the most recent database startup. If you need to monitor the database activity during a time of unusual activity—such as during a stress test—then you should either use the utlbstat/utlestat scripts or shut down and restart the database (to re-zero the system statistics) prior to the start of the test, and use the scripts provided in this chapter to identify potential problem areas.

Transaction Management

Every transaction uses a set of internal database objects to record and manage the transaction. If the database objects supporting the transaction are not properly sized or tuned, the transaction may fail, perform poorly, or wait forever for a needed lock. In this chapter, you will see scripts for managing the objects involved in managing transactions.

The major scripts presented in this chapter are:

mon_rol.sql	Monitor the number of rollback segments needed
mon_rsiz.sql	Monitor the size of rollback segments
mon_rext.sql	Monitor the rollback segment extent size
rol_users.sql	Monitor who is using which rollback segment
transsiz.sql	Monitor the size of rollback segment entries per transaction
sho_dead.sql	Show the sessions involved in deadlocks
termwait.sql	Generate the session termination commands for sessions waiting for locks
termhold.sql	Generate the session termination commands for sessions holding requested locks
lockdtab.sql	Show the tables being locked by deadlocked transactions
lock_sql.sql	Show the SQL associated with deadlocked transactions
switches.sql	Show the log switch history of the online redo log files

In the first section, you will see scripts for managing rollback segments. The scripts will allow you to determine which user is using a particular rollback segment, how the rollback segment's space is being managed, and how large you should make your rollback segments. You will also see how to measure the amount of rollback space required by a transaction.

In the second section, you will see scripts related to locking. The scripts will allow you to see which sessions are currently holding locks or waiting for locks to be released. You will also be able to see the objects being locked, the text of the SQL used in the locking transactions, and the scripts needed to kill the sessions holding or waiting for the locks.

In the final section, you will see how to determine whether your online redo log files are properly sized. The combination of environmental diagnostics (properly sized online redo log files and rollback segments) and utilities (to detect the SQL text of locks and generate session kill scripts) provided in this chapter allows you to create a database environment that supports your transactions, while providing ad hoc management capabilities as well.

Rollback Segments

Rollback segments store the "before" image of data—the data as it existed prior to the beginning of a transaction. You need to have enough rollback segments in your database to support all of the concurrent transactions. When managing rollback segments, you need to manage their number and their space allocations.

If you have too few rollback segments, new transactions attempting to write data to the rollback segments will be forced to wait temporarily. You can use the scripts in this section to monitor the rollback header waits and determine if you have enough rollback segments in your database.

If the rollback segments are too small, then transactions may fail. If a large transaction requires more space than the rollback segment has already allocated, the rollback segment will extend into the free space remaining in the tablespace. If the rollback segment requires more space than is available in the tablespace, then the transaction causing the rollback segment to extend will fail. You can monitor the number of times the rollback segments had to extend to support the database transaction load.

If the extents within the rollback segment are too small, then the transaction will "wrap" from one extent to another within the rollback segment. Ideally, a transaction's rollback segment entry will fit entirely within one extent of the rollback segment, thereby minimizing the performance and internal space management issues associated with wraps. You can monitor the number of times the rollback segment entries wrap from one extent to another within the rollback segment.

In this section, you will see scripts that can be used to diagnose problems with the rollback segment's space allocation and number. You will also see how to determine which users are currently using which rollback segments and how to predict the rollback segment usage for a transaction.

Monitor the Number of Rollback Segments

mon_rol.sql

A single rollback segment can contain data from many different transactions. As each transaction begins to allocate space within a rollback segment, the transaction must first create an entry in the rollback segment's header. If you have many users executing many small transactions (as is common in an on-line transaction processing application), then transactions may have to wait in order to access the rollback segment header.

To avoid rollback segment header waits, you should create more rollback segments. If the transactions do not reference a specific rollback segment, then the transactions should be evenly divided among the available rollback segments. For example, if there are four rollback segments available for users (excluding the SYSTEM rollback segment), then the first 12 transactions may be distributed as shown in the following listing.

Transaction Number	Rollback Segment
1	R1
2	R2
3	R3
4	R4
5	R1

Transaction Number	Rollback Segment
6	R2
7	R3
8	R4
9	R1
10	R2
11	R3
12	R4

If the number of rollback segments changes, the number of transactions supported per rollback segment will change. In the preceding listing, four rollback segments supported 12 transactions—three transactions per rollback segment. If you reduce the number of available rollback segments from four to three, then the number of transactions supported per rollback segment in the prior example will increase from three to four.

The size of the transactions is not considered when the transactions are assigned to rollback segments, so if you have large transactions, you should use the **set transaction use rollback segment** command to force a transaction to use a specific rollback segment. Regardless of the size of the transactions, you need to verify that you have enough rollback segments to support the number of transactions without incurring rollback segment header waits. In the following script, the V$WAITSTAT and V$ROLLSTAT views are queried. The V$ROLLSTAT dynamic performance view records statistics about rollback segments, and in this script is used to determine how many rollback segments are available. The Count statistic of V$WAITSTAT is queried for the rollback segment header waits ("undo header") statistic value.

```
REM   Do you have enough rollback segments?
REM
select COUNT(V$ROLLSTAT.USN)  Num_Rollbacks,
       V$WAITSTAT.Count        Rollback_Header_Waits
  from V$WAITSTAT, V$ROLLSTAT
 where V$ROLLSTAT.Status = 'ONLINE'
   and V$WAITSTAT.Class = 'undo header'
 group by V$WAITSTAT.Count;
```

Sample output from the preceding script is shown in the following listing.

```
NUM_ROLLBACKS ROLLBACK_HEADER_WAITS
------------- ---------------------
            3                     6
```

The script will generate a single line of output. As shown in the preceding listing, the output shows the number of online rollback segments (in this example, three), and the number of rollback header waits that have occurred since the database was last opened. You will seldom see a value of zero rollback segment header waits.

ANNOTATIONS

You should monitor your applications to determine an acceptable number of rollback segment header waits per application. For batch applications, you should see few rollback segment header waits; for OLTP applications, the number of rollback segment header waits will depend on the number of concurrent transactions. Once you have determined the acceptable number of rollback segment header waits for your application, you can add a threshold value to the query by adding the following limiting condition.

```
and V$WAITSTAT.Count > &threshold
```

The full text of the revised query is shown in the following listing.

```
REM    Rollback segments count check - with threshold
REM
select COUNT(V$ROLLSTAT.USN)  Num_Rollbacks,
       V$WAITSTAT.Count        Rollback_Header_Waits
  from V$WAITSTAT, V$ROLLSTAT
 where V$ROLLSTAT.Status = 'ONLINE'
   and V$WAITSTAT.Class = 'undo header'
   and V$WAITSTAT.Count > &threshold
 group by V$WAITSTAT.Count;
```

When the revised query is executed, you will be prompted for the threshold number of rollback segment header waits. If the number of waits is less than the threshold, no record will be returned by the query.

The query in the preceding listing does not join the two views in its **where** clause. The V$WAITSTAT view is restricted by limiting conditions so it will return only one row.

mon_rsiz.sql

Monitor Rollback Segment Size

All transactions, regardless of their size, compete for the same rollback segments. Unless you specifically use the **set transaction use rollback segment** command *after every* **commit**, you have no control over which rollback segment will be used during your transaction. If you use the **set transaction use rollback segment** command to support a large transaction, you should create a rollback segment that is specially sized for the transaction. If you do not use the **set transaction use rollback segment** command, a rollback segment will be assigned to your transaction in a round-robin fashion. Since most rollback segment assignments for transactions are random, you should use a standard size for all of your rollback segments (except for those that specifically support large transactions).

A single rollback segment can store the data from multiple transactions. Any of the entries within the rollback segment can force the rollback segment to extend; thus, a rollback segment extension may be caused by many concurrent small transactions rather than a single large transaction.

To control the extension of rollback segments, you can set an *optimal* size for the rollback segment. Use the *optimal* parameter of the **storage** clause to set the value when executing the **create rollback segment** or **alter rollback segment** commands. The value of the rollback segment's *optimal* parameter setting, like other rollback segment statistics, can be queried via the V$ROLLSTAT dynamic performance view. The V$ROLLSTAT view records cumulative statistics regarding all rollback segment usage since the database was last started.

If you have set an *optimal* size for your rollback segments, then rollback segments that have extended beyond their *optimal* size can "shrink." The *optimal* size should be set to minimize the number of extensions and shrinks required for the rollback segment to support the size and volume of transactions.

In the following script, V$ROLLSTAT is queried along with V$ROLLNAME. The V$ROLLNAME view shows the names of the online rollback segments; in V$ROLLSTAT, the rollback segments are identified only by their USN (Undo Segment Number) value. The query in the following listing will list the *optimal* size, number of shrinks, average size per shrink, and number of extensions per rollback segment.

```
REM   Rollback Segment Extensions
REM
column Name format A20
select Name, OptSize, Shrinks, AveShrink, Extends
  from V$ROLLSTAT, V$ROLLNAME
 where V$ROLLSTAT.USN=V$ROLLNAME.USN;
```

Sample output for the V$ROLLSTAT query is shown in the following listing.

NAME	OPTSIZE	SHRINKS	AVESHRINK	EXTENDS
SYSTEM		0	0	0
R01	10485760	4	41943040	32
R02	10485760	2	44564480	17

As shown in the preceding output listing, there are three active rollback segments in the database. The SYSTEM rollback segment is used for data dictionary transactions. Users' transactions are assigned to either the R01 or R02 rollback segment. Each of the user rollback segments has an *optimal* size of 10MB (10,485,760 bytes). Each user rollback segment has extended beyond its *optimal* value and has been forced to shrink back to its *optimal* size.

The rollback segments have shrunk by an average of almost 40MB each time they have shrunk. Thus, the R01 and R02 rollback segments are not properly sized for the transactions they are supporting. They are frequently extending (49 times since the last database startup) and extend, on average, to five times their *optimal* size. If a rollback segment has to constantly extend beyond its *optimal* setting and then shrink back to its *optimal* setting, it is performing a great deal of unnecessary space management work. To reduce the number of rollback segment extensions, you should modify the rollback segments' *optimal* settings, increasing them to at least 40MB. After modifying the rollback segments' storage settings, you can periodically re-execute the script to determine the impact of the changes.

ANNOTATIONS

When a rollback segment extends beyond its *optimal* setting the first time, the rollback segment will not shrink. The second time the rollback segment extends beyond its *optimal* setting, the rollback segment will shrink—provided the second transaction forced the rollback segment to allocate a new extent. Setting a value for the *optimal* parameter will not prevent all space management issues, but can help limit the space management issues associated with rollback segments.

Because of the manner in which rollback segments extend and shrink, the number of "Extends" in the previous script's output should always exceed the number of "Shrinks." For example, if the rollback segment started with a size less than its *optimal* setting, acquiring new extents would increment the "Extends" statistic value but no "Shrink" would be necessary. Once a rollback exceeds its *optimal* setting in size, it only shrinks at the end of a transaction—and that transaction may have forced multiple extensions.

As of ORACLE7.2, you can use the **alter rollback segment** command to shrink rollback segments to a size of your choosing. The rollback segments will still have a minimum of two extents. If you do not specify a size to shrink to, the rollback segment will shrink to its *optimal* size. In the following listing, the R01 rollback segment is shrunk back to its *optimal* size.

```
alter rollback segment R01 shrink;
```

mon_rext.sql

Monitor Rollback Segment Extent Size

To simplify the management of multiple rollback segment entries within a rollback segment, you should size the rollback segment so that each of its extents is large enough to support a typical transaction.

When a transaction's rollback segment entry cannot be stored within a single extent, the entry wraps into a second extent within the rollback segment. The extents within a rollback segment are assigned cyclically, so a rollback segment entry can wrap from the last extent of the rollback segment to its first extent—provided there is not an active rollback segment entry already in the first extent. If there is an active rollback segment entry already in the first extent, the rollback segment will extend.

You can query the V$ROLLSTAT dynamic performance view to see the number of wraps that have occurred in each rollback segment since the last time the database was started. If there have been no wraps in the rollback segment, then its extents are properly sized for the transactions it supports. If there is a non-zero value for the number of wraps, then you should recreate the rollback segments with larger extent sizes.

```
REM    Rollback Segment Wraps Check
REM
column Name format A20
select Name, OptSize, Shrinks, AveShrink, Wraps, Extends
  from V$ROLLSTAT, V$ROLLNAME
 where V$ROLLSTAT.USN=V$ROLLNAME.USN;
```

Like the query for rollback segment extension, the script in the preceding listing queries statistics from V$ROLLSTAT along with the rollback segment names from V$ROLLNAME. Sample output from the preceding query is shown in the following listing.

NAME	OPTSIZE	SHRINKS	AVESHRINK	WRAPS	EXTENDS
SYSTEM		0	0	0	0
R01	10485760	4	41943040	41	32
R02	10485760	2	44564480	26	17

The sample query output shows that 67 wraps have occurred since the last time the database was started. Given the number of extensions that have occurred, the number of wraps is not surprising (since extensions usually require wraps). The extensions indicate that the rollback segments are handling larger transactions than they were designed for; and if the entire rollback segment cannot handle a transaction's rollback information, a single extent will not be able to hold it either. Thus, rollback segments which extend will frequently have high numbers of wraps.

A second set of sample output is shown in the following listing. This output is slightly modified from the preceding output—there are no extensions, but there are wraps.

NAME	OPTSIZE	SHRINKS	AVESHRINK	WRAPS	EXTENDS
SYSTEM		0	0	0	0
R01	10485760	0	0	41	0
R02	10485760	0	0	26	0

If there are wraps but no extensions, as shown in the preceding listing, then the rollback segment has the proper *optimal* setting, but its extent sizes are too small.

That is, the rollback segment is large enough to support its transactions without extending; however, the transaction entries require multiple extents within the rollback segment. If you have wraps with no extensions, then you should recreate your rollback segments using the same *optimal* setting but larger extent sizes.

rol_usrs.sql

Monitor Who Is Using Which Rollback Segment

While monitoring user activity, you can determine which users are currently writing data to the online rollback segments. You can use this information to track users' transactions and isolate the cause of rollback segment extensions. For example, you could monitor the rollback segments periodically to determine which users' transactions are repeatedly shown using the same rollback segment— and thus run the longest.

The script shown in the following listing uses the V$LOCK dynamic performance view to relate V$SESSION (user sessions) to V$ROLLNAME (rollback segment names).

```
REM  Users in rollback segments
REM
column rr heading 'RB Segment' format a18
column us heading 'Username' format a15
column os heading 'OS User' format a10
column te heading 'Terminal' format a10
select R.Name rr,
       NVL(S.Username,'no transaction') us,
       S.Osuser os,
       S.Terminal te
  from V$LOCK L, V$SESSION S, V$ROLLNAME R
 where L.Sid = S.Sid(+)
   and TRUNC(L.Id1/65536) = R.USN
   and L.Type = 'TX'
   and L.Lmode = 6
order by R.Name
/
```

Sample output for the preceding query is shown in the following listing.

```
RB Segment          Username        OS User     Terminal
-----------------   --------------- ----------  ----------
R01                 APPL1_BAT       georgehj    ttypc
R02                 APPL1_BAT       detmerst    ttypb
```

The query output in the preceding listing shows that two separate operating system users—GEORGEHJ and DETMERST—have active transactions in the database's rollback segments. The GEORGEHJ user is the only user writing to the R01 rollback segment, and DETMERST is writing to the R02 rollback segment. Both operating system users are using the same database account (APPL1_BAT).

ANNOTATIONS

This script uses locking information to identify rollback segment activity. A 'TX' lock is a transaction lock on a table; it indicates that the transaction has locked at least one row of the table. The Id1 value is used to determine to which rollback segment the transaction is writing. A locking mode of 6 indicates an exclusive lock. The limiting conditions related to locking in the query are shown in the following listing.

```
and TRUNC(L.Id1/65536) = R.USN
and L.Type = 'TX'
and L.Lmode = 6
```

You can expand the query to include additional session-related information from V$SESSION. You could also display rollback segment statistics from V$ROLLSTAT, since the script refers to V$ROLLNAME and there is a 1-to-1 relationship between V$ROLLSTAT and V$ROLLNAME. For example, you could add V$ROLLSTAT to the **from** clause:

```
from V$LOCK L, V$SESSION S, V$ROLLNAME R, V$ROLLSTAT RS
```

and add a limiting condition to join V$ROLLSTAT to V$ROLLNAME in the **where** clause:

```
and RS.USN = R.USN
```

The statistics available in V$ROLLSTAT include the *optimal* size of the rollback segment (the OptSize column) and the number of extensions (the Extends column).

transsiz.sql

Monitor Size of Rollback Segment Entries Per Transaction

The ORACLE RDBMS maintains statistics recording the cumulative activity against each rollback segment. If you can isolate a transaction so that it is the only transaction occurring in a specific rollback segment at a given time, then you can determine exactly how much rollback segment space the transaction requires.

The V$ROLLSTAT dynamic performance view maintains a Writes statistic that reflects the number of bytes written to each rollback segment. The query in the following listing will display the number of writes per rollback segment. Each rollback segment is identified by its USN.

```
select USN,
       Writes
  from V$ROLLSTAT;
```

Sample output from the preceding query is shown in the following listing.

```
    USN      WRITES
---------- ----------
         0       1060
         2     191530
         3     279052
```

The output in the preceding listing shows that there are three online rollback segments. The rollback segment with the USN value of 0 is the SYSTEM rollback segment. If you run this query repeatedly and the Writes value remains unchanged, you can verify that there is no activity occurring in the database.

In the following listing, a sample update is executed against the EMPLOYEE table.

```
update EMPLOYEE
   set State_Code = 1
 where Emplid =1;
```

```
1 row updated.
```

Following the **update**, query V$ROLLSTAT again, as shown in the following listing.

```
select USN,
       Writes
  from V$ROLLSTAT;
```

The output of the V$ROLLSTAT query reflects the rollback segment activity generated by the **update**, as shown in the following listing.

```
    USN      WRITES
---------- ----------
         0       1060
         2     191530
         3     279556
```

The number of Writes in rollback segment 3 have increased from 279,052 to 279,556. Thus, the transaction generated 504 bytes of data in its rollback segment entry. A subsequent **commit** does not increase the number of bytes written to the rollback segments.

To effectively use the technique described in this section, you must be able to isolate the transaction to be tested at a time when no other transactions are occurring. For example, if another transaction had taken place at the same time, it would have altered the statistics that were queried. For this reason, you should avoid storing the "before" and "after" statistics values in a table—since inserting the rows into a table generates a transaction in the database, which in turn generates rollback segment activity!

LOCKING

When users share access to database tables, they may prevent each other from completing transactions because of the manner in which their table locks are managed. A user who locks a table—or a single record during an **update**—may prevent other transactions from acquiring the locks they need to complete. As a result, the transactions enter into a *wait* state. Once a transaction has entered a wait state, it must either: (1) acquire the lock it is waiting for, which requires that the lock holder either complete or be manually terminated; or (2) cancel its transaction, thus cancelling its need for the lock.

If there are multiple transactions in wait states, it is possible for the locks to be unresolvable. For example, if transaction A cannot complete until it acquires a lock used by transaction B, and transaction B cannot complete until it acquires a lock used by transaction A, then neither transaction can complete—they are in a *deadlock* state, and neither can complete unless the other is terminated. In the scripts in this section, you will see how to determine which transactions are in wait or deadlock states. You can use the scripts provided here to automatically generate the SQL commands needed to kill either the waiting transactions or the lock-holding transactions. You will also see scripts that show the SQL commands being executed by the locking transactions and the tables they are accessing. Throughout this section, the focus is on diagnosis and resolution of situations in which a requested lock has not immediately been obtained by a transaction.

sho_dead.sql

Show Sessions Involved in Lock Waits

The following script will show all sessions that are waiting for locks, as well as the sessions that are holding the locks in question. The script combines information from V$SESSION, which shows session-specific information such as Username, and V$LOCK, which shows data regarding the status of locks in the database. The script uses the **DECODE** function to interpret the lock states. Following the script, you will see sample output and an annotated walk-through of the script.

```
REM   Show deadlocks
REM
column Username format   A15
column Sid       format   9990      heading SID
column Type      format   A4
column Lmode     format   990       heading 'HELD'
column Request   format   990       heading 'REQ'
column Id1       format   9999990
column Id2       format   9999990
break on Id1 skip 1 dup
select SN.Username,
       M.Sid,
       M.Type,
```

```
          DECODE(M.Lmode, 0, 'None',
                          1, 'Null',
                          2, 'Row Share',
                          3, 'Row Excl.',
                          4, 'Share',
                          5, 'S/Row Excl.',
                          6, 'Exclusive',
                  Lmode, LTRIM(TO_CHAR(Lmode,'990'))) Lmode,
          DECODE(M.Request, 0, 'None',
                            1, 'Null',
                            2, 'Row Share',
                            3, 'Row Excl.',
                            4, 'Share',
                            5, 'S/Row Excl.',
                            6, 'Exclusive',
                  Request, LTRIM(TO_CHAR(M.Request,
                                   '990'))) Request,
        M.Id1, M.Id2
  from V$SESSION SN, V$LOCK M
 where (SN.Sid = M.Sid
        and M.Request != 0)
   or (SN.Sid = M.Sid
        and M.Request = 0 and Lmode != 4
        and (id1, id2) in
          (select S.Id1, S.Id2
             from V$LOCK S
            where Request != 0
              and S.Id1 = M.Id1
              and S.Id2 = M.Id2)  )
order by Id1, Id2, M.Request;

clear breaks
clear columns
```

Sample output from the lock detection script is shown in the following listing.

```
USERNAME          SID TYPE HELD        REQ              ID1      ID2
--------------- ----- ---- ----------- ----------- -------- --------
OPS$GEORGE        8 TX   Exclusive   None          655398    19328
OPS$BERTHA        7 TX   None        Exclusive     655398    19328
```

The script output shows that session 7, with an ORACLE username of OPS$BERTHA, is waiting for a lock. The OPS$BERTHA user has requested an exclusive lock (the "Req" column) that is held by the OPS$GEORGE user (the "Held" column). To resolve the situation, you must either kill one of the transactions or wait for OPS$GEORGE's transaction to complete.

If the lock is held at the table level, the Id2 column value will usually be left blank. Since the Id2 column has a value, the lock contention is most likely due to a row-level lock—two users attempting to **update** the same row at the same time.

ANNOTATIONS

The first part of the script defines the **column** and **break** settings to be used for the report.

```
column Username format  A15
column Sid       format  9990      heading SID
column Type      format  A4
column Lmode     format  990       heading 'HELD'
column Request   format  990       heading 'REQ'
column Id1       format  9999990
column Id2       format  9999990
break on Id1 skip 1 dup
```

The first part of the query selects the username, the session's SID value, and the type of lock. Because of the limiting conditions used in the query, the types of locks displayed are limited; you will only see lock waiters and holders.

```
select SN.Username,
       M.Sid,
       M.Type,
```

The next section of the query decodes the information in the Lmode column of the V$LOCK dynamic performance view. The Lmode column describes the lock mode for the locks currently held by the session.

```
       DECODE(M.Lmode, 0, 'None',
                       1, 'Null',
                       2, 'Row Share',
                       3, 'Row Excl.',
                       4, 'Share',
                       5, 'S/Row Excl.',
                       6, 'Exclusive',
              Lmode, LTRIM(TO_CHAR(Lmode,'990'))) Lmode,
```

The next section of the query shows the lock mode for the locks requested, but not held, by the session.

```
       DECODE(M.Request, 0, 'None',
                         1, 'Null',
                         2, 'Row Share',
                         3, 'Row Excl.',
                         4, 'Share',
                         5, 'S/Row Excl.',
```

```
                6, 'Exclusive',
      Request, LTRIM(TO_CHAR(M.Request,
                      '990'))) Request,
```

The last columns selected by the query show the Id1 and Id2 values for the resource against which a lock is requested.

```
      M.Id1, M.Id2
from V$SESSION SN, V$LOCK M
```

The limiting conditions for the query are in two sections. The first section selects all of the waiters—all those sessions for whom the Request value in V$LOCK is a non-zero value. Once the requested lock is held, the Request value changes to zero.

```
where (SN.Sid = M.Sid
        and M.Request != 0)
```

The second section of limiting conditions queries V$LOCK to determine the holder of locks that other sessions are requesting. The Id1 and Id2 columns are used by the query to determine which sessions are holding locks that other sessions need.

```
   or (SN.Sid = M.Sid
        and M.Request = 0 and Lmode != 4
        and (id1, id2) in
          (select S.Id1, S.Id2
             from V$LOCK S
           where Request != 0
             and S.Id1 = M.Id1
             and S.Id2 = M.Id2)  )
order by Id1, Id2, M.Request;

clear breaks
clear columns
```

The sample output is shown in the following listing. The record for OPS$BERTHA was generated via the first section in the limiting conditions—the Request value is non-zero, and is decoded to a value of "Exclusive." The OPS$GEORGE entry was generated via the second section in the limiting conditions—it is holding the lock requested by the OPS$BERTHA user.

```
USERNAME          SID TYPE HELD         REQ              ID1       ID2
--------------- ----- ---- ----------- ----------- -------- --------
OPS$GEORGE        8 TX   Exclusive    None          655398    19328
OPS$BERTHA        7 TX   None         Exclusive     655398    19328
```

In the following sections, you will see how to display the SQL used by the locked transactions and how to automatically generate the commands needed to kill all of the waiters or all of the lock holders.

termwait.sql

Generate Commands to Terminate Waiting Sessions

You can terminate a session via the **alter system kill session** command. To execute an **alter system** command, you must have been granted either the DBA role or the ALTER SYSTEM system privilege. In order to kill the session, you must know the session ID and serial number for the session. The session ID and serial number can be queried from the V$SESSION dynamic performance view; you can join V$SESSION to V$LOCK to retrieve the session ID and serial number for only those sessions that are waiting to obtain locks.

During the resolution of lock wait scenarios, you may need to kill the waiting sessions. For example, a user who encounters a deadlock may start a second session, which encounters the same deadlock. The number of transactions locked in this fashion may grow rapidly, and the waiting transactions may be interdependent. In such a situation, the only way to untangle the locked sessions may be to selectively kill the sessions.

The script in the following listing generates a SQL script which you can run to kill waiting sessions. It does not execute the script that it generates; you should check the accuracy of the generated script prior to executing it. The SQL script is generated by selecting the SQL commands as literal character strings, combined with the session ID and serial number variables.

```
REM   Generate SQL commands to kill waiting sessions
REM
set newpage 0 pagesize 0
select 'alter system kill session '||''''
        ||M.Sid||','||SN.Serial#||''''||'; /*'
        ||SN.Username||'*/'
  from V$SESSION SN, V$LOCK M
 where (SN.Sid = M.Sid and M.Request != 0)
 order by M.Sid

spool kill_waits.sql
/
spool off
```

Sample output, which is written to the kill_waits.sql script, is shown in the following listing.

```
alter system kill session '7,924'; /* OPS$BERTHA */
```

The OPS$BERTHA session, with a session ID of 7 and a serial number of 924, was shown in the previous section of this chapter to be waiting for a lock. The **alter system** command shown, when executed, will terminate the OPS$BERTHA session. The session username at the end of the command is not necessary for the completion of the command; it is provided solely for your reference when validating the script prior to its execution.

ANNOTATIONS

Within the script, the SQL command is built by selecting literal characters and database values. First, the **alter system kill session** text is selected as a literal string of characters.

```
select 'alter system kill session '
```

Next, a single quote is selected. In order to have a single quote written to the output, you need to use two single quotes in succession—and these must be placed within two single quotes. Thus, to write a single quote to the output file following the **alter system kill session** text, select four successive single quotes.

```
select 'alter system kill session '||''''
```

The session ID (Sid) and serial number (Serial#) are next selected, since those values are required by the command. Following those values, a closing single quote is created, along with the semicolon to execute the command and the comment at the end of the command. The generation of this information for the command is shown in the following listing.

```
        ||M.Sid||','||SN.Serial#||''''||'; /*'
        ||SN.Username||'*/'
from V$SESSION SN, V$LOCK M
```

The final part of the query uses the criteria from the previous section to detect sessions waiting for locks. If the Request column of the V$LOCK dynamic performance view contains a non-zero value, then the session is waiting for a lock and will be selected by this query.

Following the **order by** clause, the query is not immediately executed. Instead, an output file is opened via the **spool** command, and then the query is executed. The query output will be written to the output file and the file will then be closed.

PROGRAMMER'S NOTE
*There must be a blank line preceding the **spool** command, or the database will assume that the **spool** command is part of the query.*

```
where (SN.Sid = M.Sid and M.Request != 0)
order by M.Sid

spool kill_waits.sql
```

```
/
spool off
```

termhold.sql

Generate Commands to Terminate Sessions Holding Locks

You can terminate a session via the **alter system kill session** command. In order to kill the session, you must know the session ID and serial number for the session. The session ID and serial number can be queried from the V$SESSION dynamic performance view; you can join V$SESSION to V$LOCK to retrieve the session ID and serial number for only those sessions that are presently holding locks that other sessions are waiting to acquire.

During the resolution of lock wait scenarios, you may need to kill the sessions that are holding locks. For example, in a deadlock scenario, two sessions hold locks that prevent each other's transactions from completing. To resolve the deadlock, you will need to terminate at least one of the sessions involved in the deadlock.

The script in the following listing generates a SQL script which you can run to terminate sessions that are presently holding locks that other sessions are waiting to acquire. It does not execute the script that it generates; you should check the accuracy of the generated script prior to executing it. The SQL script is generated by selecting the SQL commands as literal character strings, combined with the session ID and serial number variables.

```
REM   Generate SQL commands to kill waiting sessions
REM
set newpage 0 pagesize 0
select 'alter system kill session '||''''
        ||M.Sid||','||SN.Serial#||''''||'; /*'
        ||SN.Username||'*/'
  from V$SESSION SN, V$LOCK M
 where SN.Sid = M.Sid
        and M.Request = 0 and Lmode != 4
        and (id1, id2) in
          (select S.Id1, S.Id2
             from V$LOCK S
            where Request != 0
              and S.Id1 = M.Id1
              and S.Id2 = M.Id2)
   order by M.Sid

spool kill_holds.sql
/
spool off
```

Sample output from the script is shown in the following listing. When the script is run, the output is written to the kill_holds.sql file.

```
alter system kill session '8,3098'; /* OPS$GEORGE */
```

The kill_holds.sql script, when executed, will kill the OPS$GEORGE session identified as holding a lock in the previous sections of this chapter. The only sessions listed in the file will be those that are holding locks that other sessions are waiting to acquire. If a session is holding no locks that other sessions are waiting to acquire, that session will not be returned by the query.

ANNOTATIONS

Within the script, the SQL command is built by selecting literal characters and database values. The construction of the SQL command is identical to the method described in the previous section on automatically generating the session termination commands for sessions waiting for locks. The only difference between the preceding script and the script in this section is the **where** clause.

For this script, you only want to return records that are holding locks (thus, with a Request value of 0) for which other sessions are waiting. The ID values of the V$LOCK dynamic performance view are used to determine which sessions are holding requested resources. The **where** clause for the script is shown in the following listing.

```
where SN.Sid = M.Sid
        and M.Request = 0 and Lmode != 4
        and (Id1, Id2) in
        (select S.Id1, S.Id2
            from V$LOCK S
          where Request != 0
            and S.Id1 = M.Id1
            and S.Id2 = M.Id2)
```

PROGRAMMER'S NOTE
*There is no semicolon at the end of the query because the query should not be executed until after the output file has been created via the **spool** command. There must be a blank line preceding the **spool** command, or the database will assume that the **spool** command is part of the query.*

lockdtab.sql

Show the Tables Being Locked

You can query the V$ACCESS table to see the names of the objects that are currently locked. The V$ACCESS information can be added to the deadlock query shown earlier in this chapter. In the following listing, the Owner and Object columns are selected from V$ACCESS; because of the limiting conditions on the query, you will only see those sessions currently waiting for locks or holding locks that another session is attempting to acquire.

```
REM   Show tables being locked
REM
column Username format   A15
column Sid       format   9990      heading SID
column Type      format   A4
column Lmode     format   990       heading 'HELD'
column Request   format   990       heading 'REQ'
column Id1       format   9999990
column Id2       format   9999990
column Owner     format   A20
column Object    format   A32
break on Id1 skip 1 dup
select SN.Username,
       M.Sid,
       M.Type,
       A.Owner,
       A.Object,
       DECODE(M.Lmode, 0,  'None',
                       1,  'Null',
                       2,  'Row Share',
                       3,  'Row Excl.',
                       4,  'Share',
                       5,  'S/Row Excl.',
                       6,  'Exclusive',
              Lmode, LTRIM(TO_CHAR(Lmode,'990'))) Lmode,
       DECODE(M.Request, 0,  'None',
                         1,  'Null',
                         2,  'Row Share',
                         3,  'Row Excl.',
                         4,  'Share',
                         5,  'S/Row Excl.',
                         6,  'Exclusive',
              Request, LTRIM(TO_CHAR(M.Request,
                                      '990'))) Request,
       M.Id1, M.Id2
  from V$SESSION SN, V$LOCK M, V$ACCESS A
 where SN.Sid = A.Sid and A.Owner <> 'SYS'
   and ((SN.Sid = M.Sid
         and M.Request != 0)
      or (SN.Sid = M.Sid
         and M.Request = 0 and Lmode != 4
         and (id1, id2) in
           (select S.Id1, S.Id2
             from V$LOCK S
```

```
                    where Request != 0
                      and S.Id1 = M.Id1
                      and S.Id2 = M.Id2)  ) )
order by Id1, Id2, M.Request;


clear breaks
clear columns
```

Sample output for the preceding script is shown in the following listing.

```
USERNAME          SID TYPE OWNER                    OBJECT
--------------- ----- ---- -------------------- -------------------------------
HELD         REQ            ID1     ID2
-----------  -----------  --------  --------
OPS$GEORGE      8 TX    APPOWNER             EMPLOYEE
Exclusive    None         655398   19328

OPS$BERTHA      7 TX    APPOWNER             EMPLOYEE
None         Exclusive    655398   19328
```

The query output shows that the OPS$GEORGE account has a lock on a row of the APPOWNER.EMPLOYEE table. Due to the width of the output, each row of output spans two lines. For the OPS$GEORGE user, the SID value is 8, the table being locked is APPOWNER.EMPLOYEE, an Exclusive lock is held, and no lock is requested. For the OPS$BERTHA user, the same object is desired, but the Held column value is None—showing that the OPS$BERTHA user still does not hold the requested lock.

ANNOTATIONS

In order to show the tables being locked, the V$ACCESS dynamic performance view was added to the script. The changes involved adding V$ACCESS to the **from** clause:
```
from V$SESSION SN, V$LOCK M, V$ACCESS A
```

adding its columns to the **column** formatting commands:
```
column Owner     format   A20
column Object    format   A32
```

adding its columns to the **select** list:
```
select SN.Username,
       M.Sid,
       M.Type,
       A.Owner,
       A.Object,
```

and modifying the **where** clause:
```
where SN.Sid = A.Sid and A.Owner <> 'SYS'
```

In order to preserve the logic of the remainder of the **where** clause, a set of parentheses was placed around the two limiting conditions used in the query. The clause

```
A.Owner <> 'SYS'
```

is necessary because V$ACCESS shows all locks in the database—including the locks
that the database obtains against the tables owned by SYS. If you do not exclude the
SYS-owned tables from the query, then the output will show all of the recursive data
dictionary locks currently held by the sessions in question—making it difficult to
find the records you care about among the records in the output.

lock_sql.sql

Show the SQL Associated with Locks

You can build on the scripts used in the preceding sections of this chapter. For
example, since you know the session information for the sessions that are waiting
for or holding locks, you can determine the SQL text associated with each lock that
is associated with a wait or deadlock state.

The script shown in the following listing queries the V$SQLTEXT dynamic
performance view for the SQL text for sessions. The sessions to be displayed are
determined by their lock status—they are either waiting for locks or holding locks
that other sessions are waiting to acquire.

```
REM   Show SQL text associated with locked sessions
REM
column username format    A15
column sid       format   9990      heading SID
column type      format   A4
column lmode     format   990       heading HELD
column request   format   990       heading REQ
column id1       format   9999990
column id2       format   9999990
break on Sid
select  SN.Username,
        M.Sid,
        SN.Serial#,
        M.Type,
        DECODE(M.Lmode, 0, 'None',
                        1, 'Null',
                        2, 'Row Share',
                        3, 'Row Excl.',
                        4, 'Share',
                        5, 'S/Row Excl.',
                        6, 'Exclusive',
Lmode, LTRIM(TO_CHAR(Lmode,'990'))) Lmode,
        DECODE(M.Request, 0, 'None',
                          1, 'Null',
                          2, 'Row Share',
                          3, 'Row Excl.',
                          4, 'Share',
                          5, 'S/Row Excl.',
                          6, 'Exclusive',
                Request, LTRIM(TO_CHAR(M.Request,
                                '990'))) Request,
        M.Id1,
        M.Id2,
        T.Sql_Text sql
```

```
  from V$SESSION SN, V$LOCK M , V$SQLTEXT T
 where T.Address = SN.Sql_Address
   and T.Hash_Value = SN.Sql_Hash_Value
   and ( (SN.Sid = M.Sid
           and M.Request != 0)
     or (SN.Sid = M.Sid
           and M.Request = 0 and Lmode != 4
           and (id1, id2) in
              (select S.Id1, S.Id2
                  from V$LOCK S
               where Request != 0
                  and S.Id1 = M.Id1
                  and S.Id2 = M.Id2)  ) )
order by SN.Username, SN.Sid, T.Piece;

clear breaks
clear columns
```

Sample output for the preceding script is shown in the following listing.

```
USERNAME          SID    SERIAL# TYPE HELD         REQ           ID1      ID2
--------------- ----- ---------- ---- ----------- ----------- -------- --------
SQL
----------------------------------------------------------------
OPS$BERTHA          7        924 TX   None         Exclusive    655398    19328
update employee set dept_code = 1 where emplid = 1

OPS$GEORGE          8       3098 TX   Exclusive    None         655398    19328
update employee set dept_code = 1, job_code = 10, state_code = 2

OPS$GEORGE                  3098 TX   Exclusive    None         655398    19328
, start_date = sysdate where emplid = 1
```

The output in the preceding listing shows the SQL commands being executed by both the locking transaction (OPS$GEORGE, with a SID value of 8) and the waiting transaction (OPS$BERTHA, SID 7). The locking information from the previous sections of this chapter is repeated here so there will be no question regarding which session is holding the lock and which is waiting for the lock. Since the OPS$GEORGE user is not waiting for any locks (the Req value is None), that user is holding a lock that another user—OPS$BERTHA—is waiting to acquire.

The text of SQL commands in the V$SQLTEXT dynamic performance view spans multiple records. As seen in the preceding output listing, there are two records returned for the OPS$GEORGE user—but there is only one command!
Each text segment in V$SQLTEXT is limited to 64 characters; thus, to determine the command issued by OPS$GEORGE, you need to combine the multiple records selected from V$SQLTEXT.

The command issued by the OPS$GEORGE user was

```
update employee
   set dept_code = 1,
       job_code = 10,
       state_code = 2,
```

```
        start_date = sysdate
 where emplid = 1;
```

When this command was executed, a row-level lock was acquired on the
EMPLOYEE row with an Emplid value of 1. After this command was executed,
and prior to the **commit** of the updated record, the OPS$BERTHA user executed
the following command:

```
update employee
   set dept_code = 1
 where emplid = 1;
```

Since the EMPLOYEE record associated with an Emplid value of 1 was already
locked for update by the OPS$GEORGE user, the OPS$BERTHA user's **update**
command failed to immediately obtain the lock it required.

Deadlocks and waits for locks typically arise in the following situations:

◆ *The application locks more records than necessary, or sooner than necessary.* For
   example, if the application locks all records **for update** when the records
   are first selected, then your users may acquire locks they never use.

◆ *Users initiate multiple sessions, and lock themselves.* If a client-server user's client
   process terminates abnormally, the database may not immediately detect that
   the related server session should be terminated. If the server session remains
   active, all of the locks held by the server session remain in effect—and the
   user, on reconnecting, will be unable to lock the records he or she was previously locking.

◆ *Multiple users own the same business process.* In the example shown in this
   section, two users were updating the EMPLOYEE table. Whenever multiple
   users own the same business process (in this case, updating the EMPLOYEE
   table information for employees with a Dept_Code value of 1), lock waits or
   deadlocks are possible. The more you separate business process ownership
   among users, the more you reduce the chances for lock wait situations.

A fourth possible cause of lock wait situations applies mainly to databases using
a pre-ORACLE7.1.5 version of the ORACLE RDBMS. In those versions, you needed
to be sure to index foreign key columns to avoid unnecessary table locks during
updates. A script that can be used to detect this problem is provided in Chapter 4.

ANNOTATIONS

The script in this section joins V$SQLTEXT to V$SESSION based on two values—an
address and a SQL hash value. The **where** clause used to join V$SQLTEXT (aliased
as "T") and V$SESSION (aliased as "SN") is shown in the following listing.

```
where T.Address = SN.Sql_Address
  and T.Hash_Value = SN.Sql_Hash_Value
```

When displaying the records from V$SQLTEXT, you need to order them by the Piece column (a numeric identifier for each piece of text in a SQL command), which is not selected via the query. The **order by** clause for the query, shown in the following listing, will list the records by username, session ID, and text piece number.

```
order by SN.Username, SN.Sid, T.Piece;
```

If you do not order by Piece, then the text strings will not be displayed in an order that allows you to read the combined SQL easily.

switches.sql

Redo Logs

When you create an ORACLE database, you specify the number of online redo log files available to the database. The online redo log files should be sized to support the volume of transactions within the database.

Since the online redo log files record the transactions within a database, the space requirements of the online redo log files depend on the transaction activity within the database. When an online redo log file fills, a *log switch* occurs. In an OLTP system, you should have enough online redo log files so that a log switch will occur no more often than every 20 to 30 minutes; if log switches occur more rapidly than that, then the maintenance of the online redo log files may impact the overall performance of the transactions. For a high availability database, where minimal or no loss of data is acceptable, you may wish to sacrifice some performance for more frequent log switches.

To view how often log switches occur in your system, you can query V$LOG_HISTORY, which records the time of each log switch in the database for the most recent 100 log switches. You can determine the cumulative time for the last 100 log switches by selecting the minimum Time value from V$LOG_HISTORY. The difference between the current system time and the minimum Time value will be the cumulative time required for the last 100 log switches in days, as selected by the query in the following listing.

```
REM  Online Redo Log File switch rate
REM
ttitle Frequency of log switches
alter session set nls_date_format='MM/DD/YY HH24:MI:SS'
REM
select SysDate - MIN(TO_DATE(Time, 'MM/DD/YY HH24:MI:SS'))
```

```
          Days_For_Last_100_Switches
 from V$LOG_HISTORY;
```

When running this script under some versions of ORACLE8, you will need to change the **from** clause to

```
from V_$LOG_HISTORY;
```

since a synonym for V$LOG_HISTORY is not always created. Sample output for the preceding query is shown in the following listing.

```
Frequency of log switches

DAYS_FOR_LAST_100_SWITCHES
--------------------------
                 13.1193866
```

PROGRAMMER'S NOTE   *The preceding query assumes that there have been at least 100 log switches since the database was created. To verify this, you can execute the following command:*

```
select count(*) from V$LOG_HISTORY;
```

If the count from V$LOG_HISTORY is less than 100, then the preceding query's results will show the number of days between the first log switch and today.

The output shows that for the sample database, there have been 100 log switches in just over 13 days—an average of around 8 log switches per day. On average, there is a log switch every three hours.

The preceding query will show if your online redo log files are too small. However, how do you know if you have enough online redo log files? As a general rule, you should create extra online redo log files when creating the database—for example, use six online redo log files instead of the default of three online redo log files. Having additional online redo log files has a small impact on your database's space requirements, but may help you avoid performance problems during transaction-intensive database activity.

If your database is running in ARCHIVELOG mode, then the contents of an online redo log file must be written to the archive log directory before the online redo log file can be reused. If you have too few online redo log files, then the database may need to reuse an online redo log file before it has been fully archived. If that occurs, then you will see messages in your database's alert log that resemble the following listing (with warning messages shown in bold).

```
Mon Feb 13 19:05:21
Thread 1 advanced to log sequence 941
  Current log# 2 seq# 941 mem# 0: /db04/oracle/APP1/log2a.rdo
Mon Feb 13 19:06:14
Thread 1 cannot allocate new log, sequence 942
Checkpoint not complete
```

```
   Current log# 2 seq# 941 mem# 0: /db04/oracle/APP1/log2a.rdo
Thread 1 advanced to log sequence 942
   Current log# 3 seq# 942 mem# 0: /db03/oracle/APP1/log3a.rdo
Mon Feb 13 19:07:05
```

In the example shown in the listing, the database was not able to complete a log switch because the online redo log file was still being archived. The transaction must wait until the space is freed within the online redo log file, resulting in a performance penalty for the application. The more online redo log files you have, the greater the transaction volume required to fill all of the online redo log files—and thus, the individual online redo log files are more seldom used, making the warning shown in the preceding listing rarer.

ANNOTATIONS

In addition to seeing the cumulative time required for the last 100 log switches, you can use the V$LOG_HISTORY dynamic performance view to see trends in the transaction rate within the database. Usually, the rate of transactions varies throughout the day, influenced by the running of batch transactions and the number of concurrent online users.

The query shown in the following listing will display all 100 of the records from V$LOG_HISTORY. The records will be listed from the most recent log switch to the earliest.

```
alter session set nls_date_format='MM/DD/YY HH24:MI:SS'
select TO_CHAR(TO_DATE(Time, 'MM/DD/YY HH24:MI:SS'),
             'HH24:MI:SS')
  from V$LOG_HISTORY
 order by TO_DATE(Time, 'MM/DD/YY HH24:MI:SS')  desc;
```

The log switch timing information is also printed in the alert log. When running this script under some versions of ORACLE8, you will need to change the **from** clause to

```
from V_$LOG_HISTORY;
```

since a synonym for V$LOG_HISTORY is not always created.

Querying V$LOG_HISTORY for the times of each log switch may illustrate a need for larger online redo log files even if the cumulative statistics do not show that. For example, the cumulative statistics may show that five days were needed for the last 100 log switches. But if two of those days were on the weekend, and the log switches were concentrated around short periods of high usage, you may need to increase the size of the logs to relieve the high usage periods of the performance impact of many log switches.

If you have the proper number of properly sized online redo log files, then the online redo log files should not affect your transaction performance. You can use the scripts provided earlier in this chapter to make sure your rollback segments are properly sized. The lock information scripts will help you to manage situations in which multiple users contend for access to the same resources. If you create a stable transaction environment and use the ad hoc management scripts provided in this chapter, you can effectively manage the transactions within your database.

Data Management

depends.sql

usr_fkys.sql

usr_pkys.sql

no_pks.sql

obj_chng.sql

usr_cons.sql

fk_index.sql

rows_fil.sql

del_comt.sql

hextodec.sql

bus_days.sql

random.sql

I f you are not careful, the management of your data structures can become a burden on your database administrators and developers. In this chapter, you will see scripts that simplify the management of your data objects. For example, the diagnostic scripts in this chapter will verify that your data structures have been created properly and all dependencies among objects will be displayed. You can use the utilities presented in this chapter to dynamically break large **delete**s into smaller transactions and generate random numbers within the database.

The major scripts presented in this chapter are:

depends.sql	Evaluate object dependencies
usr_fkys.sql	Identify foreign key columns
usr_pkys.sql	Identify primary key columns
no_pks.sql	Identify tables lacking primary keys
obj_chng.sql	Identify tables that changed yesterday
usr_cons.sql	List all constraints owned by a user
fk_index.sql	Ensure foreign keys are indexed
rows_fil.sql	Evaluate distribution of a table's rows per datafile
del_comt.sql	Force **commit**s during a **delete** operation
hextodec.sql	Convert a Hexadecimal value to a Decimal value
bus_days.sql	Calculate the number of business days between two dates
random.sql	Generate a random number

DIAGNOSTIC SCRIPTS

You can use the scripts in this section to determine the effectiveness of your implementation of constraints and dependencies among your database objects.

depends.sql

Object Dependencies

Objects are not usually created in isolation. Views depend on the underlying tables, tables have foreign key constraints to other tables, and packages and procedures depend on the views and tables. In order to manage the dependencies among your objects and ensure that changes to the parent object do not invalidate the dependent objects, you need to be aware of these relationships. You can use an ORACLE-provided procedure to determine the dependencies among your objects. The procedure, called DEPTREE_FILL, is created via a file called utldtree.sql. The utldtree.sql file is usually located in the /rdbms/admin subdirectory under the ORACLE software home directory.

In addition to using DEPTREE_FILL, you can query the data dictionary views DBA_DEPENDENCIES and USER_DEPENDENCIES to extract object dependency information. Querying the DBA_DEPENDENCIES data dictionary view will only show you the first level of dependencies for an object; it will not show you any additional levels of dependency. For example, if a package uses a view, then querying DBA_DEPENDENCIES will list the package as dependent on the view; however, the tables on which the view is dependent will not be displayed. To see the additional levels of dependency via the DBA_DEPENDENCIES data dictionary view, you will need to query the data dictionary repeatedly, substituting the dependent object from the prior query in order to find all levels of dependencies.

The following example shows the usage of the ORACLE-provided package.

PROGRAMMER'S NOTE   *You must have the CREATE PROCEDURE privilege in order to create the DEPTREE_FILL package.*

First, create the DEPTREE_FILL procedure in your schema by running the ORACLE-provided script in the utldtree.sql file:

```
@utldtree
```

Next, execute the DEPTREE_FILL procedure. There are three parameters for the procedure:

1. The type of object

2. The name of the schema owner for the object

3. The name of the object whose dependencies will be evaluated

A sample execution of the DEPTREE_FILL procedure (for a table named DEPTREE_TEMPTAB, which is created by the utldtree.sql script) is shown in the following listing.

```
execute DEPTREE_FILL ('table','qc_user','deptree_temptab');

PL/SQL procedure successfully completed.
```

The DEPTREE_FILL procedure **insert**s records into a table named DEPTREE. Once you have executed DEPTREE_FILL, you can select the dependency data from DEPTREE, as shown in the following listing.

```
col Nested_Level format 99 heading 'LV'
col Schema format A20

select Nested_Level,
       Type,
       Schema,
       Name
```

```
from DEPTREE
order by Seq#;
```

The output of the query is shown below:

```
LV TYPE          SCHEMA                NAME
--- ------------ -------------------   -------------------------------
  0 TABLE        QC_USER               DEPTREE_TEMPTAB
  1 PROCEDURE    QC_USER               DEPTREE_FILL
  1 VIEW         QC_USER               DEPTREE
  2 VIEW         QC_USER               IDEPTREE
```

The output shows that the base object for this analysis (the level 0 object) is DEPTREE_TEMPTAB, a table. That object has two dependencies—the DEPTREE_FILL procedure and the DEPTREE view. The IDEPTREE view is another level down the dependency tree, but it is not immediately clear from this query output on which of the level 1 objects IDEPTREE is dependent.

ORACLE provides an alternate, more easily read output listing that shows the relationships among the multiple levels of dependent objects. You can query the IDEPTREE view to see the formatted form of the dependency information.

```
select * from IDEPTREE;
```

```
DEPENDENCIES
--------------------------------------------
TABLE QC_USER.DEPTREE_TEMPTAB
   PROCEDURE QC_USER.DEPTREE_FILL
   VIEW QC_USER.DEPTREE
      VIEW QC_USER.IDEPTREE
```

The IDEPTREE output shows that the IDEPTREE view is dependent on the DEPTREE view. The output uses indenting to indicate the level of each dependency.

ANNOTATIONS

Before querying DEPTREE and IDEPTREE, you first must execute the DEPTREE_FILL procedure, filling the DEPTREE_TEMPTAB table with information to be extracted. You do not have to be the owner of the object to execute this procedure for the object; however, if you do not have permission on one of the underlying dependent objects, you will get a row of **NULL** values returned.

Once the dependency records have been **insert**ed into the DEPTREE_TEMPTAB table you can query them via the DEPTREE and IDEPTREE views. The simplest method for displaying the dependency data is to use the IDEPTREE view:

```
select * frsom IDEPTREE;
```

An alternative to using DEPTREE_FILL is to query the data dictionary view DBA_DEPENDENCIES, as shown in the following listing.

```
set term on echo on heading on linesize 80
col Type format a12
col Referenced_Type format a12 heading 'REF TYPE'
col Referenced_Owner format a20 heading 'REF OWNER'
col Name format a20
col Referenced_Name format a20 heading 'REF NAME'

select Name,
       Type,
       Referenced_Owner,
       Referenced_Name,
       Referenced_Type
  from DBA_DEPENDENCIES
 where Referenced_Name ='DEPTREE_TEMPTAB'
   and Referenced_Owner='QC_USER';
```

The output for the preceding query for the DEPTREE_TEMPTAB dependencies is shown in the following listing.

```
NAME                 TYPE          REF OWNER            REF NAME             REF TYPE
-------------------- ------------  -------------------- -------------------- ----------
DEPTREE_FILL         PROCEDURE     QC_USER              DEPTREE_TEMPTAB      TABLE
DEPTREE              VIEW          QC_USER              DEPTREE_TEMPTAB      TABLE
```

The major disadvantage to using the DBA_DEPENDENCIES data dictionary view is that only a single level of dependency is shown. To get the same results as the prior example using DEPTREE_FILL, the query will have to be run three more times, substituting DEPTREE_FILL, DEPTREE, and IDEPTREE for Referenced_Name in place of DEPTREE_TEMPTAB in the example **where** clause.

usr_fkys.sql

Foreign Key Columns

Within ORACLE, you can define foreign keys that refer to primary keys. The enforcement of referential integrity within the database can make it difficult to change tables that are referred to by other tables. If you attempt to alter a table that is referenced by foreign keys elsewhere, you will receive the following message:

```
ORA-02266: unique/primary keys in table referenced by enabled foreign keys
```

Unfortunately, this message doesn't reveal either the name of the constraint or the name of the table referencing the parent table. To effectively resolve the situation, you need to know information about the referential integrity clauses that caused the error message to be displayed. The following script will list, by parent table, all foreign key constraints, the child table, and the columns the constraint is on.

```
set pagesize 60 linesize 132 colsep ' '
col Parent_Table format a25
col Child_Table format a25
col Column_Name format a25
break on Parent_Table on Child_Table skip 1
set term on echo on heading on feedback off

select B.Table_Name Parent_Table,
       A.Table_Name Child_Table,
       C.Column_Name
  from USER_CONSTRAINTS A,
       USER_CONSTRAINTS B,
       USER_CONS_COLUMNS C
 where A.R_Constraint_Name = B.Constraint_Name
   and A.Constraint_Type='R'
   and B.Constraint_Type ='P'
   and A.Constraint_Name=C.Constraint_Name
   and A.Table_Name=C.Table_Name
 order by B.Table_Name, A.Table_Name, C.Position
/
```

Sample output for the preceding query is shown in the following listing.

PARENT_TABLE	CHILD_TABLE	COLUMN_NAME
ORDERS	ORDER_DETAILS	ORDER_NO
		ORDER_DATE
	INVOICE_DETAILS	ORDER_NO
		ORDER_DATE

The query output shows that there are two tables with two foreign keys that refer to the primary key of the ORDERS table. Both the ORDER_DETAILS table and the INVOICE_DETAILS table refer to the primary key of the ORDERS table. The columns of the foreign keys, in order, are Order_No and Order_Date .

ANNOTATIONS

The script joins the USER_CONSTRAINTS data dictionary view to itself to find the parent and child tables. The script then uses the child constraint name to extract the foreign key columns from the USER_CONS_COLUMNS data dictionary view.

In general, you should document your database from within the database itself. You can use the usr_cons.sql script, along with the script in the next section, to maintain accurate and current documentation.

usr_pkys.sql

Primary Key Columns

Creating a primary key on a table creates a unique, non-nullable index for that table. The following script will document the existing primary keys, by selected user.

```
set term on echo on heading on verify off
set colsep '' pagesize 60
break on Table_Name

select A.Table_Name,
       B.Column_Name
  from DBA_CONSTRAINTS A,
       DBA_CONS_COLUMNS B
 where A.Constraint_Type='P'
   and A.Constraint_Name=B.Constraint_Name
   and A.Owner=UPPER('&usernm')
   and B.Owner=A.Owner
 order by A.Table_Name, B.Position
/
```

When you execute this query, you will be prompted for a value for the *usernm* value—the username for which the primary keys will be displayed. Sample output for the preceding query is shown in the following listing.

```
TABLE_NAME                        COLUMN_NAME
--------------------------        -----------------------------
ORDERS                            ORDER_NO
                                  ORDER_DATE
```

The query output shows that the primary key for the ORDERS table has two columns: Order_No and Order_Date.

no_pks.sql

Tables Without Primary Keys

You can use the script in the preceding section to list all of the primary keys within your schema. You can modify that script to show the tables in your schema for which no primary keys have been defined. You may then determine what the proper primary keys are for the tables.

```
set term on echo on heading on verify off
set colsep '' pagesize 60
break on Table_Name

select Table_Name
  from USER_TABLES
 where not exists
     (select 1 from USER_CONSTRAINTS
        where USER_CONSTRAINTS.Table_Name = USER_TABLES.Table_Name
          and USER_CONSTRAINTS.Constraint_Type='P');
```

The preceding script will return the name of any table that does not have a constraint whose constraint type is 'P' (for "Primary key"). You should investigate whether there are primary keys that should be defined for such tables.

Which Objects Changed Yesterday?

obj_chng.sql

In addition to monitoring the relationships among your database objects, you may also wish to monitor when the objects change. For example, if another user alters a table that you depend on, you should be informed prior to the change being made. However, if you are not informed prior to the change, you can query the data dictionary for the record of the change after it has taken place. The script in this section will return a list of the tables that have been changed during the past day. If you run the following script daily, you will always be informed of the changes taking place in your database.

```
set term on echo on feedback off heading on
set pagesize 60 colsep ' '
col Owner format a20
col Object_Name format a30
col Ddltime format a20
break on Owner

select Owner,
       Object_Name,
       Timestamp  Ddltime
  from DBA_OBJECTS
 where Object_Type ='TABLE'
   and  SysDate - TO_DATE(TimeStamp,'YYYY-MM-DD:HH24:MI:SS') < 1
order by Owner, Object_Name
/
```

Sample output from the preceding query is shown in the following listing.

```
OWNER                   OBJECT_NAME               DDLTIME
--------------------    ------------------------  -------------------
PROD_USER               AUTH                      1998-04-11:12:01:02
PROD_USER               AUTH_CODES                1998-04-11:10:02:34
PROD_USER               CLIENTS                   1998-04-11:09:51:39
TEST_USER               LOCK_MANAGER              1998-04-11:11:39:12
QCA                     ACCOUNT                   1998-04-11:11:31:30
```

The query output shows that five tables have changed within the past day. The **where** clause of the script specifically queries for changes made to tables:

```
where Object_Type ='TABLE'
```

so only tables are shown in the query output.

ANNOTATIONS

The script uses the data dictionary view DBA_OBJECTS to monitor changes. The Timestamp column of that view is used rather than the Last_DDL_Time because the Timestamp column reflects only changes to the object's structure while Last_DDL_Time will also reflect index or view creation and **grant**s issued on that object.

The Timestamp column in the DBA_OBJECTS view is a VARCHAR2 column and must be converted to date format (via the **TO_DATE** function) for the query to succeed.

All Constraints Defined for a User's Tables

usr_cons.sql

As you manage your tables, you will often need to know the constraints that have been created on the tables. For example, you may need to know the foreign keys that exist prior to dropping a table that the foreign keys reference.

ORACLE has simplified the commands used to manage tables and their constraints. For example, you can drop a primary key constraint without knowing the name of the constraint, and you can drop the associated foreign keys at the same time. To drop the primary key constraint on a table named DEPARTMENT, you can issue the following **alter table** command:

```
alter table DEPARTMENT drop primary key;
```

If there are foreign keys that reference the DEPARTMENT table's primary key, then you must use the **cascade** clause of the **alter table** command, as shown in the following listing.

```
alter table DEPARTMENT drop primary key cascade;
```

In these examples, the names of the constraints were not specified. However, you may need to know the names of the constraints if you wish to disable or enable specific constraints or if you are trying to understand the relationships between the tables that constitute an application schema. The following script will report all constraints for the tables in the current user's schema.

```
ttitle center 'User Constraints' skip 2
column Ctabname format a15 heading 'Table Name' trunc
column Cname    format a15 heading 'Constraint Name' trunc
column Ctype    format a1
column Cdecode  format a15 heading 'Type' trunc
column On_Col   format a15 heading 'On column' trunc
column Cstatus  format a4  heading 'Status' trunc
break on Ctabname

select UC1.Table_Name Ctabname,
       UC1.Constraint_Name Cname,
       UCC1.Column_Name On_Col,
       DECODE(Constraint_Type,'C','Check',
                              'P','Prim Key',
                              'U','Unique',
                              'R','Foreign Key',
                              'V','With Chck Opt') Cdecode,
       Status Cstatus
  from USER_CONSTRAINTS UC1, USER_CONS_COLUMNS UCC1
 where UC1.Constraint_Name = UCC1.Constraint_Name(+)
   and UC1.Owner = UCC1.Owner
 order by UC1.Table_Name ;
```

Sample output for the preceding script is shown in the following listing.

```
                          User Constraints
```

Table Name	Constraint Name	On column	Type	Stat
BANK CODE	SYS_C0039844	BANK_COD	Check	ENAB
	SYS_C0039845	SYS_NAM	Check	ENAB
	SYS_C0039846	CUTOFF_TM	Check	ENAB
BRANCH	SYS_C0039847	PTY_ID	Check	ENAB
	SYS_C0039848	PTY_TYP	Check	ENAB
	SYS_C0039849	BR_TYP	Check	ENAB
	SYS_C0039850	ISO_CTRY_COD	Check	ENAB
CARDHOLDER	PK_CH_ACCT	ACCT_NUM	Prim Key	ENAB
	SYS_C0046222	ACCT_NUM	Check	ENAB
DAL_OWNER	PK_DAL_OWNER	DALNAME	Prim Key	ENAB
DAL_USER	FK_DAL_OWNER	DALNAME	Foreign Key	ENAB

TRANSACTION	PK_TRANSACTION	TRAN_NO	Prim Key	ENAB
	SYS_C0046225	TRAN_TYP	Check	ENAB
	SYS_C0046226	VERSION_NO	Check	ENAB

The status value of "ENAB" indicates that the constraints are enabled.

ANNOTATIONS

The script in this section shows all of the constraints owned by a single user. In general, constraints on a table should be created by the owner of the table. You may grant other users the ability to create constraints (and indexes) on your tables, but the more complex your constraint ownership is, the more complex the management of your constraints will be. If possible, create all constraints under the same user as the table was created.

fk_index.sql

Make Sure Foreign Key Columns Are Indexed

When you create a primary key on a table, ORACLE automatically creates a unique index on the primary key columns. When you create a foreign key, however, ORACLE does not automatically index the foreign key columns.

For example, if you have a table named DEPARTMENT with a primary key of Department_Number, then ORACLE will create a unique index on the Department_Number column. If you then create a table called EMPLOYEE with a Department_Number column that references the DEPARTMENT. Department_Number column via a foreign key, then ORACLE will not create an index on the EMPLOYEE.Department_Number column. You will need to create the index on the EMPLOYEE.Department_Number column manually.

Indexing foreign keys gives the ORACLE optimizer more options to use when resolving joins. Foreign key columns are frequently used during joins, so indexing them allows the optimizer to consider index-based access paths when resolving the join condition. In early versions of ORACLE7, the foreign key columns had to be indexed to avoid table-locking problems. Although the locking problems have been resolved, you should still index your foreign keys to improve your tuning options and your query performance.

The script in this section (fk_index.sql) checks a user's foreign keys for the following conditions:

1. All foreign key columns have indexes.

2. If the foreign key has multiple columns, then the columns in the index are in the same order as the foreign key columns.

If either of those conditions is not met, then the script will report the correct order of columns to index.

The script is shown in the following listing. Sample output is shown following the script listing. Annotations follow the sample output listing.

```
set echo off

drop table CK_LOG;
create table CK_LOG (
LineNum NUMBER,
LineMsg VARCHAR2(2000));

declare
T_Constraint_Type       USER_CONSTRAINTS.Constraint_Type%TYPE;
T_Constraint_Name       USER_CONSTRAINTS.Constraint_Name%TYPE;
T_Table_Name            USER_CONSTRAINTS.Table_Name%TYPE;
T_R_Constraint_Name     USER_CONSTRAINTS.R_Constraint_Name%TYPE;
TT_Constraint_Name      USER_CONS_COLUMNS.Constraint_Name%TYPE;
TT_Table_Name           USER_CONS_COLUMNS.Table_Name%TYPE;
TT_Column_Name          USER_CONS_COLUMNS.Column_Name%TYPE;
TT_Position             USER_CONS_COLUMNS.Position%TYPE;
TT_Dummy                NUMBER;
TT_DummyChar            VARCHAR2(2000);
L_Cons_Found_Flag       VARCHAR2(1);
Err_Table_Name          USER_CONSTRAINTS.Table_Name%TYPE;
Err_Column_Name         USER_CONS_COLUMNS.Column_Name%TYPE;
Err_Position            USER_CONS_COLUMNS.Position%TYPE;
TLineNum                NUMBER;
cursor UserTabs is
  select Table_Name
    from USER_TABLES
  order by Table_Name;
cursor TableCons is
  select Constraint_Type,
         Constraint_Name,
         R_Constraint_Name
    from USER_CONSTRAINTS
   where Owner = User
     and Table_Name = T_Table_Name
     and Constraint_Type  = 'R'
   order by Table_Name, Constraint_Name;
cursor ConColumns is
  select Constraint_Name,
         Table_Name,
         Column_Name,
```

```
        Position
    from USER_CONS_COLUMNS
  where Owner = User
    and Constraint_Name = T_Constraint_Name
  order by Position;
cursor IndexColumns is
  select Table_Name,
         Column_Name,
         Position
    from USER_CONS_COLUMNS
  where Owner = User
    and Constraint_Name = T_Constraint_Name
  order by Position;
DebugLevel      NUMBER := 99; -- >>> 99 = dump all info`
DebugFlag       VARCHAR(1) := 'N'; -- Turn Debugging off
T_Error_Found   VARCHAR(1);

begin
  tLineNum := 1000;
  open UserTabs;
  LOOP
    Fetch UserTabs into t_TABLE_NAME;
    T_Error_Found := 'N';
    exit when UserTabs%NOTFOUND;
-- Log current table
    TLineNum := TLineNum + 1;
    insert into CK_LOG ( LineNum, LineMsg ) values
      (TLineNum, NULL );
    TLineNum := TLineNum + 1;
    insert into CK_LOG ( LineNum, LineMsg ) values
      (TLineNum, 'Checking Table '||T_Table_Name);
    L_Cons_Found_Flag := 'N';
    open TableCons;
    LOOP
      FETCH TableCons into T_Constraint_Type,
                           T_Constraint_Name,
                           T_R_Constraint_Name;
      exit when TableCons%NOTFOUND;
      if ( DebugFlag = 'Y' and DebugLevel >= 99 )
      then
        begin
          TLineNum := TLineNum + 1;
          insert into CK_LOG ( LineNum, LineMsg ) values
```

```
                      (TLineNum, 'Found CONSTRAINT_NAME = '|| T_Constraint_Name);
          TLineNum := TLineNum + 1;
          insert into CK_LOG ( LineNum, LineMsg ) values
            (TLineNum, 'Found CONSTRAINT_TYPE = '|| T_Constraint_Type);
          TLineNum := TLineNum + 1;
          insert into CK_LOG ( LineNum, LineMsg ) values
            (TLineNum, 'Found R_CONSTRAINT_NAME = '|| T_R_Constraint_Name);
          commit;
        end;
    end if;
  open ConColumns;
    LOOP
    FETCH ConColumns INTO
                        TT_Constraint_Name,
                        TT_Table_Name,
                        TT_Column_Name,
                        TT_Position;
    exit when ConColumns%NOTFOUND;
    if ( DebugFlag = 'Y' and DebugLevel >= 99 )
    then
      begin
        TLineNum := TLineNum + 1;
        insert into CK_LOG ( LineNum, LineMsg ) values
          (TLineNum, NULL );
        TLineNum := TLineNum + 1;
        insert into CK_LOG ( LineNum, LineMsg ) values
          (TLineNum, 'Found CONSTRAINT_NAME = '|| TT_Constraint_Name);
        TLineNum := TLineNum + 1;
        insert into ck_log ( LineNum, LineMsg ) values
          (TLineNum, 'Found TABLE_NAME = '|| TT_Table_Name);
        TLineNum := TLineNum + 1;
        insert into CK_LOG ( LineNum, LineMsg ) values
          (TLineNum, 'Found COLUMN_NAME = '|| TT_Column_Name);
        TLineNum := TLineNum + 1;
        insert into CK_LOG ( LineNum, LineMsg ) values
          (TLineNum, 'Found POSITION = '|| TT_Position);
      commit;
      end;
    end if;
  begin
    select 1 into TT_Dummy
      from USER_IND_COLUMNS
    where Table_Name =  TT_Table_Name
```

```
      and Column_Name = TT_Column_Name
      and Column_Position = TT_Position;
  if ( DebugFlag = 'Y' and DebugLevel >= 99 )
  then
      begin
      tLineNum := tLineNum + 1;
      insert into CK_LOG ( LineNum, LineMsg ) values
      ( TLineNum, 'Row Has matching Index' );
      end;
  end if;
exception
when TOO_MANY_ROWS then
if ( DebugFlag = 'Y' and DebugLevel >= 99 ) then
    begin
      TLineNum := TLineNum + 1;
      insert into CK_LOG ( LineNum, LineMsg ) values
        (TLineNum, 'Row Has matching Index' );
    end;
end if;
when NO_DATA_FOUND then
  if ( DebugFlag = 'Y' and DebugLevel >= 99 )
  then
    begin
      TLineNum := TLineNum + 1;
      insert into CK_LOG ( LineNum, LineMsg ) values
        (TLineNum, 'NO MATCH FOUND' );
    commit;
    end;
  end if;
T_Error_Found := 'Y';
select distinct Table_Name
  into TT_DummyChar
  from USER_CONS_COLUMNS
 where Owner = User
   and Constraint_Name = T_R_Constraint_Name;
TLineNum := TLineNum + 1;
insert into CK_LOG ( LineNum, LineMsg ) values
  (TLineNum, 'Table '||TT_DummyChar||' is missing an FK index. ');
commit;
```

```
      TLineNum := TLineNum + 1;
      insert into ck_log ( LineNum, LineMsg ) values
       (TLineNum,'Create an index on the following columns: ');
      open IndexColumns ;
      LOOP
        FETCH IndexColumns into Err_Table_Name,
                                Err_Column_Name,
                                Err_Position;
        exit when IndexColumns%NOTFOUND;
        TLineNum := TLineNum + 1;
        insert into CK_LOG ( LineNum, LineMsg ) values
         (TLineNum,'Column = '||Err_Column_Name||' ('||Err_Position||')');
      end loop;
      close IndexColumns;
    end;
   end loop;
   commit;
 close ConColumns;
 end loop;
 if ( t_Error_Found = 'N' )
 then
   begin
     TLineNum := TLineNum + 1;
     insert into CK_LOG ( LineNum, LineMsg ) values
       (TLineNum,'No foreign key errors found');
   end;
 end if;
 commit;
 close TableCons;
end loop;
commit;
end;
/
```

To view the script's output, you must query the line messages from the CK_LOG table that is populated via the script:

```
select LineMsg
  from CK_LOG
 where LineMsg NOT LIKE 'Checking%'
   and LineMsg NOT LIKE 'No Probl%'
   and LineMsg NOT LIKE 'No forei%'
 order by LineNum;
```

Sample output from the query of the CK_LOG table is shown in the following listing.

```
LINEMSG
------------------------------------------------------------------
Table EMPLOYEE is missing an FK index.
Create an index on the following columns:
Column = DEPTNO (1)
Table EMPLOYEE is missing an FK index.
Create an index on the following columns:
Column = MGR (1)
Table ITEMS is missing an FK index.
Create an index on the following columns:
Column = ITEM_CAT (1)
Column = ITEM_BUS_UNIT (2)
Table ORD is missing an FK index.
Create an index on the following columns:
Column = CUSTID (1)
```

Based on the output of the query of the CK_LOG table, you should create four new indexes. The first index should be on the DeptNo column of the EMPLOYEE table. You should create the second index on the Mgr column of the EMPLOYEE table. The third index should be a concatenated index on the Item_Cat and Item_Bus_Unit columns of the ITEMS table. You should create the fourth index on the CustID column of the ORD table.

Once you create those indexes, your foreign key columns will be properly indexed. If you change any table relationships at a later date, you can re-execute this diagnostic script and any missing foreign key indexes will be reported by the script.

ANNOTATIONS

You can run the script in this section manually by repeatedly executing SQL statements. The benefit of this script is the manner in which it uses PL/SQL to navigate through the result sets of multiple queries. The first cursor generates a list of the user's tables. For each table, the next cursor generates a list of all of the foreign key constraints on the table (those constraints that have a Constraint_Type value of 'R'). For each of those constraints, the columns of the constraint are queried by the third cursor. The constraint columns are then compared to the columns of the user's indexes.

If the user does not have an index whose column definitions and positions do not match the foreign key constraints, then no rows will be returned by the query. This script uses the PL/SQL NO_DATA_FOUND error flag to capture this condition:

```
when NO_DATA_FOUND then
  if ( DebugFlag = 'Y' and DebugLevel >= 99 )
  then
    begin
      TLineNum := TLineNum + 1;
      insert into CK_LOG ( LineNum, LineMsg ) values
      (TLineNum, 'NO MATCH FOUND' );
    commit;
    end;
  end if;
```

You can use the *DebugLevel* variable shown here as a tool to assist in your debugging of long scripts. For example, you can set the *DebugLevel* within a loop and check its value after the loop completes to make sure the processing is occurring in the manner you intend.

You can write a script that generates the missing foreign key index information by querying USER_CONS_COLUMNS, USER_CONSTRAINTS, USER_TABLES, and USER_IND_COLUMNS directly, as shown in the following query.

```
ttitle 'FK columns requiring indexes'

select UCC.Table_Name,
       UCC.Column_Name,
       UCC.Position
  from USER_CONS_COLUMNS UCC,
       USER_CONSTRAINTS UC,
       USER_TABLES UT
 where UT.Table_Name = UC.Table_Name
   and UC.Constraint_Type = 'R'
   and UC.Constraint_Name = UCC.Constraint_Name
   and not exists
       (select 1
          from USER_IND_COLUMNS UIC
         where UCC.Table_Name = UIC.Table_Name
           and UCC.Column_Name = UIC.Column_Name
           and UCC.Position = UIC.Column_Position)
 order by Table_Name, Position;
```

The script in the preceding listing will return a listing of the columns that require indexes. You should note the column position within the constraint (the Position value) so the index will contain the columns in the proper order.

```
                          FK columns requiring indexes

TABLE_NAME                      COLUMN_NAME                     POSITION
------------------------------  ------------------------------  --------
EMPLOYEE                        DEPTNO                                 1
EMPLOYEE                        MGR                                    1
ITEMS                           ITEM_CAT                               1
ITEMS                           ITEM_BUS_UNIT                          2
ORD                             CUST_ID                                1
```

rows_fil.sql

Rows Per File (Striping Effectiveness of a Table)

You can query ORACLE directly to determine how your data is distributed among the datafiles of a tablespace. If your table's data is all stored in a single datafile, then you are more likely to encounter I/O bottlenecks during times of high activity for the table. If the data is distributed among multiple files, then you are less likely to encounter I/O bottlenecks during table accesses.

Since the RowID values contain information about the physical location of rows, you can query RowIDs to determine how well a table's data is distributed among multiple datafiles assigned to the table's tablespace. In the following listing, the ORACLE8 DBMS_ROWID package is used to extract file ID information about each row. The **ROWID_TO_RESTRICTED** function has two parameters: the extended RowID value and the type of conversion. Use *0* for the conversion type value, as shown in the following listing.

```
select SUBSTR(DBMS_ROWID.ROWID_TO_RESTRICTED(Rowid,0),15,4),
       COUNT(*)
from &&table
group by SUBSTR(DBMS_ROWID.ROWID_TO_RESTRICTED(Rowid,0),15,4);
```

The result of the query in the preceding listing will be the count of rows in the table for each datafile in the tablespace. This method relies on the structure of the ORACLE7 (restricted) RowID—the values in digits 15 through 18 are the Hexadecimal version of the file number.

A simpler approach may be to use the **ROWID_RELATIVE_FNO** function of the DBMS_ROWID package. The **ROWID_RELATIVE_FNO** function returns the relative file number direction from the RowID values. In the following listing,

ROWID_RELATIVE_FNO returns the number of rows per relative file number (in decimal) of the file in which the row is stored.

```
select DBMS_ROWID.ROWID_RELATIVE_FNO(Rowid),
       COUNT(*)
from &&table
group by DBMS_ROWID.ROWID_RELATIVE_FNO(Rowid);
```

You can verify the relative file number by querying the file information from DBA_DATA_FILES. When querying with the new relative file numbers, use the decimal version of the RELATIVE_FNO value. The following example shows the DBA_DATA_FILES entry for the rows queried in the preceding listing.

```
select File_Name, File_ID
  from DBA_DATA_FILES
 where Relative_FNO = 80;


FILE_NAME                                        FILE_ID
----------------------------------------- ----------
/db02/oracle/CC1/users01.dbf                           5
```

The File_ID value of 5 represents the *absolute* file number for the data file; 80 is the *relative* file number.

ANNOTATIONS

The rows_fil.sql script shown in the preceding example uses the ORACLE8 DBMS_ROWID package to convert RowID values into the "restricted" format. The restricted format of the ORACLE8 RowID is the same as the format for ORACLE7 RowIDs. Therefore, if you need to run the script against an ORACLE7 database, you must remove the reference to the DBMS_ROWID package, as shown in the following listing.

```
select SUBSTR(Rowid,15,4),
       COUNT(*)
from &&table
group by SUBSTR(Rowid,15,4);
```

The query output will be the file number, in Hexadecimal, along with the number of rows stored in the file.

UTILITIES

The scripts in this section create procedures and functions within your database. You can use these procedures and functions to manage your transactions, to manipulate data values, and to generate new data (such as a random number) in your database. Since these scripts create procedures and functions in your database, you must have the CREATE PROCEDURE system privilege in order to execute them.

DELETE_COMMIT Procedure

del_comt.sql

When you **delete** a large number of records, you may exceed the amount of rollback space available for a single transaction. If you exceed the rollback segment space available, then your **delete** transaction will fail. Therefore, you may need to make the size of the **delete** transaction smaller, or you may configure your database so you can use the **truncate** command in place of the **delete** command.

The **truncate** command deletes all of the records in the table, but it does so without using any rollback segment space. By default, the table's non-initial extents are de-allocated during a truncation.

PROGRAMMER'S NOTE *You cannot roll back a **truncate** command.*

The **truncate** command is not always a suitable alternative to the **delete** command. For example, you may not be able to support deleting all of the records from a table. If you want to **delete** only half of the records in a large table, you will need to find a way to make the transaction smaller. You can use the partitioning capabilities introduced in ORACLE8 to improve your ability to **delete** larger numbers of records in a transaction, since you can **truncate** a partition. As an example, if you create a table with two partitions, then you can **truncate** one of the partitions without affecting the other partition. Therefore, if your partitions are defined based on criteria commonly used for mass deletions, you can greatly improve your ability to manage large deletions.

However, you may not be able to use partitions, or the key columns used for partitioning may be different than those used for mass deletions. Consider a table called PROBLEM_REPORT that is used to store records of all of the calls to a helpdesk. Periodically, you will need to archive old records out of the PROBLEM_REPORT table (based on the values of its Report_Date column). For example, you may issue a command to **delete** all records from the PROBLEM_REPORT table if the records are more than one year old:

```
delete from PROBLEM_REPORT
where Report_Date < (SysDate-365);
```

If your rollback segments are not large enough to support that transaction, then the **delete** command will fail.

To divide a single **delete** transaction into multiple smaller transactions, use the procedure created by the del_comt.sql script shown in the following listing. You will see examples of its use following the script listing. When you execute the DELETE_COMMIT procedure, you pass in as variables the **delete** command and the number of records after which a **commit** should be executed. For example, if you execute DELETE_COMMIT and use 500 as the **commit** variable, then a **commit** will be executed after every 500 records have been deleted. The DELETE_COMMIT procedure uses dynamic SQL to accomplish this task.

```
create or replace procedure DELETE_COMMIT
( P_Statement              in VARCHAR2,
  P_Commit_Batch_Size      in NUMBER default 10000)
is
        CID                       INTEGER;
        Changed_Statement         VARCHAR2(2000);
        Finished                  BOOLEAN;
        Nofrows                   INTEGER;
        Lrowid                    ROWID;
        Rowcnt                    INTEGER;
        Errpsn                    INTEGER;
        Sqlfcd                    INTEGER;
        Errc                      INTEGER;
        Errm                      VARCHAR2(2000);
begin
        /* If the actual statement contains a WHERE clause, then append
           a rownum < n clause after that using AND, else use WHERE
           rownum < n clause */
        if ( UPPER(P_Statement) like '% WHERE %') then
                Changed_Statement := P_Statement||' AND rownum < '
                ||TO_CHAR(P_Commit_Batch_Size + 1);
        else
                Changed_Statement := P_Statement||' WHERE rownum < '
                ||TO_CHAR(P_Commit_Batch_Size + 1);
        end if;
        begin
    CID := DBMS_SQL.OPEN_CURSOR; -- Open a cursor for the task
                DBMS_SQL.PARSE(CID,Changed_Statement, DBMS_SQL.NATIVE);
                        -- parse the cursor.
                Rowcnt := DBMS_SQL.LAST_ROW_COUNT;
                        -- store for some future reporting
        exception
            when others then
                        Errpsn := DBMS_SQL.LAST_ERROR_POSITION;
                            -- gives the error position in the changed sql
                            -- delete statement if anything happens
                        Sqlfcd := DBMS_SQL.LAST_SQL_FUNCTION_CODE;
                            -- function code can be found in the OCI manual
```

```
                Lrowid := DBMS_SQL.LAST_ROW_ID;
                    -- store all these values for error
                    -- reporting. However all these are
                    -- really useful in a stand-alone
                    -- proc execution for DBMS_OUTPUT
                    -- to be successful, not possible
                    -- when called from a form or
                    -- front-end tool.
                Errc := SQLCODE;
                Errm := SQLERRM;
                DBMS_OUTPUT.PUT_LINE('Error '||TO_CHAR(Errc)||
                        ' Posn '||TO_CHAR(Errpsn)||
                        ' SQL fCode '||TO_CHAR(Sqlfcd)||
                        ' rowid '||ROWIDTOCHAR(Lrowid));
                RAISE_APPLICATION_ERROR(-20000,Errm);
                    -- this will ensure the display of at least
                    -- the error message if something happens,
                    -- even in a frontend tool.
end;
Finished := FALSE;
while not (Finished)
loop -- keep on executing the cursor
     -- till there is no more to process.
        begin
          Nofrows := DBMS_SQL.EXECUTE(CID);
          Rowcnt := DBMS_SQL.LAST_ROW_COUNT;
        exception
             when others then
                Errpsn := DBMS_SQL.LAST_ERROR_POSITION;
                Sqlfcd := DBMS_SQL.LAST_SQL_FUNCTION_CODE;
                Lrowid := DBMS_SQL.LAST_ROW_ID;
                Errc   := SQLCODE;
                Errm   := SQLERRM;
            DBMS_OUTPUT.PUT_LINE('Error '||TO_CHAR(Errc)||
                    ' Posn '||TO_CHAR(Errpsn)||
                    ' SQL fCode '||TO_CHAR(Sqlfcd)||
                    ' rowid '||ROWIDTOCHAR(Lrowid));
            RAISE_APPLICATION_ERROR(-20000,Errm);
        end;
        if Nofrows = 0 then
```

```
                        Finished := TRUE;
              else
               Finished := FALSE;
              end if;
              commit;
       end loop;
       begin
              DBMS_SQL.CLOSE_CURSOR(CID);
                      -- close the cursor for a clean finish
       exception
              when others then
                      Errpsn := DBMS_SQL.LAST_ERROR_POSITION;
                      Sqlfcd := DBMS_SQL.LAST_SQL_FUNCTION_CODE;
                      Lrowid := DBMS_SQL.LAST_ROW_ID;
                      Errc   := SQLCODE;
                      Errm   := SQLERRM;
              DBMS_OUTPUT.PUT_LINE('Error '||TO_CHAR(Errc)||
                      ' Posn '||TO_CHAR(Errpsn)||
                      ' SQL fCode '||TO_CHAR(Sqlfcd)||
                      ' rowid '||ROWIDTOCHAR(Lrowid));
              RAISE_APPLICATION_ERROR(-20000,Errm);
       end;
end;
/
```

Once you have created the DELETE_COMMIT procedure, you can use it to force **commit**s to occur during your **delete**s. For example, the **delete** shown earlier in this section was:

```
delete from PROBLEM_REPORT
where Report_Date < (SysDate-365);
```

You can execute this via a call of the DELETE_COMMIT procedure. The first parameter passed to the procedure is the SQL statement to execute; the second parameter is the number of records to be **commit**ted at a time. The following listing shows the DELETE_COMMIT execution for this sample **delete**.

```
execute DELETE_COMMIT('delete from PROBLEM_REPORT where Report_Date < (SysDate-365)', 500);
```

As shown in the example, you must enclose the **delete** command in single quotes. If your **delete** command contains single quotes (for example, surrounding a character string value), then you must substitute two single quotes for each single quote in your command. For example, if your **delete** command is

```
delete from PROBLEM_REPORT where Department = 'IT';
```

then the matching execution of DELETE_COMMIT will be

```
execute DELETE_COMMIT('delete from PROBLEM_REPORT where Dept= ''IT''', 500);
```

In the DELETE_COMMIT execution, the entire **delete** command is enclosed within single quotes, and each single quote surrounding a character string is changed to a set of two single quotes.

PROGRAMMER'S NOTE   *Do not put a semicolon within the text of the SQL statement you pass to DELETE_COMMIT.*

ANNOTATIONS

The DELETE_COMMIT procedure works by modifying the **delete** command you give it. When you pass DELETE_COMMIT a **delete** command, the procedure uses the **commit** batch size parameter to modify the SQL to include a **where** clause using the RowNum pseudo-column to limit the number of records affected. For example, in the previous section, the following command was shown:

```
execute DELETE_COMMIT('delete from PROBLEM_REPORT where Dept= ''IT''', 500);
```

When processed by DELETE_COMMIT, this command will be changed to:

```
delete from PROBLEM_REPORT
where Dept='IT'
and rownum < 501;
```

The **rownum < 501** clause tells ORACLE to only **delete** the first 500 rows it finds that match the criteria in the **where** clause. Once these records have been deleted, the exact same **delete** command is executed repeatedly until no rows that match the **where** clause criteria remain in the table.

There are several potential issues with this approach:

1.   *Consistency.* When you execute a single **delete** command, ORACLE guarantees that your data will be consistent throughout the transaction. When you use DELETE_COMMIT, you are executing multiple transactions, and there is no guarantee of data consistency. You should therefore execute this script at a time when you can guarantee that no other users are accessing the table. Since DELETE_COMMIT is usually used as part of a batch maintenance operation, there should not be any online users of the table during the maintenance period.

2.   *Performance.* You **must** index the columns used in the **where** clause. For example, if you use the Department_Number column in the **where** clause and

the Department_Number column is not indexed, then ORACLE will perform a full scan of the PROBLEM_REPORT table. Since the DELETE_COMMIT procedure repeatedly executes your **delete** command, you will be performing full table scans repeatedly, with a potential effect on the performance of your database. If you create an index on the Department_Number column (even if only for this **delete** operation), your deletions will perform dramatically faster.

PROGRAMMER'S NOTE   *In order to optimize the space usage within your indexes, you should rebuild indexes on any table that has had mass deletions. If you create an index that is intended solely to improve the performance of your deletions, you may drop that index following the completion of the **delete**.*

If your **delete** command does not have a **where** clause, then you should investigate the possibility of using the **truncate** command in its place. If you are unable to use the **truncate** command, then you can use DELETE_COMMIT to divide the **delete** command into smaller **delete** commands. If you do not have a **where** clause in your **delete** command, then DELETE_COMMIT will append a **where rownum <** clause to your command instead of an **and rownum <** clause, as shown in the following listing.

```
if ( UPPER(P_Statement) like '% WHERE %') then
        Changed_Statement := P_Statement||' AND rownum < '
        ||TO_CHAR(P_Commit_Batch_Size + 1);
else
        Changed_Statement := P_Statement||' WHERE rownum < '
        ||TO_CHAR(P_Commit_Batch_Size + 1);
end if;
```

Once the changed statement has been created, dynamic SQL is used to execute it. First, a cursor is opened and the statement is parsed:

```
CID := DBMS_SQL.OPEN_CURSOR; -- Open a cursor for the task
DBMS_SQL.PARSE(CID,Changed_Statement, DBMS_SQL.NATIVE);
```

Next, a binary variable named *Finished* is set to FALSE, and a While loop is used to coordinate the execution of the modified **delete** command:

```
Finished := FALSE;
while not (Finished)
loop -- keep on executing the cursor till there is no more to
     -- process.
        begin
            Nofrows := DBMS_SQL.EXECUTE(CID);
            Rowcnt := DBMS_SQL.LAST_ROW_COUNT;
```

After each execution, the deleted batch of rows is **commit**ted:

```
        commit;
end loop;
```

You can theoretically use DELETE_COMMIT to support transactions other than **delete**, but that is not its intended use. Because DELETE_COMMIT generates multiple transactions, the data processed by each transaction is not guaranteed to be consistent with the data used by any other transaction. As a result, DELETE_COMMIT is most applicable to processing **delete**s; it should not be used to process **update**s or **insert**s that depend on consistency of data throughout the entire data set processed.

hextodec.sql

Hexadecimal to Decimal Conversion

ORACLE provides a function called **HEX_TO_RAW** that converts a Hexadecimal value to a RAW datatype value. However, there is no function provided that converts Hexadecimal values to Decimal values. Database administrators and application developers may occasionally need to convert a Hexadecimal value to a Decimal value; the script in this section accomplishes that task.

The script shown in the following listing creates a stored function in the database. As a result, you can call this function within all of your SQL commands. In order to create the function, you must have the CREATE PROCEDURE system privilege.

```
create function HEXTODEC (Hexnum in CHAR)
    RETURN NUMBER IS
            X                 NUMBER;
            Digits            NUMBER;
            Result            NUMBER := 0;
            Current_Digit     CHAR(1);
            Current_Digit_Dec NUMBER;
begin
    Digits := LENGTH(Hexnum);
    for X in 1..Digits loop
        Current_Digit := UPPER(SUBSTR(Hexnum, X, 1));
        if Current_Digit in ('A','B','C','D','E','F') then
            Current_Digit_Dec := ASCII(Current_Digit) - ASCII('A') +
10;
        else
            Current_Digit_Dec := TO_NUMBER(Current_Digit);
        end if;
        Result := (Result * 16) + Current_Digit_Dec;
    end loop;
return Result;
end;
/
```

The **HEXTODEC** function has a single input variable—the Hexadecimal value to be converted to a Decimal value. Since you can execute functions within your SQL commands, you can use the **HEXTODEC** function in the same places you use functions such as **LENGTH** and **UPPER**. The following listing shows an example of the use of the **HEXTODEC** function.

```
select HEXTODEC('A3')
   from DUAL;
```

ANNOTATIONS

When evaluating a Hexadecimal value, the **HEXTODEC** function examines each digit of the value separately. The function first determines the number of digits in the value:

```
Digits := LENGTH(Hexnum);
```

and then executes a For loop to evaluate each digit in turn:

```
   for X in 1..Digits loop
```

Within the loop, each digit is examined to determine if it contains a letter value ('A' through 'F' Hexadecimal signify 10 through 15 in Decimal). If a letter is found, then the ASCII function is used to determine the proper value for the digit. The ASCII value for 'A' is subtracted from the ASCII value for the digit, and 10 is added to the difference. For example, if the digit is 'C', then the ASCII value for 'A' is subtracted from the ASCII value for 'C', leaving a difference of 2. Ten is then added to the difference, for a value of 12.

```
      if Current_Digit in ('A','B','C','D','E','F') then
         Current_Digit_Dec := ASCII(Current_Digit) - ASCII('A') + 10;
      else
         Current_Digit_Dec := TO_NUMBER(Current_Digit);
      end if;
```

Once the digit has been converted to a numeric value, the value is added to the *Result* variable. If there is already a *Result* value, then the previous value is multiplied by 16 before adding in the new value:

```
      Result := (Result * 16) + Current_Digit_Dec;
```

In the example shown earlier, the Hexadecimal value was A3. In evaluating that value, the **HEXTODEC** function first evaluates the 'A' digit. The 'A' digit is assigned the value of 10 during the first execution of the loop within **HEXTODEC**, and the *Result* variable is assigned a value of 10. The second pass through the loop evaluates the '3' digit. Since '3' is a number, there is no need to convert it before processing it. The previous value of the *Result* variable (10) is multiplied by 16 prior to adding the second digit to the Result. The function then returns 163 as the result of the Hexadecimal to Decimal conversion.

bus_days.sql

Count the Number of Business Days Between Two Given Dates

Within ORACLE, you can determine the number of days between two dates by subtracting one date from the other. However, you may need more specific information about the time lapse between the dates. In this section, you will see how to eliminate weekends and holidays from the calculation of the difference between two dates.

The **COUNT_BUSINESS_DAYS** function, shown in the following listing, counts the number of weekdays between two given dates. The function has two input parameters: a start date and an end date. The end date will be counted as one of the business days, unless it is a weekend date.

```
create function COUNT_BUSINESS_DAYS
   (Start_Date in DATE, End_Date in DATE)
return NUMBER is
   CurrDate     DATE := Start_Date;
   TheDay       VARCHAR2(10);    /* day of the week for CurrDate */
   CountBusiness   NUMBER := 0; /* counter for business days */
begin
   if end_date - start_date <= 0 then
      return (0);
   end if;
   loop
        /* go to the next day */
      CurrDate := TO_DATE(CurrDate+1);
        /* finished if End_Date is reached */
      exit when CurrDate > End_Date;
        /* what day of the week is it? */
      TheDay := TO_CHAR(CurrDate,'fmDay');
        /* count it only if it is a weekday */
      if TheDay <> 'Saturday' and TheDay <> 'Sunday' then
         CountBusiness := CountBusiness + 1;
      end if;
   end loop;
return (CountBusiness);
end;
/
```

You can execute the **COUNT_BUSINESS_DAYS** function created by the preceding script within a SQL statement, as shown in the following example.

```
select COUNT_BUSINESS_DAYS('01-JUL-98','08-JUL-98') Bus_Days
  from DUAL;


      Bus Days
    ------------
            5
```

The function's output reveals that there are five business days between the two given dates.

ANNOTATIONS

Since the script consists of only one loop, it is easy to modify. For example, you may wish to maintain a list of corporate holidays in a table within your database. You can use that list of values as part of your **COUNT_BUSINESS_DAYS** function. The ability to modify the script is important, since if a day other than a Saturday or Sunday is a non-business day for your company, you should not count that day toward the total number of business days between two dates.

For example, you could create a table named HOLIDAY:

```
create table HOLIDAY
(Hol_Date  DATE);
```

You can modify the **COUNT_BUSINESS_DAYS** function to query HOLIDAY as the function evaluates each date. The following script is a modified version of the function shown earlier; the script will only work if you have created a table named HOLIDAY as shown in the preceding listing.

```
create function NUM_BUSINESS_DAYS
    (Start_Date in DATE, End_Date in DATE)
return NUMBER is
   CurrDate      DATE := Start_Date;
   TheDay        VARCHAR2(10);     /* day of the week for CurrDate */
   CountBusiness  NUMBER := 0; /* counter for business days */
   Hol_Check    NUMBER := 0;       /* for holiday check */
begin
   if end_date - start_date <= 0 then
      return (0);
   end if;
   loop
      Hol_Check := 0;
         /* go to the next day */
      CurrDate := TO_DATE(CurrDate+1);
         /* finished if End_Date is reached */
      exit when CurrDate > End_Date;
         /* what day of the week is it? */
      TheDay := TO_CHAR(CurrDate,'fmDay');
```

```
                /* count it only if it is a weekday */
         if TheDay <> 'Saturday' and TheDay <> 'Sunday' then
              /* check to see if CurrDate is a holiday */
                 select COUNT(*) into Hol_Check
                   from HOLIDAY
                 where Hol_Date = TO_DATE(CurrDate);
              if Hol_Check <> 1 then
                 CountBusiness := CountBusiness + 1;
              end if;
           end if;
      end loop;
return (CountBusiness);
end;
/
```

The modifications to the script are shown in bold in the preceding listing. The modification adds an additional check to the *CurrDate* evaluation. If the *CurrDate* value matches a date in the HOLIDAY column, then the *CountBusiness* variable is not incremented. The value to be returned by the function is only incremented if the days are neither weekends nor holidays.

random.sql

Generate Random Numbers

You may occasionally need the ability to generate random numbers in the database. The script provided in this section will generate a random number. To simplify the script, the following assumptions have been made:

1. The numbers generated will all be non-negative integers.

2. The numbers generated will all be less than 1,000,000.

3. A new value will be generated each second.

4. Two successive generated numbers will be independent of each other.

5. If two different users execute the function at exactly the same time, they will receive different values from the function.

Given the first two criteria above, the output values are not limitless; they are, however, returned in a random order.

In the following listing, you will see the script that is used to create a function named **RANDOM**. The **RANDOM** function has a single input parameter (since it is a function), but that value is not used by the function. The function uses two "seed" values: the user's session ID value and the current time. Those two values are manipulated by the function to produce a random number between 0 and 1,000,000; that number serves as the seed value for the rest of the processing.

```
create or replace function RANDOM
    (Dummy in VARCHAR2)
return NUMBER is
    Seed1           NUMBER;
    Seed2           NUMBER;
    SeedProduct     NUMBER;
    NatLog          NUMBER;
    DecNatLog       NUMBER;
    RandomValTemp   NUMBER;
    X               NUMBER;
    ReverseVal      NUMBER;
    NatLogFinal     NUMBER;
    DecNatLogFinal  NUMBER;
    RandomValFinal  NUMBER;
begin
    select USERENV('SESSIONID')
      into Seed1 from DUAL;
    select TO_NUMBER(TO_CHAR(SysDate,'SSSSS'))
      into Seed2 from DUAL;
    SeedProduct := Seed1*Seed2;
    NatLog := LN(SeedProduct);
    DecNatLog := NatLog - TRUNC(NatLog);
    RandomValTemp := TRUNC(1000000*DecNatLog);
    ReverseVal := NULL;
    for x in 1..6 loop
      ReverseVal := ReverseVal||SUBSTR(RandomValTemp,(7-X),1);
    end loop;
    NatLogFinal := LN(ReverseVal);
    DecNatLogFinal := NatLogFinal - TRUNC(NatLogFinal);
    RandomValFinal := TRUNC(1000000*DecNatLogFinal);
return (RandomValFinal);
end;
/
```

Sample execution of the **RANDOM** function is shown in the following listing.
The results shown in the listing were achieved by executing the **RANDOM** function
once per second.

```
set heading off
select RANDOM('x') from DUAL;

    93872

/
```

```
    500579

/

    720950

/

    500488

/

    252993

/

    101697

/

    614443

/

    305343

/

    618224

/

    580892
```

The numbers are generated in a random order. You can modify the range of possible values, and the manner in which the numbers are generated, as described in the "Annotations" section. You can also automate the creation of many random numbers via a procedure, as documented in the "Annotations" section.

ANNOTATIONS

The script that creates the **RANDOM** function performs a combination of several ORACLE functions. The intent of those functions is to generate a new number that will be substantially different than the next number generated. The two "seed" values used are the user's session ID and the number of seconds that have elapsed in the current day.

The script obtains the user's session ID via the **USERENV** function:

```
select USERENV('SESSIONID')
  into Seed1 from DUAL;
```

A sample value for the session ID is shown in the following listing.

```
select USERENV('SESSIONID') from DUAL;


USERENV('SESSIONID')
--------------------
                1797
```

A user's session ID value does not change during a session. Each session has a distinct session ID, so two users who execute the **RANDOM** function at the same time will have different seed values for their random number generation.

The second seed value for the function is the number of seconds since midnight in the current day. If you execute the function twice in the same second, you will get the same output twice, since the two executions will use identical seed values.

```
    select TO_NUMBER(TO_CHAR(SysDate,'SSSSS'))
      into Seed2 from DUAL;
```

The 'SSSSS' date format of the **TO_CHAR** function returns the number of seconds since midnight. If you execute the **RANDOM** function twice in the same second, the same value will be assigned to the *Seed2* variable. If two separate sessions execute **RANDOM** at the same time, they will use the same value for *Seed2* but will have different values for *Seed1*.

PROGRAMMER'S NOTE   *There are 86,400 seconds in a day, so this function generates a maximum of 86,400 unique values for each session. See the procedure-based version of this function at the end of this chapter for additional randomization techniques.*

Once the two variables' values have been assigned, they are multiplied to generate a new value:

```
    SeedProduct := Seed1*Seed2;
```

Next, take the natural (base *e*) logarithm of that number. The purpose of this step is to generate a set of digits that is not directly related to the original seed values.

```
    NatLog := LN(SeedProduct);
```

The next step in the process is to trim off all but the decimal portion of the natural logarithm value. Since the **TRUNC** of the NatLog variable returns the integer portion of the variable's value, subtracting **TRUNC**(NatLog) from NatLog returns the decimal portion of the value.

```
DecNatLog := NatLog - TRUNC(NatLog);
```

Given the decimal value, the next step selects the first six digits and converts them into a new integer value.

```
RandomValTemp := TRUNC(1000000*DecNatLog);
```

At this point, a new number has been generated, but repeated execution of the **RANDOM** function will generate RandomValTemp values that are close together. For example, the values may be 355110, then 355135, then 355156. Since the seed values are all close together, the natural logarithms of those values are close together. However, you can use these new values to generate numbers that are significantly different. To change them, reverse them. Change 355110 to 011553, change 355135 to 531553, and change 355156 to 651553.

The code in the following listing performs the reversal of the digits. A For loop is created, and the **SUBSTR** function selects one digit at a time. The first time through the loop, the variable *X* has a value of 1, so the **SUBSTR** function starts at position 6 (7-1). The second time through the loop, the **SUBSTR** function starts at position 5 (7-2). The result is the reversal of the digits in the value. Prior to starting the loop, the *ReverseVal* variable is initialized.

```
ReverseVal := NULL;
for x in 1..6 loop
   ReverseVal := ReverseVal||SUBSTR(RandomValTemp,(7-X),1);
end loop;
```

Given these reversed values, you can now manipulate them the way the seed variables' products were manipulated earlier in the function. Take the natural log of the reversed number, and use the first six digits after the decimal as your new value. That value is the random number that is returned.

```
NatLogFinal := LN(ReverseVal);
DecNatLogFinal := NatLogFinal - TRUNC(NatLogFinal);
RandomValFinal := TRUNC(1000000*DecNatLogFinal);
return (RandomValFinal);
```

PROGRAMMER'S NOTE   *A set of random numbers may contain duplicates. The order of the values should be random. The generated values are not guaranteed to be statistically randomized.*

To increase the maximum generated value, you will need to increase:

1. The value that the *DecNatLog* variable is multiplied by.

2. The maximum value for the variable *X* in the loop control command to reflect the number of digits.

3. The value used to establish the start position for the **SUBSTR** function during the digit reversal process.

4. The value that the *DecNatLogFinal* variable is multiplied by.

For example, to increase the maximum generated value to 1,000,000,000, you must

1. Increase the value that the *DecNatLog* variable is multiplied by to 1000000000 to capture 9 digits.

2. Change the **for** command to **for X in** 1..9 **loop** to reflect the 9 digits of the value.

3. Change the **SUBSTR** command to use 10-X instead of 7-X to reflect the 9 digits reversed.

4. Increase the value that the *DecNatLogFinal* variable is multiplied by to 1000000000 to capture 9 digits.

You can convert the function into a procedure in order to programmatically insert a large number of random values into a table. In so doing, you should add a third seed value into the number generation. Determine the number of values you want to generate, and create a loop that executes a variable number of times. Since the procedure will execute the loop multiple times per second, you must use a loop counter variable in order to generate distinct seed values.

In order to store the generated values, you must first create a table. During the execution of the procedure, the generated values will be inserted into the following table:

```
create table RANDOMNESS
(RandomVal  NUMBER);
```

The procedure version of the **RANDOM** function (called RANDOM_P) is shown in the following listing. The significant changes are shown in bold.

```
create or replace procedure RANDOM_P
   (MaxCount in NUMBER)
 is
   Counter        NUMBER;
   Seed1          NUMBER;
   Seed2          NUMBER;
   SeedProduct    NUMBER;
   NatLog         NUMBER;
```

```
    DecNatLog          NUMBER;
    RandomValTemp      NUMBER;
    X                  NUMBER;
    ReverseVal         NUMBER;
    NatLogFinal        NUMBER;
    DecNatLogFinal     NUMBER;
    RandomValFinal     NUMBER;
begin
    select USERENV('SESSIONID')
        into Seed1 from DUAL;
    for Counter in 1..MaxCount loop
        select TO_NUMBER(TO_CHAR(SysDate,'SSSSS'))
            into Seed2 from DUAL;
        SeedProduct := Seed1*Seed2*Counter;
        NatLog := LN(SeedProduct);
        DecNatLog := NatLog - TRUNC(NatLog);
        RandomValTemp := TRUNC(1000000*DecNatLog);
        ReverseVal := NULL;
        for x in 1..6 loop
            ReverseVal := ReverseVal||SUBSTR(RandomValTemp,(7-X),1);
        end loop;
        NatLogFinal := LN(ReverseVal);
        DecNatLogFinal := NatLogFinal - TRUNC(NatLogFinal);
        RandomValFinal := TRUNC(1000000*DecNatLogFinal);
        insert into RANDOMNESS values (RandomValFinal);
    end loop;
commit;
end;
/
```

The procedure accepts a value into a variable named *MaxCount*. A *Counter* variable is then incremented from 1 to the *MaxCount* value. For each value of the *Counter* variable, the *Counter* value is multiplied by the two other seed values (as shown in the following listing) to determine the number evaluated by the natural logarithm function prior to the digit reversal process.

```
    SeedProduct := Seed1*Seed2*Counter;
```

When the program **insert**s multiple records per second, each execution of the loop uses a different value for the *SeedProduct* variable.

The following listing shows the generation of 100,000 random numbers inserted into the RANDOMNESS table.

```
execute RANDOM_P(100000);
```

When you execute the RANDOM_P procedure, you will likely find that the generated numbers are not all unique. Randomness and uniqueness are different concepts. If you need to generate unique numbers, you should use sequences instead of this random number generation procedure.

Several queries were run following a test load of the RANDOMNESS table in order to determine the distribution of the data values generated. The data values generated were all less than 1,000,000 because of the length constraints in the program. The following listings show the queries that were run and the results for the test.

```
select COUNT(*)
  from RANDOMNESS;


  COUNT(*)
----------
    100000
```

All 100,000 records were inserted in a single transaction. If your rollback segment cannot support that large of a transaction, you can either execute the RANDOM_P procedure multiple times or change the manner in which **commit**s are processed. You will see a discussion of the change to the **commit** processing structure following the rest of the test results.

The next test determines how many values are repeated three times or more.

```
select RandomVal, COUNT(*)
  from RANDOMNESS
 group by RandomVal
having COUNT(*)>2;


RANDOMVAL    COUNT(*)
----------  ----------
      2577           3
     57752           3
    207636           3
    230310           3
    263142           3
    485921           3
    561240           3
    664409           3
    738414           3
    786655           3
    863631           3
    897646           3
    939355           3

13 rows selected.
```

The query result shows that 13 different values appear three times each among the 100,000 generated values. As noted earlier, randomness does not imply uniqueness. A series of numbers can still be random even if it includes the same number twice in a row. The next value generated in the series is independent of the current value in the series.

The next query illustrates the range of values generated.

```
select MIN(RandomVal), MAX(RandomVal)
  from RANDOMNESS;


MIN(RANDOMVAL) MAX(RANDOMVAL)
-------------- --------------
             0         999964
```

The generated values are not confined to a small range. As shown by the preceding query output, you can generate 0 as a valid value.

All of the preceding queries have shown the generated values out of their generated order. The next query selects the first 30 values generated, in order, to illustrate the lack of relationship among consecutive generated values.

```
select RandomVal
  from RANDOMNESS
 where Rownum < 31;


 RANDOMVAL
----------
    960084
     81064
    355065
    615576
    502533
     86526
    982505
    413661
    761996
    711709
    726673
    810701
    833792
    128370
     72981
    649087
    208341
    153661
    820016
    389012
```

```
515272
548012
605694
683090
300031
751580
  6364
740070
270385
333612
```

30 rows selected.

In this random value generation program, the generated values were all non-negative integer values. You can easily modify the program to include negative numbers. For example, you could subtract 500,000 from each of the final generated values, so the range of values would then be from -500,000 to 499,999. If you want to generate character strings, you can translate each digit of a number into a character after the number has been generated. The result will be a series of random character strings.

During the execution of the RANDOM_P procedure, all of the values were inserted into the RANDOMNESS table via a single **insert** transaction. If the size of the transaction causes errors due to rollback segment space requirements, there are two alternatives to consider. First, you can execute the procedure multiple times instead of one time. For example, instead of executing

```
execute RANDOM_P(100000);
```

you could instead generate 20,000 values at a time:

```
execute RANDOM_P(20000);
execute RANDOM_P(20000);
execute RANDOM_P(20000);
execute RANDOM_P(20000);
execute RANDOM_P(20000);
```

Each execution will use different seed values than the others, since the seed value generated by the time of day will be different for each (unless they are run simultaneously). If you execute the RANDOM_P procedure multiple times, you should schedule the executions to run one after another.

A second way of reducing the rollback segment requirements for the random number **insert**s requires modifying the procedure. Move the **commit** command inside the loop that generates the numbers. Each new number will be **committed** as soon as it is **inserted**. The following listing shows the program block portion of the RANDOM_P procedure, with the moved command order shown in bold:

```
begin
    select USERENV('SESSIONID')
```

```
into Seed1 from DUAL;
   for Counter in 1..MaxCount loop
     select TO_NUMBER(TO_CHAR(SysDate,'SSSSS'))
       into Seed2 from DUAL;
     SeedProduct := Seed1*Seed2*Counter;
     NatLog := LN(SeedProduct);
     DecNatLog := NatLog - TRUNC(NatLog);
     RandomValTemp := TRUNC(1000000*DecNatLog);
     ReverseVal := NULL;
     for x in 1..6 loop
       ReverseVal := ReverseVal||SUBSTR(RandomValTemp,(7-X),1);
     end loop;
     NatLogFinal := LN(ReverseVal);
     DecNatLogFinal := NatLogFinal - TRUNC(NatLogFinal);
     RandomValFinal := TRUNC(1000000*DecNatLogFinal);
     insert into RANDOMNESS values (RandomValFinal);
     commit;
   end loop;
end;
```

The modified version of the RANDOM_P procedure **commit**s each row as it
is **insert**ed. Although this modification resolves the rollback segment problem, it
introduces a new potential problem: if your execution is interrupted, you will not
have the full set of random numbers required. If that occurs, you can query the
RANDOMNESS table to determine how many values have been generated and
then re-execute the RANDOM_P procedure to generate enough random values
to meet your needs.

Object Management

Managing the objects within your database can be an overwhelming process. How do you determine which objects are invalid and need recompilation? Can you tell what jobs are in the job queue and when they will next execute? Do you have up-to-date documentation on each object within the database, its structure and storage? In this chapter, you will see scripts that will help you to manage the objects in your database. You can use the diagnostic scripts to document your tables and jobs, and you can use the utility scripts to create a series of scripts to regenerate and document the database structure.

The major scripts presented in this chapter are:

tab_desc.sql	Fully describes a table—storage, indexes, column and constraint information
list_sub.sql	Lists submitted jobs in the job queue and their execution information
list_run.sql	Lists currently executing jobs in the job queue and their execution information
invalobj.sql	Lists all invalid objects in the database and generates a script to recompile them
pinsize.sql	Lists packages which are candidates for pinning in the SGA
revalobj.sql	Generates compilation commands to revalidate invalid objects
gen_tbl.sql	Generates a script to re-create a table and its constraints
gen_indx.sql	Generates a script to re-create indexes for a given table
gen_trig.sql	Generates a script to re-create triggers for a given table
gen_view.sql	Generates a script to re-create a view
gen_syn.sql	Generates a script to re-create synonyms for an object
gen_proc.sql	Generates a script to re-create a procedure
gen_func.sql	Generates a script to re-create a function
gen_pkg.sql	Generates a script to re-create a package
gen_seq.sql	Generates a script to re-create a sequence
gendblnk.sql	Generates a script to re-create database links
gen_grnt.sql	Generates a script to re-create grants for a given table

All the scripts in this chapter should be run from an account which has DBA privileges or which has been granted select on all the DBA_ views.

Diagnostics

You can use the scripts in this section to report on the state of various objects within your database. The diagnostic scripts in this section include reports on the status of jobs in the job queue and lists of the invalid objects within the database.

tab_desc.sql

Fully Describe a Table

While we all start out with the good intentions of keeping documentation on database tables up to date, the reality is that updating documentation is rarely a priority. Table changes are made "on the fly" to meet production needs, indexes are added to speed performance, and constraints are added (or dropped) for expediency's sake when coding.

This script will generate up-to-date documentation on the selected table, including storage parameters, column descriptions and defaults, indexes on the table, and all constraint data.

```
set echo off term on
accept table_name prompt "Enter the name of the Table: "
accept tab_owner prompt "Enter table owner: "
set heading on newpage 0
ttitle 'Table Description - Space Definition'
spool tab_desc.log

btitle off
column Nline newline
set pagesize 54
set linesize 78
set heading off embedded off verify off
accept report_comment char prompt
      'Enter a comment to identify system: '
set term off
select 'Date - '||TO_CHAR(sysdate,'Day Ddth Month YYYY HH24:MI:SS'),
'At            - '||'&&report_comment' nline,
      'Username       - '||User  nline
  from SYS.DUAL
/

prompt
```

```
set embedded on heading on

column Ts format a30
column Ta format a30
column Clu format a30
column Pcf format 99999999999990
column Pcu format 99999999999990
column Int format 99,999,999,990
column Mat format 99,999,999,990
column Inx format 99,999,999,990
column Nxt format 99,999,999,990
column Mix format 99,999,999,990
column Max format 99,999,999,990
column Pci format 99999999999990
column Num format 99,999,999,990
column Blo format 99,999,999,990
column Emp format 99,999,999,990
column Avg format 99,999,999,990
column Cha format 99,999,999,990
column Rln format 99,999,999,990
column Hdg format a30 newline
set heading off
select 'Table Name' Hdg,               Table_Name                Ta,
       'Tablespace Name' Hdg,          Tablespace_Name           Ts,
       'Cluster Name' Hdg,             Cluster_Name              Clu,
       '% Free' Hdg,                   Pct_Free                  Pcf,
       '% Used' Hdg,                   Pct_Used                  Pcu,
       'Ini Trans' Hdg,                Ini_Trans                 Int,
       'Max Trans' Hdg,                Max_Trans                 Mat,
       'Initial Extent (K)' Hdg,       Initial_Extent/1024       Inx,
       'Next Extent (K)' Hdg,          Next_Extent/1024          Nxt,
       'Min Extents' Hdg,              Min_Extents               Mix,
       'Max Extents' Hdg,              Max_Extents               Max,
       '% Increase' Hdg,               Pct_Increase              Pci,
       'Number of Rows' Hdg,           Num_Rows                  Num,
       'Number of Blocks' Hdg,         Blocks                    Blo,
       'Number of Empty Blocks' Hdg,   Empty_Blocks              Emp,
       'Average Space' Hdg,            Avg_Space                 Avg,
       'Chain Count' Hdg,              Chain_Cnt                 Cha,
       'Average Row Length' Hdg,       Avg_Row_len               Rln
  from DBA_TABLES
 where Table_Name=UPPER('&&table_name')
   and Owner=UPPER('&&tab_owner')
```

```
/
set heading on
set embedded off
column Cn format a30 heading 'Column Name'
column Fo format a15 heading 'Type'
column Nu format a8 heading 'Null'
column Nds format 99,999,999 heading 'No Distinct'
column Dfl format 9999 heading 'Dflt Len'
column Dfv format a40 heading 'Default Value'
ttitle 'Table Description - Column Definition'
select Column_Name Cn,
       Data_Type ||
       DECODE(Data_Type,
              'NUMBER',
                 '('||TO_CHAR(Data_Precision)||
                     DECODE(Data_Scale,0,'',','||
                     TO_CHAR(Data_Scale))||')',
              'VARCHAR2',
                 '('||TO_CHAR(Data_Length)||')',
              'CHAR',
                 '('||TO_CHAR(Data_Length)||')',
              'DATE','',
              'LONG','',
              '') Fo,
       DECODE(Nullable,'Y','','NOT NULL') Nu,
       Num_Distinct Nds,
       Default_Length Dfl,
       Data_Default Dfv
  from DBA_TAB_COLUMNS
 where Table_Name=UPPER('&&table_name')
   and Owner=UPPER('&&tab_owner')
 order by Column_ID
/
ttitle off
prompt
prompt TABLE CONSTRAINTS
prompt
set heading on
column Cn format a30 heading 'Primary Constraint'
column Cln format a45 heading 'Table.Column Name'
column Ct format a7 heading 'Type'
column St format a7 heading 'Status'
column Ro format a30 heading 'Ref Owner|Constraint Name'
```

```
column Se format a70 heading 'Criteria ' newline
break on Cn on St
set embedded on
prompt Primary Key
prompt
select CNS.Constraint_Name Cn,
       CNS.Table_Name||'.'||CLS.Column_Name Cln,
       INITCAP(CNS.Status) St
  from DBA_CONSTRAINTS CNS,
       DBA_CONS_COLUMNS CLS
 where CNS.Table_Name=UPPER('&&table_name')
   and CNS.Owner=UPPER('&&tab_owner')
   and CNS.Constraint_Type='P'
   and CNS.Constraint_Name=CLS.Constraint_Name
 order by CLS.Position
/
prompt Unique Key
prompt
column Cn format a30 heading 'Unique Key'
select CNS.Constraint_Name Cn,
       CNS.Table_Name||'.'||CLS.Column_Name Cln,
       INITCAP(CNS.Status) St
  from DBA_CONSTRAINTS CNS,
       DBA_CONS_COLUMNS CLS
 where CNS.Table_Name=UPPER('&&table_name')
   and CNS.Owner=UPPER('&&tab_owner')
   and CNS.Constraint_Type='U'
   and CNS.Constraint_Name=CLS.Constraint_Name
 order by CLS.Position
/
prompt Foreign Keys
prompt
column Cln format a38 heading 'Foreign Key' newline
column Clfn format a38 heading 'Parent Key'
column Cn format a40 heading 'Foreign Constraint'
break on Cn on St skip 1
select CNS.Constraint_Name Cn,
       INITCAP(CNS.Status) St,
       CLS.Table_Name||'.'||CLS.Column_Name Cln,
       CLF.Owner||'.'||CLF.Table_Name||'.'||CLF.Column_Name Clfn
  from DBA_CONSTRAINTS CNS,
```

```
            DBA_CONS_COLUMNS CLF,
            DBA_CONS_COLUMNS CLS
  where CNS.Table_Name=UPPER('&&table_name')
    and CNS.Owner=UPPER('&&tab_owner')
    and CNS.Constraint_Type='R'
    and CNS.Constraint_Name=CLS.Constraint_Name
    and CLF.Constraint_Name = CNS.R_Constraint_Name
    and CLF.Owner = CNS.Owner
    and CLF.Position = CLS.Position
  order by CNS.Constraint_Name, CLS.Position
/
prompt Check Constraints
prompt
column Cn format a40 heading 'Check Constraint'
column Se format a75 heading 'Criteria'
set arraysize 1
set long 32000
select Constraint_Name Cn,
       INITCAP(Status) St,
       Search_Condition Se
  from DBA_CONSTRAINTS
 where Table_Name=UPPER('&&table_name')
   and Owner=UPPER('&&tab_owner')
   and Constraint_Type='C'
/
prompt View Constraints
column Cn format a40 heading 'View Constraint'
select Constraint_Name Cn,
       INITCAP(Status) St,
       Search_Condition Se
  from DBA_CONSTRAINTS
 where Table_Name=UPPER('&&table_name')
   and Owner=UPPER('&&tab_owner')
   and Constraint_Type='V'
/
spool off
set arraysize 30
```

Sample output for the tab_desc.sql script is shown in the following listing. The first part of the output shows the table's storage information, followed by its column definitions and constraints.

```
Enter a comment to identify system: Orcl
Tue Jun 02                                                        page    1
                   Table Description - Space Definition


Date  -  Tuesday   02nd June     1998      17:22:41
At            -  Orcl
Username      -  APPDBA




Table Name                APP_REFERRALS
Tablespace Name           USER_DATA
Cluster Name
% Free                              10
% Used                              40
Ini Trans                            1
Max Trans                          255
Initial Extent (K)                  72
Next Extent (K)                  1,024
Min Extents                          1
Max Extents                        500
% Increase                           0
Number of Rows                     857
Number of Blocks                     9
Number of Empty Blocks               0
Average Space                    2,901
Chain Count                          0
Average Row Length                  53



Tue Jun 02                                                        page    1
                   Table Description - Column Definition

Column Name                  Type             Null     No Distinct Dflt Len
---------------------------- ---------------- -------- ----------- --------
Default Value
----------------------------------------
CODE                         VARCHAR2(3)      NOT NULL             857


REFR_TYPE                    VARCHAR2(3)      NOT NULL               1


DESCRIPTION                  VARCHAR2(25)     NOT NULL             784
```

USR_CRTD	VARCHAR2(30)	NOT NULL	1
DT_CRTD	DATE	NOT NULL	9
STATUS	VARCHAR2(3)		0
USR_MDFD	VARCHAR2(30)		2
DT_MDFD	DATE		7
REFR_CODE	VARCHAR2(3)		0
DISCOUNT	NUMBER(8,2)		17
DISCOUNT_TYPE	CHAR(1)		3

```
11 rows selected.

TABLE CONSTRAINTS

Primary Key

Primary Constraint          Table.Column Name
--------------------------- ----------------------------------------------
Status
-------
REFR_PK                     APP_REFERRALS.CODE
Enabled


Unique Key
```

```
no rows selected

Foreign Keys

Foreign Constraint                      Status
--------------------------------------- -------
Foreign Key                             Parent Key
--------------------------------------- ---------------------------------------
REFR_REFR_FK                            Enabled
APP_REFERRALS.REFR_CODE                 APP.APP_REFERRALS.CODE



Check Constraints

Check Constraint                        Status
--------------------------------------- -------
Criteria
---------------------------------------------------------------------------
SYS_C002237                             Enabled
CODE IS NOT NULL


SYS_C002238                             Enabled
REFR_TYPE IS NOT NULL


SYS_C002239                             Enabled
DESCRIPTION IS NOT NULL


SYS_C002240                             Enabled
USR_CRTD IS NOT NULL


SYS_C002241                             Enabled
DT_CRTD IS NOT NULL



View Constraints

no rows selected
```

The output is broken into sections, with information on the table storage displayed first, then the table structure, and finally the other objects that relate to this table.

ANNOTATIONS

The first section of the script does the initial setup, prompting for the table name and table owner for later use via the **accept** command, which, unlike simply using the variable with the '&' or '&&' in a SQL statement, allows you to define the datatype of the variable (the **char** in the **accept report_comment** command) and to define your own prompt for the variable. In addition, the **ttitle** statement is used to define the report heading, and the **newpage** option of the **set** command is used to tell ORACLE not to print any white space above the title. Defining the column Nline as **newline** forces a carriage return before the column is displayed.

```
set echo off term on
accept table_name prompt "Enter the name of the Table: "
accept tab_owner prompt "Enter table owner: "
set heading on newpage 0
ttitle 'Table Description - Space Definition'
spool tab_desc.log


btitle off
column Nline newline
set pagesize 54
set linesize 78
set heading off embedded off verify off
accept report_comment char prompt
      'Enter a comment to identify system: '
set term off
select 'Date -  '||TO_CHAR(sysdate,'Day Ddth Month YYYY HH24:MI:SS'),
      'At          - '||'&&report_comment' nline,
      'Username    - '||User  nline
  from SYS.DUAL
/


prompt
set embedded on heading on
```

The SQL*Plus **set** command has a variety of variables which can be defined for reporting purposes. The **embedded** option controls where on a page the report will begin. By setting **embedded** to **off** initially, the report is forced to the top of the new page. Turning it back on after the **select** from DUAL means that the remainder of the report will print immediately following the results of that select.

The **select** statement includes the pseudo-column User, which returns the name of the current user. The User value is displayed as well to indicate which userid ran the script.

Formatting the numeric columns with a "0" at the end of the format string, as shown in the following listing, forces the display of a zero rather than a blank if the column value is zero. The pseudo-column Hdg is defined with the **newline** option to force a carriage return before the column is displayed and is used for the text strings. This formatting, combined with the **set heading off** statement, is a simple way to make a report line display vertically rather than horizontally for a **select** which will return a single row.

```
column Ts format a30
column Ta format a30
column Clu format a30
column Pcf format 99999999999990
column Pcu format 99999999999990
column Int format 99,999,999,990
column Mat format 99,999,999,990
column Inx format 99,999,999,990
column Nxt format 99,999,999,990
column Mix format 99,999,999,990
column Max format 99,999,999,990
column Pci format 99999999999990
column Num format 99,999,999,990
column Blo format 99,999,999,990
column Emp format 99,999,999,990
column Avg format 99,999,999,990
column Cha format 99,999,999,990
column Rln format 99,999,999,990
column Hdg format a30 newline
set heading off
select 'Table Name' Hdg,             Table_Name           Ta,
       'Tablespace Name' Hdg,        Tablespace_Name      Ts,
       'Cluster Name' Hdg,           Cluster_Name         Clu,
       '% Free' Hdg,                 Pct_Free             Pcf,
       '% Used' Hdg,                 Pct_Used             Pcu,
       'Ini Trans' Hdg,             Ini_Trans            Int,
       'Max Trans' Hdg,             Max_Trans            Mat,
       'Initial Extent (K)' Hdg,    Initial_Extent/1024  Inx,
       'Next Extent (K)' Hdg,       Next_Extent/1024     Nxt,
       'Min Extents' Hdg,           Min_Extents          Mix,
       'Max Extents' Hdg,           Max_Extents          Max,
       '% Increase' Hdg,            Pct_Increase         Pci,
       'Number of Rows' Hdg,        Num_Rows             Num,
```

```
         'Number of Blocks' Hdg,            Blocks              Blo,
         'Number of Empty Blocks' Hdg,      Empty_Blocks        Emp,
         'Average Space' Hdg,               Avg_Space           Avg,
         'Chain Count' Hdg,                 Chain_Cnt           Cha,
         'Average Row Length' Hdg,          Avg_Row_len         Rln
   from DBA_TABLES
  where Table_Name=UPPER('&&table_name')
    and Owner=UPPER('&&tab_owner')
/
```

Sample output for the storage section of the report is shown in the following listing.

```
Table Name                    APP_REFERRALS
Tablespace Name               USER_DATA
Cluster Name
% Free                                    10
% Used                                    40
Ini Trans                                  1
Max Trans                                255
Initial Extent (K)                        72
Next Extent (K)                        1,024
Min Extents                                1
Max Extents                              500
% Increase                                 0
Number of Rows                           857
Number of Blocks                           9
Number of Empty Blocks                     0
Average Space                          2,901
Chain Count                                0
Average Row Length                        53
```

The table is not a clustered table and was defined using the standard ORACLE defaults for **pctfree, pctused, initrans, maxtrans** and **minextents**. The maximum extents value for this table has been increased to 500 extents. As of ORACLE7.3, tables can be created with an unlimited value for **maxextents**. The initial extent is 72KB and the next extent is 1MB. Since the number of blocks the table is currently using is only 9, the table has not extended and the database block size must be 8KB. There are no empty blocks in the table, so unless the table is a static table or one with low activity, it will most likely have to extend soon. The average space value is the average available free space in the table. Since the chain count is zero, there are no chained rows.

The next section of the script displays the column information for the table.

```
set heading on
set embedded off
column Cn format a30 heading 'Column Name'
```

```
column Fo format a15 heading 'Type'
column Nu format a8 heading 'Null'
column Nds format 99,999,999 heading 'No Distinct'
column Dfl format 9999 heading 'Dflt Len'
column Dfv format a40 heading 'Default Value'
ttitle 'Table Description - Column Definition'
select Column_Name Cn,
       Data_Type ||
       DECODE(Data_Type,
              'NUMBER',
                   '('||TO_CHAR(Data_Precision)||
                        DECODE(Data_Scale,0,'',','||
                        TO_CHAR(Data_Scale))||')',
              'VARCHAR2',
                   '('||TO_CHAR(Data_Length)||')',
              'CHAR',
                   '('||TO_CHAR(Data_Length)||')',
              'DATE','',
              'LONG','',
              '') Fo,
       DECODE(Nullable,'Y','','NOT NULL') Nu,
       Num_Distinct Nds,
       Default_Length Dfl,
       Data_Default Dfv
  from DBA_TAB_COLUMNS
 where Table_Name=UPPER('&&table_name')
   and Owner=UPPER('&&tab_owner')
 order by Column_ID
/
```

The **DECODE** function causes different formatting to be displayed depending on the value of the Data_Type column checked in the **DECODE**. The value of the Data_Type column determines whether the **select** statement will then look at the Data_Precision and Data_Scale columns (for a Data_Type of NUMBER), the Data_Length column (for a Data_Type of VARCHAR2 or CHAR) or no other column (for a Data_Type of DATE or LONG).

The **DECODE** function includes a "search/result" pair as well as a default value in case the expression being checked does not meet any of the explicitly defined search criteria. In this statement, the **DECODE** function is used first to search for matches on the Data_Type column values, with a non-match on the search defaulting to the string ''. It is used again within the initial **DECODE**, to determine if the NUMBER datatype has been defined with decimal places (a non-zero Data_Scale column) and if it has, the **DECODE** will format it properly.

DECODE is used again to display either 'NOT NULL' or blanks, depending on the value of the Nullable column.

The Num_Distinct column lists the number of distinct values this column has. The Default_Length and Data_Default columns refer to any default values defined for the column. In the following example output, the table has columns with datatypes of VARCHAR2, CHAR, DATE, and NUMBER. Although the first five columns are NOT NULL, the column with the most distinct values is the Code column, and this is most likely the primary key column for the table.

```
Tue Jun 02                                                      page     1
                   Table Description - Column Definition


Column Name                          Type             Null     No Distinct Dflt Len
----------------------------------   ---------------  -------- ----------- --------
Default Value
----------------------------------------------
CODE                                 VARCHAR2(3)      NOT NULL        857


REFR_TYPE                            VARCHAR2(3)      NOT NULL          1


DESCRIPTION                          VARCHAR2(25)     NOT NULL        784


USR_CRTD                             VARCHAR2(30)     NOT NULL          1


DT_CRTD                              DATE             NOT NULL          9


STATUS                               VARCHAR2(3)                        0


USR_MDFD                             VARCHAR2(30)                       2


DT_MDFD                              DATE                               7


REFR_CODE                            VARCHAR2(3)                        0
```

| DISCOUNT | NUMBER(8,2) | 17 |
| DISCOUNT_TYPE | CHAR(1) | 3 |

11 rows selected.

The next section of the script displays information on the constraints defined on the table. There are five possible types of constraints which can be defined on a table: primary key, unique key, foreign key, check, and view. If you do not explicitly name the constraint, ORACLE will generate the name, using the format 'SYS_C#####'. You should use meaningful names and name all constraints to avoid confusion and make understanding the relationships between tables easier.

```
ttitle off
prompt
prompt TABLE CONSTRAINTS
prompt
set heading on
column Cn format a30 heading 'Primary Constraint'
column Cln format a45 heading 'Table.Column Name'
column Ct format a7 heading 'Type'
column St format a7 heading 'Status'
column Ro format a30 heading 'Ref Owner|Constraint Name'
column Se format a70 heading 'Criteria ' newline
break on Cn on St
set embedded on
prompt Primary Key
prompt
select CNS.Constraint_Name Cn,
       CNS.Table_Name||'.'||CLS.Column_Name Cln,
       INITCAP(CNS.Status) St
  from DBA_CONSTRAINTS CNS,
       DBA_CONS_COLUMNS CLS
 where CNS.Table_Name=UPPER('&&table_name')
   and CNS.Owner=UPPER('&&tab_owner')
   and CNS.Constraint_Type='P'
   and CNS.Constraint_Name=CLS.Constraint_Name
 order by CLS.Position
/
```

This section lists the information on the primary key constraint on the table. A table can have one and only one primary key, although the key, like an index key, can consist of several concatenated columns, as long as this combination will point to one and only one row of the table. Primary key columns may not contain nulls.

The primary key constraint will have a constraint type of 'P.' The **INITCAP** function is used for formatting the output of the Status column of DBA_CONSTRAINTS for readability by capitalizing the first letter of each word. The status of the constraint can be either "enabled" or "disabled" (enforced or ignored on input, respectively). The **order by** clause will list the primary key columns in the order in which the key is created.

```
TABLE CONSTRAINTS


Primary Key


Primary Constraint                Table.Column Name
-------------------------         ------------------------------------
Status
-------
REFR_PK                           APP_REFERRALS.CODE
Enabled
```

In this example, the primary key is a single column and the constraint is enforced on the table.

The next section of the script checks for unique constraints. You can define multiple unique keys on a table, and their columns may contain nulls.

```
prompt Unique Key
prompt
column Cn format a30 heading 'Unique Key'
select CNS.Constraint_Name Cn,
       CNS.Table_Name||'.'||CLS.Column_Name Cln,
       INITCAP(CNS.Status) St
  from DBA_CONSTRAINTS CNS,
       DBA_CONS_COLUMNS CLS
 where CNS.Table_Name=UPPER('&&table_name')
   and CNS.Owner=UPPER('&&tab_owner')
   and CNS.Constraint_Type='U'
   and CNS.Constraint_Name=CLS.Constraint_Name
 order by CLS.Position
/
```

You cannot create a unique key on the same columns as the primary key. Adding a unique constraint on a table will also create a unique index on the constraint's columns. Creating a unique index for the table will *not* add the unique constraint to the table. Sample output for the unique constraint check on the APP_REFERRALS table is shown in the following listing.

```
Unique Key


no rows selected
```

In this example, there are no additional unique key constraints. The next section of the script checks for the existence of foreign key constraints on the table.

Foreign key constraints enforce integrity relationships between tables in the same database. A foreign key constraint may be defined on either the primary key or unique key of a table (parent table). You can define a foreign key with the **on delete cascade** clause, which will allow deletions in the parent table if there are child records and will automatically delete the dependent rows in the child table. By default, deletions are not allowed on the parent table if there are dependent rows as defined by the foreign key.

Extracting the foreign key relationships from the data dictionary is slightly more complex than extracting the primary key. In addition to knowing the name of the foreign key constraint and column(s) for the table being listed, you must know the owner, table name, and column name(s) of the table being referenced. To retrieve the information, the DBA_CONS_COLUMNS view is joined twice into the query, to extract the foreign key columns (CLS alias) and to extract the information on the primary key being referenced (CLF alias). The name of the primary key constraint being referenced by the foreign key is contained in the R_Constraint_Name column of DBA_CONSTRAINTS.

```
prompt Foreign Keys
prompt
column Cln format a38 heading 'Foreign Key' newline
column Clfn format a38 heading 'Parent Key'
column Cn format a40 heading 'Foreign Constraint'
break on Cn on St skip 1
select CNS.Constraint_Name Cn,
       INITCAP(CNS.Status) St,
       CLS.Table_Name||'.'||CLS.Column_Name Cln,
       CLF.Owner||'.'||CLF.Table_Name||'.'||CLF.Column_Name Clfn
  from DBA_CONSTRAINTS CNS,
       DBA_CONS_COLUMNS CLF,
       DBA_CONS_COLUMNS CLS
 where CNS.Table_Name=UPPER('&&table_name')
   and CNS.Owner=UPPER('&&tab_owner')
   and CNS.Constraint_Type='R'
   and CNS.Constraint_Name=CLS.Constraint_Name
```

```
   and CLF.Constraint_Name = CNS.R_Constraint_Name
   and CLF.Owner = CNS.Owner
   and CLF.Position = CLS.Position
 order by CNS.Constraint_Name, CLS.Position
/
```

Sample output for the foreign key portion of the tab_desc.sql script is shown in the following listing.

```
Foreign Keys


Foreign Constraint                             Status
---------------------------------------- ------
Foreign Key                               Parent Key
------------------------------------      -----------------------------
REFR_REFR_FK                                  Enabled
APP_REFERRALS.REFR_CODE                   APP.APP_REFERRALS.CODE
```

This constraint is self-referring, pointing back to the primary key of its own table. That is, the Refr_Code in the APP_REFERRALS table is a foreign key to the Code column in the same table.

Since foreign key columns are usually used as part of a join between the primary key table and the foreign key table in SQL statements, you should create an index on the columns of the foreign key to speed performance.

PROGRAMMER'S NOTE   *See Chapter 4 for a script that determines which foreign keys are not properly indexed.*

The next portion of the tab_desc.sql script examines the table's Check constraints.

```
prompt Check Constraints
prompt
column Cn format a40 heading 'Check Constraint'
column Se format a75 heading 'Criteria'
set arraysize 1
set long 32000
select Constraint_Name Cn,
       INITCAP(Status) St,
       Search_Condition Se
  from DBA_CONSTRAINTS
 where Table_Name=UPPER('&&table_name')
   and Owner=UPPER('&&tab_owner')
   and Constraint_Type='C'
/
```

Check constraints are used to explicitly define a condition that the column must meet for the insert or update to succeed. If you create the column as NOT NULL,

ORACLE will create a constraint for you. You can define multiple Check constraints on a column, but ORACLE will not check that they are mutually exclusive. You cannot check the values in columns in other tables when creating a Check constraint, but you can refer to columns in the same table and row.

Sample output for the Check constraint portion of the tab_desc.sql script is shown in the following listing.

```
Check Constraints

Check Constraint                         Status
-------------------------------------    -------
Criteria
----------------------------------------------------------------
SYS_C002237                              Enabled
CODE IS NOT NULL


SYS_C002238                              Enabled
REFR_TYPE IS NOT NULL


SYS_C002239                              Enabled
DESCRIPTION IS NOT NULL


SYS_C002240                              Enabled
USR_CRTD IS NOT NULL


SYS_C002241                              Enabled
DT_CRTD IS NOT NULL
```

The only Check constraints on this table are the NOT NULL constraints, with system-generated constraint names. The constraints are enabled, so **insert**s and **update**s to this table must have values for these columns.

The next portion of the script evaluates View constraints.

```
prompt View Constraints
column Cn format a40 heading 'View Constraint'
select Constraint_Name Cn,
       INITCAP(Status) St,
       Search_Condition Se
  from DBA_CONSTRAINTS
 where Table_Name=UPPER('&&table_name')
   and Owner=UPPER('&&tab_owner')
   and Constraint_Type='V'
```

```
/
spool off
```

View constraints are created when a view is created on the table using the **with check option** clause. A View constraint ensures that **insert**s and **update**s performed through the view must result in rows that the view query can **select**. The constraint will be created on the view itself, not on the underlying table.

The following listing shows the sample output for the View constraints query for the APP_REFERRALS table.

```
View Constraints

no rows selected
```

list_sub.sql

List Submitted Jobs

Which of your users have jobs running in your database and when they are scheduled to run? Are the scheduled jobs actually executing or are they broken? ORACLE supports the concept of job queues within the database, allowing users to schedule and execute "batch" jobs. The following script will display all jobs submitted to the queue, along with the information on who submitted the job, when the job will execute, and the status of the last execution.

```
set echo off term off pagesize 60
spool list_sub.log

ttitle -
  center  'List Submitted Jobs' skip 2
col Jid  format 9999   heading 'Id'
col Subu format a10    heading 'Submitter'    trunc
col Secd format a10    heading 'Security'     trunc
col Proc format a20    heading 'Job'          word_wrapped
col Lsd  format a5     heading 'Last|Ok|Date'
col Lst  format a5     heading 'Last|Ok|Time'
col Nrd  format a5     heading 'Next|Run|Date'
col Nrt  format a5     heading 'Next|Run|Time'
col Fail format 999    heading 'Errs'
col Ok   format a2     heading 'Ok'

select Job  Jid,
       Log_User Subu,
       Priv_User Secd,
       What Proc,
       TO_CHAR(Last_Date, 'MM/DD') Lsd,
```

```
        SUBSTR(Last_Sec,1,5) Lst,
        TO_CHAR(Next_Date,'MM/DD') Nrd,
        SUBSTR(Next_Sec,1,5) Nrt,
        Failures Fail,
        DECODE(Broken,'Y','N','Y') Ok
    from DBA_JOBS
/
spool off
```

Sample output for the list_sub.sql script is shown in the following listing.

```
                                List Submitted Jobs
```

Id	Submitter	Security	Job	Last Ok Date	Last Ok Time	Next Run Date	Next Run Time	Errs	Ok
353	APPDBA	APPDBA	table_analyze('APP', 'APP_TELEPHONES');			06/06	13:23	1	Y
294	APPDBA	APPDBA	table_analyze('APP', 'APP_GIFT_CERTIFICAT ES');			06/06	13:23	1	Y
256	APPDBA	APPDBA	table_analyze('APP', 'APP_CUSTOMERS');			06/06	13:23	1	Y
247	APPDBA	APPDBA	table_analyze('APP', 'APP_CREDIT_CARDS');			06/06	12:08		Y
220	APPDBA	APPDBA	table_analyze('APP', 'APP_ADDRESSES');			06/06	12:08		Y

The sample output shows that five separate jobs have been submitted, all by the APPDBA user.

ANNOTATIONS

You can use the job queue to schedule user-defined routines (procedures) and run them from the background process, at times that you define, at intervals that you define, under the same environment and user privileges and access as they were submitted. In order to run jobs in the database, the init.ora parameters

JOB_QUEUE_PROCESSES and JOB_QUEUE_INTERVAL must be set.
JOB_QUEUE_PROCESSES defines the number of background processes that will
be started to run the jobs in the job queues. At the operating system level, these
processes are created as '**ora_snp#_<SID>**', where # begins with 0.
JOB_QUEUE_INTERVAL defines the sleep time for the processes between
checking the job queue for jobs to run. You can use the job queue to schedule
database maintenance jobs at times of low user activity. Jobs are submitted to and
manipulated in the job queue using the ORACLE-provided package **DBMS_JOB**.

The first portion of the list_sub.sql script defines the column characteristics for
displaying output.

```
set echo off term off pagesize 60
spool list_sub.log


ttitle -
  center  'List Submitted Jobs' skip 2
col Jid  format 9999   heading 'Id'
col Subu format a10    heading 'Submitter'     trunc
col Secd format a10    heading 'Security'      trunc
col Proc format a20    heading 'Job'           word_wrapped
col Lsd  format a5     heading 'Last|Ok|Date'
col Lst  format a5     heading 'Last|Ok|Time'
col Nrd  format a5     heading 'Next|Run|Date'
col Nrt  format a5     heading 'Next|Run|Time'
col Fail format 999    heading 'Errs'
col Ok   format a2     heading 'Ok'
```

The **column** command has several uses besides that of formatting the column
output. The **heading** parameter will replace the default heading of the column name
with the specified heading. You can use a "|" in the heading definition to create a
multiple-line column heading. The **trunc** parameter, used for CHAR, VARCHAR2,
LONG, and DATE strings, will truncate the string after the specified format has
been displayed, rather than wrap the column value over several lines. The
word_wrapped parameter will wrap the output string within the defined column
boundaries, in this case 20 characters, and will left-justify each line.

```
select Job  Jid,
       Log_User Subu,
       Priv_User Secd,
       What Proc,
       TO_CHAR(Last_Date,'MM/DD') Lsd,
       SUBSTR(Last_Sec,1,5) Lst,
       TO_CHAR(Next_Date,'MM/DD') Nrd,
       SUBSTR(Next_Sec,1,5) Nrt,
       Failures Fail,
       DECODE(Broken,'Y','N','Y') Ok
```

```
      from DBA_JOBS
/
spool off
```

The Job column, given the alias Jid, is the unique job number assigned to the submitted job. This number is not reused, and will retain its value if the database is exported and imported. Log_User is the user who submitted the job, Priv_User is the user whose default privileges will be used to run the job, and the What column value is the PL/SQL block that will be executed when the job runs. Last_Date is the last date that the job successfully executed, Last_Sec the time of the last successful execution. Next_Date and Next_Sec are the date and time, respectively, that the job is next scheduled to run. The Failures column value is the number of times the job was started and failed since the last time it was successfully executed. The Broken column indicates whether or not the system should try to execute the job. If 16 unsuccessful attempts are made to execute the job, it will be flagged as broken. This script reverses the value of Broken via the **DECODE** command, to display a "Y" rather than an "N" if the job is executable.

List Submitted Jobs

Id	Submitter	Security	Job	Last Ok Date	Last Ok Time	Next Run Date	Next Run Time	Errs	Ok
353	APPDBA	APPDBA	table_analyze('APP', 'APP_TELEPHONES');			06/06	13:23	1	Y
294	APPDBA	APPDBA	table_analyze('APP', 'APP_GIFT_CERTIFICAT ES');			06/06	13:23	1	Y
256	APPDBA	APPDBA	table_analyze('APP', 'APP_CUSTOMERS');			06/06	13:23	1	Y
247	APPDBA	APPDBA	table_analyze('APP', 'APP_CREDIT_CARDS');			06/06	12:08		Y
220	APPDBA	APPDBA	table_analyze('APP', 'APP_ADDRESSES');			06/06	12:08		Y

In the sample output, there are five jobs waiting in the queue. Of the five, three have encountered errors once when running. All five were submitted by the same user, and will execute the same stored procedure, with different input parameters.

list_run.sql

List Running Jobs

The script in the previous section lists jobs submitted to the job queue. The list_run.sql script, shown in the following listing, lists jobs which are currently running and displays the last time they were successfully run as well as the time that the current execution began.

```
set echo off term off pagesize 60
spool listrun.log

ttitle -
  center  'List Running Jobs' skip 2
col Jid  format 9999  heading 'Id'
col Subu format a10   heading 'Submitter'    trunc
col Secd format a10   heading 'Security'     trunc
col Proc format a20   heading 'Job'          word_wrapped
col Lsd  format a5    heading 'Last|Ok|Date'
col Lst  format a5    heading 'Last|Ok|Time'
col Trd  format a5    heading 'This|Run|Date'
col Trt  format a5    heading 'This|Run|Time'
col Fail format 999   heading 'Errs'

select R.Job  Jid,
       J.Log_User Subu,
       J.Priv_User Secd,
       J.What Proc,
       TO_CHAR(R.Last_Date,'MM/DD') Lsd,
       SUBSTR(R.Last_Sec,1,5) Lst,
       TO_CHAR(R.This_Date,'MM/DD') Trd,
       SUBSTR(R.This_Sec,1,5) Trt,
       R.Failures Fail
  from DBA_JOBS_RUNNING R, DBA_JOBS J
 where R.Job = J.Job
/
spool off
```

Sample output of the list_run.sql script is shown in the following listing.

```
                              List Running Jobs

                                        Last  Last  This  This
                                        Ok    Ok    Run   Run
    Id Submitter  Security   Job         Date  Time  Date  Time  Errs
 ----- ---------- ---------- -------------------- ----- ----- ----- ----- ----
    86 APPDBA     APPDBA     table_analyze('APP',             06/06 01:17    1
                            'APP_ADDRESSES');
```

ANNOTATIONS

This script is similar to the list_sub.sql script, with the exception that it displays only jobs that are currently executing in the job queues. The maximum number of jobs that can execute at any one time is determined by the init.ora parameter JOB_QUEUE_PROCESSES. If you have a large number of jobs which will need to be run at the same time, JOB_QUEUE_PROCESSES should be set to a high number. Remember that each job queue that is created has an operating system process associated with it.

The **select** portion of the script, shown in the following listing, joins the DBA_JOBS view, which contains a list of all jobs in the job queues, with the DBA_JOBS_RUNNING view, which contains information on the currently executing jobs. The Last_Date and Last_Sec columns refer to the date and time of the last successful execution of this job; if they are blank the job has never successfully been run. The This_Date and This_Sec columns contain the date and time that the job started executing. The Failures column value is the number of times ORACLE attempted to execute the job.

Jobs can fail for a number of reasons: The table they reference may be locked, the procedure they execute may have become invalid and cannot be re-validated, or the owner of the procedure may not have the privileges needed to successfully execute the procedure. ORACLE will attempt to execute the job 16 times before marking it "broken."

```
select R.Job  Jid,
       J.Log_User Subu,
       J.Priv_User Secd,
       J.What Proc,
       TO_CHAR(R.Last_Date,'MM/DD') Lsd,
       SUBSTR(R.Last_Sec,1,5) Lst,
       TO_CHAR(R.This_Date,'MM/DD') Trd,
       SUBSTR(R.This_Sec,1,5) Trt,
       R.Failures Fail
  from DBA_JOBS_RUNNING R, DBA_JOBS J
 where R.Job = J.Job
/
```

For the sample database, the output in the following listing shows that there is only one job currently running in the job queue. ORACLE is attempting to execute the job for the second time (Errs column has a value of 1); the first attempt was unsuccessful.

List Running Jobs

Id	Submitter	Security	Job	Last Ok Date	Last Ok Time	This Run Date	This Run Time	Errs
86	APPDBA	APPDBA	table_analyze('APP', 'APP_ADDRESSES');			06/06	01:17	1

invalobj.sql

List Invalid Objects

Which objects in your database are invalid and need recompilation? Changes to a table will invalidate views, procedures, and packages that depend on that table. ORACLE does not tell you which objects are forced invalid when other objects change. The next time an invalid view, procedure, or package is executed, ORACLE will recompile it, and performance may be affected by the run-time compilation. You can avoid the performance degradation by scheduling checks and recompilation of invalid objects for low-usage times.

You can use the following script, invalobj.sql, to identify invalid objects and combine this script with the revalobj.sql script in the Utilities section of this chapter to recompile these objects, scheduling them through the ORACLE job queues to run at low-usage times.

```
set echo off verify off term off feedback off
spool invalobj.log

ttitle -
  center   'Verify Stored Procedures' skip 2

col Oown   format a10 heading 'Owner'        word_wrapped
col Oname  format a30 heading 'Object Name'  trunc
col Otype  format a12 heading 'Object Type'  trunc
col Prob   format a13 heading 'Problem'      trunc
break on Oown skip 1 on Otype
```

```
select A.Owner Oown,
       A.Object_Name Oname,
       A.Object_Type Otype,
       'Miss Pkg Body' Prob
  from DBA_OBJECTS A
 where A.Object_Type = 'PACKAGE'
   and A.Owner not in ('SYS','SYSTEM')
   and not exists
         (select 'x'
            from DBA_OBJECTS B
           where B.Object_Name = A.Object_Name
             and B.Owner = A.Owner
             and B.Object_Type = 'PACKAGE BODY')
union
select Owner Oown,
       Object_Name Oname,
       Object_Type Otype,
       'Invalid Obj' Prob
  from DBA_OBJECTS
 where Object_Type in
     ('PROCEDURE','PACKAGE','FUNCTION','TRIGGER',
      'PACKAGE BODY','VIEW')
   and Owner not in ('SYS','SYSTEM')
   and Status != 'VALID'
 order by 1,4,3,2
/
spool off
```

Sample output for the preceding script is shown in the following listing.

```
                 Verify Stored Procedures
```

Owner	Object Name	Object Type	Problem
APP	APP_A_MSG1_PRIORITY_FUNC	FUNCTION	Invalid Obj
	APP_MAST1_PRIORITY_FUNC		Invalid Obj
	APP_INSERT_CUSTOMER	PACKAGE BODY	Invalid Obj
	PKG_EXPRESS_SAVE		Invalid Obj
	PKG_ORDER_SAVE		Invalid Obj
	P_INT_ORDER_PROCESS	PROCEDURE	Invalid Obj
	REMOVE_CUSTOMER		Invalid Obj
	REMOVE_EMPLOYEE		Invalid Obj

```
        PDT_PRE_INS_DBT              TRIGGER      Invalid Obj
        PMN_PRE_INS_DBT                           Invalid Obj
        TEC_PRE_INS_DBT                           Invalid Obj

TRAIN   PKG_ORDER_SAVE              PACKAGE      Miss Pkg Body
        FINAL                       VIEW         Invalid Obj
```

The output shows that a number of database objects are currently marked as "invalid" due to missing package bodies or changes in dependent objects.

ANNOTATIONS

There are two **select** statements in the script, with their output joined by the **union** clause. This query structure allows the script to combine two different types of information, missing package bodies and invalid objects, into a single report and group the output by owner.

The first query in the **union** checks for missing package bodies by selecting for objects with a type of 'PACKAGE' (the package specification) from DBA_OBJECTS and then sub-selecting for the existence of a matching object with a type of 'PACKAGE BODY'. The **not exists** clause in the **where** clause of the **select** does not need an actual value returned; the check is just to see if the matching package body exists. If the package body exists, the **not exists** fails and the package will not be included in the output of this half of the **union** select.

```
select A.Owner Oown,
       A.Object_Name Oname,
       A.Object_Type Otype,
       'Miss Pkg Body' Prob
  from DBA_OBJECTS A
 where A.Object_Type = 'PACKAGE'
   and A.Owner not in ('SYS','SYSTEM')
   and not exists
        (select 'x'
           from DBA_OBJECTS B
          where B.Object_Name = A.Object_Name
            and B.Owner = A.Owner
            and B.Object_Type = 'PACKAGE BODY')
```

The second half of the **union** selects for invalid objects. Neither query includes objects owned by either SYS or SYSTEM.

```
union
select Owner Oown,
       Object_Name Oname,
       Object_Type Otype,
       'Invalid Obj' Prob
```

```
from DBA_OBJECTS
where Object_Type in
    ('PROCEDURE','PACKAGE','FUNCTION','TRIGGER',
     'PACKAGE BODY','VIEW')
 and Owner not in ('SYS','SYSTEM')
 and Status != 'VALID'
```

You should not use the SYSTEM user for application objects. If you think there are problems with objects owned by either SYS or SYSTEM, you can change the queries to look for objects owned specifically by these users:

```
and Owner in ('SYS','SYSTEM')
```

If you do get a report of invalid objects or missing package bodies for SYS or SYSTEM, contact ORACLE Support before attempting to correct the problem on your own.

Since the queries are **union**ed together, you must obey the formatting rules for **union**s. In each query, the columns must be of the same datatype. The datatypes and column names for the **union** query are determined by the datatypes of the first query in the **union**. You don't need to specify column names for the columns in any but the first query of the **union**.

```
 order by 1,4,3,2
/
spool off
```

This **order by** clause uses the column's ordinal positions. Prior to ORACLE7.1, you had to use ordinal positions in your **order by** clauses if you used an expression (such as in this script, since the script selects text strings instead of column values). As of ORACLE7.1, you can use the **as** clause to name a selected expression, and you can use that name in your **order by** clauses. You therefore do not need to use ordinal values in your **order by** clauses—unless you are using a **union**. If you use a **union** clause in your queries, you should use the ordinal positions of the columns in your **order by** clause. The use of ordinal positions in **order by** clauses for **union** queries is advisable because you may select different columns in each part of the query; as long as they have the same datatype, the query will succeed.

Sample output for the invalobj.sql script is shown in the following listing.

```
                    Verify Stored Procedures


Owner       Object Name                     Object Type   Problem
----------  ------------------------------  ------------  --------------
APP         APP_A_MSG1_PRIORITY_FUNC        FUNCTION      Invalid Obj
            APP_MAST1_PRIORITY_FUNC                       Invalid Obj
            APP_INSERT_CUSTOMER             PACKAGE BODY  Invalid Obj
```

	PKG_EXPRESS_SAVE		Invalid Obj
	PKG_ORDER_SAVE		Invalid Obj
	P_INT_ORDER_PROCESS	PROCEDURE	Invalid Obj
	REMOVE_CUSTOMER		Invalid Obj
	REMOVE_EMPLOYEE		Invalid Obj
	PDT_PRE_INS_DBT	TRIGGER	Invalid Obj
	PMN_PRE_INS_DBT		Invalid Obj
	TEC_PRE_INS_DBT		Invalid Obj
TRAIN	PKG_ORDER_SAVE	PACKAGE	Miss Pkg Body
	FINAL	VIEW	Invalid Obj

In this database, there are two users with problems with their objects. The first, APP, has a number of invalid objects. The functions and procedures that are invalid are independent objects, not contained within a package body. It is not possible for only a portion of a package body to become invalid—if a change to the database affects one function or procedure within the package body, the entire package body is invalidated. A package specification can become valid, and the underlying package body can become invalid. Package invalidation can occur if the package specification remains the same and the package body is changed incorrectly, or if an underlying table or view is changed.

The second user has one invalid view and is missing the package body for the package PKG_ORDER_SAVE. This error will occur if the package specification is written and created and the body has not yet been created.

Utilities

The scripts in this section can be used to generate scripts to re-create or document existing objects in the database, to recompile invalid objects to avoid run-time recompilation, and to determine which packages to pin into memory.

Running the ORACLE Import utility with "**show=y rows=n**" on a full database export will generate a log file with all the commands necessary to re-create database objects. However, this file is not very readable, is poorly organized for documentation purposes, and is not executable without extensive editing. The scripts in this section will generate readable, executable scripts to regenerate or document objects within the database.

pinsize.sql

Pinning Packages

PL/SQL objects, when used, are stored in the library cache of the shared SQL area within the SGA. If a package has already been loaded into memory by a user, other users will experience improved performance when executing that package. Thus, keeping a package "pinned" in memory decreases the response time to the user during package executions.

To improve the ability to keep large PL/SQL objects pinned in the library cache, you should load them into the SGA as soon as the database is opened. Pinning packages immediately after startup increases the likelihood that a contiguous section of memory will be available to store the package. You can use the DBMS_SHARED_POOL package to pin PL/SQL objects in the SGA.

You should pin the largest packages first. To determine the proper order, you can use the script shown in the following listing. It uses the DBA_OBJECT_SIZE view to list the order in which the objects should be pinned.

```
set term off echo off pagesize 60
col Owner format a15
col Name  format a50
col Type  format a12
col Total_Bytes format 999,999,999
spool pinsize.log
select Owner,
       Name,
       Type,
       Source_Size+Code_Size+Parsed_Size+Error_Size  Total_Bytes
  from DBA_OBJECT_SIZE
 where Type = 'PACKAGE BODY'
   and Owner not in ('SYS','SYSTEM')
 order by Total_Bytes desc
/
spool off
```

Sample output for the pinsize.sql script is shown in the following listing.

OWNER	NAME	TYPE	TOTAL_BYTES
APP	PKG_ORDER_SAVE1	PACKAGE BODY	83,171
APP	PKG_ORDER_SAVE2	PACKAGE BODY	60,767
APP	APP_NEW_CUSTOMER_PKG	PACKAGE BODY	33,210
APP	APP_EMP_WEEKLY_UPDATE_PKG	PACKAGE BODY	32,819
APP	APP_EMP_PAYROLL_PKG	PACKAGE BODY	31,175
APP	PKG_EXPRESS_SAVE	PACKAGE BODY	25,813
APP	APP_CC_PKG	PACKAGE BODY	18,377
APP	APP_EMP_SCHEDULE_PKG	PACKAGE BODY	16,995
APP	APP_TIME_CONVERSIONS_PKG	PACKAGE BODY	8,220
APP	APP_INSERT_CUSTOMER	PACKAGE BODY	7,497

APP	APP_PRINT_PKG	PACKAGE BODY	6,405
SCOTT	DEMOKIT	PACKAGE BODY	5,964
APP	APP_PRODUCTS_PKG	PACKAGE BODY	4,753
APP	APP_EMPLOYEE_PKG	PACKAGE BODY	2,555

The output shows the packages that can be stored in memory, with the largest packages listed first.

ANNOTATIONS

When a package is loaded into memory, it is not just the parsed version of the code which is loaded. In order to get an accurate determination of how much space the package will take, you must sum the Source_Size (plain text version), Code_Size (source minus comments and extraneous spaces), Parsed_Size (size of the parsed form of the object), and Error_Size (size of the error messages). This calculation is shown in the following portion of the pinsize.sql script.

```
select Owner,
       Name,
       Type,
       Source_Size+Code_Size+Parsed_Size+Error_Size   Total_Bytes
  from DBA_OBJECT_SIZE
 where Type = 'PACKAGE BODY'
   and Owner not in ('SYS','SYSTEM')
 order by Total_Bytes desc
/
```

Not every large package should be pinned. Packages which are used frequently are good candidates for pinning; packages which are used rarely should not be pinned. There are several large packages in the sample data shown in the following listing. If the packages are used rarely, or used only during low-activity times, they do not have to be pinned. Packages should not be pinned merely because they are large.

OWNER	NAME	TYPE	TOTAL_BYTES
APP	PKG_ORDER_SAVE1	PACKAGE BODY	83,171
APP	PKG_ORDER_SAVE2	PACKAGE BODY	60,767
APP	APP_NEW_CUSTOMER_PKG	PACKAGE BODY	33,210
APP	APP_EMP_WEEKLY_UPDATE_PKG	PACKAGE BODY	32,819
APP	APP_EMP_PAYROLL_PKG	PACKAGE BODY	31,175
APP	PKG_EXPRESS_SAVE	PACKAGE BODY	25,813
APP	APP_CC_PKG	PACKAGE BODY	18,377
APP	APP_EMP_SCHEDULE_PKG	PACKAGE BODY	16,995
APP	APP_TIME_CONVERSIONS_PKG	PACKAGE BODY	8,220
APP	APP_INSERT_CUSTOMER	PACKAGE BODY	7,497

APP	APP_PRINT_PKG	PACKAGE BODY	6,405
SCOTT	DEMOKIT	PACKAGE BODY	5,964
APP	APP_PRODUCTS_PKG	PACKAGE BODY	4,753
APP	APP_EMPLOYEE_PKG	PACKAGE BODY	2,555

Once you have decided which packages to pin in memory, you can use DBMS_SHARED_POOL to pin them. To use DBMS_SHARED_POOL, you first need to reference the objects that you want to pin in memory. To load a package in memory, you can reference a dummy procedure defined in the package or you can recompile the package. The core set of packages provided by ORACLE does not need to be referenced or recompiled before pinning and will be loaded the first time it is executed. You can pin a cursor by executing its SQL statement.

Once the object has been referenced, you can execute the DBMS_SHARED_POOL.KEEP procedure to pin the object. The KEEP procedure of DBMS_SHARED_POOL, as shown in the following listing, takes as its input parameters the name of the object and the type of object ('P' for packages, 'C' for cursors; the default is 'P').

```
alter package APP.PKG_ORDER_SAVE1 compile;
execute DBMS_SHARED_POOL.KEEP('APP.PKG_ORDER_SAVE1','P');
```

The example shown in the preceding listing illustrates the two-step process involved in pinning packages in memory: The package is first referenced (via the compilation step), and is then marked for keeping.

To allow a pinned object to be removed from the SGA via the normal Least Recently Used algorithm for cache management, use the UNKEEP procedure of the DBMS_SHARED_POOL package. As shown in the following listing, the UNKEEP procedure takes the same parameters the KEEP procedure took—the object name and the object type (the default is 'P' for packages).

```
execute DBMS_SHARED_POOL.UNKEEP('APP.PKG_ORDER_SAVE1');
```

UNKEEP is usually not needed, but you can use it to manage your memory allocations within the SGA if you do not have a lot of system memory available. Pinning your most-used packages in memory immediately after startup will improve your chances of acquiring contiguous space for them within the SGA.

revalobj.sql

Revalidating Objects

In the Diagnostics section, you saw the invalobj.sql script, which lists all the invalid objects in the database. The script in this section, revalobj.sql, will generate a script to recompile those invalid objects. This script can then be scheduled to run during low-peak database activity, to avoid the possible performance degradation of run-time compilation.

If you recompile a procedure successfully, the procedure becomes valid. If recompiling the procedure results in compilation errors, then ORACLE returns an error and the procedure remains invalid.

To generate a script to recompile and revalidate the invalid objects, use the following script.

```
ttitle off
set pagesize 0 feedback off verify off heading off term off echo off
spool revaldte.sql
select 'alter '||
        DECODE(Object_Type,'PACKAGE BODY','PACKAGE',Object_Type)||
        ' '||Owner ||'.'|| Object_Name ||' compile '||
        DECODE(Object_Type,'PACKAGE BODY','BODY',null)||';'
  from DBA_OBJECTS
 where Object_Type in
        ('PROCEDURE','PACKAGE','FUNCTION','TRIGGER',
             'VIEW','PACKAGE BODY')
   and Owner not in ('SYS','SYSTEM')
   and Status != 'VALID'
 order by Owner, Object_Type, Object_Name
/
spool off
```

The script will generate a script similar to the example shown in the following listing:

```
alter FUNCTION APP.APP_A_MSG1_PRIORITY_FUNC compile;
alter FUNCTION APP.APP_MAST1_PRIORITY_FUNC compile;
alter PACKAGE APP.APP_INSERT_CUSTOMER compile BODY;
alter PACKAGE APP.PKG_EXPRESS_SAVE compile BODY;
alter PACKAGE APP.PKG_ORDER_SAVE compile BODY;
alter PROCEDURE APP.P_INT_ORDER_PROCESS compile;
alter PROCEDURE APP.REMOVE_CUSTOMER compile;
alter PROCEDURE APP.REMOVE_EMPLOYEE compile;
alter TRIGGER APP.PDT_PRE_INS_DBT compile;
alter TRIGGER APP.PMN_PRE_INS_DBT compile;
alter TRIGGER APP.TEC_PRE_INS_DBT compile;
alter VIEW TRAIN.FINAL compile;
```

You can then execute the generated script to compile your invalid objects.

ANNOTATIONS

The revalobj.sql script generates a script to be executed, so its formatting eliminates the display of extraneous text. The output formatting for the script is shown in the following listing.

```
ttitle off
set pagesize 0 feedback off verify off heading off term off echo off
spool revaldte.sql
```

Setting **pagesize** to 0 will remove all page breaks and headings from the output listing. You should always **set pagesize 0** when you are running SQL to generate SQL.

```
Select 'alter '||
       DECODE(Object_Type,'PACKAGE BODY','PACKAGE',Object_Type)||
       ' '||Owner ||'.'|| Object_Name ||' compile '||
       DECODE(Object_Type,'PACKAGE BODY','BODY',null)||';'
  from DBA_OBJECTS
 where Object_Type in
       ('PROCEDURE','PACKAGE','FUNCTION','TRIGGER',
           'VIEW','PACKAGE BODY')
   and Owner not in ('SYS','SYSTEM')
   and Status != 'VALID'
 order by Owner, Object_Type, Object_Name
/
spool off
```

The syntax of the **alter** statement for recompilation is slightly different for package bodies than it is for all other types of objects. For most objects, the statement includes the object type after the **alter** command. For package bodies, the object type is **package**, and the word "body" must be included after the word "compile." In order to do this in a single **select** statement, the **DECODE** function is used twice on the Object_Type column—the first time to replace the column value 'PACKAGE BODY' with the word 'PACKAGE' and the second time to append the word 'BODY' if the column value is 'PACKAGE BODY.'

Objects owned by SYS or SYSTEM should not be automatically recompiled if they are invalid. Invalid objects owned by SYS or SYSTEM could indicate a problem within the database and you should check with ORACLE Support before attempting to fix it.

To automate the recompilation, add the line:

```
start  revaldte.sql
```

to the end of the revalobj.sql script.

gen_tbl.sql

Generate Tables

You must know what your tables actually look like and what constraints you have imposed on them to ensure that your application will work the way you want it to. While the tab_desc.sql script in the Diagnostics section of this chapter will document a table and its indexes and constraints, it does not generate executable SQL to re-create the table. As you move a table from one database to another, or change the table within the database, you may find it difficult to manually save off and re-create the table and its constraints. The script in this section, gen_tbl.sql, will generate a script to re-create a table and its constraints.

The full gen_tbl.sql script is shown in the following listing. This script is long; its method of generating the **create table** command for a table is described in the Annotations section.

PROGRAMMER'S NOTE *The script does not handle the new ORACLE8 table clause* **organization index** *in order to be generic over both ORACLE7 and ORACLE8. If you use index-organized tables, you will have to manually edit the generated SQL script to include the clause.*

```
set echo off verify off feedback off pagesize 0 term on
select 'Creating table build script...' from DUAL;

accept table_name prompt "Enter the name of the Table: "
accept tab_owner prompt "Enter table owner: "
set term off

drop table TAB_TEMP;

create table TAB_TEMP (
      Lineno NUMBER,
      Id_Owner VARCHAR2(30),
      Id_Name VARCHAR2(30),
      Text VARCHAR2(2000))
/

declare
   cursor TAB_CURSOR is
         select Owner,
                Table_Name,
                Tablespace_Name,
                Pct_Free,
                Pct_Used,
                Ini_Trans,
                Max_Trans,
                Initial_Extent,
                Next_Extent,
                Min_Extents,
                Max_Extents,
                Pct_Increase,
                Freelists,
                Freelist_Groups,
                Degree,
```

```
                 Instances
          from DBA_TABLES
         where Owner = UPPER('&&tab_owner')
           and Table_Name like UPPER('&&table_name')
         order by Table_Name;

cursor COL_CURSOR (C_Owner    VARCHAR2,
                   C_Tabname VARCHAR2) is
      select Column_Name,
             Data_Type,
             Data_Length,
             Data_Precision,
             Data_Scale,
             Nullable,
             Default_Length,
             Data_Default
        from DBA_TAB_COLUMNS
       where Owner       = C_Owner
         and Table_Name  = C_Tabname
       order by Column_ID;

cursor CONS_CURSOR (Cons_Owner      VARCHAR2,
                    Cons_Tablename VARCHAR2) is
      select A.Owner,
             A.Constraint_Name,
             A.Constraint_Type,
             A.Table_Name,
             A.Search_Condition,
             B.Column_Name,
             B.Position
        from DBA_CONSTRAINTS  A,
             DBA_CONS_COLUMNS B
       where A.Owner = B.Owner
         and A.Constraint_Name = B.Constraint_Name
         and A.Table_Name      = B.Table_Name
         and A.Constraint_Type in ('C','P')
         and A.Owner           = Cons_Owner
         and A.Table_Name      = Cons_Tablename
       order by A.Constraint_Type,
                A.Constraint_Name,
                B.Position;
```

```
cursor REF_CURSOR (R_Owner      VARCHAR2,
                   R_Tablename VARCHAR2) is
      select A.Owner,
             A.Table_Name,
             A.Constraint_Name,
             A.R_Constraint_Name,
             B.Column_Name,
             C.Owner,
             C.Table_Name,
             C.Column_Name,
             C.Position
        from DBA_CONSTRAINTS   A,
             DBA_CONS_COLUMNS B,
             DBA_CONS_COLUMNS C
       where A.Constraint_Name = B.Constraint_Name
         and A.Owner          = B.Owner
         and C.Constraint_name = A.R_Constraint_Name
         and B.Position        = C.Position
         and A.Owner           = R_Owner
         and A.Table_Name      = R_Tablename
       order by A.Constraint_Name,
                A.Owner,
                C.Position;


Lv_Table_Owner            DBA_TABLES.Owner%TYPE;
Lv_Table_Name             DBA_TABLES.Table_Name%TYPE;
Lv_Tablespace_Name        DBA_TABLES.Tablespace_Name%TYPE;
Lv_Pct_Free               DBA_TABLES.Pct_Free%TYPE;
Lv_Pct_Used               DBA_TABLES.Pct_Used%TYPE;
Lv_Initial_Trans          DBA_TABLES.Ini_Trans%TYPE;
Lv_Max_Trans              DBA_TABLES.Max_Trans%TYPE;
Lv_Initial_Extent         DBA_TABLES.Initial_Extent%TYPE;
Lv_Next_Extent            DBA_TABLES.Next_Extent%TYPE;
Lv_Min_Extents            DBA_TABLES.Min_Extents%TYPE;
Lv_Max_Extents            DBA_TABLES.Max_Extents%TYPE;
Lv_Pct_Increase           DBA_TABLES.Pct_Increase%TYPE;
Lv_Freelists              DBA_TABLES.Freelists%TYPE;
Lv_Freelist_Groups        DBA_TABLES.Freelist_Groups%TYPE;
Lv_Degree                 DBA_TABLES.Degree%TYPE;
Lv_Instances              DBA_TABLES.Instances%TYPE;
Lv_Column_Name            DBA_TAB_COLUMNS.Column_Name%TYPE;
```

```
    Lv_Column_Data_Type          DBA_TAB_COLUMNS.Data_Type%TYPE;
    Lv_Column_Data_Length        DBA_TAB_COLUMNS.Data_Length%TYPE;
    Lv_Column_Data_Precision     DBA_TAB_COLUMNS.Data_Precision%TYPE;
    Lv_Column_Data_Scale         DBA_TAB_COLUMNS.Data_Scale%TYPE;
    Lv_Column_Nullable           DBA_TAB_COLUMNS.Nullable%TYPE;
    Lv_Column_Default_Length     DBA_TAB_COLUMNS.Default_Length%TYPE;
    Lv_Column_Data_Default       DBA_TAB_COLUMNS.Data_Default%TYPE;
    Lv_Cons_Owner                DBA_CONSTRAINTS.Owner%TYPE;
    Lv_Cons_Table_Name           DBA_CONSTRAINTS.Table_Name%TYPE;
    Lv_Cons_Constraint_Name      DBA_CONSTRAINTS.Constraint_Name%TYPE;
    Lv_Cons_Constraint_Type      DBA_CONSTRAINTS.Constraint_Type%TYPE;
    Lv_Cons_Search_Cond          DBA_CONSTRAINTS.Search_Condition%TYPE;
    Lv_Cons_Column_Name          DBA_CONS_COLUMNS.Column_Name%TYPE;
    Lv_Cons_R_Constraint_Name    DBA_CONSTRAINTS.R_Constraint_Name%TYPE;
    Lv_Cons_Ref_Owner            DBA_CONSTRAINTS.Owner%TYPE;
    Lv_Cons_Ref_Table_Name       DBA_CONSTRAINTS.Table_Name%TYPE;
    Lv_Cons_Ref_Column_Name      DBA_CONS_COLUMNS.Column_Name%TYPE;
    Lv_Cons_Ref_Position         DBA_CONS_COLUMNS.Position%TYPE;
    Lv_Cons_Exists               VARCHAR2(1);
    Lv_String                    VARCHAR2(800);
    Lv_String2                   VARCHAR2(800);
    Lv_Lineno                    NUMBER := 0;

  procedure WRITE_OUT(P_Line INTEGER,  P_Owner VARCHAR2,
                      P_Name VARCHAR2, P_String VARCHAR2) is
  begin
    insert into TAB_TEMP (Lineno, Id_Owner, Id_Name, Text)
          values (P_Line,P_Owner,P_Name,P_String);
   end;

  procedure UPDATE_OUT(P_Line INTEGER,  P_Owner VARCHAR2,
                       P_Name VARCHAR2, P_String VARCHAR2) is
  begin
    update TAB_TEMP
       set Text = P_String
     where Lineno = P_Line
       and Id_Owner = P_Owner
       and Id_Name  = P_Name;
  end;

begin
  open TAB_CURSOR;
  loop
```

```
    fetch TAB_CURSOR into Lv_Table_Owner,
                         Lv_Table_Name,
                         Lv_Tablespace_Name,
                         Lv_Pct_Free,
                         Lv_Pct_Used,
                         Lv_Initial_Trans,
                         Lv_Max_Trans,
                         Lv_Initial_Extent,
                         Lv_Next_Extent,
                         Lv_Min_Extents,
                         Lv_Max_Extents,
                         Lv_Pct_Increase,
                         Lv_Freelists,
                         Lv_Freelist_Groups,
                         Lv_Degree,
                         Lv_Instances;
exit when TAB_CURSOR%NOTFOUND;

Lv_Lineno := 1;

Lv_String:= 'CREATE TABLE ' || LOWER(Lv_Table_Owner)
                            || '.'
                            || LOWER(Lv_Table_Name);
WRITE_OUT(Lv_Lineno, Lv_Table_Owner, Lv_Table_Name, Lv_String);
Lv_Lineno := Lv_Lineno + 1;

Lv_string := '(';
WRITE_OUT(Lv_Lineno, Lv_Table_Owner, Lv_Table_Name, Lv_String);
Lv_Lineno := Lv_Lineno + 1;

open COL_CURSOR (Lv_Table_Owner,Lv_Table_Name);

loop
   fetch COL_CURSOR into Lv_Column_Name,
                         Lv_Column_Data_Type,
                         Lv_Column_Data_Length,
                         Lv_Column_Data_Precision,
                         Lv_Column_Data_Scale,
                         Lv_Column_Nullable,
                         Lv_Column_Default_Length,
                         Lv_Column_Data_Default;
   exit when COL_CURSOR%NOTFOUND;
```

```
      Lv_String := '    '                           ||
               RPAD(LOWER(Lv_Column_Name),35) ||
               Lv_Column_Data_Type;

      if ( (Lv_Column_Data_Type = 'VARCHAR2' ) or
           (Lv_Column_Data_Type = 'RAW'      ) or
           (Lv_Column_Data_Type = 'CHAR'     ) )
      then
          Lv_String := Lv_String              ||
                       '('                    ||
                       Lv_Column_Data_Length ||
                       ')';
      elsif (Lv_Column_Data_Type = 'NUMBER')
      then
          if Lv_Column_Data_Precision IS NULL
          then
              Lv_Column_Data_Precision := 38;
              Lv_Column_Data_Scale     := 0;
          end if;
          Lv_String := Lv_String                ||
                       '('                       ||
                       Lv_Column_Data_Precision ||
                       ','                       ||
                       Lv_Column_Data_Scale      ||
                       ')';
      end if;

      if (Lv_Column_Data_Default IS NOT NULL)
      then
          LV_String := Lv_String || ' DEFAULT '
                                 || SUBSTR(Lv_Column_Data_Default,
                                    1,Lv_Column_Default_Length);
      end if;
      if (Lv_Column_Nullable = 'N' )
      then
          Lv_String  := Lv_String || '  NOT NULL';
      end if;

      Lv_String := Lv_String || ',';
      WRITE_OUT(Lv_Lineno, Lv_Table_Owner, Lv_Table_Name, Lv_String);
      Lv_Lineno := Lv_Lineno + 1;

end loop;
```

```
close COL_CURSOR;
Lv_Lineno   := Lv_Lineno - 1;
Lv_String   := SUBSTR(Lv_String,1,(LENGTH(Lv_String) - 1));
UPDATE_OUT(Lv_Lineno, Lv_Table_Owner, Lv_Table_Name,Lv_String);
Lv_Lineno   := Lv_Lineno + 1;



Lv_String   := ')';
WRITE_OUT(Lv_Lineno, Lv_Table_Owner, Lv_Table_Name, Lv_String);
Lv_Lineno := Lv_Lineno + 1;

Lv_String   := 'PARALLEL ( DEGREE ' || Lv_Degree
                                    || ' INSTANCES '
                                    || Lv_Instances
                                    || ' )';
WRITE_OUT(Lv_Lineno, Lv_Table_Owner, Lv_Table_Name, Lv_String);
Lv_Lineno := Lv_Lineno + 1;

Lv_String   := 'TABLESPACE ' || Lv_Tablespace_Name ;
WRITE_OUT(Lv_Lineno, Lv_Table_Owner, Lv_Table_Name, Lv_String);
Lv_Lineno := Lv_Lineno + 1;

Lv_String   := 'PCTFREE ' || Lv_Pct_Free ;
WRITE_OUT(Lv_Lineno, Lv_Table_Owner, Lv_Table_Name, Lv_String);
Lv_Lineno := Lv_Lineno + 1;

Lv_String   := 'PCTUSED ' || Lv_Pct_Used ;
WRITE_OUT(Lv_Lineno, Lv_Table_Owner, Lv_Table_Name, Lv_String);
Lv_Lineno := Lv_Lineno + 1;

Lv_String   := 'INITRANS ' || Lv_Initial_Trans ;
WRITE_OUT(Lv_Lineno, Lv_Table_Owner, Lv_Table_Name, Lv_String);
Lv_Lineno := Lv_Lineno + 1;

Lv_String   := 'MAXTRANS ' || Lv_Max_Trans ;
WRITE_OUT(Lv_Lineno, Lv_Table_Owner, Lv_Table_Name, Lv_String);
Lv_Lineno := Lv_Lineno + 1;

Lv_String   := 'STORAGE';
WRITE_OUT(Lv_Lineno, Lv_Table_Owner, Lv_Table_Name, Lv_String);
Lv_Lineno := Lv_Lineno + 1;
Lv_String   := '(';
WRITE_OUT(Lv_Lineno, Lv_Table_Owner, Lv_Table_Name, Lv_String);
```

```
    Lv_Lineno := Lv_Lineno + 1;


    Lv_String   := '   INITIAL ' || Lv_Initial_Extent ;
    WRITE_OUT(Lv_Lineno, Lv_Table_Owner, Lv_Table_Name, Lv_String);
    Lv_Lineno := Lv_Lineno + 1;


    Lv_String   := '   NEXT ' || Lv_Next_Extent ;
    WRITE_OUT(Lv_Lineno, Lv_Table_Owner, Lv_Table_Name, Lv_String);
    Lv_Lineno := Lv_Lineno + 1;


    Lv_String   := '   MINEXTENTS ' || Lv_Min_Extents ;
    WRITE_OUT(Lv_Lineno, Lv_Table_Owner, Lv_Table_Name, Lv_String);
    Lv_Lineno := Lv_Lineno + 1;


    Lv_String   := '   MAXEXTENTS ' || Lv_Max_Extents ;
    WRITE_OUT(Lv_Lineno, Lv_Table_Owner, Lv_Table_Name, Lv_String);
    Lv_Lineno := Lv_Lineno + 1;


    Lv_String   := '   PCTINCREASE ' || Lv_Pct_Increase ;
    WRITE_OUT(Lv_Lineno, Lv_Table_Owner, Lv_Table_Name, Lv_String);
    Lv_Lineno := Lv_Lineno + 1;


    Lv_String   := '   FREELISTS ' || Lv_Freelists ;
    WRITE_OUT(Lv_Lineno, Lv_Table_Owner, Lv_Table_Name, Lv_String);
    Lv_Lineno := Lv_Lineno + 1;


    Lv_String   := '   FREELIST GROUPS ' || Lv_Freelist_Groups ;
    WRITE_OUT(Lv_Lineno, Lv_Table_Owner, Lv_Table_Name, Lv_String);
    Lv_Lineno := Lv_Lineno + 1;


    Lv_String   := ')';
    WRITE_OUT(Lv_Lineno, Lv_Table_Owner, Lv_Table_Name, Lv_String);
    Lv_Lineno := Lv_Lineno + 1;


    Lv_String   := '/';
    WRITE_OUT(Lv_Lineno, Lv_Table_Owner, Lv_Table_Name, Lv_String);
    Lv_Lineno := Lv_Lineno + 1;



    Lv_Cons_Exists := 'N';

    open CONS_CURSOR(Lv_Table_Owner, Lv_Table_Name);
    loop
```

```
    fetch CONS_CURSOR into Lv_Cons_Owner,
                          Lv_Cons_Constraint_Name,
                          Lv_Cons_Constraint_Type,
                          Lv_Cons_Table_Name,
                          Lv_Cons_Search_Cond,
                          Lv_Cons_Column_Name,
                          Lv_Cons_Ref_Position;
exit when CONS_CURSOR%NOTFOUND;

if (Lv_Cons_Constraint_Type = 'C') AND
   (INSTR(Lv_Cons_Search_Cond,'NOT NULL',1) = 0)
then
    Lv_String := 'ALTER TABLE ' || Lv_Cons_Owner
                                 || '.'
                                 || Lv_Cons_Table_Name;
    WRITE_OUT(Lv_Lineno, Lv_Table_Owner, Lv_Table_Name,
             Lv_String);
    Lv_Lineno := Lv_Lineno + 1;

    Lv_String := 'ADD ';
    if  (INSTR(Lv_Cons_Constraint_Name,'SYS_C',1) = 0)
    then
        Lv_String := Lv_String || 'CONSTRAINT '
                               || Lv_Cons_Constraint_Name;
    end if;
    Lv_String := Lv_String     || ' CHECK ('
                               || Lv_Cons_Search_Cond
                               || ')';
    WRITE_OUT(Lv_Lineno, Lv_Table_Owner, Lv_Table_Name,
             Lv_String);
    Lv_Lineno := Lv_Lineno + 1;

    Lv_String := '/';
    WRITE_OUT(Lv_Lineno, Lv_Table_Owner, Lv_Table_Name,
             Lv_String);
    Lv_Lineno := Lv_Lineno + 1;
end if;

if (Lv_Cons_Constraint_Type = 'P')
then
    Lv_Cons_Exists := 'Y';
    if (Lv_Cons_Ref_Position = 1)
    then
```

```
                                Lv_String := 'ALTER TABLE ' || Lv_Cons_Owner
                                                        || '.'
                                                        || Lv_Cons_Table_Name;
                        WRITE_OUT(Lv_Lineno, Lv_Table_Owner, Lv_Table_Name,
                                    Lv_String);
                        Lv_Lineno := Lv_Lineno + 1;
                        Lv_String := 'ADD ';
                        if  (INSTR(Lv_Cons_Constraint_Name,'SYS_C') = 0)
                        then
                            Lv_String := Lv_String || 'CONSTRAINT ' ||
                                        Lv_Cons_Constraint_Name || ' ';
                        end if;

                        Lv_String := Lv_String || 'PRIMARY KEY (' ||
                                    Lv_Cons_Column_Name || ')';
                    else
                        Lv_String := REPLACE(Lv_String,')',',' ||
                                    Lv_Cons_Column_Name|| ')' );
                    end if;

                end if;
        end loop;

    if (Lv_Cons_Exists = 'Y')
    then
        WRITE_OUT(Lv_Lineno, Lv_Table_Owner, Lv_Table_Name, Lv_String);
        Lv_Lineno := Lv_Lineno + 1;

        Lv_String := '/';
        WRITE_OUT(Lv_Lineno, Lv_Table_Owner, Lv_Table_Name, Lv_String);
        Lv_Lineno := Lv_Lineno + 1;
    end if;

    close CONS_CURSOR;

    open  REF_CURSOR(Lv_Table_Owner, Lv_Table_Name);
    loop
        fetch REF_CURSOR into Lv_Cons_Owner,
                                Lv_Cons_Table_Name,
                                Lv_Cons_Constraint_Name,
                                Lv_Cons_R_Constraint_Name,
                                Lv_Cons_Column_Name,
                                Lv_Cons_Ref_Owner,
```

```
                        Lv_Cons_Ref_Table_Name,
                        Lv_Cons_Ref_Column_Name,
                        Lv_Cons_Ref_Position;

   exit when REF_CURSOR%NOTFOUND;

   if (Lv_Cons_Ref_Position = 1)
   then
      Lv_String := 'ALTER TABLE '|| Lv_Table_Owner
                              || '.'
                              || Lv_Table_Name;
      WRITE_OUT(Lv_Lineno, Lv_Table_Owner, Lv_Table_Name,
               Lv_String);
      Lv_Lineno := Lv_Lineno + 1;

      Lv_String := 'ADD ';
      if  (INSTR(Lv_Cons_Constraint_Name,'SYS_C',1) = 0)
      then
          Lv_String := Lv_String || 'CONSTRAINT '
                              || Lv_Cons_Constraint_Name
                              || ' ';
      end if;
      Lv_String  := Lv_String    || 'FOREIGN KEY ('
                              || Lv_Cons_Column_Name
                              || ')';
      WRITE_OUT(Lv_Lineno, Lv_Table_Owner, Lv_Table_Name,
               Lv_String);
      Lv_Lineno := Lv_Lineno + 1;

      Lv_String2 := '   REFERENCES ' || Lv_Cons_Ref_Owner
                              || '.'
                              || Lv_Cons_Ref_Table_Name
                              || '('
                              || Lv_Cons_Ref_Column_Name
                              || ')';
      WRITE_OUT(Lv_Lineno, Lv_Table_Owner, Lv_Table_Name,
               Lv_String2);
      Lv_Lineno := Lv_Lineno + 1;

      WRITE_OUT(Lv_Lineno, Lv_Table_Owner, Lv_Table_Name, '/');
      Lv_Lineno := Lv_Lineno + 1;
   else
      Lv_String  := REPLACE(Lv_String,  ')', ',' ||
```

```
                           Lv_Cons_Column_Name         || ')' );
            Lv_Lineno  := Lv_Lineno - 3;
            UPDATE_OUT(Lv_Lineno, Lv_Table_Owner, Lv_Table_Name,
                       Lv_String);
            Lv_Lineno  := Lv_Lineno + 1;

            Lv_String2 := REPLACE(Lv_String2, ')', ',' ||
                          Lv_Cons_Ref_Column_Name || ')' );
            UPDATE_OUT(Lv_Lineno, Lv_Table_Owner, Lv_Table_Name,
                       Lv_String2);
            Lv_Lineno  := Lv_Lineno + 2;
        end if;

    end loop;
    close REF_CURSOR;

  end loop;
  close TAB_CURSOR;
end;
/
spool cre_tbl.sql
select Text
  from TAB_TEMP
 order by Id_Owner, Id_Name, Lineno
/
spool off
```

For the APP_REFERRALS table, the script will generate the following script to re-create the table and all its constraints.

```
CREATE TABLE app.app_referrals
(
    code                          VARCHAR2(3)   NOT NULL,
    refr_type                     VARCHAR2(3)   NOT NULL,
    description                   VARCHAR2(25)  NOT NULL,
    usr_crtd                      VARCHAR2(30)  NOT NULL,
    dt_crtd                       DATE  NOT NULL,
    status                        VARCHAR2(3),
    usr_mdfd                      VARCHAR2(30),
    dt_mdfd                       DATE,
    refr_code                     VARCHAR2(3),
    discount                      NUMBER(8,2),
    discount_type                 CHAR(1)
```

```
)
PARALLEL (DEGREE 1 INSTANCES 1)
TABLESPACE USER_DATA
PCTFREE 10
PCTUSED 40
INITRANS 1
MAXTRANS 255
STORAGE
(
   INITIAL 73728
   NEXT 1048576
   MINEXTENTS 1
   MAXEXTENTS 500
   PCTINCREASE 0
   FREELISTS 1
   FREELIST GROUPS 1
)
/
ALTER TABLE APP.APP_REFERRALS
ADD CONSTRAINT REFR_PK PRIMARY KEY (CODE)
/
ALTER TABLE APP.APP_REFERRALS
ADD CONSTRAINT REFR_REFR_FK FOREIGN KEY (REFR_CODE)
   REFERENCES APP.APP_REFERRALS(CODE)
/
```

You can run the generated script to re-create the APP_REFERRALS table and its constraints.

ANNOTATIONS

Although the script as written will return information for a single table, it uses a cursor to allow you to enter a wildcard value or to modify the script to select all tables for an owner or all tables in the database. The script will generate a script to re-create the requested table and any constraints on the table. The script uses a temporary table to hold individual lines of the **create table** and **alter table** statements, writing to the table rather than using DBMS_OUTPUT.PUT_LINE so that you can extract the information for an individual table from the temporary table. Using the temporary table greatly increases the script's flexibility; using the DBMS_OUTPUT procedure would force you to save and edit the output file for the table you want.

For the sake of simplicity, all constraints will be re-created as table constraints rather than column constraints.

The first section of the script does the initial setup, prompting for the table name and table owner for later use via the **accept** command, which, unlike simply using the variable with the '&' or '&&' in a SQL statement, allows you to define your own prompt for the variable. You can enter the table name with wildcards (such as '%APP%') to generate a script for all tables with a similar name. You can enter '%' as the *table_name* variable value to generate a script for all tables for that table owner.

The SQL*Plus **set** command turns off headers (**pagesize 0**), row counts (**feedback off**) and displays of old and new values for the *table_name* and *tab_owner* variables (**verify off**).

```
set echo off verify off feedback off pagesize 0 term on
select 'Creating table build script...' from DUAL;

accept table_name prompt "Enter the name of the Table: "
accept tab_owner prompt "Enter table owner: "
set term off
```

Next, a temporary table is created to hold each **create table** command and its owner. The Lineno column preserves the ordering of the lines of the **create table** command during later queries.

```
drop table TAB_TEMP;

create table TAB_TEMP (
        Lineno NUMBER,
        Id_Owner VARCHAR2(30),
        Id_Name VARCHAR2(30),
        Text VARCHAR2(2000))
/
```

In the next section of the script, the TAB_CURSOR cursor selects the storage definition information from DBA_TABLES where the table name matches the input variable *table_name* and the table owner matches the input variable *table_owner*. Using **like** in the **where** clause allows for wildcards in the *table_name* variable.

```
declare
    cursor TAB_CURSOR is
        select Owner,
                Table_Name,
                Tablespace_Name,
                Pct_Free,
                Pct_Used,
                Ini_Trans,
                Max_Trans,
                Initial_Extent,
                Next_Extent,
```

```
              Min_Extents,
              Max_Extents,
              Pct_Increase,
              Freelists,
              Freelist_Groups,
              Degree,
              Instances
       from DBA_TABLES
      where Owner = UPPER('&&tab_owner')
        and Table_Name like UPPER('&&table_name')
      order by Table_Name;
```

In the next section of the script, the COL_CURSOR cursor selects the column definition information from DBA_TAB_COLUMNS where the table name and owner match the table name and owner passed in from the TAB_CURSOR.

```
   cursor COL_CURSOR (C_Owner    VARCHAR2,
                      C_Tabname VARCHAR2) is
       select Column_Name,
              Data_Type,
              Data_Length,
              Data_Precision,
              Data_Scale,
              Nullable,
              Default_Length,
              Data_Default
       from DBA_TAB_COLUMNS
      where Owner      = C_Owner
        and Table_Name = C_Tabname
      order by Column_ID;
```

In the next section of the script, the CONS_CURSOR cursor selects the constraint definition and column information from DBA_CONSTRAINTS and DBA_CONS_COLUMNS where the table name and owner match the table name and owner passed in from the TAB_CURSOR and the constraint is either a Check constraint or the primary key (Constraint_Type in ('C','P')). The **order by** clause ensures that if the constraint is on multiple columns, it will be re-created in the proper column order.

```
   cursor CONS_CURSOR (Cons_Owner     VARCHAR2,
                       Cons_Tablename VARCHAR2) is
       select A.Owner,
              A.Constraint_Name,
              A.Constraint_Type,
              A.Table_Name,
```

```
            A.Search_Condition,
            B.Column_Name,
            B.Position
      from DBA_CONSTRAINTS   A,
            DBA_CONS_COLUMNS B
    where A.Owner              = B.Owner
      and A.Constraint_Name = B.Constraint_Name
      and A.Table_Name       = B.Table_Name
      and A.Constraint_Type in ('C','P')
      and A.Owner            = Cons_Owner
      and A.Table_Name       = Cons_Tablename
    order by A.Constraint_Type,
              A.Constraint_Name,
              B.Position;
```

The next section of the script, shown in the following listing, extracts the foreign key relationships. Extracting the foreign key relationships from the data dictionary is slightly more complex than extracting the primary key. In addition to knowing the name of the foreign key constraint and column(s) for the requested table, you must know the owner, table name and column name(s) of the table being referenced. To retrieve the information, the DBA_CONS_COLUMNS view is joined twice into the REF_CURSOR cursor, to extract the foreign key columns (C alias) and to extract the information on the primary key being referenced (B alias). The name of the primary key constraint being referenced by the foreign key is contained in the R_Constraint_Name column of DBA_CONSTRAINTS.

```
cursor REF_CURSOR (R_Owner       VARCHAR2,
                   R_Tablename VARCHAR2) is
    select A.Owner,
           A.Table_Name,
           A.Constraint_Name,
           A.R_Constraint_Name,
           B.Column_Name,
           C.Owner,
           C.Table_Name,
           C.Column_Name,
           C.Position
      from DBA_CONSTRAINTS   A,
           DBA_CONS_COLUMNS B,
           DBA_CONS_COLUMNS C
    where A.Constraint_Name = B.Constraint_Name
      and A.Owner            = B.Owner
      and C.Constraint_Name = A.R_Constraint_Name
      and B.Position          = C.Position
```

```
        and A.Owner            = R_Owner
        and A.Table_Name       = R_Tablename
    order by A.Constraint_Name,
             A.Owner,
             C.Position;
```

The procedure variables for the cursor, shown in the following listing, are declared as TABLE_NAME.Column_Name%**TYPE**. This "anchoring" of datatypes takes the column definition from within the database itself. If the column definition changes in a different version of ORACLE, the procedure will still work because the definition of the column has not been hard-coded. The *Lv_Cons_Exists* variable indicates whether or not there is a primary key constraint on the requested table. The variable *Lv_Lineno* orders the lines of the **create** statement and is initialized to 0.

```
Lv_Table_Owner              DBA_TABLES.Owner%TYPE;
Lv_Table_Name               DBA_TABLES.Table_Name%TYPE;
Lv_Tablespace_Name          DBA_TABLES.Tablespace_Name%TYPE;
Lv_Pct_Free                 DBA_TABLES.Pct_Free%TYPE;
Lv_Pct_Used                 DBA_TABLES.Pct_Used%TYPE;
Lv_Initial_Trans            DBA_TABLES.Ini_Trans%TYPE;
Lv_Max_Trans                DBA_TABLES.Max_Trans%TYPE;
Lv_Initial_Extent           DBA_TABLES.Initial_Extent%TYPE;
Lv_Next_Extent              DBA_TABLES.Next_Extent%TYPE;
Lv_Min_Extents              DBA_TABLES.Min_Extents%TYPE;
Lv_Max_Extents              DBA_TABLES.Max_Extents%TYPE;
Lv_Pct_Increase             DBA_TABLES.Pct_Increase%TYPE;
Lv_Freelists                DBA_TABLES.Freelists%TYPE;
Lv_Freelist_Groups          DBA_TABLES.Freelist_Groups%TYPE;
Lv_Degree                   DBA_TABLES.Degree%TYPE;
Lv_Instances                DBA_TABLES.Instances%TYPE;
Lv_Column_Name              DBA_TAB_COLUMNS.Column_Name%TYPE;
Lv_Column_Data_Type         DBA_TAB_COLUMNS.Data_Type%TYPE;
Lv_Column_Data_Length       DBA_TAB_COLUMNS.Data_Length%TYPE;
Lv_Column_Data_Precision    DBA_TAB_COLUMNS.Data_Precision%TYPE;
Lv_Column_Data_Scale        DBA_TAB_COLUMNS.Data_Scale%TYPE;
Lv_Column_Nullable          DBA_TAB_COLUMNS.Nullable%TYPE;
Lv_Column_Default_Length    DBA_TAB_COLUMNS.Default_Length%TYPE;
Lv_Column_Data_Default      DBA_TAB_COLUMNS.Data_Default%TYPE;
Lv_Cons_Owner               DBA_CONSTRAINTS.Owner%TYPE;
Lv_Cons_Table_Name          DBA_CONSTRAINTS.Table_Name%TYPE;
Lv_Cons_Constraint_Name     DBA_CONSTRAINTS.Constraint_Name%TYPE;
Lv_Cons_Constraint_Type     DBA_CONSTRAINTS.Constraint_Type%TYPE;
Lv_Cons_Search_Cond         DBA_CONSTRAINTS.Search_Condition%TYPE;
Lv_Cons_Column_Name         DBA_CONS_COLUMNS.Column_Name%TYPE;
Lv_Cons_R_Constraint_Name   DBA_CONSTRAINTS.R_Constraint_Name%TYPE;
```

```
Lv_Cons_Ref_Owner            DBA_CONSTRAINTS.Owner%TYPE;
Lv_Cons_Ref_Table_Name       DBA_CONSTRAINTS.Table_Name%TYPE;
Lv_Cons_Ref_Column_Name      DBA_CONS_COLUMNS.Column_Name%TYPE;
Lv_Cons_Ref_Position         DBA_CONS_COLUMNS.Position%TYPE;
Lv_Cons_Exists               VARCHAR2(1);
Lv_String                    VARCHAR2(800);
Lv_String2                   VARCHAR2(800);
Lv_Lineno                    NUMBER := 0;
```

The next portion of the script defines two internal procedures: WRITE_OUT to do the **insert**s into the temporary table, and UPDATE_OUT to **update** rows in the table. You can use UPDATE_OUT to remove extra characters from lines once the command or section of the command has been written.

```
procedure WRITE_OUT(P_Line INTEGER,   P_Owner VARCHAR2,
                    P_Name VARCHAR2, P_String VARCHAR2) is

begin
   insert into TAB_TEMP (Lineno, Id_Owner, Id_Name, Text)
          values (P_Line,P_Owner,P_Name,P_String);
 end;


procedure UPDATE_OUT(P_Line INTEGER,   P_Owner VARCHAR2,
                     P_Name VARCHAR2, P_String VARCHAR2) is
begin
   update TAB_TEMP
      set Text = P_String
    where Lineno = P_Line
      and Id_Owner = P_Owner
      and Id_Name  = P_Name;
end;
```

The TAB_CURSOR cursor forms an outer loop for each table. *Lv_Lineno* is used in conjunction with the table name to order the rows in the temporary table TAB_TEMP so that if you prefer, you can extract the **create** statement for a single table at the end of the procedure.

```
begin
   open TAB_CURSOR;
   loop
      fetch TAB_CURSOR into Lv_Table_Owner,
                            Lv_Table_Name,
                            Lv_Tablespace_Name,
                            Lv_Pct_Free,
                            Lv_Pct_Used,
                            Lv_Initial_Trans,
                            Lv_Max_Trans,
```

```
                            Lv_Initial_Extent,
                            Lv_Next_Extent,
                            Lv_Min_Extents,
                            Lv_Max_Extents,
                            Lv_Pct_Increase,
                            Lv_Freelists,
                            Lv_Freelist_Groups,
                            Lv_Degree,
                            Lv_Instances;
        exit when TAB_CURSOR%NOTFOUND;
```

The next section of the script inserts the beginning of the **create** statement into the temporary table. The SQL function **LOWER** is used to change the case of the table owner and table name to lowercase for readability.

To perform the **insert**, the WRITE_OUT procedure is executed, and line numbers are assigned to each inserted line.

```
        Lv_Lineno := 1;

        Lv_String := 'CREATE TABLE ' || LOWER(Lv_Table_Owner)
                                      || '.'
                                      || LOWER(Lv_Table_Name);
        WRITE_OUT(Lv_Lineno, Lv_Table_Owner, Lv_Table_Name, Lv_String);
        Lv_Lineno := Lv_Lineno + 1;

        Lv_String := '(';
        WRITE_OUT(Lv_Lineno, Lv_Table_Owner, Lv_Table_Name, Lv_String);
        Lv_Lineno := Lv_Lineno + 1;
```

The COL_CURSOR cursor forms the inner loop of the script, selecting all the column names in the table from DBA_TAB_COLUMNS. Each column's data definition will be processed and added to the temporary table before the next column is fetched. The inner cursor will be opened, fetched, and closed once for each table selected by the outer cursor.

```
        open COL_CURSOR (Lv_Table_Owner, Lv_Table_Name);

    loop
        fetch COL_CURSOR into Lv_Column_Name,
                              Lv_Column_Data_Type,
                              Lv_Column_Data_Length,
                              Lv_Column_Data_Precision,
                              Lv_Column_Data_Scale,
                              Lv_Column_Nullable,
                              Lv_Column_Default_Length,
                              Lv_Column_Data_Default;
        exit when COL_CURSOR%NOTFOUND;
```

The next section begins creating the string for the column definition with the column name. To make the line more readable, **RPAD** is used to pad the column name with blanks on the right before concatenating the datatype in so that the datatypes will line up.

```
Lv_String := '          '                    ||
             RPAD(LOWER(Lv_Column_Name),35) ||
             Lv_Column_Data_Type;
```

VARCHAR2, RAW, and CHAR datatypes all have a data length associated with the column. If this column is one of these datatypes, then the following section of the script appends the length enclosed in the required "( )".

```
if ( (Lv_Column_Data_Type = 'VARCHAR2' ) or
     (Lv_Column_Data_Type = 'RAW'      ) or
     (Lv_Column_Data_Type = 'CHAR'     ) )
then
    Lv_String := Lv_String             ||
                 '('                    ||
                 Lv_Column_Data_Length ||
                 ')';
```

If the column uses the NUMBER datatype, it can be defined with both a precision and scale. If the precision is NULL, the script sets the precision to 38 (the maximum definition for a numeric column) and the scale to 0 before adding them to the column definition. DATE and LONG datatypes do not need any additional processing.

```
elsif (Lv_Column_Data_Type = 'NUMBER')
then
    if Lv_Column_Data_Precision IS NULL
    then
        Lv_Column_Data_Precision := 38;
        Lv_Column_Data_Scale     := 0;
    end if;
    Lv_String := Lv_String                ||
                 '('                       ||
                 Lv_Column_Data_Precision ||
                 ','                       ||
                 Lv_Column_Data_Scale      ||
                 ')';
end if;
```

If you have defined a default value for the column, the default value needs to be added to the column definition. Since the Data_Default column in DBA_TAB_ COLUMNS is a LONG column, the script extracts the contents of the column by using the **SUBSTR** function. Defaults are used when you want to ensure that a particular value is inserted into a column if an **insert** command does not include a value for that column.

```
if (Lv_Column_Data_Default IS NOT NULL)
then
    Lv_String := Lv_String || ' DEFAULT '
                            || SUBSTR(Lv_Column_Data_Default,
                               1, Lv_Column_Default_Length);
end if;
```

If the column is a required column, the *Lv_Column_Nullable* variable's value will be N and the phrase **NOT NULL** must be added to the string.

Add a comma to separate the columns, and write the column definition line to the temporary table. The inner loop will repeat for each column of the table.

```
if (Lv_Column_Nullable = 'N' )
then
    Lv_String := Lv_String || '  NOT NULL';
end if;

Lv_String := Lv_String || ',';
WRITE_OUT(Lv_Lineno, Lv_Table_Owner, Lv_Table_Name, Lv_String);
Lv_Lineno := Lv_Lineno + 1;


end loop;
```

Because the procedure adds a comma to the end of every line of the column definition, there is an additional, unnecessary comma at the end of the last column. The variable *Lv_Lineno* is decremented to go back to that last line, and the procedure uses the **SUBSTR** command to extract all of the line except the comma. The line is then rewritten to the temporary table by the UPDATE_OUT procedure and the *Lv_Lineno* is incremented again.

```
close COL_CURSOR;
Lv_Lineno := Lv_Lineno - 1;
Lv_String := SUBSTR(Lv_String, 1,(LENGTH(Lv_String) - 1));
UPDATE_OUT(Lv_Lineno, Lv_Table_Owner, Lv_Table_Name,Lv_String);
Lv_Lineno := Lv_Lineno + 1;
```

Now that the column definitions have been completed, that part of the **create table** command is closed with a final ')' .

```
Lv_String := ')';
WRITE_OUT(Lv_Lineno, Lv_Table_Owner, Lv_Table_Name, Lv_String);
Lv_Lineno := Lv_Lineno + 1;
```

The **parallel** clause of the **create table** command determines the degree of parallelism for an operation on a single instance (the number of query servers used in the parallel operation), and is ignored by ORACLE unless you have installed the Parallel Query Option. When you specify DEFAULT instead of an integer value, the number of query servers used is calculated from the number of CPUs and the number of devices storing the tables to be scanned in parallel. The **instances** clause within the **parallel** clause is ignored unless you are running ORACLE Parallel Server, in which case it determines the number of parallel server instances to use in the operation.

```
Lv_String := 'PARALLEL ( DEGREE ' || Lv_Degree
                                  || ' INSTANCES '
                                  || Lv_Instances
                                  || ' )';
WRITE_OUT(Lv_Lineno, Lv_Table_Owner, Lv_Table_Name, Lv_String);
Lv_Lineno := Lv_Lineno + 1;
```

Specifying **noparallel** when you create the table is the same as specifying **parallel (degree 1 instances 1)**.

The next section of the script, shown in the following listing, defines the location and internal configuration of the table and the data blocks within the table. The **tablespace** clause defines which tablespace the table will be created in; if you do not specify a tablespace in the original **create table** statement, the table will be created in your default tablespace. **pctfree** defines the percentage of space in each block that will be reserved for future **update**s of the rows. **pctused** defines the minimum percentage of used space maintained in each block. If the percentage of used space falls below the **pctused** value, rows can be **insert**ed into the block. **initrans** and **maxtrans** define the initial and maximum concurrent transactions that can **update** a data block.

```
Lv_String := 'TABLESPACE ' || Lv_Tablespace_Name ;
WRITE_OUT(Lv_Lineno, Lv_Table_Owner, Lv_Table_Name, Lv_String);
Lv_Lineno := Lv_Lineno + 1;

Lv_String := 'PCTFREE ' || Lv_Pct_Free ;
WRITE_OUT(Lv_Lineno, Lv_Table_Owner, Lv_Table_Name, Lv_String);
Lv_Lineno := Lv_Lineno + 1;

Lv_String := 'PCTUSED ' || Lv_Pct_Used ;
WRITE_OUT(Lv_Lineno, Lv_Table_Owner, Lv_Table_Name, Lv_String);
Lv_Lineno := Lv_Lineno + 1;

Lv_String := 'INITRANS ' || Lv_Initial_Trans ;
WRITE_OUT(Lv_Lineno, Lv_Table_Owner, Lv_Table_Name, Lv_String);
Lv_Lineno := Lv_Lineno + 1;

Lv_String := 'MAXTRANS ' || Lv_Max_Trans ;
WRITE_OUT(Lv_Lineno, Lv_Table_Owner, Lv_Table_Name, Lv_String);
Lv_Lineno := Lv_Lineno + 1;
```

The final section of the **create table** statement is the storage definition. **initial** and **next** define the size of the first data block allocated and the size of the next block to be allocated. If **pctincrease** is non-zero, indicating that the size of the next extent allocated should grow by this percent, the value of **next** will change as each new block is allocated to the table. **minextents** defines the number of extents that are allocated when the table is initially created. **maxextents** limits the size of the table by limiting extension to this number of extents. **freelists** are the number of lists of data blocks that can be used during **insert**s. Multiple freelists reduces contention for free blocks during concurrent updates. **freelist groups** are the number of groups of freelists, and are only used with the ORACLE Parallel Server.

```
Lv_String := 'STORAGE';
WRITE_OUT(Lv_Lineno, Lv_Table_Owner, Lv_Table_Name, Lv_String);
Lv_Lineno := Lv_Lineno + 1;
Lv_String := '(';
WRITE_OUT(Lv_Lineno, Lv_Table_Owner, Lv_Table_Name, Lv_String);
Lv_Lineno := Lv_Lineno + 1;

Lv_String := '   INITIAL ' || Lv_Initial_Extent ;
WRITE_OUT(Lv_Lineno, Lv_Table_Owner, Lv_Table_Name, Lv_String);
Lv_Lineno := Lv_Lineno + 1;

Lv_String := '   NEXT ' || Lv_Next_Extent ;
WRITE_OUT(Lv_Lineno, Lv_Table_Owner, Lv_Table_Name, Lv_String);
Lv_Lineno := Lv_Lineno + 1;

Lv_String := '   MINEXTENTS ' || Lv_Min_Extents ;
WRITE_OUT(Lv_Lineno, Lv_Table_Owner, Lv_Table_Name, Lv_String);
Lv_Lineno := Lv_Lineno + 1;

Lv_String := '   MAXEXTENTS ' || Lv_Max_Extents ;
WRITE_OUT(Lv_Lineno, Lv_Table_Owner, Lv_Table_Name, Lv_String);
Lv_Lineno := Lv_Lineno + 1;

Lv_String := '   PCTINCREASE ' || Lv_Pct_Increase ;
WRITE_OUT(Lv_Lineno, Lv_Table_Owner, Lv_Table_Name, Lv_String);
Lv_Lineno := Lv_Lineno + 1;

Lv_String := '   FREELISTS ' || Lv_Freelists ;
WRITE_OUT(Lv_Lineno, Lv_Table_Owner, Lv_Table_Name, Lv_String);
Lv_Lineno := Lv_Lineno + 1;
```

```
Lv_String := '    FREELIST GROUPS ' || Lv_Freelist_Groups ;
WRITE_OUT(Lv_Lineno, Lv_Table_Owner, Lv_Table_Name, Lv_String);
Lv_Lineno := Lv_Lineno + 1;

Lv_String := ')';
WRITE_OUT(Lv_Lineno, Lv_Table_Owner, Lv_Table_Name, Lv_String);
Lv_Lineno := Lv_Lineno + 1;

Lv_String := '/';
WRITE_OUT(Lv_Lineno, Lv_Table_Owner, Lv_Table_Name, Lv_String);
Lv_Lineno := Lv_Lineno + 1;
```

Once the storage information has been written to the temporary table, the **create table** command is ended with a /.

```
Lv_Cons_Exists := 'N';

open CONS_CURSOR(Lv_Table_Owner, Lv_Table_Name);
loop
    fetch CONS_CURSOR into Lv_Cons_Owner,
                           Lv_Cons_Constraint_Name,
                           Lv_Cons_Constraint_Type,
                           Lv_Cons_Table_Name,
                           Lv_Cons_Search_Cond,
                           Lv_Cons_Column_Name,
                           Lv_Cons_Ref_Position;
    exit when CONS_CURSOR%NOTFOUND;
```

The next section of the script determines if there are any Check or primary key constraints on the table, and if there are, generates the SQL statements to create them. The CONS_CURSOR cursor will fetch any constraints with a constraint type of 'C' or 'P.' The *Lv_Cons_Exists* variable determines whether or not you have extracted a primary key constraint. The first check will be for Check constraints.

```
        if (Lv_Cons_Constraint_Type = 'C') AND
           (INSTR(Lv_Cons_Search_Cond,'NOT NULL',1) = 0)
```

Defining a column as NOT NULL adds a Check constraint to the data dictionary. Since we have already dealt with NOT NULL columns in the **create table** statement, we can ignore them here.

The next section of the script generates the constraint creation script using the **alter table** command.

```
        then
            Lv_String := 'ALTER TABLE ' || Lv_Cons_Owner
                                         || '.'
                                         || Lv_Cons_Table_Name;
```

```
            WRITE_OUT(Lv_Lineno, Lv_Table_Owner, Lv_Table_Name,
                     Lv_String);
         Lv_Lineno := Lv_Lineno + 1;
```

   Constraints can be named or unnamed. Unnamed constraints are named by
ORACLE and all these constraint names begin with 'SYS_C.' If the constraint name
does not begin with this string, we need to add the **constraint** *constraint_name* clause
to the string before writing it to the temporary table.

```
         Lv_String := 'ADD ';
         if  (INSTR(Lv_Cons_Constraint_Name,'SYS_C',1) = 0)
         then
             Lv_String := Lv_String || 'CONSTRAINT '
                                    || Lv_Cons_Constraint_Name;
         end if;
         Lv_String := Lv_String      || ' CHECK ('
                                    || Lv_Cons_Search_Cond
                                    || ')';
         WRITE_OUT(Lv_Lineno, Lv_Table_Owner, Lv_Table_Name,
                     Lv_String);
         Lv_Lineno := Lv_Lineno + 1;
```

   The next portion of the script completes the **alter table** statement for a Check
constraint by writing a '/' to execute the statement when the generated script is run.

```
         Lv_String := '/';
         WRITE_OUT(Lv_Lineno, Lv_Table_Owner, Lv_Table_Name,
                     Lv_String);
         Lv_Lineno := Lv_Lineno + 1;
      end if;
```

   The next section of the procedure will generate the statements to re-create the
primary key constraint on the table if one exists. Since the script builds the statement
as a single string, you need to set a flag to determine whether or not there is a
primary key constraint to write to the temporary table at the end of the cursor loop.
The **order by** clause of the cursor definition, by placing Constraint_Type as the first
column to sort on, puts the primary key constraint, if it exists, as the last row fetched
from the cursor.

```
      if (Lv_Cons_Constraint_Type = 'P')
      then
          Lv_Cons_Exists := 'Y';

          if (Lv_Cons_Ref_Position = 1)
          then
              Lv_String := 'ALTER TABLE ' || Lv_Cons_Owner
                                          || '.'
```

```
                                  || Lv_Cons_Table_Name;
        WRITE_OUT(Lv_Lineno, Lv_Table_Owner, Lv_Table_Name,
                  Lv_String);
        Lv_Lineno := Lv_Lineno + 1;
```

The *Lv_Cons_Ref_Position* cursor variable holds the column position within the primary key. If the column being processed is the first column, the beginning of the **alter table** statement is written to the temporary table.

Since this script is still processing the first column in the primary key, the second part of the primary key constraint clause, **add**, must be concatenated to the string. As with Check constraints, primary key constraints can be named or unnamed. Unnamed constraints are named by ORACLE and all these constraint names begin with 'SYS_C.' If the constraint name does not begin with this string, we need to start the string with the **constraint** *constraint_name* clause.

```
        Lv_String := 'ADD ';
        if  (INSTR(Lv_Cons_Constraint_Name,'SYS_C') = 0)
        then
            Lv_String := Lv_String || 'CONSTRAINT ' ||
                         Lv_Cons_Constraint_Name || ' ';
        end if;
```

Since this is still processing the first column in the primary key, the second part of the primary key constraint clause, **primary key**, must be concatenated to the string along with the column name.

```
        Lv_String := Lv_String || 'PRIMARY KEY (' ||
                     Lv_Cons_Column_Name || ')';
```

The constraint clause is closed with a ')' after each column is concatenated to the string. If there are multiple columns in the constraint, the ')' is replaced by a comma with the **REPLACE** function before the next column name is added in and the clause is closed again.

```
        else
            Lv_String := REPLACE(Lv_String,')',',' ||
                         Lv_Cons_Column_Name|| ')' );
        end if;

    end if;
end loop;
```

The loop will repeat until all Check constraints and the primary key constraint have been processed.

If the variable *Lv_Cons_Exists* has been set to 'Y,' then there is a primary key constraint on the table and the string has to be written to the temporary table.

```
    if (Lv_Cons_Exists = 'Y')
    then
```

```
      WRITE_OUT(Lv_Lineno, Lv_Table_Owner, Lv_Table_Name, Lv_String);
      Lv_Lineno := Lv_Lineno + 1;


      Lv_String := '/';
      WRITE_OUT(Lv_Lineno, Lv_Table_Owner, Lv_Table_Name, Lv_String);
      Lv_Lineno := Lv_Lineno + 1;
    end if;


    close CONS_CURSOR;
```

The final constraint type to check for is the foreign key constraint. There can be multiple foreign key constraints defined on a table, so a cursor, REF_CURSOR, is needed.

```
    open   REF_CURSOR(Lv_Table_Owner, Lv_Table_Name);
    loop
        fetch REF_CURSOR into Lv_Cons_Owner,
                              Lv_Cons_Table_Name,
                              Lv_Cons_Constraint_Name,
                              Lv_Cons_R_Constraint_Name,
                              Lv_Cons_Column_Name,
                              Lv_Cons_Ref_Owner,
                              Lv_Cons_Ref_Table_Name,
                              Lv_Cons_Ref_Column_Name,
                              Lv_Cons_Ref_Position;
        exit when REF_CURSOR%NOTFOUND;
```

The *Lv_Cons_Ref_Position* cursor variable holds the column position within the foreign key. If the column being processed is the first column, the beginning of the **alter table** statement is written to the temporary table.

```
        if (Lv_Cons_Ref_Position = 1)
        then
            Lv_String := 'ALTER TABLE '|| Lv_Table_Owner
                                       || '.'
                                       || Lv_Table_Name;
            WRITE_OUT(Lv_Lineno, Lv_Table_Owner, Lv_Table_Name,
                      Lv_String);
            Lv_Lineno := Lv_Lineno + 1;
```

Since this script is still processing the first column in the foreign key, the second part of the foreign key constraint clause, **add**, must be concatenated to the string. As with Check and primary key constraints, foreign key constraints can be named or unnamed. Unnamed constraints are named by ORACLE and all these constraint names begin with 'SYS_C.' If the constraint name does not begin with this string, we need to start the string with the **constraint** *constraint_name* clause.

```
       Lv_String := 'ADD ';
if   (INSTR(Lv_Cons_Constraint_Name,'SYS_C',1) = 0)
then
        Lv_String := Lv_String || 'CONSTRAINT '
                                || Lv_Cons_Constraint_Name
                                || ' ';
end if;
```

The next section of the script concatenates the last parts of the foreign key constraint clause, **foreign key** and **references**, to the strings along with the column name. In order to keep the two clauses in sync, the script uses two string variables, *Lv_String* and *Lv_String2*.

```
Lv_String := Lv_String      || 'FOREIGN KEY ('
                            || Lv_Cons_Column_Name
                            || ')';
WRITE_OUT(Lv_Lineno, Lv_Table_Owner, Lv_Table_Name,
          Lv_String);
Lv_Lineno := Lv_Lineno + 1;

Lv_String2 := '    REFERENCES ' || Lv_Cons_Ref_Owner
                            || '.'
                            || Lv_Cons_Ref_Table_Name
                            || '('
                            || Lv_Cons_Ref_Column_Name
                            || ')';
WRITE_OUT(Lv_Lineno, Lv_Table_Owner, Lv_Table_Name,
          Lv_String2);
Lv_Lineno := Lv_Lineno + 1;

WRITE_OUT(Lv_Lineno, Lv_Table_Owner, Lv_Table_Name, '/');
Lv_Lineno := Lv_Lineno + 1;
```

Each part of the constraint clause is closed with a ')' after the foreign key column and the referenced column are concatenated to the strings. If there are multiple columns in the constraint, the ')' is replaced by a comma with the **REPLACE** function before the next column name is added in and the clause is closed again. Because the **foreign key** clause, the **references** clause, and the '/' are written separately to the temporary table for each column, the procedure backs up three lines to update the **foreign key** clause and then forward one line to update the **references** clause, and finally forward two lines to re-position to the end of the **alter table** command.

```
        else
          Lv_String   := REPLACE(Lv_String,  ')', ',' ||
                                Lv_Cons_Column_Name    || ')' );
          Lv_Lineno   := Lv_Lineno -3;
          UPDATE_OUT(Lv_Lineno, Lv_Table_Owner, Lv_Table_Name,
                     Lv_String);
          Lv_Lineno   := Lv_Lineno + 1;

          Lv_String2 := REPLACE(Lv_String2, ')', ',' ||
                                Lv_Cons_Ref_Column_Name || ')' );
          UPDATE_OUT(Lv_Lineno, Lv_Table_Owner, Lv_Table_Name,
                     Lv_String2);
          Lv_Lineno   := Lv_Lineno + 2;

        end if;

    end loop;
    close REF_CURSOR;
```

The loop will repeat until all foreign key constraints have been processed. Once all constraints on the table have been processed, the outer loop on TAB_CURSOR will repeat until all tables have been processed.

```
  end loop;
  close TAB_CURSOR;
end;
/
spool cre_tbl.sql
select Text
  from TAB_TEMP
 order by Id_Owner, Id_Name, Lineno
/
spool off
```

Once the **create** and **alter** statements for the table and all the constraints have been generated, they are spooled to a file for later execution. The following listing shows sample output for the APP_REFERRALS table.

```
CREATE TABLE app.app_referrals
(
    code                             VARCHAR2(3)   NOT NULL,
    refr_type                        VARCHAR2(3)   NOT NULL,
    description                      VARCHAR2(25)  NOT NULL,
    usr_crtd                         VARCHAR2(30)  NOT NULL,
    dt_crtd                          DATE  NOT NULL,
    status                           VARCHAR2(3),
```

```
        usr_mdfd                    VARCHAR2(30),
        dt_mdfd                     DATE,
        refr_code                   VARCHAR2(3),
        discount                    NUMBER(8,2),
        discount_type               CHAR(1)
)
PARALLEL (DEGREE 1 INSTANCES 1)
TABLESPACE USER_DATA
PCTFREE 10
PCTUSED 40
INITRANS 1
MAXTRANS 255
STORAGE
(
    INITIAL 73728
    NEXT 1048576
    MINEXTENTS 1
    MAXEXTENTS 500
    PCTINCREASE 0
    FREELISTS 1
    FREELIST GROUPS 1
)
/
ALTER TABLE APP.APP_REFERRALS
CONSTRAINT REFR_PK ADD PRIMARY KEY (CODE)
/
ALTER TABLE APP.APP_REFERRALS
ADD CONSTRAINT REFR_REFR_FK FOREIGN KEY (REFR_CODE)
    REFERENCES APP.APP_REFERRALS(CODE)
/
```

The APP_REFERRALS table has several columns defined as NOT NULL, no default values for any columns, one primary key constraint, and one foreign key constraint.

As an alternative, if you want to use this script to document all the tables for a particular owner, remove the **accept** *table_name* statement at the beginning of the script and change the **where** clause for the TAB_CURSOR cursor to:

```
where Owner  = UPPER('&&tab_owner')
```

If you want to document all tables in your database that are not owned by SYS, remove the two **accept** statements from the beginning of the script and change the **where** clause for the TAB_CURSOR cursor to:

```
where Owner != 'SYS'
```

gen_indx.sql

Generate Indexes

Losing an index on a table can be a catastrophe in terms of performance. As you move a table from one database to another, or change the table itself within the database, it is difficult to manually save off and re-create indexes. The gen_indx.sql script, shown in the following listing, will generate a script to re-create all the indexes of a given table. Following the gen_indx.sql listing, you will see a sample set of generated index creation scripts.

PROGRAMMER'S NOTE   *In order to be generic over both ORACLE7 and ORACLE8, the script does not handle reverse indexes. If you use reverse indexes, you will need to manually edit the generated SQL script.*

```
set echo off verify off term on feedback off pagesize 0

select 'Creating index build script...' from DUAL;
prompt
accept table_name prompt "Enter the name of the Table: "
accept tab_owner prompt "Enter table owner: "
set term off

drop table I_TEMP;
create table I_TEMP (
        Lineno NUMBER,
        Id_Owner VARCHAR2(30),
        Id_Name VARCHAR2(30),
        Text VARCHAR2(800))
/

declare
    cursor IND_CURSOR is
        select Owner,
                Index_Name,
                Table_Owner,
                Table_Name,
                Uniqueness,
                Tablespace_Name,
                Ini_Trans,
                Max_Trans,
                Initial_Extent,
                Next_Extent,
                Min_Extents,
                Max_Extents,
                Pct_Increase,
```

```
            Pct_Free
        from DBA_INDEXES
      where Owner = UPPER('&&tab_owner')
        and Table_Name like UPPER('&&table_name')
        and Index_Name not like 'SYS_%'
        and not exists (select 'x'
                            from DBA_CONSTRAINTS
                            where Constraint_Name = Index_Name
                            and Table_Owner       =
                                UPPER('&&tab_owner'))
      order by Index_Name;

cursor COL_CURSOR (I_Own VARCHAR2,
                   C_Ind VARCHAR2,
                   C_Tab VARCHAR2) is
      select Column_Name
        from DBA_IND_COLUMNS
      where Index_Owner = I_Own
        and Index_Name  = C_Ind
        and Table_Name  = C_Tab
      order by Column_Position;

Lv_Index_Owner        DBA_INDEXES.Owner%TYPE;
Lv_Index_Name         DBA_INDEXES.Index_Name%TYPE;
Lv_Table_Owner        DBA_INDEXES.Table_Owner%TYPE;
Lv_Table_Name         DBA_INDEXES.Table_Name%TYPE;
Lv_Uniqueness         DBA_INDEXES.Uniqueness%TYPE;
Lv_Tablespace_Name    DBA_INDEXES.Tablespace_Name%TYPE;
Lv_Ini_Trans          DBA_INDEXES.Ini_Trans%TYPE;
Lv_Max_Trans          DBA_INDEXES.Max_Trans%TYPE;
Lv_Initial_Extent     DBA_INDEXES.Initial_Extent%TYPE;
Lv_Next_Extent        DBA_INDEXES.Next_Extent%TYPE;
Lv_Min_Extents        DBA_INDEXES.Min_Extents%TYPE;
Lv_Max_Extents        DBA_INDEXES.Max_Extents%TYPE;
Lv_Pct_Increase       DBA_INDEXES.Pct_Increase%TYPE;
Lv_Pct_Free           DBA_INDEXES.Pct_Free%TYPE;
Lv_Column_Name        DBA_IND_COLUMNS.Column_Name%TYPE;
Lv_First_Rec          BOOLEAN;
Lv_String             VARCHAR2(800);
Lv_Lineno             NUMBER := 0;

procedure WRITE_OUT(P_Line INTEGER, P_Owner varchar2, P_Name
```

```
                               VARCHAR2, P_String VARCHAR2) is
    begin
       insert into I_TEMP (Lineno, Id_Owner, Id_Name, Text)
                values (P_Line,P_Owner,P_Name,P_String);
    end;

begin
    open IND_CURSOR;
    loop
       fetch IND_CURSOR into Lv_Index_Owner,
                              Lv_Index_Name,
                              Lv_Table_Owner,
                              Lv_Table_Name,
                              Lv_Uniqueness,
                              Lv_Tablespace_Name,
                              Lv_Ini_Trans,
                              Lv_Max_Trans,
                              Lv_Initial_Extent,
                              Lv_Next_Extent,
                              Lv_Min_Extents,
                              Lv_Max_Extents,
                              Lv_Pct_Increase,
                              Lv_Pct_Free;
       exit when IND_CURSOR%NOTFOUND;
       Lv_Lineno := 1;
       Lv_First_Rec := TRUE;
       if (Lv_Uniqueness = 'UNIQUE')
       then
          Lv_String:= 'CREATE UNIQUE INDEX ' || LOWER(Lv_Index_Owner) ||
                      '.' || LOWER(Lv_Index_Name);
       else
          Lv_String:= 'CREATE INDEX ' || LOWER(LV_INDEX_OWNER) || '.' ||
                      LOWER(Lv_Index_Name);
       end if;
        WRITE_OUT(Lv_Lineno, Lv_Index_Owner, Lv_Index_Name, Lv_String);
        Lv_Lineno := Lv_Lineno + 1;

       open COL_CURSOR(Lv_Index_Owner,Lv_Index_Name,Lv_Table_Name);
       loop
          fetch COL_CURSOR into Lv_Column_Name;
          exit when COL_CURSOR%NOTFOUND;
          if (Lv_First_Rec)
          then
```

```
            Lv_String := '    ON '|| LOWER(Lv_Table_Owner) || '.' ||
                         LOWER(Lv_Table_Name)||' (';
            Lv_First_Rec := FALSE;
          else
            Lv_String := Lv_String || ',';
          end if;
          Lv_String := Lv_String || LOWER(Lv_Column_Name);
        end loop;
        close COL_CURSOR;
        Lv_String := Lv_String || ')';
        WRITE_OUT(Lv_Lineno, Lv_Index_Owner, Lv_Index_Name, Lv_String);
        Lv_Lineno := Lv_Lineno + 1;
        Lv_String := null;
        Lv_String := 'PCTFREE ' || TO_CHAR(Lv_Pct_Free);
        WRITE_OUT(Lv_Lineno, Lv_Index_Owner, Lv_Index_Name, Lv_String);
        Lv_Lineno := Lv_Lineno + 1;
        Lv_String := 'INITRANS ' || TO_CHAR(Lv_Ini_Trans) ||
                     ' MAXTRANS ' || TO_CHAR(Lv_Max_Trans);
        WRITE_OUT(Lv_Lineno, Lv_Index_Owner, Lv_Index_Name, Lv_String);
        Lv_Lineno := Lv_Lineno + 1;
        Lv_String := 'TABLESPACE ' || Lv_Tablespace_Name || ' STORAGE (';
        WRITE_OUT(Lv_Lineno, Lv_Index_Owner, Lv_Index_Name, Lv_String);
        Lv_Lineno := Lv_Lineno + 1;
        Lv_String := 'INITIAL ' || TO_CHAR(Lv_Initial_Extent) ||
                     ' NEXT ' || TO_CHAR(Lv_Next_Extent);
        WRITE_OUT(Lv_Lineno, Lv_Index_Owner, Lv_Index_Name, Lv_String);
        Lv_Lineno := Lv_Lineno + 1;
        Lv_String := 'MINEXTENTS ' || TO_CHAR(Lv_Min_Extents) ||
                     ' MAXEXTENTS ' || TO_CHAR(Lv_Max_Extents) ||
                     ' PCTINCREASE ' || TO_CHAR(Lv_Pct_Increase) || ')';

        WRITE_OUT(Lv_Lineno, Lv_Index_Owner, Lv_Index_Name, Lv_String);
        Lv_Lineno := Lv_Lineno + 1;
        Lv_String := '/';
        WRITE_OUT(Lv_Lineno, Lv_Index_Owner, Lv_Index_Name, Lv_String);
        Lv_Lineno := Lv_Lineno + 1;
        Lv_Lineno := Lv_Lineno + 1;
        Lv_String:='                                            ';
        WRITE_OUT(Lv_Lineno, Lv_Index_Owner, Lv_Index_Name, Lv_String);
      end loop;
      close IND_CURSOR;
end;
```

```
/

spool cre_indx.sql
set heading off recsep off
col Text format a80 word_wrap

select Text
  from I_TEMP
 order by Id_Owner, Id_Name, Lineno;
spool off
```

Sample output for the gen_indx.sql script is shown in the following listing. The gen_indx.sql script will generate the following script to re-create all indexes for the given table and owner.

```
CREATE INDEX app.terminals_cpy_fk_I
ON app.app_terminals (cpy_abbr)
PCTFREE 0
INITRANS 2 MAXTRANS 255
TABLESPACE USER_INDEX STORAGE (
INITIAL 1048576 NEXT 516096
MINEXTENTS 1 MAXEXTENTS 300 PCTINCREASE 0)
/


CREATE INDEX app.terminals_epe_fk_i
ON app.app_terminals (epe_code)
PCTFREE 0
INITRANS 2 MAXTRANS 255
TABLESPACE USER_INDEX STORAGE (
INITIAL 1048576 NEXT 516096
MINEXTENTS 1 MAXEXTENTS 300 PCTINCREASE 0)
/


CREATE INDEX app.terminals_terminals_fk_i
ON app.app_terminals (terminals_terminal_no)
PCTFREE 0
INITRANS 2 MAXTRANS 255
TABLESPACE USER_INDEX STORAGE (
INITIAL 1048576 NEXT 516096
MINEXTENTS 1 MAXEXTENTS 300 PCTINCREASE 0)
/
```

The output, shown in the preceding listing, is a set of three **create index** commands for the APP_TERMINALS table. You can use the gen_indx.sql script to generate the **create index** commands for multiple tables and schemas.

ANNOTATIONS

The gen_indx.sql script generates all indexes created against a given table, excluding indexes named by ORACLE (SYS_C#####) and named indexes created by a constraint declared on the table. Indexes are named by ORACLE when a constraint is declared on the table or a column without naming the constraint. Re-creating these indexes manually can cause a conflict with a system-allocated name. Indexes created by a constraint are re-created when the constraint is re-created. SQL to re-create constraints is part of the gen_tbl.sql script in the preceding section of this chapter.

The script uses a temporary table to hold individual lines of the **create index** statement, writing to the table rather than using DBMS_OUTPUT.PUT_LINE so that you can extract the information for an individual index or for all indexes on the table from the temporary table. Using the DBMS_OUTPUT procedure would force you to save and edit the output file for the index you want.

The first section of the script does the initial setup, prompting for the table name and table owner for later use via the **accept** command, which, unlike simply using the variable with the '&' or '&&' in a SQL statement, allows you to define your own prompt for the variable. You can enter *'%table_name%'* to generate a script for all indexes on tables with a similar name, or enter '%' to generate all indexes on all tables owned by *tab_owner*.

The SQL*Plus **set** command turns off headers (**pagesize 0**), row counts (**feedback off**), and displays of old and new values for the *table_name* and *tab_owner* variables (**verify off**).

```
set echo off verify off term on feedback off pagesize 0

select 'Creating index build script...' from DUAL;
prompt
accept table_name prompt "Enter the name of the Table: "
accept tab_owner prompt "Enter table owner: "
set term off
```

The next section of the script creates a temporary table to hold each **create index** command and its owner. The Lineno column is used for ordering of the lines of the **create index** command by index name.

```
drop table I_TEMP;
create table I_TEMP (
        Lineno NUMBER,
        Id_Owner VARCHAR2(30),
```

```
        Id_Name VARCHAR2(30),
        Text VARCHAR2(800))
/
```

The IND_CURSOR cursor, defined in the next section of the script, selects the storage information from DBA_INDEXES where the table name matches the input variable *table_name* and the table owner matches the input variable *tab_owner*. By selecting for Table_Name rather than Index_Name, all indexes on the table will be processed. Using **like** instead of = in the **where** clause allows for wildcards. The check for index names that are not like 'SYS_%' removes all indexes with ORACLE-generated names from the rows returned. The **not exists** in the **where** clause of the **select** does not need an actual value returned; the check is just to see if the index was created by a constraint. If the index was created by a constraint, the **not exists** fails and the index will not be included in the generated SQL. Use the gen_tbl.sql script shown in the preceding section of this chapter to generate the SQL necessary to re-create those indexes.

```
declare
    cursor IND_CURSOR is
        select Owner,
                Index_Name,
                Table_Owner,
                Table_Name,
                Uniqueness,
                Tablespace_Name,
                Ini_Trans,
                Max_Trans,
                Initial_Extent,
                Next_Extent,
                Min_Extents,
                Max_Extents,
                Pct_Increase,
                Pct_Free
          from DBA_INDEXES
        where Owner = UPPER('&&tab_owner')
          and Table_Name like UPPER('&&table_name')
          and Index_Name not like 'SYS_%'
          and not exists (select 'x'
                            from DBA_CONSTRAINTS
                          where Constraint_Name = Index_Name
                            and Table_Owner     =
                                UPPER('&&tab_owner'))
        order by Index_Name;
```

In the next section of the script, the COL_CURSOR cursor selects the column name from DBA_IND_COLUMNS for each index selected by the IND_CURSOR cursor. The results are ordered by Column_Position, so that indexes created on multiple columns will be re-created in the proper column order.

```
cursor COL_CURSOR (I_Own VARCHAR2,
                   C_Ind VARCHAR2,
                   C_Tab VARCHAR2) is
      select Column_Name
        from DBA_IND_COLUMNS
       where Index_Owner = I_Own
         and Index_Name  = C_Ind
         and Table_Name  = C_Tab
       order by Column_Position;
```

The procedure variables for the cursor are declared as TABLE_NAME.Column_Name%**TYPE**. This anchoring of the datatypes takes the column definition from within the database itself. If the column definition changes in a different version of ORACLE, the procedure will still work because the definition of the column has not been hard-coded. The variable *Lv_Lineno* orders the lines of the **create** statement and is initialized to 0.

```
Lv_Index_Owner        DBA_INDEXES.Owner%TYPE;
Lv_Index_Name         DBA_INDEXES.Index_Name%TYPE;
Lv_Table_Owner        DBA_INDEXES.Table_Owner%TYPE;
Lv_Table_Name         DBA_INDEXES.Table_Name%TYPE;
Lv_Uniqueness         DBA_INDEXES.Uniqueness%TYPE;
Lv_Tablespace_Name    DBA_INDEXES.Tablespace_Name%TYPE;
Lv_Ini_Trans          DBA_INDEXES.Ini_Trans%TYPE;
Lv_Max_Trans          DBA_INDEXES.Max_Trans%TYPE;
Lv_Initial_Extent     DBA_INDEXES.Initial_Extent%TYPE;
Lv_Next_Extent        DBA_INDEXES.Next_Extent%TYPE;
Lv_Min_Extents        DBA_INDEXES.Min_Extents%TYPE;
Lv_Max_Extents        DBA_INDEXES.Max_Extents%TYPE;
Lv_Pct_Increase       DBA_INDEXES.Pct_Increase%TYPE;
Lv_Pct_Free           DBA_INDEXES.Pct_Free%TYPE;
Lv_Column_Name        DBA_IND_COLUMNS.Column_Name%TYPE;
Lv_First_Rec          BOOLEAN;
Lv_String             VARCHAR2(800);
Lv_Lineno             NUMBER := 0;
```

An internal procedure named WRITE_OUT will perform the **insert**s into the temporary table. The values inserted into the temporary table will later be queried to generate the **create index** command.

```
procedure WRITE_OUT(P_Line INTEGER, P_Owner varchar2, P_Name
                    VARCHAR2, P_String VARCHAR2) is
```

```
begin
    insert into I_TEMP (Lineno, Id_Owner, Id_Name, Text)
            values (P_Line,P_Owner,P_Name,P_String);
end;
```

In the first part of the Executable Commands section of the script, shown in the following listing, the IND_CURSOR cursor forms an outer loop for each index for the requested table. *Lv_Lineno* is used in conjunction with the index name to order the rows in the temporary table I_TEMP so you can extract the **create index** command for a single index at the end of the procedure if you wish. *Lv_First_Rec* is a Boolean variable that distinguishes between the first column in the index, which is preceded by '(', and the remaining columns in the index, which are preceded by ','. *Lv_First_Rec* is initialized to TRUE to indicate that the procedure is beginning to process the index.

```
begin
    open IND_CURSOR;
    loop
        fetch IND_CURSOR into Lv_Index_Owner,
                              Lv_Index_Name,
                              Lv_Table_Owner,
                              Lv_Table_Name,
                              Lv_Uniqueness,
                              Lv_Tablespace_Name,
                              Lv_Ini_Trans,
                              Lv_Max_Trans,
                              Lv_Initial_Extent,
                              Lv_Next_Extent,
                              Lv_Min_Extents,
                              Lv_Max_Extents,
                              Lv_Pct_Increase,
                              Lv_Pct_Free;
        exit when IND_CURSOR%NOTFOUND;
        Lv_Lineno := 1;
        Lv_First_Rec := TRUE;
```

Based on the value of the Uniqueness column, the next portion of the gen_indx.sql script generates the proper **create** string and writes it to the temporary table. The **LOWER** function changes the text to all lowercase to make the output more readable.

```
    if (Lv_Uniqueness = 'UNIQUE')
    then
        Lv_String:= 'CREATE UNIQUE INDEX ' || LOWER(Lv_Index_Owner) ||
                    '.' || LOWER(Lv_Index_Name);
    else
```

```
        Lv_String:= 'CREATE INDEX ' || LOWER(LV_INDEX_OWNER) || '.' ||
                    LOWER(Lv_Index_Name);
    end if;
    WRITE_OUT(Lv_Lineno, Lv_Index_Owner, Lv_Index_Name, Lv_String);
    Lv_Lineno := Lv_Lineno + 1;
```

In the next section of the script, shown in the following listing, COL_CURSOR forms the inner loop, selecting all the column names in the index from DBA_IND_COLUMNS and concatenating them together to form the index key. The Boolean *Lv_First_Rec* is used here to determine whether to prefix the column name with the **on** *table_owner.table_name* clause for the first column in the index or with ',' for all other columns in the index. Once all the column names have been selected and concatenated, the cursor is closed and the SQL statement is finished by appending ')' before it is written to the temporary table.

The inner cursor will be opened, fetched, and closed once for each index selected by the outer cursor.

```
open COL_CURSOR(Lv_Index_Owner,Lv_Index_Name,Lv_Table_Name);
    loop
        fetch COL_CURSOR into Lv_Column_Name;
        exit when COL_CURSOR%NOTFOUND;
        if (Lv_First_Rec)
        then
            Lv_String := '   ON '|| LOWER(Lv_Table_Owner) || '.' ||
                            LOWER(Lv_Table_Name)||' (';
            Lv_First_Rec := FALSE;
        else
            Lv_String := Lv_String || ',';
        end if;
        Lv_String := Lv_String || LOWER(Lv_Column_Name);
    end loop;
    close COL_CURSOR;
    Lv_String := Lv_String || ')';
    WRITE_OUT(Lv_Lineno, Lv_Index_Owner, Lv_Index_Name, Lv_String);
    Lv_Lineno := Lv_Lineno + 1;
```

The next section of the script creates the storage information clauses for the index. The numeric columns **pctfree, initrans, maxtrans, initial, next, minextents, maxextents** and **pctincrease** are converted to character using the **TO_CHAR** function. Their values can then be concatenated into the string variable to be inserted into the temporary table. The **storage** clauses are written to the temporary table and a '/' is written to the table to execute the **create** statement generated.

```
    Lv_String := null;
    Lv_String := 'PCTFREE ' || TO_CHAR(Lv_Pct_Free);
    WRITE_OUT(Lv_Lineno, Lv_Index_Owner, Lv_Index_Name, Lv_String);
```

```
    Lv_Lineno := Lv_Lineno + 1;
    Lv_String := 'INITRANS ' || TO_CHAR(Lv_Ini_Trans) ||
                 ' MAXTRANS ' || TO_CHAR(Lv_Max_Trans);
    WRITE_OUT(Lv_Lineno, Lv_Index_Owner, Lv_Index_Name, Lv_String);
    Lv_Lineno := Lv_Lineno + 1;
    Lv_String := 'TABLESPACE ' || Lv_Tablespace_Name || ' STORAGE (';
    WRITE_OUT(Lv_Lineno, Lv_Index_Owner, Lv_Index_Name, Lv_String);
    Lv_Lineno := Lv_Lineno + 1;
    Lv_String := 'INITIAL ' || TO_CHAR(Lv_Initial_Extent) ||
                 ' NEXT ' || TO_CHAR(Lv_Next_Extent);
    WRITE_OUT(Lv_Lineno, Lv_Index_Owner, Lv_Index_Name, Lv_String);
    Lv_Lineno := Lv_Lineno + 1;
    Lv_String := 'MINEXTENTS ' || TO_CHAR(Lv_Min_Extents) ||
                 ' MAXEXTENTS ' || TO_CHAR(Lv_Max_Extents) ||
                 ' PCTINCREASE ' || TO_CHAR(Lv_Pct_Increase) || ')';
    WRITE_OUT(Lv_Lineno, Lv_Index_Owner, Lv_Index_Name, Lv_String);
    Lv_Lineno := Lv_Lineno + 1;
    Lv_String := '/';
    WRITE_OUT(Lv_Lineno, Lv_Index_Owner, Lv_Index_Name, Lv_String);
    Lv_Lineno := Lv_Lineno + 1;
```

A final line of blanks is written to make the output file generated at the end of the procedure more readable. The outer cursor loop ends and the procedure will loop back through the IND_CURSOR and COL_CURSOR inner loop until all indexes for the requested table have been generated. Then the outer cursor is closed and the procedure exits.

```
    Lv_Lineno := Lv_Lineno + 1;
    Lv_String:='                                                ';
    WRITE_OUT(Lv_Lineno, Lv_Index_Owner, Lv_Index_Name, Lv_String);
  end loop;
  close IND_CURSOR;
end;
/
```

Once the **create** statements for all the indexes have been generated, they are spooled to a file for later execution. The SQL*Plus **set** command parameter **recsep** defines the character(s) that will be displayed between selected columns. Setting it to **off** means that there will be no separation between columns.

```
spool cre_indx.sql
set heading off recsep off
col Text format a80 word_wrap
```

```
select Text
  from I_TEMP
 order by Id_Owner, Id_Name, Lineno;
spool off
```

As shown in the following sample output, the table in this example has three indexes which are not created by constraints. All of the indexes are single column indexes.

```
CREATE INDEX app.terminals_cpy_fk_I
ON app.app_terminals (cpy_abbr)
PCTFREE 0
INITRANS 2 MAXTRANS 255
TABLESPACE USER_INDEX STORAGE (
INITIAL 1048576 NEXT 516096
MINEXTENTS 1 MAXEXTENTS 300 PCTINCREASE 0)
/


CREATE INDEX app.terminals_epe_fk_i
ON app.app_terminals (epe_code)
PCTFREE 0
INITRANS 2 MAXTRANS 255
TABLESPACE USER_INDEX STORAGE (
INITIAL 1048576 NEXT 516096
MINEXTENTS 1 MAXEXTENTS 300 PCTINCREASE 0)
/


CREATE INDEX app.terminals_terminals_fk_i
ON app.app_terminals (terminals_terminal_no)
PCTFREE 0
INITRANS 2 MAXTRANS 255
TABLESPACE USER_INDEX STORAGE (
INITIAL 1048576 NEXT 516096
MINEXTENTS 1 MAXEXTENTS 300 PCTINCREASE 0)
/
```

As an alternative, you can use this script to document all the indexes on all tables for a particular owner. To document all of the indexes for a user, remove the **accept** *table_name* statement at the beginning of the script and change the **where** clause for the IND_CURSOR cursor to:

```
where Owner = UPPER('&&tab_owner')
        and Index_Name not like 'SYS_%'
        and not exists (select 'x'
                        from DBA_CONSTRAINTS
```

```
                    where Constraint_Name = Index_Name
                      and Table_Owner       =
                          UPPER('&&tab_owner'))
```

If you want to document all indexes in your database that are not owned by SYS, remove the two **accept** statements from the beginning of the script and change the **where** clause for the IND_CURSOR cursor to:

```
where Owner != 'SYS'
        and Index_Name not like 'SYS_%'
        and not exists (select 'x'
                          from DBA_CONSTRAINTS
                          where Constraint_Name = Index_Name
                            and Table_Owner     = Owner)
```

gen_trig.sql

Generate Triggers

Tables can have many types of triggers defined on them, including **before row**, **after row**, **before statement**, and **after statement** for **delete**, **insert**, and **update**. Managing all possible types and ensuring that they are documented is complex. As you move a table from one database to another, or change the table itself within the database, it is difficult to manually save off and re-create triggers. The gen_trig.sql script, shown in the following listing, will generate a script to re-create all the triggers of a given table.

You will see an annotated walk-through of the gen_trig.sql script following the script listing and sample output.

```
set echo off term on verify off feedback off long 30000 pagesize 0
select 'Creating trigger build script...' from DUAL;

accept table_name prompt "Enter the name of the Table: "
accept tab_owner prompt "Enter table owner: "
set term off

drop table TRIG_TEMP;

create table TRIG_TEMP (
        Lineno   NUMBER,
        Id_Owner VARCHAR2(30),
        Id_Name  VARCHAR2(30),
        Text     LONG)
/

declare
   cursor TRIG_CURSOR is
```

```
     select Owner,
            Trigger_Name,
            Trigger_Type,
            Triggering_Event,
            Table_Owner,
            Table_Name,
            Referencing_Names,
            When_Clause,
            Status,
            Description,
            Trigger_Body
       from DBA_TRIGGERS
      where Table_Owner  = UPPER('&&tab_owner')
        and Table_Name like UPPER('&&table_name')
      order by Trigger_Name;

cursor TRIG_COL_CURSOR (A_Trigger_Owner VARCHAR2,
                        A_Trigger_Name  VARCHAR2) is
     select Table_Owner,
            Table_Name,
            Column_Name
       from DBA_TRIGGER_COLS
      where Trigger_Owner = A_Trigger_Owner
        and Trigger_Name  = A_Trigger_Name
        and Column_List   = 'YES';

Lv_Trig_Owner             DBA_TRIGGERS.Owner%TYPE;
Lv_Trig_Name              DBA_TRIGGERS.Trigger_Name%TYPE;
Lv_Trig_Type              DBA_TRIGGERS.Trigger_Type%TYPE;
Lv_Trig_Event             DBA_TRIGGERS.Triggering_Event%TYPE;
Lv_Trig_Table_Owner       DBA_TRIGGERS.Table_Owner%TYPE;
Lv_Trig_Table_Name        DBA_TRIGGERS.Table_Name%TYPE;
Lv_Trig_Referencing_Names DBA_TRIGGERS.Referencing_Names%TYPE;
Lv_Trig_When_Clause       DBA_TRIGGERS.When_Clause%TYPE;
Lv_Trig_Status            DBA_TRIGGERS.Status%TYPE;
Lv_Description            DBA_TRIGGERS.Description%TYPE;
Lv_Trig_Body              DBA_TRIGGERS.Trigger_Body%TYPE;
Lv_Col_Tab_Owner          DBA_TRIGGER_COLS.Trigger_Owner%TYPE;
Lv_Col_Tab_Name           DBA_TRIGGER_COLS.Table_Name%TYPE;
Lv_Col_Tab_Col_Name       DBA_TRIGGER_COLS.Column_Name%TYPE;


Lv_String                 VARCHAR2(800);
Lv_String2                VARCHAR2(80);
```

```
   Lv_Of_Count                    INTEGER;
   Lv_Lineno                      NUMBER := 0;


   procedure WRITE_OUT(P_Line INTEGER,   P_Owner VARCHAR2,
                    P_Name VARCHAR2, P_String VARCHAR2) is
   begin
      insert into TRIG_TEMP (Lineno, Id_Owner, Id_Name, Text)
            values (P_Line,P_Owner,P_Name,P_String);
   end;

begin
   open TRIG_CURSOR;
   loop
      fetch TRIG_CURSOR into Lv_Trig_Owner,
                             Lv_Trig_Name,
                             Lv_Trig_Type,
                             Lv_Trig_Event,
                             Lv_Trig_Table_Owner,
                             Lv_Trig_Table_Name,
                             Lv_Trig_Referencing_Names,
                             Lv_Trig_When_Clause,
                             Lv_Trig_Status,
                             Lv_Description,
                             Lv_Trig_Body;
      exit when TRIG_CURSOR%NOTFOUND;


      Lv_Lineno := 1;

      Lv_String:= 'CREATE OR REPLACE TRIGGER ' || LOWER(Lv_Trig_Owner)
                                   || '.'
                                   || LOWER(Lv_Trig_Name);
      WRITE_OUT(Lv_Lineno, Lv_Trig_Owner, Lv_Trig_Name, Lv_String);
      Lv_Lineno := Lv_Lineno + 1;

      Lv_String2:= SUBSTR(Lv_Trig_Type,1,INSTR(Lv_Trig_Type,' '));
      if (Lv_String2 = 'INSTEAD ')
      then
          LV_String2 := Lv_String2 || 'OF ';
      end if;

      Lv_String := Lv_String2 || Lv_Trig_Event;
      WRITE_OUT(Lv_Lineno, Lv_Trig_Owner, Lv_Trig_Name, Lv_String);
      Lv_Lineno := Lv_Lineno + 1;
```

```
Lv_Of_Count := 0;
open TRIG_COL_CURSOR (Lv_Trig_Owner,Lv_Trig_Name);
loop
   fetch TRIG_COL_CURSOR into    Lv_Col_Tab_Owner,
                                 Lv_Col_Tab_Name,
                                 Lv_Col_Tab_Col_Name;
   exit when TRIG_COL_CURSOR%NOTFOUND;
   Lv_Of_Count := Lv_Of_Count + 1;

   If ( Lv_Of_Count = 1 )
   then
        Lv_String  := '  OF ' || LOWER(Lv_Col_Tab_Col_Name);
   else
        Lv_String  := '    ,' ||LOWER(Lv_Col_Tab_Col_Name);
   end if;
   WRITE_OUT(Lv_Lineno, Lv_Trig_Owner, Lv_Trig_Name, Lv_String);
   Lv_Lineno := Lv_Lineno + 1;
end loop;
close TRIG_COL_CURSOR;

Lv_String := 'ON '                       ||
             LOWER(Lv_Trig_Owner)        ||
             '.'                         ||
             LOWER(Lv_Trig_Table_Name);

WRITE_OUT(Lv_Lineno, Lv_Trig_Owner, Lv_Trig_Name, Lv_String);
Lv_Lineno := Lv_Lineno + 1;

WRITE_OUT(Lv_Lineno, Lv_Trig_Owner, Lv_Trig_Name,
          Lv_Trig_Referencing_Names);
Lv_Lineno := Lv_Lineno + 1;

if (INSTR(Lv_Trig_Type,'EACH ROW') > 0)
then
    Lv_String := 'FOR EACH ROW';
    WRITE_OUT(Lv_Lineno, Lv_Trig_Owner, Lv_Trig_Name, Lv_String);
    Lv_Lineno := Lv_Lineno + 1;
end if;

if (Lv_Trig_When_Clause IS NOT NULL)
then
    Lv_String := 'WHEN (' || Lv_Trig_When_Clause || ')';
```

```
        WRITE_OUT(Lv_Lineno, Lv_Trig_Owner, Lv_Trig_Name, Lv_String);
        Lv_Lineno := Lv_Lineno + 1;
      end if;

    WRITE_OUT(Lv_Lineno, Lv_Trig_Owner, Lv_Trig_Name, Lv_Trig_Body);
    Lv_Lineno := Lv_Lineno + 1;

    WRITE_OUT(Lv_Lineno, Lv_Trig_Owner, Lv_Trig_Name, '/');
    Lv_Lineno := Lv_Lineno + 1;

  end loop;
  close TRIG_CURSOR;
end;
/
spool cre_trig.sql
select Text
  from TRIG_TEMP
 order by Id_Owner, Id_Name, Lineno
/
spool off
```

The gen_trig.sql script generates a script to re-create all triggers for the given table and owner. Sample output for the gen_trig.sql script is shown in the following listing.

```
CREATE OR REPLACE TRIGGER app.ref_pre_upd_dbt
BEFORE UPDATE
ON app.app_referrals
REFERENCING NEW AS NEW OLD AS OLD
FOR EACH ROW
DECLARE
begin
BEGIN
set_audit_proc('U', :new.usr_crtd, :new.dt_crtd,
        :new.usr_mdfd, :new.dt_mdfd);
  END;
END;

/
CREATE OR REPLACE TRIGGER app.ref_pre_ins_dbt
BEFORE INSERT
ON app.app_referrals
REFERENCING NEW AS NEW OLD AS OLD
```

```
FOR EACH ROW
DECLARE
BEGIN
begin
set_audit_proc('I', :new.usr_crtd, :new.dt_crtd,
        :new.usr_mdfd, :new.dt_mdfd);
   END;
END;
```

```
/
```

The generated script provides the commands necessary to re-create the two triggers on the APP_REFERRALS table.

ANNOTATIONS

The gen_trig.sql script generates the code for all triggers created against a given table. Triggers can be used to enforce business rules that cannot be enforced with check or referential integrity constraints or to generate more detailed auditing information than ORACLE auditing provides. Triggers can enforce referential integrity across the different nodes of a distributed database. Triggers can be defined on both a row and statement level, to be executed before or after the DML operation executes, and can be defined on one or more of the DML operations. As of ORACLE8, triggers can be configured to execute instead of the SQL operation that causes the trigger to fire.

The gen_trig.sql script uses a temporary table to hold individual lines of the **create trigger** statement, writing to the table rather than using DBMS_OUTPUT.PUT_LINE so that you can extract the information for an individual trigger or for all triggers on the table. Using the DBMS_OUTPUT procedure would force you to save and edit the output file for the trigger you want.

The first section of the script does the initial setup, prompting for the table name and table owner for later use via the **accept** command. You can enter '%table_name%' to generate a script for all triggers on tables with a similar name, or enter '%' at the table name prompt to generate a script for all triggers on all tables for that owner.

The SQL*Plus **set** command turns off headers (**pagesize 0**), row counts (**feedback off**), and displays of old and new values for the *table_name* and *tab_owner* variables (**verify off**).

```
set echo off term on verify off feedback off long 30000 pagesize 0
select 'Creating trigger build script...' from DUAL;

accept table_name prompt "Enter the name of the Table: "
accept tab_owner prompt "Enter table owner: "
set term off
```

In the next part of the script, a temporary table is created to hold each **create trigger** command and its owner. The Lineno column provides ordering for the lines of the **create trigger** command by trigger name.

```
drop table TRIG_TEMP;

create table TRIG_TEMP (
        Lineno    NUMBER,
        Id_Owner  VARCHAR2(30),
        Id_Name   VARCHAR2(30),
        Text      LONG)
/
```

The next section of the script creates the main cursor for the script, TRIG_CURSOR. TRIG_CURSOR cursor selects the information from DBA_TRIGGERS where the table name matches the input variable *table_name* and the table owner matches the input variable *tab_owner*. By selecting for Table_Name rather than Trigger_Name, all triggers on the table will be processed. Using **like** in the **where** clause instead of = allows for wildcards.

```
declare
   cursor TRIG_CURSOR is
        select Owner,
                Trigger_Name,
                Trigger_Type,
                Triggering_Event,
                Table_Owner,
                Table_Name,
                Referencing_Names,
                When_Clause,
                Status,
                Description,
                Trigger_Body
          from DBA_TRIGGERS
         where Table_Owner  = UPPER('&&tab_owner')
           and Table_Name like UPPER('&&table_name')
         order by Trigger_Name;
```

The cursor TRIG_COL_CURSOR, in the following listing, selects the name of any column listed in an **update** trigger. Update triggers have a slightly different syntax than **insert** and **delete** triggers, including the name of the column or columns that cause the trigger to fire. If Column_List in the DBA_TRIGGER_COLS table is 'YES,' that column is part of an **update** trigger.

```
   cursor TRIG_COL_CURSOR (A_Trigger_Owner VARCHAR2,
                           A_Trigger_Name  VARCHAR2) is
        select Table_Owner,
```

```
            Table_Name,
            Column_Name
     from DBA_TRIGGER_COLS
    where Trigger_Owner = A_Trigger_Owner
      and Trigger_Name  = A_Trigger_Name
      and Column_List   = 'YES';
```

In the next section of the script, the procedure variables for the cursor are declared as TABLE_NAME.Column_Name%**TYPE**. This anchoring of datatypes takes the column definition from within the database itself. If the column definition changes in a different version of ORACLE, the procedure will still work because the definition of the column has not been hard-coded. *Lv_Of_Count* counts the columns in the **of** clause of an **update** trigger statement to include or remove commas from that clause of the statement. The variable *Lv_Lineno* orders the lines of the **create** statement and is initialized to 0.

```
    Lv_Trig_Owner               DBA_TRIGGERS.Owner%TYPE;
    Lv_Trig_Name                DBA_TRIGGERS.Trigger_Name%TYPE;
    Lv_Trig_Type                DBA_TRIGGERS.Trigger_Type%TYPE;
    Lv_Trig_Event               DBA_TRIGGERS.Triggering_Event%TYPE;
    Lv_Trig_Table_Owner         DBA_TRIGGERS.Table_Owner%TYPE;
    Lv_Trig_Table_Name          DBA_TRIGGERS.Table_Name%TYPE;
    Lv_Trig_Referencing_Names   DBA_TRIGGERS.Referencing_Names%TYPE;
    Lv_Trig_When_Clause         DBA_TRIGGERS.When_Clause%TYPE;
    Lv_Trig_Status              DBA_TRIGGERS.Status%TYPE;
    Lv_Description              DBA_TRIGGERS.Description%TYPE;
    Lv_Trig_Body                DBA_TRIGGERS.Trigger_Body%TYPE;
    Lv_Col_Tab_Owner            DBA_TRIGGER_COLS.Trigger_Owner%TYPE;
    Lv_Col_Tab_Name             DBA_TRIGGER_COLS.Table_Name%TYPE;
    Lv_Col_Tab_Col_Name         DBA_TRIGGER_COLS.Column_Name%TYPE;
    Lv_String                   VARCHAR2(800);
    Lv_String2                  VARCHAR2(80);
    Lv_Of_Count                 INTEGER;
    Lv_Lineno                   NUMBER := 0;
```

The internal procedure WRITE_OUT is defined to do the **insert** into the temporary table. WRITE_OUT will be called later in the script to help build the **create table** script.

```
    procedure WRITE_OUT(P_Line INTEGER,  P_Owner VARCHAR2,
                        P_Name VARCHAR2, P_String VARCHAR2) is
    begin
       insert into TRIG_TEMP (Lineno, Id_Owner, Id_Name, Text)
            values (P_Line,P_Owner,P_Name,P_String);
    end;
```

The next section of the script begins the executable commands. TRIG_CURSOR forms an outer loop for each trigger for the requested table. The *Lv_Lineno* variable, in conjunction with the trigger name, orders the rows in the temporary table TRIG_TEMP so that if you prefer, you can extract the **create trigger** statement for a single trigger at the end of the procedure.

```
begin
   open TRIG_CURSOR;
   loop
      fetch TRIG_CURSOR into Lv_Trig_Owner,
                             Lv_Trig_Name,
                             Lv_Trig_Type,
                             Lv_Trig_Event,
                             Lv_Trig_Table_Owner,
                             Lv_Trig_Table_Name,
                             Lv_Trig_Referencing_Names,
                             Lv_Trig_When_Clause,
                             Lv_Trig_Status,
                             Lv_Description,
                             Lv_Trig_Body;
      exit when TRIG_CURSOR%NOTFOUND;

      Lv_Lineno := 1;
```

The script generates the proper **create** string and writes it to the temporary table. Using the **create or replace** syntax ensures that if the trigger exists, no error will be generated when the script is run. The **LOWER** function changes the text to all lowercase to make the output more readable.

```
      Lv_String:= 'CREATE OR REPLACE TRIGGER ' || LOWER(Lv_Trig_Owner)
                                      || '.'
                                      || LOWER(Lv_Trig_Name);
      WRITE_OUT(Lv_Lineno, Lv_Trig_Owner, Lv_Trig_Name, Lv_String);
      Lv_Lineno := Lv_Lineno + 1;
```

The *Lv_Trig_Type* variable value contains the type of trigger. The syntax of a **create trigger** statement only needs the word **before** or **after** at this point, not the full type of the trigger. The portion of the script in the following listing will extract the required word, keeping the blank after it so that a blank does not need to be concatenated in, and concatenate it with the triggering event, the DML operation, before writing it to the temporary table.

The **SUBSTR** function trims the *Lv_Trig_Type* value based on the location of the first space in the value. The **INSTR** function determines the location of the first space in the *Lv_Trig_Type* variable's value, and **SUBSTR** uses that location when determining the number of characters to select. A new trigger type, **INSTEAD OF**, was introduced in ORACLE8. This trigger is used to **delete**, **update**, or **insert** into views which are not inherently modifiable. These views are created by:

- ◆ set operators
- ◆ group functions
- ◆ **group by**, **connect by**, or **start with** clauses
- ◆ the DISTINCT operator
- ◆ joins (a subset of join views are updatable)

Because the script extracts the trigger type only up to the first space, it will miss the full syntax of the new trigger type. It will check for the new trigger type and add the **OF** back into the string.

```
Lv_String2:= SUBSTR(Lv_Trig_Type,1,INSTR(Lv_Trig_Type,' '));
Lv_String := Lv_String2 || Lv_Trig_Event;
WRITE_OUT(Lv_Lineno, Lv_Trig_Owner, Lv_Trig_Name, Lv_String);
Lv_Lineno := Lv_Lineno + 1;

if (Lv_String2 = 'INSTEAD ')
then
    LV_String2 := Lv_String2 || 'OF ';
end if;
```

If the trigger is an **update** trigger, the columns that cause it to fire are stored in the DBA_TRIGGERING_COLS table, referenced by the TRIG_COL_CURSOR. As shown in the following listing, the columns are retrieved by the cursor and, depending on whether or not the column is the first one, are prefixed by either 'OF' or ','. Each column is written to the temporary table. The **LOWER** function makes the output more readable.

```
Lv_Of_Count := 0;
open TRIG_COL_CURSOR (Lv_Trig_Owner,Lv_Trig_Name);
loop
    fetch TRIG_COL_CURSOR into     Lv_Col_Tab_Owner,
                                   Lv_Col_Tab_Name,
                                   Lv_Col_Tab_Col_Name;
    exit when TRIG_COL_CURSOR%NOTFOUND;
    Lv_Of_Count := Lv_Of_Count + 1;

    If ( Lv_Of_Count = 1 )
    then
        Lv_String := '  OF ' || LOWER(Lv_Col_Tab_Col_Name);
    else
```

```
                Lv_String  :=  '      ,'  ||LOWER(Lv_Col_Tab_Col_Name);
          end if;
          WRITE_OUT(Lv_Lineno, Lv_Trig_Owner, Lv_Trig_Name, Lv_String);
          Lv_Lineno := Lv_Lineno + 1;
     end loop;
     close TRIG_COL_CURSOR;
```

The next section of the script adds the lines defining the table owner and table and the correlation names to the temporary table. The correlation names allow you to refer to both the old and new values of a column in the trigger.

```
Lv_String := 'ON '                       ||
             LOWER(Lv_Trig_Owner)        ||
             '.'                         ||
             LOWER(Lv_Trig_Table_Name);

WRITE_OUT(Lv_Lineno, Lv_Trig_Owner, Lv_Trig_Name, Lv_String);
Lv_Lineno := Lv_Lineno + 1;


WRITE_OUT(Lv_Lineno, Lv_Trig_Owner, Lv_Trig_Name,
          Lv_Trig_Referencing_Names);
Lv_Lineno := Lv_Lineno + 1;
```

At this point in the script, the type of trigger (row or statement) needs to be added to the **create trigger** command in the temporary table. By default, triggers are created as statement triggers, and nothing needs to be added to the temporary table. Statement triggers fire once for the DML statement, regardless of the number of rows affected. Row-level triggers fire for each row affected by the DML operation.

```
if (INSTR(Lv_Trig_Type,'EACH ROW') > 0)
then
    Lv_String := 'FOR EACH ROW';
    WRITE_OUT(Lv_Lineno, Lv_Trig_Owner, Lv_Trig_Name, Lv_String);
    Lv_Lineno := Lv_Lineno + 1;
end if;
```

The next portion of the script determines if any **when** clauses affect the trigger's execution. You can limit when a trigger will fire based on a SQL condition. You can only specify this restriction on row-level triggers.

```
if (Lv_Trig_When_Clause IS NOT NULL)
then
    Lv_String := 'WHEN (' || Lv_Trig_When_Clause || ')';
    WRITE_OUT(Lv_Lineno, Lv_Trig_Owner, Lv_Trig_Name, Lv_String);
    Lv_Lineno := Lv_Lineno + 1;
end if;
```

The final section of the script re-creates the actual PL/SQL block that will execute if the trigger fires. The trigger body is written to the temporary table, and the **create trigger** statement is ended with a '/' so that it will execute when you run the generated script. The cursor loop will repeat for each trigger on the requested table.

Once the final entry has been inserted into the temporary table, the script selects the command syntax from the temporary table.

```
      WRITE_OUT(Lv_Lineno, Lv_Trig_Owner, Lv_Trig_Name, Lv_Trig_Body);
      Lv_Lineno := Lv_Lineno + 1;

      WRITE_OUT(Lv_Lineno, Lv_Trig_Owner, Lv_Trig_Name, '/');
      Lv_Lineno := Lv_Lineno + 1;

   end loop;
   close TRIG_CURSOR;
end;
/

spool cre_trig.sql
select Text
  from TRIG_TEMP
 order by Id_Owner, Id_Name, Lineno
/
spool off
```

Once the **create trigger** commands for all the triggers have been generated, they are spooled to a file for later execution.

A sample-generated **create trigger** script is shown in the following listing.

```
CREATE OR REPLACE TRIGGER app.ref_pre_upd_dbt
BEFORE UPDATE
ON app.app_referrals
REFERENCING NEW AS NEW OLD AS OLD
FOR EACH ROW
DECLARE
begin
BEGIN
set_audit_proc('U', :new.usr_crtd, :new.dt_crtd,
        :new.usr_mdfd, :new.dt_mdfd);
   END;
END;

/
CREATE OR REPLACE TRIGGER app.ref_pre_ins_dbt
BEFORE INSERT
ON app.app_referrals
```

```
REFERENCING NEW AS NEW OLD AS OLD
FOR EACH ROW
DECLARE
BEGIN
begin
set_audit_proc('I', :new.usr_crtd, :new.dt_crtd,
        :new.usr_mdfd, :new.dt_mdfd);
   END;
END;

/
```

The sample table has two triggers, a **before update** and a **before insert** on each row. The **referencing new as new old as old** clause allows the PL/SQL block in the trigger to refer to the new column values and the old column values in the same procedure by prefixing the column names with **:new** or **:old**.

As an alternative, if you want to use this script to document all the triggers on all tables for a particular owner, remove the **accept** *table_name* statement at the beginning of the script and change the **where** clause for the TRIG_CURSOR cursor to:

```
where Table_Owner  = UPPER('&&tab_owner')
```

If you want to document all indexes in your database that are not owned by SYS, remove the two **accept** statements from the beginning of the script and change the **where** clause for the TRIG_CURSOR cursor to:

```
where Table_Owner != 'SYS'
```

gen_view.sql

Generate Views

Views present a tailored picture of the data in the database. You can create views that are exact replicas of the underlying table, to allow for table modifications without creating problems in application code, or that show selected columns and rows of one or more tables. You can use views to rename columns and to restrict access to certain columns or the data they contain. The following script, gen_view.sql, will generate a script to re-create a view.

```
set echo off verify off term on feedback off pagesize 0 long 20000
select 'Creating view build script...' from DUAL;


accept view_name prompt "Enter the name of the View: "
accept view_owner prompt "Enter view owner: "
set term off


drop   table VIEW_TEMP
/
```

```
create table VIEW_TEMP (
       Lineno NUMBER,
       Id_Owner VARCHAR2(30),
       Id_Name VARCHAR2(30),
       Text LONG)
/

declare
   cursor VIEW_CURSOR is
        select Owner,
               View_Name,
               Text_Length,
               Text
          from DBA_VIEWS
         where Owner = UPPER('&&view_owner')
           and View_Name like UPPER('&&view_name')
         order by Owner, View_Name;

   cursor VIEW_COLS_CURSOR (V_Name VARCHAR2, V_Owner VARCHAR2) is
        select Column_Name
          from DBA_TAB_COLUMNS
         where Table_Name = V_Name
           and Owner = V_Owner
         order by Column_ID;

   Lv_Owner              DBA_VIEWS.Owner%TYPE;
   Lv_View_Name          DBA_VIEWS.View_Name%TYPE;
   Lv_Text_Length        DBA_VIEWS.Text_Length%TYPE;
   Lv_Text               DBA_VIEWS.Text%TYPE;

   Lv_Column_Name        DBA_TAB_COLUMNS.Column_Name%TYPE;
   Lv_Separator          VARCHAR2(1);

   Lv_Substr_Start       NUMBER;
   Lv_Substr_Len         NUMBER;
   Lv_String             VARCHAR2(32760);
   Lv_Lineno             NUMBER := 0;

   procedure WRITE_OUT(P_Line INTEGER, P_Owner VARCHAR2, P_Name VARCHAR2,
                       P_String VARCHAR2) is
   begin
      insert into VIEW_TEMP (Lineno, Id_Owner, Id_Name, Text)
            values (P_Line,P_Owner,P_Name,P_String);
   end;
```

```
begin
   open VIEW_CURSOR;
   loop
      fetch VIEW_CURSOR into Lv_Owner,
                             Lv_View_Name,
                             Lv_Text_Length,
                             Lv_Text;
      exit when VIEW_CURSOR%NOTFOUND;

      Lv_Lineno := 1;

      Lv_String:= 'CREATE OR REPLACE VIEW ' || LOWER(Lv_Owner)
                                            || '.'
                                            || LOWER(Lv_View_Name);
      WRITE_OUT(Lv_Lineno, Lv_Owner, Lv_View_Name, Lv_String);
      Lv_Lineno := Lv_Lineno + 1;

      Lv_String := '';
      Lv_Separator := ',';
      Open VIEW_COLS_CURSOR (Lv_View_Name, Lv_Owner);

      loop
         fetch VIEW_COLS_CURSOR into Lv_Column_Name;
         exit when VIEW_COLS_CURSOR%NOTFOUND;

         Lv_String := Lv_Separator
                      || Lv_Column_Name;
         Lv_Separator := ',';
         WRITE_OUT(Lv_Lineno, Lv_Owner, Lv_View_Name, Lv_String);
         Lv_Lineno := Lv_Lineno + 1;

      end loop;

      Lv_String := ')';
      WRITE_OUT(Lv_Lineno, Lv_Owner, Lv_View_Name, Lv_String);
      Lv_Lineno := Lv_Lineno + 1;
      close VIEW_COLS_CURSOR;

      Lv_String := 'AS';
      WRITE_OUT(Lv_Lineno, Lv_Owner, Lv_View_Name, Lv_String);
      Lv_Lineno := Lv_Lineno + 1;

      Lv_Substr_Start := 1;
```

```
        Lv_Substr_Len    := Lv_Text_Length;
        if Lv_Substr_Len > 32760
        then
            Lv_Substr_Len := 32760;
        end if;

        loop
            Lv_String := SUBSTR(Lv_Text,Lv_Substr_Start, Lv_Substr_Len);
            WRITE_OUT(Lv_Lineno, Lv_Owner, Lv_View_Name, Lv_String);
            Lv_Lineno := Lv_Lineno + 1;

            Lv_Substr_Start := Lv_Substr_Start + Lv_Substr_Len;
            if (Lv_Substr_Start + Lv_Substr_Len) > Lv_Text_Length
            then
                Lv_Substr_Len := Lv_Text_Length -
                                (Lv_Substr_Start + Lv_Substr_Len);
            end if;
            exit when Lv_Substr_Start > Lv_Text_Length;
        end loop;

        Lv_String  := '/';
        WRITE_OUT(Lv_Lineno, Lv_Owner, Lv_View_Name, Lv_String);
        Lv_Lineno := Lv_Lineno + 1;

    end loop;
    close VIEW_CURSOR;
end;
/
spool cre_view.sql
select Text
  from VIEW_TEMP
 order by Id_Owner, Id_Name, Lineno
/
spool off
/
```

Sample output for the gen_view.sql script is shown in the following listing.

```
CREATE OR REPLACE VIEW demo.sales
(SALESPERSON_ID
,CUSTOMER_ID
,CUSTOMER
,PRODUCT_ID
```

```
,PRODUCT
,AMOUNT
)
AS
SELECT SALESPERSON_ID, SALES_ORDER.CUSTOMER_ID, CUSTOMER.NAME CUSTOMER,
       PRODUCT.PRODUCT_ID, DESCRIPTION PRODUCT, SUM(ITEM.TOTAL) AMOUNT
FROM SALES_ORDER, ITEM, CUSTOMER, PRODUCT
WHERE SALES_ORDER.ORDER_ID = ITEM.ORDER_ID
AND SALES_ORDER.CUSTOMER_ID = CUSTOMER.CUSTOMER_ID
AND ITEM.PRODUCT_ID = PRODUCT.PRODUCT_ID
GROUP BY SALESPERSON_ID, SALES_ORDER.CUSTOMER_ID, CUSTOMER.NAME,
       PRODUCT.PRODUCT_ID, DESCRIPTION

/
```

The generated script is automatically saved to a file which you can edit and execute.

ANNOTATIONS

Although all information about a view is stored in a single row of the DBA_VIEWS view, the script uses a cursor to allow you to enter a wildcard value or to modify the script to select all views for an owner or all views in the database. The gen_view.sql script uses a temporary table to hold individual lines of the **create view** statement, writing to the table rather than using DBMS_OUTPUT.PUT_LINE so that you can extract the information for an individual view or for all views. Using the DBMS_OUTPUT procedure would force you to save and edit the output file for the view you want.

The first section of the script does the initial setup, prompting for the view name and view owner for later use via the **accept** command. You can enter the view name with the '%' wildcard to generate a script for all views with a similar name.

The SQL*Plus **set** command turns off headers (**pagesize 0**), row counts (**feedback off**), and displays of old and new values for the *view_name* and *view_owner* variables (**verify off**).

```
set echo off verify off term on feedback off pagesize 0 long 2000
select 'Creating view build script...' from DUAL;
accept view_name prompt "Enter the name of the View: "
accept view_owner prompt "Enter view owner: "
set term off
```

The next section of the script, shown in the following listing, creates a temporary table to hold each **create view** command and its owner. The Lineno column orders the lines of the **create view** command. Since the Text column of DBA_VIEWS is defined with a LONG datatype, the Text column of the temporary table is also defined LONG, to allow the sections of the view definition to be stored.

```
drop    table VIEW_TEMP
/

create table VIEW_TEMP (
        Lineno NUMBER,
        Id_Owner VARCHAR2(30),
        Id_Name VARCHAR2(30),
        Text LONG)
/
```

The next section of the script defines the VIEW_CURSOR cursor. The VIEW_CURSOR cursor selects the storage information from DBA_VIEWS where the view name matches the input variable *view_name* and the table owner matches the input variable *view_owner*. While a cursor is not needed if you are running the script for a single view, using the cursor with **like** in the **where** clause allows you to enter a wildcard value ('%*view_name*%' or '%') to match more than one view name.

```
declare
    cursor VIEW_CURSOR is
        select Owner,
                View_Name,
                Text_Length,
                Text
          from DBA_VIEWS
         where Owner = UPPER('&&view_owner')
           and View_Name like UPPER('&&view_name')
         order by Owner, View_Name;
```

The next section of the script defines the VIEW_COLS_CURSOR. You can create views with column names that do not match those of the underlying tables. One use for this is a view that takes a column with the same name from 2 different tables. Since you can't create duplicate column names in a table or view, you have to rename one or both of the columns. Column names for views are stored in the DBA_TAB_COLUMNS data dictionary view. This cursor will extract all column names for each view selected. No distinction is made between renamed columns and those whose names match the underlying table columns.

```
Cursor VIEW_COLS_CURSOR (V_Name VARCHAR2, V_Owner VARCHAR2) is
        select Column_Name
          from DBA_TAB_COLUMNS
         where Table_Name = V_Name
           and Owner = V_Owner
         order by Column_ID;
```

The procedure variables for the cursor are declared as TABLE_NAME.Column_Name**%TYPE**. The anchoring of datatypes takes the column definition from within the database itself. If the column definition changes in a different version of ORACLE, the procedure will still work because the definition of the column has not been hard-coded.

Since the Text column in DBA_VIEWS is a LONG datatype, containing the entire view definition, the script needs to allow for long values. You cannot define a PL/SQL variable as a LONG, so the insert string variable, *Lv_String*, is defined as VARCHAR2(32760) and *Lv_Substr_Start* and *Lv_Substr_Len* will help break the Text column into several lines that can be handled by the PL/SQL variable *Lv_String*. The variable *Lv_Lineno* is used to order the lines of the **create view** statement and is initialized to 0.

```
Lv_Owner              DBA_VIEWS.Owner%TYPE;
Lv_View_Name          DBA_VIEWS.View_Name%TYPE;
Lv_Text_Length        DBA_VIEWS.Text_Length%TYPE;
Lv_Text               DBA_VIEWS.Text%TYPE;

Lv_Column_Name        DBA_TAB_COLUMNS.Column_Name%TYPE;
Lv_Separator          VARCHAR2(1);

Lv_Substr_Start       NUMBER;
Lv_Substr_Len         NUMBER;
Lv_String             VARCHAR2(32760);
Lv_Lineno             NUMBER := 0;
```

The next section of the script creates WRITE_OUT, an internal procedure that performs the **insert** into the temporary table.

```
procedure WRITE_OUT(P_Line INTEGER, P_Owner VARCHAR2, P_Name VARCHAR2,
                    P_String VARCHAR2) is
begin
   insert into VIEW_TEMP (Lineno, Id_Owner, Id_Name, Text)
          values (P_Line,P_Owner,P_Name,P_String);
end;
```

In the next section of the gen_view.sql script, shown in the following listing, the VIEW_CURSOR is executed. A cursor is used in this section of the script to allow for wildcards in the entered *view_name* and to allow for changes to the script to select all views for a given user or all views in the database.

```
begin
   open VIEW_CURSOR;
   loop
      fetch VIEW_CURSOR into Lv_Owner,
```

```
                          Lv_View_Name,
                          Lv_Text_Length,
                          Lv_Text;
        exit when VIEW_CURSOR%NOTFOUND;
```

The next section of the script begins the generation of the **create view** command script. The **create or replace** clause retains all grants on a view that is being replaced. If you were to drop the view and then create it, all grants would be lost.

```
        Lv_Lineno := 1;
        Lv_String:= 'CREATE OR REPLACE VIEW ' || LOWER(Lv_Owner)
                                              || '.'
                                              || LOWER(Lv_View_Name);
        WRITE_OUT(Lv_Lineno, Lv_Owner, Lv_View_Name, Lv_String);
        Lv_Lineno := Lv_Lineno + 1;
```

The next section of the script processes the column names for the view. No distinction is made between view columns whose names match those of the underlying table columns and those who have been renamed. View columns, like table columns, are listed in the DBA_TAB_COLUMNS data dictionary view. The column names are fetched by the VIEW_COLS_CURSOR inserted into the temporary table one by one.

```
        Lv_String := '';
        Lv_Separator := '(';
        open VIEW_COLS_CURSOR (Lv_View_Name, Lv_Owner);

        loop
            fetch VIEW_COLS_CURSOR into Lv_Column_Name;
            exit when VIEW_COLS_CURSOR%NOTFOUND;

            Lv_String := Lv_Separator
                            || Lv_Column_Name
            Lv_Separator := ',';
            WRITE_OUT(Lv_Lineno, Lv_Owner, Lv_View_Name, Lv_String;
            Lv_Lineno := Lv_Lineno + 1;

        end loop;

        Lv_String := ')';
        WRITE_OUT(Lv_Lineno, Lv_Owner, Lv_View_Name, Lv_String);
        Lv_Lineno := Lv_Lineno + 1;
        close VIEW_COLS_CURSOR;
```

```
Lv_String := 'AS';
WRITE_OUT(Lv_Lineno, Lv_Owner, Lv_View_Name, Lv_String);
Lv_Lineno := Lv_Lineno + 1;
```

The next portion of the script, shown in the following listing, selects the view's base query from the data dictionary. Since that column in the data dictionary is defined with a LONG datatype, you need to modify the manner in which you select the data.

PL/SQL variables can be defined to a maximum length of 32767, but LONG columns can contain text up to 2GB. To capture the entire view definition if it is longer than 32767 bytes, a loop is used and the text is **SUBSTR**ed out in chunks of 32760 bytes and written to the temporary table before the next chunk is extracted. The **SUBSTR** start variable, *Lv_Substr_Start*, is incremented by the length of the previous substring, *Lv_Substr_Len*, and, if the next chunk will go past the end of the Text column, the **SUBSTR** length variable is reset to the number of bytes remaining. The loop ends when the start point is greater than the total length of the view text.

Unfortunately, it isn't possible to guarantee that the text will break on a space. If your views tend to be extremely long, review the generated script for valid line breaks before running it.

```
Lv_Substr_Start := 1;
Lv_Substr_Len    := Lv_Text_Length;
if Lv_Substr_Len > 32760
then
    Lv_Substr_Len := 32760;
end if;

loop
    Lv_String := SUBSTR(Lv_Text,Lv_Substr_Start, Lv_Substr_Len);
    WRITE_OUT(Lv_Lineno, Lv_Owner, Lv_View_Name, Lv_String);
    Lv_Lineno := Lv_Lineno + 1;

    Lv_Substr_Start := Lv_Substr_Start + Lv_Substr_Len;
    if (Lv_Substr_Start + Lv_Substr_Len) > Lv_Text_Length
    then
        Lv_Substr_Len := Lv_Text_Length -
                         (Lv_Substr_Start + Lv_Substr_Len);
    end if;
    exit when Lv_Substr_Start > Lv_Text_Length;
end loop;
```

In the final portion of the script, the cursor loop ends and the procedure will loop back through the VIEW_CURSOR until all views have been generated. Then the cursor closes and the procedure exits.

```
        Lv_String   := '/';
        WRITE_OUT(Lv_Lineno, Lv_Owner, Lv_View_Name, Lv_String);
        Lv_Lineno := Lv_Lineno + 1;

    end loop;
    close VIEW_CURSOR;
end;
/

spool cre_view.sql
select   Text
  from   VIEW_TEMP
order by Id_Owner, Id_Name, Lineno
/
spool off
```

Once the **create** statements for all the views have been generated, they are
spooled to a file called cre_view.sql for later execution. The following listing shows a
sample cre_view.sql file.

```
CREATE OR REPLACE VIEW demo.sales
 (SALESPERSON_ID
,CUSTOMER_ID
,CUSTOMER
,PRODUCT_ID
,PRODUCT
,AMOUNT
)
AS
SELECT SALESPERSON_ID, SALES_ORDER.CUSTOMER_ID, CUSTOMER.NAME CUSTOMER,
       PRODUCT.PRODUCT_ID, DESCRIPTION PRODUCT, SUM(ITEM.TOTAL) AMOUNT
FROM SALES_ORDER, ITEM, CUSTOMER, PRODUCT
WHERE SALES_ORDER.ORDER_ID = ITEM.ORDER_ID
AND SALES_ORDER.CUSTOMER_ID = CUSTOMER.CUSTOMER_ID
AND ITEM.PRODUCT_ID = PRODUCT.PRODUCT_ID
GROUP BY SALESPERSON_ID, SALES_ORDER.CUSTOMER_ID, CUSTOMER.NAME,
         PRODUCT.PRODUCT_ID, DESCRIPTION

/
```

The gen_view.sql script will generate a script for a single view. As an alternative,
if you want to use this script to document all the views for a particular owner,
remove the **accept** *view_name* statement at the beginning of the script and change the
where clause for the VIEW_CURSOR cursor to:

```
where Owner = UPPER('&&view_owner')
```

If you want to document all views in your database that are not owned by SYS, remove the two **accept** statements from the beginning of the script and change the **where** clause for the VIEW_CURSOR cursor to:

```
where Owner != 'SYS'
```

gen_syn.sql

Generate Synonyms

Synonyms mask the real name and owner of an object. Synonyms simplify SQL statements and simplify public access to an object. You can use synonyms to hide the location and ownership of an object, and to move an object without forcing re-coding of the application.

You can create both public and private synonyms in your database. Public synonyms are accessible to all users, but you will still need to grant object privileges to the users before they can execute the procedure or view the data in the table. If you use roles in your database, you should create public synonyms for the objects that will be accessed, since roles cannot own synonyms. You can grant the object privileges to the role. If you have the CREATE PUBLIC SYNONYM privilege or the DBA role, you can create synonyms for other users.

When evaluating the name and permissions to an object, ORACLE first checks to see if the user owns an object of that name, then checks to see if the user owns a private synonym with that name, and finally checks to see if there is a public synonym with that name. You should keep track of both private and public synonyms so that you don't have duplicates for the same object.

The script in this section, gen_syn.sql, generates the SQL commands needed to re-create all synonyms, public or private, for a specified object. Synonyms can be created for tables, views, sequences, database links, packages, procedures, and functions.

In the following listing, you will see the full gen_syn.sql script.

```
set echo off term on verify off feedback off pagesize 0
select 'Creating synonym build script...' from DUAL;

accept syn_object prompt "Enter the synonym object: "
accept syn_owner prompt "Enter the object owner: "
set term off

drop    table SYN_TEMP
/

create table SYN_TEMP (
        Lineno NUMBER,
        Id_Owner VARCHAR2(30),
        Id_Name VARCHAR2(30),
```

```
            Text VARCHAR2(350))
/

declare
    cursor SYN_CURSOR is
        select Owner,
                Synonym_Name,
                Table_Owner,
                Table_Name,
                Db_Link
          from DBA_SYNONYMS
         where Table_Owner = UPPER('&&syn_owner')
           and Table_Name like UPPER('&&syn_object')
         order by Owner, Table_Owner, Table_Name;

    Lv_Owner            DBA_SYNONYMS.Owner%TYPE;
    Lv_Synonym_Name     DBA_SYNONYMS.Synonym_Name%TYPE;
    Lv_Table_Owner      DBA_SYNONYMS.Table_Owner%TYPE;
    Lv_Table_Name       DBA_SYNONYMS.Table_Name%TYPE;
    Lv_DBLink           DBA_SYNONYMS.DB_Link%TYPE;
    Lv_String           VARCHAR2(350);
    Lv_Lineno           NUMBER := 0;

    procedure WRITE_OUT(P_Line INTEGER, P_Owner VARCHAR2, P_Name VARCHAR2,
                        P_String VARCHAR2) is
    begin
        insert into SYN_TEMP (Lineno, Id_Owner, Id_Name, Text)
            values (P_Line,P_Owner,P_Name,P_String);
    end;

begin
    open SYN_CURSOR;
    Lv_Lineno  := 1;
    loop
        fetch SYN_CURSOR into    Lv_Owner,
                                 Lv_Synonym_Name,
                                 Lv_Table_Owner,
                                 Lv_Table_Name,
                                 Lv_DBLink;
        exit when SYN_CURSOR%NOTFOUND;

        if ( Lv_Owner = 'PUBLIC' )
        then
```

```
            Lv_String   := 'CREATE PUBLIC SYNONYM '  || Lv_Synonym_Name
                                                      || ' FOR '
                                                      || Lv_Table_Owner
                                                      || '.'
                                                      || Lv_Table_Name;
        else
            Lv_String   := 'CREATE SYNONYM '          || Lv_Owner
                                                      || '.'
                                                      || Lv_Synonym_Name
                                                      || ' FOR '
                                                      || Lv_Table_Owner
                                                      || '.'
                                                      || Lv_Table_Name;
        end if;

        if (Lv_DBLink is NOT NULL)
        then
            Lv_String := Lv_String || ' ' || Lv_DBLink;
        end if;

        WRITE_OUT(Lv_Lineno, Lv_Owner, Lv_Table_Name, Lv_String);
        Lv_Lineno := Lv_Lineno + 1;
        WRITE_OUT(Lv_Lineno, Lv_Owner, Lv_Table_Name, '/');
        Lv_Lineno := Lv_Lineno + 1;
    end loop;

    close SYN_CURSOR;
end;
/
spool cre_syn.sql
select Text
  from SYN_TEMP
 order by Id_Owner, Id_Name, Lineno
/
spool off
```

Sample generated output for this script is shown in the following listing.

```
CREATE PUBLIC SYNONYM EMP_ADDRESSES FOR APP.EMP_ADDRESSES
/
CREATE SYNONYM QCUSER1.EMP_ADDRESSES FOR APP.EMP_ADDRESSES
/
```

ORACLE will write the script's output to a file named cre_syn.sql, which you can edit and execute.

ANNOTATIONS

Because there can be multiple synonyms for the same object, the script uses a cursor both to extract the synonym information and to allow you to enter a wildcard value for the table name. The script uses a temporary table to hold individual lines of the **create synonym** statement, writing to the table rather than using DBMS_OUTPUT.PUT_LINE so that you can extract the information for an individual synonym on the object. Using the DBMS_OUTPUT procedure would force you to save and edit the output file for the synonym you want.

The first section of the script does the initial setup, prompting for the object name and object owner for later use via the **accept** command, which, unlike simply using the variable with the '&' or '&&' in a SQL statement, allows you to define your own prompt for the variable. You can enter the object name with '%' to generate a script for all synonyms for all objects with a similar name.

The SQL*Plus **set** command turns off headers (**pagesize 0**), row counts (**feedback off**), and displays of old and new values for the *object_name* and *object_owner* variables (**verify off**).

```
set echo off term on verify off feedback off pagesize 0
select 'Creating synonym build script...' from DUAL;

accept syn_object prompt "Enter the synonym object: "
accept syn_owner prompt "Enter the object owner: "
set term off
```

The next section of the script, shown in the following listing, creates a temporary table to hold each **create synonym** command and its owner. The Lineno column orders the lines of the **create synonym** command.

```
drop    table SYN_TEMP
/

create table SYN_TEMP (
        Lineno NUMBER,
        Id_Owner VARCHAR2(30),
        Id_Name VARCHAR2(30),
        Text VARCHAR2(350))
/
```

The SYN_CURSOR cursor, shown in the following listing, selects the information from DBA_SYNONYMS where the table name matches the input variable *object_name* and the table owner matches the input variable *object_owner*. The column names in DBA_SYNONYMS are misleading because synonyms can be created on objects other than tables. Using **like** in the **where** clause instead of = allows for wildcards.

```
declare
   cursor SYN_CURSOR is
         select Owner,
                Synonym_Name,
                Table_Owner,
                Table_Name,
                Db_Link
            from DBA_SYNONYMS
           where Table_Owner = UPPER('&&syn_owner')
             and Table_Name like UPPER('&&syn_object')
           order by Owner, Table_Owner, Table_Name;
```

In the next section of the script, the procedure variables for the cursor are declared as TABLE_NAME.Column_Name%TYPE. Anchoring the variable definitions in this manner takes the column definition from within the database itself. If the column definition changes in a different version of ORACLE, the procedure will still work because the definition of the column has not been hard-coded. The variable *Lv_Lineno*, which orders the lines of the **create synonym** command, is initialized to 0.

```
   Lv_Owner                 DBA_SYNONYMS.Owner%TYPE;
   Lv_Synonym_Name          DBA_SYNONYMS.Synonym_Name%TYPE;
   Lv_Table_Owner           DBA_SYNONYMS.Table_Owner%TYPE;
   Lv_Table_Name            DBA_SYNONYMS.Table_Name%TYPE;
   Lv_DBLink                DBA_SYNONYMS.DB_Link%TYPE;
   Lv_String                VARCHAR2(350);
   Lv_Lineno                NUMBER := 0;
```

The next section of the script creates an internal procedure named WRITE_OUT to **insert** rows into the temporary table the script uses.

```
   procedure WRITE_OUT(P_Line INTEGER, P_Owner VARCHAR2, P_Name VARCHAR2,
                       P_String VARCHAR2) is
   begin
      insert into SYN_TEMP (Lineno, Id_Owner, Id_Name, Text)
            values (P_Line,P_Owner,P_Name,P_String);
   end;
```

You can create multiple synonyms for a single database object. The cursor SYN_CURSOR, shown in the following listing, extracts all the synonyms, public and private. *Lv_Lineno* is used in conjunction with the object name to order the rows in the temporary table SYN_TEMP so that if you prefer, you can extract the **create synonym** statement for a single synonym at the end of the procedure.

```
begin
   open SYN_CURSOR;
   Lv_Lineno   := 1;
   loop
      fetch SYN_CURSOR into      Lv_Owner,
                                 Lv_Synonym_Name,
                                 Lv_Table_Owner,
                                 Lv_Table_Name,
                                 Lv_DBLink;
      exit when SYN_CURSOR%NOTFOUND;
```

There is a very slight variation in the syntax for creating public and private synonyms. Since there is no real user named PUBLIC in the database, any synonym owned by PUBLIC is accessible to all. The section of the script shown in the following listing creates the proper syntax for public synonyms.

```
if ( Lv_Owner = 'PUBLIC' )
then
     Lv_String  := 'CREATE PUBLIC SYNONYM ' || Lv_Synonym_Name
                                             || ' FOR '
                                             || Lv_Table_Owner
                                             || '.'
                                             || Lv_Table_Name;
   else
     Lv_String  := 'CREATE SYNONYM '        || Lv_Owner
                                             || '.'
                                             || Lv_Synonym_Name
                                             || ' FOR '
                                             || Lv_Table_Owner
                                             || '.'
                                             || Lv_Table_Name;
   end if;
```

In addition to being able to create a synonym for a database link, synonyms can be created for objects that exist on remote databases, using a database link to define the object. If the object does not exist in the local database, the link information is added to the **create synonym** string by the following section of the script.

```
if (Lv_DBLink is NOT NULL)
then
     Lv_String := Lv_String || ' ' || Lv_DBLink;
   end if;
```

The generated **create synonym** string is written to the temporary table, and the loop repeats until all synonyms have been processed. Once all synonyms have been processed, the cursor closes and the procedure exits.

```
        WRITE_OUT(Lv_Lineno, Lv_Owner, Lv_Table_Name, Lv_String);
        Lv_Lineno := Lv_Lineno + 1;
        WRITE_OUT(Lv_Lineno, Lv_Owner, Lv_Table_Name, '/');
        Lv_Lineno := Lv_Lineno + 1;
    end loop;
    close SYN_CURSOR;
end;
/
spool cre_syn.sql
select Text
  from SYN_TEMP
 order by Id_Owner, Id_Name, Lineno
/
spool off
```

Once the **create** statements for all the synonyms have been generated, they are spooled to a file named cre_syn.sql for later execution. A sample cre_syn.sql output file is shown in the following listing.

```
CREATE PUBLIC SYNONYM EMP_ADDRESSES FOR APP.EMP_ADDRESSES
/
CREATE SYNONYM QCUSER1.EMP_ADDRESSES FOR APP.EMP_ADDRESSES
/
```

There is one public synonym in this listing, making the underlying object accessible to all users. One user has his own synonym, with the same name as that of the public one. You should avoid creating multiple synonyms for the same object (such as is the case in this example). Using multiple synonyms for the same object makes managing the database objects and users more difficult.

If you want to use this script to document all the synonyms for all the objects for a particular owner, remove the **accept** *object_name* statement at the beginning of the script and change the **where** clause for the SYN_CURSOR cursor to:

```
where Owner  = UPPER('&&object_owner')
```

If you want to document all synonyms in your database that are not owned by SYS, remove the two **accept** statements from the beginning of the script and change the **where** clause for the SYN_CURSOR cursor to:

```
where Owner != 'SYS'
```

gen_proc.sql

Generate Procedures

When you use stored procedures, you keep compiled PL/SQL code within the database, avoiding performance degradation from run-time compilation. Unlike anonymous PL/SQL blocks, stored procedures can also be pinned in the SGA, again improving performance. The following script, gen_proc.sql, generates a script to re-create a stored procedure.

```
set echo off verify off term on feedback off pagesize 0
select 'Creating procedure build script...' from DUAL;

accept procedure_name prompt "Enter the name of the procedure: "
accept procedure_owner prompt "Enter procedure owner: "
set term off

drop    table PROC_TEMP
/

create table PROC_TEMP (
        Lineno NUMBER,
        Id_Owner VARCHAR2(30),
        Id_Name VARCHAR2(30),
        Text VARCHAR2(2000))
/

declare
    cursor PROC_CURSOR is
        select Owner,
               Name,
               Type,
               Line,
               Text
          from DBA_SOURCE
         where Type  = 'PROCEDURE'
           and Owner = UPPER('&&procedure_owner')
           and Name  like UPPER('&&procedure_name')
         order by Owner, Name, Type, Line;

    Lv_Owner             DBA_SOURCE.Owner%TYPE;
    Lv_Name              DBA_SOURCE.Name%TYPE;
    Lv_Type              DBA_SOURCE.Type%TYPE;
    Lv_Text              DBA_SOURCE.Text%TYPE;
    Lv_Line              DBA_SOURCE.Line%TYPE;

    Lv_String            VARCHAR2(2000);
    Lv_String2           VARCHAR2(2000);
    Lv_Lineno            NUMBER := 0;

    procedure WRITE_OUT(P_Line INTEGER, P_Owner VARCHAR2, P_Name VARCHAR2,
                    P_String VARCHAR2) is
    begin
```

```
            insert into PROC_TEMP (Lineno, Id_Owner, Id_Name, Text)
                    values (P_Line,P_Owner,P_Name,P_String);
        end;

begin
    open PROC_CURSOR;
    Lv_Lineno  := 1;
    loop
        fetch PROC_CURSOR into Lv_Owner,
                               Lv_Name,
                               Lv_Type,
                               Lv_Line,
                               Lv_Text;
        exit when PROC_CURSOR%NOTFOUND;

        if (Lv_Line = 1)
        then
            Lv_String  := 'CREATE OR REPLACE PROCEDURE ';
            WRITE_OUT(Lv_Lineno, Lv_Owner, Lv_Name, Lv_String);
            Lv_Lineno  := Lv_Lineno + 1;

            Lv_String  := SUBSTR(Lv_Text,LENGTH(Lv_Type)+1,
                           (LENGTH(Lv_Text) - LENGTH(Lv_Type)));
            Lv_String  := Lv_Owner || '.' || LTRIM(Lv_String);
            WRITE_OUT(Lv_Lineno, Lv_Owner, Lv_Name, Lv_String);
            Lv_Lineno   := Lv_Lineno + 1;
        else
            WRITE_OUT(Lv_Lineno, Lv_Owner, Lv_Name, Lv_Text);
            Lv_Lineno := Lv_Lineno + 1;
        end if;
    end loop;
    WRITE_OUT(Lv_Lineno, Lv_Owner, Lv_Name, '/');
    close PROC_CURSOR;
end;
/
spool cre_proc.sql
select Text
  from PROC_TEMP
 order by Id_Owner, Id_Name, Lineno
/
spool off
```

The following listing shows a sample output file (named cre_proc.sql) generated by the gen_proc.sql script.

```
CREATE OR REPLACE PROCEDURE
APP.remove_customer(
  p_temp_cust_id IN number )
IS
BEGIN

    delete from app_account_payments where cust_id = p_temp_cust_id;
    delete from app_customer_mailers where cust_id = p_temp_cust_id;
    delete from app_customer_points where cust_id = p_temp_cust_id;
    delete from app_gift_certificates where cust_id = p_temp_cust_id;
    delete from app_orders where cust_id = p_temp_cust_id;
    delete from app_unfound_orders where cust_id = p_temp_cust_id;
    delete from app_credit_cards where cust_id = p_temp_cust_id;
    delete from app_telephones where cust_id = p_temp_cust_id;
    delete from app_addresses where cust_id = p_temp_cust_id;
    delete from app_customers where id = p_temp_cust_id;
    commit;
END remove_customer;
/
```

The generated script is written to the cre_proc.sql file. You can edit the cre_proc.sql file prior to executing it.

ANNOTATIONS

Because each line of a procedure is stored as a separate row in DBA_SOURCE, the script uses a cursor both to extract the procedure information and to allow you to enter a wildcard value or to modify the script to select all procedures for an owner or all procedures in the database. The script generates an output file containing the commands necessary to re-create the requested stored procedure. The gen_proc.sql script uses a temporary table to hold individual lines of the **create procedure** statement, writing to the table rather than using DBMS_OUTPUT.PUT_LINE so that you can extract the information for an individual procedure from the temporary table. Using the DBMS_OUTPUT procedure would force you to save and edit the output file for the procedure you want.

The first section of the script, shown in the following listing, does the initial setup, prompting for the procedure name and procedure owner for later use via the **accept** command, which, unlike simply using the variable with '&' or '&&' in a SQL statement, allows you to define your own prompt for the variable. You can enter the procedure name with '%' to generate a script for all procedures with a similar name.

The SQL*Plus **set** command turns off headers (**pagesize 0**), row counts (**feedback off**), and displays of old and new values for the *procedure_name* and *procedure_owner* variables (**verify off**).

```
set echo off verify off term on feedback off pagesize 0
select 'Creating procedure build script...' from DUAL;


accept procedure_name prompt "Enter the name of the procedure: "
accept procedure_owner prompt "Enter procedure owner: "
set term off
```

The next section of the script, shown in the following listing, creates a temporary table to hold each **create procedure** command and its owner. The Lineno column orders the lines of the **create procedure** command.

```
drop    table PROC_TEMP
/

create table PROC_TEMP (
        Lineno NUMBER,
        Id_Owner VARCHAR2(30),
        Id_Name VARCHAR2(30),
        Text VARCHAR2(2000))
/
```

The PROC_CURSOR cursor, shown in the following listing, selects the information from DBA_SOURCE where the procedure name matches the input variable *procedure_name* and the procedure owner matches the input variable *procedure_owner*. Using **like** in the **where** clause instead of = allows for wildcards.

```
declare
    cursor PROC_CURSOR is
        select Owner,
               Name,
               Type,
               Line,
               Text
         from DBA_SOURCE
        where Type  = 'PROCEDURE'
          and Owner = UPPER('&&procedure_owner')
          and Name like UPPER('&&procedure_name')
        order by Owner, Name, Type, Line;
```

In the next portion of the script, the procedure variables for the cursor are declared as TABLE_NAME.Column_Name%**TYPE**. Anchoring the variables via the %**TYPE** operator takes the column definition from within the database itself. If the column definition changes in a different version of ORACLE, the procedure will still work because the definition of the column has not been hard-coded. The variable *Lv_Lineno* orders the lines of the **create procedure** statement and is initialized to 0.

```
Lv_Owner                DBA_SOURCE.Owner%TYPE;
Lv_Name                 DBA_SOURCE.Name%TYPE;
Lv_Type                 DBA_SOURCE.Type%TYPE;
Lv_Text                 DBA_SOURCE.Text%TYPE;
Lv_Line                 DBA_SOURCE.Line%TYPE;
Lv_String               VARCHAR2(2000);
Lv_String2              VARCHAR2(2000);
Lv_Lineno               NUMBER := 0;
```

The next section of the script creates an internal procedure to perform the **insert** into the temporary table used by the gen_proc.sql script.

```
procedure WRITE_OUT(P_Line INTEGER, P_Owner VARCHAR2, P_Name VARCHAR2,
                    P_String VARCHAR2) is
begin
    insert into PROC_TEMP (Lineno, Id_Owner, Id_Name, Text)
            values (P_Line,P_Owner,P_Name,P_String);
end;
```

Unlike triggers and views, the lines of a stored procedure are stored as separate lines in the data dictionary. The cursor PROC_CURSOR extracts all the lines of the stored procedure. *Lv_Lineno* is used in conjunction with the procedure name to order the rows in the temporary table PROC_TEMP so that if you prefer, you can extract the **create procedure** statement for a single procedure at the end of the script.

```
begin
    open PROC_CURSOR;
    Lv_Lineno   := 1;
    loop
        fetch PROC_CURSOR into Lv_Owner,
                               Lv_Name,
                               Lv_Type,
                               Lv_Line,
                               Lv_Text;
        exit when PROC_CURSOR%NOTFOUND;
```

The **create or replace** clause, used in the next section of gen_proc.sql, retains all grants on a procedure that is being replaced. If you drop a procedure and then create it, all grants are lost.

```
        if (Lv_Line = 1)
        then
            Lv_String   := 'CREATE OR REPLACE PROCEDURE ';
            WRITE_OUT(Lv_Lineno, Lv_Owner, Lv_Name, Lv_String);
            Lv_Lineno   := Lv_Lineno + 1;
```

ORACLE stores the first line of a procedure as **PROCEDURE** *procedure_name*. Because the script concatenates the owner's name to the name of the stored procedure in the generated script, the word PROCEDURE has to be removed from the first line of the stored source code. The **SUBSTR** function, along with the **LENGTH** of the variable *Lv_Type* (which contains the type of source code), extracts the rest of the line and places it in the string variable *Lv_String* to be written to the temporary table. The **LTRIM** function removes any leading spaces before concatenating the string with the owner's name.

```
Lv_String   := SUBSTR(Lv_Text,LENGTH(Lv_Type)+1,
                    (LENGTH(Lv_Text) - LENGTH(Lv_Type)));
Lv_String   := Lv_Owner || '.' || LTRIM(Lv_String);
WRITE_OUT(Lv_Lineno, Lv_Owner, Lv_Name, Lv_String);
Lv_Lineno   := Lv_Lineno + 1;
```

If this is not the first line of the stored procedure in DBA_SOURCE, the text as read from the database is inserted into the temporary table. The cursor loop ends and the procedure will loop back through the PROC_CURSOR until all procedures have been generated. Then the cursor closes and the procedure exits.

```
    else
        WRITE_OUT(Lv_Lineno, Lv_Owner, Lv_Name, Lv_Text);
        Lv_Lineno := Lv_Lineno + 1;
    end if;
  end loop;
  WRITE_OUT(Lv_Lineno, Lv_Owner, Lv_Name, '/');
  close PROC_CURSOR;
end;
/
spool cre_proc.sql
select Text
  from PROC_TEMP
 order by Id_Owner, Id_Name, Lineno
/
spool off
```

Once the **create** statements for all the procedures have been generated, they are spooled to a file name cre_proc.sql for later execution. A sample cre_proc.sql file is shown in the following listing.

```
CREATE OR REPLACE PROCEDURE
APP.remove_customer(
  p_temp_cust_id IN number )
IS
BEGIN

    delete from app_account_payments where cust_id = p_temp_cust_id;
```

```
      delete from app_customer_mailers where cust_id = p_temp_cust_id;
      delete from app_customer_points where cust_id = p_temp_cust_id;
      delete from app_gift_certificates where cust_id = p_temp_cust_id;
      delete from app_orders where cust_id = p_temp_cust_id;
      delete from app_unfound_orders where cust_id = p_temp_cust_id;
      delete from app_credit_cards where cust_id = p_temp_cust_id;
      delete from app_telephones where cust_id = p_temp_cust_id;
      delete from app_addresses where cust_id = p_temp_cust_id;
      delete from app_customers where id = p_temp_cust_id;
      commit;
END remove_customer;
/
```

To use this script to document all the stored procedures for a particular owner, remove the **accept** *procedure_name* command at the beginning of the script and change the **where** clause for the PROC_CURSOR cursor to:

```
where Owner  = UPPER('&&procedure_owner')
```

If you want to document all procedures in your database that are not owned by SYS, remove the two **accept** statements from the beginning of the script and change the **where** clause for the PROC_CURSOR cursor to:

```
where Owner != 'SYS'
```

gen_func.sql

Generate Functions

When you use functions, you keep compiled PL/SQL code within the database, avoiding performance degradation from run-time compilation. A function is identical to a procedure except that functions always return a single value while procedures return nothing. The following script, gen_func.sql, generates a script to re-create a function.

```
set echo off verify off term on feedback off pagesize 0
select 'Creating function build script...' from DUAL;

accept function_name prompt "Enter the name of the function: "
accept function_owner prompt "Enter function owner: "
set term off

drop   table FUNC_TEMP
/

create table FUNC_TEMP (
       Lineno NUMBER,
       Id_Owner VARCHAR2(30),
```

```
        Id_Name VARCHAR2(30),
        Text VARCHAR2(2000))
/


declare
    cursor FUNC_CURSOR is
        select Owner,
               Name,
               Type,
               Line,
               Text
          from DBA_SOURCE
         where Type  = 'FUNCTION'
           and Owner = UPPER('&&function_owner')
           and Name  like UPPER('&&function_name')
         order by Owner, Name, Type, Line;

    Lv_Owner                DBA_SOURCE.Owner%TYPE;
    Lv_Name                 DBA_SOURCE.Name%TYPE;
    Lv_Type                 DBA_SOURCE.Type%TYPE;
    Lv_Text                 DBA_SOURCE.Text%TYPE;
    Lv_Line                 DBA_SOURCE.Line%TYPE;

    Lv_String               VARCHAR2(2000);
    Lv_String2              VARCHAR2(2000);
    Lv_Lineno               NUMBER := 0;

    procedure WRITE_OUT(P_Line INTEGER, P_Owner VARCHAR2, P_Name VARCHAR2,
                    P_String VARCHAR2) is
    begin
       insert into FUNC_TEMP (Lineno, Id_Owner, Id_Name, Text)
            values (P_Line,P_Owner,P_Name,P_String);
     end;

begin
   open FUNC_CURSOR;
   Lv_Lineno  := 1;
   loop
      fetch FUNC_CURSOR into Lv_Owner,
                             Lv_Name,
                             Lv_Type,
                             Lv_Line,
                             Lv_Text;
```

```
    exit when FUNC_CURSOR%NOTFOUND;

    if (Lv_Line = 1)
    then
        Lv_String  := 'CREATE OR REPLACE FUNCTION ';
        WRITE_OUT(Lv_Lineno, Lv_Owner, Lv_Name, Lv_String);
        Lv_Lineno  := Lv_Lineno + 1;

        Lv_String  := SUBSTR(Lv_Text,LENGTH(Lv_Type)+1,
                      (LENGTH(Lv_Text) - LENGTH(Lv_Type)));
        Lv_String  := Lv_Owner || '.' || LTRIM(Lv_String);
        WRITE_OUT(Lv_Lineno, Lv_Owner, Lv_Name, Lv_String);
        Lv_Lineno  := Lv_Lineno + 1;
    else
        WRITE_OUT(Lv_Lineno, Lv_Owner, Lv_Name, Lv_Text);
        Lv_Lineno := Lv_Lineno + 1;
    end if;
  end loop;
  WRITE_OUT(Lv_Lineno, Lv_Owner, Lv_Name, '/');
  close FUNC_CURSOR;
end;
/

spool cre_func.sql
select Text
  from FUNC_TEMP
 order by Id_Owner, Id_Name, Lineno
/
spool off
```

Sample output for the script is shown in the following listing.

```
CREATE OR REPLACE FUNCTION
APP.f_date(
t_date IN varchar2 )
RETURN date IS
BEGIN
  BEGIN
    DECLARE
    tmp_dt date;
    BEGIN
    IF lower(t_date) in ('sun', 'mon', 'tue',
                         'wed', 'thu', 'fri', 'sat')
```

```
    THEN
        tmp_dt:= next_day(sysdate, t_date);
    ELSE
        IF substr(t_date,5,2) BETWEEN 0 AND 49 THEN
          tmp_dt := to_date(substr(t_date, 1, 2)||'/'||
                               substr(t_date, 3, 2)||'/'||
                               '20'||substr(t_date, 5, 2), 'mm/dd/yyyy');
        ELSE
          tmp_dt := to_date(substr(t_date, 1, 2)||'/'||
                               substr(t_date, 3, 2)||'/'||
                               '19'||substr(t_date, 5, 2),
                                          'mm/dd/yyyy');
        END IF;
      END IF;
       return(tmp_dt);
      END;
   END f_date;
END f_date;
/
```

The output is written to a file called cre_func.sql. You can edit or execute the cre_func.sql file.

ANNOTATIONS

Because each line of a function is stored as a separate row in DBA_SOURCE, the gen_func.sql script uses a cursor both to extract the function information and to allow you to enter a wildcard value. You can also modify the script to select all functions for an owner or all functions in the database. The gen_func.sql script generates an output file containing a script to re-create the requested function. The gen_func.sql script uses a temporary table to hold individual lines of the **create function** statement, writing to the table rather than using DBMS_OUTPUT.PUT_LINE so that you can extract the information for an individual function from the table. Using the DBMS_OUTPUT procedure would force you to save and edit the output file for the function you want.

The first section of the script, shown in the following listing, does the initial setup, prompting for the function name and function owner for later use via the **accept** command. Unlike simply using the variable with the '&' or '&&' in a SQL statement, **accept** allows you to define your own prompt for the variable. You can enter the function name with '%' to generate a script for all functions with a similar name.

The SQL*Plus **set** command turns off headers (**pagesize 0**), row counts (**feedback off**), and displays of old and new values for the *function_name* and *function_owner* variables (**verify off**).

```
set echo off verify off term on feedback off pagesize 0
select 'Creating function build script...' from DUAL;

accept function_name prompt "Enter the name of the function: "
accept function_owner prompt "Enter function owner: "
set term off
```

The next portion of the script creates a temporary table to hold each **create function** command and its owner. The Lineno column orders the lines of the **create function** command.

```
drop    table FUNC_TEMP
/

create table FUNC_TEMP (
        Lineno NUMBER,
        Id_Owner VARCHAR2(30),
        Id_Name VARCHAR2(30),
        Text VARCHAR2(2000))
/
```

The next portion of the script creates the FUNC_CURSOR cursor. The FUNC_CURSOR cursor selects the information from DBA_SOURCE where the function name matches the input variable *function_name* and the function owner matches the input variable *function_owner*. Using **like** in the **where** clause instead of = allows for wildcards.

```
declare
  cursor FUNC_CURSOR is
        select Owner,
               Name,
               Type,
               Line,
               Text
          from DBA_SOURCE
         where Type  = 'FUNCTION'
           and Owner = UPPER('&&function_owner')
           and Name  like UPPER('&&function_name')
         order by Owner, Name, Type, Line;
```

The procedure variables for the cursor are declared as TABLE_NAME.Column_Name%TYPE. Anchoring the datatypes in this manner takes the column definition from within the database itself. If the column definition changes in a different version of ORACLE, the procedure will still work because the definition of the column has not been hard-coded. The variable *Lv_Lineno* orders the lines of the **create function** statement and is initialized to 0.

```
Lv_Owner              DBA_SOURCE.Owner%TYPE;
Lv_Name               DBA_SOURCE.Name%TYPE;
Lv_Type               DBA_SOURCE.Type%TYPE;
Lv_Text               DBA_SOURCE.Text%TYPE;
Lv_Line               DBA_SOURCE.Line%TYPE;
Lv_String             VARCHAR2(2000);
Lv_String2            VARCHAR2(2000);
Lv_Lineno             NUMBER := 0;
```

The next section of the script creates WRITE_OUT, an internal procedure to **insert** rows into the temporary table used by the gen_func.sql script.

```
procedure WRITE_OUT(P_Line INTEGER, P_Owner VARCHAR2, P_Name VARCHAR2,
                    P_String VARCHAR2) is
begin
   insert into FUNC_TEMP (Lineno, Id_Owner, Id_Name, Text)
          values (P_Line,P_Owner,P_Name,P_String);
   end;
```

As with stored procedures, the lines of a function are stored as separate lines in the data dictionary. The cursor FUNC_CURSOR extracts all the lines of the function. *Lv_Lineno*, in conjunction with the function name, orders the rows in the temporary table FUNC_TEMP so you can extract the **create function** statement for a single function at the end of the procedure.

```
begin
   open FUNC_CURSOR;
   Lv_Lineno  := 1;
   loop
      fetch FUNC_CURSOR into Lv_Owner,
                             Lv_Name,
                             Lv_Type,
                             Lv_Line,
                             Lv_Text;
      exit when FUNC_CURSOR%NOTFOUND;
```

The **create or replace** clause retains all grants on a function that is being replaced. If you drop the function and then create it, all grants are lost.

```
      if (Lv_Line = 1)
      then
          Lv_String  := 'CREATE OR REPLACE FUNCTION ';
          WRITE_OUT(Lv_Lineno, Lv_Owner, Lv_Name, Lv_String);
          Lv_Lineno  := Lv_Lineno + 1;
```

ORACLE stores the first line of a function as **FUNCTION** *function_name*. Because the script concatenates the owner's name to the name of the function in the generated script, it has to remove the word **"FUNCTION"** from the first line of the stored source code. In the following section of the script, the **SUBSTR** function, along with the **LENGTH** of the variable *Lv_Type*, extracts the rest of the line and places it in the string variable *Lv_String* to be written to the temporary table. The **LTRIM** function removes any leading spaces before concatenating the string with the owner's name.

```
Lv_String   := SUBSTR(Lv_Text,LENGTH(Lv_Type)+1,
                   (LENGTH(Lv_Text) - LENGTH(Lv_Type)));
Lv_String   := Lv_Owner || '.' || LTRIM(Lv_String);
WRITE_OUT(Lv_Lineno, Lv_Owner, Lv_Name, Lv_String);
Lv_Lineno   := Lv_Lineno + 1;
```

The final section of the script completes the entries into the temporary table. If this is not the first line of the function in DBA_SOURCE, the text as read from the database is inserted into the temporary table. The cursor loop ends and the procedure will loop back through the FUNC_CURSOR until all functions have been generated, at which point the cursor closes and the procedure exits.

Once the **create function** statements for all the functions have been generated, they are spooled to a file for later execution.

```
    else
        WRITE_OUT(Lv_Lineno, Lv_Owner, Lv_Name, Lv_Text);
        Lv_Lineno := Lv_Lineno + 1;
    end if;
  end loop;
  WRITE_OUT(Lv_Lineno, Lv_Owner, Lv_Name, '/');
  close FUNC_CURSOR;
end;
/

spool cre_func.sql
select Text
  from FUNC_TEMP
 order by Id_Owner, Id_Name, Lineno
/
spool off
```

The following listing shows a sample cre_func.sql file for a function called F_DATE.

```
CREATE OR REPLACE FUNCTION
APP.f_date(
t_date IN varchar2 )
RETURN date IS
BEGIN
```

```
BEGIN
  DECLARE
  tmp_dt date;
  BEGIN
  IF lower(t_date) in ('sun', 'mon', 'tue',
                        'wed', 'thu', 'fri', 'sat')
  THEN
     tmp_dt:= next_day(sysdate, t_date);
  ELSE
     IF substr(t_date,5,2) BETWEEN 0 AND 49 THEN
        tmp_dt := to_date(substr(t_date, 1, 2)||'/'||
                          substr(t_date, 3, 2)||'/'||
                          '20'||substr(t_date, 5, 2), 'mm/dd/yyyy');
     ELSE
        tmp_dt := to_date(substr(t_date, 1, 2)||'/'||
                          substr(t_date, 3, 2)||'/'||
                          '19'||substr(t_date, 5, 2),
                                      'mm/dd/yyyy');
     END IF;
  END IF;
   return(tmp_dt);
  END;
 END f_date;
END f_date;
/
```

As an alternative, if you want to use this script to document all the functions for a particular owner, remove the **accept** *function_name* statement at the beginning of the script and change the **where** clause for the FUNC_CURSOR cursor to:

```
where Owner  = UPPER('&&function_owner')
```

If you want to document all functions in your database that are not owned by SYS, remove the two **accept** statements from the beginning of the script and change the **where** clause for the FUNC_CURSOR cursor to:

```
where Owner != 'SYS'
```

gen_pkg.sql

Generate Packages

Packages provide a means of grouping together related functions and procedures and storing them as a unit in the database. Like procedures and functions, they are stored as compiled code, and the procedures and functions in a package are loaded into memory once, improving performance. Like procedures, they can be pinned in memory. Unlike procedures and functions, packages are stored as two objects in the database—the package specification and the package body. The following script, gen_pkg.sql, generates a script to re-create both the package specification and package body.

```
set echo off verify off feedback off pagesize 0
set term on
select 'Creating package build script...' from DUAL;

accept package_name prompt "Enter the name of the package: "
accept package_owner prompt "Enter package owner: "
set term off

drop    table PACK_TEMP
/

create table PACK_TEMP (
        Lineno NUMBER,
        Id_Owner VARCHAR2(30),
        Id_Name VARCHAR2(30),
        text VARCHAR2(2000))
/

declare
    cursor PACK_CURSOR is
        select Owner,
                Name,
                Type,
                Line,
                Text
            from DBA_SOURCE
            where Type in ('PACKAGE','PACKAGE BODY')
              and Owner = UPPER('&&package_owner')
              and Name like UPPER('&&package_name')
            order by Owner, Name, Type, Line;

    Lv_Owner            DBA_SOURCE.Owner%TYPE;
    Lv_Name             DBA_SOURCE.Name%TYPE;
    Lv_Type             DBA_SOURCE.Type%TYPE;
    Lv_Text             DBA_SOURCE.Text%TYPE;
    Lv_Line             DBA_SOURCE.Line%TYPE;
    Lv_String           VARCHAR2(2100);
    Lv_String2          VARCHAR2(2100);
    Lv_Lineno           NUMBER := 0;
```

```
   procedure WRITE_OUT(P_Line INTEGER, P_Owner VARCHAR2, P_Name VARCHAR2,

                    P_String VARCHAR2) is
begin
   insert into PACK_TEMP (Lineno, Id_Owner, Id_Name, Text)
         values (P_Line,P_Owner,P_Name,P_String);
   end;

begin
   open PACK_CURSOR;
   Lv_Lineno  := 1;
   loop
      fetch PACK_CURSOR into Lv_Owner,
                             Lv_Name,
                             Lv_Type,
                             Lv_Line,
                             Lv_Text;
      exit when PACK_CURSOR%NOTFOUND;

      if (Lv_Line = 1)
      then
          if (Lv_Type = 'PACKAGE BODY')
          then
              WRITE_OUT(Lv_Lineno, Lv_Owner, Lv_Name, '/');
              Lv_Lineno  := Lv_Lineno + 1;
          end if;

          Lv_String  := 'CREATE OR REPLACE ' || UPPER(Lv_Type)  || ' ';
          WRITE_OUT(Lv_Lineno, Lv_Owner, Lv_Name, Lv_String);
          Lv_Lineno  := Lv_Lineno + 1;

          Lv_String  := SUBSTR(Lv_Text,LENGTH(Lv_Type)+1,
                         (LENGTH(Lv_Text) - LENGTH(Lv_Type)));
          Lv_String  := Lv_Owner || '.' || LTRIM(Lv_String);
          WRITE_OUT(Lv_Lineno, Lv_Owner, Lv_Name, Lv_String);
          Lv_Lineno  := Lv_Lineno + 1;
      else
          WRITE_OUT(Lv_Lineno, Lv_Owner, Lv_Name, Lv_Text);
          Lv_Lineno := Lv_Lineno + 1;
      end if;
   end loop;
```

```
    WRITE_OUT(Lv_Lineno, Lv_Owner, Lv_Name, '/');
    close PACK_CURSOR;
end;
/
spool cre_pkg.sql
select Text
  from PACK_TEMP
 order by Id_Owner, Id_Name, Lineno
/
spool off
```

Sample output for the gen_pkg.sql script is shown in the following listing.

```
CREATE OR REPLACE PACKAGE
APP.APP_EMPLOYEE_PKG IS
  PROCEDURE APP_EMP_SWITCH_UPDATE(
  EMP_ID IN VARCHAR2 )
;
PROCEDURE APP_EMPL_ACT_DETAILS_PROC(
  EMP_ID IN CHAR ,
  ACT_DESC IN CHAR ,
  START_TIME IN DATE ,
  PROJ IN CHAR ,
  DUR IN NUMBER )
;

END APP_EMPLOYEE_PKG;
/
CREATE OR REPLACE PACKAGE BODY
APP.APP_EMPLOYEE_PKG IS
 /* If an employee goes on a project then the necessary info is recorded
 in the app_employee_activity_details table for use by the supervisor
 */

  PROCEDURE APP_EMP_SWITCH_UPDATE(
  EMP_ID IN VARCHAR2 )
  IS
  BEGIN
   update app_employee_time_records_1
     set status='I',clock_out=sysdate
      where epe_code=emp_id AND STATUS='A' AND PAYTIMTYPE_CODE='T';
        commit;
    IF SQL%NOTFOUND THEN
```

```
        NULL;
      END IF;
  END;

  PROCEDURE APP_EMPL_ACT_DETAILS_PROC(
  EMP_ID IN CHAR ,
  ACT_DESC IN CHAR ,
  START_TIME IN DATE ,
  PROJ IN CHAR ,
  DUR IN NUMBER )
  IS
      M_ID          NUMBER(10);
      ACT_CODE      APP_EMPLOYEE_ACTIVITY_DETAILS.ACTIVITY%TYPE;
      M_END_TIME    DATE;
  BEGIN
      /* Sequence no is generated */
      SELECT APP_ID_SEQ.NEXTVAL INTO M_ID FROM DUAL;
 /* Using duration and start_date/time the end_date/time is evaluated*/
      M_END_TIME :=START_TIME +(DUR/24/60);
      INSERT INTO
APP_EMPLOYEE_ACTIVITY_DETAILS(EPE_CODE,ACTIVITY,START_DATE,ID,
      ACTIVITY_CODE,END_DATE,SPECIAL)
      VALUES(EMP_ID,PROJ,START_TIME,M_ID,'PROJ',M_END_TIME,ACT_DESC);
      COMMIT;
  END;
END APP_EMPLOYEE_PKG;
/
```

The gen_pkg.sql script writes its output to a file called cre_pkg.sql. You can edit or execute the cre_pkg.sql file.

ANNOTATIONS

ORACLE enforces certain restrictions on functions and procedures that can be called from SQL statements. For functions and procedures stored as standalones, ORACLE can enforce the restrictions by checking the function or procedure body directly. In packages, however, only the specification of the function or procedure is visible. Therefore, for functions and procedures which will be called outside of the package itself, you must use the pragma (compiler directive) RESTRICT_REFERENCES to enforce the rules. The pragma tells the PL/SQL compiler to deny the packaged function read/write access to database tables, packaged variables, or both. If you try to compile a function body that violates the pragma, you get a compilation error. For details on how to code the pragma, see the appendix.

Because each line of a package is stored as a separate row in DBA_SOURCE, the script uses a cursor both to extract the package information and to allow you to enter a wildcard value for the package name (*%package_name%*) or to modify the script to select all packages for an owner or all packages in the database. The gen_pkg.sql script generates a script to re-create the requested package. The gen_pkg.sql script uses a temporary table to hold individual lines of the **create package** and **create package body** statements, writing to the table rather than using DBMS_OUTPUT.PUT_LINE so that you can extract the information for an individual package from the table. Using the DBMS_OUTPUT procedure would force you to save and edit the output file for the package you want.

The first section of the script, shown in the following listing, does the initial setup, prompting for the package name and package owner for later use via the **accept** command, which, unlike simply using the variable with the '&' or '&&' in a SQL statement, allows you to define your own prompt for the variable. You can enter a value for the package name with '%' to generate a script for all packages with a similar name.

The SQL*Plus **set** command turns off headers (**pagesize 0**), row counts (**feedback off**), and displays of old and new values for the *package_name* and *package_owner* variables (**verify off**).

```
set echo off verify off feedback off pagesize 0
set term on
select 'Creating package build script...' from DUAL;

accept package_name prompt "Enter the name of the package: "
accept package_owner prompt "Enter package owner: "
set term off
```

The next section of the script creates a temporary table to hold each **create package** and associated **create package body** command and owner. The Lineno column orders the lines of the **create package** and **create package body** command.

```
drop    table PACK_TEMP
/

create table PACK_TEMP (
        Lineno NUMBER,
        Id_Owner VARCHAR2(30),
        Id_Name VARCHAR2(30),
        text VARCHAR2(2000))
/
```

The next section of the script, shown in the following listing, creates the PACK_CURSOR cursor. The PACK_CURSOR cursor selects the information from DBA_SOURCE where the package name matches the input variable *package_name* and the package owner matches the input variable *package_owner*. Using **like** in the **where** clause instead of = allows for wildcards. Selecting for **Type in ('PACKAGE','PACKAGE BODY')** selects all the lines for both the package specification and the package body. The **order by** clause orders by Type before Line, so all lines of the package specification will be returned before any line of the package body.

```
declare
   cursor PACK_CURSOR is
        select Owner,
               Name,
               Type,
               Line,
               Text
          from DBA_SOURCE
         where Type in ('PACKAGE','PACKAGE BODY')
           and Owner = UPPER('&&package_owner')
           and Name like UPPER('&&package_name')
         order by Owner, Name, Type, Line;
```

The procedure variables for the cursor are declared as TABLE_NAME.Column_Name%**TYPE**. Anchoring the variable declarations to columns takes the column definition from within the database itself. If the column definition changes in a different version of ORACLE, the procedure will still work because the definition of the column has not been hard-coded. The variable *Lv_Lineno* orders the lines of the **create package** statement and is initialized to 0.

```
Lv_Owner              DBA_SOURCE.Owner%TYPE;
Lv_Name               DBA_SOURCE.Name%TYPE;
Lv_Type               DBA_SOURCE.Type%TYPE;
Lv_Text               DBA_SOURCE.Text%TYPE;
Lv_Line               DBA_SOURCE.Line%TYPE;
Lv_String             VARCHAR2(2000);
Lv_String2            VARCHAR2(2000);
Lv_Lineno             NUMBER := 0;
```

The next section of the script creates WRITE_OUT, an internal procedure to perform the **insert**s into the temporary table.

```
procedure WRITE_OUT(P_Line INTEGER, P_Owner VARCHAR2, P_Name VARCHAR2,
                    P_String VARCHAR2) is
begin
   insert into PACK_TEMP (Lineno, Id_Owner, Id_Name, Text)
          values (P_Line,P_Owner,P_Name,P_String);
  end;
```

The lines of a package specification or package body are stored as separate lines in the data dictionary. The cursor PACK_CURSOR extracts all the lines of both the package specification and the package body. *Lv_Lineno,* in conjunction with the package name, orders the rows in the temporary table PACK_TEMP so you can extract the **create package** command for a single package at the end of the procedure.

```
begin
    open PACK_CURSOR;
    Lv_Lineno   := 1;
    loop
        fetch PACK_CURSOR into Lv_Owner,
                               Lv_Name,
                               Lv_Type,
                               Lv_Line,
                               Lv_Text;
        exit when PACK_CURSOR%NOTFOUND;
```

The **order by** clause of **PACK_CURSOR** ensures that all the lines of the package specification are returned before the lines of the package body. Because the script is creating two SQL statements, a '/' is inserted before the second statement (for the package body) is created.

```
        if (Lv_Line = 1)
        then
            if (Lv_Type = 'PACKAGE BODY')
            then
                WRITE_OUT(Lv_Lineno, Lv_Owner, Lv_Name, '/');
                Lv_Lineno   := Lv_Lineno + 1;
            end if;
```

The **create or replace** clause retains all grants on a package that is being replaced. If you drop the package and then create it, all grants are lost.

```
            Lv_String   := 'CREATE OR REPLACE ' || UPPER(Lv_Type) || ' ';
            WRITE_OUT(Lv_Lineno, Lv_Owner, Lv_Name, Lv_String);
            Lv_Lineno   := Lv_Lineno + 1;
```

ORACLE stores the first line of each part of a package as **PACKAGE [BODY]** *package_name.* Because the script concatenates the owner's name to the name of the package in the generated script, it has to remove the term "**PACKAGE**" or "**PACKAGE BODY**" from the first line of the stored source code. The **SUBSTR** function, along with the variable *Lv_Type,* extracts the rest of the line and places it in the string variable *Lv_String* to be written to the temporary table. The **LTRIM** function removes extra blanks from the beginning of the string.

```
Lv_String   := SUBSTR(Lv_Text,LENGTH(Lv_Type)+1,
                     (LENGTH(Lv_Text) - LENGTH(Lv_Type)));
Lv_String   := Lv_Owner || '.' || LTRIM(Lv_String);
WRITE_OUT(Lv_Lineno, Lv_Owner, Lv_Name, Lv_String);
Lv_Lineno   := Lv_Lineno + 1;
```

If this is not the first line of the package or package body in DBA_SOURCE, the text as read from the database is inserted into the temporary table. The cursor loop ends and the procedure will loop back through the PACK_CURSOR until all packages have been generated. The cursor then closes and the procedure exits. Once the **create** statements for all the packages and package bodies have been generated, they are spooled to a file for later execution.

```
    else
        WRITE_OUT(Lv_Lineno, Lv_Owner, Lv_Name, Lv_Text);
        Lv_Lineno := Lv_Lineno + 1;
    end if;
  end loop;
  WRITE_OUT(Lv_Lineno, Lv_Owner, Lv_Name, '/');
  close PACK_CURSOR;
end;
/

spool cre_pkg.sql
select Text
  from PACK_TEMP
 order by Id_Owner, Id_Name, Lineno
/
spool off
```

The following listing shows a sample cre_pkg.sql file generated by the gen_pkg.sql script.

```
CREATE OR REPLACE PACKAGE
APP.APP_EMPLOYEE_PKG IS
  PROCEDURE APP_EMP_SWITCH_UPDATE(
  EMP_ID IN VARCHAR2 )
;
PROCEDURE APP_EMPL_ACT_DETAILS_PROC(
  EMP_ID IN CHAR ,
  ACT_DESC IN CHAR ,
  START_TIME IN DATE ,
  PROJ IN CHAR ,
  DUR IN NUMBER )
;

END APP_EMPLOYEE_PKG;
```

```
/
CREATE OR REPLACE PACKAGE BODY
APP.APP_EMPLOYEE_PKG IS
 /* If an employee goes on a project then the necessary info is recorded
 in the app_employee_activity_details table for use by the supervisor
 */

   PROCEDURE APP_EMP_SWITCH_UPDATE(
   EMP_ID IN VARCHAR2 )
   IS
   BEGIN
    update app_employee_time_records_1
      set status='I',clock_out=sysdate
       where epe_code=emp_id AND STATUS='A' AND PAYTIMTYPE_CODE='T';
         commit;
     IF SQL%NOTFOUND THEN
      NULL;
      END IF;
   END;

   PROCEDURE APP_EMPL_ACT_DETAILS_PROC(
   EMP_ID IN CHAR ,
   ACT_DESC IN CHAR ,
   START_TIME IN DATE ,
   PROJ IN CHAR ,
   DUR IN NUMBER )
   IS
      M_ID          NUMBER(10);
      ACT_CODE      APP_EMPLOYEE_ACTIVITY_DETAILS.ACTIVITY%TYPE;
      M_END_TIME    DATE;
   BEGIN
      /* Sequence no is generated */
      SELECT APP_ID_SEQ.NEXTVAL INTO M_ID FROM DUAL;
  /* Using duration and start_date/time the end_date/time is evaluated*/
      M_END_TIME :=START_TIME +(DUR/24/60);
      INSERT INTO
APP_EMPLOYEE_ACTIVITY_DETAILS(EPE_CODE,ACTIVITY,START_DATE,ID,
      ACTIVITY_CODE,END_DATE,SPECIAL)
      VALUES(EMP_ID,PROJ,START_TIME,M_ID,'PROJ',M_END_TIME,ACT_DESC);
      COMMIT;
   END;
END APP_EMPLOYEE_PKG;
/
```

As an alternative, if you want to use this script to document all the packages for a particular owner, remove the **accept** *package_name* statement at the beginning of the script and change the **where** clause for the PACK_CURSOR cursor to:

```
where Owner  = UPPER('&&package_owner')
```

If you want to document all packages in your database that are not owned by SYS, remove the two **accept** statements from the beginning of the script and change the **where** clause for the PACK_CURSOR cursor to:

```
where Owner != 'SYS'
```

gen_seq.sql

Generate Sequences

A sequence is a database object used to generate unique integers. You can use sequences to automatically generate primary key values or as part of a timestamp. Sequences can have groups of values cached in the SGA for faster retrieval, although any values stored in the cache will be lost if the database is shut down or if the shared pool is flushed. If you need consecutive numbers with no gaps, do not cache sequence values. The following listing shows the full gen_seq.sql script.

```
set echo off term on verify off feedback off pagesize 0
select 'Creating sequences build script...' from DUAL;

accept sequence_name prompt "Enter the name of the sequence: "
accept sequence_owner prompt "Enter sequence owner: "
set term off

drop    table SEQ_TEMP
/

create table SEQ_TEMP (
        Lineno NUMBER,
        Id_Owner VARCHAR2(30),
        Id_Name VARCHAR2(30),
        Text VARCHAR2(300))
/
declare
   cursor SEQ_CURSOR is
        select Sequence_Owner,
                Sequence_Name,
                Min_Value,
                Max_Value,
                Increment_By,
                Cycle_Flag,
```

```
              Order_Flag,
              Cache_Size,
              Last_Number
           from DBA_SEQUENCES
          where Sequence_Owner = UPPER('&&sequence_owner')
            and Sequence_Name like UPPER('&&sequence_name')
          order by Sequence_Owner, Sequence_Name;

     Lv_Seq_Owner          DBA_SEQUENCES.Sequence_Owner%TYPE;
     Lv_Seq_Name           DBA_SEQUENCES.Sequence_Name%TYPE;
     Lv_Seq_Min_Value      DBA_SEQUENCES.Min_Value%TYPE;
     Lv_Seq_Max_Value      DBA_SEQUENCES.Max_Value%TYPE;
     Lv_Seq_Increment_By   DBA_SEQUENCES.Increment_By%TYPE;
     Lv_Seq_Cycle_Flag     DBA_SEQUENCES.Cycle_Flag%TYPE;
     Lv_Seq_Order_Flag     DBA_SEQUENCES.Order_Flag%TYPE;
     Lv_Seq_Cache_Size     DBA_SEQUENCES.Cache_Size%TYPE;
     Lv_Seq_Last_Number    DBA_SEQUENCES.Last_Number%TYPE;
     Lv_String             VARCHAR2(2000);
     Lv_Lineno             NUMBER := 0;
     Lv_Start_No           INTEGER;

     procedure WRITE_OUT(P_Line INTEGER, P_Owner VARCHAR2, P_Name VARCHAR2,
                    P_String VARCHAR2) is
     begin
        insert into SEQ_TEMP (Lineno, Id_Owner, Id_Name, Text)
              values (P_Line,P_Owner,P_Name,P_String);
      end;

begin
    open SEQ_CURSOR;
    Lv_Lineno  := 1;
    loop
       fetch SEQ_CURSOR into Lv_Seq_Owner,
                             Lv_Seq_Name,
                             Lv_Seq_Min_Value,
                             Lv_Seq_Max_Value,
                             Lv_Seq_Increment_By,
                             Lv_Seq_Cycle_Flag,
                             Lv_Seq_Order_Flag,
                             Lv_Seq_Cache_Size,
                             Lv_Seq_Last_Number;
       exit when SEQ_CURSOR%NOTFOUND;
```

```
        Lv_Start_No := Lv_Seq_Last_Number + Lv_Seq_Increment_By;
        Lv_String  := 'CREATE SEQUENCE '  || LOWER(Lv_Seq_Owner)
                                          || '.'
                                          || LOWER(Lv_Seq_Name)
                                          || ' START WITH '
                                          || Lv_Start_No;
     WRITE_OUT(Lv_Lineno, Lv_Seq_Owner, Lv_Seq_Name, Lv_String);
     Lv_Lineno  := Lv_Lineno + 1;

     Lv_String := 'MAXVALUE ' || Lv_Seq_Max_Value ;
     Lv_String := Lv_String   || ' MINVALUE '       || Lv_Seq_Min_Value;
     Lv_String := Lv_String   || ' INCREMENT BY '  || Lv_Seq_Increment_By;

     if ( Lv_Seq_Cycle_Flag = 'Y' )
     then
         Lv_String := Lv_String || ' CYCLE ';
     else
         Lv_String := Lv_String || ' NOCYCLE ';
     end if;

     if ( Lv_Seq_Order_Flag = 'Y' )
     then
         Lv_String := Lv_String || ' ORDER ';
     else
         Lv_String := Lv_String || ' NOORDER ';
     end if;

     if ( Lv_Seq_Cache_Size = 0 )
     then
         Lv_String := Lv_String || ' NOCACHE ';
     else
         Lv_String := Lv_String || ' CACHE ' || Lv_Seq_Cache_Size;
     end if;
     WRITE_OUT(Lv_Lineno, Lv_Seq_Owner, Lv_Seq_Name, Lv_String);
     Lv_Lineno  := Lv_Lineno + 1;

     WRITE_OUT(Lv_Lineno, Lv_Seq_Owner, Lv_Seq_Name, '/');
     Lv_Lineno  := Lv_Lineno + 1;

  end loop;
  close SEQ_CURSOR;
end;
/
```

```
spool cre_seq.sql
select Text
  from SEQ_TEMP
 order by Id_Owner, Id_Name, Lineno
/
spool off
```

Sample output for the gen_seq.sql script is shown in the following listing.

```
CREATE SEQUENCE scott.chess_saveid START WITH 2
MAXVALUE 999999999999999999999999999 MINVALUE 1 INCREMENT BY 1 NOCYCLE   NOORDER CACHE 20
/
```

By default, the gen_seq.sql script writes its output to a file named cre_seq.sql.

ANNOTATIONS

Although the script as written will return information for a single sequence, it uses a cursor to allow you to enter a wildcard value or to modify the script to select all sequences for an owner or all sequences in the database. The gen_seq.sql script generates a script to re-create the requested sequence. The gen_seq.sql script uses a temporary table to hold individual lines of the **create sequence** statement, writing to the table rather than using DBMS_OUTPUT.PUT_LINE so that you can extract the information for an individual sequence from the table. Using the DBMS_OUTPUT procedure would force you to save and edit the output file for the sequence you want.

The first section of the script, shown in the following listing, does the initial setup, prompting for the sequence name and sequence owner for later use via the **accept** command, which, unlike simply using the variable with the '&' or '&&' in a SQL statement, allows you to define your own prompt for the variable. You can enter a value for the sequence name with '%' to generate a script for all sequences with a similar name.

The SQL*Plus **set** command turns off headers (**pagesize 0**), row counts (**feedback off**), and displays of old and new values for the *sequence_name* and *sequence_owner* variables (**verify off**).

```
set echo off term on verify off feedback off pagesize 0
select 'Creating sequences build script...' from DUAL;

accept sequence_name prompt "Enter the name of the sequence: "
accept sequence_owner prompt "Enter sequence owner: "
set term off
```

The next section of the script, shown in the following listing, creates a temporary table to hold each **create sequence** command and its owner. The Lineno column orders the lines of the **create sequence** command.

```
drop    table SEQ_TEMP
/

create table SEQ_TEMP (
        Lineno NUMBER,
        Id_Owner VARCHAR2(30),
        Id_Name VARCHAR2(30),
        Text VARCHAR2(300))
/
```

The SEQ_CURSOR cursor selects the information from DBA_SEQUENCES where the sequence name matches the input variable *sequence_name* and the sequence owner matches the input variable *sequence_owner*. Using **like** in the **where** clause instead of = allows for wildcards in the sequence name.

```
declare
    cursor SEQ_CURSOR is
        select Sequence_Owner,
                Sequence_Name,
                Min_Value,
                Max_Value,
                Increment_By,
                Cycle_Flag,
                Order_Flag,
                Cache_Size,
                Last_Number
            from DBA_SEQUENCES
          where Sequence_Owner = UPPER('&&sequence_owner')
            and Sequence_Name like UPPER('&&sequence_name')
          order by Sequence_Owner, Sequence_Name;
```

The procedure variables for the cursor are declared as TABLE_NAME.Column_Name%**TYPE**. Anchoring the variables' datatypes takes the column definition from within the database itself. If the column definition changes in a different version of ORACLE, the procedure will still work because the definition of the column has not been hard-coded. The variable *Lv_Lineno* orders the lines of the **create sequence** statement and is initialized to 0. The variable *Lv_Start_No* holds what will be the next value of the sequence so that you will not overwrite a value already used.

```
    Lv_Seq_Owner          DBA_SEQUENCES.Sequence_Owner%TYPE;
    Lv_Seq_Name           DBA_SEQUENCES.Sequence_Name%TYPE;
    Lv_Seq_Min_Value      DBA_SEQUENCES.Min_Value%TYPE;
    Lv_Seq_Max_Value      DBA_SEQUENCES.Max_Value%TYPE;
    Lv_Seq_Increment_By   DBA_SEQUENCES.Increment_By%TYPE;
    Lv_Seq_Cycle_Flag     DBA_SEQUENCES.Cycle_Flag%TYPE;
```

```
Lv_Seq_Order_Flag        DBA_SEQUENCES.Order_Flag%TYPE;
Lv_Seq_Cache_Size        DBA_SEQUENCES.Cache_Size%TYPE;
Lv_Seq_Last_Number       DBA_SEQUENCES.Last_Number%TYPE;
Lv_String                VARCHAR2(2000);
Lv_Lineno                NUMBER := 0;
Lv_Start_No              INTEGER;
```

The next portion of the script creates an internal procedure to do the **insert** into the temporary table.

```
procedure WRITE_OUT(P_Line INTEGER, P_Owner VARCHAR2, P_Name VARCHAR2,
                    P_String VARCHAR2) is
begin
   insert into SEQ_TEMP (Lineno, Id_Owner, Id_Name, Text)
          values (P_Line,P_Owner,P_Name,P_String);
   end;
```

The cursor SEQ_CURSOR extracts all the information about the sequences. *Lv_Lineno*, in conjunction with the sequence name, orders the rows in the temporary table SEQ_TEMP so that if you prefer, you can extract the **create sequence** statement for a single sequence at the end of the procedure.

```
begin
   open SEQ_CURSOR;
   Lv_Lineno  := 1;
   loop
      fetch SEQ_CURSOR into Lv_Seq_Owner,
                            Lv_Seq_Name,
                            Lv_Seq_Min_Value,
                            Lv_Seq_Max_Value,
                            Lv_Seq_Increment_By,
                            Lv_Seq_Cycle_Flag,
                            Lv_Seq_Order_Flag,
                            Lv_Seq_Cache_Size,
                            Lv_Seq_Last_Number;
      exit when SEQ_CURSOR%NOTFOUND;
```

The *Lv_Seq_Last_Number* variable contains the last sequence number written to disk. If a sequence uses caching, this number is the last number placed in the sequence cache in the SGA and is likely to be greater than the last sequence number that was really used. Because it is possible for this number to equal the last sequence value actually used, the start number for the **create sequence** statement is generated by incrementing this number by the sequence increment value. If you are using the sequence to generate consecutive numbers, and cannot have any missing values, you should not cache the sequence.

```
Lv_Start_No := Lv_Seq_Last_Number + Lv_Seq_Increment_By;
```

The next section of the script, shown in the following listing, inserts the beginning of the **create** statement into the temporary table. The **LOWER** function converts the text to lowercase to improve its readability. The generated start number is added to the string and written to the temporary table.

```
Lv_String  := 'CREATE SEQUENCE '   || LOWER(Lv_Seq_Owner
                                   || '.'
                                   || LOWER(Lv_Seq_Name)
                                   || ' START WITH '
                                   || Lv_Start_No;
    WRITE_OUT(Lv_Lineno, Lv_Seq_Owner, Lv_Seq_Name, Lv_String);
    Lv_Lineno  := Lv_Lineno + 1;
```

If you create a sequence with **nomaxvalue**, ORACLE will specify a maximum value of 10^{27} for an ascending sequence and −1 for a descending sequence. Since the script cannot distinguish between a specified value of 10^{27} using the keyword **maxvalue** and the keyword **nomaxvalue**, the keyword **maxvalue** is always used. **minvalue** specifies the lowest allowable value for a sequence and has no use unless the sequence has been generated to wrap back to the beginning number once the **maxvalue** has been reached. If the sequence is generated to wrap back, **minvalue** specifies the minimum value the sequence can have. **increment by** can be positive or negative, but cannot be zero. If it is negative, the sequence will generate descending numbers; if it is positive, the sequence will generate ascending numbers.

```
Lv_String := 'MAXVALUE ' || Lv_Seq_Max_Value ;
Lv_String := Lv_String   || ' MINVALUE '   || Lv_Seq_Min_Value;
Lv_String := Lv_String   || ' INCREMENT BY '  || Lv_Seq_Increment_By;
```

The next section of the script examines the **cycle** setting for the sequence. If **nocycle** is specified, the sequence will stop generating numbers once the maximum value (for ascending sequences) or minimum value (for descending sequences) has been reached. If you create a sequence with **cycle**, the sequence will wrap back to its beginning value once the maximum or minimum value has been reached.

```
if ( Lv_Seq_Cycle_Flag = 'Y' )
then
    Lv_String := Lv_String || ' CYCLE ';
else
    Lv_String := Lv_String || ' NOCYCLE ';
end if;
```

The **order** clause guarantees that sequence numbers will be generated in the order that they are requested and is not essential for primary keys, where only a unique value is needed. If you are using the sequence to generate consecutive numbers, like invoice or check numbers, you should specify **order** for the sequence.

```
if ( Lv_Seq_Order_Flag = 'Y' )
then
```

```
        Lv_String := Lv_String || ' ORDER ';
    else
        Lv_String := Lv_String || ' NOORDER ';
    end if;
```

The **cache** clause specifies how many values ORACLE will pre-generate and keep in memory for the sequence. Caching sequence values improves performance, but values that are cached are lost when the database is shut down and when the shared pool is flushed. The minimum number of values you can cache is two. The section of the gen_seq.sql script shown in the following listing generates the proper **nocache** or **cache** setting for the sequence.

```
    if ( Lv_Seq_Cache_Size = 0 )
    then
        Lv_String := Lv_String || ' NOCACHE ';
    else
        Lv_String := Lv_String || ' CACHE ' || Lv_Seq_Cache_Size;
    end if;
```

The final portion of the script writes the generated commands to the temporary table. The cursor loop ends and the procedure will loop back through the SEQ_CURSOR until all sequences have been generated. Once the **create** statements for all the sequences have been generated, they are spooled to a file named cre_seq.sql for later execution.

```
        WRITE_OUT(Lv_Lineno, Lv_Seq_Owner, Lv_Seq_Name, Lv_String);
        Lv_Lineno   := Lv_Lineno + 1;

        WRITE_OUT(Lv_Lineno, Lv_Seq_Owner, Lv_Seq_Name, '/');
        Lv_Lineno   := Lv_Lineno + 1;
    end loop;
    close SEQ_CURSOR;
end;
/
spool cre_seq.sql
select Text
  from SEQ_TEMP
 order by Id_Owner, Id_Name, Lineno
/
spool off
```

A sample cre_seq.sql script is shown in the following listing.

```
CREATE SEQUENCE scott.chess_saveid START WITH 2
MAXVALUE 999999999999999999999999999 MINVALUE 1 INCREMENT BY 1 NOCYCLE  NOORDER CACHE 20
/
```

As an alternative, if you want to use this script to document all the sequences for a particular owner, remove the **accept** *sequence_name* statement at the beginning of the script and change the **where** clause for the SEQ_CURSOR cursor to:

```
where Owner  = UPPER('&&sequence_owner')
```

If you want to document all sequences in your database that are not owned by SYS, remove the two **accept** statements from the beginning of the script and change the **where** clause for the SEQ_CURSOR cursor to:

```
where Owner != 'SYS'
```

gendblnk.sql

Generate Database Links

Database links are used to connect to another database and access data contained within the remote database. You can use database links to separate data while maintaining location transparency when accessing data. The gendblnk.sql script shown in the following listing generates a script to document the existing database links in your database. With some minor editing, the generated script can be run to re-create these links.

```
set term on echo off feedback off verify off heading off pagesize 0
select 'Creating database link build script...' from DUAL;
set term off

create table DL_TEMP (Lineno NUMBER, Grantor_Owner VARCHAR2(20),
                   Text VARCHAR2(800));
declare
   cursor LINK_CURSOR is
        select U.Name,
               L.Name,
               L.Userid,
               L.Password,
               L.Host
          from SYS.LINK$ L,
               SYS.USER$ U
         where L.Owner# = U.User#
         order by L.Name;

   Lv_Owner     SYS.USER$.Name%TYPE;
   Lv_Db_Link   SYS.LINK$.Name%TYPE;
   Lv_Username  SYS.LINK$.Userid%TYPE;
   Lv_Password  SYS.LINK$.Password%TYPE;
   Lv_Host      SYS.LINK$.Host%TYPE;
   Lv_String    VARCHAR2(800);
```

```
   Lv_User      VARCHAR2(255);
   Lv_Connect   VARCHAR2(255);
   Lv_Text      VARCHAR2(800);

   procedure WRITE_OUT(P_String VARCHAR2) is
   begin
      insert into DL_TEMP (Grantor_Owner, Text)
               values (Lv_Owner,P_String);
   end;

begin
   open LINK_CURSOR;
   loop
      fetch LINK_CURSOR into Lv_Owner,
                             Lv_Db_Link,
                             Lv_Username,
                             Lv_Password,
                             Lv_Host;
      exit when LINK_CURSOR%NOTFOUND;
      if (Lv_Owner = 'PUBLIC')
      then
         Lv_String := ('CREATE PUBLIC DATABASE LINK '||
              LOWER(Lv_Db_Link));
      else
         Lv_String := ('CREATE DATABASE LINK '||
              LOWER(Lv_Db_Link));
      end if;
      if (Lv_Username is not null)
      then
         Lv_User := ('CONNECT TO '||LOWER(Lv_Username)||
                  ' IDENTIFIED BY '||LOWER(Lv_Password));
      end if;
      if (Lv_Host is not null)
      then
         Lv_Connect := ('USING '''||Lv_Host||''''||';');
      end if;
      Lv_Text := Lv_String || ' ' || Lv_User || ' ' || Lv_Connect;
      WRITE_OUT(Lv_Text);
      Lv_User := ' ';
      Lv_Connect := ' ';
   end loop;
```

```
    close link_cursor;
end;
/
define cr=chr(10)
spool credblnk.sql
break on Downer skip 1
col Text format a60 word_wrap
select 'connect ' || DECODE (Grantor_Owner, 'PUBLIC', 'SYS',
          Grantor_Owner)|| '/' Downer,
        &cr||Text
  from DL_TEMP
 order by Downer
/
spool off
drop table DL_TEMP;
```

Sample output for the gendblnk.sql script is shown in the following listing.
```
connect APP/

CREATE DATABASE LINK myprod.world CONNECT TO app IDENTIFIED BY
appowner USING 'PROD';

CREATE DATABASE LINK mytest.world CONNECT TO app IDENTIFIED BY
appowner USING 'TEST';

connect SYS/

CREATE DATABASE LINK deve.world CONNECT TO app IDENTIFIED BY appowner
USING 'DEVE';

CREATE DATABASE LINK test.world CONNECT TO app IDENTIFIED BY appowner
USING 'TEST';

CREATE DATABASE LINK prod.world CONNECT TO app IDENTIFIED BY appowner
USING 'PROD';

connect SYSTEM/

CREATE DATABASE LINK sdeve.world CONNECT TO system IDENTIFIED BY
manager USING 'DEVE';
```

The generated file contains incomplete commands—the **connect** commands do not specify the passwords for the accounts. You will need to modify the created file (called credblnk.sql) in order to re-create the database links.

ANNOTATIONS

Since a DBA cannot create a private database link on behalf of a user, the output script will contain **connect** commands before each **create database link** command. In order for the database links to be created under the correct schema, you must add each user's password to the **connect** command.

PUBLIC database links require you to **connect** as 'SYS' or any user with the DBA role or with the CREATE PUBLIC DATABASE LINK system privilege.

The first portion of the gendblnk.sql script, shown in the following listing, sets up the environment for the gendblnk.sql script. The gendblnk.sql script does not prompt the user for any variables. After the environment is configured, the script creates a temporary table to hold each **create database link** command and its owner. The Grantor_Owner column generates the **connect** command before each **create** command.

```
set term on echo off feedback off verify off heading off pagesize 0
select 'Creating database link build script...' from DUAL;
set term off

create table DL_TEMP (Lineno NUMBER, Grantor_Owner VARCHAR2(20),
                      Text VARCHAR2(800));
```

The LINK_CURSOR cursor, shown in the following listing, uses the SYS.LINK$ table rather than the data dictionary view DBA_DB_LINKS because the password for the user you are connecting to in the link is not stored in clear text in the view, but is in the SYS.LINK$ table. The password is needed for the **connect to** clause of the **create database link** statement. The SYS.LINK$ table is joined to the SYS.USER$ table to extract the name of the owner of the database link.

```
declare
    cursor LINK_CURSOR is
            select U.Name,
                   L.Name,
                   L.Userid,
                   L.Password,
                   L.Host
              from SYS.LINK$ L,
                   SYS.USER$ U
             where L.Owner# = U.User#
             order by L.Name;
```

In the following listing, the procedure variables for the cursor are declared as TABLE_NAME.Column_Name%**TYPE**. Anchoring the variable definitions takes the column definition from within the database itself. If the column definition changes in a different version of ORACLE, the procedure will still work because the definition of the column has not been hard-coded.

```
Lv_Owner      SYS.USER$.Name%TYPE;
Lv_Db_Link    SYS.LINK$.Name%TYPE;
Lv_Username   SYS.LINK$.Userid%TYPE;
Lv_Password   SYS.LINK$.Password%TYPE;
Lv_Host       SYS.LINK$.Host%TYPE;
Lv_String     VARCHAR2(800);
Lv_User       VARCHAR2(255);
Lv_Connect    VARCHAR2(255);
Lv_Text       VARCHAR2(800);
```

The next portion of the gendblnk.sql script creates WRITE_OUT, an internal procedure to do the **insert** into the temporary table:

```
procedure WRITE_OUT(P_String VARCHAR2) is
begin
    insert into DL_TEMP (Grantor_Owner, Text)
            values (Lv_Owner,P_String);
end;
```

Public database links are owned by a pseudo-user named PUBLIC. The syntax for the **create database link** command differs depending on whether the link is public or private. The portion of the gendblnk.sql script shown in the following listing generates the proper **create** syntax. The SQL function **LOWER** is used to change the database link name to lowercase for readability.

```
begin
    open LINK_CURSOR;
    loop
        fetch LINK_CURSOR into Lv_Owner,
                               Lv_Db_Link,
                               Lv_Username,
                               Lv_Password,
                               Lv_Host;
        exit when LINK_CURSOR%NOTFOUND;

        if (Lv_Owner = 'PUBLIC')
        then
            Lv_String := ('CREATE PUBLIC DATABASE LINK '||
                LOWER(Lv_Db_Link));
```

```
      else
         Lv_String := ('CREATE DATABASE LINK '||
                LOWER(Lv_Db_Link));
      end if;
```

The next section of the gendblnk.sql script generates the **connect** clause for the link. If there is no username to connect to specified in the database link, the connection is made using the username and password of the userid accessing the link. Thus, each user also needs a userid and password on the remote database.

```
      if (Lv_Username is not null)
      then
         Lv_User := ('CONNECT TO '||LOWER(Lv_Username)||
                   ' IDENTIFIED BY '||LOWER(Lv_Password));
      end if;
```

The final portion of the gendblnk.sql script, shown in the following listing, generates the **using** clause for the link. The *Lv_Host* value is the database specification for the remote database.

Following the **using** clause generation, the script inserts the information on this database link into the temporary table, and initializes the variables for the next link to be processed.

```
      if (Lv_Host is not null)
      then
         Lv_Connect := ('USING '''||Lv_Host||''''||';');
      end if;
      Lv_Text := Lv_String || ' ' || Lv_User || ' ' || Lv_Connect;
      WRITE_OUT(Lv_Text);
      Lv_User := ' ';
      Lv_Connect := ' ';
   end loop;
   close link_cursor;
end;
/
define cr=chr(10)
```

The SQL*Plus command **define** allows you to assign a value to an internal variable and use it later with the '&' or '&&' feature to substitute the value into a command. In this section of the gendblnk.sql script, the variable *cr* is assigned the ASCII value of 10, or carriage return.

Now that all the links have been read and processed, the script extracts the information into a file to document the database links. Public database links are owned by SYS so the **DECODE** function is used to replace the owner PUBLIC with SYS in the **connect** command. If you prefer, you can substitute the name of any userid with either the DBA role or CREATE PUBLIC DATABASE LINK privilege for SYS.

The **break** on Downer in the following listing suppresses the display of repeated values for the column. If there are multiple database links owned by this user, the **connect** command will be generated only once. The **skip 1** of the **break** command forces a new line after the '/'. Concatenating the *cr* variable with the text string forces a new line for every database link displayed.

```
spool credblnk.sql
break on Downer skip 1
col Text format a60 word_wrap
select    'connect ' || DECODE (Grantor_Owner, 'PUBLIC', 'SYS',
                          Grantor_Owner)|| '/' Downer,
          &cr||Text
from      DL_TEMP
order by Downer
/
spool off
drop table DL_TEMP;
```

The following listing shows a sample credblnk.sql file.

```
connect APP/

CREATE DATABASE LINK myprod.world CONNECT TO app IDENTIFIED BY
appowner USING 'PROD';

CREATE DATABASE LINK mytest.world CONNECT TO app IDENTIFIED BY
appowner USING 'TEST';

connect SYS/

CREATE DATABASE LINK deve.world CONNECT TO app IDENTIFIED BY appowner
USING 'DEVE';

CREATE DATABASE LINK test.world CONNECT TO app IDENTIFIED BY appowner
USING 'TEST';

CREATE DATABASE LINK prod.world CONNECT TO app IDENTIFIED BY appowner
USING 'PROD';

connect SYSTEM/

CREATE DATABASE LINK sdeve.world CONNECT TO system IDENTIFIED BY
manager USING 'DEVE';
```

The output cannot be run without minor editing. Since you cannot create a database link for someone else, there has to be a **connect** for each database link owner in the credblnk.sql file. You must edit the output file to include the passwords before running credblnk.sql. There is only one **connect** statement per database link owner because of the **break** command.

Each of the database link names has the default domain, .WORLD, included as part of the name. You can create a database link name without specifying the default domain and ORACLE will append it to your database link name. You should not specify the default domain name in the **using** clause.

gen_grnt.sql

Generate Object Grants

In order for someone else to use an object you own, you have to grant them the privilege to use it. You can grant access to tables, views, sequences, synonyms, and snapshots. You can also grant the right to execute packages, procedures, and functions. In addition, you can grant another user the right to grant access to your object with the **with grant option** clause. Unless you have been granted access **with grant option**, you cannot grant access to another user's objects, even if you have been given the DBA role. Be very cautious about using **with grant option**; if you revoke the privilege from the user who has the grant option, the revoke cascades and the privilege is revoked from any user that he has granted the privilege to as well.

Grants can be made to PUBLIC, which allows all users in the database to access the object. However, before another user can write a package, procedure, or function which accesses an object you own, you must specifically grant him or her access to the object. Privileges inherited through a role, even the PUBLIC role, are not sufficient.

The object privileges you can grant are: **ALTER**, **SELECT**, **INSERT**, **UPDATE**, **DELETE**, **INDEX**, and **REFERENCES**. The last two apply to tables only: **INDEX** allows the user to create an index on the table and **REFERENCES** allows the user to create a constraint on the table. **REFERENCES** cannot be granted to a role. You can grant the **EXECUTE** privilege to packages, procedures, and functions. In ORACLE8, there is a new privilege, **READ**, which refers to permission to access operating system directories.

The following script, gen_grnt.sql, generates a script to document the grants on a table. With some minor editing of the output file to include the appropriate password, the script can be run to re-create the grants.

```
set echo off term off verify off feedback off pagesize 0

set term on
select 'Creating grants build script...' from DUAL;
accept table_name  prompt "Enter the name of the table: "
```

```
accept tab_owner prompt "Enter table owner              : "
set term off

drop    table GRANT_TEMP
/

create table GRANT_TEMP
    (
        Lineno        NUMBER,
        Table_Owner   VARCHAR2(30),
        Table_Name    VARCHAR2(30),
        Text          VARCHAR2(800)
    )
/
declare
    cursor GRANT_CURSOR is
        select Grantee,
               Grantor,
               Owner,
               Table_Name,
               Privilege,
               Grantable
          from DBA_TAB_PRIVS
         where Owner      = UPPER('&&tab_owner')
           and Table_Name like UPPER('&&table_name')
         order by Owner,Table_Name,Grantor,Grantee,Privilege,Grantable;

    Lv_TP_Grantee         SYS.DBA_TAB_PRIVS.Grantee%TYPE;
    Lv_TP_Grantor         SYS.DBA_TAB_PRIVS.Grantor%TYPE;
    Lv_TP_Owner           SYS.DBA_TAB_PRIVS.Owner%TYPE;
    Lv_TP_Table_Name      SYS.DBA_TAB_PRIVS.Table_Name%TYPE;
    Lv_TP_Privilege       SYS.DBA_TAB_PRIVS.Privilege%TYPE;
    Lv_TP_Grantable       SYS.DBA_TAB_PRIVS.Grantable%TYPE;
    Prior_Grantor         SYS.DBA_TAB_PRIVS.Grantor%TYPE;
    Lv_String             VARCHAR2(2000);
    Lv_Lineno             NUMBER := 0;

    procedure WRITE_OUT(P_Line INTEGER, P_Owner VARCHAR2, P_Name VARCHAR2,
                        P_String VARCHAR2) is
    begin
       insert into GRANT_TEMP (Lineno, Table_Owner, Table_Name, Text)
             values (P_Line,P_Owner,P_Name,P_String);
    end;
```

```
begin
    Prior_Grantor := ' ';
    Lv_Lineno := 1;
    open GRANT_CURSOR;

    loop
        fetch GRANT_CURSOR into      Lv_TP_Grantee,
                                     Lv_TP_Grantor,
                                     Lv_TP_Owner,
                                     Lv_TP_Table_Name,
                                     Lv_TP_Privilege,
                                     Lv_TP_Grantable;
        exit when GRANT_CURSOR%NOTFOUND;

        if (Prior_Grantor != Lv_TP_Grantor)
        then
            Prior_Grantor := Lv_TP_Grantor;
            Lv_String  := 'CONNECT ' || Lv_TP_Grantor || '/PASSWORD';
            WRITE_OUT(Lv_Lineno, Lv_TP_Grantor, Lv_TP_Table_Name, Lv_String);
            Lv_Lineno  := Lv_Lineno + 1;
        end if;

        Lv_String := 'GRANT '          ||
                     Lv_TP_Privilege  ||
                     ' ON '           ||
                     Lv_TP_Owner      ||
                     '.'              ||
                     Lv_TP_Table_Name ||
                     ' TO '           ||
                     Lv_TP_Grantee;

        if (Lv_TP_Grantable = 'YES' )
        then
            Lv_String := Lv_String     || ' WITH GRANT OPTION';
        end if;

        WRITE_OUT(Lv_Lineno, Lv_TP_Owner, Lv_TP_Table_Name, Lv_String);
        Lv_Lineno     := Lv_Lineno + 1;
        WRITE_OUT(Lv_Lineno, Lv_TP_Owner, Lv_TP_Table_Name, '/');
        Lv_Lineno     := Lv_Lineno + 1;
```

```
   end loop;

   close GRANT_CURSOR;
end;
/

spool cre_grnt.sql
select Text
  from GRANT_TEMP
 order by Lineno
/
spool off
```

Sample output for the gen_grnt.sql script is shown in the following listing.

```
CONNECT DEMO/PASSWORD
GRANT SELECT ON DEMO.JOB TO PUBLIC
/
GRANT SELECT ON DEMO.JOB TO QC_USER
/
GRANT SELECT ON DEMO.JOB TO SCOTT WITH GRANT OPTION
/
CONNECT SCOTT/PASSWORD
GRANT SELECT ON DEMO.JOB TO QC_USER
/
```

Prior to running the cre_grnt.sql script, you must provide the passwords for each of the accounts used.

ANNOTATIONS

Since a DBA cannot create a grant on behalf of a user unless specifically granted the privilege **with grant option**, the output script will contain **connect** clauses before the **grant** statement(s) if the grantor changes. In order for the privileges to be granted, you must replace the word "PASSWORD" with the correct user's password in the **connect** clause.

Although the script as written will return grants for a single object, it uses a cursor because there can be multiple grants on an object. In addition, using a cursor also allows you to enter a wildcard value or to modify the script to select all objects for an owner or all objects in the database. The script will generate a script to re-create the grants on the requested object. It uses a temporary table to hold individual lines of the **connect** and **grant** statements, writing to the table rather than using DBMS_OUTPUT.PUT_LINE so that you can extract the information for an individual grant on the table. Using the DBMS_OUTPUT procedure would force you to save and edit the output file for the grant you want.

The first section of the script, shown in the following listing, does the initial setup, prompting for the table name and table owner for later use via the **accept** command. The **accept** command, unlike the '&' or '&&' operators, allows you to define your own prompt for the variable. You can enter the table name with the '%' wildcard to generate a script for all grants on objects with a similar name.

Although the prompt asks for the table name and owner, the word "table" is misleading and is used merely to be consistent with ORACLE's terminology in the DBA_TAB_PRIVS data dictionary view. You can issue grants on tables, views, sequences, synonyms, snapshots, packages, procedures, functions, and, as of ORACLE8, directories.

The SQL*Plus **set** command turns off headers (**pagesize 0**), row counts (**feedback off**), and displays of old and new values for the *table_name* and *table_owner* variables (**verify off**).

```
set echo off term off verify off feedback off pagesize 0

set term on
select 'Creating grants build script...' from DUAL;

accept table_name  prompt "Enter the name of the table: "
accept tab_owner   prompt "Enter table owner          : "
set term off
```

The next section of the gen_grnt.sql script, shown in the following listing, creates a temporary table to hold each **connect** and **grant** command and its owner. The Lineno column orders the lines of the **connect** and **grant** commands.

```
drop    table GRANT_TEMP
/

create table GRANT_TEMP
    (
        Lineno       NUMBER,
        Table_Owner  VARCHAR2(30),
        Table_Name   VARCHAR2(30),
        Text         VARCHAR2(800)
    )
/
```

The next section of the script, shown in the following listing, defines the GRANT_CURSOR cursor. The GRANT_CURSOR cursor selects the information from DBA_TAB_PRIVS where the table name matches the input variable *table_name* and the table owner matches the input variable *tab_owner*. Using **like** in the **where** clause instead of = allows for wildcards.

Both the owner and the grantor are selected from the view. In most cases, the grantor and the owner will be the same. The grantor can be a user other than the owner if a user has been granted the privilege **with grant option**.

```
declare
    cursor GRANT_CURSOR is
            select Grantee,
                   Grantor,
                   Owner,
                   Table_Name,
                   Privilege,
                   Grantable
             from DBA_TAB_PRIVS
            where Owner      = UPPER('&&tab_owner')
              and Table_Name like UPPER('&&table_name')
            order by Owner,Table_Name,Grantor,Grantee,Privilege,Grantable;
```

The procedure variables for the cursor are declared as TABLE_NAME.Column_Name%**TYPE**. Anchoring the variables' definitions takes the column definition from within the database itself. If the column definition changes in a different version of ORACLE, the procedure will still work because the definition of the column has not been hard-coded. The variable *Prior_Grantor* determines when a new **connect** statement is required. The variable *Lv_Lineno* orders the lines of the **connect** and **grant** statements and is initialized to 0.

```
    Lv_TP_Grantee           SYS.DBA_TAB_PRIVS.Grantee%TYPE;
    Lv_TP_Grantor           SYS.DBA_TAB_PRIVS.Grantor%TYPE;
    Lv_TP_Owner             SYS.DBA_TAB_PRIVS.Owner%TYPE;
    Lv_TP_Table_Name        SYS.DBA_TAB_PRIVS.Table_Name%TYPE;
    Lv_TP_Privilege         SYS.DBA_TAB_PRIVS.Privilege%TYPE;
    Lv_TP_Grantable         SYS.DBA_TAB_PRIVS.Grantable%TYPE;
    Prior_Grantor           SYS.DBA_TAB_PRIVS.Grantor%TYPE;
    Lv_String               VARCHAR2(2000);
    Lv_Lineno               NUMBER := 0;
```

The next section of the script creates WRITE_OUT, an internal procedure to **insert** the generated text into the temporary table.

```
    procedure WRITE_OUT(P_Line INTEGER, P_Owner VARCHAR2, P_Name VARCHAR2,
                    P_String VARCHAR2) is
```

```
begin
    insert into GRANT_TEMP (Lineno, Table_Owner, Table_Name, Text)
            values (P_Line,P_Owner,P_Name,P_String);
end;
```

Granted privileges are stored as separate rows in the DBA_TAB_PRIVS view. Even if you **grant all** to a user, ORACLE converts that to the individual privileges and stores them separately. Additionally, you can **grant** privileges on an object to more than one user. Because of this, the cursor GRANT_CURSOR is used to extract all the granted privileges on the object. *Lv_Lineno* is used to order the rows in the temporary table GRANT_TEMP so that if you prefer, you can extract the **connect** and **grant** statements for a single grantee at the end of the procedure.

```
begin
    Prior_Grantor := ' ';
    Lv_Lineno := 1;
    open GRANT_CURSOR;

    loop
        fetch GRANT_CURSOR into     Lv_TP_Grantee,
                                    Lv_TP_Grantor,
                                    Lv_TP_Owner,
                                    Lv_TP_Table_Name,
                                    Lv_TP_Privilege,
                                    Lv_TP_Grantable;
        exit when GRANT_CURSOR%NOTFOUND;
```

Each time the grantor changes, a new **connect** statement is necessary. The variable *Prior_Grantor* tracks when the grantor changes. The following section of the gen_grnt.sql script generates the proper **connect** command.

```
        if (Prior_Grantor != Lv_TP_Grantor)
        then
            Prior_Grantor := Lv_TP_Grantor;
            Lv_String   := 'CONNECT ' || Lv_TP_Grantor || '/PASSWORD';
            WRITE_OUT(Lv_Lineno, Lv_TP_Grantor, Lv_TP_Table_Name, Lv_String);
            Lv_Lineno   := Lv_Lineno + 1;
        end if;
```

The next section of the script generates the **grant** command, and, if the privilege has been granted **with grant option**, that information is added to the statement before it is written to the table. There will be one **grant** command for each privilege.

```
        Lv_String := 'GRANT '           ||
                        Lv_TP_Privilege  ||
                        ' ON '           ||
                        Lv_TP_Owner      ||
```

```
                    '.'                ||
                    Lv_TP_Table_Name ||
                    ' TO '             ||
                    Lv_TP_Grantee;

          if (Lv_TP_Grantable = 'YES' )
          then
              Lv_String := Lv_String    || ' WITH GRANT OPTION';
          end if;
```

In the final section of the script, the statement is written to the file and a '/' is added to complete the SQL command.

The cursor loop ends and the procedure will loop back through the GRANT_CURSOR until **grant** statements for all privileges on the object have been generated. The cursor then closes and the procedure exits.

```
          WRITE_OUT(Lv_Lineno, Lv_TP_Owner, Lv_TP_Table_Name, Lv_String);
          Lv_Lineno      := Lv_Lineno + 1;
          WRITE_OUT(Lv_Lineno, Lv_TP_Owner, Lv_TP_Table_Name, '/');
          Lv_Lineno      := Lv_Lineno + 1;
       end loop;

       close GRANT_CURSOR;
end;
/
spool cre_grnt.sql
select Text
  from GRANT_TEMP
 order by Lineno
 /
spool off
```

Once the **connect** and **grant** statements for all the privileges have been generated, they are spooled to a file for later execution. By default, the output file is named cre_grnt.sql. A sample cre_grnt.sql file is shown in the following listing.

```
CONNECT DEMO/PASSWORD
GRANT SELECT ON DEMO.JOB TO PUBLIC
/
GRANT SELECT ON DEMO.JOB TO QC_USER
/
GRANT SELECT ON DEMO.JOB TO SCOTT WITH GRANT OPTION
/
CONNECT SCOTT/PASSWORD
GRANT SELECT ON DEMO.JOB TO QC_USER
/
```

In the sample output in the preceding listing, the **SELECT** privilege has been **grant**ed directly to PUBLIC, QC_USER and to SCOTT **with grant option**. In addition, SCOTT has in turn granted the **SELECT** privilege directly to QC_USER. Should the DEMO user **revoke** the **SELECT** privilege from SCOTT, the QC_USER will also lose that privilege from SCOTT but will keep it from DEMO. Because of this cascading **revoke**, you should be very careful when using **with grant option**.

As an alternative, if you want to use this script to document all the privileges on all objects for a particular owner, remove the **accept** *table_name* statement at the beginning of the script and change the **where** clause for the GRANT_CURSOR cursor to:

```
where Owner  = UPPER('&&table_owner')
```

If you want to document all privileges on objects in your database that are not owned by SYS, remove the two **accept** statements from the beginning of the script and change the **where** clause for the GRANT_CURSOR cursor to:

```
where Owner != 'SYS'
```

Space
Management

Management of the space used by your data requires you to understand how your data is stored, where it is stored, and how new space is acquired. In this chapter, you will see scripts that simplify the management of the space available to your objects. For example, you can use the diagnostic scripts in this chapter to see how the current space is allocated, and you can use the utility scripts to estimate the space requirements of new objects.

The major scripts presented in this chapter are:

free_ext.sql	List available space within each datafile and tablespace
fragment.sql	List contiguous extents within each datafile of a tablespace
file_ext.sql	List the tablespace datafiles and extension information
free_spc.sql	Report on free space percentages within each tablespace
usr_quot.sql	List by user and by tablespace the resources used and the quota allocated
def_stor.sql	List the default storage values for objects created within tablespaces
seg_spac.sql	List the space used and the next extent for all segments owned by a user
seg_info.sql	List the default storage for a segment and all the extents allocated to this segment
temp_seg.sql	List the size and number of extents of all temporary segments in the database
max_exts.sql	List the segments that do not have maxextents set to unlimited
coalesce.sql	Force a tablespace to be coalesced
len_long.sql	Measure the length of a LONG value
len_lob.sql	Measure the length of a LOB value
len_row.sql	Measure the average row length for a table
size_tab.sql	Estimate the storage requirements for a table
size_ind.sql	Estimate the storage requirements for an index

Diagnostics

You can use the scripts in this section to determine how the space in your database is allocated. The diagnostic scripts in this section include reports of space used by objects (such as tables and temporary segments) as well as free space.

free_ext.sql

Space Available in the Database

How large is your database? How many tablespaces do you have and how many datafiles are there within the tablespaces? How much space within each of the tablespaces is still available? Rather than finding out this information when users are getting errors, it is important to monitor the available space within the tablespaces as well as the database as a whole. This allows you to allocate additional datafiles or defragment existing datafiles before users begin to have problems.

The following script will tell you the total space allocated and the total space remaining by datafile within the tablespace for every datafile and tablespace in the database.

```
set feedback off term off echo off pagesize 60 linesize 80 newpage 0
spool free_space.log
ttitle center 'DATABASE REMAINING SPACE BY TABLESPACE '
col Tablespace_Name heading 'TABLESPACE|NAME' format a15
col File_Name heading 'FILE' format a30
col File_Len heading 'SIZE' format 9,999,999
col Remaining heading 'BLOCKS|REMAINING' format 9,999,999
col Total_Space heading 'TOTAL|SPACE' format 9,999,999
break on report on Tablespace_Name skip 1 on File_Name on Total_Space
compute sum of Remaining on Tablespace_Name
compute sum of Remaining on report
compute sum of Total_Space on Tablespace_Name
compute sum of Total_Space on report

select FS.Tablespace_Name,
       File_Name,
       SUM(FS.Blocks) Remaining,
       DF.Blocks Total_Space
  from DBA_FREE_SPACE FS, DBA_DATA_FILES DF
 where FS.File_Id = DF.File_Id
 group by FS.Tablespace_Name,
       File_Name, DF.Blocks
order by FS.Tablespace_Name,File_Name
/
spool off
```

Sample output for the preceding script is shown in the following listing.

DATABASE REMAINING SPACE BY TABLESPACE

TABLESPACE NAME	FILE	BLOCKS REMAINING	TOTAL SPACE
IDX1	/home01/oracle/indx_1_test	426,218	511,744
	/home01/oracle/indx_2_test	146,228	511,744
**************	*****************************	----------	----------
sum		572,446	1,023,488
RBS	/home01/oracle/rbs_test	508,543	511,744
**************	*****************************	----------	----------
sum		508,543	511,744
SYSTEM	/home01/oracle/sys_test	5,427	25,344
**************	*****************************	----------	----------
sum		5,427	25,344
TEMP	/home01/oracle/temp2_test	511,743	511,744
	/home01/oracle/temp_test	25,343	25,344
**************	*****************************	----------	----------
sum		537,086	537,088
TEMP_TABLES	/home01/oracle/temptbl.dbf	1,279	1,280
**************	*****************************	----------	----------
sum		1,279	1,280
USR1	/home01/oracle/user_1_test	13,446	511,744
	/home01/oracle/user_2_test	15,893	511,744
**************	*****************************	----------	----------
sum		29,339	1,023,488
		----------	----------
sum		1,654,120	3,122,432

The output lists not only the space available within the tablespace but also within each datafile in the tablespace. A tablespace can have a large amount of free space remaining and still not have enough room for the next extent requested. This is caused by a large number of datafiles with only a small amount of space available in each one. The USR1 tablespace is an example of this.

The TEMP tablespace shows almost the entire allocated space as free space. This indicates that the report was run when there was little activity in the database, or there would be temporary segments in use and the tablespace would not be totally available.

Even if no space has been allocated within a datafile, there will always be one block in use for the datafile header block.

ANNOTATIONS

The free_ext.sql script uses the SQL*Plus reporting capabilities to format the output for readability. The **break on** command suppresses the display of duplicate values in a column. If you omit an action with the **break on** command, it also marks the place in the report that SQL*Plus will perform the computation you specify in a corresponding **compute** command.

```
set feedback off term off echo off pagesize 60 linesize 80 newpage 0
spool free_space.log
ttitle center 'DATABASE REMAINING SPACE BY TABLESPACE '
col Tablespace_Name heading 'TABLESPACE|NAME' format a15
col File_Name heading 'FILE' format a30
col File_Len heading 'SIZE' format 9,999,999
col Remaining heading 'BLOCKS|REMAINING' format 9,999,999
col Total_Space heading 'TOTAL|SPACE' format 9,999,999
break on report on Tablespace_Name skip 1 on File_Name on Total_Space
```

If multiple **on** clauses are used in a **break** command, the breaks are processed from left to right (outermost break to innermost) with a break at the outermost level superceding the break on an inner level.

This section of the script instructs SQL*Plus to compute the values of all columns in a **compute** command at the end of the script (on report); to skip a line each time the tablespace name changes (on Tablespace_Name skip 1); to compute the values of all columns in a **compute** command each time the tablespace name changes and to suppress the printing of the tablespace name if there is more than one data file associated with it (on Tablespace_Name); and to suppress the printing of the total space used by the tablespace each time the filename changes, by having that clause (on Total_Space) follow the File_Name break.

```
compute sum of Remaining on Tablespace_Name
compute sum of Remaining on report
compute sum of Total_Space on Tablespace_Name
compute sum of Total_Space on report
```

This section will compute subtotals and totals of the remaining and total space each time the tablespace name or report breaks. For the **compute** command to be processed, the column it references in the **on** clause must be part of the select command and also part of the most recent **break** command.

```
select FS.Tablespace_Name,
       File_Name,
       SUM(FS.Blocks) Remaining,
       DF.Blocks Total_Space
  from DBA_FREE_SPACE FS, DBA_DATA_FILES DF
 where FS.File_Id = DF.File_Id
 group by FS.Tablespace_Name,
       File_Name, DF.Blocks
order by FS.Tablespace_Name,File_Name
/
spool off
```

The DBA_FREE_SPACE view contains a row for every free extent in the database. It is neither practical nor useful to list every free extent available. In order to display a summary row of data per data file, the **group by** clause of the **select** command is used. The selected columns in a **select** statement with the **group by** clause must either be a group function (such as **SUM**) or be listed in the **group by** clause itself.

DATABASE REMAINING SPACE BY TABLESPACE

TABLESPACE NAME	FILE	BLOCKS REMAINING	TOTAL SPACE
IDX1	/home01/oracle/indx_1_test	426,218	511,744
	/home01/oracle/indx_2_test	146,228	511,744
****************	****************************	----------	----------
sum		572,446	1,023,488
RBS	/home01/oracle/rbs_test	508,543	511,744
****************	****************************	----------	----------
sum		508,543	511,744
SYSTEM	/home01/oracle/sys_test	5,427	25,344
****************	****************************	----------	----------
sum		5,427	25,344
TEMP	/home01/oracle/temp2_test	511,743	511,744
	/home01/oracle/temp_test	25,343	25,344
****************	****************************	----------	----------
sum		537,086	537,088

```
TEMP_TABLES      /home01/oracle/temptbl.dbf          1,279       1,280
***************  *****************************  ----------  ----------
sum                                                  1,279       1,280


USR1             /home01/oracle/user_1_test         13,446     511,744
                 /home01/oracle/user_2_test         15,893     511,744
***************  *****************************  ----------  ----------
sum                                                 29,339   1,023,488


                                               ----------  ----------
sum                                             1,654,120   3,122,432
```

You can use this report to track how space usage is growing within your database. By comparing reports over time, you can see how quickly tablespaces are filling and add datafiles before your applications start getting space allocation errors.

The space allocated and used is stated in database blocks and is relative to the database block size of your database (set by the DB_BLOCK_SIZE init.ora parameter during database creation). In the preceding example, the initial datafile in the SYSTEM tablespace has 5,427 database blocks remaining, an indication that it is time to add another datafile to SYSTEM, especially if there are a large number of stored procedures being developed for this application. Stored procedure source code is stored in SYS.SOURCE$ and other data dictionary tables. You cannot move those data dictionary tables out of the SYSTEM tablespace, so you must maintain adequate free space in the SYSTEM tablespace.

fragment.sql

Tablespace Fragmentation

While the prior section shows you the total amount of space available within each datafile and tablespace, it does not tell you how fragmented that space is. You can have a large amount of space available and still get space allocation errors if your tablespace is very fragmented. The PL/SQL script below will display the extents available within your tablespace and the size of each extent.

To run the PL/SQL script, you first have to create a table to hold the intermediate results.

```
create table FREESP (
Fname   VARCHAR2(513),
Tspace  VARCHAR2(30),
First   NUMBER(10),
Blocks  NUMBER(10),
Last    NUMBER(10))
/
```

Rather than create this table each time the PL/SQL script is run (and further fragment the tablespace), FREESP is created once and **truncate**d before each use in the fragment.sql script.

```
set feedback off term off verify off pagesize 60 newpage 0 linesize 66
truncate table FREESP;
declare
  Fileid    NUMBER(9);
  Filename  VARCHAR2(513);
  Tsname    VARCHAR2(30);
  Cursor Tablespaces is
     select File_Name, File_ID, Tablespace_Name
       from DBA_DATA_FILES
       where Tablespace_Name = upper('&1');
begin
open tablespaces;
loop
  fetch Tablespaces into Filename, Fileid, Tsname;
  exit when Tablespaces%NOTFOUND;
declare
  First   NUMBER(10);
  Blocks  NUMBER(10);
  Last    NUMBER(10);
  Tfirst  NUMBER(10);
  Tblocks NUMBER(10);
  Tlast   NUMBER(10);
  Cursor Free is
    select Block_ID a, Blocks b, Block_ID+Blocks c
      from DBA_FREE_SPACE
    where File_ID = Fileid
    order by Block_ID;
begin
  open Free;
  fetch Free into First, Blocks, Last;
  if Free%NOTFOUND
   then
       goto close_free;
  end if;
  loop
    fetch Free into Tfirst, Tblocks, Tlast;
    exit when Free%NOTFOUND;
    if Tfirst = Last
      then
        Blocks := Blocks + Tblocks;
```

```
        Last := Tlast;
      else
        insert into FREESP
          values (Filename, Tsname, First, Blocks, Last-1);
        commit;
        First := Tfirst;
        Blocks := Tblocks;
        Last := Tlast;
    end if;
  end loop;
      insert into FREESP
          values (Filename, Tsname, First, Blocks, Last-1);
  commit;
<<close_free>>
  close Free;
end;
end loop;
commit;
close Tablespaces;
end;
/

set term off echo off
col Db_Name new_value Instance
select 'INSTANCE NAME' Description, value Db_name from V$PARAMETER
   where UPPER(Name) = 'DB_NAME'
/
ttitle center Instance ' TABLESPACE FRAGMENTATION REPORT'
col Tspace heading 'TABLESPACE|NAME' format a10 trunc
col Fname heading 'FILE' format A30 trunc
col First heading 'START|BLOCK' format 999,999
col Blocks heading 'BLOCKS|REMAINING' format 99,999,999
break on report on Tspace skip 1 on Fname skip 1
compute sum of Blocks on Fname
compute sum of Blocks on report

spool fragmentation.rpt
select Tspace, Fname, First, Blocks
  from FREESP
 order by Tspace,Fname,First;

spool off
```

The script runs for a single tablespace and expects the tablespace name as input. The output of the script is shown in the following listing.

```
                        test TABLESPACE FRAGMENTATION REPORT
```

TABLESPACE NAME	FILE	START BLOCK	BLOCKS REMAINING
USR1	/home01/oracle/user_1_test	3,215	3
		4,065	40
		5,586	75
		8,475	145
		10,080	110
		10,545	100
		21,832	3,215
		50,563	85
		61,054	111
		85,045	1,420
		95,996	7
		108,526	70
		121,503	121
		125,689	275
		127,250	450
		131,418	58
		151,903	895
		159,394	50
		171,876	325
		270,022	665
		292,477	18
		328,862	50
		328,922	85
		334,617	110
		344,614	285
		359,493	670
		360,328	675
		365,297	125
		366,197	325
		366,567	435
		369,117	33
		371,945	13
		372,033	220
		372,833	155
		375,651	150
		423,382	195
		425,657	100

```
                                       431,110               72
                                       434,692            1,905
                                       481,830               40
          ******************************                 ----------
          sum                                            13,881

          /home01/oracle/user_2_test      4,812              125
                                         10,849               50
                                         10,924               40
                                         26,151              102
                                         28,888              360
                                         29,758              455
                                         31,909              355
                                         51,235              105
                                        135,832              145
                                        136,197              325
                                        166,270               18
                                        186,381              590
                                        202,906            2,503
```

test TABLESPACE FRAGMENTATION REPORT

TABLESPACE NAME	FILE	START BLOCK	BLOCKS REMAINING
USR1	/home01/oracle/user_2_test	258,757	2,910
		346,192	50
		401,162	1,705
		442,167	40
		468,537	1,090
		476,277	1,205
		478,717	50
		481,342	110
		481,477	1,450
		483,367	235
		487,142	915
		502,107	345

```
          ******************************                 ----------
          sum                                            15,278


          **********                                     ----------
          sum                                            29,159
```

This tablespace is badly fragmented, and while it might seem that there is plenty of space left, most of the extents are less than 500 blocks. Unless this tablespace is either read-only or contains tables which are updated infrequently, another datafile should be added.

ANNOTATIONS

The fragment.sql script will read the DBA_FREE_SPACE data dictionary view, sum up contiguous extents if necessary, store the results in a temporary table, and report, by datafile, on the fragmentation in your tablespace. Unless you have set the **pctincrease** for the tablespace to non-zero, ORACLE will not automatically coalesce this space until you either coalesce it manually (via the **coalesce** option of the **alter tablespace** command) or force ORACLE to dynamically coalesce extents by requesting an extent that is larger than any of the ones that are available.

ORACLE does not merge contiguous free extents unless there is no other alternative; thus the tablespace becomes more and more fragmented as ORACLE first allocates space from the largest free extent it encounters in the tablespace before reusing and coalescing the smaller free extents created as objects are dropped. Figure 6-1 illustrates available extents within a tablespace before and after a request for an extent has been allocated.

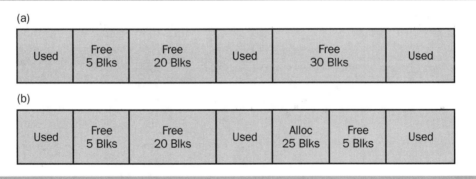

FIGURE 6-1. (a) Tablespace fragmentation before 25-block extent request
(b) Tablespace fragmentation after 25-block extent request allocated

In order to run the fragment.sql script, you must first build a table called FREESP, which is used to store information about the datafiles and extents. If your tablespace has a non-zero **pctincrease**, the data in this table will be the same as that in DBA_FREE_SPACE, since SMON periodically coalesces the free space in tablespaces with non-zero **pctincrease** settings.

To create the FREESP table, execute the following script:

```
create table FREESP (
Fname   VARCHAR2(513),
Tspace VARCHAR2(30),
First  NUMBER(10),
Blocks NUMBER(10),
Last   NUMBER(10))
/
```

The first section of the fragment.sql script will read through the DBA_DATA_FILES view for the datafiles associated with the requested tablespace. For each datafile found, the script loops through DBA_FREE_SPACE to extract the extent information.

```
set feedback off term off verify off pagesize 60 newpage 0 linesize 66
truncate table FREESP;
declare
  Fileid     NUMBER(9);
  Filename   VARCHAR2(513);
  Tsname     VARCHAR2(30);
  Cursor Tablespaces is
     select File_Name, File_ID, Tablespace_Name
       from DBA_DATA_FILES
      where Tablespace_Name = upper('&1');
begin
open tablespaces;
loop
  fetch Tablespaces into Filename, Fileid, Tsname;
  exit when Tablespaces%NOTFOUND;
```

For every datafile found, the script will open a cursor and read through DBA_FREE_SPACE, summing up the contiguous extents as it goes. Separate extents are contiguous if the Block_ID value plus the number of blocks minus 1 equals the next Block_ID found. If the extents are contiguous, the number of blocks is added to a holding variable and the next Block_ID is read. If the extents are not contiguous, the holding information is inserted into the FREESP table and the holding variables are reset. Once all the extents for a datafile have been processed, the inner cursor is closed and the next datafile information is gotten. Once all datafiles have been processed, the outer cursor is closed and the data in the intermediate table FREESP is reported.

```
declare
  First   NUMBER(10);
  Blocks  NUMBER(10);
```

```
    Last    NUMBER(10);
    Tfirst  NUMBER(10);
    Tblocks NUMBER(10);
    Tlast   NUMBER(10);
    Cursor Free is
      select Block_ID a, Blocks b, Block_ID+Blocks c
        from DBA_FREE_SPACE
       where File_ID = Fileid
       order by Block_ID;
begin
  open Free;
  fetch Free into First, Blocks, Last;
  if Free%NOTFOUND
   then
        goto close_free;
  end if;
  loop
    fetch Free into Tfirst, Tblocks, Tlast;
    exit when Free%NOTFOUND;
    if Tfirst = Last
      then
        Blocks := Blocks + Tblocks;
        Last := Tlast;
      else
        insert into FREESP
          values (Filename, Tsname, First, Blocks, Last-1);
        commit;
        First := Tfirst;
        Blocks := Tblocks;
        Last := Tlast;
    end if;
  end loop;
      insert into FREESP
          values (Filename, Tsname, First, Blocks, Last-1);
  commit;
<<close_free>>
  close Free;
end;
end loop;
commit;
close Tablespaces;
end;
/
```

Once all the datafiles have been checked, the information gathered in the FREESP table is displayed via SQL*Plus reporting commands. Using the **value** parameter, the instance name is captured for display in all page headers. The **break** and **compute** commands are used to create subtotal, total, and grand total values.

```
set term off echo off
col Db_Name new_value Instance
select 'INSTANCE NAME' Description, value Db_name from V$PARAMETER
   where UPPER(Name) = 'DB_NAME'
/
ttitle center Instance ' TABLESPACE FRAGMENTATION REPORT'
col Tspace heading 'TABLESPACE|NAME' format a10 trunc
col Fname heading 'FILE' format A30 trunc
col First heading 'START|BLOCK' format 999,999
col Blocks heading 'BLOCKS|REMAINING' format 99,999,999
break on report on Tspace skip 1 on Fname skip 1
compute sum of Blocks on Fname
compute sum of Blocks on report

spool fragmentation.rpt
select Tspace, Fname, First, Blocks
  from FREESP
 order by Tspace,Fname,First;

spool off
```

The output in the following listing shows that the tablespace USR1 in the TEST database is extremely fragmented. Although there are 29,159 total blocks available in the USR1 tablespace, the largest single extent that can be allocated is 3,215 blocks, with most of the extents much smaller. This tablespace may appear to have a good deal of space left, based on the total blocks available, but closer examination indicates possible problems. Monitoring the changes in this report over several days or weeks will show when additional datafiles will be needed.

```
            test TABLESPACE FRAGMENTATION REPORT

TABLESPACE                                  START      BLOCKS
NAME        FILE                            BLOCK    REMAINING
----------  ------------------------------ --------  -----------
USR1        /home01/oracle/user_1_test      3,215           3
                                            4,065          40
                                            5,586          75
                                            8,475         145
                                           10,080         110
                                           10,545         100
```

```
                                                     21,832        3,215
                                                     50,563           85
                                                     61,054          111
                                                     85,045        1,420
                                                     95,996            7
                                                    108,526           70
                                                    121,503          121
                                                    125,689          275
                                                    127,250          450
                                                    131,418           58
                                                    151,903          895
                                                    159,394           50
                                                    171,876          325
                                                    270,022          665
                                                    292,477           18
                                                    328,862           50
                                                    328,922           85
                                                    334,617          110
                                                    344,614          285
                                                    359,493          670
                                                    360,328          675
                                                    365,297          125
                                                    366,197          325
                                                    366,567          435
                                                    369,117           33
                                                    371,945           13
                                                    372,033          220
                                                    372,833          155
                                                    375,651          150
                                                    423,382          195
                                                    425,657          100
                                                    431,110           72
                                                    434,692        1,905
                                                    481,830           40
*******************************                              -----------
sum                                                              13,881

/home01/oracle/user_2_test            4,812          125
                                     10,849           50
                                     10,924           40
                                     26,151          102
                                     28,888          360
                                     29,758          455
                                     31,909          355
```

51,235	105
135,832	145
136,197	325
166,270	18
186,381	590
202,906	2,503

test TABLESPACE FRAGMENTATION REPORT

TABLESPACE NAME	FILE	START BLOCK	BLOCKS REMAINING
USR1	/home01/oracle/user_2_test	258,757	2,910
		346,192	50
		401,162	1,705
		442,167	40
		468,537	1,090
		476,277	1,205
		478,717	50
		481,342	110
		481,477	1,450
		483,367	235
		487,142	915
		502,107	345
*****************************			-----------
sum			15,278

**********	-----------
sum	29,159

If you periodically coalesce your tablespaces, or you have set the **pctincrease** to a non-zero value, you can run the fragment.sql script below without having to create a permanent FREESP table to store the intermediate information on fragmentation. The script reads through the DBA_FREE_SPACE view and reports the same information as the fragment.sql script. Since tablespaces with a non-zero **pctincrease** will not be coalesced, they are excluded from the report for readability. In general, it is not a good idea for the temporary tablespace to have a non-zero **pctincrease**.

The following script will generate the same output as the original script, as long as the requested tablespace has a non-zero **pctincrease**.

```
set term off echo off feedback off verify off pagesize 60 newpage 0
set linesize 66
col DB_Name new_value instance
```

```
select 'INSTANCE NAME' Description, Value DB_Name
  from V$PARAMETER
 where UPPER(name) = 'DB_NAME'
/
ttitle center instance ' TABLESPACE FRAGMENTATION REPORT'
col Tablespace_Name heading 'TABLESPACE|NAME' format a10 trunc
col File_Name heading 'FILE' format a30 trunc
col Block_ID heading 'START|BLOCK' format 999,999
col Blocks heading 'BLOCKS|REMAINING' format 99,999,999
break on report on Tablespace_Name skip 1 on File_Name skip 1
compute sum of blocks on File_Name
compute sum of blocks on report
spool fragment.rpt

select A.Tablespace_Name, File_Name, Block_ID, B.Blocks
  from DBA_DATA_FILES A, DBA_FREE_SPACE B, DBA_TABLESPACES C
 where C.Pct_Increase > 0
   and A.Tablespace_Name=C.Tablespace_Name
   and A.File_ID=B.File_ID
   and A.Tablespace_Name = upper('&1')
 order by A.Tablespace_Name, A.File_ID, Block_ID;

spool off
```

The output of this script is below. This output is identical to the output of the prior script. However, if the tablespace selected does not have a non-zero **pctincrease**, this script will return an empty report while the prior one will return data.

                    test TABLESPACE FRAGMENTATION REPORT

TABLESPACE NAME	FILE	START BLOCK	BLOCKS REMAINING
USR1	/home01/oracle/user_1_test	3,215	3
		4,065	40
		5,586	75
		8,475	145
		10,080	110
		10,545	100
		21,832	3,215
		50,563	85
		61,054	111
		85,045	1,420
		95,996	7

	108,526	70
	121,503	121
	125,689	275
	127,250	450
	131,418	58
	151,903	895
	159,394	50
	171,876	325
	270,022	665
	292,477	18
	328,862	50
	328,922	85
	334,617	110
	344,614	285
	359,493	670
	360,328	675
	365,297	125
	366,197	325
	366,567	435
	369,117	33
	371,945	13
	372,033	220
	372,833	155
	375,651	150
	423,382	195
	425,657	100
	431,110	72
	434,692	1,905
	481,830	40
******************************		-----------
sum		13,881
/home01/oracle/user_2_test	4,812	125
	10,849	50
	10,924	40
	26,151	102
	28,888	360
	29,758	455
	31,909	355
	51,235	105
	135,832	145
	136,197	325
	166,270	18
	186,381	590

```
                                             202,906        2,503

               test TABLESPACE FRAGMENTATION REPORT

TABLESPACE                                     START        BLOCKS
NAME          FILE                             BLOCK      REMAINING
----------    ------------------------------ --------    -----------
USR1          /home01/oracle/user_2_test      258,757        2,910
                                               346,192           50
                                               401,162        1,705
                                               442,167           40
                                               468,537        1,090
                                               476,277        1,205
                                               478,717           50
                                               481,342          110
                                               481,477        1,450
                                               483,367          235
                                               487,142          915
                                               502,107          345
              ****************************                 -----------
              sum                                             15,278


**********                                                 -----------
sum                                                           29,159
```

file_ext.sql

Which Files Can Extend

As of ORACLE7.2, you can set datafiles within a tablespace to automatically extend when they run out of space. Although implementing this option will make sure that users never run out of space (unless you run out of space on the disk that stores the datafile), you should use automatic extensions cautiously and monitor your space usage closely. Datafile extension is an indication that the objects within the database are not sized correctly and can mask a more serious problem within the application.

Autoextend can be implemented at the time you create the datafile via the **alter tablespace** or **create tablespace** command, or can be added to an existing datafile via the **alter database datafile** command.

To turn **autoextend** on, use the clause:

```
autoextend on [next [K/M] maxsize [UNLIMITED/integer [K/M]]]
```

The **autoextend** clause specifies the maximum size to which the datafile can expand and the size of each incremental extension. If you leave off the **next** and

maxsize parameters, the default for **maxsize** is UNLIMITED, and the default for **next** is one data block. Turning **autoextend off** sets **maxsize** and **next** to zero, and they must be reset if **autoextend** is turned back on. **Autoextend** cannot be used when using raw partitions. There are no flags within the database to indicate when a datafile has **autoextend**ed.

The following script will list which datafiles can extend and the extension sizes.

PROGRAMMER'S NOTE *If no tablespace has ever had **autoextend** turned on, the SYS.FILEXT$ table will not have been created and the script will fail.*

```
set term off verify off echo off feedback off
set linesize 80 pagesize 60
col Value new_value blksz noprint
col Maxext format 9999999999 heading 'MAXIMUM|EXTENDED SIZE'
col Incr format 999999999 heading 'EXTENSION|INCREMENT'
col Tablespace_Name format a15 heading 'TABLESPACE'
col File_Name format a30 heading 'FILE NAME'

select Value
  from V$PARAMETER
 where Name = 'db_block_size';

set term on

select Tablespace_Name,
       File_Name,
       Maxextend*&&blksz Maxext,
       Inc*&&blksz Incr
  from DBA_DATA_FILES, SYS.FILEXT$
 where File_Id=File#(+)
 order by Tablespace_Name, File_Name
/
```

Sample output for the preceding query is shown in the following listing.

TABLESPACE	FILE NAME	MAXIMUM EXTENDED SIZE	EXTENSION INCREMENT
ROLLBACK_DATA	D:\ORANT\DATABASE\RBS1ORCL.ORA		
SYSTEM	D:\ORANT\DATABASE\SYS1ORCL.ORA	209715200	10485760
TEMPORARY_DATA	D:\ORANT\DATABASE\TMP1ORCL.ORA	157286400	5242880
USER_DATA	D:\ORANT\DATABASE\USR1ORCL.ORA	157286400	5242880

A NULL value for the maximum size and increment indicates that the datafile does not have **autoextend** turned on.

ANNOTATIONS

The **column** command for the Value column will store the value of Value in the *blksz* variable for later use in the script. The **noprint** clause keeps the result of the query from displaying.

```
set term off verify off echo off feedback off
set linesize 80 pagesize 60
col Value new_value blksz noprint
col Maxext format 9999999999 heading 'MAXIMUM|EXTENDED SIZE'
col Incr format 999999999 heading 'EXTENSION|INCREMENT'
col Tablespace_Name format a15 heading 'TABLESPACE'
col File_Name format a30 heading 'FILE NAME'

select Value
  from V$PARAMETER
 where Name = 'db_block_size';

set term on
```

Maximum extension size and extent increments are stored in the database in a number of database blocks. In order to convert these to meaningful numbers, they are multiplied by the value of the database block size, stored in the variable *blksz*, and extracted in the prior **select** statement. For a database with a 4KB blocksize, setting **maxsize** to UNLIMITED translates to 17,179,860,992 (17GB).

This query displays all datafiles, whether or not they are **autoextend**able. Datafiles which are not in the SYS.FILEXT$ table and which are therefore not extendable are included in the output by the use of the outer join '**(+)**' clause. If you only want to display datafiles that can extend, remove the outer join clause from the query.

```
select Tablespace_Name,
       File_Name,
       Maxextend*&&blksz Maxext,
       Inc*&&blksz Incr
  from DBA_DATA_FILES, SYS.FILEXT$
 where File_Id=File#(+)
 order by Tablespace_Name, File_Name
/
```

If no datafile has been created with **autoextend** ON, the SYS.FILEXT$ table will not exist. This table does not get dropped once created, even if all datafiles have **autoextend** turned OFF.

TABLESPACE	FILE NAME	MAXIMUM EXTENDED SIZE	EXTENSION INCREMENT
ROLLBACK_DATA	D:\ORANT\DATABASE\RBS1ORCL.ORA		
SYSTEM	D:\ORANT\DATABASE\SYS1ORCL.ORA	209715200	10485760
TEMPORARY_DATA	D:\ORANT\DATABASE\TMP1ORCL.ORA	157286400	5242880
USER_DATA	D:\ORANT\DATABASE\USR1ORCL.ORA	157286400	5242880

The output listing shows that the SYSTEM, TEMPORARY_DATA and USER_DATA tablespaces have **autoextend** set to ON. The USER_DATA tablespace can grow to a maximum of 150MB, in 5MB increments.

As of ORACLE8, the data dictionary view DBA_DATA_FILES has been modified to contain the **autoextend** information. The columns for the ORACLE8 DBA_DATA_FILES view are shown in Table 6-1. The following query will return the same results as the prior query, but accesses only one view.

The Autoextensible column has possible values of YES or NO. If Autoextensible is NO, the MaxBytes, MaxBlocks, and Increment_By columns will contain zeros.

```
set term off verify off echo off feedback off
set linesize 80 pagesize 60
col Value new_value blksz noprint
col Maxext format a13 heading 'MAXIMUM|EXTENDED SIZE'
col Incr format a10 heading 'EXTENSION|INCREMENT'
col Tablespace_Name format a15 heading 'TABLESPACE'
col File_Name format a30 heading 'FILE NAME'

select Value
  from V$PARAMETER
 where Name = 'db_block_size';

set term on

select Tablespace_Name,
       File_Name,
       LPAD(DECODE(Maxblocks,0,' ',Maxblocks*&&blksz),15) Maxext,
       LPAD(DECODE(Increment_By,0,' ',Increment_By*&&blksz),10) Incr
  from DBA_DATA_FILES
 order by Tablespace_Name, File_Name
/
```

Column	Description
FILE_NAME	Name of the database file
FILE_ID	ID of the database file
TABLESPACE_NAME	Name of the tablespace to which the file belongs
BYTES	Size of the file in bytes
BLOCKS	Size of the file in ORACLE blocks
STATUS	File status: AVAILABLE or INVALID
RELATIVE_FNO	Relative file number (relative to the tablespace)
AUTOEXTENSIBLE	Indicates whether or not this datafile has **autoextend** enabled
MAXBYTES	Maximum file size in bytes
MAXBLOCKS	Maximum file size in blocks
INCREMENT_BY	Autoextension increment

TABLE 6-1.   ORACLE8 DBA_DATA_FILES View

Sample output for the preceding query is shown in the following listing.

```
                                               MAXIMUM    EXTENSION
TABLESPACE       FILE NAME                   EXTENDED SIZE  INCREMENT
---------------  ----------------------------  ------------- ----------
ROLLBACK_DATA    D:\ORANT\DATABASE\RBS1ORCL.ORA
SYSTEM           D:\ORANT\DATABASE\SYS1ORCL.ORA   209715200   10485760
TEMPORARY_DATA   D:\ORANT\DATABASE\TMP1ORCL.ORA   157286400    5242880
USER_DATA        D:\ORANT\DATABASE\USR1ORCL.ORA   157286400    5242880
```

ANNOTATIONS

The difference in the two scripts is in the following section of the **select** statement:

```
     LPAD(DECODE(Maxblocks,0,' ',Maxblocks*&&blksz),15) Maxext,
     LPAD(DECODE(Increment_By,0,' ',Increment_By*&&blksz),10) Incr
from DBA_DATA_FILES
```

The **DECODE** function replaces the zero value in the nonextendable rows with a NULL to make the output more readable. The **LPAD** function inserts leading blanks to right-justify the numeric values.

If you allow ORACLE8 to create the database for you (via the ORACLE installer), the SYSTEM and temporary tablespaces will be created with **autoextend** ON.

Free Space Within the Database

free_spc.sql

The queries in the preceding sections showed the total amount of space allocated to the database, and the greatest possible extension of each datafile. In this section, you will see queries that report on the free space within the database. Free space within datafiles has not yet been allocated by any extents in that datafile.

The free space query shown below uses the **from** clause subquery feature to group two queries separately and then join the result sets on the Tablespace_Name value. The query will show the largest free extent in the tablespace, the number of free extents in the tablespace, the total free space in the tablespace, and the percentage of the tablespace's available space that is free.

PROGRAMMER'S NOTE *Since this query uses a subquery within the **from** clause, it will only work in ORACLE7.2 and above.*

```
column Tablespace_Name format A20
column Pct_Free format 999.99

select Tablespace_Name,
       Max_Blocks,
       Count_Blocks,
       Sum_Free_Blocks,
       100*Sum_Free_Blocks/Sum_Alloc_Blocks AS Pct_Free
  from (select Tablespace_Name, SUM(Blocks) Sum_Alloc_Blocks
          from DBA_DATA_FILES
         group by Tablespace_Name),
       (select Tablespace_Name FS_TS_NAME,
               MAX(Blocks) AS Max_Blocks,
               COUNT(Blocks) AS Count_Blocks,
               SUM(Blocks) AS Sum_Free_Blocks
          from DBA_FREE_SPACE
         group by Tablespace_Name)
 where Tablespace_Name = FS_TS_NAME;
```

Sample output for the preceding query is shown in the following listing.

TABLESPACE_NAME	MAX_BLOCKS	COUNT_BLOCKS	SUM_FREE_BLOCKS	PCT_FREE
IDX1	487198	29	965726	94.36
RBS	452943	243	501343	97.97
SYSTEM	2763	4	3195	12.61
TEMP	460943	283	537086	100.00
TEMP_TABLES	634	1	634	49.53
USR1	293683	145	501372	48.99

The output shows the structure of the free space within each tablespace. In the USR1 tablespace, for example, there are 501,372 free database blocks (the Sum_Free_Blocks column). Those 501,372 blocks of free space are in 145 separate sections (the Count_Blocks column). The largest single free extent is 293,683 blocks in length (the Max_Blocks column). The free space within the USR1 tablespace accounts for 48.99 percent of the space in that tablespace (the Pct_Free column).

ANNOTATIONS

The query selects the tablespace name within each of the **from** clause subqueries. In the first **from** clause subquery, the Tablespace_Name column is selected from the DBA_DATA_FILES data dictionary view. An alias of Sum_Alloc_Blocks is given to the summation of the Blocks column in the DBA_DATA_FILES view. The Sum_Alloc_Blocks column's value will reflect the total number of allocated blocks in the database.

```
from (select Tablespace_Name, SUM(Blocks) Sum_Alloc_Blocks
        from DBA_DATA_FILES
        group by Tablespace_Name),
```

The second query in the **from** clause selects free space statistics from the DBA_FREE_SPACE view. In this query, the Tablespace_Name column is given the alias Fs_Ts_Name in order to avoid ambiguity with the Tablespace_Name column previously selected from the DBA_DATA_FILES data dictionary view. The maximum free extent size, number of free extents, and total free space statistics are selected and given aliases.

```
(select Tablespace_Name FS_TS_NAME,
        MAX(Blocks) AS Max_Blocks,
        COUNT(Blocks) AS Count_Blocks,
        SUM(Blocks) AS Sum_Free_Blocks
   from DBA_FREE_SPACE
   group by Tablespace_Name)
```

The Sum_Free_Blocks column from the second **from** clause subquery, divided by the Sum_Alloc_Blocks from the first **from** clause subquery, generates the value for the Pct_Free for each tablespace:

```
100*Sum_Free_Blocks/Sum_Alloc_Blocks AS Pct_Free
```

The two Tablespace_Name values are joined; the Fs_Ts_Name alias assigned in the second **from** clause subquery provides the join value for the DBA_FREE_SPACE portion of the join.

```
where Tablespace_Name = FS_TS_NAME;
```

The Max_Blocks column lists the largest available extent in the tablespace. The Count_Blocks column value is the number of free extents in the tablespace.

Sum_Free_Blocks is the total amount of space available in the tablespace. The Pct_Free column shows how close you are to needing to add another datafile to the tablespace. In the output in the following listing, the SYSTEM tablespace is dangerously low on space.

TABLESPACE_NAME	MAX_BLOCKS	COUNT_BLOCKS	SUM_FREE_BLOCKS	PCT_FREE
IDX1	487198	29	965726	94.36
RBS	452943	243	501343	97.97
SYSTEM	2763	4	3195	12.61
TEMP	460943	283	537086	100.00
TEMP_TABLES	634	1	634	49.53
USR1	293683	145	501372	48.99

Rollback and temporary tablespaces will tend to have a high Pct_Free as the extents are released when not immediately needed for sorts and rollback segments.

usr_quot.sql

Space Usage Within the Database by User

You can use the DBA_TS_QUOTAS view to display the allocated space, by user, in each tablespace, along with the space quota for each user. If a user has an unlimited quota in a tablespace, the quota will be displayed as a negative value. Querying DBA_TS_QUOTAS is a great way to quickly see which users own objects in which tablespaces and how close users are to their quotas. The following script queries the space quota and usage data from DBA_TS_QUOTAS.

```
set heading on linesize 66
set pagesize 60 term off echo off feedback off
col Username format a20 heading 'USER'
col Tablespace_Name format a20 heading 'RESOURCE|TBS'
col Blocks format 999,999,999 heading 'USED|BLOCKS'
col Max_Blocks format 999,999,999 heading 'QUOTA|BLOCKS'
break on Username skip 1
ttitle center 'USER QUOTAS BY TABLESPACE'
btitle left 'QUOTA OF -1 SIGNIFIES UNLIMITED QUOTA'

select Username, Tablespace_Name, Blocks, Max_Blocks
  from DBA_TS_QUOTAS
 order by Username, Tablespace_Name
/
```

Sample output for the preceding query is shown in the following listing.

```
                    USER QUOTAS BY TABLESPACE

                  RESOURCE                    USED        QUOTA
USER              TBS                       BLOCKS       BLOCKS
----------------  --------------------  ------------  ------------
DEMO              USR1                       10,345            -1

QC_USER           IDX1                       10,240            -1
                  USR1                       23,855            -1

QUOTA OF -1 SIGNIFIES UNLIMITED QUOTA
```

The output shows, by user, the tablespaces in which resource quotas have been
allocated or used. The quotas are expressed in database blocks. Since all of the
quotas in this example are -1, the users have unlimited resources available in the
tablespaces.

def_stor.sql

Default Storage for Objects

Unless you include the **storage** clause when executing a **create** statement, an object
will be created with the default storage parameters of the tablespace in which it is
created. To see the default storage by tablespace, run the following SQL statement.

```
col Tablespace_Name format a20
col Pct_Increase format 999 heading 'PCT|INCR'
select Tablespace_Name,
       Initial_Extent,
       Next_Extent,
       Min_Extents,
       Max_Extents,
       Pct_Increase
  from DBA_TABLESPACES;
```

Sample output for the preceding query is shown in the following listing.

TABLESPACE_NAME	INITIAL_EXTENT	NEXT_EXTENT	MIN_EXTENTS	MAX_EXTENTS	PCT INCR
SYSTEM	12288	12288	1	249	50
RBS	819200	819200	20	249	0
TEMP	819200	8192000	1	249	0

USR1	20480	20480	1	2147483645	50
TEMP_TABLES	20480	20480	1	249	50
IDX1	20480	20480	1	249	50

The output shows the default storage parameters (such as the initial extent size) for any new segment created. The storage parameters specified during object creation override the tablespaces' default values. Changing the default parameters does not affect the storage parameters of previously created objects.

ANNOTATIONS

If a tablespace is created without the **default storage** clause, the **initial** and **next** extent size default to 5 blocks and the **pctincrease** defaults to 50 percent. As of ORACLE7, it is possible to set the rollback segment maximum extents to UNLIMITED, although in practice this defaults to 2,147,483,645.

As of ORACLE7.3. you can designate a tablespace as either PERMANENT or TEMPORARY. A tablespace whose contents are designated as TEMPORARY can contain only temporary segments. Dedicating a tablespace to temporary segments can improve sorting performance if your application frequently uses temporary segments for sorting, as the temporary segments do not disappear once the sort is done. Tablespaces designated as TEMPORARY should also have an **initial** and **next** extent size that are equal, as well as a **pctincrease** of 0. This will result in identically sized segments and will ensure reusability of the extents once the temporary segment is dropped. All tablespaces are created as PERMANENT by default.

To check the status and contents of a tablespace, run the following query:

```
select Tablespace_Name,
       Status,
       Contents
  from DBA_TABLESPACES;
```

The output follows:

TABLESPACE_NAME	STATUS	CONTENTS
SYSTEM	ONLINE	PERMANENT
RBS	ONLINE	PERMANENT
TEMP	ONLINE	TEMPORARY
USR1	ONLINE	PERMANENT
TEMP_TABLES	ONLINE	PERMANENT
IDX1	ONLINE	PERMANENT

As with the DBA_DATA_FILES view, the DBA_TABLESPACES view has been modified for ORACLE8 to provide more information. The columns of DBA_TABLESPACES are shown in Table 6-2.

Column	Description
TABLESPACE_NAME	Tablespace name
INITIAL_EXTENT	Default initial extent size for objects created within this tablespace
NEXT_EXTENT	Default next extent size
MIN_EXTENTS	Default minimum number of extents
MAX_EXTENTS	Default maximum number of extents
PCT_INCREASE	Default percent increase for extent size
MIN_EXTLEN	Minimum extent size for the tablespace
STATUS	Tablespace status: ONLINE, OFFLINE, READONLY
CONTENTS	Tablespace contents: PERMANENT or TEMPORARY
LOGGING	Default logging attribute

TABLE 6-2.   DBA_TABLESPACES Columns

Several of the columns listed in Table 6-2 were introduced with ORACLE8. They are:

- MIN_EXTLEN which, when set, ensures that every used and/or free extent size in the tablespace is at least as large as and is a multiple of this value. This parameter is used to control free space fragmentation.

- LOGGING which defines whether or not certain DML and DDL operations are logged. Operations which can support **nologging** are:
  - DML: direct-load INSERT and Direct path SQL*Loader
  - DDL: **create table ... as select**

    create index

    alter index ... rebuild

    alter index ... rebuild partition

    alter index ... split partition

    alter table ... split partition

    alter table ... move partition

In general, operations which are simpler and faster to recreate from the beginning are ideal candidates for **nologging**. The **logging** attribute of a tablespace can be overridden for tables, indexes, and partitions, just as the **storage** parameters can be.

Changing the **logging** attribute of a tablespace does not affect the **logging** attributes of existing objects within the tablespace.

To view the new columns, modify the query above to read:

```
select Tablespace_Name,
       Contents,
       Logging
  from DBA_TABLESPACES;
```

The output of the modified query is below.

```
TABLESPACE_NAME CONTENTS  LOGGING
--------------- --------- ---------
SYSTEM          PERMANENT LOGGING
USER_DATA       PERMANENT LOGGING
ROLLBACK_DATA   PERMANENT LOGGING
TEMPORARY_DATA  TEMPORARY NOLOGGING
```

As the name indicates, the tablespace TEMPORARY_DATA can contain only temporary segments and, since temporary segments do not contain data needed for recovery, the tablespace has been set to **nologging**.

seg_spac.sql

Space Usage of a Segment

In addition to knowing how much space a tablespace and its associated datafiles is using, you should monitor and track the individual segment sizes within the database. The following query will display, by selected user, the segment name, the tablespace it resides in, the type of segment, allocated size of the segment in both bytes and blocks, the number of extents allocated to the segment, and the size of the next extent to be allocated when needed.

```
col Segment_Name format a20
col Segment_Type format a5 heading 'TYPE'
col Tablespace_Name format a10 heading 'TABLESPACE'
col Bytes format 999,999,999
col Blocks format 9,999,999
col Extents format 999,999
col Next_Extent format 999,999,999
set linesize 100 pagesize 60

select Segment_Name,
       Segment_Type,
       Tablespace_Name,
       Bytes,
       Blocks,
       Extents,
       Next_Extent
```

```
from DBA_SEGMENTS
where Owner = UPPER('&owner')
order by Segment_Name;
```

Sample output for the preceding query is shown in the following listing.

SEGMENT_NAME	TYPE	TABLESPACE	BYTES	BLOCKS	EXTENTS	NEXT_EXTENT
BRANCH	TABLE	USR1	20,480	5	1	20,480
CARDHOLDER	TABLE	USR1	1,761,280	430	10	860,160
CH_IDX	INDEX	USR1	348,160	85	6	167,936
CK_LOG	TABLE	USR1	20,480	5	1	20,480
DEPTREE_TEMPTAB	TABLE	USR1	20,480	5	1	20,480
HOLIDAY	TABLE	USR1	20,480	5	1	20,480
PK_CH_ACCT	INDEX	USR1	348,160	85	6	167,936
PK_TRANSACTION	INDEX	USR1	20,480	5	1	20,480
PK_TRANS_ID	INDEX	USR1	348,160	85	6	167,936
RANDOMNESS	TABLE	USR1	1,269,760	310	60	20,480
TEMPOPRIV	TABLE	USR1	2,621,440	640	11	1,290,240
TEMPSPRIV	TABLE	USR1	20,480	5	1	20,480
TRANSACTION	TABLE	USR1	20,480	5	1	20,480

Segments are objects which take up physical space within the database. The Bytes column lists the number of bytes the segment is currently allocated within the tablespace. The Blocks column lists the number of database blocks allocated. The Extents column contains the number of extents allocated to the segment. In general, it is more efficient to keep the number of extents small. The Next_Extent column lists the number of contiguous bytes that will be needed the next time the segment needs more space. In the example above, the TEMPOPRIV table will need an extent of 1,290,240 bytes, and the request may fail, depending on how fragmented the tablespace is.

ANNOTATIONS

On running the seg_spac.sql query, the user will be prompted for the name of the segment owner to populate the &*owner* variable. To run this query for all users in the database, remove the **where** clause:

```
where Owner = UPPER('&owner')
```

and change the **order by** to

```
order by Owner, Segment_Name
```

If you run the report for multiple owners, you should add the following **break** for readability:

```
break on Owner
```

You can list segments within a tablespace in descending order of size to determine if there is enough space in the tablespace for growth and to determine if an object should be moved to another tablespace. To list the segments in descending order of size, change the **order by** clause to:

```
order by Next_Extent desc, Segment_Name
```

If you are running the report for multiple owners, then you must add Owner to the **order by** clause, as shown in the following listing. This report may become extremely lengthy, depending on the number of owners and number of segments each owner has.

```
order by Owner, Next_Extent desc, Segment_Name
```

The initial output, re-run with the **order by** Next_Extent desc, Segment_Name clause is shown in the following listing:

SEGMENT_NAME	TYPE	TABLESPACE	BYTES	BLOCKS	EXTENTS	NEXT_EXTENT
TEMPOPRIV	TABLE	USR1	2,621,440	640	11	1,290,240
CARDHOLDER	TABLE	USR1	1,761,280	430	10	860,160
CH_IDX	INDEX	USR1	348,160	85	6	167,936
PK_CH_ACCT	INDEX	USR1	348,160	85	6	167,936
PK_TRANS_ID	INDEX	USR1	348,160	85	6	167,936
BRANCH	TABLE	USR1	20,480	5	1	20,480
CK_LOG	TABLE	USR1	20,480	5	1	20,480
DEPTREE_TEMPTAB	TABLE	USR1	20,480	5	1	20,480
HOLIDAY	TABLE	USR1	20,480	5	1	20,480
PK_TRANSACTION	INDEX	USR1	20,480	5	1	20,480
RANDOMNESS	TABLE	USR1	1,269,760	310	60	20,480
TEMPSPRIV	TABLE	USR1	20,480	5	1	20,480
TRANSACTION	TABLE	USR1	20,480	5	1	20,480

In general, you should keep all the data within a table within one extent. The more extents a segment has, the more work is involved in retrieving data from it and administering it. A table can be resized via the Export/Import utilities using the COMPRESS=Y flag. Compressing a table via Export/Import will result in a table with a single extent equal to the allocated size of the original table. If there are no free extents in the tablespace that can support the compressed size of the segment, then the Import command will fail when it attempts to create the table. In such cases, you will not be able to compress the extents unless you create a large enough free extent by adding a new datafile, extending an existing datafile, or reorganizing the entire tablespace to compress free extents.

Extents Showing Increasing Extent Size and Location

seg_info.sql   In addition to monitoring the overall space usage of a segment, you can monitor how the extents are allocated and the size of each of the extents. The following queries will list the default storage for a segment and all the extents allocated to this segment. When you execute these queries, you will be prompted for values for the *owner* and *segment_name* variables.

```
undefine owner
undefine segment_name
set verify off
select Segment_Name,
       Initial_Extent,
       Next_Extent,
       Pct_Increase
  from DBA_SEGMENTS
 where Segment_Name = UPPER('&&segment_name')
   and Owner=UPPER('&&owner');

select Tablespace_Name,
       File_ID,
       Block_ID,
       Blocks
  from DBA_EXTENTS
 where Owner = UPPER('&&owner')
   and Segment_Name = UPPER('&&segment_name')
 order by File_ID, Block_ID;

undefine owner
undefine segment_name
```

Sample output for the preceding script is shown in the following listing.

SEGMENT_NAME	INITIAL_EXTENT	NEXT_EXTENT	PCT_INCREASE
RANDOMNESS	20480	860,160	50

TABLESPACE_NAME	FILE_ID	BLOCK_ID	BLOCKS
USR1	4	53123	45
USR1	4	53168	65
USR1	4	53233	95
USR1	4	132321	5
USR1	5	37995	5
USR1	5	38000	15
USR1	5	38015	20
USR1	5	38035	35
USR1	5	64164	140

The output in the preceding listing shows the results for the query when run for a database user who owns a segment named RANDOMNESS. The result of the first query in the script shows that the segment's extent size increases by 50 percent with each extension. The initial extent size is 20,480 bytes—20 KB. The database block size for this example is 4KB, so the initial extent is 5 blocks in size. The 5KB entry in the second query's output is the first extent of the segment.

The segment's **next** extent value must have initially been set at 20KB (5 blocks). The segment's second extent is 5 blocks in size. The segment's third extent should be 50 percent greater than 5 blocks—7.5 blocks. However, ORACLE will never allocate fractions of blocks, and will usually round block sizes up to the nearest multiple of five (to improve the chances for reusing dropped extents). Therefore, the third extent should be 10 blocks in size. However, in this case ORACLE has found a free extent of 15 blocks available. Instead of taking 10 of those blocks and leaving only 5, ORACLE allocates all 15 blocks.

Because the table's **pctincrease** value is non-zero, the segment's extent sizes increase in a geometric fashion after the second extent has been allocated. The initial extent size is only 20,480 bytes. The next extent to be allocated (and the tenth overall for the segment) will be 860,160 bytes!

ANNOTATIONS

The first query is run to show the initial extent size, next extent size, and percent increase for the segment. If this query is not run, the implications of the second query's output are difficult to interpret. Without knowing the **pctincrease** set for the segment, you cannot estimate the growth pattern of that segment.

Before the first query is executed, any previous settings for the *owner* and *segment_name* variables are undefined. The **set verify off** command eliminates the writing of "old" and "new" values to the output every time a value is substituted for a variable. The variables are defined with double ampersands (&&) so the user will not be prompted for the same values multiple times. The **undefine** commands are repeated at the end of the script so that any values assigned to the variables will be undefined for the rest of the user's session.

```
undefine owner
undefine segment_name
set verify off

select Segment_Name,
       Initial_Extent,
       Next_Extent,
       Pct_Increase
  from DBA_SEGMENTS
 where Segment_Name = UPPER('&&segment_name')
   and Owner=UPPER('&&owner');
```

The second query extracts the locations and sizes of the extents in the segment.

```
select Tablespace_Name,
       File_ID,
       Block_ID,
       Blocks
  from DBA_EXTENTS
 where Owner = UPPER('&&owner')
   and Segment_Name = UPPER('&&segment_name')
 order by File_ID, Block_ID;
```

The output from the second query shows that the segment's extents are stored in two separate files: four extents in file #4 and five extents in file #5.

SEGMENT_NAME	INITIAL_EXTENT	NEXT_EXTENT	PCT_INCREASE
RANDOMNESS	20480	860,160	50

TABLESPACE_NAME	FILE_ID	BLOCK_ID	BLOCKS
USR1	4	53123	45
USR1	4	53168	65
USR1	4	53233	95
USR1	4	132321	5
USR1	5	37995	5
USR1	5	38000	15

USR1	5	38015	20
USR1	5	38035	35
USR1	5	64164	140

Looking at the listing, there is no way to determine which file will be used to store the next extent of the table. You can tell how large the next extent will be (via the Next_Extent value in the first query's output), but there is no discernible pattern to the file assignments for the extent allocations. By allowing the table to extend, and by using a non-zero value for **pctincrease**, the table owner has given up the ability to predictably manage space allocation for the table.

temp_seg.sql

Size of Temporary Segments

During operations that involve sorts (such as index creations, or **order by** operations), ORACLE allocates space in memory to perform the sort. The memory area used to perform the sort is called the *sort area*. If the sort area is not large enough to store all of the data used for the sort, then the sort data is written to a disk area called a *temporary segment*. The temporary segment is dropped once the sort has completed unless you have designated the tablespace as a TEMPORARY tablespace. If you designate a tablespace as a TEMPORARY tablespace, then the temporary segment is not dropped once the sort operation has completed.

While a sort is underway, you can view information about its temporary segment by querying the DBA_SEGMENTS data dictionary view. The following query will list the current size and number of extents for each of the temporary segments currently in use in your database.

```
col Segment_Name format a20
col Tablespace_Name format a10 heading 'TABLESPACE'
col Bytes format 999,999,999
col Blocks format 9,999,999
col Extents format 999,999
col Next_Extent format 999,999,999
set linesize 100 pagesize 60
select Owner,
       Segment_Name,
       Tablespace_Name
       Bytes,
       Blocks,
       Extents,
       Next_Extent
  from DBA_SEGMENTS
 where Segment_Type = 'TEMPORARY'
 order by Owner, Segment_Name;
```

If there are no sort operations currently underway in your database, then the preceding query will return no records.

max_exts.sql

Segments Not Set to maxextents unlimited

Setting the **maxextents** parameter for a segment to UNLIMITED means you will never have to worry that the segment will run out of extents. While it is tempting to set **maxextents** unlimited on all segments, it is not a good idea. Temporary segment tablespaces and rollback segments should not have unlimited extents since runaway transactions that continue for a long time will continue to extend the rollback segment or temporary segment until the disk is full.

The query shown in the following listing will generate a listing of all of the segments owned by a specific user for which the **maxextents** value has not been set to UNLIMITED.

```
col Segment_Name format a20
col Segment_Type format a5 heading 'TYPE'
col Tablespace_Name format a10 heading 'TABLESPACE'
col Bytes format 999,999,999
col Blocks format 9,999,999
col Extents format 999,999
col Next_Extent format 999,999,999
set linesize 100 pagesize 60

select Segment_Name,
       Segment_Type,
       Tablespace_Name,
       Bytes,
       Blocks,
       Extents,
       Next_Extent
  from DBA_SEGMENTS
 where Owner = UPPER('&owner')
   and Max_Extents < 2147483645
 order by Segment_Name;
```

The **where** clause limits the rows returned based on the value of the Max_Extents column of the DBA_SEGMENTS data dictionary view. If you set a segment's **maxextents** value to UNLIMITED, then ORACLE assigns a **maxextents** value of 2147483645 to the segment. Any value less than this satisfies the **where** clause and the row is returned. If a segment has a **maxextents** value other than UNLIMITED, then it may potentially reach its maximum number of extents.

The output of the query is next.

SEGMENT_NAME	TYPE	TABLESPACE	BYTES	BLOCKS	EXTENTS	NEXT_EXTENT
BRANCH	TABLE	USR1	20,480	5	1	20,480
CARDHOLDER	TABLE	USR1	1,761,280	430	10	860,160
CH_IDX	INDEX	USR1	348,160	85	6	167,936
CK_LOG	TABLE	USR1	20,480	5	1	20,480
DEPTREE_TEMPTAB	TABLE	USR1	20,480	5	1	20,480
HOLIDAY	TABLE	USR1	20,480	5	1	20,480
PK_CH_ACCT	INDEX	USR1	348,160	85	6	167,936
PK_TRANSACTION	INDEX	USR1	20,480	5	1	20,480
PK_TRANS_ID	INDEX	USR1	348,160	85	6	167,936
RANDOMNESS	TABLE	USR1	1,269,760	310	60	20,480
TEMPOPRIV	TABLE	USR1	2,621,440	640	11	1,290,240
TEMPSPRIV	TABLE	USR1	20,480	5	1	20,480
TRANSACTION	TABLE	USR1	20,480	5	1	20,480

Utilities

In the following sections, you will see scripts that you can use to alter the manner in which data is stored in your database. The scripts in this section provide means of coalescing free space and estimating space usage of new objects.

coalesce.sql

Force Coalesce of Free Space in a Tablespace

The extents of a segment are marked as free extents when the segment is dropped. If the extents are next to each other, they can be coalesced into a single free extent. The coalesced extent will be larger than either of the two separate free extents, and thus will be more likely to be reused. Figure 6-2 illustrates the extent allocations before and after a tablespace coalesce is performed.

(a)

| Used | Free 10 Blks | Free 25 Blks | Used | Free 30 Blks | Used |

(b)

| Used | Free 35 Blks | Used | Free 30 Blks | Used |

FIGURE 6-2.   (a) Extent allocation before tablespace coalesce
(b) extent allocation after tablespace coalesce

The SMON background process periodically coalesces neighboring free extents into larger free extents. However, there is a potential problem with the SMON-based free space coalesce implementation.

The SMON background process only coalesces free extents in tablespaces whose default **pctincrease** storage parameter is non-zero. Since temporary and rollback segment tablespaces typically use a **pctincrease** of 0, the free space in their tablespaces will not be coalesced. If you have set the default **pctincrease** to 0 for a data tablespace, you may be experiencing free space fragmentation in the tablespace. You may think that SMON is coalescing the tablespace's free space, but in fact it will skip the tablespace.

There are several solutions available to resolve the free space coalescing problem. First, you can size your extents properly. If this is done, the reuse of free extents will be maximized and the impact of noncoalesced free extents will be minimized. Second, you can set the default **pctincrease** value for your data and index tablespaces to a non-zero value. You could, for example, set the default **pctincrease** for each tablespace to a value of 1, and then override the default setting when creating objects within the tablespace. Third, as of ORACLE7.3, you can manually coalesce the free space in a tablespace. Other users of the tablespace will not be affected by the free space coalesce.

To determine if a tablespace needs to be coalesced, you can use a new data dictionary view, DBA_FREE_SPACE_COALESCED. The columns of the DBA_FREE_SPACE_COALESCED data dictionary view are listed in Table 6-3.

Ideally, the Percent_Blocks_Coalesced column of DBA_FREE_SPACE_COALESCED should be 100 percent. You can display the free space coalescence percentage for the tablespaces using the following query.

```
select Tablespace_Name,
       Percent_Blocks_Coalesced
  from DBA_FREE_SPACE_COALESCED
 order by Percent_Blocks_Coalesced
/
```

Sample output for the preceding query is shown in the following listing.

TABLESPACE_NAME	PERCENT_BLOCKS_COALESCED
TEMP	.074475968
RBS	.629248657
SYSTEM	100
USR1	100
TEMP_TABLES	100
IDX1	100

Column	Description
TABLESPACE_NAME	Name of the tablespace
TOTAL_EXTENTS	Number of free extents in the tablespace
EXTENTS_COALESCED	Number of coalesced free extents in the tablespace
PERCENT_EXTENTS_COALESCED	Percentage of coalesced free extents in the tablespace
TOTAL_BYTES	Number of free bytes in the tablespace
BYTES_COALESCED	Number of coalesced free bytes in the tablespace
TOTAL_BLOCKS	Number of free database blocks in the tablespace
BLOCKS_COALESCED	Number of coalesced database blocks in the tablespace
PERCENT_BLOCKS_COALESCED	Percentage of the coalesced free blocks in the tablespace

TABLE 6-3.   Columns in the DBA_FREE_SPACE_COALESCED View

The output shows the percentage of each tablespace's free extents that are coalesced. A value of 100 means that all of the tablespace's free extents are coalesced—that is, there are no neighboring free extents.

ANNOTATIONS

The tablespace with the lowest percentage of free extents coalesced will be displayed first due to the **order by** clause specified.

```
select Tablespace_Name,
       Percent_Blocks_Coalesced
  from DBA_FREE_SPACE_COALESCED
 order by Percent_Blocks_Coalesced
/
```

Use the **alter tablespace** command shown in the following listing to coalesce the free extents in a tablespace. If a tablespace frequently has uncoalesced free extents, you should check the default **pctincrease** value for the tablespace and the extent sizes for the segments stored in the tablespace.

```
alter tablespace TEMP coalesce;
```

Executing the query in the test database yields the following results after the TEMP tablespace has been coalesced.

TABLESPACE_NAME	PERCENT_BLOCKS_COALESCED
RBS	.629248657
SYSTEM	100
TEMP	100
USR1	100
TEMP_TABLES	100
IDX1	100

The tablespace TEMP now has all the free extents coalesced into a single extent, with no fragmentation in the tablespace at all.

How Long Is a LONG?

len_long.sql

If you use ORACLE's LONG datatype for one of your columns, you are restricted in the ways in which you can use the column. For example, consider a table with two columns, one of which uses a LONG datatype:

```
create table TOY
(Toy_ID      NUMBER,
Description  LONG);
```

In the TOY table, the Description column uses the LONG datatype. If you try to use any function on the Description column, your query will fail:

```
select LENGTH(Description)
  from TOY;


select LENGTH(Description)
               *
ERROR at line 1:
ORA-00932: inconsistent datatypes
```

The "inconsistent datatypes" error is raised because you are attempting to perform a function on a column (Description) defined by a LONG datatype. If you had used a VARCHAR2 datatype instead, the preceding query would have succeeded—but the text storage would have been limited by the VARCHAR2 datatype. In ORACLE7, VARCHAR2 can only store 2,000 characters; in ORACLE8, 4,000 characters. Thus, if you want to store more than 4,000 characters of text per column, you can't use a VARCHAR2 for your text searches.

As of ORACLE8, you can use the LOB datatypes (described in the next section) for storing long data. The LONG datatype is supported in both ORACLE7 and ORACLE8, and the inability to perform functions on LONG columns makes managing LONG columns difficult. In this section, you will see how to use PL/SQL variables to perform functions on the LONG data.

The following script, len_long.sql, evaluates the length of the LONG column in the TOY table via an anonymous PL/SQL block. The output of the block is displayed via the execution of the DBMS_OUTPUT package.

For this example, a single record was inserted into TOY, with a description 21 characters in length. The script shown in the following listing was then executed.

```
set serveroutput on

declare
  length_var    NUMBER;
  cursor TOY_CURSOR is
      select * from TOY;
  toy_val TOY_CURSOR%ROWTYPE;
begin
  open TOY_CURSOR;
  fetch TOY_CURSOR into toy_val;
    length_var := LENGTH(toy_val.Description);
    DBMS_OUTPUT.PUT_LINE('Length of Description: '||length_var);
  close TOY_CURSOR;
end;
/
```

The output for the sample data is shown in the following listing.
```
Length of Description: 21

PL/SQL procedure successfully completed.
```

Because the script uses the DBMS_OUTPUT package, it includes the **set serveroutput on** command to enable the writing of output from within the PL/SQL block.
```
set serveroutput on
```

The TOY_CURSOR cursor defines the query against the TOY table—in this case, since only one record is in the table, no **where** clause is necessary. The **declare** portion of the PL/SQL block also contains a variable named *length_var* to hold the length value prior to displaying the value.

```
declare
  length_var    NUMBER;
  cursor TOY_CURSOR is
      select * from TOY;
  toy_val TOY_CURSOR%ROWTYPE;
```

Within the PL/SQL block's executable section, the cursor is opened and the record is fetched into the *toy_val* variable. The *toy_val* variable's definition is anchored to the *toy_cursor* results via the %ROWTYPE flag. The next step of the script executes the **LENGTH** function on the Description column of the *toy_val* variable and returns that value via the DBMS_OUTPUT execution.

```
begin
  open TOY_CURSOR;
  fetch TOY_CURSOR into toy_val;
    length_var := LENGTH(toy_val.Description);
    DBMS_OUTPUT.PUT_LINE('Length of Description: '||length_var);
  close TOY_CURSOR;
end;
/
```

PROGRAMMER'S NOTE *When you select the values into PL/SQL variables, the Description column's value is selected into a PL/SQL string variable. Since VARCHAR2 datatypes in PL/SQL cannot exceed 32,767 characters in length, this script will only work if the Description column's value fits within that length.*

You can expand this script to report the lengths of multiple LONG values, by using a loop within your PL/SQL block. You will see the use of a cursor FOR loop within your PL/SQL block in the "Annotations" section. In addition to this modification, you could make the query a variable as well, via the use of dynamic SQL. See the DELETE_COMMIT procedure in Chapter 4 for an example of dynamic SQL.

ANNOTATIONS

The len_long.sql script acts on only one record. You can modify the script to use a cursor FOR loop so multiple records can be evaluated. Since multiple length values will be returned by the script, the modified script selects the Toy_ID values as well as the lengths of the Description fields.

In a cursor FOR loop, the results of a query are used to dynamically determine the number of times the loop is executed. In a cursor FOR loop, the opening, fetching, and closing of cursors are performed implicitly; you do not need to explicitly command these actions.

The following listing shows a cursor FOR loop that queries the Toy_ID and Description values from the TOY table. For each row returned, the DBMS_OUTPUT package is called to display the results.

```
set serveroutput on

declare
  length_var    NUMBER;
  cursor TOY_CURSOR is
      select * from TOY;
  toy_val TOY_CURSOR%ROWTYPE;
begin
  for toy_val in TOY_CURSOR
    loop
      length_var := LENGTH(toy_val.Description);
      DBMS_OUTPUT.PUT_LINE('ID: '||toy_val.Toy_ID);
      DBMS_OUTPUT.PUT_LINE('Length of Description: '||length_var);
    end loop;
end;
/
```

Sample output for the cursor FOR loop is shown in the following listing.

```
ID: 1
Length of Description: 21
ID: 2
Length of Description: 27


PL/SQL procedure successfully completed.
```

In a cursor FOR loop, there is no **open** or **fetch** command. The

```
for toy_val in TOY_CURSOR
```

command implicitly opens the TOY_CURSOR cursor and fetches a value into the *toy_val* variable. When there are no more records in the cursor, the loop is exited and the cursor is closed. In a cursor FOR loop, there is no need for a **close** command.

The loop is controlled by the existence of a fetchable record in the TOY_CURSOR cursor. There is no need to check the cursor's %NOTFOUND attribute—that is automated via the cursor FOR loop. Within the loop, the *length_var* variable is defined and the DBMS_OUTPUT package is executed to display the results. Both executions of the DBMS_OUTPUT package use the PUT_LINE procedure, so each value is displayed on a new line.

```
      length_var := LENGTH(toy_val.Description);
      DBMS_OUTPUT.PUT_LINE('ID: '||toy_val.Toy_ID);
      DBMS_OUTPUT.PUT_LINE('Length of Description: '||length_var);
```

len_lob.sql

How Long Is a LOB?

As of ORACLE8, you can use LOB (large object) datatypes. LOB datatypes include BLOB (for binary large objects), CLOB (for character string large objects), and BFILE (for binary files stored external to the database). LOB datatype columns are much more easily managed than LONG datatype columns. For example, you are limited to a single LONG datatype column per table; you can have multiple LOB columns. You cannot perform functions on LONG columns; ORACLE provides functions that you can execute on columns that use LOB datatypes. In this section, you will see an example of the use of the **GETLENGTH** function of the DBMS_LOB package.

For the examples in this section, the TOY table will be created using a CLOB datatype for the Description column. A CLOB datatype column can be up to 4GB in length; the data is stored within the database.

```
create table TOY
(Toy_ID      NUMBER,
Description   CLOB);
```

The data for LOB columns, whether stored inside or outside the database, is not always physically stored with the table. Within the TOY table, ORACLE stores locator values that point to data locations. For BFILE data types, the locator points to an external file; for BLOB and CLOB data types, the locator points to a separate data location that the database creates to hold the LOB data. Thus, the LOB data is not necessarily stored directly with the rest of the data in the TOY table.

When you execute functions on the LOB data, you must select the locator value for the LOB and pass that value as a parameter to the function. In this example, the goal is to determine the length of the LOB value, so the script will execute the **GETLENGTH** function of the DBMS_LOB package. You cannot use the **LENGTH** function on LOB values.

The **GETLENGTH** function of the DBMS_LOB package has only one input parameter: the locator value for the LOB. In the following listing, variables are declared to hold the locator value and the output value. The **GETLENGTH** function is then executed, and the result is reported via the PUT_LINE procedure.

```
declare
   locator_var    CLOB;
   length_var     INTEGER;
begin
  select Description into locator_var
    from TOY
   where Toy_ID = 1;
  length_var := DBMS_LOB.GETLENGTH(locator_var);
  DBMS_OUTPUT.PUT_LINE('Length of LOB: '|| length_var);
end;
/
```

The output for this script is shown in the following listing.

```
Length of LOB: 21

PL/SQL procedure successfully completed.
```

If the LOB value is NULL, then the **GETLENGTH** function will return a value of NULL.

ANNOTATIONS

The first section of the PL/SQL block defines two variables. The script uses the first variable, *locator_var*, to store the locator value for the Description column value. The *locator_var* variable has the same datatype (CLOB) as the Description column. The second variable, *length_var*, is an integer value that will store the length of the Description value.

```
declare
    locator_var     CLOB;
    length_var      INTEGER;
```

Once those two variables have been defined, the Description column's value is selected into the *locator_var* variable for a particular record.

```
begin
  select Description into locator_var
    from TOY
  where Toy_ID = 1;
```

The **GETLENGTH** function of the DBMS_LOB procedure is executed next, using the *locator_var* variable as its only input. The output of the **GETLENGTH** function is then displayed via the PUT_LINE procedure of the DBMS_OUTPUT package.

```
  length_var := DBMS_LOB.GETLENGTH(locator_var);
  DBMS_OUTPUT.PUT_LINE('Length of LOB: '|| length_var);
end;
/
```

In addition to the **GETLENGTH** function, the DBMS_LOB package contains the **INSTR** function and the **SUBSTR** function. You cannot use the SQL **INSTR** function on LOB columns; the **INSTR** function of the DBMS_LOB package provides this capability. The **SUBSTR** function of the DBMS_LOB package performs **SUBSTR** operations on LOB columns.

len_row.sql

How to Measure Row Length

When performing calculations of the actual and estimated space used by data, you will often need to know the length of each row. In this section, you will see how to automatically generate scripts that report the average space used for each row and each column of a table.

The examples in this section evaluate the space usage of rows in the STUDENT table. The **create table** command for the STUDENT table is shown in the following listing.

```
create table STUDENT
(Student_ID    NUMBER,
 First_Name    VARCHAR2(25),
 Middle_Init   CHAR(1),
 Last_Name     VARCHAR2(25),
 Birth_Date    DATE);
```

The STUDENT table contains columns using the NUMBER, VARCHAR2, CHAR, and DATE datatypes.

PROGRAMMER'S NOTE *The row length queries in this section will not work for columns defined with LONG or LOB datatypes. See the preceding sections of this chapter for ways to calculate the actual length of LONG and LOB columns.*

The script in the following listing, len_row.sql, generates a SQL command. The only parameter for the script is the name of the table.

```
set pagesize 0
set verify off
set feedback off
undefine tablename
column ordercol noprint

select '1' ordercol,
       'select ' textcol
  from USER_TABLES
 where Table_Name = '&&tablename'
union
select '2',
       ' AVG(VSIZE('||Column_Name||')), '
  from USER_TAB_COLUMNS
 where Column_ID <
       (select MAX(Column_ID)
          from USER_TAB_COLUMNS
         where Table_Name = '&&tablename')
   and Table_Name = '&&tablename'
union
select '3',
```

```
        ' AVG(VSIZE('||Column_Name||')) '
  from USER_TAB_COLUMNS
 where Column_ID =
        (select MAX(Column_ID)
           from USER_TAB_COLUMNS
          where Table_Name = '&&tablename')
   and Table_Name = '&&tablename'
union
select '4',
        ' from '||'&&tablename'||'; '
  from USER_TABLES
 where Table_Name = '&&tablename'
order by 1, 2

spool vsizes.sql
/
spool off
undefine tablename
set pagesize 20
```

Sample output for the preceding script is shown in the following listing. In the listing, the STUDENT table is supplied as input when the script prompts the user for a value for the *tablename* variable.

```
Enter value for tablename: STUDENT
select
 AVG(VSIZE(FIRST_NAME)),
 AVG(VSIZE(LAST_NAME)),
 AVG(VSIZE(MIDDLE_INIT)),
 AVG(VSIZE(STUDENT_ID)),
 AVG(VSIZE(BIRTH_DATE))
 from STUDENT;
```

The output shown in the preceding listing contains the following SQL statement:

```
select
 AVG(VSIZE(FIRST_NAME)),
 AVG(VSIZE(LAST_NAME)),
 AVG(VSIZE(MIDDLE_INIT)),
 AVG(VSIZE(STUDENT_ID)),
 AVG(VSIZE(BIRTH_DATE))
from STUDENT;
```

The generated SQL statement selects the average space used (the **VSIZE** function) for each column in the table. The **spool** commands create a file called vsizes.sql to store the generated SQL script.

You can now execute the vsizes.sql script. The following listing shows the execution of the vsizes.sql script along with sample output for data in the STUDENT table.

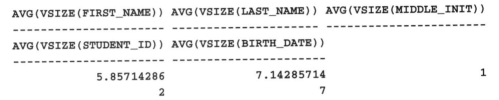

```
@vsizes

AVG(VSIZE(FIRST_NAME))  AVG(VSIZE(LAST_NAME))  AVG(VSIZE(MIDDLE_INIT))
----------------------  ---------------------  -----------------------
AVG(VSIZE(STUDENT_ID))  AVG(VSIZE(BIRTH_DATE))
----------------------  ---------------------
            5.85714286             7.14285714                        1
                     2                      7
```

The query output shows the average length of each column in the STUDENT table. The **VSIZE** function returns the actual space used, not the maximum space used. If you have only used 3 characters of a 25-character VARCHAR2 column, then **VSIZE** returns a 3, not 25.

PROGRAMMER'S NOTE   *Since the vsizes.sql script has no input parameters, you can alter the len_row.sql script to automatically execute the vsizes.sql script as soon as len_row.sql completes.*

The output shown in the preceding listing illustrates several important space usage facts:

◆ **CHAR columns use their maximum width.** If you define a column with a CHAR datatype, then a **VSIZE** of that column will return the maximum width as the actual width.

◆ **VARCHAR2 columns use their exact size.** If you define a column with a VARCHAR2 datatype, then a **VSIZE** of that column will return the number of used characters, not the defined length.

◆ **DATE columns use 7 bytes.** Regardless of the date value, DATE datatypes in ORACLE always use 7 bytes (one each for century, year, month, day, hour, minute, and second). If you write out a date in the standard DD-MON-YY format, you use 9 characters; ORACLE's internal storage of DATEs is independent of the format used for displaying the values.

◆ **NUMBER datatypes are stored efficiently.** Internally, ORACLE uses a method called "exponent in excess of 64 notation" that allows it to store numbers in few bytes. In the sample data used for the STUDENT table, some of the numbers were over 1,000. On average, ORACLE used just 2 bytes to store each numeric value.

ANNOTATIONS

The len_row.sql script builds the vsizes.sql script based on data retrieved from data dictionary views. In order to construct the SQL statement properly, the len_row.sql script uses a hidden column. A column named OrderCol is defined as hidden via the **noprint** clause of the **column** command, as shown in the following listing.

```
column ordercol noprint
```

Each section of the script specifies a value for the OrderCol column. For example, the first part of the script uses an OrderCol value of 1:

```
select '1' ordercol,
       'select ' textcol
  from USER_TABLES
 where Table_Name = '&&tablename'
```

Since the display of the OrderCol column is suppressed via the **noprint** clause, the output of this query will be the word 'select '. The next section of the script retrieves the column names for all but the last column in the table. The column names have a comma appended to them; if you appended a comma to the last column, then the SQL would be improperly formatted.

```
union
select '2',
       ' AVG(VSIZE('||Column_Name||')), '
  from USER_TAB_COLUMNS
 where Column_ID <
       (select MAX(Column_ID)
          from USER_TAB_COLUMNS
         where Table_Name = '&&tablename')
   and Table_Name = '&&tablename'
```

Since the queries are **union**ed together, you must obey the formatting rules for **union**s. In each query, the columns must be of the same datatype. The datatypes and column names for the **union** query are determined by the datatypes of the first query in the **union**. You don't need to specify column names for the columns in any but the first query of the **union**.

The third section of the len_row.sql script retrieves the column name of the last column in the table; no comma is appended to it. The fourth section of the len_row.sql script generates the **from** clause for the generated query. At the end of the query, the rows returned are ordered by their OrderCol values (even though that column's value is not displayed).

```
order by 1, 2
```

This **order by** clause uses the column's ordinal positions. Prior to ORACLE7.1, you had to use ordinal positions in your **order by** clauses if you used an expression (such as in this script, since the script selects text strings instead of column values). As of ORACLE7.1, you can use the **as** clause to name a selected expression, and you can use that name in your **order by** clauses. You therefore do not need to use ordinal values in your **order by** clauses—unless you are using a **union**. If you use a **union** clause in your queries, you should use the ordinal positions of the columns in your **order by** clause. The use of ordinal positions in **order by** clauses for **union** queries is advisable because you may select different columns in each part of the query; as long as they have the same datatype, the query will succeed.

PROGRAMMER'S NOTE   *The results of the **VSIZE** function may be inconsistent for columns defined via abstract datatypes.*

At the beginning of the script, **verify** and **feedback** are turned **off**, suppressing the variable value display (for the *tablename* variable) and the display of the number of records returned. The **pagesize** control is set to 0, disabling the display of page and column headings. At the end of the len_row.sql script, **pagesize** is set to 20, re-enabling the column headings for the vsizes.sql report output.

The len_row.sql script shows the average length of each column value individually. Instead of adding the column lengths manually, you can alter the query to force ORACLE to add them for you. Instead of appending commas to the end of each generated column value, append a plus sign (+), as shown in the following listing.

```
set pagesize 0
set verify off
set feedback off
column TotalSize format 999,999.99 heading "TotalSize"
undefine tablename
column ordercol noprint

select '1' ordercol,
       'select ' textcol
  from USER_TABLES
 where Table_Name = '&&tablename'
union
select '2',
       ' AVG(VSIZE('||Column_Name||'))+ '
  from USER_TAB_COLUMNS
 where Table_Name = '&&tablename'
union
select '3',
       '0 totalsize from '||'&&tablename'||'; '
```

```
   from USER_TABLES
 where Table_Name = '&&tablename'

spool vsizes.sql
/
spool off
undefine tablename
set pagesize 20
```

The query shown in the preceding listing has three sections instead of four. Each column (including the last column) has a '+' appended to its generated value. The text generated in the last section of the **union** query starts with a zero, so the column's total average length will have zero added to it. The total average column length will be unaffected by the addition, allowing the script to be simplified.

Sample output for the preceding script is shown in the following listing. The output is generated for the STUDENT table.

```
Enter value for tablename: STUDENT
select
 AVG(VSIZE(BIRTH_DATE))+
 AVG(VSIZE(FIRST_NAME))+
 AVG(VSIZE(LAST_NAME))+
 AVG(VSIZE(MIDDLE_INIT))+
 AVG(VSIZE(STUDENT_ID))+
0 totalsize from STUDENT;
```

As with the len_row.sql script's output, this output is written to a file named vsizes.sql. A sample execution of the preceding vsizes.sql script is shown in the following listing.

```
unknown command beginning "Enter valu..." - rest of line ignored.

   TotalSize
 -----------
      23.00
```

The error shown at the start of the output listing is generated by the presence of the

```
Enter value for tablename: STUDENT
```

line in the vsizes.sql file. The output shows that the total average length of a row in the STUDENT table is 23 bytes.

You can modify the script again, generating both the individual column lengths and the total length in a single SQL script. The following script expands len_row.sql in this manner.

```
set pagesize 0
set verify off
set feedback off
column TotalSize format 999,999.99 heading "TotalSize"
undefine tablename
column ordercol noprint

select '1' ordercol,
       'select ' textcol
  from USER_TABLES
 where Table_Name = '&&tablename'
union
select '2',
       ' AVG(VSIZE('||Column_Name||')), '
  from USER_TAB_COLUMNS
 where Table_Name = '&&tablename'
union
select '3',
       ' AVG(VSIZE('||Column_Name||'))+ '
  from USER_TAB_COLUMNS
 where Table_Name = '&&tablename'
union
select '4',
       '0 totalsize from '||'&&tablename'||'; '
  from USER_TABLES
 where Table_Name = '&&tablename'

spool vsizes.sql
/
spool off
undefine tablename
set pagesize 20
```

The first section, which generates the 'select' command, is left unchanged.

```
select '1' ordercol,
       'select ' textcol
  from USER_TABLES
 where Table_Name = '&&tablename'
```

The second part of the original len_row.sql script is modified to include all columns of the table by removing the limiting condition on the Column_ID value.

```
select '2',
       ' AVG(VSIZE('||Column_Name||')), '
  from USER_TAB_COLUMNS
 where Table_Name = '&&tablename'
```

The third part of the new query generates the addition section, totalling the average sizes of the columns.

```
select '3',
       ' AVG(VSIZE('||Column_Name||'))+ '
  from USER_TAB_COLUMNS
 where Table_Name = '&&tablename'
```

As with the previous addition query, a zero is added to the output prior to the **from** clause generation.

```
select '4',
       '0 totalsize from '||'&&tablename'||'; '
  from USER_TABLES
 where Table_Name = '&&tablename'
```

The modified query generates a vsizes.sql script that will, when executed, calculate the average size of each column and the total average size of a row in the table. Sample output for the modified query is shown in the following listing.

```
Enter value for tablename: STUDENT
select
 AVG(VSIZE(BIRTH_DATE)),
 AVG(VSIZE(FIRST_NAME)),
 AVG(VSIZE(LAST_NAME)),
 AVG(VSIZE(MIDDLE_INIT)),
 AVG(VSIZE(STUDENT_ID)),
 AVG(VSIZE(BIRTH_DATE))+
 AVG(VSIZE(FIRST_NAME))+
 AVG(VSIZE(LAST_NAME))+
 AVG(VSIZE(MIDDLE_INIT))+
 AVG(VSIZE(STUDENT_ID))+
0 totalsize from STUDENT;
```

When you run this version of vsizes.sql, your output will show the average size of each column as well as the average size of each row.

SIZE ISSUES FOR OIDS AND REFS

As of ORACLE8, the system generates a unique identifier called an *OID* (object ID) for each row in an object table. The OID generator is a network function that generates a globally unique identifier (RAW(16)) based on network address, current time, and so on. An OID is referenced via a *REF*. In this section, you will see how to estimate the size of the automatically generated data for OIDs and their associated REFs.

Object tables have a hidden column, SYS_NC_OID$, that stores the system-generated OID and is always 16 bytes long. As of ORACLE8, you can define object views over relational tables; object views will not have this system-generated OID. In object views, the OID is synthesized based on a primary key that the view definer specifies. These primary key-based OIDs (called *PKOIDs*) can be as long as the primary key value itself. In ORACLE8, PKOIDs are never stored.

Object tables maintain relationships via REF datatypes and do not directly retrieve and manipulate OID values. The REF value contains the OID and other items, such as the identifier of the object table or view in which the row object with the OID may be found.

OIDs are assigned to row objects and to metadata objects such as object tables and abstract datatypes. These identifiers assigned to object table and type enable identifying and sharing object tables and types across databases.

A system-generated OID is 16 bytes long. A PKOID can be as long as the primary-key values. Correspondingly, REF values stored in the database can be of varying size. REFs contain 2 length bytes + 2 bytes of flags + 16 bytes for the object table OID + 16 bytes OID (or length of PKOID) + optionally, 10 bytes RowID. When a REF value is stored in a column, if the column is not declared to be scoped nor declared to store the RowID, then the REF that is stored is stripped of its RowID. If the REF column is declared as scoped, then in ORACLE8, only the OID of the referenced row object is stored; that is, the REF is completely stripped of its overhead bytes and the object table's OID. If the REF column is unscoped and declared to store the RowID, then the entire REF is stored in the column. Note that in ORACLE8, the primary key-based REF is not allowed to be stored.

size_tab.sql

How to Size a Table

The more accurately you size your tables and indexes, the less administrative work you will have to perform as the tables and indexes grow. In this section, you will see scripts related to the calculation of space requirements for tables. In the next section, you will see scripts related to the space requirements of indexes. Each of these sections requires that you be able to calculate the average length of the rows and columns involved; see the prior sections in this chapter for scripts related to row length calculations.

The following script, when executed, will prompt you for five variables. Those five variables, combined with database block size information from the database, determine the space required for your table's data.

```
set verify off
undefine pctfree
undefine avg_row_length
```

```
undefine number_of_columns
undefine number_of_cols_over_250_bytes
undefine number_of_rows

select &&number_of_rows/
  (((100-&&pctfree)*(Value-90))
    /(100*(&&avg_row_length + 3 + &&number_of_columns
          + &&number_of_cols_over_250_bytes))) Blocks_Required
  from V$PARAMETER
 where Name = 'db_block_size';
```

When you execute the script, you will be prompted for values for the five variables, as shown in the following listing. The query will use those variable values, along with the database block size, to calculate the table's storage requirements, as shown in the following listing.

```
Enter value for number_of_rows: 100000
Enter value for pctfree: 10
Enter value for avg_row_length: 23
Enter value for number_of_columns: 5
Enter value for number_of_cols_over_250_bytes: 0


BLOCKS_REQUIRED
---------------
      859.821379
```

The output shows that for the given table parameters, ORACLE will require about 860 blocks to store the table's data.

PROGRAMMER'S NOTE *The storage calculations are estimates. Develop a set of standard extent sizes (such as 1MB, 2MB, 4MB, 8MB, etc.) and round the storage requirements up so they make the best use of your standard extent sizes.*

When you execute the size_tab.sql script, you are prompted for five variables:

◆ *number_of_rows* Enter the number of rows you expect to store in this table. For this example, 100,000 rows were used.

◆ *pctfree* Enter the **pctfree** setting for the table. The space set aside via **pctfree** is used during **update**s of rows already stored in the block.

◆ *avg_row_length* Enter the average row length of the table. For this example, the STUDENT table's statistics were used—the average row length for rows in STUDENT is 23; see the section on average row length earlier in this chapter for details on calculating average row length.

◆ *number_of_columns*   Enter the number of columns in the table. For this example, the STUDENT table was used; it has five columns.

◆ *number_of_cols_over_250_bytes*   Enter the number of columns whose average length exceeds 250. If a column length exceeds 250 bytes, ORACLE will need an additional length byte for row overhead.

Your settings for these five parameters are re-initialized each time you execute the size_tab.sql script, so you can execute the script repeatedly to determine the impact of different variable settings on your table's space requirements.

ANNOTATIONS

The completed size_tab.sql script contains many variables; if you only wish to see specific information about your database blocks, you can run portions of the script, as shown in the following listings.

Before executing the individual scripts, you should first re-initialize the variables, as shown in the following listing.

```
set verify off
undefine pctfree
undefine avg_row_length
undefine number_of_columns
undefine number_of_cols_over_250_bytes
undefine number_of_rows
```

To see the space available for a table in a database block, execute the following query. This query uses an estimate of 90 bytes for the block header within a database block. The resulting number is given the alias "Space_in_Block."

```
select Value-90    Space_in_Block
  from V$PARAMETER
where Name = 'db_block_size';
```

Sample output for the preceding query is shown in the following listing. In this example, the database block size is 4KB.

```
SPACE_IN_BLOCK
--------------
          4006
```

Of the 4,096 bytes in the database block, 4,006 are available for use. Next, you need to take into account the **pctfree** setting. The **pctfree** setting determines the percentage of the space in the block (not including the 90 bytes for the block header) that is not used during **insert**s of new rows. The free space is used when previously **insert**ed rows in the block are **update**d. The more you **update** your rows, the more

free space you need to maintain in your blocks. The query shown in the following
listing returns the space that is available for **insert**s.

```
REM Available space - take pctfree into account

select ((100-&&pctfree)*(Value-90))/100    Available_Space
  from V$PARAMETER
 where Name = 'db_block_size';
```

Sample output from the preceding query is shown in the following listing. For
this example, the database block size is 4KB. During the execution of this query,
you will be prompted for a value for the *pctfree* variable. The *pctfree* variable here
is set to 10.

```
Enter value for pctfree: 10


AVAILABLE_SPACE
---------------
         3605.4
```

As shown by the output, 90 percent of the available space in the block
(4096-90)*0.90 is available for **insert**s of new rows. For consistency, the *pctfree*
variable setting will not be altered for the remaining queries shown in this section.

Next, you can calculate the number of rows that will fit into the available space. A
row's space requirements come from several sources:

◆ 3 bytes for row overhead

◆ the total average number of bytes used for each row

◆ the number of columns in the table (1 byte is needed for each to indicate the
length of the value)

◆ the number of columns in the table whose data exceeds 250 bytes in length
(and thus require an additional byte to store the length information)

In the following query, these four factors are combined to determine the number
of bytes required per row. The calculation from the previous query provides the
total number of bytes available per block. By dividing the available bytes by
the bytes per row, you can determine the number of rows that can be stored in
each block.

```
REM  Calculate rows per block

select ((100-&&pctfree)*(Value-90))/
       (100*(&&avg_row_length + 3 + &&number_of_columns
          + &&number_of_cols_over_250_bytes)) Rows_Per_Block
  from V$PARAMETER
 where Name = 'db_block_size';
```

Sample output from the preceding query is shown in the following listing. When you execute the query, you will be prompted for values for the *avg_row_length*, *number_of_columns*, and *number_of_cols_over_250_bytes* variables. The *pctfree* variable will use the value (10) set in the earlier example.

```
Enter value for avg_row_length: 23
Enter value for number_of_columns: 5
Enter value for number_of_cols_over_250_bytes: 0


ROWS_PER_BLOCK
--------------
     116.303226
```

The output shows that 116 rows can be stored in each block. ORACLE does not store partial rows per block for **insert**s unless a row is larger than the database block size (4KB)—a condition called a *spanned row*.

For this example, the sizing information for the STUDENT table is used: the average row length is 23 bytes, there are five columns, and none of the columns has an average row length exceeding 250 bytes. The better you can estimate your average row length, the more accurately you can forecast your table's space requirements.

You can now combine the previous queries into the size_tab.sql script, as shown in the following listing. The combined script divides the number of rows you expect for the table by the average number of rows per block.

```
set verify off
select &&number_of_rows/
  (((100-&&pctfree)*(Value-90))
     /(100*(&&avg_row_length + 3 + &&number_of_columns
            + &&number_of_cols_over_250_bytes))) Blocks_Required
  from V$PARAMETER
 where Name = 'db_block_size';
```

When you execute the preceding query in this sequence, the only undefined parameter is the *number_of_rows* parameter. In the sample output shown in the following listing, the space requirement is calculated based on an estimate of 100,000 rows for the table.

```
Enter value for number_of_rows: 100000


BLOCKS_REQUIRED
---------------
     859.821379
```

Although ORACLE calculates the number of blocks required to multiple places after the decimal, partial blocks are never allocated for tables. Round the result up to a value that makes sense for your environment and sizing standards. ORACLE may dynamically change your space requirements when you create the table, based on the size of the available free extents in your tablespace.

size_ind.sql

How to Estimate the Size of an Index

The more accurately you size your tables and indexes, the less administrative work you will have to perform as the tables and indexes grow. In this section, you will see scripts related to the calculation of space requirements for indexes. The scripts in this sections require that you be able to calculate the average length of the columns involved; see the prior sections in this chapter for scripts related to column and row length calculations.

The following script, when executed, will prompt you for five variables. Those five variables, combined with database block size information from the database, determine the space required for your index's data.

```
set verify off
undefine pctfree
undefine avg_length_of_indexed_cols
undefine number_of_indexed_cols
undefine num_of_ind_cols_over_127_bytes
undefine number_of_rows

select &&number_of_rows/(((100-&&pctfree)*(Value-161))
  /(100*(&&avg_length_of_indexed_cols+8+&&number_of_indexed_cols
  + &&num_of_ind_cols_over_127_bytes))) Blocks_Required
  from V$PARAMETER
 where Name = 'db_block_size';
```

When you execute the script, you will be prompted for values for the five variables, as shown in the following listing. The query will use those variable values, along with the database block size, to calculate the index's storage requirements, as shown in the following listing.

```
Enter value for number_of_rows: 100000
Enter value for pctfree: 2
Enter value for avg_length_of_indexed_cols: 15
Enter value for number_of_indexed_cols: 2
Enter value for num_of_ind_cols_over_127_bytes: 0


BLOCKS_REQUIRED
---------------
    648.289811
```

The output shows that for the given parameters, ORACLE will require about 650 blocks to store the index data.

PROGRAMMER'S NOTE *The storage calculations are estimates. Develop a set of standard extent sizes (such as 1MB, 2MB, 4MB, 8MB, etc.) and round the storage requirements up so they make the best use of your standard extent sizes.*

When you execute the size_ind.sql script, you are prompted for five variables:

◆ *number_of_rows* Enter the number of rows you expect to store in this table for which the index will have a value. For this example, 100,000 rows were used.

◆ *pctfree* Enter the **pctfree** setting for the index. The space set aside via **pctfree** is used during **update**s of rows already stored in the block. Since ORACLE does not **update** index entries in place (instead, a **delete** and **insert** is performed), you should set **pctfree** to a very low value (such as 1 or 2) for your indexes.

◆ *avg_length_of_indexed_cols* Enter the total average row length of the columns to be indexed. For this example, a two-column index will be used as the basis for calculations. The two columns' average length, added together, will be assumed to be 15 bytes. See the section on average row length earlier in this chapter for details on calculating average column length.

◆ *number_of_indexed_cols* Enter the number of columns in the index. For this example, the index is a concatenated index of two columns.

◆ *num_of_ind_cols_over_127_bytes* Enter the number of columns in the index whose average length exceeds 127 bytes. If a column length exceeds 127 bytes, ORACLE will need an additional length byte for index entry overhead.

Your settings for these five parameters are re-initialized each time you execute the size_ind.sql script, so you can execute the script repeatedly to determine the impact of different variable settings on your index's space requirements.

ANNOTATIONS

The completed size_ind.sql script contains many variables; if you only wish to see specific information about your database blocks, you can run portions of the script, as shown in the following listings.

Before executing the individual scripts, you should first re-initialize the variables, as shown in the following listing.

```
set verify off
undefine pctfree
undefine avg_length_of_indexed_cols
```

```
undefine number_of_indexed_cols
undefine num_of_ind_cols_over_127_bytes
undefine number_of_rows
```

To see the space available for an index in a database block, execute the following query. This query uses an estimate of 161 bytes for the index block header within a database block. The resulting number is given the alias "Space_in_Block."

```
select Value-161 Space_in_Block
  from V$PARAMETER
 where Name = 'db_block_size';
```

Sample output for the preceding query is shown in the following listing. In this example, the database block size is 4KB. For the sake of simplicity, the index's *initrans* parameter is assumed to be the default value of 1.

```
SPACE_IN_BLOCK
--------------
          3935
```

Of the 4,096 bytes in the database block, 3,935 are available for use. Next, you need to take into account the **pctfree** setting. The **pctfree** setting determines the percentage of the space in the block (not including the 161 bytes for the block header) that is not used during **insert**s of new index entries. Since ORACLE does not **update** index entries in place, you need very little space reserved via **pctfree**. The query shown in the following listing returns the space that is available for **insert**s of new index entries.

```
REM  Available space in the block

select ((100-&&pctfree)*(Value-161))/100  Available_Space
  from V$PARAMETER
 where Name = 'db_block_size';
```

Sample output from the preceding query is shown in the following listing. For this example, the database block size is 4KB. During the execution of this query, you will be prompted for a value for the *pctfree* variable. The *pctfree* variable here is set to 2.

```
Enter value for pctfree: 2

AVAILABLE_SPACE
---------------
         3856.3
```

As shown by the output, 98 percent of the available space in the block (4096-161)*0.98 is available for **insert**s of new rows. For consistency, the *pctfree* variable setting will not be altered for the remaining queries shown in this section.

Next, you can calculate the number of index entries that will fit into the available space. An index entry's space requirements come from several sources:

◆ 8 bytes for entry overhead

◆ the total average number of bytes used for each entry

◆ the number of columns in the index (1 byte is needed for each column to indicate the length of the value)

◆ the number of columns in the table whose data exceeds 127 bytes in length (and thus require an additional byte to store the length information)

In the following query, these four factors are combined to determine the number of bytes required per index entry. The calculation from the previous query provides the total number of bytes available per block. By dividing the available bytes by the bytes per row, you can determine the number of rows that can be stored in each block.

```
REM    Calculate Entries per Block

select ((100-&&pctfree)*(value-161))/
  (100*(&&avg_length_of_indexed_cols+8+&&number_of_indexed_cols
      + &&num_of_ind_cols_over_127_bytes)) Entries_Per_Block
  from V$PARAMETER
 where Name = 'db_block_size';
```

Sample output from the preceding query is shown in the following listing. When you execute the query, you will be prompted for values for the *avg_length_of_ indexed_cols*, *number_of_indexed_cols*, and *number_of_cols_over_127_bytes* variables. The *pctfree* variable will use the value (2) set in the earlier example.

```
Enter value for avg_length_of_indexed_cols: 15
Enter value for number_of_indexed_cols: 2
Enter value for num_of_ind_cols_over_127_bytes: 0


ENTRIES_PER_BLOCK
-----------------
          154.252
```

The output shows that 154 index entries can be stored in each block. ORACLE does not store partial index entries in a block.

You can now combine the previous queries into the size_ind.sql script, as shown in the following listing. The combined script divides the number of rows you expect for the table by the average number of index entries per block.

```
select &&number_of_rows/(((100-&&pctfree)*(Value-161))/
  (100*(&&avg_length_of_indexed_cols+8+&&number_of_indexed_cols
       + &&num_of_ind_cols_over_127_bytes))) Blocks_Required
  from V$PARAMETER
 where Name = 'db_block_size';
```

When you execute the preceding query in this sequence, the only undefined parameter is the *number_of_rows* parameter. In the sample output shown in the following listing, the space requirement is calculated based on an estimate of 100,000 rows for the table.

```
Enter value for number_of_rows: 100000

BLOCKS_REQUIRED
---------------
       648.289811
```

As shown by the query output, you can store 100,000 of the index entries in approximately 650 blocks. Although ORACLE calculates the number of blocks required to multiple places after the decimal, partial blocks are never allocated for indexes. Round the result up to a value that makes sense for your environment and sizing standards. ORACLE may dynamically change your space requirements based on the size of the available free extents in your tablespace.

User Management

E very database user account has characteristics that define and limit it. In this chapter, you will see scripts for managing your database users. You can use the scripts to re-create users, to list the grants each user has, and to determine the activity of current users. You will also see scripts that you can use to re-create roles. These scripts complement the capabilities already provided via tools such as Oracle Enterprise Manager.

The major scripts presented in this chapter are:

user_obj.sql	Users who own objects
obj_typs.sql	Types of objects owned
usr_sprv.sql	Users' system and role privileges
usr_oprv.sql	Users' object privileges
usr_sesn.sql	User session information
usr_quot.sql	User resource quotas
pas_cmpx.sql	Enforce password complexity
cr8_usr.sql	Re-create users
gen_grnt.sql	Generate grant commands
gen_role.sql	Generate commands to create roles

In the first section of this chapter, you will see diagnostic scripts you can use to identify the characteristics of the users in your database. In the second part of this chapter, you will see utilities you can use when re-creating users, privileges, and roles.

DIAGNOSTIC SCRIPTS

In the following sections, you will see scripts that report on the users already created in the database. This set of scripts relies on queries of the data dictionary tables to display commonly needed diagnostic information about your users.

user_obj.sql

Users Who Own Objects

The DBA_USERS data dictionary view lists all of the users in the database, along with their assigned default tablespace and temporary tablespace; you can also see the encrypted version of each user's password. If you are encountering a database for the first time, you will need to know which of these users own objects. The more you know about the object ownership within a database application, the better you will be able to support the application.

The following script selects from the data dictionary all object owners other than SYS. The SYS owner is not selected for several reasons. First, the objects owned by SYS should be the same across instances. Second, the SYS owner owns many objects (such as tables, views, and synonyms) that are not part of your application; listing them with the rest of the output will not add to your knowledge of the application.

The script, shown in the following listing, queries DBA_OBJECTS for all types of objects owned by any user other than SYS. The objects shown in the output will include tables, indexes, views, synonyms, and sequences.

```
select distinct Owner
  from DBA_OBJECTS
 where Owner <> 'SYS'
 order by Owner asc;
```

Sample output from the query is shown in the following listing.

```
OWNER
------------------------------
DBSNMP
PUBLIC
SCOTT
SYSTEM
```

obj_typs.sql

Types of Objects Owned

In addition to listing the users who own objects, you can list the objects themselves. Before doing a full listing of the objects, you should generate a summary that shows the number and type of objects owned.

The following query displays the number of objects owned, by owner and object type.

```
select Owner,
       Object_Type,
       COUNT(*)
  from DBA_OBJECTS
 where Owner <> 'SYS'
 group by Owner, Object_Type;
```

Sample output from the preceding query is shown in the following listing.

OWNER	OBJECT_TYPE	COUNT(*)
DBSNMP	SYNONYM	4
PUBLIC	SYNONYM	586
SCOTT	TABLE	5
SYSTEM	INDEX	15
SYSTEM	SEQUENCE	1
SYSTEM	SYNONYM	8

SYSTEM	TABLE	14
SYSTEM	UNDEFINED	9
SYSTEM	VIEW	3

ANNOTATIONS

In the query output in the preceding listing, an Object_Type value of 'UNDEFINED' was displayed for 9 objects owned by the SYSTEM user. The UNDEFINED object type was introduced in ORACLE8; it refers to LOB segments. When you create a table that uses an internal LOB datatype (such as BLOB or CLOB), the LOB data is not usually stored with the base data. Instead, the base table contains a *LOB locator* value that points to a separate storage area that contains the LOB data. When you create a table using a BLOB or CLOB datatype, ORACLE dynamically creates and manages a separate storage area for the LOB data.

What kind of structure is the LOB storage area? It's not truly a table, since it is not created via a **create table** command. LOB storage areas appear as UNDEFINED in the DBA_OBJECTS output, as shown in the previous listing. The SYSTEM user in this database appears to have nine internal LOBs.

The preceding query tells you how many objects of each type are owned by each non-SYS user. You can select further information about the objects. DBA_OBJECTS is the only data dictionary view that shows the date on which an object was created (the Created column) or last modified (the Last_DDL_Time column). For example, the following query will return the creation date for each table owned by the user named SCOTT:

```
select Object_Name,
       Created
  from DBA_OBJECTS
 where Owner = 'SCOTT'
   and Object_Type = 'TABLE';
```

PROGRAMMER'S NOTE

The Last_DDL_Time column will also reflect changes to privileges granted on the object, as well as the creation of constraints if the object is a table. To see the time when the structure of the object was last changed, query the Timestamp column.

usr_sprv.sql

Users' System and Role Privileges

What system privileges and roles do your users have? And which of your users' roles inherit privileges from other roles? Since there can be a hierarchical relationship among roles, you will need to use the **connect by** operator during your query. Due to the different types of privileges you can have and the restrictions on the way in which the **connect by** is used, a temporary work table will be created for use by the script in this section.

The following script should be saved as a single file (called usr_sprv.sql). When executed, it will prompt you for the name of the user account to examine. The script annotations follow the sample output provided.

```
set verify off head off  feedback off pagesize 20
undefine usernm
accept usernm char prompt 'Enter username for system privileges report: '

set termout off echo off
drop table TEMPSPRIV;
create table TEMPSPRIV
(Grantee,Granted_Role,PrivType)
tablespace TEMP_TABLES
as
select Grantee,Granted_Role,'R'
  from DBA_ROLE_PRIVS;

insert into TEMPSPRIV
select distinct Grantee,
       DECODE(Grantee, 'DBA', 'DBA-role (+- 80 privs)',
               'IMP_FULL_DATABASE','Role of 35 privs',
               'EXP_FULL_DATABASE','Role of 2 privs',
               privilege),
       'P'
from DBA_SYS_PRIVS;

set termout on heading on
col Title format a30 heading "UserID/Role" trunc
col Privtype format a40 heading "System Privilege"
prompt SYSTEM PRIVILEGES
break on title

select LPAD(Grantee,LENGTH(Grantee)+Level*3) title,
       DECODE (PrivType,'R',NULL,'P',Granted_Role) Privtype
  from TEMPSPRIV
connect by Grantee = prior Granted_Role
 start with Grantee = UPPER('&usernm');
```

When the script is executed, you will be prompted for the username to show, and the output will then be displayed:

```
SQL> @usr_sprv
Enter username to show SYSTEM privileges of: DBSNMP
```

```
SYSTEM PRIVILEGES

UserID/Role                      System Privilege
----------------------------     ---------------------------------
DBSNMP
        CONNECT                  ALTER SESSION
                                 CREATE CLUSTER
                                 CREATE DATABASE LINK
                                 CREATE SEQUENCE
                                 CREATE SESSION
                                 CREATE SYNONYM
                                 CREATE TABLE
                                 CREATE VIEW
DBSNMP
        RESOURCE                 CREATE CLUSTER
                                 CREATE PROCEDURE
                                 CREATE SEQUENCE
                                 CREATE TABLE
                                 CREATE TRIGGER
                                 CREATE TYPE
DBSNMP
        SNMPAGENT                ANALYZE ANY
DBSNMP                           CREATE PUBLIC SYNONYM
DBSNMP                           UNLIMITED TABLESPACE
```

The output shows several related columns presented as a single column of data. The far-left data is the username—in this example, DBSNMP. If the privileges are obtained via a role, then the role name will be shown indented under the username. In this example, the DBSNMP user has been granted three roles: CONNECT, RESOURCE, and SNMPAGENT.

For each role, the privileges associated with the role are shown on the far-right column of data in the output. For example, the RESOURCE role gives the DBSNMP user the following system privileges: CREATE CLUSTER, CREATE PROCEDURE, CREATE SEQUENCE, CREATE TABLE, CREATE TRIGGER, and CREATE TYPE.

PROGRAMMER'S NOTE

The CREATE TYPE system privilege was introduced with ORACLE8; you will not see that privilege if you run this script under ORACLE7.

If a system-level privilege has been granted directly to the user, then that privilege is shown without a role associated with it. For example, in the preceding output listing, the CREATE PUBLIC SYNONYM privilege has been granted directly to the DBSNMP user; that privilege allows the DBSNMP user to create a public synonym without requiring the DBA role. The second privilege directly granted to the user is the UNLIMITED TABLESPACE privilege; that privilege cannot be granted via a role.

ANNOTATIONS

The script has three separate parts. In the first part of the script, shown in the following listing, the temporary work table that will hold the role privileges data is created and populated with role-related data.

```
set verify off head off  feedback off pagesize 20
undefine usernm
accept usernm char prompt 'Enter username for system privileges report: '

set termout off echo off
drop table TEMPSPRIV;
create table TEMPSPRIV
(Grantee,Granted_Role,PrivType)
tablespace TEMP_TABLES
as
select Grantee,Granted_Role,'R'
  from DBA_ROLE_PRIVS;
```

As a consequence of running this script, the user executing the script will have a table named TEMPSPRIV left in his or her schema. The script does not first attempt to see if the TEMPSPRIV table already exists. If the TEMPSPRIV table does not already exist, the **drop table** command will fail, but the failure will not be reported as an error to the user because of the **set termout off** setting that precedes it. Because repeatedly running this script will cause the table to be dropped and re-created multiple times, you should create a tablespace to store the table apart from your SYSTEM tablespace.

When the data from DBA_ROLE_PRIVS is inserted into the TEMPSPRIV table, its PrivType value is set to "R" to indicate that those records are associated with roles. The PrivType designations are used as part of the query that generates the final report output.

The second part of the script, shown in the following listing, generates the entries for directly granted privileges. Roles are directly granted to users, so the script uses the **DECODE** function to add entries and avoid listing all privileges for those three roles.

```
insert into TEMPSPRIV
select distinct Grantee,
       DECODE(Grantee, 'DBA', 'DBA-role (+- 80 privs)',
              'IMP_FULL_DATABASE','Role of 35 privs',
              'EXP_FULL_DATABASE','Role of 2 privs',
              privilege),
       'P'
  from DBA_SYS_PRIVS;
```

After this **insert** completes, the TEMPSPRIV table contains roles granted directly to the user, privileges granted directly to the user, and privileges granted directly to roles. You can now select the data from the TEMPSPRIV table and use the **connect by** clause to show the relationship between the roles and privileges.

```
set termout on heading on
col Title format a30 heading "UserID/Role" trunc
col Privtype format a40 heading "System Privilege"
prompt SYSTEM PRIVILEGES
break on title

select LPAD(Grantee,LENGTH(Grantee)+Level*3) title,
       DECODE (PrivType,'R',NULL,'P',Granted_Role)
  from TEMPSPRIV
connect by Grantee = prior Granted_Role
 start with Grantee = UPPER('&usernm');
```

```
undefine usernm
```

The **insert**s inserted into TEMPSPRIV *all* of the roles and *all* of the system privileges in the database. The final query is the only point at which the username is used as a limiting condition on the output. After the query completes, the *usernm* variable is undefined. Thus, you could run the final query again, using a different value for the *usernm* variable. When you enter a slash (/) on the SQL*Plus command line, the last SQL command in the buffer will be executed. Since the last SQL command is the query from TEMPSPRIV, the query will be re-executed. Since the *usernm* variable has been undefined, you will be prompted for a new *usernm* value.

usr_oprv.sql

Users' Object Privileges

What table privileges do your users have, and which of your users' table privileges come via roles? In this section, you will see a script that generates a listing of a user's table privileges—both those that are directly granted and those that are granted via roles. Since there can be a hierarchical relationship among roles, you will need to use the **connect by** operator during your query. Due to the different types of privileges you can have and the restrictions on the way in which the **connect by** is used, a temporary work table will be created for use by the script in this section.

Since table privileges may be granted via roles, you need to query DBA_ROLE_PRIVS, just as was done in the previous section. When displaying table privileges, you will need to query DBA_TAB_PRIVS for the information. However, you need to know more about table privileges than you do about system privileges. For example, you need to know what type of table privilege has been granted to a user, and whether or not the user was granted the privilege **with grant option**. Thus, the temporary work table used by the queries in this section will contain columns that were not a part of the temporary work table used in the preceding section.

The following script should be saved as a single file (called usr_oprv.sql). When executed, it will prompt you for the name of the user account to examine. The script annotations follow the sample output provided.

```
set verify off head off  feedback off pagesize 20
undefine usernm
accept usernm char prompt 'Enter username for obj privileges report: '

set termout off echo off
drop table TEMPOPRIV;
create table TEMPOPRIV
(Grantee,Granted_Role,PrivType,TableName,Grantable)
tablespace TEMP_TABLES
as
select Role,
       Privilege,
       'P',
       Table_Name,
       Grantable
  from ROLE_TAB_PRIVS;

insert into TEMPOPRIV
select Grantee,
       Granted_Role,
       'R',
       NULL,
       NULL
  from DBA_ROLE_PRIVS;

insert into TEMPOPRIV
select distinct Grantee,
       Privilege,
       'P',
       Table_Name,
       Grantable
  from DBA_TAB_PRIVS;

set termout on heading on
col Title format a30 heading "UserID/Role" trunc
col Privtype format a10 heading "Object Privilege"
col Grantable format a10
prompt OBJECT PRIVILEGES
```

```
break on title

select LPAD(Grantee,LENGTH(Grantee)+Level*3) title,
       TableName,
       DECODE (PrivType,'R',NULL,'P',Granted_Role) Privtype,
       Grantable
  from TEMPOPRIV
connect by Grantee = prior Granted_Role
 start with Grantee = UPPER('&usernm');
```

This script is similar to the usr_sprv.sql script in the previous section. The primary differences are the data dictionary views queried, the columns in the temporary work table, and the number of **insert** statements. In this script, three sets of records are inserted into the TEMPOPRIV table: the role grants, the table privileges granted to the roles, and the table privileges granted directly to users.

ANNOTATIONS

In the first part of the usr_tprv.sql script, the temporary work table TEMPOPRIV is created:

```
drop table TEMPOPRIV;
create table TEMPOPRIV
(Grantee,Granted_Role,PrivType,TableName,Grantable)
tablespace TEMP_TABLES
as
select Role,
       Privilege,
       'P',
       Table_Name,
       Grantable
  from ROLE_TAB_PRIVS;
```

The code does not check to see if a TEMPOPRIV table already exists prior to executing the **drop table** command. If a table with that name already exists in your schema, then it will be dropped when you run the script. When the script completes, the TEMPOPRIV table is not dropped. The TEMPOPRIV table, which contains all of the role and table privilege information for your database, remains in your schema and all of its data remains in the database. As with the script in the prior section, the table that stores the data is stored in the TEMP_TABLES tablespace to avoid fragmenting the SYSTEM tablespace.

During the TEMPOPRIV data load process, you may **insert** many records into the table; the number of records depends on the number of user accounts and objects maintained in your database, and on the extent to which you use roles to manage table privileges. Since these **insert**s are transactions, ORACLE will maintain rollback segment entries for the transactions. If the rollback segment entry sizes exceed the available space in your rollback segments, you have two options available to you. First, you could add a **commit** command following each **insert** command in the script. Second, you could use the **nologging** option when the table is created (this option is available as of ORACLE8; this is an enhanced version of the **unrecoverable** option introduced in ORACLE7.2).

You may wish to run both reports together, which would allow you to see a user's system privileges and table privileges. In that case, you could simply create a single SQL script that calls the other two:

```
start usr_sprv
start usr_tprv
```

You'll be prompted for the *usernm* variable value twice (once by each script) unless you remove the **undefine** command from the end of the usr_sprv.sql script and the beginning of the usr_tprv.sql script. In order for a SQL*Plus variable to maintain its value, you need to change the single ampersand values (&) to double ampersands (&&). Change the *&usernm* variable reference to *&&usernm* in both scripts and the variable will maintain its value throughout your session (until an **undefine** command is executed).

You can also grant privileges at the column level. For example, you can grant a user UPDATE privilege on only certain columns of a table. Since the column privilege data dictionary views' structure closely parallels the structure of the table privilege data dictionary views, you can easily modify the usr_tprv.sql script shown in this section to support the display of column-level privileges. For example, DBA_COL_PRIVS contains the same columns as DBA_TAB_PRIVS, with the addition of a Column_Name column.

If you do not have DBA privileges, you can execute modified versions of the privilege scripts shown in this section and the preceding section. If you replace DBA_ROLE_PRIVS with USER_ROLE_PRIVS, then you will see the role privilege information for all roles which have been granted to you. If you replace DBA_TAB_PRIVS with ALL_TAB_PRIVS, then you will see the table privileges for all tables which you own or to which you have been granted access.

Active Roles and Privileges

How can you tell which privileges and roles are currently active for a user? Privileges that are directly granted to a user are always active, but privileges granted via a role are only active during the user's session while the role is enabled for the user. Roles are enabled for users via the **set role** command; a user may also have default roles that are enabled on login.

Two views, each with a single column, list the privileges and roles currently enabled for the current session, as shown here:

SESSION_PRIVS   The Privilege column lists all system privileges available
                               to the session, whether granted directly or via roles.

SESSION_ROLES   The Role column lists all roles that are currently enabled
                               for the session.

You do not have to be a DBA to access these views; SESSION_PRIVS and
SESSION_ROLES are available to all users.

How Many Users Have Logged In?

In order to determine how many users have logged into your database, you could
use ORACLE's auditing features. However, the auditing features do not provide
data that easily shows you the number of concurrent users who were active. To see
that information, you should query the V$LICENSE dynamic view.

The following listing shows a query of the V$LICENSE view, along with sample
output.

```
select *
  from V$LICENSE;


SESSIONS_MAX SESSIONS_WARNING SESSIONS_CURRENT SESSIONS_HIGHWATER  USERS_MAX
------------ ---------------- ---------------- ------------------ ----------
           0                0               12                 55          0
```

Currently, there are 12 sessions accessing the database. The highest number of
concurrent sessions (as displayed in the Sessions_Highwater column) was 55. The
Sessions_Max, Sessions_Warning, and Max_Users columns reflect the settings of
parameters in the database's init.ora file.

To limit the number of named users in a database, set a value for the
LICENSE_MAX_USERS parameter in the database's init.ora file. The setting
in the following example sets the maximum number of named users to 100:

```
LICENSE_MAX_USERS = 100
```

If you already have created more than 100 users in your database, starting
ORACLE with a LICENSE_MAX_USERS setting of 100 will cause a warning to
be displayed (a warning will also be written to the alert log for the database). To
avoid the error, set the LICENSE_MAX_USERS parameter value to a value that
properly reflects your usage and database usage licensing.

To change the maximum named users limit while a database is open, use the
alter system command with the **license_max_users** clause. The following example
changes the maximum number of named users to 200:

```
alter system set LICENSE_MAX_USERS = 200;
```

To set the maximum number of concurrent sessions for an instance, set a value
for the LICENSE_MAX_SESSIONS init.ora parameter, as shown in the following
listing.

```
LICENSE_MAX_SESSIONS = 80
```

You can also set a warning limit for the number of concurrent sessions; if the warning limit is exceeded, then a warning message will be written to the database's alert log. To set a warning limit, set a value for the LICENSE_SESSIONS_WARNING init.ora parameter, as shown in the following listing.

```
LICENSE_SESSIONS_WARNING = 70
```

You can change both the LICENSE_MAX_SESSIONS parameter value and the LICENSE_SESSIONS_WARNING parameter value while the database is open. The **alter system** command contains clauses that manipulate these settings, as shown in the following listing.

```
alter system set LICENSE_MAX_SESSIONS = 64;
alter system set LICENSE_SESSIONS_WARNING = 54;
```

To change either of these parameter values permanently, change the value of the parameter in the init.ora file.

When you query from the V$LICENSE view, the output shows both the system usage and the current parameter settings, as shown in the following listing.

```
select *
  from V$LICENSE;
```

SESSIONS_MAX	SESSIONS_WARNING	SESSIONS_CURRENT	SESSIONS_HIGHWATER	USERS_MAX
0	0	12	55	0

The Sessions_Max column value is the value of the LICENSE_MAX_SESSIONS parameter; none has been specified, so ORACLE reports a value of 0 for the value. The value is not really 0, since such a setting would prevent ORACLE from starting. ORACLE will report a value of 0 for a license parameter for which a value has not been set. The Sessions_Warning column corresponds to the LICENSE_SESSIONS_WARNING parameter setting. The Users_Max column corresponds to the LICENSE_MAX_USERS setting.

User Session Information

usr_sesn.sql

You can query V$SESSION to see information about current active sessions in the database. In this section, you will see a script that retrieves and formats the data from V$SESSION in an easy-to-use manner.

The following script, usr_sesn.sql, queries V$SESSION and embeds character strings in the output. In order to make the output more readable, the script places carriage returns in the output by concatenating an ASCII character (via the **CHR**(10) function) at the proper places in the output.

```
col "Session Info" form a80

select ' Sid, Serial#, Aud sid : '|| S.sid||
    ' , '||S.Serial#||' , '|| S.audsid||CHR(10)||
```

```
'DB User / OS User : '||S.Username||
     '    /   '||S.OSuser||CHR(10)||
     '    Machine - Terminal : '|| S.Machine||
     '  - '|| S.Terminal||CHR(10)||
     '        OS Process Ids : '|| S.Process||
     ' (Client)  '||P.Spid||' (Server)'|| CHR(10)||
     '    Client Program Name : '||S.Program "Session Info"
 from V$PROCESS P, V$SESSION S
where P.Addr = S.Paddr
  and S.Audsid = USERENV('SESSIONID');
```

Sample output is shown in the following listing.

```
Session Info
-----------------------------------------------------------
Sid, Serial#, Aud sid : 8 , 251 , 1044
    DB User / OS User : BONNIE   /   appadmin
  Machine - Terminal : myhost1  -   ttyp4
        OS Process Ids : 12100 (Client)  12103 (Server)
  Client Program Name : sqlplus@myhost1 (TNS V1-V3)
```

usr_quot.sql

User Resource Quotas

You can query the DBA_TS_QUOTAS data dictionary view to see the current and maximum space allocation per tablespace. In the following listing, all of the columns are selected from DBA_TS_QUOTAS, ordered by tablespace name and username.

```
select * from DBA_TS_QUOTAS
order by Tablespace_Name, Username;
```

Sample output is shown in the following listing. Because of the length of the lines of output, the output is wrapped across two lines per row returned.

TABLESPACE_NAME	USERNAME	BYTES
MAX_BYTES	BLOCKS	MAX_BLOCKS

TABLESPACE_NAME / MAX_BYTES	USERNAME / BLOCKS	BYTES / MAX_BLOCKS
APP_D1	APPLOADER	1.1889E+10
-1	1451241	-1
APP_D2	APPLOADER	0
52428800	0	6400
APP_I1	APPLOADER	7503986688
-1	916014	-1
APP_I2	APPLOADER	7474888704
-1	912462	-1

The output shows the tablespace quotas and usage for a single user over four tablespaces. The APPLOADER user has no maximum space quota on three of the tablespaces (those for which the Max_Bytes column displays a value of -1). For the APP_D2 tablespace, a quota of 52,428,800 bytes (50MB) has been established. The database block size is 8KB, as you can tell by dividing one of the Bytes values by its matching Blocks value.

The Bytes and Blocks values reflect the current allocated space within each tablespace for each user. Thus, in the APP_I1 tablespace, the APPLOADER user has allocated 916,014 database blocks. There is no space quota for the APPLOADER user in the APP_I1 tablespace, so the user's space allocation in that tablespace is limited only by the size of the tablespace's datafiles.

PROGRAMMER'S NOTE

*You can alter a user's quota on a tablespace at any time via the **alter user** command. If you change the quota to a value below the user's current space allocation, the user will not be able to create new tables or indexes and will encounter an error when attempting to acquire more space for an existing object. Objects already created and extents already obtained will not be dropped to reduce the user's allocated space.*

ANNOTATIONS

You can allow your datafiles to extend. When you configure the extension parameters for your datafiles, you specify an extent size to acquire and the maximum size to which the file can extend. You cannot specify the maximum number of extents your file will acquire.

If any of the datafiles in your database can extend, then there will be records in the table SYS.FILEXT$. If your datafiles cannot extend, then this table will not exist in your database.

You can determine which users own objects in which tablespaces (and datafiles) by querying the data dictionary views. For scripts that map objects to tablespaces, see Chapter 6.

UTILITIES

In the first section of this chapter, you saw scripts that report on the current status of the users in the database. In this section, the scripts provided will modify the users in the database or will generate code that will help you manage your users.

pas_cmpx.sql

Password Complexity

As of ORACLE8, you can use profiles to manage the expiration, reuse, and complexity of passwords. For example, you can limit the lifetime of a password and lock an account whose password is too old. You can also force a password to be at least moderately complex and lock any account that has repeated failed login attempts.

ORACLE provides a script file called utlpwdmg.sql (usually found in the /rdbms/admin directory under the ORACLE software home directory) that provides a good basis for enforcing password complexity. In this section, you will see a modified version of the script provided in the utlpwdmg.sql file. The script forces users' passwords to meet standards for complexity. For example, you can require that passwords be a minimum length, that they not be simple words, and that they contain at least one number or punctuation mark.

Once the script has been run (and the password complexity verification function has been created) you can assign the function to one of the profiles in the database. The standard file provided by ORACLE alters the default profile for the database. The script provided in this section does not alter the default profile; instead, it creates a new profile and assigns the password complexity verification function to the new profile. You can use the **password_verify_function** parameter of the **create profile** and **alter profile** commands to associate a password complexity verification function with a profile. If a user who has that profile tries to set a password that does not meet the criteria, the password will not be not accepted.

In the following listing, the modified version of the utlpwdmg.sql file is shown. The command should be executed when logged into ORACLE as SYS. Annotations follow the listing.

```
REM Modified version of utlpwdmg.sql
REM Based on original utlpwd.mg.sql script provided by Oracle
create or replace function PASSWORD_COMPLEXITY
   (username     varchar2,
    password     varchar2,
    old_password varchar2)
   RETURN boolean IS
    n          boolean;
    m          integer;
    differ     integer;
    isdigit    boolean;
    ischar     boolean;
    ispunct    boolean;
    digitarray varchar2(20);
    punctarray varchar2(25);
    chararray  varchar2(52);

BEGIN
    digitarray:= '0123456789';
    chararray:= 'abcdefghijklmnopqrstuvwxyzABCDEFGHIJKLMNOPQRSTUVWXYZ';
    punctarray:='!"#$%&()``*+,-/:;<=>?_';

    -- Check if the password is same as the username
    IF password = username THEN
```

```
   raise_application_error(-20001, 'Password same as user');
END IF;


-- Check for the minimum length of the password
IF length(password) < 8 THEN
   raise_application_error(-20002, 'Password length less than 8');
END IF;


-- Check if the password is too simple. A dictionary of words may be
-- maintained and a check may be made so as not to allow the words
-- that are too simple for the password.
IF password IN ('welcome', 'password', 'oracle', 'computer', 'abcd') THEN
   raise_application_error(-20003, 'Password too simple');
END IF;


-- Check if the password contains at least one letter, one digit and one
-- punctuation mark.
-- 1. Check for the digit
isdigit:=FALSE;
m := length(password);
FOR i IN 1..10 LOOP
   FOR j IN 1..m LOOP
      IF substr(password,j,1) = substr(digitarray,i,1) THEN
         isdigit:=TRUE;
          GOTO findchar;
      END IF;
   END LOOP;
END LOOP;
IF isdigit = FALSE THEN
   raise_application_error(-20004, 'Password should contain at least one
          digit, one character and one punctuation');
END IF;
-- 2. Check for the character
<<findchar>>
ischar:=FALSE;
FOR i IN 1..length(chararray) LOOP
   FOR j IN 1..m LOOP
      IF substr(password,j,1) = substr(chararray,i,1) THEN
         ischar:=TRUE;
          GOTO findpunct;
      END IF;
   END LOOP;
END LOOP;
IF ischar = FALSE THEN
   raise_application_error(-20004, 'Password should contain at least one \
          digit, one character and one punctuation');
END IF;
-- 3. Check for the punctuation
```

```
<<findpunct>>
ispunct:=FALSE;
FOR i IN 1..length(punctarray) LOOP
    FOR j IN 1..m LOOP
        IF substr(password,j,1) = substr(punctarray,i,1) THEN
            ispunct:=TRUE;
            GOTO endsearch;
        END IF;
    END LOOP;
END LOOP;
IF ispunct = FALSE THEN
    raise_application_error(-20004, 'Password should contain at least one \
            digit, one character and one punctuation');
END IF;

<<endsearch>>
-- Check that there is an old password
IF old_password = '' THEN
    raise_application_error(-20005, 'Old password is null');
END IF;
-- Everything is fine; return TRUE ;
RETURN(TRUE);END;
/

create profile APPLICATION_USERS limit
PASSWORD_LIFE_TIME    60
PASSWORD_GRACE_TIME   10
PASSWORD_REUSE_TIME   1800
PASSWORD_REUSE_MAX    UNLIMITED
FAILED_LOGIN_ATTEMPTS 3
PASSWORD_LOCK_TIME     1/1440
PASSWORD_VERIFY_FUNCTION password_complexity;
```

When this script is executed, a profile named APPLICATION_USERS will be created. You can assign this profile to a user via the **profile** clause of the **alter user** command, as shown in the following listing.

```
alter user BONNIE
profile APPLICATION_USERS;
```

The next time that the user BONNIE changes her password, her new password will have to meet the password complexity criteria specified by the **PASSWORD_COMPLEXITY** function created by the script.

The other parameters specified in the **create profile** command shown in the preceding listing are described in the Annotations section.

ANNOTATIONS

The first three **if** clauses in the **PASSWORD_COMPLEXITY** function check if the password is the same as the username, if the password is less than eight characters, and if the password is in a set of specific words. You can modify any of these checks or add your own. For example, your corporate security guideline may call for passwords to have a minimum of six characters; simply update that portion of the script prior to running it.

The first **if** clause checks to see if the password is the same as the username.

```
IF password = username THEN
   raise_application_error(-20001, 'Password same as user');
END IF;
```

The preceding password checks use two of the three input parameters for the **PASSWORD_COMPLEXITY** function. When you create a password complexity verification function, you can use the username, password, and old password as input values. You can use the **RAISE_APPLICATION_ERROR** function to create an error number and a matching error message. The error numbers you use should be in the range -20,000 to -20,999 (all error numbers are negative numbers). If a user attempts to use a password that is the same as the username, a "Password same as user" message will be displayed.

The second **if** clause checks the length of the password. If the password is less than eight characters long, then the password is rejected.

```
IF length(password) < 8 THEN
   raise_application_error(-20002, 'Password length less than 8');
END IF;
```

The third **if** clause checks to see if the new password is in a list of common, easily guessable words. You can add additional values to the list of words to check.

```
IF password IN ('welcome', 'password', 'oracle', 'computer', 'abcd') THEN
   raise_application_error(-20003, 'Password too simple');
END IF;
```

The next major section of the function is a three-part check of the contents of the password string. In order to pass these checks, the password must contain at least one character, number, and punctuation mark. As with the earlier checks, these can be edited.

The first section uses a variable named *digitarray* that is defined at the start of the script as having the value 0123456789. In this section, the character values of the password are checked one at a time against the values in the *digitarray* value. If there is a match between a character in the password and a character in the *digitarray* variable, then the new password contains at least one number, the *isdigit* variable is set to TRUE and the **goto** command is used to go to the "findchar" section, which checks for characters in the new password.

```
isdigit:=FALSE;
m := length(password);
FOR i IN 1..10 LOOP
    FOR j IN 1..m LOOP
        IF substr(password,j,1) = substr(digitarray,i,1) THEN
            isdigit:=TRUE;
            GOTO findchar;
        END IF;
    END LOOP;
END LOOP;
IF isdigit = FALSE THEN
    raise_application_error(-20004, 'Password should contain at least one
            digit, one character and one punctuation');
END IF;
```

In the "findchar" section (marked by the <<findchar>> label), the
PASSWORD_COMPLEXITY function uses a parameter called *chararray*,
which is defined at the beginning of the script. The *chararray* variable
contains all of the letters in the alphabet, in both uppercase and lowercase.
If any of the characters in the password matches any of the characters
in the *chararray* variable, then the *ischar* variable is set to TRUE and the
"findpunct" section of the script is called.

```
<<findchar>>
ischar:=FALSE;
FOR i IN 1..length(chararray) LOOP
    FOR j IN 1..m LOOP
        IF substr(password,j,1) = substr(chararray,i,1) THEN
            ischar:=TRUE;
            GOTO findpunct;
        END IF;
    END LOOP;
END LOOP;
IF ischar = FALSE THEN
    raise_application_error(-20004, 'Password should contain at least one \
            digit, one character and one punctuation');
END IF;
```

In the "findpunct" section, the **if** clause checks to see if any character in the
password matches any of the values in the *punctarray* variable defined at the
start of the script. If there are no punctuation characters in the password, then
the password is not accepted as a valid password.

```
<<findpunct>>
ispunct:=FALSE;
FOR i IN 1..length(punctarray) LOOP
    FOR j IN 1..m LOOP
        IF substr(password,j,1) = substr(punctarray,i,1) THEN
            ispunct:=TRUE;
```

```
            GOTO endsearch;
        END IF;
    END LOOP;
END LOOP;
IF ispunct = FALSE THEN
    raise_application_error(-20004, 'Password should contain at least one \
            digit, one character and one punctuation');
END IF;
```

If you do not require your users to have punctuation in their passwords, then you should skip this section. To skip this section, change the **goto findpunct** command in the "findchar" section to **goto endsearch.** After the **create function** command completes, a profile is created to use the new function:

```
create profile APPLICATION_USERS limit
PASSWORD_LIFE_TIME      60
PASSWORD_GRACE_TIME     10
PASSWORD_REUSE_TIME     1800
PASSWORD_REUSE_MAX      UNLIMITED
FAILED_LOGIN_ATTEMPTS 3
PASSWORD_LOCK_TIME      1/1440
PASSWORD_VERIFY_FUNCTION password_complexity;
```

The last line of the **create profile** command associates the **PASSWORD_COMPLEXITY** function with the profile named APPLICATION_USERS. The other parameters control the frequency with which the password must be changed and the way ORACLE handles failed login attempts.

To force a user to change his or her password, set a value for the PASSWORD_LIFE_TIME variable. In this example, any user who has the APPLICATION_USERS profile will have to select a new password every 60 days. Once the user logs in following the password expiration date, the grace period (PASSWORD_GRACE_TIME) for the old password begins. In this example, users of the APPLICATION_USERS profile will have 10 days to change their old passwords once they log in following the expiration of the old password.

To prevent a password from being reused, you can use one of two profile parameters: PASSWORD_REUSE_MAX or PASSWORD_REUSE_TIME. These two parameters are mutually exclusive; if you set a value for one of them, then the other must be set to UNLIMITED. In this example, the PASSWORD_REUSE_TIME parameter is used, while PASSWORD_REUSE_MAX is set to UNLIMITED.

The PASSWORD_REUSE_TIME parameter specifies the number of days that must pass before a password can be reused. In this example, PASSWORD_REUSE_TIME is set to 1,800, so users with this profile cannot reuse the same password within 1,800 days.

The PASSWORD_REUSE_MAX parameter specifies the number of password changes that must occur before a password can be reused. If you attempt to reuse the password before the limit is reached, ORACLE will reject your password change.

Password histories are stored in the table named USER_HISTORY$ under the SYS schema. In this table, ORACLE stores the userid, encrypted password value, and the date/timestamp for the creation of the password. When the PASSWORD_REUSE_TIME value is exceeded or the number of changes exceeds PASSWORD_REUSE_MAX, the old password records are deleted from the SYS.USER_HISTORY$ table. If a new encryption matches an existing encryption, the new password is rejected.

Because the old passwords are stored in a table owned by SYS, the data is stored in the SYSTEM tablespace. Therefore, if you will maintain a very large password history for a very large number of users who are forced to change passwords frequently, the space requirements of the password history table (SYS.USER_HISTORY$) may impact the space requirements of your SYSTEM tablespace.

You can use the FAILED_LOGIN_ATTEMPTS parameter to lock an account that has repeated failed login attempts. In this example, the FAILED_LOGIN_ATTEMPTS parameter is set to three, so three consecutive failed login attempts will cause the account to be locked and no logins will be allowed until the account is unlocked. You can unlock an account manually (via the **account unlock** clause of the **alter user** command) or you can have the account automatically unlock itself. The time before the account is unlocked is expressed in days via the PASSWORD_LOCK_TIME parameter. In this example, the PASSWORD_LOCK_TIME parameter is set to 1/1,440 of a day, or 1 minute.

You can use profiles to restrict other aspects of user activities. For example, you can restrict the number of concurrent logins that are permitted using the same username. For a list of all of the resource-related parameters and their values for a profile, query the DBA_PROFILES data dictionary view. Users without DBA authority can query the USER_RESOURCE_LIMITS data dictionary view to see the resource limits for their profile and USER_PASSWORD_LIMITS to see the password-related restrictions for their profile. The DBA_PROFILES data dictionary view contains entries for both types of restriction (the Resource_Type column of DBA_PROFILES has a value of PASSWORD for restrictions related to passwords and KERNEL for all other restrictions).

cr8_usr.sql

Re-creating Users

You can use the information in the data dictionary to generate a **create user** command that will reflect the current settings for each user. For example, if you have changed a user's default tablespace since the user was created, this script will capture the current setting of that parameter. The script will even capture the user's password (via an undocumented option of the **create user** command).

The script is in three parts. The first part generates the **create user** command. The second part generates the **alter user** commands that will assign resource quotas for the user. The third part uses a PL/SQL loop to generate the **alter user** command that will set the proper default roles for the user. The annotations of the script follow the sample output.

```
set heading off verify off feedback off echo off term on
column X format a40 word_wrapped
undefine usernm

select 'create user '||Username||
       ' identified '||
           DECODE(Password,NULL, 'EXTERNALLY',
            ' by values '||''''||Password||'''')||
       ' default tablespace '||Default_Tablespace||
       ' temporary tablespace '||Temporary_Tablespace||
       ' profile '||Profile||'; ' X
  from DBA_USERS
 where Username = UPPER('&&usernm');

select 'alter user '||Username||
       ' quota '||DECODE(Max_Bytes,-1,'UNLIMITED',Max_Bytes)||
       ' on '||Tablespace_Name||'; '
  from DBA_TS_QUOTAS
 where Username = UPPER('&&usernm');

set serveroutput on
declare
  usernam    VARCHAR2(32) := '&&usernm';
  roles_list VARCHAR2(32767) := 'NONE';
  cursor roles_cursor is
      select *
        from DBA_ROLE_PRIVS
       where (Grantee = UPPER(usernam) or Grantee = 'PUBLIC')
         and Default_Role = 'YES';
  role_val roles_cursor%ROWTYPE;
begin
open roles_cursor;
  loop
    fetch roles_cursor into role_val;
    exit when roles_cursor%NOTFOUND;
      roles_list := roles_list||','||role_val.Granted_Role;
  end loop;
if LENGTH(roles_list)>5 THEN
  roles_list:=SUBSTR(roles_list,6);
end if;
```

```
DBMS_OUTPUT.PUT_LINE('alter user '||usernam||' default role '
||roles_list||';');
end;
.
/
```

When you execute the cr8_usr.sql script, you should save the output to a file via the **spool** command. Sample generated output is shown in the following listing.

```
SQL> @cr8_usr
Enter value for usernm: BONNIE

create user BONNIE identified by
values '8808AD4E97AAAF0E' default
tablespace SOURCE_D1 temporary
tablespace LOAD_TEMP profile DEFAULT;


alter user BONNIE quota UNLIMITED on APP_IP1;
alter user BONNIE quota UNLIMITED on APP_DA1;
alter user BONNIE quota UNLIMITED on APP_D1;
alter user BONNIE quota UNLIMITED on APP_I1;

alter user BONNIE default role
ATLOADER_SEL_ROLE,CONNECT,DIMLOADER_SEL_ROLE,DPCLOADER_SEL_ROLE;

PL/SQL procedure successfully completed.
```

The output contains three separate sets of SQL commands. The first SQL command in the output is the **create user** command that specifies the default and temporary tablespace for the user. The user's encrypted password is also captured; the password encryption setting is described in the "Annotations" section. The second set of SQL commands alters the user by applying the space quotas the user has been granted. There is one **alter user** command for each tablespace for which the user has a space quota. The third part of the output shows the command that will specify the user's default roles (since not all roles may be assigned as default roles).

ANNOTATIONS

The cr8_user.sql script uses a number of tricks and techniques. First, it makes use of the way in which the Import utility assigns passwords to users when it creates users. When a user is created in a database via Import, the Import utility uses the **identified by values** clause of the **create user** command to specify the encrypted version of the user's password. The cr8_usr.sql script uses this same technique—if the user has a password, then the encrypted version of the password is selected as part of the **create user** command generation:

```
set heading off verify off feedback off echo off term on
column X format a40 word_wrapped
undefine usernm

select 'create user '||Username||
       ' identified '||
          DECODE(Password,NULL, 'EXTERNALLY',
           ' by values '||''''||Password||'''')||
       ' default tablespace '||Default_Tablespace||
       ' temporary tablespace '||Temporary_Tablespace||
       ' profile '||Profile||'; ' X
  from DBA_USERS
 where Username = UPPER('&&usernm');
```

In the first part of the script, four output settings are turned off: heading, feedback, echo, and verify. The **set heading off** command will suppress the display of the column headings in output. The **set feedback off** command will suppress the display of messages such as "4 rows selected." The **set verify off** command will suppress the display of "old" and "new" values for a variable when a variable has a value assigned to it. The **set echo off** command will suppress the display of the SQL statements being processed. The **set term on** command ensures that the results of the SQL statements are displayed.

The first part of the script surrounds the encrypted password value with single quotes by concatenating strings of four single quotes before and after the password value. A string of four single quotes is interpreted as a single quote: the outer two quotes signal that the string is a character string, and the inner two quotes are transformed into a single quote.

The second part of the script is the simplest of the three parts. In the second part of the script, one row is generated for each tablespace for which the user has been granted a space quota.

```
select 'alter user '||Username||
       ' quota '||DECODE(Max_Bytes,-1,'UNLIMITED',Max_Bytes)||
       ' on '||Tablespace_Name||'; '
  from DBA_TS_QUOTAS
 where Username = UPPER('&&usernm');
```

There is no requirement that all of the space quota commands be specified in a single command, so this section of the script generates a separate **alter user** command for each tablespace. When you select multiple rows from a table, ORACLE normally tells you how many rows were retrieved; this display is suppressed via the **set feedback off** command at the beginning of the script.

The third part of the script generates a single command that specifies the default roles for your user. All of the default roles for a user must be specified in a single **alter user** command, so this part of the script must generate a single command based on the output of multiple rows in the DBA_ROLE_PRIVS data dictionary view. To create a single command from multiple rows, a PL/SQL loop is used.

First, the **set serveroutput on** command is executed to enable display of the values generated within the PL/SQL block. Next, four variables are declared. The variables are the username, whose value is inherited from the *usernm* variable used earlier in the script; the list of default roles; a cursor that selects data from DBA_ROLE_PRIVS; and a variable that has the same structure as the cursor.

```
set serveroutput on
declare
   usernam    VARCHAR2(32) := '&&usernm';
   roles_list VARCHAR2(32767) := 'NONE';
   cursor roles_cursor is
      select *
        from DBA_ROLE_PRIVS
       where (Grantee = UPPER(usernam) or Grantee = 'PUBLIC')
         and Default_Role = 'YES';
   role_val roles_cursor%ROWTYPE;
```

By default, the *roles_list* parameter is set to NONE. If a user has no default roles, the command **alter user** *username* **default role NONE;** will be generated by this script. The *usernam* variable in the PL/SQL block will have as its default value the value of the *usernm* variable used in the first two parts of the script.

In the next section of the PL/SQL block, a simple loop is created. The cursor that queries DBA_ROLE_PRIVS is opened. For each record that is retrieved, the value of the Granted_Role column is appended to the *roles_list* variable's value. When no more rows are returned by the cursor, the loop is exited.

```
begin
open roles_cursor;
  loop
    fetch roles_cursor into role_val;
    exit when roles_cursor%NOTFOUND;
      roles_list := roles_list||','||role_val.Granted_Role;
  end loop;
```

If any rows have been returned by the cursor, then the value of the *roles_list* variable will begin with NONE, followed by the default roles. To remove the NONE part of the command, check the length of the *roles_list* variable, as shown in the following listing. If the length is greater than five characters, then the user has at least one default role and the NONE section at the start of the variable's value is stripped. To strip out the first five characters of the *roles_list* variable value, use the **SUBSTR**(roles_list,6) function. The "6" in that function tells ORACLE to begin the

SUBSTR function at the sixth character of the string. Since no length parameter is specified for the **SUBSTR** function, the entire rest of the string will be selected.

```
if LENGTH(roles_list)>5 THEN
  roles_list:=SUBSTR(roles_list,6);
end if;
```

You can now output the list of default roles via the **PUT_LINE** function of the DBMS_OUTPUT package, as shown in the following listing.

```
DBMS_OUTPUT.PUT_LINE('alter user '||usernam||' default role '
||roles_list||';');
end;
.
/
```

When the script has completed, the *usernm* variable still has a value assigned to it. The *usernm* variable will retain its value until you undefine it (via the **undefine** command) or until you run the cr8_usr.sql command again (since it contains an **undefine** command in its first section).

gen_grnt.sql

Generate Grant Commands

You can use the information in the data dictionary views to generate the commands necessary to re-create system and object privileges. In most cases, you should use the Export and Import utilities to re-create grants. However, you can generate the SQL scripts needed to re-create the grants you need.

To use the Export/Import method, perform a full Export of the database while using the ROWS=N and GRANTS=Y parameters. All of the object definitions will be exported along with all of the **grant** commands that apply to those objects. When you re-create the object elsewhere, you can use the Export dump file to retrieve all of the object grants. Since **grant**s on a table can be made by multiple users, the Export/Import method allows you to re-create all grants no matter who made them. However, you may wish to generate the privilege creation scripts yourself.

As long as the privilege structure is not tiered, you can easily re-create the **grant** commands by querying the data dictionary. That is, if you have not granted privileges on an object via an account other than the object owner account, then you can generate the proper **grant** commands by querying the necessary data from DBA_TAB_PRIVS, DBA_COL_PRIVS, and DBA_ROLE_PRIVS. See the user diagnostics section in the first section of this chapter for examples of privilege diagnostics queries.

You can generate the system privilege commands as well. For example, the following script generates the **grant** commands for system privileges. The basic system-level roles such as CONNECT and RESOURCE are not displayed in the output; only user-created roles and individual users will be shown. As with the script in the prior section, you should save the script output to a file via the **spool** command.

```
set verify off feedback off termout on echo off pagesize 0

select 'grant ' || RPAD(Privilege,30) || ' to ' || Grantee ||
       DECODE(Admin_Option,'YES',' with admin option;',';')
  from DBA_SYS_PRIVS
 where Grantee not in ('CONNECT','RESOURCE','DBA',
            'EXP_FULL_DATABASE','IMP_FULL_DATABASE')
 order by Grantee;
```

Sample output is shown in the following listing.

```
grant CREATE SESSION                 to BOB;
grant CREATE SESSION                 to BONNIE;
grant CREATE SYNONYM                 to CAROLYN;
grant CREATE PUBLIC SYNONYM          to DBSNMP;
grant UNLIMITED TABLESPACE           to DBSNMP;
```

As you can see from the preceding listing, there is one **grant** command generated for each distinct privilege for each user.

gen_role.sql

Generate Roles

In addition to re-creating users and **grant** commands, you can re-create the **create role** commands. The script provided in this section will generate the commands necessary to create all the roles in the database. This script will not generate the **create role** commands for the basic ORACLE roles such as CONNECT, RESOURCE, and DBA.

```
REM  For Oracle7, the column name in USER$ is   Type
REM  For Oracle8, the column name in USER$ is   Type#
set echo off verify off feedback off pagesize 0

select 'create role ' || Role || ' not identified;'
  from DBA_ROLES
 where Role not in ('CONNECT','RESOURCE','DBA', 'EXP_FULL_DATABASE',

                    'IMP_FULL_DATABASE')
   and Password_Required='NO' ;

select 'create role ' || Role || ' identified by values ' ||
       '''' || Password || '''' || ';'
```

```
   from DBA_ROLES, sys.USER$
 where Role not in ('CONNECT','RESOURCE','DBA', 'EXP_FULL_DATABASE',
                    'IMP_FULL_DATABASE')
   and Password_Required='YES'
   and DBA_ROLES.Role=USER$.Name
   and USER$.Type=0 ;

select 'grant ' || Granted_Role || ' to ' || Grantee ||
       ' with admin option;'
  from DBA_ROLE_PRIVS
 where Admin_Option='YES'
   and Granted_Role not in ('CONNECT','RESOURCE','DBA',
                            'EXP_FULL_DATABASE', 'IMP_FULL_DATABASE')

  order by Grantee ;
```

Sample output from the preceding script is shown in the following listing.

```
create role APP_USER_ROLE not identified;
create role LOADER_ROLE not identified;
create role APP_ADMIN_ROLE not identified;
create role SNMPAGENT not identified;
grant APP_USER_ROLE to BONNIE with admin option;
grant LOADER_ROLE to BONNIE with admin option;
grant APP_ADMIN_ROLE to BONNIE with admin option;
grant SNMPAGENT to SYS with admin option;
```

ANNOTATIONS

The output shows the **create role** commands for four roles. Each of the roles has been created without an associated password, so they are created with the **not identified** clause. The commands for roles with no passwords are created via the first part of the script:

```
select 'create role ' || Role || ' not identified;'
  from DBA_ROLES
 where Role not in ('CONNECT','RESOURCE','DBA', 'EXP_FULL_DATABASE',
                    'IMP_FULL_DATABASE')
   and Password_Required='NO' ;
```

The second part of the script queries the data dictionary for information on roles that have passwords associated with them. The passwords for roles are stored in the SYS.USER$ table. Each role has an entry in SYS.USER$; its password is stored

encrypted, and the USER$.Type# (USER$.Type in ORACLE7) column has a value
of 0 for each role.

```
select 'create role ' || Role || ' identified by values ' ||
       '''' || Password || '''' || ';'
  from DBA_ROLES, SYS.USER$
 where Role not in ('CONNECT','RESOURCE','DBA', 'EXP_FULL_DATABASE',
                      'IMP_FULL_DATABASE')
   and Password_Required='YES'
   and DBA_ROLES.Role=USER$.Name
   and USER$.Type=0 ;
```

The query of SYS.USER$ uses the same technique shown in the preceding section
on re-creating users to capture a user's password. In this case, it is the role's password.

The third section of the script captures any roles that have been granted **with
admin option**:

```
select 'grant ' || Granted_Role || ' to ' || Grantee ||
       ' with admin option;'
  from DBA_ROLE_PRIVS
 where Admin_Option='YES'
   and Granted_Role not in ('CONNECT','RESOURCE','DBA',
                              'EXP_FULL_DATABASE', 'IMP_FULL_DATABASE')
 order by Grantee ;
```

The **with admin option** clause gives the recipient the ability to grant the role to
other users. In general, you can simplify your role maintenance by always creating
roles under the SYSTEM user and always granting access to them via a single
DBA-privileged user. In this example, the user BONNIE has been granted **with
admin option** on each of her roles. As a result, she can grant those roles to other
users. If she grants those roles to other users, then re-creating the role and privilege
structure in your database becomes much more difficult. The simpler you keep the
privilege structure in your database, the simpler it will be to re-create your users
and their privilege structure.

Database Management

lstfiles.sql	gen_tbs.sql
audopts.sql	gen_tbs8.sql
audit.sql	gen_dbse.sql

C an you re-create your database if you have to? Do you know which parameters in your init.ora file are not set to the ORACLE defaults? Do you know the location of all the datafiles, control files, and redo logs in your database? In this chapter, you will see scripts that will help you to understand your database. You can use the diagnostic scripts to document auditing, tablespaces, redo logs and their history, and your control files, and you can use the utility scripts to help you to document or create a copy of your database.

The major scripts presented in this chapter are:

lstfiles.sql	Lists all the control, log, and datafiles in the database
audopts.sql	Lists all auditing options enabled for the database
audit.sql	Reports on all auditable actions captured
gen_tbs.sql	Generates a script to re-create a tablespace
gen_tbs8.sql	Generates a script to re-create a tablespace with new ORACLE8 features
gen_dbse.sql	Generates a script to re-create a database and its init.ora file

All the scripts in this chapter should be run from an account with DBA privileges.

Diagnostics

You can use the scripts in this section to report on the overall state of your database. The diagnostic scripts include reports on which objects and SQL statements are being audited, as well as the results of the auditing, a report on which init.ora parameters are not the defaults, and a list of all control files, log files and datafiles currently being used in your database.

lstfiles.sql

List All Files in the Database

We all attempt to make sure that our documentation is up to date, that we update every affected script each time we make a change in the database. Unfortunately, we don't always manage to do this. The lstfiles.sql script, shown in the following listing, reads the database system tables and generates a list of every control file, log file, and datafile. You can use the list of files as input to backup and recovery scripts to automate the capture of these files.

```
set term off echo off pagesize 0 trimspool on feedback off linesize 500
col tbspce format a15
spool lstfiles.log
select ' ' tbspce,Name
  from SYS.V_$CONTROLFILE
union
select ' ' tbspce, Member
  from SYS.V_$LOGFILE
union
select Tablespace_Name tbspce, File_Name
  from DBA_DATA_FILES
/
spool off
```

The script produces the following listing:

```
                   /usr/ORADATA41/TEST/controlTEST02.ctl
                   /usr/ORADATA41/TEST/redoTEST02.log
                   /usr/ORADATA53/TEST/controlTEST03.ctl
                   /usr/ORADATA53/TEST/redoTEST03.log
                   /usr/ORADATA55/TEST/controlTEST01.ctl
                   /usr/ORADATA55/TEST/redoTEST01.log
RBS1               /usr/ORADATA40/TEST/rbs1_TEST_01.dbf
RBS2               /usr/ORADATA51/TEST/rbs2_TEST_01.dbf
SYSTEM             /usr/ORADATA54/TEST/system_TEST_01.dbf
TEMP               /usr/ORADATA41/TEST/temp_TEST_01.dbf
TOOLS              /usr/ORADATA40/TEST/tools_TEST_01.dbf
USERS              /usr/ORADATA41/TEST/users_TEST_01.dbf
USER_DATA          /usr/ORADATA29/TEST/user_data_TEST_01.dbf
USER_DATA          /usr/ORADATA29/TEST/user_data_TEST_04.dbf
USER_DATA          /usr/ORADATA29/TEST/user_data_TEST_07.dbf
USER_DATA          /usr/ORADATA45/TEST/user_data_TEST_03.dbf
USER_DATA          /usr/ORADATA45/TEST/user_data_TEST_06.dbf
USER_DATA          /usr/ORADATA48/TEST/user_data_TEST_02.dbf
USER_DATA          /usr/ORADATA48/TEST/user_data_TEST_05.dbf
USER_DATA          /usr/ORADATA48/TEST/user_data_TEST_08.dbf
USER_INDEX         /usr/ORADATA42/TEST/user_index_TEST_03.dbf
USER_INDEX         /usr/ORADATA42/TEST/user_index_TEST_06.dbf
USER_INDEX         /usr/ORADATA43/TEST/user_index_TEST_02.dbf
USER_INDEX         /usr/ORADATA43/TEST/user_index_TEST_05.dbf
USER_INDEX         /usr/ORADATA49/TEST/user_index_TEST_01.dbf
USER_INDEX         /usr/ORADATA49/TEST/user_index_TEST_04.dbf
```

ANNOTATIONS

Besides its use for documentation, the file list can help you automate your backup and recovery process. In the lstfiles.sql script, the SQL*Plus **set** command turns off headers (**pagesize 0**) and row counts (**feedback off**) and removes trailing blanks at the end of each spooled line (**trimspool on**). The length of the output line is set to 500 characters (**linesize 500**) to accommodate the longer filenames allowed under ORACLE8.

There are three types of online files that ORACLE needs for a complete database: control files, online redo log files, and datafiles. Information about the log and control files is stored in the V$ dynamic performance tables; information about the datafiles is retrieved from a data dictionary view to include the tablespace name. For a complete listing, the three **select** statements are joined by the **union** operator. Because a **union** requires the same number of columns in each **select** statement, and because the script selects the tablespace name when selecting the datafile names, each of the other **select** statements must include a dummy column to make the column lists match. The tablespace name is included for use with an online backup operating system script. Online backups must first **alter** the tablespace into BEGIN BACKUP mode before backing up the datafiles, so you need the tablespace name. If you only back up the database when the database has been shut down (offline backup), you can remove the Tablespace_Name column and the dummy columns from the **select**s.

```
set term off echo off pagesize 0 trimspool on feedback off linesize 500
col tbspce format a15
spool lstfiles.log
select '   ' tbspce,Name
  from SYS.V_$CONTROLFILE
union
select '   ' tbspce, Member
  from SYS.V_$LOGFILE
union
select Tablespace_Name tbspce, File_Name
  from DBA_DATA_FILES
/
spool off
```

The output listing has blanks for the Tablespace_Name column values for the control files and online redo log files. Since no pseudocolumn has been introduced to order the output, ORACLE sorts on the columns in column order, sorting all the rows returned from the **union**, not each group of rows returned from the individual **select** statements. Due to the physical locations of the control and online redo log files, the output listing has the control files and online redo log files intermixed, not grouped separately by type. Again, because of this sorting order, the datafiles that make up the USER_DATA and USER_INDEX tablespaces are listed out of the order in which they were created.

```
                         /usr/ORADATA41/TEST/controlTEST02.ctl
                         /usr/ORADATA41/TEST/redoTEST02.log
                         /usr/ORADATA53/TEST/controlTEST03.ctl
                         /usr/ORADATA53/TEST/redoTEST03.log
                         /usr/ORADATA55/TEST/controlTEST01.ctl
                         /usr/ORADATA55/TEST/redoTEST01.log
RBS1                     /usr/ORADATA40/TEST/rbs1_TEST_01.dbf
RBS2                     /usr/ORADATA51/TEST/rbs2_TEST_01.dbf
SYSTEM                   /usr/ORADATA54/TEST/system_TEST_01.dbf
TEMP                     /usr/ORADATA41/TEST/temp_TEST_01.dbf
TOOLS                    /usr/ORADATA40/TEST/tools_TEST_01.dbf
USERS                    /usr/ORADATA41/TEST/users_TEST_01.dbf
USER_DATA                /usr/ORADATA29/TEST/user_data_TEST_01.dbf
USER_DATA                /usr/ORADATA29/TEST/user_data_TEST_04.dbf
USER_DATA                /usr/ORADATA29/TEST/user_data_TEST_07.dbf
USER_DATA                /usr/ORADATA45/TEST/user_data_TEST_03.dbf
USER_DATA                /usr/ORADATA45/TEST/user_data_TEST_06.dbf
USER_DATA                /usr/ORADATA48/TEST/user_data_TEST_02.dbf
USER_DATA                /usr/ORADATA48/TEST/user_data_TEST_05.dbf
USER_DATA                /usr/ORADATA48/TEST/user_data_TEST_08.dbf
USER_INDEX               /usr/ORADATA42/TEST/user_index_TEST_03.dbf
USER_INDEX               /usr/ORADATA42/TEST/user_index_TEST_06.dbf
USER_INDEX               /usr/ORADATA43/TEST/user_index_TEST_02.dbf
USER_INDEX               /usr/ORADATA43/TEST/user_index_TEST_05.dbf
USER_INDEX               /usr/ORADATA49/TEST/user_index_TEST_01.dbf
USER_INDEX               /usr/ORADATA49/TEST/user_index_TEST_04.dbf
```

If you want to see the files listed by type, add an additional column to each of the **select** statements in the query to force an ordering. Using the SQL*Plus **column** command, **noprint** suppresses printing of the new column, but still allows you to use it to order the output of the query and group the files listed by type of file.

```
set term off echo off pagesize 0 trimspool on feedback off linesize 500
col tbspce format a15
col orderby noprint
spool lstfiles.log
select '1' orderby, '   ' tbspce,Name
  from SYS.V_$CONTROLFILE
union
select '2' orderby, '   ' tbspce, Member
  from SYS.V_$LOGFILE
```

```
union
select '3' orderby, Tablespace_Name tbspce, File_Name
  from DBA_DATA_FILES
 order by orderby
/
spool off
```

The new script produces the following output, with all control files listed, followed by the log files and finally the tablespace datafiles.

```
                    /usr/ORADATA41/TEST/control02.ctl
                    /usr/ORADATA53/TEST/control03.ctl
                    /usr/ORADATA55/TEST/control01.ctl
                    /usr/ORADATA41/TEST/redoTEST02.log
                    /usr/ORADATA53/TEST/redoTEST03.log
                    /usr/ORADATA55/TEST/redoTEST01.log
RBS1                /usr/ORADATA40/TEST/rbs1_TEST_01.dbf
RBS2                /usr/ORADATA51/TEST/rbs2_TEST_01.dbf
SYSTEM              /usr/ORADATA54/TEST/system01.dbf
TEMP                /usr/ORADATA41/TEST/temp_TEST_01.dbf
TOOLS               /usr/ORADATA40/TEST/tools_TEST_01.dbf
USERS               /usr/ORADATA41/TEST/users_TEST_01.dbf
USER_DATA           /usr/ORADATA29/TEST/user_data_TEST_01.dbf
USER_DATA           /usr/ORADATA29/TEST/user_data_TEST_04.dbf
USER_DATA           /usr/ORADATA29/TEST/user_data_TEST_07.dbf
USER_DATA           /usr/ORADATA45/TEST/user_data_TEST_03.dbf
USER_DATA           /usr/ORADATA45/TEST/user_data_TEST_06.dbf
USER_DATA           /usr/ORADATA48/TEST/user_data_TEST_02.dbf
USER_DATA           /usr/ORADATA48/TEST/user_data_TEST_05.dbf
USER_DATA           /usr/ORADATA48/TEST/user_data_TEST_08.dbf
USER_INDEX          /usr/ORADATA42/TEST/user_index_TEST_03.dbf
USER_INDEX          /usr/ORADATA42/TEST/user_index_TEST_06.dbf
USER_INDEX          /usr/ORADATA43/TEST/user_index_TEST_02.dbf
USER_INDEX          /usr/ORADATA43/TEST/user_index_TEST_05.dbf
USER_INDEX          /usr/ORADATA49/TEST/user_index_TEST_01.dbf
USER_INDEX          /usr/ORADATA49/TEST/user_index_TEST_04.dbf
```

You can further order the query by selecting the File_ID of each of the datafiles that make up the tablespaces. The File_ID is the unique ID number of the datafile within the database. By adding this column to the query, again using the **noprint** parameter on the SQL*Plus **column** command, you can change the output to list the files by type, tablespace, and order in which they were added to the tablespace. Since the File_ID column of DBA_DATA_FILES is numeric, the placeholder column in the first two **select**s of the **union** query is a number.

```
set term off echo off pagesize 0 trimspool on feedback off linesize 500
col tbspce format a15
col orderby noprint
col fileid noprint
spool lstfiles.log
select '1' orderby, 1 fileid, ' ' tbspce,Name
  from SYS.V_$CONTROLFILE
union
select '2' orderby, 2 fileid, ' ' tbspce, Member
  from SYS.V_$LOGFILE
union
select '3' orderby, File_ID fileid, Tablespace_Name tbspce, File_Name
  from DBA_DATA_FILES
 order by orderby,tbspce,fileid
/
spool off
```

The output of this new query, with the datafiles now listed in the order in which they were added to the tablespace, is shown below.

```
                   /usr/ORADATA41/TEST/control02.ctl
                   /usr/ORADATA53/TEST/control03.ctl
                   /usr/ORADATA55/TEST/control01.ctl
                   /usr/ORADATA41/TEST/redoTEST02.log
                   /usr/ORADATA53/TEST/redoTEST03.log
                   /usr/ORADATA55/TEST/redoTEST01.log
RBS1               /usr/ORADATA40/TEST/rbs1_TEST_01.dbf
RBS2               /usr/ORADATA51/TEST/rbs2_TEST_01.dbf
SYSTEM             /usr/ORADATA54/TEST/system01.dbf
TEMP               /usr/ORADATA41/TEST/temp_TEST_01.dbf
TOOLS              /usr/ORADATA40/TEST/tools_TEST_01.dbf
USERS              /usr/ORADATA41/TEST/users_TEST_01.dbf
USER_DATA          /usr/ORADATA29/TEST/user_data_TEST_01.dbf
USER_DATA          /usr/ORADATA48/TEST/user_data_TEST_02.dbf
USER_DATA          /usr/ORADATA45/TEST/user_data_TEST_03.dbf
USER_DATA          /usr/ORADATA29/TEST/user_data_TEST_04.dbf
USER_DATA          /usr/ORADATA48/TEST/user_data_TEST_05.dbf
USER_DATA          /usr/ORADATA45/TEST/user_data_TEST_06.dbf
USER_DATA          /usr/ORADATA29/TEST/user_data_TEST_07.dbf
USER_DATA          /usr/ORADATA48/TEST/user_data_TEST_08.dbf
USER_INDEX         /usr/ORADATA49/TEST/user_index_TEST_01.dbf
USER_INDEX         /usr/ORADATA43/TEST/user_index_TEST_02.dbf
USER_INDEX         /usr/ORADATA42/TEST/user_index_TEST_03.dbf
USER_INDEX         /usr/ORADATA49/TEST/user_index_TEST_04.dbf
USER_INDEX         /usr/ORADATA43/TEST/user_index_TEST_05.dbf
USER_INDEX         /usr/ORADATA42/TEST/user_index_TEST_06.dbf
```

audopts.sql

Report on Enabled Auditing Options

You can use database auditing to track who is doing what to what, and what privileges they are using to do it. ORACLE supports three types of auditing: statement, privilege, and object. Statement-level auditing monitors specific SQL statements, without regard to the object they affect. Privilege-level auditing monitors the use of the system privileges. Object-level auditing monitors access to specific schema objects. If you want to record the old and new values of columns for the objects, you should use database triggers rather than auditing. All types of auditing can be set to record when the statement executes successfully, unsuccessfully, or both. Statement and privilege auditing can be set for all users or only specific users.

The audopts.sql script, shown in the following listing, lists all audit options in effect in your database.

```
set term on
accept obj_owner prompt "Enter the owner for object auditing: "
set term off echo off pagesize 60 linesize 132
set trimspool on verify off feedback off
col User_Name format a10
col Privilege format a15
col Success format a10
col Failure format a10
col Audit_Option format a15
col Owner format a10
col Object_Name format a25
col Object_Type format a12
spool audopts.log
prompt
prompt *** System Privilege Auditing
prompt
select *
  from DBA_PRIV_AUDIT_OPTS
/
prompt
prompt *** SQL Statement Auditing
prompt
select *
  from DBA_STMT_AUDIT_OPTS
/
prompt
prompt *** Object Auditing
prompt
```

```
select *
  from DBA_OBJ_AUDIT_OPTS
 where Owner like UPPER('&&obj_owner')
/
spool off
```

Sample output for the audopts.sql script is shown in the following listing.

```
*** System Privilege Auditing

USER_NAME  PRIVILEGE        SUCCESS    FAILURE
---------- ---------------- ---------- ----------
           CREATE SESSION   BY ACCESS  NOT SET


*** SQL Statement Auditing

USER_NAME  AUDIT_OPTION     SUCCESS    FAILURE
---------- ---------------- ---------- ----------
           TRIGGER          BY ACCESS  NOT SET
QC_USER    TRIGGER          BY ACCESS  BY ACCESS
           CREATE SESSION   BY ACCESS  NOT SET


*** Object Auditing

OWNER      OBJECT_NAME              OBJECT_TYPE  ALT AUD COM DEL GRA IND INS LOC REN SEL UPD REF EXE CRE REA WRI
---------- ------------------------ ------------ --- --- --- --- --- --- --- --- --- --- --- --- --- --- --- ---
QC_USER    CUSTOMERS_PA             TABLE        -/- -/- -/- -/- -/- -/- S/- -/- -/- A/A -/- -/- -/- -/- -/- -/-
QC_USER    CUSTOMERS_SJ             TABLE        -/- -/- -/- -/- -/- -/- -/- -/- -/- -/- -/- -/- -/- -/- -/- -/-
QC_USER    FREESP                   TABLE        -/- -/- -/- -/- -/- -/- -/- -/- -/- -/- -/- -/- -/- -/- -/- -/-
QC_USER    STUDENT                  TABLE        -/- -/- -/- -/- -/- -/- -/- -/- -/- -/- -/- -/- -/- -/- -/- -/-
QC_USER    TOY                      TABLE        -/- -/- -/- -/- -/- -/- -/- -/- -/- -/- -/- -/- -/- -/- -/- -/-
QC_USER    ALL_CUSTOMERS            VIEW         -/- -/- -/- -/- -/- -/- -/- -/- -/- -/- -/- -/- -/- -/- -/- -/-
```

In the Annotations section, you will see how to interpret the script's output.

ANNOTATIONS

You should use auditing with caution and monitor the results closely. Audit records go into the SYS.AUD$ table, which is stored in the SYSTEM tablespace by default. If auditing is turned on, the size of the SYS.AUD$ table and the amount of free space left in the SYSTEM tablespace must be checked on a regular basis. ORACLE allows you to delete records from this table. To ensure that the results of auditing are not removed from this table by an unauthorized user, you can audit the SYS.AUD$ table itself using the following SQL statement:

audit insert, update, delete on SYS.AUD$ by access;

For every row added, removed, or changed in this table, another row will be added, showing who made the change. The table can, however, be **truncate**d without the access added to SYS.AUD$, so you should not give out the DELETE ANY TABLE privilege, which enables a user to **truncate** any table.

PROGRAMMER'S NOTE   *As of ORACLE8, users with the DELETE_CATALOG_ROLE role can delete rows from SYS.AUD$.*

The audopts.sql script first executes the initial setup, prompting for the object owner for later use via the **accept** command, which allows you to define your own prompt for the variable. You can enter the object owner with wildcards (such as '%QC%') to extract auditing information for all objects owned by users with similar names. You can enter '%' as the *obj_owner* variable value to extract auditing information on all objects owned by all users in the database.

The SQL*Plus **set** command sets the number of lines on the page (**pagesize 60**), sets the length of each line (**linesize 132**), turns off the display of row counts (**feedback off**), removes trailing blanks at the end of each spooled line (**trimspool on**), and turns off displays of old and new values for the *obj_owner* variable (**verify off**). The **col** command formats the columns for a more readable output listing.

```
set term on
accept obj_owner prompt "Enter the owner for object auditing: "
set term off echo off pagesize 60 linesize 132
set trimspool on verify off feedback off
col User_Name format a10
col Privilege format a15
col Success format a10
col Failure format a10
col Audit_Option format a15
col Owner format a10
col Object_Name format a25
col Object_Type format a12
spool audopts.log
```

ORACLE retrieves information on what is being audited from three data dictionary views: DBA_PRIV_AUDIT_OPTS, DBA_STMT_AUDIT_OPTS, and DBA_OBJ_AUDIT_OPTS. Unlike the first two, which contain rows only for those privileges or SQL statements being audited, DBA_OBJ_AUDIT_OPTS contains one row for every schema object for every user, including SYS and SYSTEM, and therefore needs the **where** clause to make the output listing more manageable.

The **prompt** command creates a separator section between each of the **select** statements and identifies the information being extracted.

```
prompt
prompt *** System Privilege Auditing
prompt
select *
  from DBA_PRIV_AUDIT_OPTS
/
prompt
prompt *** SQL Statement Auditing
```

```
prompt
select *
  from DBA_STMT_AUDIT_OPTS
/
prompt
prompt *** Object Auditing
prompt
select *
  from DBA_OBJ_AUDIT_OPTS
 where Owner like UPPER('&&obj_owner')
/
spool off
```

The first section of the output lists all system privileges being audited. In this database, the DBA has decided to record all successful attempts at connecting to the database (the CREATE SESSION action).

```
*** System Privilege Auditing
```

USER_NAME	PRIVILEGE	SUCCESS	FAILURE
	CREATE SESSION	BY ACCESS	NOT SET

The second section of the output lists all SQL statement privileges being monitored. Any user who successfully **create**s, **alter**s, **enable**s, **disable**s or **drop**s a trigger will have a record inserted into SYS.AUD$. In addition, the QC_USER will have a record inserted into SYS.AUD$ whenever he attempts to **create** or modify a trigger, whether he is successful or not.

As shown in the following listing, the **create session** command is listed in DBA_STMT_AUDIT_OPTS as well as in the view describing privilege auditing (DBA_PRIV_AUDIT_OPTS).

```
*** SQL Statement Auditing
```

USER_NAME	AUDIT_OPTION	SUCCESS	FAILURE
	TRIGGER	BY ACCESS	NOT SET
QC_USER	TRIGGER	BY ACCESS	BY ACCESS
	CREATE SESSION	BY ACCESS	NOT SET

The final section of the output listing shows the auditing options set on all objects owned by the QC_USER. Auditing is turned on only for one object, the CUSTOMERS_PA table. All **insert**s will be audited by session, and only when successful. All **select**s will be audited by access, whether successful or not. The audit actions are read as follows: the character before the '/' indicates that auditing will be done if the action is successful; the character after the '/' refers to unsuccessful actions. 'S' indicates audit by session, while 'A' indicates audit by access. This listing, run against an ORACLE8 database, has more auditable actions than an ORACLE7 database will.

```
*** Object Auditing

OWNER      OBJECT_NAME              OBJECT_TYPE   ALT AUD COM DEL GRA IND INS LOC REN SEL UPD REF EXE CRE REA WRI
---------- ------------------------ ------------  --- --- --- --- --- --- --- --- --- --- --- --- --- --- --- ---
QC_USER    CUSTOMERS_PA             TABLE         -/- -/- -/- -/- -/- -/- S/- -/- -/- A/A -/- -/- -/- -/- -/- -/-
QC_USER    CUSTOMERS_SJ             TABLE         -/- -/- -/- -/- -/- -/- -/- -/- -/- -/- -/- -/- -/- -/- -/- -/-
QC_USER    FREESP                   TABLE         -/- -/- -/- -/- -/- -/- -/- -/- -/- -/- -/- -/- -/- -/- -/- -/-
QC_USER    STUDENT                  TABLE         -/- -/- -/- -/- -/- -/- -/- -/- -/- -/- -/- -/- -/- -/- -/- -/-
QC_USER    TOY                      TABLE         -/- -/- -/- -/- -/- -/- -/- -/- -/- -/- -/- -/- -/- -/- -/- -/-
QC_USER    ALL_CUSTOMERS            VIEW          -/- -/- -/- -/- -/- -/- -/- -/- -/- -/- -/- -/- -/- -/- -/- -/-
```

audit.sql

Report on Auditing Results

Once you've turned auditing on in your database by setting the init.ora parameter AUDIT_DB to DB, enabled various audit options via the SQL **audit** command, and reviewed the enabled auditing options using the audopts.sql script from the previous section, you have to monitor the results of those audits.

The audit.sql script, shown in the following listing, displays the audit records from SYS.AUD$ via the DBA_AUDIT_TRAIL data dictionary view.

```
set term off echo off feedback off pagesize 60 linesize 132 trimspool on
col Username format a10 heading 'USER'
col Owner format a10 heading 'OWNER'
col Action_Name format a20 heading 'ACTION'
col Obj_Name format a25 heading 'OBJECT NAME'
col Result format a8 heading 'RESULTS'
spool audit.log
select Username,
       Owner,
       Obj_Name,
       Action_Name,
       Ses_Actions,
       DECODE(Returncode,0,'Success','Failure') Result
  from SYS.DBA_AUDIT_TRAIL
/
spool off
```

For the enabled audit options listed in the prior section, the audit.sql script produces the following:

```
USER       OWNER      OBJECT NAME              ACTION                SES_ACTIONS          RESULTS
---------- ---------- ------------------------ -------------------- -------------------- --------
QC_USER                                        LOGOFF                                    Success
QC_USER    QC_USER    CUSTOMERS_PA             SESSION REC          ------S--S------     Success
QC_USER    QC_USER    TEST                     DROP TRIGGER                              Failure
SYSTEM                                         LOGOFF                                    Success
SYS                                            LOGOFF                                    Success
SYSTEM                                         LOGOFF                                    Success
SYSTEM     QC_USER    TEST_TRIG                DROP TRIGGER                              Success
```

The Ses_Actions column is a shorthand description of the session summary, with each character in the string (11 characters in ORACLE7, 16 in ORACLE8) representing an action type. In order, the action types are: ALTER, AUDIT, COMMENT, DELETE, GRANT, INDEX, INSERT, LOCK, RENAME, SELECT, and UPDATE for ORACLE7. ORACLE added two new action types in ORACLE8: REFERENCES and EXECUTE. The last three characters in the ORACLE8 string are currently unused. Each character can take on one of four values: - for none, S for success, F for failure, and B for both.

The SES_ACTIONS column will only have values in it when the Action value is SESSION REC (session record).

ANNOTATIONS

All audit information is stored in the SYS.AUD$ table in the SYSTEM tablespace. You should closely monitor the size of this table and purge out older audit records before you begin to run out of space in SYSTEM. You should **audit** delete, insert, and update actions on the SYS.AUD$ table.

The SQL*Plus **set** command sets the number of lines on the page (**pagesize 60**), sets the length of each line (**linesize 132**), turns off the display of row counts (**feedback off**), and removes trailing blanks at the end of each spooled line (**trimspool on**). The **col** command formats the columns for a more readable output listing and sets the heading for each column. The column Result is an alias used for the **DECODE** expression in the query, to allow for formatting and a heading.

```
set term off echo off feedback off pagesize 60 linesize 132 trimspool on
col Username format a10 heading 'USER'
col Owner format a10 heading 'OWNER'
col Action_Name format a20 heading 'ACTION'
col Obj_Name format a25 heading 'OBJECT NAME'
col Result format a8 heading 'RESULTS'
spool audit.log
```

The data dictionary view DBA_AUDIT_TRAIL has many columns, capturing information for all possible types of auditing. For readability, the columns referring to the most common types of auditing are displayed in this report. The Username column is the user performing the audited action, Owner is the owner of the object, Action_Name is the audited action, and Ses_Actions refers to the auditable object privileges listed by the script in the previous section. A value of – indicates no action, S indicates success, F indicates failure, and B indicates both. ORACLE stores 0 for a successful action in the Returncode column; any other value indicates that the audited statement failed. A **DECODE** function translates the numeric values to Success or Failure indicators.

If you **grant** and **audit** other types of privileges, you should modify the script to include the other columns in DBA_AUDIT_TRAIL.

```
select Username,
       Owner,
       Obj_Name,
       Action_Name,
       Ses_Actions,
       DECODE(Returncode,0,'Success','Failure') Result
  from SYS.DBA_AUDIT_TRAIL
/
spool off
```

In this database, the **create session** command is audited whenever a user successfully connects to the database. During the time auditing was enabled in this database, several users successfully connected to the database. Note that even the SYS account is audited and that a successful connection is indicated by an action value of LOGOFF.

In addition to auditing connections to the database, auditing has been enabled for: certain DML actions on the QC_USER.CUSTOMERS_PA table; any action, successful or not, on a trigger by the user QC_USER; and any successful action on a trigger by any other user.

The Ses_Actions column is a shorthand description of the session summary, with each character in the string (11 characters in ORACLE7, 16 in ORACLE8) representing an action type: ALTER, AUDIT, COMMENT, DELETE, GRANT, INDEX, INSERT, LOCK, RENAME, SELECT, and UPDATE for ORACLE7 and additionally, REFERENCES and EXECUTE in ORACLE8. The output shows that the QC_USER successfully **insert**ed and **select**ed from the CUSTOMERS_PA table (S in the seventh and tenth positions in the Ses_Actions value), but does not show the number of rows or values. If you want to capture the actual values **insert**ed, **update**d, or **delete**d from a table, you should create a trigger on the table, rather than audit it.

Finally, the QC_USER attempted to drop a trigger named TEST that he owned but failed, most probably because the trigger did not exist. The SYSTEM user was able to successfully drop the QC_USER.TEST_TRIG trigger.

USER	OWNER	OBJECT NAME	ACTION	SES_ACTIONS	RESULTS
QC_USER			LOGOFF		Success
QC_USER	QC_USER	CUSTOMERS_PA	SESSION REC	------S--S------	Success
QC_USER	QC_USER	TEST	DROP TRIGGER		Failure
SYSTEM			LOGOFF		Success
SYS			LOGOFF		Success
SYSTEM			LOGOFF		Success
SYSTEM	QC_USER	TEST_TRIG	DROP TRIGGER		Success

Utilities

You can use the scripts in this section to generate scripts to re-create or document tablespaces or the database structure, including rollback segments and the init.ora parameter file. In addition, a "fast" database copy method is explained.

Running the ORACLE Import utility with "**show=y rows=n**" on a full database export will generate a log file with all the commands necessary to re-create your database, rollback segments, and tablespaces. However, the Import log file is not very readable, is poorly organized for documentation purposes, and is not executable without extensive editing. The scripts in this section will generate readable, executable scripts to regenerate or document your database.

Generate Tablespaces

gen_tbs.sql
gen_tbs8.sql

A tablespace is an allocation of space in the database that can contain objects. Tablespaces can be used to group like objects, such as tables or indexes, onto different disks to reduce I/O contention. You can segregate applications into separate tablespaces and take the tablespaces offline or online for backup or recovery.

With ORACLE7.2, ORACLE introduced the ability to allow datafiles to autoextend their disk allocations. When you turn **autoextend on** for the first time, the table SYS.FILEXT$ is created. The gen_tbs.sql script requires the existence of this table to compile properly. If you have never turned on **autoextend** in your database, you must run the following script once before using the gen_tbs.sql script.

```
create tablespace temp_xyz
datafile '<full_datafile_specification>' size 2k autoextend on;
alter tablespace temp_xyz offline;
drop tablespace temp_xyz;
```

The preceding script will force the creation of the SYS.FILEXT$ table. Once you have dropped the tablespace, you can remove the physical file it creates. Before running the script, substitute a valid path and filename for *<full_datafile_specification>*.

PROGRAMMER'S NOTE *If you allow ORACLE8 to create your database for you, several of the tablespaces will be created with **autoextend on** and you won't need to run the above script.*

The gen_tbs.sql script, shown in the following listing, generates the **create tablespace** command for one or more existing tablespaces.

```
set echo off term on verify off feedback off pagesize 0
select 'Creating tablespace build script...' from DUAL;

accept tablespace_name prompt "Enter the name of the tablespace: "
set term off

drop table TSPACE_TEMP;
```

```
create table TSPACE_TEMP (
       Lineno       NUMBER,
       Tspace_Name VARCHAR2(30),
       Text         VARCHAR2(500))
/

declare
   cursor TSPACE_CURSOR is
         select Tablespace_Name,
                Initial_Extent,
                Next_Extent,
                Min_Extents,
                Max_Extents,
                Pct_Increase,
                Status,
                Contents
           from DBA_TABLESPACES
          where Tablespace_Name != 'SYSTEM';

   cursor DFILE_CURSOR (C_Tablespace_Name VARCHAR2) is
         select A.Maxextend,
                A.Inc,
                B.File_Name,
                B.File_ID,
                B.Bytes,
                B.Status
           from SYS.FILEXT$    A,
                DBA_DATA_FILES B
          where B.File_ID = A.File#(+)
            and Tablespace_Name = C_Tablespace_Name
          order by File_ID;

   Lv_TS_Tablespace_Name        DBA_TABLESPACES.Tablespace_Name%TYPE;
   Lv_TS_Initial_Extent         DBA_TABLESPACES.Initial_Extent%TYPE;
   Lv_TS_Next_Extent            DBA_TABLESPACES.Next_Extent%TYPE;
   Lv_TS_Min_Extents            DBA_TABLESPACES.Min_Extents%TYPE;
   Lv_TS_Max_Extents            DBA_TABLESPACES.Max_Extents%TYPE;
   Lv_TS_Pct_Increase           DBA_TABLESPACES.Pct_Increase%TYPE;
   Lv_TS_Status                 DBA_TABLESPACES.Status%TYPE;
   Lv_TS_Contents               DBA_TABLESPACES.Contents%TYPE;
   Lv_DF_MaxExtend              SYS.FILEXT$.MaxExtend%TYPE;
   Lv_DF_Inc                    SYS.FILEXT$.Inc%TYPE;
   Lv_DF_File_Name              DBA_DATA_FILES.File_Name%TYPE;
```

```
   Lv_DF_File_ID                    DBA_DATA_FILES.File_ID%TYPE;
   Lv_DF_Bytes                      DBA_DATA_FILES.Bytes%TYPE;
   Lv_DF_Status                     DBA_DATA_FILES.Status%TYPE;

   Lv_String                        VARCHAR2(800);
   Lv_Lineno                        NUMBER   := 0;
   Lv_DF_Count                      NUMBER;
   Lv_Block_Size                    NUMBER;

   procedure WRITE_OUT(P_Line INTEGER,   P_Tablespace VARCHAR2,
                   P_String VARCHAR2)
   is
   begin
      insert into TSPACE_TEMP (Lineno, Tspace_name, Text)
            values (P_Line,P_Tablespace,P_String);
   end;

begin

   select Value
     into Lv_Block_Size
     from SYS.V_$PARAMETER
    where UPPER(Name) = 'DB_BLOCK_SIZE';

   open TSPACE_CURSOR;
   loop
      fetch TSPACE_CURSOR into Lv_TS_Tablespace_Name,
                               Lv_TS_Initial_Extent,
                               Lv_TS_Next_Extent,
                               Lv_TS_Min_Extents,
                               Lv_TS_Max_Extents,
                               Lv_TS_Pct_Increase,
                               Lv_TS_Status,
                               Lv_TS_Contents;
      exit when TSPACE_CURSOR%NOTFOUND;

      Lv_Lineno := 1;
      Lv_DF_Count := 0;
      Lv_String := 'CREATE TABLESPACE ' ||
                  LOWER(Lv_TS_Tablespace_Name);
      WRITE_OUT(Lv_Lineno, Lv_TS_Tablespace_Name, Lv_String);
      Lv_Lineno := Lv_Lineno + 1;
      open DFILE_CURSOR (Lv_TS_Tablespace_Name);
```

```
loop
    fetch DFILE_CURSOR into       Lv_DF_MaxExtend,
                                  Lv_DF_Inc,
                                  Lv_DF_File_Name,
                                  Lv_DF_File_ID,
                                  Lv_DF_Bytes,
                                  Lv_DF_Status;
    exit when DFILE_CURSOR%NOTFOUND;
    Lv_DF_Count := Lv_DF_Count + 1;

    if (Lv_DF_Count > 1)
    then
        Lv_String := '           ,''';
    else
        Lv_String := 'DATAFILE ''';
    end if;

    Lv_String := Lv_String || Lv_DF_File_Name
                           || ''' SIZE '
                           || (Lv_DF_Bytes)/1024 ||'K' ;

    Lv_String := Lv_String || ' REUSE ';
    WRITE_OUT(Lv_Lineno, Lv_TS_Tablespace_Name, Lv_String);
    Lv_Lineno := Lv_Lineno + 1;

    if (Lv_DF_MaxExtend IS NOT NULL)
    then
        Lv_String := 'AUTOEXTEND ON NEXT '
                          || (Lv_DF_Inc * Lv_Block_Size)/1024
                          || 'K MAXSIZE '
                          || (Lv_DF_MaxExtend *
                             Lv_Block_Size)/1024
                          || 'K';

WRITE_OUT(Lv_Lineno, Lv_TS_Tablespace_Name, Lv_String);
        Lv_Lineno := Lv_Lineno + 1;
    end if;
end loop;
close DFILE_CURSOR;

Lv_String := 'DEFAULT STORAGE ';
WRITE_OUT(Lv_Lineno, Lv_TS_Tablespace_Name, Lv_String);
Lv_Lineno := Lv_Lineno + 1;
```

```
Lv_String := '(';
    WRITE_OUT(Lv_Lineno, Lv_TS_Tablespace_Name, Lv_String);
    Lv_Lineno := Lv_Lineno + 1;
    Lv_String := '    INITIAL     ' || Lv_TS_Initial_Extent/1024 || 'K';
    WRITE_OUT(Lv_Lineno, Lv_TS_Tablespace_Name, Lv_String);
    Lv_Lineno := Lv_Lineno + 1;

    Lv_String := '    NEXT        ' || Lv_TS_Next_Extent/1024 || 'K';
    WRITE_OUT(Lv_Lineno, Lv_TS_Tablespace_Name, Lv_String);
    Lv_Lineno := Lv_Lineno + 1;

    Lv_String := '    MINEXTENTS ' || Lv_TS_Min_Extents;
    WRITE_OUT(Lv_Lineno, Lv_TS_Tablespace_Name, Lv_String);
    Lv_Lineno := Lv_Lineno + 1;

    Lv_String := '    MAXEXTENTS ' || Lv_TS_Max_Extents;
    WRITE_OUT(Lv_Lineno, Lv_TS_Tablespace_Name, Lv_String);
    Lv_Lineno := Lv_Lineno + 1;

    Lv_String := '    PCTINCREASE ' || Lv_TS_Pct_Increase;
    WRITE_OUT(Lv_Lineno, Lv_TS_Tablespace_Name, Lv_String);
    Lv_Lineno := Lv_Lineno + 1;

    Lv_String := ')';
    WRITE_OUT(Lv_Lineno, Lv_TS_Tablespace_Name, Lv_String);
    Lv_Lineno := Lv_Lineno + 1;

    Lv_String := Lv_TS_Status || ' ' || Lv_TS_Contents;
    WRITE_OUT(Lv_Lineno, Lv_TS_Tablespace_Name, Lv_String);
    Lv_Lineno := Lv_Lineno + 1;

    Lv_String := '/';
    WRITE_OUT(Lv_Lineno, Lv_TS_Tablespace_Name, Lv_String);
    Lv_Lineno := Lv_Lineno + 1;

  end loop ;
  close TSPACE_CURSOR;

end;
/

set trimspool on
spool cre_tbs.sql
select Text
```

```
  from TSPACE_TEMP
 where Tspace_Name like UPPER('&&tablespace_name');
 order by Tspace_Name, Lineno
/
spool off
```

For the USER_DATA tablespace, the script will generate the following script to
re-create the tablespace.

```
CREATE TABLESPACE user_data
DATAFILE '/usr/ORADATA29/TEST/user_data_TEST_01.dbf' SIZE 512000K REUSE
        ,'/usr/ORADATA48/TEST/user_data_TEST_02.dbf' SIZE 512000K REUSE
        ,'/usr/ORADATA45/TEST/user_data_TEST_03.dbf' SIZE 512000K REUSE
        ,'/usr/ORADATA29/TEST/user_data_TEST_04.dbf' SIZE 512000K REUSE
        ,'/usr/ORADATA48/TEST/user_data_TEST_05.dbf' SIZE 512000K REUSE
        ,'/usr/ORADATA45/TEST/user_data_TEST_06.dbf' SIZE 512000K REUSE
        ,'/usr/ORADATA29/TEST/user_data_TEST_07.dbf' SIZE 512000K REUSE
        ,'/usr/ORADATA48/TEST/user_data_TEST_08.dbf' SIZE 512000K REUSE
DEFAULT STORAGE
(
    INITIAL    400K
    NEXT       400K
    MINEXTENTS 1
    MAXEXTENTS 5000
    PCTINCREASE 0
)
ONLINE PERMANENT
/
```

ANNOTATIONS

With ORACLE8, ORACLE added several new clauses to the **create tablespace**
command. If you don't use the new clauses (**minimum extent** and **logging**,
described at the end of this section), the gen_tbs.sql script will work for both
ORACLE7 and ORACLE8. If you use these new features, an ORACLE8 version of
the script, gen_tbs8.sql, with the differences highlighted, is included at the end
of this section.

The gen_tbs.sql script returns information for all tablespaces except the SYSTEM
tablespace. SYSTEM is excluded so that the script can be used with the gen_dbse.sql
script in a later section, to re-create all tablespaces for your database. The gen_tbs.sql
script uses the *tablespace_name* variable to allow you to enter a single tablespace
name or a wildcard value so you can extract the **create tablespace** statements for
only the tablespaces you want. The gen_tbs.sql script generates a script to re-create
the requested tablespace(s). The gen_tbs.sql script uses a temporary table to hold
individual lines of the **create tablespace** statement, writing to the table rather than

using DBMS_OUTPUT.PUT_LINE so that you can extract the information for an individual tablespace from the table. Using the DBMS_OUTPUT procedure would force you to save and edit the output file for the tablespace you want.

The first section of the script, shown in the following listing, performs the initial setup, prompting for the tablespace name for later use via the **accept** command. You can enter the tablespace name with wildcards (such as '%DATA%') to generate a script for all tablespaces with a similar name. You can enter '%' as the *tablespace_name* variable value to generate a script for all tablespaces in the database except the SYSTEM tablespace.

The SQL*Plus **set** command turns off headers (**pagesize 0**), row counts (**feedback off**), and displays of old and new values for the *tablespace_name* variable (**verify off**).

```
set echo off term on verify off feedback off pagesize 0
select 'Creating tablespace build script...' from DUAL;

accept tablespace_name prompt "Enter the name of the tablespace: "
set term off
```

The next section of the gen_tbs.sql script creates a temporary table to hold each **create tablespace** command. Unlike the temporary tables created in the generate scripts in Chapter 5, no Owner column is needed since a tablespace has no defined owner other than ORACLE. The Lineno column preserves the ordering of the lines of the **create tablespace** command during later queries.

```
drop table TSPACE_TEMP;

create table TSPACE_TEMP (
        Lineno       NUMBER,
        Tspace_Name  VARCHAR2(30),
        Text         VARCHAR2(500))
/
```

In the next section of the script, the TSPACE_CURSOR cursor selects the information from DBA_TABLESPACES for all tablespaces except the SYSTEM tablespace. Unless you have an extremely large number of tablespaces, extracting the information for all of them at once will not have a performance impact. The cursor extracts the default storage information defined for the tablespace.

```
declare
    cursor TSPACE_CURSOR is
        select Tablespace_Name,
               Initial_Extent,
               Next_Extent,
               Min_Extents,
               Max_Extents,
               Pct_Increase,
               Status,
```

```
        Contents
  from DBA_TABLESPACES
  where Tablespace_Name !='SYSTEM';
```

The next cursor, the DFILE_CURSOR, selects information from DBA_DATAFILES and SYS.FILEXT$ where the tablespace name matches the tablespace name passed in from the TSPACE_CURSOR. An outer join, (+), ensures that all rows in the DBA_DATA_FILES view are returned, even if there is no matching row in SYS.FILEXT$. If an outer join were not used, only the datafiles which are in SYS.FILEXT$ would be returned by the cursor and the tablespace definition would not be complete. The outer join is placed on the more restrictive table selection.

The DFILE_CURSOR cursor extracts the physical disk space information for each datafile, including the extension information for datafiles which have **autoextend** turned on. The **order by** clause ensures that the datafiles will be re-created in the same order as they were originally created.

```
cursor DFILE_CURSOR (C_Tablespace_Name VARCHAR2) is
    select A.Maxextend,
           A.Inc,
           B.File_Name,
           B.File_ID,
           B.Bytes,
           B.Status
      from SYS.FILEXT$     A,
           DBA_DATA_FILES B
     where B.File_ID = A.File#(+)
       and Tablespace_Name = C_Tablespace_Name
     order by File_ID;
```

The procedure variables for the cursor, shown in the following listing, are declared as TABLE_NAME.Column_Name%**TYPE**. This "anchoring" of datatypes takes the column definition from within the database itself. If the column definition changes in a different version of ORACLE, the procedure will still work because the definition of the column has not been hard-coded. The *Lv_DF_Count* variable tracks the order of the datafile being processed (first, second, etc.). The variable *Lv_Lineno* orders the lines of the **create** statement and is initialized to 0. The *Lv_Block_Size* variable holds the database block size for converting datafile **autoextend** definitions from ORACLE blocks to kilobytes.

```
Lv_TS_Tablespace_Name    DBA_TABLESPACES.Tablespace_Name%TYPE;
Lv_TS_Initial_Extent     DBA_TABLESPACES.Initial_Extent%TYPE;
Lv_TS_Next_Extent        DBA_TABLESPACES.Next_Extent%TYPE;
Lv_TS_Min_Extents        DBA_TABLESPACES.Min_Extents%TYPE;
Lv_TS_Max_Extents        DBA_TABLESPACES.Max_Extents%TYPE;
Lv_TS_Pct_Increase       DBA_TABLESPACES.Pct_Increase%TYPE;
```

```
Lv_TS_Status                 DBA_TABLESPACES.Status%TYPE;
Lv_TS_Contents               DBA_TABLESPACES.Contents%TYPE;
Lv_DF_MaxExtend              SYS.FILEXT$.MaxExtend%TYPE;
Lv_DF_Inc                    SYS.FILEXT$.Inc%TYPE;
Lv_DF_File_Name              DBA_DATA_FILES.File_Name%TYPE;
Lv_DF_File_ID                DBA_DATA_FILES.File_ID%TYPE;
Lv_DF_Bytes                  DBA_DATA_FILES.Bytes%TYPE;
Lv_DF_Status                 DBA_DATA_FILES.Status%TYPE;

Lv_String                    VARCHAR2(800);
Lv_Lineno                    NUMBER   := 0;
Lv_DF_Count                  NUMBER;
Lv_Block_Size                NUMBER;
```

The next portion of the script defines an internal procedure, WRITE_OUT, to do the **insert**s into the temporary table.

```
procedure WRITE_OUT(P_Line INTEGER,  P_Tablespace VARCHAR2,
                    P_String VARCHAR2)
is
begin
   insert into TSPACE_TEMP (Lineno, Tspace_name, Text)
         values (P_Line,P_Tablespace,P_String);
end;
```

If **autoextend** is on for a datafile, the next and maximum file size information is stored in SYS.FILEXT$ in ORACLE blocks. The next section of the script extracts the database block size so it can convert the **autoextend** information to kilobytes.

```
begin

   select Value
     into Lv_Block_Size
     from SYS.V_$PARAMETER
    where UPPER(Name) = 'DB_BLOCK_SIZE';
```

The TSPACE_CURSOR cursor, shown in the following listing, forms an outer loop for each tablespace. *Lv_Lineno* is used in conjunction with the tablespace name to order the rows in the temporary table TSPACE_TEMP so that if you prefer, you can extract the **create** statement for a single tablespace at the end of the procedure. *Lv_DF_Count* distinguishes the first datafile in the inner cursor loop from the others.

```
   open TSPACE_CURSOR;
   loop
      fetch TSPACE_CURSOR into Lv_TS_Tablespace_Name,
                               Lv_TS_Initial_Extent,
                               Lv_TS_Next_Extent,
```

```
                              Lv_TS_Min_Extents,
                              Lv_TS_Max_Extents,
                              Lv_TS_Pct_Increase,
                              Lv_TS_Status,
                              Lv_TS_Contents;
            exit when TSPACE_CURSOR%NOTFOUND;


            Lv_Lineno := 1;
            Lv_DF_Count := 0;
```

The next section of the script **insert**s the beginning of the **create** statement into the temporary table. The **LOWER** function changes the case of the tablespace name to lowercase for readability.

To perform the **insert**, the WRITE_OUT procedure is executed, and line numbers are assigned to each inserted line.

```
    Lv_String := 'CREATE TABLESPACE ' || LOWER(Lv_TS_Tablespace_Name);
    WRITE_OUT(Lv_Lineno, Lv_TS_Tablespace_Name, Lv_String);
    Lv_Lineno := Lv_Lineno + 1;
```

The DFILE_CURSOR cursor, shown in the following listing, forms an inner loop for each tablespace, selecting all the datafiles that make up the tablespace from DBA_DATA_FILES and SYS.FILEXT$. Each datafile's physical location and space allocations will be processed and added to the temporary table before the next datafile is fetched. The inner cursor will be opened, fetched, and closed once for each tablespace selected by the outer cursor.

```
    open DFILE_CURSOR (Lv_TS_Tablespace_Name);


    loop
        fetch DFILE_CURSOR into      Lv_DF_MaxExtend,
                                     Lv_DF_Inc,
                                     Lv_DF_File_Name,
                                     Lv_DF_File_ID,
                                     Lv_DF_Bytes,
                                     Lv_DF_Status;
            exit when DFILE_CURSOR%NOTFOUND;
            Lv_DF_Count := Lv_DF_Count + 1;
```

The next section begins creating the datafile definition string by checking the value of *Lv_DF_Count* and adding either the word 'DATAFILE' (for the first datafile fetched) or a comma (for a delimiter for all other datafiles). The datafile specification must be enclosed in single quotes in the string. Because the string definition itself must be enclosed in single quotes, the script uses three single quotes to indicate to ORACLE that one of them should be part of the string itself.

```
if (Lv_DF_Count > 1)
  then
                Lv_String := '              ,''';
  else
                Lv_String := 'DATAFILE ''';
  end if;
```

The filename information in DBA_DATA_FILES contains the full path and file specification for the physical location of this datafile. Again, the three single quotes resolve to the closing quote on the file specification. While the datafile size is stored in bytes and could be specified that way, the script converts the **size** of the datafile to kilobytes for consistency with the **autoextend** clause. Because the scripts document an existing datafile, **reuse** must be added to the string or the generated script will fail when run. The **reuse** clause tells ORACLE that the file already exists and can be overwritten. Without the **reuse** clause, the creation of the tablespace would fail if the file already exists. Once the datafile name and size definition are complete, the script writes the line to the temporary table.

```
Lv_String := Lv_String || Lv_DF_File_Name
                       || ''' SIZE '
                       || (Lv_DF_Bytes)/1024 ||'K' ;

Lv_String := Lv_String || ' REUSE ';
WRITE_OUT(Lv_Lineno, Lv_TS_Tablespace_Name, Lv_String);
Lv_Lineno := Lv_Lineno + 1;
```

The next section of the script checks to see if the datafile has been created with **autoextend on**. The outer join in the DFILE_CURSOR cursor ensures that all datafiles are selected from DBA_DATA_FILES and SYS.FILEXT$, even those which are not extendable. If the datafile does not have **autoextend on**, the outer join returns nulls in the fields selected from SYS.FILEXT$ and the script tests for a maximum extended size of null to decide whether or not to include the **autoextend** clause.

SYS.FILEXT$ stores the sizes of the next extent and maximum extended size in ORACLE blocks. The script uses the database block size, stored in the variable *Lv_Block_Size* earlier in the script, to convert these sizes to bytes and then divides by 1,024 to convert them to a more readable kilobytes number. Once the **autoextend** clause is completed, it is written to the temporary table. The inner cursor loop will repeat for each datafile in the tablespace.

```
if (Lv_DF_MaxExtend IS NOT NULL)
then
    Lv_String := 'AUTOEXTEND ON NEXT '
                    || (Lv_DF_Inc * Lv_Block_Size)/1024
                    || 'K MAXSIZE '
                    || (Lv_DF_MaxExtend * Lv_Block_Size)/1024
                    || 'K';
```

```
        WRITE_OUT(Lv_Lineno, Lv_TS_Tablespace_Name, Lv_String);
        Lv_Lineno := Lv_Lineno + 1;
    end if;


        end loop;
```

Now that the definitions of all the datafiles have been added to the temporary table, the **default storage** clause must be added to the **create tablespace** command. The **default storage** clause sets the storage definitions of any objects created in this tablespace that do not have their own storage options defined at creation. The **initial** and **next** extent size values are stored in DBA_TABLESPACES in bytes; the script converts them to kilobytes for readability and consistency with the other size definitions.

```
    close DFILE_CURSOR;

    Lv_String := 'DEFAULT STORAGE ';
    WRITE_OUT(Lv_Lineno, Lv_TS_Tablespace_Name, Lv_String);
    Lv_Lineno := Lv_Lineno + 1;

    Lv_String := '(';
    WRITE_OUT(Lv_Lineno, Lv_TS_Tablespace_Name, Lv_String);
    Lv_Lineno := Lv_Lineno + 1;
    Lv_String := '    INITIAL    ' || Lv_TS_Initial_Extent/1024 || 'K';
    WRITE_OUT(Lv_Lineno, Lv_TS_Tablespace_Name, Lv_String);
    Lv_Lineno := Lv_Lineno + 1;

    Lv_String := '    NEXT       ' || Lv_TS_Next_Extent/1024 || 'K';
    WRITE_OUT(Lv_Lineno, Lv_TS_Tablespace_Name, Lv_String);
    Lv_Lineno := Lv_Lineno + 1;

    Lv_String := '    MINEXTENTS ' || Lv_TS_Min_Extents;
    WRITE_OUT(Lv_Lineno, Lv_TS_Tablespace_Name, Lv_String);
    Lv_Lineno := Lv_Lineno + 1;

    Lv_String := '    MAXEXTENTS ' || Lv_TS_Max_Extents;
    WRITE_OUT(Lv_Lineno, Lv_TS_Tablespace_Name, Lv_String);
    Lv_Lineno := Lv_Lineno + 1;

    Lv_String := '    PCTINCREASE ' || Lv_TS_Pct_Increase;
    WRITE_OUT(Lv_Lineno, Lv_TS_Tablespace_Name, Lv_String);
    Lv_Lineno := Lv_Lineno + 1;

    Lv_String := ')';
    WRITE_OUT(Lv_Lineno, Lv_TS_Tablespace_Name, Lv_String);
    Lv_Lineno := Lv_Lineno + 1;
```

The next section of the script adds the final clauses to the **create tablespace** command. A tablespace can be created as ONLINE or OFFLINE (Status column of DBA_TABLESPACES). Tablespaces which are online are available to users for object creation and access.

As of ORACLE7.3, you can designate a tablespace as either PERMANENT or TEMPORARY (Contents column of DBA_TABLESPACES). A tablespace whose contents are designated as TEMPORARY can contain only temporary segments. Dedicating a tablespace to temporary segments can improve sorting performance if your application frequently uses temporary segments for sorting as the temporary segments are not dropped once the sort is complete.

```
Lv_String := Lv_TS_Status || ' ' || Lv_TS_Contents;
WRITE_OUT(Lv_Lineno, Lv_TS_Tablespace_Name, Lv_String);
Lv_Lineno := Lv_Lineno + 1;
```

The next portion of the script completes the **create tablespace** command by writing a '/' to execute the statement when the generated script is run. The outer cursor loop repeats for all tablespaces selected.

```
Lv_String := '/';
WRITE_OUT(Lv_Lineno, Lv_TS_Tablespace_Name, Lv_String);
Lv_Lineno := Lv_Lineno + 1;

  end loop ;
  close TSPACE_CURSOR;

end;
/
```

The **trimspool on** option of the **set** command allows SQL*Plus to remove trailing blanks at the end of each spooled line. The **spool** command and the **select** from the TSPACE_TEMP table write the generated script to a file named cre_tbs.sql. Because the TSPACE_CURSOR cursor selects all tablespaces except SYSTEM, the **where** clause lets you select only those tablespaces whose name matches the input variable *tablespace_name*. Using **like** in the **where** clause instead of = allows for wildcards.

```
set trimspool on
spool cre_tbs.sql
select Text
  from TSPACE_TEMP
 where Tablespace_Name like UPPER('&&tablespace_name')
 order by Tspace_Name, Lineno
/
spool off
```

For the USER_DATA tablespace, the gen_tbs.sql script will generate the following script to re-create the tablespace. The tablespace contains eight datafiles each sized the same, and they have been striped over three different disks. The tablespace has been defined as **permanent**, so objects can be created within it. The tablespace does not have **autoextend on**, so the DBA will have to monitor space usage within the tablespace to ensure that the application does not run out of space.

```
CREATE TABLESPACE user_data
DATAFILE '/usr/ORADATA29/TEST/user_data_TEST_01.dbf' SIZE 512000K REUSE
        ,'/usr/ORADATA48/TEST/user_data_TEST_02.dbf' SIZE 512000K REUSE
        ,'/usr/ORADATA45/TEST/user_data_TEST_03.dbf' SIZE 512000K REUSE
        ,'/usr/ORADATA29/TEST/user_data_TEST_04.dbf' SIZE 512000K REUSE
        ,'/usr/ORADATA48/TEST/user_data_TEST_05.dbf' SIZE 512000K REUSE
        ,'/usr/ORADATA45/TEST/user_data_TEST_06.dbf' SIZE 512000K REUSE
        ,'/usr/ORADATA29/TEST/user_data_TEST_07.dbf' SIZE 512000K REUSE
        ,'/usr/ORADATA48/TEST/user_data_TEST_08.dbf' SIZE 512000K REUSE
DEFAULT STORAGE
(
    INITIAL     400K
    NEXT        400K
    MINEXTENTS 1
    MAXEXTENTS 5000
    PCTINCREASE 0
)
ONLINE PERMANENT
/
```

As of ORACLE8, you can now define the **minimum extent** size for a tablespace. **minimum extent** ensures that every extent in a tablespace is at least as large as or is a multiple of the size of the minimum extent. Setting a **minimum extent** size helps to reduce free space fragmentation by standardizing the size of the available extents in the tablespace.

Also new in ORACLE8 is the ability to turn **logging** on or off for a tablespace. **logging** specifies the default logging attributes for all objects within the tablespace which do not explicitly define their own logging attributes. **nologging** is supported for:

◆ DML: direct-load **insert** and Direct path SQL*Loader

◆ DDL: **create table ... as select**
   create index
   alter index ... rebuild
   alter index ... rebuild partition
   alter index ... split partition
   alter table ... split partition
   alter table ... move partition

nologging speeds up these operations because no redo information is generated. If you change the **logging** attribute for a tablespace, it does not change the attribute for objects which already exist.

In addition, the ORACLE8 DBA_DATA_FILES data dictionary view has been modified to include the **autoextend** information, removing the need to join with the SYS.FILEXT$ table in the DFILE_CURSOR cursor. To allow for the new options on the **create tablespace** command and the new data dictionary view, the gen_tbs.sql script has been modified into the gen_tbs8.sql script, as shown in the following listing:

```
set echo off term on verify off feedback off pagesize 0
select 'Creating tablespace build script...' from DUAL;

accept tablespace_name prompt "Enter the name of the tablespace: "
set term off

drop table TSPACE_TEMP;

create table TSPACE_TEMP (
        Lineno       NUMBER,
        Tspace_Name VARCHAR2(30),
        Text         VARCHAR2(500))
/

declare
   cursor TSPACE_CURSOR is
        select Tablespace_Name,
               Initial_Extent,
               Next_Extent,
               Min_Extents,
               Max_Extents,
               Pct_Increase,
               Min_Extlen,
               Status,
               Contents,
               Logging
          from DBA_TABLESPACES
         where Tablespace_Name !='SYSTEM';

   cursor DFILE_CURSOR (C_Tablespace_Name VARCHAR2) is
        select Maxbytes,
               Increment_By,
```

```
                    File_Name,
                    Bytes,
                    Status,
                    Autoextensible
                from DBA_DATA_FILES
             where Tablespace_Name = C_Tablespace_Name
             order by File_ID;


   Lv_TS_Tablespace_Name        DBA_TABLESPACES.Tablespace_Name%TYPE;
   Lv_TS_Initial_Extent         DBA_TABLESPACES.Initial_Extent%TYPE;
   Lv_TS_Next_Extent            DBA_TABLESPACES.Next_Extent%TYPE;
   Lv_TS_Min_Extents            DBA_TABLESPACES.Min_Extents%TYPE;
   Lv_TS_Max_Extents            DBA_TABLESPACES.Max_Extents%TYPE;
   Lv_TS_Pct_Increase           DBA_TABLESPACES.Pct_Increase%TYPE;
   Lv_TS_Min_Extlen             DBA_TABLESPACES.Min_Extlen%TYPE;
   Lv_TS_Status                 DBA_TABLESPACES.Status%TYPE;
   Lv_TS_Contents               DBA_TABLESPACES.Contents%TYPE;
   Lv_TS_Logging                DBA_TABLESPACES.Logging%TYPE;

   Lv_DF_Maxbytes               DBA_DATA_FILES.Maxbytes%TYPE;
   Lv_DF_Increment_By           DBA_DATA_FILES.Increment_By%TYPE;
   Lv_DF_File_Name              DBA_DATA_FILES.File_Name%TYPE;
   Lv_DF_Bytes                  DBA_DATA_FILES.Bytes%TYPE;
   Lv_DF_Status                 DBA_DATA_FILES.Status%TYPE;
   Lv_DF_Autoextensible         DBA_DATA_FILES.Autoextensible%TYPE;

   Lv_String                    VARCHAR2(800);
   Lv_Lineno                    NUMBER   := 0;
   Lv_DF_Count                  NUMBER;
   Lv_Block_Size                NUMBER;

   procedure WRITE_OUT(P_Line INTEGER,   P_Tablespace VARCHAR2,
                     P_String VARCHAR2)
   is
   begin
      insert into TSPACE_TEMP (Lineno, Tspace_name, Text)
            values (P_Line,P_Tablespace,P_String);
   end;

begin
```

```
select Value
  into Lv_Block_Size
  from SYS.V_$PARAMETER
 where UPPER(Name) = 'DB_BLOCK_SIZE';


open TSPACE_CURSOR;
loop
   fetch TSPACE_CURSOR into Lv_TS_Tablespace_Name,
                            Lv_TS_Initial_Extent,
                            Lv_TS_Next_Extent,
                            Lv_TS_Min_Extents,
                            Lv_TS_Max_Extents,
                            Lv_TS_Pct_Increase,
                            Lv_TS_Min_Extlen,
                            Lv_TS_Status,
                            Lv_TS_Contents,
                            Lv_TS_Logging;
   exit when TSPACE_CURSOR%NOTFOUND;

   Lv_Lineno := 1;
   Lv_DF_Count := 0;
   Lv_String := 'CREATE TABLESPACE ' || LOWER(Lv_TS_Tablespace_Name);
   WRITE_OUT(Lv_Lineno, Lv_TS_Tablespace_Name, Lv_String);
   Lv_Lineno := Lv_Lineno + 1;


   open DFILE_CURSOR (Lv_TS_Tablespace_Name);

   loop
      fetch DFILE_CURSOR into    Lv_DF_Maxbytes,
                                 Lv_DF_Increment_By,
                                 Lv_DF_File_Name,
                                 Lv_DF_Bytes,
                                 Lv_DF_Status,
                                 Lv_DF_Autoextensible;
      exit when DFILE_CURSOR%NOTFOUND;
      Lv_DF_Count := Lv_DF_Count + 1;

      if (Lv_DF_Count > 1)
      then
          Lv_String := '          ,''';
      else
```

```
                    Lv_String := 'DATAFILE ''';
      end if;

      Lv_String := Lv_String || Lv_DF_File_Name
                               || ''' SIZE '
                               || (Lv_DF_Bytes)/1024 ||'K' ;

      Lv_String := Lv_String || ' REUSE ';

      WRITE_OUT(Lv_Lineno, Lv_TS_Tablespace_Name, Lv_String);
      Lv_Lineno := Lv_Lineno + 1;

      if (Lv_DF_Autoextensible = 'YES')
      then
           Lv_String := 'AUTOEXTEND ON NEXT '
                               || (Lv_DF_Increment_By * Lv_Block_Size)/1024
                               || 'K MAXSIZE '
                               || (Lv_DF_Maxbytes/1024)
                               || 'K';

           WRITE_OUT(Lv_Lineno, Lv_TS_Tablespace_Name, Lv_String);
           Lv_Lineno := Lv_Lineno + 1;
      end if;
end loop;
close DFILE_CURSOR;

Lv_String := 'DEFAULT STORAGE ';
WRITE_OUT(Lv_Lineno, Lv_TS_Tablespace_Name, Lv_String);
Lv_Lineno := Lv_Lineno + 1;

Lv_String := '(';
WRITE_OUT(Lv_Lineno, Lv_TS_Tablespace_Name, Lv_String);
Lv_Lineno := Lv_Lineno + 1;

Lv_String := '   INITIAL    ' || Lv_TS_Initial_Extent;
        WRITE_OUT(Lv_Lineno, Lv_TS_Tablespace_Name, Lv_String);
        Lv_Lineno := Lv_Lineno + 1;

Lv_String := '   NEXT       ' || Lv_TS_Next_Extent;
WRITE_OUT(Lv_Lineno, Lv_TS_Tablespace_Name, Lv_String);
Lv_Lineno := Lv_Lineno + 1;

Lv_String := '   MINEXTENTS ' || Lv_TS_Min_Extents;
```

```
        WRITE_OUT(Lv_Lineno, Lv_TS_Tablespace_Name, Lv_String);
        Lv_Lineno := Lv_Lineno + 1;


        Lv_String := '    MAXEXTENTS ' || Lv_TS_Max_Extents;
        WRITE_OUT(Lv_Lineno, Lv_TS_Tablespace_Name, Lv_String);
        Lv_Lineno := Lv_Lineno + 1;


        Lv_String := '    PCTINCREASE ' || Lv_TS_Pct_Increase;
        WRITE_OUT(Lv_Lineno, Lv_TS_Tablespace_Name, Lv_String);
        Lv_Lineno := Lv_Lineno + 1;


        Lv_String := ')';
        WRITE_OUT(Lv_Lineno, Lv_TS_Tablespace_Name, Lv_String);
        Lv_Lineno := Lv_Lineno + 1;


        if (Lv_TS_Min_Extlen > 0)
        then
            Lv_String := 'MINIMUM EXTENT '||Lv_TS_Min_Extlen||' ';
        else
            Lv_String := '';
        end if;


        Lv_String := Lv_String || Lv_TS_Status || ' '
                     || Lv_TS_Contents || ' ' || Lv_TS_Logging;
        WRITE_OUT(Lv_Lineno, Lv_TS_Tablespace_Name, Lv_String);
        Lv_Lineno := Lv_Lineno + 1;


        Lv_String := '/';
        WRITE_OUT(Lv_Lineno, Lv_TS_Tablespace_Name, Lv_String);
        Lv_Lineno := Lv_Lineno + 1;


    end loop ;
    close TSPACE_CURSOR;

end;
/
set trimspool on
spool cre_tbs8.sql
select Text
  from TSPACE_TEMP
 order by Tspace_Name, Lineno
/
spool off
```

The major changes to the script are in the DFILE_CURSOR cursor, which now reads only from the DBA_DATA_FILES view:

```
cursor DFILE_CURSOR (C_Tablespace_Name VARCHAR2) is
        select Maxbytes,
                Increment_By,
                File_Name,
                Bytes,
                Status,
                Autoextensible
         from DBA_DATA_FILES
         where Tablespace_Name = C_Tablespace_Name
         order by File_ID;
```

and the associated code which creates the **autoextend** clause:

```
        if (Lv_DF_Autoextensible = 'YES')
        then
            Lv_String := 'AUTOEXTEND ON NEXT '
                          || (Lv_DF_Increment_By * Lv_Block_Size)/1024
                          || 'K MAXSIZE '
                          || (Lv_DF_Maxbytes/1024)
                          || 'K';

            WRITE_OUT(Lv_Lineno, Lv_TS_Tablespace_Name, Lv_String);
            Lv_Lineno := Lv_Lineno + 1;
        end if;
```

New code is added to check for the **minimum extent** setting:

```
        if (Lv_TS_Min_Extlen > 0)
        then
            Lv_String := 'MINIMUM EXTENT '||Lv_TS_Min_Extlen||' ';
        else
            Lv_String := '';
        end if;
```

And finally, the **logging** attribute is added to the end of the **create tablespace** command:

```
        Lv_String := Lv_String || Lv_TS_Status || ' '
                      || Lv_TS_Contents || ' ' || Lv_TS_Logging;
```

The gen_tbs8.sql script, run with an input to the *tablespace_name* prompt of '%data%', generates the following cre_tbs.sql script. The TEMPORARY_DATA tablespace has been created as **temporary**, so no objects other than temporary segments can be created in this tablespace. Because the tablespace is temporary, it makes sense to turn on **nologging** as well. Both tablespaces have been created with

autoextend on. You should very carefully monitor the sizes of autoextendable tablespaces because ORACLE does not keep a record within the database if the datafile has extended and you will not be able to tell if you need to resize the objects in your tablespace. The USER_DATA tablespace has also been created with a **minimum extent** of 40960. The **initial** and **next** extent sizes, however, are not multiples of 40960. ORACLE will allow you to create the tablespace this way, but will round up the allocated extent sizes to the next larger multiple of 40960 for any object you create in this tablespace, whether or not you specify the storage clause. The **initial** and **next** extent sizes stored in the DBA_SEGMENTS data dictionary view will be either the tablespace default or actual specifed sizes, depending on how you create the object, but the actual allocated blocks will be a multiple of the **minimum extent** size.

```
CREATE TABLESPACE temporary_data
DATAFILE 'D:\ORANT\DATABASE\TMP1ORCL.ORA' SIZE 2048K REUSE
AUTOEXTEND ON NEXT 10240K MAXSIZE 153600K
DEFAULT STORAGE
(
    INITIAL     10240
    NEXT        10240
    MINEXTENTS  1
    MAXEXTENTS  121
    PCTINCREASE 50
)
ONLINE TEMPORARY NOLOGGING
/
CREATE TABLESPACE user_data
DATAFILE 'D:\ORANT\DATABASE\USR1ORCL.ORA' SIZE 8192K REUSE
AUTOEXTEND ON NEXT 5120K MAXSIZE 153600K
DEFAULT STORAGE
(
    INITIAL     10240
    NEXT        10240
    MINEXTENTS  1
    MAXEXTENTS  121
    PCTINCREASE 50
)
MINIMUM EXTENT 40960 ONLINE PERMANENT LOGGING
/
```

gen_dbse.sql

Generate a Database

Have you ever wanted to make an empty copy of your production database for testing purposes? Do you know all the init.ora parameters that you've changed from

ORACLE's default values? To answer these questions, you can use the gen_dbse.sql script to generate two scripts. The two files created as output include a copy of your current init.ora and the **create database** script to re-create your database.

Before you can run the gen_dbse.sql script, you need to run the ORACLE-provided script utlfiles.sql which is in the /rdbms/admin directory under your ORACLE software home directory. The utlfiles.sql script creates the UTL_FILE package, which lets you access an operating system flat file from within a PL/SQL procedure. In conjunction with the utlfiles.sql script, you must modify your init.ora to include the *utl_file_dir* parameter, which points to the operating system directory or directories that the UTL_FILE package is able to write to. Finally, in order to make sure that all the tablespaces in the database are captured in the script, you must run the gen_tbs.sql or gen_tbs8.sql script discussed in the prior section. When running the gen_tbs.sql script, you can enter '%' as the tablespace name at the prompt. The gen_tbs.sql script fills the TSPACE_TEMP table, accessed in this script, with **create tablespace** commands for all tablespaces except SYSTEM.

The gen_dbse.sql script is shown in the following listing:

```
set echo off term on verify off feedback off pagesize 0 trimspool on
select 'Creating database build script...' from DUAL;
accept ORACLE_sid prompt "Enter the SID of the database: "
accept init_loc prompt "Enter the location for the init.ora file: "
set term off

drop table DBASE_TEMP;

create table DBASE_TEMP (
        Lineno NUMBER,
        Text VARCHAR2(100));

declare
    cursor PARAM_CURSOR is
            select Name,
                   Value,
                   Description
              from V$PARAMETER
             where Isdefault = 'FALSE'
             order by Name;

    cursor LOGFILE_CURSOR (LF_Group_Num IN VARCHAR2) is
            select A.Group#,
                   A.Bytes,
                   A.Members,
                   B.Member
              from V$LOG A,
```

```
                V$LOGFILE B
        where A.Group# = B.Group#
          and A.Group# = LF_Group_Num
        order by A.Group#;

cursor DFILE_CURSOR is
      select A.Maxextend,
             A.Inc,
             B.File_Name,
             B.Bytes
        from SYS.FILEXT$ A,
             DBA_DATA_FILES B
       where B.File_ID = A.File#(+)
         and Tablespace_Name = 'SYSTEM'
     order by File_ID;

cursor TSPACE_CURSOR is
      select Text
        from TSPACE_TEMP
       order by Tspace_Name, Lineno;

cursor TEMP_SPACE_CURSOR is
      select Username,
             Default_Tablespace,
             Temporary_Tablespace
        from DBA_USERS
       where Username in ('SYS','SYSTEM');

cursor ROLLBACK_SEGS_CURSOR is
      select A.Segment_Name,
             A.Owner,
             A.Tablespace_Name,
             A.Initial_Extent,
             A.Next_Extent,
             A.Min_Extents,
             A.Max_Extents,
             A.Pct_Increase,
             A.Status,
             B.Optsize
        from DBA_ROLLBACK_SEGS A,
             V$ROLLSTAT         B
       where A.Segment_Id = B.USN(+)
```

```
        and A.Segment_id > 0
        and A.Segment_Name != 'RB_TEMP'
    order by A.Owner, A.Segment_Name;


Lv_PC_Name                  V$PARAMETER.Name%TYPE;
Lv_PC_Value                 V$PARAMETER.Value%TYPE;
Lv_PC_Description           V$PARAMETER.Description%TYPE;
Lv_LF_Group_Num             V$LOG.Group#%TYPE;
Lv_LF_Bytes                 V$LOG.Bytes%TYPE;
Lv_LF_Members               V$LOG.Members%TYPE;
Lv_LF_Member                V$LOGFILE.Member%TYPE;
Lv_DF_MaxExtend             SYS.FILEXT$.MaxExtend%TYPE;
Lv_DF_Inc                   SYS.FILEXT$.Inc%TYPE;
Lv_DF_File_Name             DBA_DATA_FILES.File_Name%TYPE;
Lv_DF_Bytes                 DBA_DATA_FILES.Bytes%TYPE;
Lv_TS_Text                  TSPACE_TEMP.Text%TYPE;
Lv_TE_Temp_Tspace           DBA_USERS.Temporary_Tablespace%TYPE;
Lv_TE_Deflt_Tspace          DBA_USERS.Default_Tablespace%TYPE;
Lv_TE_Username              DBA_USERS.Username%TYPE;
Lv_RB_Segment_Name          DBA_ROLLBACK_SEGS.Segment_Name%TYPE;
Lv_RB_Owner                 DBA_ROLLBACK_SEGS.Owner%TYPE;
Lv_RB_Tablespace_Name       DBA_ROLLBACK_SEGS.Tablespace_Name%TYPE;
Lv_RB_Initial_Extent        DBA_ROLLBACK_SEGS.Initial_Extent%TYPE;
Lv_RB_Next_Extent           DBA_ROLLBACK_SEGS.Next_Extent%TYPE;
Lv_RB_Min_Extents           DBA_ROLLBACK_SEGS.Min_Extents%TYPE;
Lv_RB_Max_Extents           DBA_ROLLBACK_SEGS.Max_Extents%TYPE;
Lv_RB_Pct_Increase          DBA_ROLLBACK_SEGS.Pct_Increase%TYPE;
Lv_RB_Status                DBA_ROLLBACK_SEGS.Status%TYPE;
Lv_RB_Optsize               V$ROLLSTAT.Optsize%TYPE;


Lv_FileHandle               UTL_FILE.FILE_TYPE;


Lv_String                   VARCHAR2(2000);
Lv_Lineno                   NUMBER := 0;
Lv_First_Time               BOOLEAN;
Lv_Size                     NUMBER;
Lv_No_Of_Groups             INTEGER;
Lv_InitOra_Location         VARCHAR2(40);
Lv_InitOra_Name             VARCHAR2(30);
Lv_Database_Name            VARCHAR2(8);
Lv_MaxLogFiles              INTEGER;
Lv_MaxLogMembers            INTEGER;


Lv_LogMode                  VARCHAR2(15);
```

```
     Lv_CharacterSet              VARCHAR2(64);
     Lv_Group                     INTEGER;
     Lv_Members                   INTEGER;
     Lv_Block_Size                NUMBER;
     Lv_DF_Count                  NUMBER   := 0;
     Lv_Platform_Slash            VARCHAR2(1);

     procedure WRITE_OUT(P_Line INTEGER, P_String VARCHAR2) is
     begin
        insert into DBASE_TEMP (Lineno, Text)
              values (P_Line,P_String);
      end;

begin

   Lv_Lineno := 1;
   Lv_InitOra_Location := '&&init_loc';
   Lv_InitOra_Name      := 'init'                 ||
                           '&&ORACLE_sid'||
                           '.ora';

   Lv_FileHandle :=
            UTL_FILE.FOPEN(Lv_InitOra_Location,Lv_InitOra_Name,'W');

   open PARAM_CURSOR;
   loop
      fetch PARAM_CURSOR
      into  Lv_PC_Name,
           Lv_PC_Value,
           Lv_PC_Description;
      exit when PARAM_CURSOR%NOTFOUND;

      if (UPPER(Lv_PC_Name) = 'DB_NAME')
      then
          Lv_Database_Name := Lv_PC_Value;
      end if;

      Lv_String := '# ' || Lv_PC_Description;
      UTL_FILE.PUTF(Lv_FileHandle,'%s\n',Lv_String);

      Lv_String := RPAD(Lv_PC_Name,45) || ' = ' || Lv_PC_Value;
      UTL_FILE.PUTF(Lv_FileHandle,'%s\n\n',Lv_String);
```

```
end loop;

close PARAM_CURSOR;
UTL_FILE.FCLOSE(Lv_FileHandle);

Lv_Lineno := 1;

Lv_String := 'CREATE DATABASE ' || Lv_Database_Name;
WRITE_OUT(Lv_Lineno,Lv_String);

Lv_Lineno := Lv_Lineno + 1;
Lv_String := LPAD(' ',5) || 'CONTROLFILE REUSE';
WRITE_OUT(Lv_Lineno,Lv_String);

select MAX(Group#)
  into Lv_No_Of_Groups
  from V$LOG;

Lv_Lineno := Lv_Lineno + 1;
WRITE_OUT(Lv_Lineno,LPAD(' ',5) ||'LOGFILE');
Lv_First_Time := TRUE;

for Lv_Index IN  1 .. Lv_No_Of_Groups
loop
   open  LOGFILE_CURSOR (Lv_Index);
   loop
       fetch LOGFILE_CURSOR
       into  Lv_LF_Group_Num,
             Lv_LF_Bytes,
             Lv_LF_Members,
             Lv_LF_Member;
       exit when LOGFILE_CURSOR%NOTFOUND;

       Lv_Size := Lv_LF_Bytes / 1024;

       if (Lv_First_Time = TRUE)
       then
          Lv_String     := '      ';
          Lv_First_Time := FALSE;
       else
          Lv_String     := '    ,';
       end if;
```

```
    if (Lv_LF_Members = 1)
    then
       Lv_String := Lv_String                     ||
                    'GROUP '                       ||
                    LPAD(Lv_LF_Group_Num,3)        ||
                    ' '''                          ||
                    Lv_LF_Member                   ||
                    ''''                           ||
                    ' SIZE '                       ||
                    Lv_Size                        ||
                    'K REUSE';

       Lv_Lineno := Lv_Lineno + 1;
       WRITE_OUT(Lv_Lineno,Lv_String);
    else
       if  (LOGFILE_CURSOR%ROWCOUNT = 1)
       then
           Lv_String := Lv_String                     ||
                        'GROUP '                       ||
                        LPAD(Lv_LF_Group_Num,3)        ||
                        ' ('''                         ||
                        Lv_LF_Member                   ||
                        '''' ;
           Lv_Lineno := Lv_Lineno + 1;
           WRITE_OUT(Lv_Lineno,Lv_String);
       else
           Lv_String := LPAD(' ',15)    ||
                        ',''            ||
                        Lv_LF_Member   ||
                        '''';
           if (LOGFILE_CURSOR%ROWCOUNT = Lv_LF_Members)
           then
               Lv_String := Lv_String ||
                            ') SIZE ' ||
                            Lv_Size   ||
                            'K REUSE';
           end if;
           Lv_Lineno := Lv_Lineno + 1;
```

```
                    WRITE_OUT(Lv_Lineno, Lv_String);
              end if;

        end if;
    end loop;
    CLOSE LOGFILE_CURSOR;
end loop;

select Value
  into Lv_Block_Size
  from SYS.V_$PARAMETER
 where UPPER(Name) = 'DB_BLOCK_SIZE';


open DFILE_CURSOR;

loop
      fetch DFILE_CURSOR into    Lv_DF_MaxExtend,
                                 Lv_DF_Inc,
                                 Lv_DF_File_Name,
                                 Lv_DF_Bytes;
      exit when DFILE_CURSOR%NOTFOUND;
      Lv_DF_Count := Lv_DF_Count + 1;

      if (Lv_DF_Count > 1)
      then
          Lv_String := '          ,''';
      else
          Lv_String := 'DATAFILE ''';
      end if;

      Lv_String := LPAD(' ',5)          ||
                   Lv_String            ||
                   Lv_DF_File_Name      ||
                   ''' SIZE '           ||
                   (Lv_DF_Bytes)/1024   ||
                   'K REUSE' ;

      WRITE_OUT(Lv_Lineno, Lv_String);
      Lv_Lineno := Lv_Lineno + 1;

      if (Lv_DF_MaxExtend IS NOT NULL)
      then
          Lv_String := LPAD(' ',12)                       ||
                    'AUTOEXTEND ON NEXT '                 ||
                    (Lv_DF_Inc * Lv_Block_Size) / 1024    ||
```

```
                              'K MAXSIZE '                                ||
                              (Lv_DF_MaxExtend * Lv_Block_Size) / 1024    ||
                              'K';

                WRITE_OUT(Lv_Lineno, Lv_String);
                Lv_Lineno := Lv_Lineno + 1;
           end if;
end loop;
close DFILE_CURSOR;

select MAX(Group#),
       MAX(Members)
  into Lv_Group,
       Lv_Members
  from SYS.V_$LOG;

Lv_MaxLogFiles   := Lv_Group   * Lv_Members * 4;
Lv_MaxLogMembers := Lv_Members * 2;

Lv_Lineno := Lv_Lineno + 1;
Lv_String := LPAD(' ',5) || 'MAXLOGFILES ' || Lv_MaxLogFiles;
WRITE_OUT(Lv_Lineno,Lv_String);

Lv_Lineno := Lv_Lineno + 1;
Lv_String := LPAD(' ',5) || 'MAXLOGMEMBERS ' || Lv_MaxLogMembers;
WRITE_OUT(Lv_Lineno,Lv_String);

Lv_Lineno := Lv_Lineno + 1;
WRITE_OUT(Lv_Lineno,LPAD(' ',5) || 'MAXLOGHISTORY 160');

Lv_Lineno := Lv_Lineno +1;
WRITE_OUT(Lv_Lineno,LPAD(' ',5) || 'MAXDATAFILES 255');

Lv_Lineno := Lv_Lineno + 1;
WRITE_OUT(Lv_Lineno,LPAD(' ',5) || 'MAXINSTANCES 1');

select Log_Mode
  into Lv_LogMode
  from SYS.V_$DATABASE;

Lv_Lineno := Lv_Lineno + 1;
WRITE_OUT(Lv_Lineno,LPAD(' ',5) || Lv_LogMode);
```

```
select Value
    into Lv_CharacterSet
    from V$NLS_PARAMETERS
   where UPPER(Parameter) = 'NLS_CHARACTERSET';

  Lv_Lineno := Lv_Lineno + 1;
  Lv_String := LPAD(' ',5)      ||
               'CHARACTER SET ' ||
               Lv_CharacterSet ||
               ';';
  WRITE_OUT(Lv_Lineno,Lv_String);
  Lv_Lineno := Lv_Lineno + 1;
  WRITE_OUT(Lv_Lineno, ' ');
  Lv_Lineno := Lv_Lineno + 1;
  WRITE_OUT(Lv_Lineno, 'Rem ------------------------------------');
  Lv_Lineno := Lv_Lineno + 1;
  WRITE_OUT(Lv_Lineno, 'Rem Create a Temporary Rollback Segment');
  Lv_Lineno := Lv_Lineno + 1;
  WRITE_OUT(Lv_Lineno, 'Rem ------------------------------------');
  Lv_Lineno := Lv_Lineno + 1;
  WRITE_OUT(Lv_Lineno, ' ');

  Lv_Lineno := Lv_Lineno + 1;
  WRITE_OUT(Lv_Lineno, 'Create Rollback Segment rb_temp;');
  Lv_Lineno := Lv_Lineno + 1;
  WRITE_OUT(Lv_Lineno, 'Alter  Rollback Segment rb_temp Online;');
  Lv_Lineno := Lv_Lineno + 1;
  WRITE_OUT(Lv_Lineno, 'commit;');

  if (INSTR(Lv_DF_File_Name,'/',1) > 0)
  then
      Lv_Platform_Slash := '/';
  else
      Lv_Platform_Slash := '\';
  end if;

  Lv_Lineno := Lv_Lineno + 1;
  WRITE_OUT(Lv_Lineno, ' ');
  Lv_Lineno := Lv_Lineno + 1;
  WRITE_OUT(Lv_Lineno, 'Rem ------------------------------------');
  Lv_Lineno := Lv_Lineno + 1;
  WRITE_OUT(Lv_Lineno, 'Rem Start catalog.sql script');
```

```
Lv_Lineno := Lv_Lineno + 1;
WRITE_OUT(Lv_Lineno, 'Rem -----------------------------------');
Lv_Lineno := Lv_Lineno + 1;
WRITE_OUT(Lv_Lineno, '  ');


Lv_String := '@$ORACLE_HOME'       ||
             Lv_Platform_Slash ||
             'rdbms'               ||
             Lv_Platform_Slash ||
             'admin'               ||
             Lv_Platform_Slash ||
             'catalog.sql;';
Lv_Lineno := Lv_Lineno + 1;
WRITE_OUT(Lv_Lineno, Lv_String);
Lv_Lineno := Lv_Lineno + 1;
WRITE_OUT(Lv_Lineno, 'commit;');


WRITE_OUT(Lv_Lineno, 'Rem -----------------------------------');
Lv_Lineno := Lv_Lineno + 1;
WRITE_OUT(Lv_Lineno, 'Rem Start catproc.sql script');
Lv_Lineno := Lv_Lineno + 1;
WRITE_OUT(Lv_Lineno, 'Rem -----------------------------------');
Lv_Lineno := Lv_Lineno + 1;
WRITE_OUT(Lv_Lineno, '  ');


Lv_String := '@$ORACLE_HOME'       ||
             Lv_Platform_Slash ||
             'rdbms'               ||
             Lv_Platform_Slash ||
             'admin'               ||
             Lv_Platform_Slash ||
             'catproc.sql;';
Lv_Lineno := Lv_Lineno + 1;
WRITE_OUT(Lv_Lineno, Lv_String);
Lv_Lineno := Lv_Lineno + 1;
WRITE_OUT(Lv_Lineno, 'commit;');

Lv_Lineno := Lv_Lineno + 1;
WRITE_OUT(Lv_Lineno, '  ');
Lv_Lineno := Lv_Lineno + 1;
WRITE_OUT(Lv_Lineno, 'Rem -----------------------------------');
Lv_Lineno := Lv_Lineno + 1;

WRITE_OUT(Lv_Lineno, 'Rem Create Tablespaces');
Lv_Lineno := Lv_Lineno + 1;
```

```
      WRITE_OUT(Lv_Lineno, 'Rem ----------------------------------');
   Lv_Lineno := Lv_Lineno + 1;
   WRITE_OUT(Lv_Lineno, '  ');

   open TSPACE_CURSOR;
   loop
      fetch TSPACE_CURSOR
      into  Lv_TS_Text;
      exit when TSPACE_CURSOR%NOTFOUND;

      Lv_Lineno := Lv_Lineno + 1;
      WRITE_OUT(Lv_Lineno,Lv_TS_Text);
   end loop;
close TSPACE_CURSOR;

   Lv_Lineno := Lv_Lineno + 1;
   WRITE_OUT(Lv_Lineno, '  ');
   Lv_Lineno := Lv_Lineno + 1;
   WRITE_OUT(Lv_Lineno, 'Rem ----------------------------------');
   Lv_Lineno := Lv_Lineno + 1;
   WRITE_OUT(Lv_Lineno, 'Rem Alter sys and system ');
   Lv_Lineno := Lv_Lineno + 1;
   WRITE_OUT(Lv_Lineno, 'Rem ----------------------------------');
   Lv_Lineno := Lv_Lineno + 1;
   WRITE_OUT(Lv_Lineno, '  ');

   open TEMP_SPACE_CURSOR;
   loop
      fetch TEMP_SPACE_CURSOR
      into  Lv_TE_Username,
            Lv_TE_Deflt_Tspace,
            Lv_TE_Temp_Tspace;
      exit when TEMP_SPACE_CURSOR%NOTFOUND;

      Lv_String := 'Alter user '            ||
                   Lv_TE_Username           ||
                 ' default tablespace '     ||
                   Lv_TE_Deflt_Tspace       ||
                 ' temporary tablespace '   ||
                   Lv_TE_Temp_Tspace        ||
                 ';';
      Lv_Lineno := Lv_Lineno + 1;
      WRITE_OUT(Lv_Lineno,Lv_String);
```

```
end loop;
close TEMP_SPACE_CURSOR;

 Lv_Lineno := Lv_Lineno + 1;

 WRITE_OUT(Lv_Lineno, '  ');
 Lv_Lineno := Lv_Lineno + 1;
 WRITE_OUT(Lv_Lineno, 'Rem ----------------------------------');
 Lv_Lineno := Lv_Lineno + 1;
 WRITE_OUT(Lv_Lineno, 'Rem Create Rollback segments');
 Lv_Lineno := Lv_Lineno + 1;
 WRITE_OUT(Lv_Lineno, 'Rem ----------------------------------');
 Lv_Lineno := Lv_Lineno + 1;
 WRITE_OUT(Lv_Lineno, '  ');

 open ROLLBACK_SEGS_CURSOR;
 loop
    fetch ROLLBACK_SEGS_CURSOR
    into  Lv_RB_Segment_Name,
          Lv_RB_Owner,
          Lv_RB_Tablespace_Name,
          Lv_RB_Initial_Extent,
          Lv_RB_Next_Extent,
          Lv_RB_Min_Extents,
          Lv_RB_Max_Extents,
          Lv_RB_Pct_Increase,
          Lv_RB_Status,
          Lv_RB_Optsize;
    exit when ROLLBACK_SEGS_CURSOR%NOTFOUND;

    if (UPPER(Lv_RB_Owner) = 'PUBLIC')
    then
       Lv_String := 'CREATE PUBLIC ROLLBACK SEGMENT ';
    else
       Lv_String := 'CREATE ROLLBACK SEGMENT ';
    end if;

    Lv_String := Lv_String              ||
                 Lv_RB_Segment_Name;
   Lv_Lineno := Lv_Lineno + 1;
   WRITE_OUT(Lv_Lineno,Lv_String);

   Lv_String := '          '            ||
                'TABLESPACE '           ||
```

```
                   Lv_RB_Tablespace_Name ;
Lv_Lineno := Lv_Lineno + 1;
WRITE_OUT(Lv_Lineno,Lv_String);


Lv_Lineno := Lv_Lineno + 1;
WRITE_OUT(Lv_Lineno,'            STORAGE (');

Lv_String := '                 '            ||
             'Initial      '               ||
             (Lv_RB_Initial_Extent) / 1024 ||
             ' K' ;
Lv_Lineno := Lv_Lineno + 1;
WRITE_OUT(Lv_Lineno,Lv_String);

Lv_String := '                 '            ||
             'Next       '                  ||
             (Lv_RB_Next_Extent) / 1024     ||
             ' K' ;
Lv_Lineno := Lv_Lineno + 1;
WRITE_OUT(Lv_Lineno,Lv_String);

Lv_String := '                 '            ||
             'Minextents     '              ||
             Lv_RB_Min_Extents;
Lv_Lineno := Lv_Lineno + 1;
WRITE_OUT(Lv_Lineno,Lv_String);

Lv_String := '                 '            ||
             'Maxextents    '               ||
             Lv_RB_Max_Extents;
Lv_Lineno := Lv_Lineno + 1;
WRITE_OUT(Lv_Lineno,Lv_String);

if ( Lv_RB_Optsize is NOT NULL)
then
   Lv_String := '               '          ||
                'Optimal      '             ||
                (Lv_RB_Optsize);
   Lv_Lineno := Lv_Lineno + 1;
   WRITE_OUT(Lv_Lineno,Lv_String);
end if;


Lv_Lineno := Lv_Lineno + 1;
```

```
      WRITE_OUT(Lv_Lineno,'                );');

      Lv_String := 'Alter Rollback Segment '        ||
                   Lv_RB_Segment_Name              ||
                   ' '                             ||
                   Lv_RB_STATUS                    ||
                   ';';
      Lv_Lineno := Lv_Lineno + 1;
      WRITE_OUT(Lv_Lineno,Lv_String);


  end loop;
  close ROLLBACK_SEGS_CURSOR;

exception
    WHEN NO_DATA_FOUND
    THEN
        DBMS_OUTPUT.PUT_LINE ('Reached end of file');

    WHEN UTL_FILE.INTERNAL_ERROR
    THEN
        DBMS_OUTPUT.PUT_LINE ('Internal File Error');

    WHEN UTL_FILE.INVALID_FILEHANDLE
    THEN
        DBMS_OUTPUT.PUT_LINE ('Invalid File Handle');

    WHEN UTL_FILE.INVALID_MODE
    THEN
        DBMS_OUTPUT.PUT_LINE ('Invalid file mode specified');

    WHEN UTL_FILE.INVALID_OPERATION
    THEN
        DBMS_OUTPUT.PUT_LINE ('Invalid file operation specified');

    WHEN UTL_FILE.INVALID_PATH
    THEN
        DBMS_OUTPUT.PUT_LINE ('Invalid file path specified');

    WHEN UTL_FILE.WRITE_ERROR
    THEN
        DBMS_OUTPUT.PUT_LINE ('A Write error occurred');
```

```
    WHEN UTL_FILE.READ_ERROR
    THEN
        DBMS_OUTPUT.PUT_LINE ('A file read error occurred');

    WHEN OTHERS
    THEN
        DBMS_OUTPUT.PUT_LINE ('An unknown exception occurred');
end;
/
set trimspool on
spool init.sql
select text
  from DBASE_TEMP
 order by Lineno
/
spool off
```

The two scripts created by gen_dbse.sql are shown in the following listings. The first file is the init.ora parameter file. This file contains only the initialization parameters which have been changed from the ORACLE default values. Some of these values are not listed in the original init.ora, but are derived from other parameters. As an example, the parameter *GC_RELEASABLE_LOCKS* is not set in the original init.ora and, in fact, is not applicable to this database because that parameter is used only for ORACLE Parallel Server. *GC_RELEASABLE_LOCKS* takes its default value from the parameter *DB_BLOCK_BUFFERS*, and because the *DB_BLOCK_BUFFERS* value has been changed, *GC_RELEASABLE_LOCKS* has also been changed. Since this database does not use the ORACLE Parallel Server, setting *GC_RELEASABLE_LOCKS* has no effect in this case. There are several other parameters which will take their default values from other init.ora parameters.

```
# always use this anti-join when possible
always_anti_join = NESTED_LOOPS

# enable system auditing
audit_trail = NONE

# Detached process dump directory
background_dump_dest = /usr/app/ORACLE/admin/TEST/bdump

# maximum size of table or piece to be cached (in blocks)
cache_size_threshold = 4000
```

```
# create a separate checkpoint process
checkpoint_process = TRUE

# no. of undo entries to apply per transaction cleanup
cleanup_rollback_entries = 75

# Database will be completely compatible with this software version
compatible = 7.3.4

# control file names list
control_files = /usr/ORADATA55/TEST/control01.ctl,
/usr/ORADATA41/TEST/control02.ctl, /usr/ORADATA53/TEST/control03.ctl

# Core dump directory
core_dump_dest = /usr/app/ORACLE/admin/TEST/cdump

# number of cpu's for this instance
cpu_count = 16

# Number of database blocks cached in memory
db_block_buffers = 40000

# number of lru latches
db_block_lru_latches = 8

# Size of database block in bytes
db_block_size = 4096

# db block to be read each IO
db_file_multiblock_read_count = 16

# max allowable # db files
db_files = 150

# database name specified in CREATE DATABASE
db_name = TEST

# max. number of concurrent distributed transactions
distributed_transactions = 137
```

```
# dml locks - one for each table modified in a transaction
dml_locks = 800

# resources for enqueues
enqueue_resources = 1035

# # freelist groups locks in (DFS)
gc_freelist_groups = 50

# # releasable DB locks (DFS)
gc_releasable_locks = 40000

# enable/disable hash join
hash_join_enabled = FALSE

# include file in init.ora
ifile = /usr/app/ORACLE/admin/TEST/pfile/configTEST.ora

# number of job queue processes to start
job_queue_processes = 10

# redo circular buffer size
log_buffer = 8192000

# # redo blocks checkpoint threshold
log_checkpoint_interval = 40000

# number of simultaneous copies into redo buffer(# of copy latches
log_simultaneous_copies = 16

# Maximum size (blocks) of dump file
max_dump_file_size = 10240

# max. number of rollback segments in SGA cache
max_rollback_segments = 50

# max # cursors per process
open_cursors = 5000

# optimizer mode
optimizer_mode = CHOOSE
```

```
# user processes
processes = 500

# password file usage parameter
remote_login_passwordfile = NONE

# undo segment list
rollback_segments = r01, r02, r03, r04, r05, r06, r08, r09, r10

# number of sequence cache hash buckets
sequence_cache_hash_buckets = 10

# user and system sessions
sessions = 500

# size in bytes of shared pool
shared_pool_size = 200000000

# size of in-memory sort work area retained between fetch calls
sort_area_retained_size = 100000000

# size of in-memory sort work area
sort_area_size = 100000000

# use direct write
sort_direct_writes = AUTO

# temporary table locks
temporary_table_locks = 500

# max. number of concurrent active transactions
transactions = 550

# number of active transactions per rollback segment
transactions_per_rollback_segment = 34

# allow unlimited extents for rollback segments
unlimited_rollback_segments = TRUE

# User process dump directory
user_dump_dest = /usr/app/ORACLE/admin/TEST/udump

# utl_file accessible directories list
utl_file_dir = /usr/utlfiles
```

The second file created by the gen_dbse.sql script is the actual **create datatabase** script.

```
CREATE DATABASE TEST
     CONTROLFILE REUSE
     LOGFILE
     GROUP    1 '/usr/ORADATA55/TEST/redoTEST01.log' SIZE 5120K REUSE
    ,GROUP    2 '/usr/ORADATA41/TEST/redoTEST02.log' SIZE 5120K REUSE
    ,GROUP    3 '/usr/ORADATA53/TEST/redoTEST03.log' SIZE 5120K REUSE
     DATAFILE '/usr/ORADATA54/TEST/system01.dbf' SIZE 512000K REUSE
     MAXLOGFILES 12
     MAXLOGMEMBERS 2
     MAXLOGHISTORY 160
     MAXDATAFILES 255
     MAXINSTANCES 1
     NOARCHIVELOG
     CHARACTER SET US7ASCII;


Rem -----------------------------------
Rem Create a Temporary Rollback Segment
Rem -----------------------------------

Create Rollback Segment rb_temp;
Alter  Rollback Segment rb_temp Online;
commit;


Rem -----------------------------------
Rem Start catalog.sql script
Rem -----------------------------------

@$ORACLE_HOME/rdbms/admin/catalog.sql;
commit;
Rem -----------------------------------
Rem Start catproc.sql script
Rem -----------------------------------

@$ORACLE_HOME/rdbms/admin/catproc.sql;
commit;


Rem -----------------------------------
Rem Create Tablespaces
Rem -----------------------------------

CREATE TABLESPACE rbs1
```

```
DATAFILE '/usr/ORADATA40/TEST/rbs1_TEST_01.dbf' SIZE 307200K REUSE
DEFAULT STORAGE
(
    INITIAL     800K
    NEXT        800K
    MINEXTENTS 20
    MAXEXTENTS 500
    PCTINCREASE 50
)
ONLINE PERMANENT
/
CREATE TABLESPACE rbs2
DATAFILE '/usr/ORADATA51/TEST/rbs2_TEST_01.dbf' SIZE 307200K REUSE
DEFAULT STORAGE
(
    INITIAL     800K
    NEXT        800K
    MINEXTENTS 20
    MAXEXTENTS 500
    PCTINCREASE 50
)
ONLINE PERMANENT
/
CREATE TABLESPACE temp
DATAFILE '/usr/ORADATA41/TEST/temp_TEST_01.dbf' SIZE 512000K REUSE
DEFAULT STORAGE
(
    INITIAL     800K
    NEXT        800K
    MINEXTENTS 1
    MAXEXTENTS 500
    PCTINCREASE 0
)
ONLINE TEMPORARY
/
CREATE TABLESPACE tools
DATAFILE '/usr/ORADATA40/TEST/tools_TEST_01.dbf' SIZE 20480K REUSE
DEFAULT STORAGE
(
    INITIAL     40K
    NEXT        40K
    MINEXTENTS 1
    MAXEXTENTS 249
```

```
   PCTINCREASE 0
)
ONLINE PERMANENT
/
CREATE TABLESPACE users
DATAFILE '/usr/ORADATA41/TEST/users_TEST_01.dbf' SIZE 102400K REUSE
DEFAULT STORAGE
(
   INITIAL    40K
   NEXT       40K
   MINEXTENTS 1
   MAXEXTENTS 249
   PCTINCREASE 0
)
ONLINE PERMANENT
/
CREATE TABLESPACE user_data
DATAFILE '/usr/ORADATA29/TEST/user_data_TEST_01.dbf' SIZE 512000K REUSE
        ,'/usr/ORADATA48/TEST/user_data_TEST_02.dbf' SIZE 512000K REUSE
        ,'/usr/ORADATA45/TEST/user_data_TEST_03.dbf' SIZE 512000K REUSE
        ,'/usr/ORADATA29/TEST/user_data_TEST_04.dbf' SIZE 512000K REUSE
        ,'/usr/ORADATA48/TEST/user_data_TEST_05.dbf' SIZE 512000K REUSE
        ,'/usr/ORADATA45/TEST/user_data_TEST_06.dbf' SIZE 512000K REUSE
        ,'/usr/ORADATA29/TEST/user_data_TEST_07.dbf' SIZE 512000K REUSE
        ,'/usr/ORADATA48/TEST/user_data_TEST_08.dbf' SIZE 512000K REUSE
DEFAULT STORAGE
(
   INITIAL    400K
   NEXT       400K
   MINEXTENTS 1
   MAXEXTENTS 5000
   PCTINCREASE 0
)
ONLINE PERMANENT
/
CREATE TABLESPACE user_index
DATAFILE '/usr/ORADATA49/TEST/user_index_TEST_01.dbf' SIZE 512000K REUSE
        ,'/usr/ORADATA43/TEST/user_index_TEST_02.dbf' SIZE 512000K REUSE
        ,'/usr/ORADATA42/TEST/user_index_TEST_03.dbf' SIZE 512000K REUSE
        ,'/usr/ORADATA49/TEST/user_index_TEST_04.dbf' SIZE 512000K REUSE
        ,'/usr/ORADATA43/TEST/user_index_TEST_05.dbf' SIZE 512000K REUSE
        ,'/usr/ORADATA42/TEST/user_index_TEST_06.dbf' SIZE 512000K REUSE
```

```
DEFAULT STORAGE
(
   INITIAL     400K
   NEXT        400K
   MINEXTENTS 1
   MAXEXTENTS 5000
   PCTINCREASE 0
)
ONLINE PERMANENT
/


Rem ----------------------------------
Rem Alter sys and system
Rem ----------------------------------

Alter user SYSTEM default tablespace USERS temporary tablespace TEMP;
Alter user SYS default tablespace SYSTEM temporary tablespace TEMP;


Rem ----------------------------------
Rem Create Rollback segments
Rem ----------------------------------

CREATE ROLLBACK SEGMENT R0
        TABLESPACE SYSTEM
            STORAGE (
                    Initial      16 K
                    Next         16 K
                    Minextents   2
                    Maxextents   20
            );
Alter Rollback Segment R0 OFFLINE;
CREATE ROLLBACK SEGMENT R01
        TABLESPACE RBS1
            STORAGE (
                    Initial      800 K
                    Next         800 K
                    Minextents   10
                    Maxextents   500
                    Optimal      8192000
            );
Alter Rollback Segment R01 ONLINE;
CREATE ROLLBACK SEGMENT R10
        TABLESPACE RBS2
            STORAGE (
```

```
                    Initial      800 K
                    Next         800 K
                    Minextents   10
                    Maxextents   500
                    Optimal      8192000
        );
Alter Rollback Segment R10 ONLINE;
CREATE ROLLBACK SEGMENT R02
        TABLESPACE RBS2
            STORAGE (
                    Initial      800 K
                    Next         800 K
                    Minextents   10
                    Maxextents   500
                    Optimal      8192000
            );
Alter Rollback Segment R02 ONLINE;
CREATE ROLLBACK SEGMENT R03
        TABLESPACE RBS1
            STORAGE (
                    Initial      800 K
                    Next         800 K
                    Minextents   10
                    Maxextents   500
                    Optimal      8192000
            );
Alter Rollback Segment R03 ONLINE;
CREATE ROLLBACK SEGMENT R04
        TABLESPACE RBS2
            STORAGE (
                    Initial      800 K
                    Next         800 K
                    Minextents   10
                    Maxextents   500
                    Optimal      8192000
            );
Alter Rollback Segment R04 ONLINE;
CREATE ROLLBACK SEGMENT R05
        TABLESPACE RBS1
            STORAGE (
                    Initial      800 K
                    Next         800 K
                    Minextents   10
```

```
                    Maxextents    500
                    Optimal       8192000
          );
Alter Rollback Segment R05 ONLINE;
CREATE ROLLBACK SEGMENT R06
      TABLESPACE RBS2
         STORAGE (
                    Initial       800 K
                    Next          800 K
                    Minextents    10
                    Maxextents    500
                    Optimal       8192000
          );
Alter Rollback Segment R06 ONLINE;
CREATE ROLLBACK SEGMENT R07
      TABLESPACE RBS1
         STORAGE (
                    Initial       800 K
                    Next          800 K
                    Minextents    10
                    Maxextents    500
                    Optimal       8192000
          );
Alter Rollback Segment R07 OFFLINE;
CREATE ROLLBACK SEGMENT R08
      TABLESPACE RBS2
         STORAGE (
                    Initial       800 K
                    Next          800 K
                    Minextents    10
                    Maxextents    500
                    Optimal       8192000
          );
Alter Rollback Segment R08 ONLINE;
CREATE ROLLBACK SEGMENT R09
      TABLESPACE RBS1
         STORAGE (
                    Initial       800 K
                    Next          800 K
                    Minextents    10
                    Maxextents    500
                    Optimal       8192000
          );
Alter Rollback Segment R09 ONLINE;
```

ANNOTATIONS

The gen_dbse.sql script documents your init.ora parameter file and generates a script to re-create your database. You can use the gen_dbse.sql script to document your tablespaces, rollback segments, and overall database configuration, or to create an empty copy of your database for testing purposes. You can edit the tablespace locations and sizes if you wish, to map to disk space availability on a different server, or edit the init.ora file to change the database block size, then run the script and reload your database from a full database export.

The script uses the *ORACLE_sid* variable to allow you to enter the correct SID (instance) to name the init.ora parameter file as init*ORACLE_sid*.ora to follow ORACLE conventions. The *init_loc* variable is used in conjunction with the UTL_FILE package to create the init*ORACLE_sid*.ora file in this directory. The script uses a temporary table to hold individual lines of the various **create** and **alter** statements, writing to the table rather than using DBMS_OUTPUT.PUT_LINE. Using the DBMS_OUTPUT procedure would force you to save and edit the output file for the tablespace you want.

The first section of the script does the initial setup, prompting for the ORACLE SID and init.ora location for later use via the **accept** command, which, unlike simply using the variable with the '&' or '&&' in a SQL statement, allows you to define your own prompt for the variable. The value entered for *init_loc* must be one of the directories defined by the init.ora parameter *utl_file_dir*, or the init*ORACLE_sid*.ora file will not be created.

The SQL*Plus **set** command turns off headers (**pagesize 0**), row counts (**feedback off**), and displays of old and new values for the *ORACLE_sid* and *init_loc* variables (**verify off**), and removes trailing blanks at the end of each spooled line (**trimspool on**).

```
set echo off term on verify off feedback off pagesize 0 trimspool on
select 'Creating database build script...' from DUAL;
accept ORACLE_sid prompt "Enter the SID of the database: "
accept init_loc prompt "Enter the location for the init.ora file: "
set term off
```

Next, a temporary table is created to hold all the commands used to create an empty database. Unlike the temporary tables created in the generate scripts in Chapter 5, no Owner column is needed since a database has no defined owner other than ORACLE. The Lineno column preserves the ordering of the lines of the **create** and **alter** commands during later queries.

```
drop table DBASE_TEMP;

create table DBASE_TEMP (
       Lineno NUMBER,
       Text VARCHAR2(100));
```

In the next section of the script, the PARAM_CURSOR cursor selects the information from the V$PARAMETER table where the values are not the ORACLE-supplied default values in order to build a copy of the init.ora file.

```
declare
  cursor PARAM_CURSOR is
        select Name,
               Value,
               Description
          from V$PARAMETER
         where Isdefault = 'FALSE'
         order by Name;
```

The next cursor to be defined is the LOGFILE_CURSOR, which extracts the information necessary to re-create the online redo log file groups and members.

```
  cursor LOGFILE_CURSOR (LF_Group_Num IN VARCHAR2) is
        select A.Group#,
               A.Bytes,
               A.Members,
               B.Member
          from V$LOG A,
               V$LOGFILE B
         where A.Group# = B.Group#
           and A.Group# = LF_Group_Num
         order by A.Group#;
```

The DFILE_CURSOR cursor extracts all the information needed to re-create the SYSTEM tablespace. An outer join, (+), ensures that all rows in the DBA_DATA_FILES view are returned, even if there is no matching row in SYS.FILEXT$. If an outer join were not used, only the datafiles which are in SYS.FILEXT$ would be returned by the cursor and the tablespace definition would not be complete. The outer join is placed on the more restrictive table selection.

The DFILE_CURSOR cursor extracts the physical disk space information for each datafile, including the extension information for datafiles which have **autoextend** turned on. The **order by** clause ensures that the datafiles will be re-created in the same order as they were originally created.

Although the DBA_DATA_FILES view in ORACLE8 contains the **autoextend** information in the view itself, the join to SYS.FILEXT$ makes this script generic for both ORACLE7 and ORACLE8.

```
  cursor DFILE_CURSOR is
        select A.Maxextend,
               A.Inc,
               B.File_Name,
               B.Bytes
          from SYS.FILEXT$ A,
```

```
                    DBA_DATA_FILES B
          where B.File_ID = A.File#(+)
            and Tablespace_Name = 'SYSTEM'
          order by File_ID;
```

The TSPACE_CURSOR cursor extracts the **create tablespace** command generated by the gen_tbs.sql or gen_tbs8.sql script.

```
    cursor TSPACE_CURSOR is
         select Text
           from TSPACE_TEMP
          order by Tspace_Name, Lineno;
```

The TEMP_SPACE_CURSOR cursor extracts the default and temporary tablespace locations for the SYS and SYSTEM userids to alter the user's default and temporary tablespaces, created as SYSTEM by the **create database** command, to the correct one as defined in the database being documented.

```
    cursor TEMP_SPACE_CURSOR is
         select Username,
                Default_Tablespace,
                Temporary_Tablespace
           from DBA_USERS
          where Username in ('SYS','SYSTEM');
```

The final cursor defined, ROLLBACK_SEGS_CURSOR, extracts the information needed to re-create all the rollback segments in the database. The V$ROLLSTAT table is joined to the DBA_ROLLBACK_SEGS view to include the **optimal** information, if it exists. The outer join ensures that all rollback segments will be fetched by the cursor, even if they do not have an **optimal** size set. The SYSTEM rollback segment, created by the **create database** command, has a Segment_ID of 0 and you do not need to re-create it. Because ORACLE requires you to create a rollback segment other than the SYSTEM rollback segment before you can create additional tablespaces, the script manually creates a rollback segment named RB_TEMP and it can be excluded from the cursor.

```
    cursor ROLLBACK_SEGS_CURSOR is
         select A.Segment_Name,
                A.Owner,
                A.Tablespace_Name,
                A.Initial_Extent,
                A.Next_Extent,
                A.Min_Extents,
                A.Max_Extents,
                A.Pct_Increase,
                A.Status,
                B.Optsize
```

```
     from DBA_ROLLBACK_SEGS A,
          V$ROLLSTAT         B
    where A.Segment_Id = B.USN(+)
      and A.Segment_id > 0
      and A.Segment_Name != 'RB_TEMP'
    order by A.Owner, A.Segment_Name;
```

The procedure variables for the cursor, shown in the following listing, are declared as TABLE_NAME.Column_Name%**TYPE**. This "anchoring" of datatypes takes the column definition from within the database itself. If the column definition changes in a different version of ORACLE, the procedure will still work because the definition of the column has not been hard-coded. The *Lv_FileHandle* variable takes its definition from the UTL_FILE package record definition **FILE_TYPE**.

```
Lv_PC_Name                  V$PARAMETER.Name%TYPE;
Lv_PC_Value                 V$PARAMETER.Value%TYPE;
Lv_PC_Description           V$PARAMETER.Description%TYPE;
Lv_LF_Group_Num             V$LOG.Group#%TYPE;
Lv_LF_Bytes                 V$LOG.Bytes%TYPE;
Lv_LF_Members               V$LOG.Members%TYPE;
Lv_LF_Member                V$LOGFILE.Member%TYPE;
Lv_DF_MaxExtend             SYS.FILEXT$.MaxExtend%TYPE;
Lv_DF_Inc                   SYS.FILEXT$.Inc%TYPE;
Lv_DF_File_Name             DBA_DATA_FILES.File_Name%TYPE;
Lv_DF_Bytes                 DBA_DATA_FILES.Bytes%TYPE;
Lv_TS_Text                  TSPACE_TEMP.Text%TYPE;
Lv_TE_Temp_Tspace           DBA_USERS.Temporary_Tablespace%TYPE;
Lv_TE_Deflt_Tspace          DBA_USERS.Default_Tablespace%TYPE;
Lv_TE_Username              DBA_USERS.Username%TYPE;
Lv_RB_Segment_Name          DBA_ROLLBACK_SEGS.Segment_Name%TYPE;
Lv_RB_Owner                 DBA_ROLLBACK_SEGS.Owner%TYPE;
Lv_RB_Tablespace_Name       DBA_ROLLBACK_SEGS.Tablespace_Name%TYPE;
Lv_RB_Initial_Extent        DBA_ROLLBACK_SEGS.Initial_Extent%TYPE;
Lv_RB_Next_Extent           DBA_ROLLBACK_SEGS.Next_Extent%TYPE;
Lv_RB_Min_Extents           DBA_ROLLBACK_SEGS.Min_Extents%TYPE;
Lv_RB_Max_Extents           DBA_ROLLBACK_SEGS.Max_Extents%TYPE;
Lv_RB_Pct_Increase          DBA_ROLLBACK_SEGS.Pct_Increase%TYPE;
Lv_RB_Status                DBA_ROLLBACK_SEGS.Status%TYPE;
Lv_RB_Optsize               V$ROLLSTAT.Optsize%TYPE;

Lv_FileHandle               UTL_FILE.FILE_TYPE;
```

The *Lv_DF_Count* variable tracks the order of the datafile being processed (first, second, etc.). The variable *Lv_Lineno* orders the lines of the **create** statement and is initialized to 0. The *Lv_Block_Size* variable holds the database block size for converting datafile **autoextend** definitions from ORACLE blocks to kilobytes. *Lv_Platform_Slash* contains either a forward or backward slash, depending on which is appropriate for the platform this database is on. *Lv_InitOra_Location* and *Lv_InitOra_Name* are used with the input parameter *ORACLE_sid* to create the init.ora file. The *Lv_No_of_Groups* variable is the number of log groups in the database and controls the loop creating the log groups. **maxlogfiles** and **maxlogmembers** are parameters to the **create database** command but are not stored within the database itself. For the purposes of generating the script, they will be set by selecting the maximum number of log files and members of log file groups into *Lv_MaxLogFiles* and *Lv_MaxLogMembers* respectively. **maxloghistory** is also not stored and for the purposes of the script is set to 160. If you want these variables set to a different value, edit the generated script. *Lv_LogMode* is the ARCHIVELOG mode the database is currently running in and *Lv_CharacterSet* is the character set.

```
Lv_String               VARCHAR2(2000);
Lv_Lineno               NUMBER := 0;
Lv_First_Time           BOOLEAN;
Lv_Size                 NUMBER;
Lv_No_Of_Groups         INTEGER;
Lv_InitOra_Location     VARCHAR2(40);
Lv_InitOra_Name         VARCHAR2(30);
Lv_Database_Name        VARCHAR2(8);
Lv_MaxLogFiles          INTEGER;
Lv_MaxLogMembers        INTEGER;
Lv_LogMode              VARCHAR2(15);
Lv_CharacterSet         VARCHAR2(64);
Lv_Group                INTEGER;
Lv_Members              INTEGER;
Lv_Block_Size           NUMBER;
Lv_DF_Count             NUMBER   := 0;
Lv_Platform_Slash       VARCHAR2(1);
```

The next portion of the script defines an internal procedure, WRITE_OUT, to do the **inserts** into the temporary table.

```
procedure WRITE_OUT(P_Line INTEGER, P_String VARCHAR2) is
begin
   insert into DBASE_TEMP (Lineno, Text)
          values (P_Line,P_String);
end;
```

First, the script will create an init.ora file. Using the location (*init_loc*) and ORACLE SID (*ORACLE_sid*) from the prompts at the beginning of the script as input to the UTL_FILE package, the physical disk file is opened for writing.

```
begin
 Lv_Lineno := 1;

  Lv_InitOra_Location := '&&init_loc';
  Lv_InitOra_Name     := 'init'          ||
                         '&&ORACLE_sid'   ||
                         '.ora';


  Lv_FileHandle :=
         UTL_FILE.FOPEN(Lv_InitOra_Location,Lv_InitOra_Name,'W');
```

Looping through the PARAM_CURSOR cursor, all the init.ora parameters that are not set to the ORACLE-defined defaults are fetched and written to the disk file along with their descriptions as comments. The database name will be needed later on in the script so it is saved in the *Lv_Database_Name* variable to save an additional database access. The PUTF procedure in the UTL_FILE package writes formatted text including special characters and line feeds to a file.

```
open PARAM_CURSOR;
   loop
      fetch PARAM_CURSOR
      into  Lv_PC_Name,
            Lv_PC_Value,
            Lv_PC_Description;
      exit when PARAM_CURSOR%NOTFOUND;

      if (UPPER(Lv_PC_Name) = 'DB_NAME')
      then
          Lv_Database_Name := Lv_PC_Value;
      end if;

      Lv_String := '# ' || Lv_PC_Description;
      UTL_FILE.PUTF(Lv_FileHandle,'%s\n',Lv_String);

      Lv_String := RPAD(Lv_PC_Name,45) || ' = ' || Lv_PC_Value;
      UTL_FILE.PUTF(Lv_FileHandle,'%s\n\n',Lv_String);
   end loop;

   close PARAM_CURSOR;
   UTL_FILE.FCLOSE(Lv_FileHandle);
```

Once all the changed parameters have been written to the file, the cursor and disk file are closed. At this point, the gen_dbse.sql script starts creating the second of the two files, the actual **create database** script. The names of the control files are defined in the init.ora file. By adding **controlfile reuse** to the **create database** command, the files will be reused if they exist. If the word **reuse** were not there, the **create database** command would error out if the files exist.

```
Lv_Lineno := 1;

Lv_String := 'CREATE DATABASE ' || Lv_Database_Name;
WRITE_OUT(Lv_Lineno,Lv_String);

Lv_Lineno := Lv_Lineno + 1;
Lv_String := LPAD(' ',5) || 'CONTROLFILE REUSE';
WRITE_OUT(Lv_Lineno,Lv_String);
```

The next part of the **create database** command is the online redo log file information. The script first determines the number of online redo log groups to create by selecting the highest group number from the current groups in V$LOG; this number controls the loop creating the online redo log file groups.

```
select MAX(Group#)
    into Lv_No_Of_Groups
    from V$LOG;

Lv_Lineno := Lv_Lineno + 1;
WRITE_OUT(Lv_Lineno,LPAD(' ',5) ||'LOGFILE');
Lv_First_Time := TRUE;
```

For each group, the LOGFILE_CURSOR cursor is opened and the member information is fetched and added to the temporary table for each member in the group.

```
for Lv_Index IN  1 .. Lv_No_Of_Groups
loop
   open  LOGFILE_CURSOR (Lv_Index);
   loop
       fetch LOGFILE_CURSOR
       into  Lv_LF_Group_Num,
             Lv_LF_Bytes,
             Lv_LF_Members,
             Lv_LF_Member;
       exit when LOGFILE_CURSOR%NOTFOUND;
```

For consistency, all file sizes are translated into kilobytes. If this is the first member of the first group, the log file name is preceded by a blank; otherwise, it is preceded by a comma.

```
       Lv_Size := Lv_LF_Bytes / 1024;

       if (Lv_First_Time = TRUE)
       then
```

```
    Lv_String     := '       ';
    Lv_First_Time := FALSE;
else
    Lv_String     := '     ,';
end if;
```

If there is only one online redo log file in the group, then the script adds the information about the group number, name, and size of the log file to the string and writes it to the temporary table. Again, the **reuse** parameter is added to ensure the command won't fail if the log files already exist.

```
if (Lv_LF_Members = 1)
then
    Lv_String := Lv_String                ||
                 'GROUP '                  ||
                 LPAD(Lv_LF_Group_Num,3)   ||
                 ' ''                      ||
                 Lv_LF_Member              ||
                 '' ''                     ||
                 ' SIZE '                  ||
                 Lv_Size                   ||
                 'K REUSE';

    Lv_Lineno := Lv_Lineno + 1;
    WRITE_OUT(Lv_Lineno,Lv_String);
else
```

If there are multiple members in the log group, the member information has to be enclosed in parentheses and separated by commas. There are several types of cursor attributes available (see Appendix A). The %ROWCOUNT attribute is similar to the RowNum pseudovariable in SQL in that it returns the number of rows fetched so far. Rather than set and check another Boolean, the script uses this cursor attribute to decide if this is the first member in the group and processes the first member and all other members, appropriately.

```
if  (LOGFILE_CURSOR%ROWCOUNT = 1)
then
    Lv_String := Lv_String                  ||
                 'GROUP '                    ||
                 LPAD(Lv_LF_Group_Num,3)     ||
                 ' (''                       ||
                 Lv_LF_Member                ||
                 '' ' ;
    Lv_Lineno := Lv_Lineno + 1;
    WRITE_OUT(Lv_Lineno,Lv_String);
else
```

```
Lv_String := LPAD(' ',15)   ||
             ',''           ||
             Lv_LF_Member   ||
             '''';
```

Again, using the %ROWCOUNT attribute, the script checks for the last member in the group and closes the **group** clause.

```
if (LOGFILE_CURSOR%ROWCOUNT = Lv_LF_Members)
then
    Lv_String := Lv_String  ||
                 ') SIZE '   ||
                 Lv_Size     ||
                 'K REUSE';
end if;
Lv_Lineno := Lv_Lineno + 1;
WRITE_OUT(Lv_Lineno, Lv_String);
    end if;

  end if;
end loop;
```

Once all members in the group have been processed and added to the temporary table, the LOGFILE_CURSOR cursor is closed and the next group is processed. Once all groups have been processed, the loop ends and the script continues on to the next clause of the **create database** command.

```
    close LOGFILE_CURSOR;
end loop;
```

The script needs the database block size to translate the autoextend size information, in case **autoextend** has been turned on for the datafiles in the SYSTEM tablespace.

```
select Value
  into Lv_Block_Size
  from SYS.V_$PARAMETER
 where UPPER(Name) = 'DB_BLOCK_SIZE';
```

The gen_dbse.sql script loops through the DFILE_CURSOR cursor, selecting all the datafiles that make up the SYSTEM tablespace from DBA_DATA_FILES and SYS.FILEXT$. Each datafile's physical location, space allocations, and autoextend information will be processed and added to the temporary table before the next datafile is fetched. Because the script is processing only the SYSTEM tablespace, the variable *Lv_DF_Count* is initialized to 0 in the declarations section and does not need to be re-initialized within the cursor loop itself.

```
open DFILE_CURSOR;

loop
     fetch DFILE_CURSOR into      Lv_DF_MaxExtend,
                                  Lv_DF_Inc,
                                  Lv_DF_File_Name,
                                  Lv_DF_Bytes;
         exit when DFILE_CURSOR%NOTFOUND;
         Lv_DF_Count := Lv_DF_Count + 1;
```

The script uses the datafile counter to decide how each line of the datafile specifications should be prefixed. All lines other than the first are prefixed with a comma to separate them from the one previous.

```
     if (Lv_DF_Count > 1)
     then
         Lv_String := '          ,''';
     else
         Lv_String := 'DATAFILE ''';
     end if;
```

The datafile name and size specification are added to the string and written to the temporary table. Again, for consistency, the datafile size is converted to kilobytes. **reuse** is specified to ensure that the generated script won't error out if the datafile already exists. The **reuse** clause has no effect if the datafile does not exist.

```
     Lv_String := LPAD(' ',5)         ||
                     Lv_String         ||
                     Lv_DF_File_Name   ||
                     ''' SIZE '        ||
                     (Lv_DF_Bytes)/1024 ||
                     'K REUSE' ;


     WRITE_OUT(Lv_Lineno, Lv_String);
     Lv_Lineno := Lv_Lineno + 1;
```

The script next checks to see if the datafile has **autoextend** turned on, and if it does, adds the **autoextend** clause to the temporary table. The **increment by** value and the maximum file size value are stored in the SYS.FILEXT$ table in database blocks; the script converts them to bytes and then to kilobytes for consistency with all other size declarations.

Once all datafiles in the SYSTEM tablespace are processed, the cursor loop ends and the DFILE_CURSOR cursor is closed.

```
     if (Lv_DF_MaxExtend IS NOT NULL)
     then
         Lv_String := LPAD(' ',12)                    ||
```

```
                                  'AUTOEXTEND ON NEXT '                    ||
                                  (Lv_DF_Inc * Lv_Block_Size) / 1024       ||
                                  'K MAXSIZE '                             ||
                                  (Lv_DF_MaxExtend * Lv_Block_Size) / 1024 ||
                                  'K';

                   WRITE_OUT(Lv_Lineno, Lv_String);
                   Lv_Lineno := Lv_Lineno + 1;
              end if;
         end loop;
         close DFILE_CURSOR;
```

The **maxlogfiles**, **maxlogmembers**, **maxloghistory**, **maxdatafiles**, and **maxinstances** values are defined at database creation and stored only within the control file. In the next section of this chapter, you will see how to extract the control file information. In order to include this information in the script, an artificial value for each of these is generated. **maxlogfiles** specifies the maximum number of online redo log file groups that can ever be created for this database and is set to the highest log group number times the largest number of members in any log group times 4. **maxlogmembers** specifies the largest number of members in any online redo log file group that can be created in this database and is set to the largest number of members in any online redo log group times 2. **maxloghistory** is only useful if you are using ORACLE Parallel Server in parallel mode and specifies the maximum number of archived redo log files for automatic media recovery. **maxloghistory** is included in this script for completeness and is set to an arbitrary value of 160. **maxdatafiles** is the maximum number of datafiles that can ever be created for this database and is arbitrarily set to its maximum value of 255. **maxinstances** is the maximum number of instances that can simultaneously have this database open and mounted; the script uses the ORACLE default value of 1. ORACLE uses these values to help determine the size of the control file(s).

PROGRAMMER'S NOTE   *If any of these values is larger than the value used to create the database originally, the* **create database** *statement will return an error if the control files already exist and you are reusing them. You should either remove the line* **controlfile reuse** *and delete the existing control files or you should extract the correct values from the control file (see the next section) and edit the generated script with the right values.*

```
     select MAX(Group#),
            MAX(Members)
       into Lv_Group,
            Lv_Members
       from SYS.V_$LOG;

     Lv_MaxLogFiles    := Lv_Group    * Lv_Members * 4;
     Lv_MaxLogMembers  := Lv_Members * 2;
```

```
Lv_Lineno := Lv_Lineno + 1;
Lv_String := LPAD(' ',5) || 'MAXLOGFILES ' || Lv_MaxLogFiles;
WRITE_OUT(Lv_Lineno,Lv_String);

Lv_Lineno := Lv_Lineno + 1;
Lv_String := LPAD(' ',5) || 'MAXLOGMEMBERS ' || Lv_MaxLogMembers;
WRITE_OUT(Lv_Lineno,Lv_String);

Lv_Lineno := Lv_Lineno + 1;
WRITE_OUT(Lv_Lineno,LPAD(' ',5) || 'MAXLOGHISTORY 160');

Lv_Lineno := Lv_Lineno +1;
WRITE_OUT(Lv_Lineno,LPAD(' ',5) || 'MAXDATAFILES 255');

Lv_Lineno := Lv_Lineno + 1;
WRITE_OUT(Lv_Lineno,LPAD(' ',5) || 'MAXINSTANCES 1');
```

The final clauses of the **create database** command to be added are the initial ARCHIVELOG mode and character set to be used to store data. The ARCHIVELOG mode can be changed once the database has been created by changing the init.ora parameter *LOG_ARCHIVE_START* or by executing the SQL command **alter database [no]archivelog**. Once the database has been created, you cannot change the character set without re-creating the database.

```
select Log_Mode
  into Lv_LogMode
  from SYS.V_$DATABASE;

Lv_Lineno := Lv_Lineno + 1;
WRITE_OUT(Lv_Lineno,LPAD(' ',5) || Lv_LogMode);

select Value
  into Lv_CharacterSet
  from V$NLS_PARAMETERS
 where UPPER(Parameter) = 'NLS_CHARACTERSET';

Lv_Lineno := Lv_Lineno + 1;
Lv_String :=  LPAD(' ',5)      ||
              'CHARACTER SET ' ||
              Lv_CharacterSet ||
              ';';
WRITE_OUT(Lv_Lineno,Lv_String);
```

Since the generated script is long, the gen_dbse.sql script inserts some comments to make the output more readable.

```
Lv_Lineno := Lv_Lineno + 1;
WRITE_OUT(Lv_Lineno, '   ');
Lv_Lineno := Lv_Lineno + 1;
WRITE_OUT(Lv_Lineno, 'Rem ----------------------------------');
Lv_Lineno := Lv_Lineno + 1;
WRITE_OUT(Lv_Lineno, 'Rem Create a Temporary Rollback Segment');
Lv_Lineno := Lv_Lineno + 1;
WRITE_OUT(Lv_Lineno, 'Rem ----------------------------------');
Lv_Lineno := Lv_Lineno + 1;
WRITE_OUT(Lv_Lineno, '   ');
```

When ORACLE creates the initial database, it creates a SYSTEM rollback segment in the SYSTEM tablespace which is reserved for ORACLE's use only. Before you can create any other tablespaces, you must create a second rollback segment. By default, this rollback segment will be created in SYSTEM. The second rollback segment should be used only for the initial creation of tablespaces and other rollback segments and should be altered offline once that is done. Leaving this rollback segment available for general use can fragment your SYSTEM tablespace.

```
Lv_Lineno := Lv_Lineno + 1;
WRITE_OUT(Lv_Lineno, 'Create Rollback Segment rb_temp;');
Lv_Lineno := Lv_Lineno + 1;
WRITE_OUT(Lv_Lineno, 'Alter  Rollback Segment rb_temp Online;');
Lv_Lineno := Lv_Lineno + 1;
WRITE_OUT(Lv_Lineno, 'commit;');
```

The gen_dbse.sql script includes the running of the catalog.sql and other ORACLE-provided scripts. In order to properly generate the **start** command for these scripts, the direction of the directory separator character (forward slash or backward slash) is calculated by looking at the name of the last datafile processed in the SYSTEM tablespace.

```
if (INSTR(Lv_DF_File_Name,'/',1) > 0)
then
    Lv_Platform_Slash := '/';
else
    Lv_Platform_Slash := '\';
end if;
```

Again, for readability of the generated script, comments are inserted before the **start** command for the catalog.sql script. Catalog.sql is located in the ORACLE_HOME/rdbms/admin directory on UNIX systems and generates the data dictionary views. The **commit** is added to the temporary table to ensure that DML operations performed in the catalog scripts are committed to the database.

```
Lv_Lineno := Lv_Lineno + 1;
WRITE_OUT(Lv_Lineno, '   ');
```

```
Lv_Lineno := Lv_Lineno + 1;
WRITE_OUT(Lv_Lineno, 'Rem ----------------------------------');
Lv_Lineno := Lv_Lineno + 1;
WRITE_OUT(Lv_Lineno, 'Rem Start catalog.sql script');
Lv_Lineno := Lv_Lineno + 1;
WRITE_OUT(Lv_Lineno, 'Rem ----------------------------------');
Lv_Lineno := Lv_Lineno + 1;
WRITE_OUT(Lv_Lineno, '   ');

Lv_String := '@$ORACLE_HOME'    ||
              Lv_Platform_Slash ||
              'rdbms'            ||
              Lv_Platform_Slash ||
              'admin'            ||
              Lv_Platform_Slash ||
              'catalog.sql;';
Lv_Lineno := Lv_Lineno + 1;
WRITE_OUT(Lv_Lineno, Lv_String);
Lv_Lineno := Lv_Lineno + 1;
WRITE_OUT(Lv_Lineno, 'commit;');
```

Again, for readability of the generated script, comments are inserted before the **start** command for the catproc.sql script. Catproc.sql is located in the ORACLE_HOME/rdbms/admin directory on UNIX systems and runs all the SQL scripts for the procedural option. The **commit** is added to the temporary table to ensure that DML operations performed in the catproc scripts are committed to the database.

```
Lv_Lineno := Lv_Lineno + 1;
WRITE_OUT(Lv_Lineno, '   ');
Lv_Lineno := Lv_Lineno + 1;
WRITE_OUT(Lv_Lineno, 'Rem ----------------------------------');
Lv_Lineno := Lv_Lineno + 1;
WRITE_OUT(Lv_Lineno, 'Rem Start catproc.sql script');
Lv_Lineno := Lv_Lineno + 1;
WRITE_OUT(Lv_Lineno, 'Rem ----------------------------------');
Lv_Lineno := Lv_Lineno + 1;
WRITE_OUT(Lv_Lineno, '   ');

Lv_String := '@$ORACLE_HOME'    ||
              Lv_Platform_Slash ||
              'rdbms'            ||
              Lv_Platform_Slash ||
              'admin'            ||
              Lv_Platform_Slash ||
```

```
                      'catproc.sql;';
     Lv_Lineno := Lv_Lineno + 1;
     WRITE_OUT(Lv_Lineno, Lv_String);
     Lv_Lineno := Lv_Lineno + 1;
     WRITE_OUT(Lv_Lineno, 'commit;');
```

At this point, you can re-create all the other tablespaces in the database. The output of the gen_tbs.sql or gen_tbs8.sql script that you ran before running gen_dbse.sql is stored in the TSPACE_TEMP table and is added to the temporary table by looping through the TSPACE_CURSOR cursor. Again, comments are added to document what is happening.

```
     Lv_Lineno := Lv_Lineno + 1;
     WRITE_OUT(Lv_Lineno, '  ');
     Lv_Lineno := Lv_Lineno + 1;
     WRITE_OUT(Lv_Lineno, 'Rem ----------------------------------');
     Lv_Lineno := Lv_Lineno + 1;
     WRITE_OUT(Lv_Lineno, 'Rem Create a User Tablespaces');
     Lv_Lineno := Lv_Lineno + 1;
     WRITE_OUT(Lv_Lineno, 'Rem ----------------------------------');
     Lv_Lineno := Lv_Lineno + 1;
     WRITE_OUT(Lv_Lineno, '  ');

open TSPACE_CURSOR;
loop
    fetch TSPACE_CURSOR
    into  Lv_TS_Text;
    exit when TSPACE_CURSOR%NOTFOUND;

    Lv_Lineno := Lv_Lineno + 1;
    WRITE_OUT(Lv_Lineno,Lv_TS_Text);
end loop;
close TSPACE_CURSOR;
```

When ORACLE creates the default userids SYS and SYSTEM, it sets their default and temporary tablespaces to SYSTEM, since there are no other tablespaces available at that point. In general, just as it is not a good idea to keep rollback segments in the SYSTEM tablespace, it is not good to have any user's default or temporary tablespace be SYSTEM. Now that other tablespaces have been created, we can alter the SYS and SYSTEM users' default and temporary tablespaces to whatever they are set to in the original database we are documenting. Again, comments are added for readability before looping through the TEMP_SPACE_CURSOR cursor and altering the default and temporary tablespaces for SYS and SYSTEM.

```
Lv_Lineno := Lv_Lineno + 1;
WRITE_OUT(Lv_Lineno, '  ');
Lv_Lineno := Lv_Lineno + 1;
WRITE_OUT(Lv_Lineno, 'Rem ----------------------------------');
Lv_Lineno := Lv_Lineno + 1;
WRITE_OUT(Lv_Lineno, 'Rem Alter sys and system ');
Lv_Lineno := Lv_Lineno + 1;
WRITE_OUT(Lv_Lineno, 'Rem ----------------------------------');
Lv_Lineno := Lv_Lineno + 1;
WRITE_OUT(Lv_Lineno, '  ');

open TEMP_SPACE_CURSOR;
loop
   fetch TEMP_SPACE_CURSOR
   into  Lv_TE_Username,
         Lv_TE_Deflt_Tspace,
         Lv_TE_Temp_Tspace;
   exit when TEMP_SPACE_CURSOR%NOTFOUND;

   Lv_String := 'Alter user '           ||
                  Lv_TE_Username         ||
                ' default tablespace '   ||
                  Lv_TE_Deflt_Tspace     ||
                ' temporary tablespace ' ||
                  Lv_TE_Temp_Tspace      ||
                  ';';
   Lv_Lineno := Lv_Lineno + 1;
   WRITE_OUT(Lv_Lineno,Lv_String);
end loop;
close TEMP_SPACE_CURSOR;
Lv_Lineno := Lv_Lineno + 1;
```

Before we can drop the TEMP_RB rollback segment we created in the SYSTEM tablespace so that we could generate the other tablespaces, we must create other rollback segments in one or more different tablespaces. The ROLLBACK_SEGS_CURSOR cursor fetches one row for every rollback segment currently defined in the database, with the exception of the SYSTEM and RB_TEMP rollback segments.

```
WRITE_OUT(Lv_Lineno, '  ');
Lv_Lineno := Lv_Lineno + 1;
WRITE_OUT(Lv_Lineno, 'Rem ----------------------------------');
Lv_Lineno := Lv_Lineno + 1;
WRITE_OUT(Lv_Lineno, 'Rem Create Rollback segments');
```

```
Lv_Lineno := Lv_Lineno + 1;
WRITE_OUT(Lv_Lineno, 'Rem ------------------------------------');
Lv_Lineno := Lv_Lineno + 1;
WRITE_OUT(Lv_Lineno, ' ');

open ROLLBACK_SEGS_CURSOR;
loop
   fetch ROLLBACK_SEGS_CURSOR
   into   Lv_RB_Segment_Name,
          Lv_RB_Owner,
          Lv_RB_Tablespace_Name,
          Lv_RB_Initial_Extent,
          Lv_RB_Next_Extent,
          Lv_RB_Min_Extents,
          Lv_RB_Max_Extents,
          Lv_RB_Pct_Increase,
          Lv_RB_Status,
          Lv_RB_Optsize;
      exit when ROLLBACK_SEGS_CURSOR%NOTFOUND;
```

Rollback segments can be created as either public or private rollback segments. Private rollback segments are only available to an instance that includes that rollback segment name in the ROLLBACK_SEGMENTS init.ora parameter. Public rollback segments are available to any instance that accesses that database and are used for ORACLE Parallel Server, although each instance in the Parallel Server can also have private rollback segments. If you are not running OPS, public and private rollback segments are identical.

```
if (upper(Lv_RB_Owner) = 'PUBLIC')
then
   Lv_String := 'CREATE PUBLIC ROLLBACK SEGMENT ';
else
   Lv_String := 'CREATE ROLLBACK SEGMENT ';
end if;

Lv_String := Lv_String              ||
             Lv_RB_Segment_Name;
Lv_Lineno := Lv_Lineno + 1;
WRITE_OUT(Lv_Lineno,Lv_String);
```

Rollback segments, like tables and indexes, have a tablespace and storage definition. You can create a rollback segment in a tablespace and allow it to use the default storage options of that tablespace. However, unlike other objects, you cannot specify a **pctincrease** value at all and you must specify a **minextents** value greater than 1. ORACLE uses the first extent in a rollback segment as the header block and stores and manages the information about which transactions are active in that rollback segment there. You should define the **initial** and **next** extent sizes to be the same to reduce fragmentation in your rollback tablespace. ORACLE suggests creating rollback segments with 10 to 20 equally sized extents for optimal rollback I/O performance.

Again, for consistency, all rollback segment sizes are converted to kilobytes.

```
Lv_String := '              '                ||
             'TABLESPACE '                   ||
             Lv_RB_Tablespace_Name ;
Lv_Lineno := Lv_Lineno + 1;
WRITE_OUT(Lv_Lineno,Lv_String);


Lv_Lineno + 1;
WRITE_OUT(Lv_Lineno,'            STORAGE (');

Lv_String := '                    '          ||
             'Initial       '                ||
             (Lv_RB_Initial_Extent) / 1024  ||
             ' K' ;
Lv_Lineno := Lv_Lineno + 1;
WRITE_OUT(Lv_Lineno,Lv_String);

Lv_String := '                    '          ||
             'Next          '                ||
             (Lv_RB_Next_Extent) / 1024      ||
             ' K' ;
Lv_Lineno := Lv_Lineno + 1;
WRITE_OUT(Lv_Lineno,Lv_String);

Lv_String := '                   '           ||
             'Minextents     '               ||
             Lv_RB_Min_Extents;
Lv_Lineno := Lv_Lineno + 1;
WRITE_OUT(Lv_Lineno,Lv_String);

Lv_String := '                   '           ||
             'Maxextents     '               ||
             Lv_RB_Max_Extents;
Lv_Lineno := Lv_Lineno + 1;
WRITE_OUT(Lv_Lineno,Lv_String);

if ( Lv_RB_Optsize is NOT NULL)
then
```

```
        Lv_String := '                      '           ||
                      'Optimal        '                  ||
                      (Lv_RB_Optsize);
        Lv_Lineno := Lv_Lineno + 1;
        WRITE_OUT(Lv_Lineno,Lv_String);
      end if;


      Lv_Lineno := Lv_Lineno + 1;
      WRITE_OUT(Lv_Lineno,'              );');
```

By default, rollback segments are created with a status of 'OFFLINE,' and must be altered online to be available to the database. Because we are copying an existing database, the rollback segment will be altered to its state in the original database. The script will continue looping through the ROLLBACK_SEGS_CURSOR cursor until all the rollback segments defined in the database have been processed.

```
      Lv_String := 'Alter Rollback Segment '   ||
                    Lv_RB_Segment_Name          ||
                    ' '                         ||
                    Lv_RB_STATUS                ||
                    ';';
      Lv_Lineno := Lv_Lineno + 1;
      WRITE_OUT(Lv_Lineno,Lv_String);


  end loop;
  close ROLLBACK_SEGS_CURSOR;
```

At this point, everything that is necessary to create a standard database has been completed. You may wish to add a section here to generate the SQL commands to run the ORACLE-provided dbms*XXXX*.sql scripts that you need for your specific application.

The **exception** clause handles errors that may occur during execution of the script. You can use exception conditions to trap for errors and present your own explicit error message or error handling and then exit cleanly from the script. The **when others** exception will capture any other error that has not been explicitly defined. In general, you should always include a **when others** exception. Most of the exceptions defined here will capture errors from ORACLE's UTL_FILE package.

```
exception
    WHEN NO_DATA_FOUND
    THEN
        DBMS_OUTPUT.PUT_LINE ('Reached end of file');


    WHEN UTL_FILE.INTERNAL_ERROR
    THEN
        DBMS_OUTPUT.PUT_LINE ('Internal File Error');
```

```
    WHEN UTL_FILE.INVALID_FILEHANDLE
    THEN
        DBMS_OUTPUT.PUT_LINE ('Invalid File Handle');

    WHEN UTL_FILE.INVALID_MODE
    THEN
        DBMS_OUTPUT.PUT_LINE ('Invalid file mode specified');

    WHEN UTL_FILE.INVALID_OPERATION
    THEN
        DBMS_OUTPUT.PUT_LINE ('Invalid file operation specified');

    WHEN UTL_FILE.INVALID_PATH
    THEN
        DBMS_OUTPUT.PUT_LINE ('Invalid file path specified');

    WHEN UTL_FILE.WRITE_ERROR
    THEN
        DBMS_OUTPUT.PUT_LINE ('A Write error occurred');

    WHEN UTL_FILE.READ_ERROR
    THEN
        DBMS_OUTPUT.PUT_LINE ('A file read error occurred');

    WHEN OTHERS
    THEN
        DBMS_OUTPUT.PUT_LINE ('An unknown exception occurred');
end;
/
```

The **trimspool on** option of the **set** command tells SQL*Plus to remove trailing blanks at the end of each spooled line. The **spool** command and the **select** from the DBASE_TEMP table write the generated script to a file named init.sql. You can use the init.sql file, with the init*ORACLE_sid*.ora file from this script, to create an empty copy of the current database.

```
set trimspool on
spool init.sql
select text
  from DBASE_TEMP
 order by Lineno
/
spool off
```

The init.ora file generated from the gen_dbse.sql script shows only those init.ora parameters which are not the ORACLE-supplied defaults. Some of these values are not listed in the original init.ora, but are derived from other parameters. As an example, the parameter *GC_RELEASABLE_LOCKS* is not set in the original init.ora and, in fact, is not applicable to this database because that parameter is used only for ORACLE Parallel Server. *GC_RELEASABLE_LOCKS* takes its default value from the parameter *DB_BLOCK_BUFFERS*, and because the *DB_BLOCK_BUFFERS* value has been changed, *GC_RELEASABLE_LOCKS* has also been changed. Since this database does not use the ORACLE Parallel Server, setting *GC_RELEASABLE_LOCKS* has no effect in this case. There are several other parameters which will take their default values from other init.ora parameters.

```
# always use this anti-join when possible
always_anti_join = NESTED_LOOPS

# enable system auditing
audit_trail = NONE

# Detached process dump directory
background_dump_dest = /usr/app/ORACLE/admin/TEST/bdump

# maximum size of table or piece to be cached (in blocks)
cache_size_threshold = 4000

# create a separate checkpoint process
checkpoint_process = TRUE

# no. of undo entries to apply per transaction cleanup
cleanup_rollback_entries = 75

# Database will be completely compatible with this software version
compatible = 7.3.4

# control file names list
control_files = /usr/ORADATA55/TEST/control01.ctl,
/usr/ORADATA41/TEST/control02.ctl, /usr/ORADATA53/TEST/control03.ctl

# Core dump directory
core_dump_dest = /usr/app/ORACLE/admin/TEST/cdump

# number of cpu's for this instance
cpu_count = 16
```

```
# Number of database blocks cached in memory
db_block_buffers = 40000

# number of lru latches
db_block_lru_latches = 8

# Size of database block in bytes
db_block_size = 4096

# db block to be read each IO
db_file_multiblock_read_count = 16

# max allowable # db files
db_files = 150

# database name specified in CREATE DATABASE
db_name = TEST

# max. number of concurrent distributed transactions
distributed_transactions = 137

# dml locks - one for each table modified in a transaction
dml_locks = 800

# resources for enqueues
enqueue_resources = 1035

# # freelist groups locks in (DFS)
gc_freelist_groups = 50

# # releasable DB locks (DFS)
gc_releasable_locks = 40000

# enable/disable hash join
hash_join_enabled = FALSE

# include file in init.ora
ifile = /usr/app/ORACLE/admin/TEST/pfile/configTEST.ora

# number of job queue processes to start
job_queue_processes = 10
```

```
# redo circular buffer size
log_buffer = 8192000

# # redo blocks checkpoint threshold
log_checkpoint_interval = 40000

# number of simultaneous copies into redo buffer(# of copy latches
log_simultaneous_copies = 16

# Maximum size (blocks) of dump file
max_dump_file_size = 10240

# max. number of rollback segments in SGA cache
max_rollback_segments = 50

# max # cursors per process
open_cursors = 5000

# optimizer mode
optimizer_mode = CHOOSE

# user processes
processes = 500

# password file usage parameter
remote_login_passwordfile = NONE

# undo segment list
rollback_segments = r01, r02, r03, r04, r05, r06, r08, r09, r10

# number of sequence cache hash buckets
sequence_cache_hash_buckets = 10

# user and system sessions
sessions = 500

# size in bytes of shared pool
shared_pool_size = 200000000

# size of in-memory sort work area retained between fetch calls
sort_area_retained_size = 100000000

# size of in-memory sort work area
sort_area_size = 100000000
```

```
# use direct write
sort_direct_writes = AUTO

# temporary table locks
temporary_table_locks = 500

# max. number of concurrent active transactions
transactions = 550

# number of active transactions per rollback segment
transactions_per_rollback_segment = 34

# allow unlimited extents for rollback segments
unlimited_rollback_segments = TRUE

# User process dump directory
user_dump_dest = /usr/app/ORACLE/admin/TEST/udump

# utl_file accessible directories list
utl_file_dir = /usr/utlfiles
```

The **create database** script shows that there are three log file groups, with one member in each group. Because we used an artificial calcuation to arrive at **maxlogfiles**, **maxlogmembers**, **maxloghistory**, **maxdatafiles**, and **maxinstances**, these numbers should be checked against the actual values in the control file and corrected if necessary.

```
CREATE DATABASE TEST
    CONTROLFILE REUSE
    LOGFILE
    GROUP    1 '/usr/ORADATA55/TEST/redoTEST01.log' SIZE 5120K REUSE
    ,GROUP   2 '/usr/ORADATA41/TEST/redoTEST02.log' SIZE 5120K REUSE
    ,GROUP   3 '/usr/ORADATA53/TEST/redoTEST03.log' SIZE 5120K REUSE
    DATAFILE '/usr/ORADATA54/TEST/system01.dbf' SIZE 512000K REUSE
    MAXLOGFILES 12
    MAXLOGMEMBERS 2
    MAXLOGHISTORY 160
    MAXDATAFILES 255
    MAXINSTANCES 1
    NOARCHIVELOG
    CHARACTER SET US7ASCII;

Rem ------------------------------------
Rem Create a Temporary Rollback Segment
Rem ------------------------------------
```

```
Create Rollback Segment rb_temp;
Alter  Rollback Segment rb_temp Online;
commit;


Rem ---------------------------------
Rem Start catalog.sql script
Rem ---------------------------------

@$ORACLE_HOME/rdbms/admin/catalog.sql;
commit;
Rem ---------------------------------
Rem Start catproc.sql script
Rem ---------------------------------

@$ORACLE_HOME/rdbms/admin/catproc.sql;
commit;
```

Every tablespace in the database with the exception of SYSTEM is now created. The tablespaces named RBS1 and RBS2 are most likely rollback segment tablespaces, based on the names, and the **pctincrease** value in the default storage will be ignored if a rollback segment is created in these databases using the tablespace's default storage. The tablespace named TEMP is created with a Contents value of TEMPORARY and can only hold temporary segments.

```
Rem ---------------------------------
Rem Create Tablespaces
Rem ---------------------------------

CREATE TABLESPACE rbs1
DATAFILE '/usr/ORADATA40/TEST/rbs1_TEST_01.dbf' SIZE 307200K REUSE
DEFAULT STORAGE
(
    INITIAL    800K
    NEXT       800K
    MINEXTENTS 20
    MAXEXTENTS 500
    PCTINCREASE 50
)
ONLINE PERMANENT
/
CREATE TABLESPACE rbs2
DATAFILE '/usr/ORADATA51/TEST/rbs2_TEST_01.dbf' SIZE 307200K REUSE
DEFAULT STORAGE
(
```

```
    INITIAL      800K
    NEXT         800K
    MINEXTENTS 20
    MAXEXTENTS 500
    PCTINCREASE 50
)
ONLINE PERMANENT
/
CREATE TABLESPACE temp
DATAFILE '/usr/ORADATA41/TEST/temp_TEST_01.dbf' SIZE 512000K REUSE
DEFAULT STORAGE
(
    INITIAL      800K
    NEXT         800K
    MINEXTENTS 1
    MAXEXTENTS 500
    PCTINCREASE 0
)
ONLINE TEMPORARY
/
CREATE TABLESPACE tools
DATAFILE '/usr/ORADATA40/TEST/tools_TEST_01.dbf' SIZE 20480K REUSE
DEFAULT STORAGE
(
    INITIAL      40K
    NEXT         40K
    MINEXTENTS 1
    MAXEXTENTS 249
    PCTINCREASE 0
)
ONLINE PERMANENT
/
CREATE TABLESPACE users
DATAFILE '/usr/ORADATA41/TEST/users_TEST_01.dbf' SIZE 102400K REUSE
DEFAULT STORAGE
(
    INITIAL      40K
    NEXT         40K
    MINEXTENTS 1
    MAXEXTENTS 249
    PCTINCREASE 0
)
```

```
ONLINE PERMANENT
/
CREATE TABLESPACE user_data
DATAFILE '/usr/ORADATA29/TEST/user_data_TEST_01.dbf' SIZE 512000K REUSE
        ,'/usr/ORADATA48/TEST/user_data_TEST_02.dbf' SIZE 512000K REUSE
        ,'/usr/ORADATA45/TEST/user_data_TEST_03.dbf' SIZE 512000K REUSE
        ,'/usr/ORADATA29/TEST/user_data_TEST_04.dbf' SIZE 512000K REUSE
        ,'/usr/ORADATA48/TEST/user_data_TEST_05.dbf' SIZE 512000K REUSE
        ,'/usr/ORADATA45/TEST/user_data_TEST_06.dbf' SIZE 512000K REUSE
        ,'/usr/ORADATA29/TEST/user_data_TEST_07.dbf' SIZE 512000K REUSE
        ,'/usr/ORADATA48/TEST/user_data_TEST_08.dbf' SIZE 512000K REUSE
DEFAULT STORAGE
(
   INITIAL    400K
   NEXT       400K
   MINEXTENTS 1
   MAXEXTENTS 5000
   PCTINCREASE 0
)
ONLINE PERMANENT
/
CREATE TABLESPACE user_index
DATAFILE '/usr/ORADATA49/TEST/user_index_TEST_01.dbf' SIZE 512000K REUSE
        ,'/usr/ORADATA43/TEST/user_index_TEST_02.dbf' SIZE 512000K REUSE
        ,'/usr/ORADATA42/TEST/user_index_TEST_03.dbf' SIZE 512000K REUSE
        ,'/usr/ORADATA49/TEST/user_index_TEST_04.dbf' SIZE 512000K REUSE
        ,'/usr/ORADATA43/TEST/user_index_TEST_05.dbf' SIZE 512000K REUSE
        ,'/usr/ORADATA42/TEST/user_index_TEST_06.dbf' SIZE 512000K REUSE


DEFAULT STORAGE
(
   INITIAL    400K
   NEXT       400K
   MINEXTENTS 1
   MAXEXTENTS 5000
   PCTINCREASE 0
)
ONLINE PERMANENT
/
```

When you initially create a database, ORACLE sets the default and temporary tablespaces for the SYS and SYSTEM users to SYSTEM, since there are no other tablespaces at that point in time. In general, you should change the default and temporary tablespaces for SYS and SYSTEM to something other than SYS. In this database, the temporary tablespaces have been changed to TEMP and SYSTEM's default tablespace has been changed to USERS.

```
Rem ----------------------------------
Rem Alter sys and system
Rem ----------------------------------

Alter user SYSTEM default tablespace USERS temporary tablespace TEMP;
Alter user SYS default tablespace SYSTEM temporary tablespace TEMP;
```

The R0 rollback segment is created in the SYSTEM tablespace and is most likely the rollback segment that was created to allow for other tablespaces to be created. This rollback segment is left **offline** and will not be used by the database. The R0 rollback segment can be dropped since there are other rollback segments. Dropping R0 can prevent it from being accidentally altered online and causing problems in the SYSTEM tablespace.

All the other rollback segments have been created with an **optimal** parameter, which will allow ORACLE to shrink them back to this size if they extend past it. The **optimal** setting helps to prevent space problems in the rollback tablespace(s). In addition, the rollback segments have a **maxextents** of 500, which is larger than the maximum number of extents generally allowed in a database with a 4K database block size. The tablespace has not been created with unlimited extents, but the new (as of ORACLE7.3.3) init.ora parameter UNLIMITED_ROLLBACK_SEGMENTS has been set to TRUE, and this allows you to create a rollback segment with a larger maximum extents value.

```
Rem ----------------------------------
Rem Create Rollback segments
Rem ----------------------------------

CREATE ROLLBACK SEGMENT R0
        TABLESPACE SYSTEM
            STORAGE (
                    Initial         16 K
                    Next            16 K
                    Minextents      2
                    Maxextents      20
            );
Alter Rollback Segment R0 OFFLINE;
CREATE ROLLBACK SEGMENT R01
        TABLESPACE RBS1
            STORAGE (
                    Initial         800 K
                    Next            800 K
```

```
                        Minextents    10
                        Maxextents    500
                        Optimal       8192000
            );
Alter Rollback Segment R01 ONLINE;
CREATE ROLLBACK SEGMENT R10
        TABLESPACE RBS2
            STORAGE (
                        Initial       800 K
                        Next          800 K
                        Minextents    10
                        Maxextents    500
                        Optimal       8192000
            );
Alter Rollback Segment R10 ONLINE;
CREATE ROLLBACK SEGMENT R02
        TABLESPACE RBS2
            STORAGE (
                        Initial       800 K
                        Next          800 K
                        Minextents    10
                        Maxextents    500
                        Optimal       8192000
            );
Alter Rollback Segment R02 ONLINE;
CREATE ROLLBACK SEGMENT R03
        TABLESPACE RBS1
            STORAGE (
                        Initial       800 K
                        Next          800 K
                        Minextents    10
                        Maxextents    500
                        Optimal       8192000
            );
Alter Rollback Segment R03 ONLINE;
CREATE ROLLBACK SEGMENT R04
        TABLESPACE RBS2
            STORAGE (
                        Initial       800 K
                        Next          800 K
                        Minextents    10
                        Maxextents    500
                        Optimal       8192000
            );
```

```
Alter Rollback Segment R04 ONLINE;
CREATE ROLLBACK SEGMENT R05
        TABLESPACE RBS1
                STORAGE (
                        Initial         800 K
                        Next            800 K
                        Minextents      10
                        Maxextents      500
                        Optimal         8192000
                );
Alter Rollback Segment R05 ONLINE;
CREATE ROLLBACK SEGMENT R06
        TABLESPACE RBS2
                STORAGE (
                        Initial         800 K
                        Next            800 K
                        Minextents      10
                        Maxextents      500
                        Optimal         8192000
                );
Alter Rollback Segment R06 ONLINE;
CREATE ROLLBACK SEGMENT R07
        TABLESPACE RBS1
                STORAGE (
                        Initial         800 K
                        Next            800 K
                        Minextents      10
                        Maxextents      500
                        Optimal         8192000
                );
Alter Rollback Segment R07 OFFLINE;
CREATE ROLLBACK SEGMENT R08
        TABLESPACE RBS2
                STORAGE (
                        Initial         800 K
                        Next            800 K
                        Minextents      10
                        Maxextents      500
                        PctIncrease     0
                        Optimal         8192000
                );
Alter Rollback Segment R08 ONLINE;
CREATE ROLLBACK SEGMENT R09
        TABLESPACE RBS1
```

```
STORAGE (
        Initial      800 K
        Next         800 K
        Minextents   10
        Maxextents   500
        PctIncrease  0
        Optimal      8192000
);
Alter Rollback Segment R09 ONLINE;
```

Rename/Copy a Database

Have you ever wanted to rename your database or make an exact copy of it, data and all, on another machine? You can use the following command:

alter database backup controlfile to trace [resetlogs/noresetlogs];

to make a readable, editable copy of the commands needed to create a new control file and open the database. You can use this file, along with a copy of the init.ora, log files, and datafiles, to create a new copy of your database or to rename an existing database. You can run this command from either Server Manager or SQL*Plus, by a userid with DBA privileges.

When you run the **alter database backup controlfile to trace** command, it creates a trace file in your udump directory (as defined in your init.ora parameter file). The trace file is created with the standard ORACLE trace filename; on UNIX, this is ora_<sid>_<UNIX process id>.trc. You should rename this file to a more meaningful filename as soon as you create it so that it does not get lost in the other trace files generated by ORACLE.

Once you have generated this trace file, you can edit it and make the changes you need to rename the database or to move it.

If you specify **noresetlogs**, the database commands generated in the trace file are **recover database** and **alter database open**. The log sequence number and redo log files are left in their current state in the control file and you will have to perform database recovery to open the database. If you specify **resetlogs**, the database commands generated are **recover database using backup controlfile** and **alter database open resetlogs** and no recovery is needed. The default is **noresetlogs**. Unless you are certain that the database has been shut down normally and that you have a cold backup of all the redo log files and datafiles, you should not override the default.

A sample trace file, for a UNIX-based database, follows.

```
Dump file /usr/app/ORACLE/admin/TEST/udump/ora_TEST_23730.trc
ORACLE7 Server Release 7.3.4.0.0 - Production
With the distributed and parallel query options
PL/SQL Release 2.3.4.0.0 - Production
ORACLE_HOME = /usr/app/ORACLE/product/7.3.4
```

```
System name:   test
Node name:     test
Release: 4.0
Version: 3.0
Machine: 4850
Instance name: TEST
Redo thread mounted by this instance: 1
ORACLE process number: 143
Unix process pid: 23730, image: ORACLETEST


*** SESSION ID:(219.9617) 1998.07.27.09.49.30.000
*** 1998.07.27.09.49.30.000
# The following commands will create a new control file and use it
# to open the database.
# No data other than log history will be lost. Additional logs may
# be required for media recovery of offline data files. Use this
# only if the current version of all online logs are available.
STARTUP NOMOUNT
CREATE CONTROLFILE REUSE DATABASE "TEST" NORESETLOGS NOARCHIVELOG
    MAXLOGFILES 32
    MAXLOGMEMBERS 2
    MAXDATAFILES 62
    MAXINSTANCES 8
    MAXLOGHISTORY 800
LOGFILE
  GROUP 1 '/usr/ORADATA55/TEST/redoTEST01.log'  SIZE 5M,
  GROUP 2 '/usr/ORADATA41/TEST/redoTEST02.log'  SIZE 5M,
  GROUP 3 '/usr/ORADATA53/TEST/redoTEST03.log'  SIZE 5M
DATAFILE
  '/usr/ORADATA54/TEST/system01.dbf',
  '/usr/ORADATA40/TEST/rbs1_TEST_01.dbf',
  '/usr/ORADATA51/TEST/rbs2_TEST_01.dbf',
  '/usr/ORADATA41/TEST/temp_TEST_01.dbf',
  '/usr/ORADATA41/TEST/users_TEST_01.dbf',
  '/usr/ORADATA29/TEST/user_data_TEST_01.dbf',
  '/usr/ORADATA48/TEST/user_data_TEST_02.dbf',
  '/usr/ORADATA45/TEST/user_data_TEST_03.dbf',
  '/usr/ORADATA29/TEST/user_data_TEST_04.dbf',
  '/usr/ORADATA48/TEST/user_data_TEST_05.dbf',
  '/usr/ORADATA45/TEST/user_data_TEST_06.dbf',
  '/usr/ORADATA29/TEST/user_data_TEST_07.dbf',
  '/usr/ORADATA48/TEST/user_data_TEST_08.dbf',
  '/usr/ORADATA49/TEST/user_index_TEST_01.dbf',
  '/usr/ORADATA43/TEST/user_index_TEST_02.dbf',
```

```
  '/usr/ORADATA42/TEST/user_index_TEST_03.dbf',
  '/usr/ORADATA49/TEST/user_index_TEST_04.dbf',
  '/usr/ORADATA43/TEST/user_index_TEST_05.dbf',
  '/usr/ORADATA42/TEST/user_index_TEST_06.dbf',
  '/usr/ORADATA40/TEST/tools_TEST_01.dbf'
;
# Recovery is required if any of the datafiles are restored backups,
# or if the last shutdown was not normal or immediate.
RECOVER DATABASE
# Database can now be opened normally.
ALTER DATABASE OPEN;
```

The trace file contains the entire **create controlfile** command for the database.

ANNOTATIONS

The steps involved in renaming an existing database are simple:

1. Generate the trace file to create the new control file using the **alter database backup controlfile to trace** command.

2. Edit the trace file and init.ora files to change the database name.

3. Shut down the existing database.

4. Change the environment variables to point to the new instance.

5. If you want to rename or move the datafiles or log files as well, edit their locations in the trace file and move the physical datafiles after you shut down the database. Additionally change any files that include the full specification, such as backup scripts.

6. Run the trace file in Server Manager, connected as internal.

7. Run the **alter database rename global_name** to *<newdb>* command.

8. Rename the init.ora and config.ora files to reflect the new database name.

9. Edit the configuration files that are instance name specific, such as oratab, listener.ora and tnsnames.ora.

You only need to do step 6 above if your database is part of a global network. The global name, also referred to as a service name, is defined as the database name and a domain name, and is used in database links in remote databases to access your database. Changing the global name of the new database does not change it at any remote site that references it and it is up to the remote database administrator to change the references to your database.

To make a copy of an existing database, you need to make a backup of the database in addition to editing the control file. If you have the time to make a cold backup with the database shutdown normally, you can use the **resetlogs** clause. If you have a hot backup of the database, including the archive logs, use the **noresetlogs** clause and do recovery on the new database.

Before you can use the trace file generated by the **alter database backup controlfile to trace** command, you will need to edit the file. The first section contains information about the system and database versions and should either be edited or commented out before running the script.

```
Dump file /usr/app/ORACLE/admin/TEST/udump/ora_TEST_23730.trc
ORACLE7 Server Release 7.3.4.0.0 - Production
With the distributed and parallel query options
PL/SQL Release 2.3.4.0.0 - Production
ORACLE_HOME = /usr/app/ORACLE/product/7.3.4
System name:   test
Node name:     test
Release: 4.0
Version: 3.0
Machine: 4850
Instance name: TEST
Redo thread mounted by this instance: 1
ORACLE process number: 143
Unix process pid: 23730, image: ORACLETEST

*** SESSION ID:(219.9617) 1998.07.27.09.49.30.000
*** 1998.07.27.09.49.30.000
```

The next section mounts the database and creates the new control file. The **create controlfile** command in this example has the **noresetlogs** parameter, so recovery has to be done on the database before it can be re-opened. The **reuse** clause tells ORACLE to reuse the existing control files, overwriting any information in them. If you want to generate new control files, edit the init.ora parameter **control_files** and remove the word **reuse** from this line. If you want to change the database name, add the word **set** before the clause **database "**<*database name*>**"**, replace the original database name with the new one, and change the name of the database in the init.ora file.

The control file is the only place where the **maxlogfiles**, **maxlogmembers**, **maxdatafiles**, **maxinstances**, and **maxloghistory** values are stored for a database,

and it is a good idea, even if you do not want to rename the database, to run the
alter database backup controlfile to trace command to document this information.
If you want to change these values for your database, you can edit the script and
change them at this point.

```
# The following commands will create a new control file and use it
# to open the database.
# No data other than log history will be lost. Additional logs may
# be required for media recovery of offline data files. Use this
# only if the current version of all online logs are available.
STARTUP NOMOUNT
CREATE CONTROLFILE REUSE DATABASE "TEST" NORESETLOGS NOARCHIVELOG
    MAXLOGFILES 32
    MAXLOGMEMBERS 2
    MAXDATAFILES 62
    MAXINSTANCES 8
    MAXLOGHISTORY 800
```

The next section of the trace file lists every online redo log file in your current
database. If you wish to move a log file, you can edit this portion of the script.
Because this version of the trace file is going to perform recovery, you cannot change
the size of the log files.

```
LOGFILE
  GROUP 1 '/usr/ORADATA55/TEST/redoTEST01.log'  SIZE 5M,
  GROUP 2 '/usr/ORADATA41/TEST/redoTEST02.log'  SIZE 5M,
  GROUP 3 '/usr/ORADATA53/TEST/redoTEST03.log'  SIZE 5M
```

The next section lists every datafile in your database, in the order in which they
were added to the database. If you want to move the datafiles, or if you are creating
a new database, you can edit the file and change the locations of the files. Before you
run this script, make sure you copy or move the datafiles to the new locations, with
the new names. You cannot change the size of the datafiles.

```
DATAFILE
  '/usr/ORADATA54/TEST/system01.dbf',
  '/usr/ORADATA40/TEST/rbs1_TEST_01.dbf',
  '/usr/ORADATA51/TEST/rbs2_TEST_01.dbf',
  '/usr/ORADATA41/TEST/temp_TEST_01.dbf',
  '/usr/ORADATA41/TEST/users_TEST_01.dbf',
  '/usr/ORADATA29/TEST/user_data_TEST_01.dbf',
  '/usr/ORADATA48/TEST/user_data_TEST_02.dbf',
  '/usr/ORADATA45/TEST/user_data_TEST_03.dbf',
  '/usr/ORADATA29/TEST/user_data_TEST_04.dbf',
  '/usr/ORADATA48/TEST/user_data_TEST_05.dbf',
  '/usr/ORADATA45/TEST/user_data_TEST_06.dbf',
  '/usr/ORADATA29/TEST/user_data_TEST_07.dbf',
```

```
  '/usr/ORADATA48/TEST/user_data_TEST_08.dbf',
  '/usr/ORADATA49/TEST/user_index_TEST_01.dbf',
  '/usr/ORADATA43/TEST/user_index_TEST_02.dbf',
  '/usr/ORADATA42/TEST/user_index_TEST_03.dbf',
  '/usr/ORADATA49/TEST/user_index_TEST_04.dbf',
  '/usr/ORADATA43/TEST/user_index_TEST_05.dbf',
  '/usr/ORADATA42/TEST/user_index_TEST_06.dbf',
  '/usr/ORADATA40/TEST/tools_TEST_01.dbf'
;
```

The final section of the script does the database recovery and then opens the database. Recovery is necessary because the new control file is created with **noresetlogs**, so the log sequence numbers and redo information are retained.

```
# Recovery is required if any of the datafiles are restored backups,
# or if the last shutdown was not normal or immediate.
RECOVER DATABASE
# Database can now be opened normally.
ALTER DATABASE OPEN;
```

The generated trace file, run against the same database but with the **resetlogs** clause on the **alter database** command, follows.

```
Dump file /usr/app/ORACLE/admin/TEST/udump/ora_TEST_23419.trc
ORACLE7 Server Release 7.3.4.0.0 - Production
With the distributed and parallel query options
PL/SQL Release 2.3.4.0.0 - Production
ORACLE_HOME = /usr/app/ORACLE/product/7.3.4
System name:  test
Node name:    test
Release: 4.0
Version: 3.0
Machine: 4850
Instance name: TEST
Redo thread mounted by this instance: 1
ORACLE process number: 146
Unix process pid: 23419, image: ORACLETEST


*** SESSION ID:(194.12011) 1998.07.27.09.49.01.000
*** 1998.07.27.09.49.01.000
# The following commands will create a new control file and use it
# to open the database.
# The contents of online logs will be lost and all backups will
# be invalidated. Use this only if online logs are damaged.
STARTUP NOMOUNT
CREATE CONTROLFILE REUSE DATABASE "TEST" RESETLOGS NOARCHIVELOG
```

```
    MAXLOGFILES 32
    MAXLOGMEMBERS 2
    MAXDATAFILES 62
    MAXINSTANCES 8
    MAXLOGHISTORY 800
LOGFILE
  GROUP 1 '/usr/ORADATA55/TEST/redoTEST01.log'   SIZE 5M,
  GROUP 2 '/usr/ORADATA41/TEST/redoTEST02.log'   SIZE 5M,
  GROUP 3 '/usr/ORADATA53/TEST/redoTEST03.log'   SIZE 5M
DATAFILE
  '/usr/ORADATA54/TEST/system01.dbf',
  '/usr/ORADATA40/TEST/rbs1_TEST_01.dbf',
  '/usr/ORADATA51/TEST/rbs2_TEST_01.dbf',
  '/usr/ORADATA41/TEST/temp_TEST_01.dbf',
  '/usr/ORADATA41/TEST/users_TEST_01.dbf',
  '/usr/ORADATA29/TEST/user_data_TEST_01.dbf',
  '/usr/ORADATA48/TEST/user_data_TEST_02.dbf',
  '/usr/ORADATA45/TEST/user_data_TEST_03.dbf',
  '/usr/ORADATA29/TEST/user_data_TEST_04.dbf',
  '/usr/ORADATA48/TEST/user_data_TEST_05.dbf',
  '/usr/ORADATA45/TEST/user_data_TEST_06.dbf',
  '/usr/ORADATA29/TEST/user_data_TEST_07.dbf',
  '/usr/ORADATA48/TEST/user_data_TEST_08.dbf',
  '/usr/ORADATA49/TEST/user_index_TEST_01.dbf',
  '/usr/ORADATA43/TEST/user_index_TEST_02.dbf'
  '/usr/ORADATA42/TEST/user_index_TEST_03.dbf',
  '/usr/ORADATA49/TEST/user_index_TEST_04.dbf',
  '/usr/ORADATA43/TEST/user_index_TEST_05.dbf',
  '/usr/ORADATA42/TEST/user_index_TEST_06.dbf',
  '/usr/ORADATA40/TEST/tools_TEST_01.dbf'
  ;
# Recovery is required if any of the datafiles are restored backups,
# or if the last shutdown was not normal or immediate.
RECOVER DATABASE USING BACKUP CONTROLFILE
# Database can now be opened zeroing the online logs.
ALTER DATABASE OPEN RESETLOGS;
```

There are only minor differences between the two trace files. The **create controlfile** command has the **resetlogs** clause rather than the **noresetlogs** clause. You should use this version of the command cautiously, only when you are sure you have a cold backup of the database or have been able to shut down the database normally. Although there is no difference in the generated script for log file definitions, using **resetlogs** lets you change the size of the log files because ORACLE will ignore the existing information if the log files exist and create them if they do not. If you are not moving the log files but are changing the size, you should delete the original log files before running this script.

```
CREATE CONTROLFILE REUSE DATABASE "TEST" RESETLOGS NOARCHIVELOG
```

The other differences are in the **recover** command and in the **alter database open** command. The **recover** command includes the clause **using backup controlfile**. Because the database is being opened with resetlogs, which ORACLE sees as incomplete recovery, the **using backup controlfile** clause is required. ORACLE assumes that a backup of the control file or a re-created control file is being used. The last change is the **alter database open resetlogs** command. The command resets the current log sequence number to 1 and ignores any redo information. The **resetlogs** option will discard all changes to the database that have not been applied, possibly leaving you with inconsistent data in your database. Again, this version of the backup control file should be used with caution.

```
# Recovery is required if any of the datafiles are restored backups,
# or if the last shutdown was not normal or immediate.
RECOVER DATABASE USING BACKUP CONTROLFILE
# Database can now be opened zeroing the online logs.
ALTER DATABASE OPEN RESETLOGS;
```

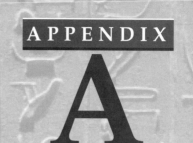

APPENDIX
A

PL/SQL, Dynamic PL/SQL, and Procedures

T he code archives in this book use SQL*Plus and PL/SQL techniques to achieve one of two goals: evaluating diagnostic statistics or generating useful scripts. In this appendix, you will see an overview of PL/SQL, including its implementation within stored procedures, functions, and packages. You will also see how to customize exception handling and how to implement dynamic SQL within your PL/SQL code.

PL/SQL is Oracle's procedural language (PL) superset of structured query language (SQL). You can use PL/SQL to codify your business rules through the creation of stored procedures and packages, to trigger database events to occur, or to add programming logic to the execution of SQL commands. In the first part of this appendix, you will see the basic structures and syntax used in PL/SQL.

PL/SQL Overview

PL/SQL code is grouped into structures called *blocks*. If you create a stored procedure or package, you give the block of PL/SQL code a name; if the block of PL/SQL code is not given a name, then it is called an *anonymous* block. The examples in this appendix will feature anonymous blocks of PL/SQL code; the following sections of this appendix illustrate the creation of named blocks.

A block of PL/SQL code contains three sections, as listed in Table A-1.

Within a PL/SQL block, the first section is the Declarations section. Within the Declarations section, you define the variables and cursors that the block will use. The Declarations section starts with the keyword **declare** and ends when the Executable Commands section starts (as indicated by the keyword **begin**). The Executable Commands section is followed by the Exception Handling section; the **exception** keyword signals the start of the Exception Handling section. The PL/SQL block is terminated by the **end** keyword.

The structure of a typical PL/SQL block is shown in the following listing:

```
declare
   <declarations section>
begin
   <executable commands>
 exception
   <exception handling>
end;
```

In the following sections of this appendix, you will see descriptions of each section of the PL/SQL block.

Section	Description
Declarations	Defines and initializes the variables and cursors used in the block
Executable Commands	Uses flow control commands (such as **if** commands and loops) to execute the commands and assign values to the declared variables
Exception Handling	Provides customized handling of error conditions

TABLE A-1. Sections of an Anonymous PL/SQL Block

Declarations Section

The Declarations section begins a PL/SQL block. The Declarations section starts with the **declare** keyword, followed by a list of variable and cursor definitions. You can define variables to have constant values, and variables can inherit datatypes from existing columns and query results, as shown in the following examples.

In the following examples, the area of a circle is calculated. The result is stored in a table named AREAS. The script for creating the AREAS table is shown in the following listing.

```
create table AREAS
(Radius      NUMBER(5),
 Area        NUMBER(14,2));
```

The AREAS table has two columns: Radius for the radius of the circle, and Area for the corresponding area of the circle. The AREAS table will be populated by executing the example scripts in this appendix. The area of the circle is calculated by squaring the value for the circle's radius and multiplying that value times the constant *pi*. The example in the following listing calculates the area of a circle whose radius has a value of 3. The initial Radius value and the resulting Area value are stored in the AREAS table.

```
declare
  pi      constant NUMBER(9,7) := 3.1415926;
  radius INTEGER(5);
  area    NUMBER(14,2);
begin
  radius := 3;
  area := pi*power(radius,2);
  insert into AREAS values (radius, area);
end;
.
/
```

The '.' signals the end of the PL/SQL block, and the '/' executes the PL/SQL block. When the PL/SQL block is executed, you will receive the following response from ORACLE:

```
PL/SQL procedure successfully completed.
```

To verify that that PL/SQL block completed correctly, you can select from the database the rows that were inserted by the PL/SQL code. The query and results in the following listing show the row the PL/SQL block created in the AREAS table:

```
select *
  from AREAS;


    RADIUS        AREA
---------- ----------
         3       28.27
```

The output shows that a single row was inserted into the AREAS table by the PL/SQL block. Only one row was created because only one radius value was specified.

In the first section of the PL/SQL block, shown in the following listing, three variables are declared. You must declare the variables that will be used in the Executable Commands section of the PL/SQL block.

```
declare
  pi     constant NUMBER(9,7) := 3.1415926;
  radius INTEGER(5);
  area   NUMBER(14,2);
```

The first variable declared is *pi*, which is set to a constant value via the **constant** keyword. The value is assigned via the := operator:

```
  pi     constant NUMBER(9,7) := 3.1415926;
```

The next two variables are defined, but are not given default values:

```
  radius INTEGER(5);
  area   NUMBER(14,2);
```

You can assign an initial value to a variable in the Declarations section. To set an initial value for a variable, simply follow its datatype specification with the value assignment, as shown in the following listing:

```
  radius INTEGER(5)   := 3;
```

In the example, the datatypes included NUMBER and INTEGER. PL/SQL datatypes include all of the valid SQL datatypes as well as complex datatypes based on query structures.

In the following example, a cursor is declared to retrieve a record from the RADIUS_VALS table. The structure for the RADIUS_VALS table is shown in the following listing.

```
create table RADIUS_VALS
(Radius       NUMBER(5));
```

The RADIUS_VALS table has a single column named Radius. The following examples will query the Radius column of the RADIUS_VALS table for input values when calculating the areas of circles. In the following example, a cursor is declared in the Declarations section of the PL/SQL block, and a variable named *rad_val* is declared with a datatype based on the cursor's results.

```
declare
  pi      constant NUMBER(9,7) := 3.1415926;
  area    NUMBER(14,2);
  cursor rad_cursor is
      select * from RADIUS_VALS;
  rad_val rad_cursor%ROWTYPE;
begin
  open rad_cursor;
  fetch rad_cursor into rad_val;
    area := pi*power(rad_val.radius,2);
    insert into AREAS values (rad_val.radius, area);
  close rad_cursor;
end;
.
/
```

For this example, the table RADIUS_VALS contains a single column (named Radius) and a single row (with a Radius value of 3).

In the first part of the Declarations section, the *pi* and *area* variables are defined, as they were in the examples earlier in this appendix. The *radius* variable is not defined; instead, a cursor named "rad_cursor" is defined. The cursor definition consists of a cursor name ("rad_cursor") and a query. A cursor holds the results of a query for processing by other commands within the PL/SQL block:

```
declare
  pi      constant NUMBER(9,7) := 3.1415926;
  area    NUMBER(14,2);
  cursor rad_cursor is
      select * from RADIUS_VALS;
```

A final declaration creates a variable whose structure is inherited from the cursor's result set:

```
  rad_val rad_cursor%ROWTYPE;
```

The *rad_val* variable will be able to reference each column of the query's result set. In this example, the query only returns a single column, but if the table contained multiple columns you would be able to reference all of them via the *rad_val* variable.

In addition to the %ROWTYPE declaration, you can also use the %TYPE declaration to inherit datatype information. If you use the %ROWTYPE declaration, the variable inherits the column and datatype information for all of the columns in the cursor's result set. If you use the %TYPE declaration, then the variable only inherits the definition of the column used to define it. You can even base %TYPE definitions on cursors, as shown in the following example:

```
cursor rad_cursor is
    select * from RADIUS_VALS;
rad_val rad_cursor%ROWTYPE;
rad_val_radius  rad_val.Radius%TYPE;
```

In the preceding listing, the *rad_val* variable inherits the datatypes of the result set of the "rad_cursor" cursor. The *rad_val_radius* variable inherits the datatype of the Radius column within the *rad_val* variable.

The advantage of datatype inheritance using %ROWTYPE and %TYPE definitions is that it makes the datatype definitions in your PL/SQL code independent of the underlying data structures. If the RADIUS_VALS.Radius column is changed from a NUMBER(5) datatype to a NUMBER(4,2) datatype, you do not need to modify your PL/SQL code; the datatype assigned to the associated variables will be determined dynamically at runtime.

Executable Commands Section

In the Executable Commands section, you manipulate the variables and cursors declared in the Declarations section of your PL/SQL block. The Executable Commands section always starts with the keyword **begin**. In the following listing, the first PL/SQL block example from the Declarations section is repeated: the area of a circle is calculated, and the results are inserted into the AREAS table.

```
declare
  pi      constant NUMBER(9,7) := 3.1415926;
  radius INTEGER(5);
  area    NUMBER(14,2);
begin
  radius := 3;
  area := pi*power(radius,2);
  insert into AREAS values (radius, area);
end;
.
/
```

In the preceding listing, the Executable Commands section is

```
begin
  radius := 3;
  area := pi*power(radius,2);
  insert into AREAS values (radius, area);
end;
```

Following the **begin** keyword, the PL/SQL block's work is begun. First, a value is assigned to the *radius* variable, and the *radius* variable and the *pi* constant value are used to determine the value of the *area* variable. The *radius* and *area* values are then inserted into the AREAS table.

The Executable Commands section of the PL/SQL block may contain commands that execute the cursors declared in the Declarations section. In the following example (from the previous section of this appendix), the Executable Commands section features several commands concerning the "rad_cursor" cursor:

```
declare
  pi      constant NUMBER(9,7) := 3.1415926;
  area    NUMBER(14,2);
  cursor rad_cursor is
      select * from RADIUS_VALS;
  rad_val rad_cursor%ROWTYPE;
begin
  open rad_cursor;
  fetch rad_cursor into rad_val;
    area := pi*power(rad_val.radius,2);
    insert into AREAS values (rad_val.radius, area);
  close rad_cursor;
end;
.
/
```

In the first command involving the cursor, the **open** command is used:

```
open rad_cursor;
```

When the "rad_cursor" cursor is **open**ed, the query declared for that cursor is executed and the records to be returned are identified. Next, records are **fetch**ed from the cursor:

```
fetch rad_cursor into rad_val;
```

In the Declarations section, the *rad_val* variable was declared to inherit its datatypes from the "rad_cursor" cursor:

```
cursor rad_cursor is
    select * from RADIUS_VALS;
rad_val rad_cursor%ROWTYPE;
```

When you **fetch** a record from the cursor into the *rad_val* variable, you can still address each column value selected via the cursor's query. When the cursor's data is no longer needed, you can **close** the cursor, as shown in the following listing:

```
close rad_cursor;
```

The Executable Commands section may contain conditional logic such as **if** commands and loops. In the following sections, you will see examples of each of the major types of flow control operations permitted in PL/SQL. You can use the flow control operations to alter the manner in which the executable commands are executed.

Conditional Logic

Within PL/SQL, you can use **if**, **else**, and **elsif** commands to control the flow of commands within the Executable Commands section. The formats of the available conditional logic commands (excluding loops, which are covered in the next section) are shown in the following listing:

```
if    <some condition>
   then   <some command>
elsif  <some condition>
   then   <some command>
else   <some command>
end if;
```

You can nest **if** conditions within each other, as shown in the following listing:

```
if    <some condition>
   then
     if   <some condition>
       then   <some command>
     end if;
else   <some command>
end if;
```

By nesting **if** conditions, you can quickly develop complex logic flows within your Executable Commands section. When nesting **if** conditions, make sure you are not making the flow control more complex than it needs to be; always check to see if logical conditions can be combined into simpler orders.

The area of a circle example used in the previous section will now be modified to include conditional logic. In the following listing, the Executable Commands section of the PL/SQL block has been modified to include **if** and **then** commands.

```
declare
   pi     constant NUMBER(9,7) := 3.1415926;
```

```
area    NUMBER(14,2);
cursor rad_cursor is
    select * from RADIUS_VALS;
rad_val rad_cursor%ROWTYPE;
begin
  open rad_cursor;
  fetch rad_cursor into rad_val;
    area := pi*power(rad_val.radius,2);
    if  area >30
    then
      insert into AREAS values (rad_val.radius, area);
    end if;
  close rad_cursor;
end;
.
/
```

In the preceding listing, an **if** condition is used to control the flow of commands within the Executable Commands section of the PL/SQL block. The flow control commands are shown in the following listing:

```
if  area >30
then
   insert into AREAS values (rad_val.radius, area);
end if;
```

The flow control commands in this example begin after the *area* variable's value has been determined. If the value of *area* is greater than 30, then a record will be inserted into the AREAS table; if the value is less than 30, then no record will be inserted into the AREAS table. You can use this sort of flow control to determine which of several SQL statements are executed, based on the conditions in your **if** conditions. The following listing shows syntax for flow control involving SQL commands:

```
if  area > 30
  then  <some command>
elsif  area < 10
  then  <some command>
else <some command>
end if;
```

Loops

You can use loops to process multiple records within a single PL/SQL block.
PL/SQL supports three types of loops:

Simple loop	A loop that keeps repeating until an **exit** or **exit when** statement is reached within the loop
FOR loop	A loop that repeats a specified number of times
WHILE loop	A loop that repeats until a condition is met

In the following sections, you will see examples of each type of loop. The loop
examples will use as their starting point the PL/SQL blocks used previously in this
appendix. You can use loops to process multiple records from a cursor.

SIMPLE LOOPS

In the following listing, a simple loop is used to generate multiple rows in the
AREAS table. The loop is started by the **loop** keyword, and the **exit when** clause is
used to determine when the loop should be exited. An **end loop** clause signals the
end of the loop.

```
declare
  pi      constant NUMBER(9,7) := 3.1415926;
  radius INTEGER(5);
  area    NUMBER(14,2);
begin
  radius := 3;
  loop
    area := pi*power(radius,2);
      insert into AREAS values (radius, area);
    radius := radius+1;
    exit when area >100;
  end loop;
end;
.
/
```

The loop section of the example establishes the flow control for the commands in
the Executable Commands section of the PL/SQL block. The steps within the loop
are described in the following commented version of the loop commands:

```
loop
    /* Calculate the area, based on the radius value.   */
  area := pi*power(radius,2);
    /* Insert the current values into the AREAS table.   */
```

```
insert into AREAS values (radius, area);
   /* Increment the radius value by 1.                   */
 radius := radius+1;
   /* Evaluate the last calculated area.  If the value */
   /* exceeds 100, then exit.  Otherwise, repeat the   */
   /* loop using the new radius value.                 */
 exit when area >100;
   /* Signal the end of the loop.                        */
end loop;
```

The loop should generate multiple entries in the AREAS table. The first record will be the record generated by a *radius* value of 3. Once an *area* value exceeds 100, no more records will be inserted into the AREAS table.

Sample output following the execution of the PL/SQL block is shown in the following listing:

```
select *
  from AREAS
 order by Radius;


    RADIUS        AREA
---------- ----------
         3      28.27
         4      50.27
         5      78.54
         6      113.1
```

Since the Area value for a Radius value of 6 exceeds 100, the **exit** command executes, no further Radius values are processed, and the PL/SQL block completes.

SIMPLE CURSOR LOOPS

You can use the attributes of a cursor—such as whether or not there are any rows remaining to be fetched—as the exit criteria for a loop. In the following example, a cursor is executed until no more rows are returned by the query. To determine the status of the cursor, the cursor's attributes are checked. Cursors have four attributes you can use in your program:

%FOUND	A record can be fetched from the cursor.
%NOTFOUND	No more records can be fetched from the cursor.
%ISOPEN	The cursor has been opened.
%ROWCOUNT	The number of rows fetched from the cursor so far.

The %FOUND, %NOTFOUND, and %ISOPEN cursor attributes are Booleans; they are either set to TRUE or FALSE. Because they are Boolean attributes, you can evaluate their settings without explicitly matching them to values of TRUE or FALSE. For example, the following command will cause an exit to occur when rad_cursor%NOTFOUND is TRUE:

```
exit when rad_cursor%NOTFOUND;
```

In the following listing, a simple loop is used to process multiple rows from a cursor:

```
declare
  pi      constant NUMBER(9,7) := 3.1415926;
  area    NUMBER(14,2);
  cursor rad_cursor is
      select * from RADIUS_VALS;
  rad_val rad_cursor%ROWTYPE;
begin
  open rad_cursor;
  loop
    fetch rad_cursor into rad_val;
    exit when rad_cursor%NOTFOUND;
      area := pi*power(rad_val.radius,2);
      insert into AREAS values (rad_val.radius, area);
  end loop;
  close rad_cursor;
end;
.
/
```

The loop section of the PL/SQL block performs the same processing as the simple loop shown in the previous section, with one exception. Instead of basing the exit criteria on the *area* value, the cursor's %NOTFOUND attribute is checked. If no more rows are found in the cursor, then %NOTFOUND will be TRUE—and thus, the loop will be exited. The commented version of the loop is shown in the following listing:

```
loop
    /*  Within the loop, fetch a record.         */
    fetch rad_cursor into rad_val;
    /*  If the fetch attempt reveals no more      */
    /*  records in the cursor, then exit the loop. */
    exit when rad_cursor%NOTFOUND;
    /*  If the fetch attempt returned a record,    */
    /*  then process the radius value and insert   */
    /*  a record into the AREAS table.             */
```

```
      area := pi*power(rad_val.radius,2);
      insert into AREAS values (rad_val.radius, area);
      /*  Signal the end of the loop.                    */
   end loop;
```

When the preceding PL/SQL block is executed, every record in the RADIUS_VALS table will be processed by the loop. In previous examples, the RADIUS_VALS table only contained one record—a Radius value of 3. Prior to executing the PL/SQL block for this section, add two new Radius values to the RADIUS_VALS table: 4 and 10.

The following listing shows the addition of the new records to the RADIUS_VALS table:

```
insert into RADIUS_VALS values (4);
insert into RADIUS_VALS values (10);
commit;

select *
  from RADIUS_VALS
 order by Radius;


    RADIUS
----------
         3
         4
        10
```

Once the new records have been added to the RADIUS_VALS table, execute the PL/SQL block shown earlier in this section. The output of the PL/SQL block is shown in the following listing:

```
select *
  from AREAS
 order by Radius;

    RADIUS        AREA
---------- ----------
         3       28.27
         4       50.27
        10      314.16
```

The query of the AREAS table shows that every record in the RADIUS_VALS table was fetched from the cursor and processed. Once there were no more records to process in the cursor, the exit condition was met, the loop was exited, and the PL/SQL block completed.

FOR LOOPS

In simple loops, the loop executes until an **exit** condition is met. In a FOR loop, the loop executes a specified number of times. An example of a FOR loop is shown in the following listing. The FOR loop's start is indicated by the keyword **for**, followed by the criteria used to determine when the processing should exit the loop. Since the number of times the loop is executed is set when the loop is begun, there is no need for an **exit** command within the loop.

In the following example, the areas of circles are calculated based on *radius* values ranging from 1 through 7, inclusive:

```
declare
   pi       constant NUMBER(9,7) := 3.1415926;
   radius INTEGER(5);
   area     NUMBER(14,2);
begin
   for radius in 1..7 loop
     area := pi*power(radius,2);
        insert into AREAS values (radius, area);
     end loop;
end;
.
/
```

The steps involved in processing the loop are shown in the following commented listing:

```
    /*  Specify the criteria for the number of loop    */
    /*  executions.                                     */
  for radius in 1..7 loop
    /*  Calculate the area using the current Radius     */
    /*  value.                                          */
    area := pi*power(radius,2);
    /*  Insert the area and radius values into the AREAS */
    /*  table.                                          */
      insert into AREAS values (radius, area);
    /*  Signal the end of the loop.                     */
  end loop;
```

Note that there is no line that says

```
radius := radius+1;
```

in the FOR loop. Since the specification of the loop specifies

```
for radius in 1..7 loop
```

the *radius* values are already specified. For each value, all of the commands within the loop are executed (these commands can include other conditional logic, such as **if** conditions). Once the loop has completed processing a Radius value, the limits on the **for** clause are checked, and either the next Radius value is used or the loop execution is complete.

Sample output from the FOR loop execution is shown in the following listing:

```
select *
  from AREAS
 order by Radius;


    RADIUS        AREA
---------- ----------
         1        3.14
         2       12.57
         3       28.27
         4       50.27
         5       78.54
         6       113.1
         7      153.94

7 rows selected.
```

In this example, the values of the *radius* variable ranged from 1 to 7, in ascending order. Loops can be executed in descending order as well. If the **for** clause read

```
for radius in 7..1 loop
```

then the *radius* value would start at 7 and descend to 1.

CURSOR FOR LOOPS

In FOR loops, the loop executes a specified number of times. In a cursor FOR loop, the results of a query are used to dynamically determine the number of times the loop is executed. In a cursor FOR loop, the opening, fetching, and closing of cursors is performed implicitly; you do not need to explicitly command these actions.

The following listing shows a cursor FOR loop that queries the RADIUS_VALS table and inserts records into the AREAS table.

```
declare
   pi      constant NUMBER(9,7) := 3.1415926;
   area    NUMBER(14,2);
   cursor rad_cursor is
       select * from RADIUS_VALS;
   rad_val rad_cursor%ROWTYPE;
begin
   for rad_val in rad_cursor
     loop
        area := pi*power(rad_val.radius,2);
        insert into AREAS values (rad_val.radius, area);
```

```
      end loop;
end;
.
/
```

In a cursor FOR loop, there is no **open** or **fetch** command. The

```
for rad_val in rad_cursor
```

command implicitly opens the "rad_cursor" cursor and fetches a value into the *rad_val* variable. When there are no more records in the cursor, the loop is exited and the cursor is closed. In a cursor FOR loop, there is no need for a **close** command.

The loop portion of the PL/SQL block is shown in the following listing, with comments to indicate the flow of control. The loop is controlled by the existence of a fetchable record in the "rad_cursor" cursor. There is no need to check the cursor's %NOTFOUND attribute—that is automated via the cursor FOR loop.

```
    /*  If a record can be fetched from the cursor,     */
    /*  then fetch it into the rad_val variable.  If     */
    /*  no rows can be fetched, then skip the loop.      */
  for rad_val in rad_cursor
    /*  Begin the loop commands.                         */
    loop
        /*  Calculate the area based on the radius value */
        /*  and insert a record into the AREAS table.    */
      area := pi*power(rad_val.radius,2);
      insert into AREAS values (rad_val.radius, area);
    /*  Signal the end of the loop commands.             */
    end loop;
```

Sample output is shown in the following listing. For this example, the RADIUS_VALS table has three records, with Radius values of 3, 4, and 10:

```
select *
  from RADIUS_VALS
 order by Radius;


    RADIUS
----------
         3
         4
        10
```

The execution of the PL/SQL block with the cursor FOR loop will generate the following records in the AREAS table:

```
select *
  from AREAS
 order by Radius;
```

```
   RADIUS        AREA
---------- ----------
        3       28.27
        4       50.27
       10      314.16
```

WHILE LOOPS

In a WHILE loop, the loop is processed until an exit condition is met. Instead of specifying the exit condition via an **exit** command within the loop, the exit condition is specified in the **while** command that initiates the loop.

In the following listing, a WHILE loop is created so that multiple *radius* values will be processed. If the current value of the *radius* variable meets the **while** condition in the loop's specification, then the loop's commands are processed. Once a *radius* value fails the **while** condition in the loop's specification, the loop's execution is terminated.

```
declare
  pi       constant NUMBER(9,7) := 3.1415926;
  radius INTEGER(5);
  area     NUMBER(14,2);
begin
  radius := 3;
  while radius <= 7
    loop
      area := pi*power(radius,2);
      insert into AREAS values (radius, area);
    radius := radius+1;
  end loop;
end;
.
/
```

The WHILE loop is similar in structure to the Simple loop, since it terminates the loop based on a variable's value. The following listing shows the steps involved in the loop, with embedded comments:

```
    /*  Set an initial value for the Radius variable.   */
  radius := 3;
    /*  Establish the criteria for the termination of   */
    /*  the loop.  If the condition is met, execute the  */
    /*  commands within the loop.  If the condition is   */
    /*  not met, then terminate the loop.                */
  while radius <= 7
```

```
    /*  Begin the commands to be executed.            */
  loop
      /*  Calculate the area based on the current      */
      /*  Radius value and insert a record in the      */
      /*  AREAS table.                                 */
   area := pi*power(radius,2);
   insert into AREAS values (radius, area);
      /*  Set a new value for the Radius variable.  The  */
      /*  new value of Radius will be evaluated against  */
      /*  the termination criteria and the loop commands */
      /*  will be executed for the new Radius value or   */
      /*  the loop will terminate.                     */
   radius := radius+1;
      /*  Signal the end of the commands within the loop. */
  end loop;
```

When executed, the PL/SQL block in the previous listing will generate records in the AREAS table. The output of the PL/SQL block is shown in the following listing:

```
select *
  from AREAS
 order by Radius;


    RADIUS        AREA
---------- ----------
         3       28.27
         4       50.27
         5       78.54
         6      113.1
         7      153.94
```

Because of the value assigned to the *radius* variable prior to the loop, the loop is forced to execute at least once. You should verify that your variable assignments meet the conditions used to limit the loop executions.

goto Statements

A **goto** statement forces the flow of the commands to be immediately diverted to another set of commands. In order to use **goto**, you must first create labels for sets of commands. A **goto** command cannot transfer control to a block nested within the current block or inside a FOR loop or within an **if** condition.

A label is created by enclosing the label name in angle brackets, as shown in the following listing.

```
<<area_of_circle>>
  radius := 3;
```

```
while radius <= 7
  loop
    area := pi*power(radius,2);
    insert into AREAS values (radius, area);
  radius := radius+1;
end loop;
```

In the preceding listing, the <<area_of_circle>> label names the set of commands that follow it. If another command within the Executable Commands section read

```
goto area_of_circle;
```

then the commands within the <<area_of_circle>> label would begin to be executed.

When possible, you should try to use loops or **if** conditions instead of **goto** commands. Loops and **if** conditions, by their nature, document the logical rules applied to the flow of control among the commands. A **goto** command, on the other hand, requires no documentation of the reason for branching to another set of commands. Since **goto** commands are not self-documenting, you may find it easier to maintain PL/SQL code written with **if** conditions and loops.

Exception Handling Section

When user-defined or system-related exceptions (errors) are encountered, the control of the PL/SQL block shifts to the Exception Handling section. Within the Exception Handling section, the **when** clause is used to evaluate which exception is to be "raised"—that is, executed.

If an exception is raised within the Executable Commands section of your PL/SQL block, the flow of commands immediately leaves the Executable Commands section and searches the Exception Handling section for an exception matching the error encountered. PL/SQL provides a set of system-defined exceptions and allows you to add your own exceptions. Examples of user-defined exceptions are shown in the "Procedures" section later in this appendix.

The Exception Handling section always begins with the keyword **exception**, and it precedes the **end** command that terminates the Executable Commands section of the PL/SQL block. The placement of the Exception Handling section within the PL/SQL block is shown in the following listing:

```
declare
  <declarations section>
begin
  <executable commands>
 exception
  <exception handling>
end;
```

The Exception Handling section of a PL/SQL block is optional—none of the PL/SQL blocks shown previously in this appendix included an Exception Handling section. However, the examples shown in this appendix have been based on a very small set of known input values with very limited processing performed.

In the following listing, the simple loop for calculating the area of a circle is shown, with two modifications (shown without boldfacing). A new variable named *some_variable* is declared in the Declarations section, and a calculation to determine the variable's value is created in the Executable Commands section.

```
declare
  pi      constant NUMBER(9,7) := 3.1415926;
  radius INTEGER(5);
  area    NUMBER(14,2);
  some_variable    NUMBER(14,2);
begin
  radius := 3;
  loop
    some_variable := 1/(radius-4);
    area := pi*power(radius,2);
      insert into AREAS values (radius, area);
    radius := radius+1;
    exit when area >100;
  end loop;
end;
.
/
```

Because the calculation for *some_variable* involves division, you may encounter a situation in which the calculation attempts to divide by zero—an error condition. The first time through the loop, the *radius* variable (with an initial value of 3) is processed and a record is inserted into the AREAS table. The second time through the loop, the *radius* variable has a value of 4—and the calculation for *some_variable* encounters an error:

```
declare
*
ERROR at line 1:
ORA-01476: divisor is equal to zero
ORA-06512: at line 9
```

Since an error was encountered, the first row inserted into AREAS is rolled back, and the PL/SQL block terminates.

You can modify the processing of the error condition by adding an Exception Handling section to the PL/SQL block, as shown in the following listing:

```
declare
  pi      constant NUMBER(9,7) := 3.1415926;
  radius INTEGER(5);
  area    NUMBER(14,2);
  some_variable    NUMBER(14,2);
begin
  radius := 3;
  loop
    some_variable := 1/(radius-4);
    area := pi*power(radius,2);
      insert into AREAS values (radius, area);
    radius := radius+1;
    exit when area >100;
  end loop;
exception
  when ZERO_DIVIDE
   then insert into AREAS values (0,0);
end;
.
/
```

The Exception Handling section of the PL/SQL block is repeated in the following listing:

```
exception
  when ZERO_DIVIDE
   then insert into AREAS values (0,0);
```

When the PL/SQL block encounters an error, it scans the Exception Handling section for the defined exceptions. In this case, it finds the ZERO_DIVIDE exception, which is one of the system-defined exceptions available in PL/SQL. In addition to the system-defined exceptions and user-defined exceptions, you can use the **when others** clause to address all exceptions not defined within your Exception Handling section. The command within the Exception Handling section for the matching exception is executed and a row is inserted into the AREAS table. The output of the PL/SQL block is shown in the following listing:

```
select *
from AREAS;

    RADIUS        AREA
---------- ----------
         3       28.27
         0           0
```

The output shows that the first *radius* value (3) was processed, and the exception was encountered on the second pass through the loop.

PROGRAMMER'S NOTE *Once an exception is encountered, you cannot return to your normal flow of command processing within the Executable Commands section. You cannot use a **goto** command to go from the Exception Handling section to the Executable Commands section of your PL/SQL block. If you need to maintain control within the Executable Commands section, you should use **if** conditions to test for possible exceptions before they are encountered by the program.*

The available system-defined exceptions are listed in Table A-2. Examples of user-defined exceptions are shown in the "Procedures" section later in this appendix.

Exception	Condition
ACCESS_INTO_NULL	Attempting assignment of values to the attributes of an uninitialized object.
COLLECTION_IS_NULL	Attempting use of collection methods other than **exists** to an uninitialized (atomically null) nested table or varying array, or trying to assign values to the elements of an uninitialized nested table or varying array.
CURSOR_ALREADY_OPEN	Attempting opening of an already open cursor. You must close a cursor before you can reopen it. A cursor **for** loop automatically opens the cursor to which it refers.
DUP_VAL_ON_INDEX	Attempting to store duplicate values in a database column that is constrained by a unique index.
INVALID_CURSOR	Attempting an illegal cursor operation such as closing an unopened cursor.
INVALID_NUMBER	Failing a conversion of character string to a number because the character string does not represent a valid number. In procedural statements, VALUE_ERROR is raised.
LOGIN_DENIED	Attempting to login to ORACLE with an invalid username and/or password.
NO_DATA_FOUND	Executing a **select into** statement returns no rows, or referencing a deleted element in a nested table, or referencing an uninitialized element in an index-by table. The **fetch** statement is expected to return no rows eventually, so when that happens, no exception is raised. SQL group functions such as **AVG** and **SUM** always return a value or a null. A **select into** statement that calls a group function will never raise NO_DATA_FOUND.
NOT_LOGGED_ON	Attempting to issue a database call without being connected to ORACLE.

TABLE A-2. System-Defined Exception Conditions

Exception	Condition
PROGRAM_ERROR	An internal PL/SQL problem.
ROWTYPE_MISMATCH	Using a host cursor variable and PL/SQL cursor variable in an assignment with incompatible return types. When you pass an open host cursor variable to a stored subprogram, the return types of the actual and formal parameters must be compatible.
STORAGE_ERROR	Occurs when PL/SQL runs out of memory or memory is corrupted.
SUBSCRIPT_BEYOND_COUNT	Attempting to reference a nested table or varying array element using an index number larger than the number of elements in the collection.
SUBSCRIPT_OUTSIDE_LIMIT	Attempting to reference a nested table or varying array element using an index number that is outside the legal range.
TIMEOUT_ON_RESOURCE	Occurs when a timeout occurs while ORACLE is waiting for a resource.
TOO_MANY_ROWS	Occurs when a **select into** statement returns more than one row.
VALUE_ERROR	Occurs when an arithmetic, conversion, truncation, or size-constraint error occurs. For example, when you select a column value into a character variable, if the value is longer than the declared length of the variable, PL/SQL aborts the assignment and raises VALUE_ERROR. In procedural statements, VALUE_ERROR is raised if the conversion of a character string to a number fails. In SQL statements, INVALID_NUMBER is raised.
ZERO_DIVIDE	Attempting to divide a number by zero.

TABLE A-2.   System-Defined Exception Conditions (*continued*)

Procedures, Functions, and Packages

Sophisticated business rules and application logic can be stored as *procedures* within ORACLE. Stored procedures—groups of SQL and PL/SQL statements—allow you to move code that enforces business rules from your application to your database. As a result, the code will be stored once for use by multiple applications. Because ORACLE supports stored procedures, the code within your applications should become more consistent and easier to maintain.

For example, consider the following PL/SQL code shown in the first section of this appendix:

```
declare
   pi       constant NUMBER(9,7) := 3.1415926;
```

```
  radius INTEGER(5);
  area    NUMBER(14,2);
begin
  radius := 3;
  area := pi*power(radius,2);
  insert into AREAS values (radius, area);
end;
.
/
```

The code shown in the preceding listing inserts a single record into the AREAS table, based on a calculation of the area of a circle. You can create a *function* that performs the calculation. You can call that function directly from SQL—the same way you call functions like **UPPER** and **SUBSTR**. The code shown in the following listing creates the F_CALCULATE_CIRCLE_AREA function.

```
create function F_CALCULATE_CIRCLE_AREA (Radius IN number)
  RETURN NUMBER
  IS
  pi      constant NUMBER(9,7) := 3.1415926;
  area    NUMBER(14,2);
begin
  area := pi*power(radius,2);
  RETURN(area);
end;
/
```

The F_CALCULATE_CIRCLE_AREA function has a single input variable: the *radius* of the circle. The Declarations section of the function defines the other variables, and the Executable Commands section calculates the *area* value and returns it to the user. You can call the F_CALCULATE_CIRCLE_AREA function in your SQL commands, as shown in the following examples:

```
select F_CALCULATE_CIRCLE_AREA(3) from DUAL;


F_CALCULATE_CIRCLE_AREA(3)
--------------------------
                     28.27


select F_CALCULATE_CIRCLE_AREA(12) from DUAL;


F_CALCULATE_CIRCLE_AREA(12)
---------------------------
                    452.39
```

The preceding examples execute the F_CALCULATE_CIRCLE_AREA function while selecting a record from DUAL (a single-row, single-column table). You may group functions, procedures, and other PL/SQL commands into *packages.* In the following sections, you will see implementation details and recommendations for packages, procedures, and functions.

You may experience performance gains when using procedures, for two reasons. First, the processing of complex business rules may be performed within the database—and therefore by the server. In client-server or three-tier applications, shifting complex processing from the application (on the client) to the database (on the server) may dramatically improve your performance. Second, since the procedural code is stored within the database and is fairly static, you may also benefit from the reuse of the same queries within the database. The Shared SQL Area in the System Global Area will store the parsed versions of the executed commands in memory. Thus, the second time a procedure is executed, it may be able to take advantage of the parsing that was previously performed, improving the performance of the procedure's execution.

In addition to these advantages, your application development efforts may also benefit. Business rules that have been consolidated within the database no longer need to be written into each application, saving time during application creation and simplifying the maintenance process.

Required System Privileges

In order to create a procedural object, you must have the CREATE PROCEDURE system privilege (which is part of the RESOURCE role). If the procedural object will be in another user's schema, then you must have CREATE ANY PROCEDURE system privilege.

In order to create a procedural object that accesses a table, you must have been granted explicit access to the object. You cannot create a procedural object using privileges acquired via roles. Therefore, if you are creating procedural objects based on tables and views not residing within your schema, the table owner must explicitly **grant** you the proper access to those tables.

Executing Procedures

Once you have created a procedure or function, you can execute it. When a procedural object is executed, it relies on the table privileges of its owner, *not* those of the user who is executing it. A user executing a procedure does not need to have been granted access to the tables that the procedure accesses.

To allow other users to execute your procedural object, **grant** them EXECUTE privilege on that object, as shown in the following example:

```
grant execute on MY_PROCEDURE to George;
```

The user George will now be able to execute the procedure named MY_PROCEDURE—even if he does not have privileges on any of the tables that MY_PROCEDURE uses. If you do not **grant** EXECUTE privilege to users, then they must have the EXECUTE ANY PROCEDURE system privilege in order to execute the procedure.

When executed, procedures usually have variables passed to them. For example, a procedure that interacts with the RADIUS_VALS table may accept a value for the Radius column as its input. In the following example, the procedure creates a new record in the AREAS table for each *radius* value specified. This procedure can be called from any application within the database (provided the user calling the procedure has been granted EXECUTE privilege for it).

The syntax used to execute a procedure depends on the environment from which the procedure is being called. From within SQL*Plus, a procedure can be executed by using the **execute** command, followed by the procedure name. Any arguments to be passed to the procedure must be enclosed in parentheses following the procedure name, as shown in the following example (which uses a procedure called P_CALCULATE_CIRCLE_AREA):

```
execute P_CALCULATE_CIRCLE_AREA(5);
```

The command shown in the preceding example will execute the P_CALCULATE_CIRCLE_AREA procedure, passing to it the value 5.

From within another procedure, function, package, or trigger, a procedure can be called without the **execute** command. If the P_CALCULATE_CIRCLE_AREA procedure is called from a trigger on the MATH table, then the body of that trigger may include the command

```
P_CALCULATE_CIRCLE_AREA(:new.Radius);
```

In this example, the P_CALCULATE_CIRCLE_AREA procedure will be executed using the new value of the Radius column as its input.

To execute a procedure owned by another user, you must either create a synonym for that procedure or reference the owner's name during the execution, as shown in the following listing.

```
execute Dora.P_CALCULATE_CIRCLE_AREA(5);
```

The command shown in the preceding example will execute the P_CALCULATE_CIRCLE_AREA procedure owned by Dora. Alternatively, a synonym for the procedure could be created using the command

```
create synonym P_CALCULATE_CIRCLE_AREA
    for Dora.P_CALCULATE_CIRCLE_AREA;
```

The owner of that synonym would then no longer need to refer to the procedure's owner in order to execute the procedure. You could simply enter the command

```
execute P_CALCULATE_CIRCLE_AREA(5);
```

and the synonym would point to the proper procedure.

When executing remote procedures, the name of a database link must be specified. The name of the database link must be specified after the procedure's name but before the variables, as shown in the following example:

```
execute P_CALCULATE_CIRCLE_AREA@REMOTE_CONNECT(5);
```

The command shown in the preceding example uses the REMOTE_CONNECT database link to access a procedure called P_CALCULATE_CIRCLE_AREA in a remote database. To make the location of the procedure transparent to the user, a synonym may be created for the remote procedure, as shown in the following example:

```
create synonym P_CALCULATE_CIRCLE_AREA
   for P_CALCULATE_CIRCLE_AREA@REMOTE_CONNECT;
```

Once this synonym has been created, the user may refer to the remote procedure by using the name of the synonym. ORACLE assumes that all remote procedure calls involve updates in the remote database; therefore, you must have installed the distributed option in order to call remote procedures.

Required Table Privileges

Procedural objects may reference tables. In order for the objects to execute properly, the owner of the procedure, package, or function being executed must have privileges on the tables the procedure, package, or function uses. The user who is executing the procedural object does not need privileges on its underlying tables; such a user only needs to have EXECUTE privilege on the procedural object.

PROGRAMMER'S NOTE *The privileges needed for procedures, packages, and functions cannot come from roles; they must be granted directly to the owner of the procedure, package, or function.*

Procedures vs. Functions

Unlike procedures, functions can return a value to the caller (as shown in the F_CALCULATE_CIRCLE_AREA example earlier in this appendix). Values are returned from functions through the use of the **return** keyword within the function. If you use procedures, then you must either store the generated values in tables or display them by executing the DBMS_OUTPUT package's procedures.

Procedures vs. Packages

Packages are groups of procedures, functions, variables, and SQL statements grouped together into a single unit. To execute a procedure within a package, you must first list the package name, then the procedure name, as shown in the following example:

```
execute RADIUS_PACKAGE.P_CALCULATE_CIRCLE_AREA(3);
```

In the preceding example, the P_CALCULATE_CIRCLE_AREA procedure within the RADIUS_PACKAGE package is executed with an input value of 3.

Packages allow multiple procedures to use the same variables and cursors. Procedures within packages may be available to the public (as the P_CALCULATE_CIRCLE_AREA procedure is in the prior example) or they may be private, in which case they are only accessible via commands from within the package (such as calls from other procedures). Examples of packages will be shown in the "create package Syntax" section later in this appendix.

Procedures may also include commands that are to be executed each time the package is called, regardless of the procedure or function called within the package. Thus, they not only group procedures but also give you the ability to execute commands that are not procedure-specific. See the "Initializing Packages" section later in this appendix for an example of code that is executed each time a package is called.

create procedure Syntax

The syntax for the **create procedure** command is

```
create [or replace] procedure [user.] procedure
[(argument [IN|OUT|IN OUT] datatype
[,argument [IN|OUT|IN OUT] datatype]...)]
{IS|AS} {block | external program};
```

Both the header and the body of the procedure are created by this command. The P_CALCULATE_CIRCLE_AREA procedure is created by the command shown in the following listing:

```
create procedure P_CALCULATE_CIRCLE_AREA (Radius in NUMBER)
AS
  pi      constant NUMBER(9,7) := 3.1415926;
  area    NUMBER(14,2);
begin
  area := pi*power(radius,2);
  insert into AREAS values (radius, area);
end;
/
```

The P_CALCULATE_CIRCLE_AREA procedure shown in this example will accept a *radius* value as its input. The procedure can be called from any application. The procedure inserts a record into the AREAS table. The following listing shows an example of the execution of the P_CALCULATE_CIRCLE_AREA procedure.

```
execute P_CALCULATE_CIRCLE_AREA(5);

PL/SQL procedure successfully completed.
```

You can verify the execution of the procedure by querying the AREAS table, as shown in the following listing.

```
select *
  from AREAS;

    RADIUS       AREA
---------- ----------
         5      78.54
```

If a procedure already exists, you may replace it via the **create or replace procedure** command. The benefit of using this command (instead of dropping and recreating the old procedure) is that any **execute** grants previously made on the procedure will remain in place.

The IN qualifier is used for arguments for which values must be specified when calling the procedure. In the P_CALCULATE_CIRCLE_AREA example, the Radius argument would be declared as IN.

The OUT qualifier signifies that the procedure passes a value back to the caller through this argument.

The IN OUT qualifier signifies that the argument is both an IN and an OUT: a value must be specified for this argument when the procedure is called, and the procedure will return a value to the caller via this argument.

If no qualifier type is specified, then the default value is IN.

As of ORACLE8, you can call external procedures via the **create procedure** command. An external procedure is part of a program stored outside of the ORACLE database (such as a C program). The syntax for the **external program** clause (replacing the PL/SQL block in a typical procedure) is:

```
external library [user.]library_name
  [name external_proc_name]
  [language language_name]
  [calling standard [c | pascal]
  parameters (external_parameter_list) [with context]
```

The library must have been previously created via the **create library** command. The **create library** command simply assigns a library name to a shared library in the operating system. For example, the following listing shows the creation of a library named MY_LIB, pointing to a library named "/ora/progs.so."

```
create library MY_LIB as '/ora/progs.so';
```

Once the library has been created, you can use its programs as part of the **create procedure** command. You must have EXECUTE privilege on the library.

create function Syntax

The syntax for the **create function** command is very similar to the syntax for the **create procedure** command. It is

```
create [or replace] function [user.] function
[(argument [IN|OUT|IN OUT] datatype
[,argument [IN|OUT|IN OUT] datatype]...)]
RETURN datatype
{IS|AS} {block | external body};
```

Both the header and the body of the function are created by this command.

The **return** keyword specifies the datatype of the function's return value. This can be any valid PL/SQL datatype. Every function must have a **return** clause, since the function must, by definition, return a value to the calling environment.

The following example shows a function that calculates the volume of a sphere, given the sphere's radius. The volume of a sphere is the radius cubed, multiplied by *pi*, multiplied by 4/3.

```
create function F_CALCULATE_SPHERE_VOLUME (Radius IN number)
   RETURN NUMBER
   IS
   pi      constant NUMBER(9,7) := 3.1415926;
   volume   NUMBER(14,2);
begin
   volume := (4/3)*pi*power(radius,3);
   RETURN(volume);
end;
/
```

In the following listing, the F_CALCULATE_SPHERE_VOLUME function is executed along with the F_CALCULATE_CIRCLE_AREA function during a SQL command execution.

```
select F_CALCULATE_SPHERE_VOLUME(3),
       F_CALCULATE_CIRCLE_AREA(3)
   from DUAL;
```

```
F_CALCULATE_SPHERE_VOLUME(3) F_CALCULATE_CIRCLE_AREA(3)
---------------------------- ----------------------------
                      113.1                        28.27
```

If a function already exists, you may replace it via the **create or replace function** command. If you use the **or replace** clause, then any EXECUTE grants previously made on the function will remain in place.

If the function is to be created in a different account (also known as a *schema*), then you must have the CREATE ANY PROCEDURE system privilege. If no schema is specified, then the function will be created in your schema. In order to create a function in your schema, you must have been granted the CREATE PROCEDURE system privilege (which is part of the RESOURCE role). Having the privilege to create procedures gives you the privilege to create functions and packages as well.

Referencing Remote Tables in Procedures

You can access remote tables in the SQL statements within your procedures and functions. You can access a remote table via a database link in the procedure, as shown in the following example. In this example, the P_CALCULATE_CIRCLE_AREA procedure inserts a record into the AREAS table in the database defined by the REMOTE_CONNECT database link, which is not bold in the following listing:

```
create or replace procedure P_CALCULATE_CIRCLE_AREA (Radius in NUMBER)
AS
  pi      constant NUMBER(9,7) := 3.1415926;
  area    NUMBER(14,2);
begin
  area := pi*power(radius,2);
  insert into AREAS@REMOTE_CONNECT values (radius, area);
end;
/
```

Data manipulation in remote databases—such as the **insert** shown in the preceding example—will usually require that the distributed option be installed in your database.

Procedures may also make use of local synonyms. For example, you may create a local synonym for a remote table, as shown in the following listing:

```
create synonym AREAS for AREAS@REMOTE_CONNECT;
```

You can then rewrite your procedure to remove the database link specifications:

```
create or replace procedure P_CALCULATE_CIRCLE_AREA (Radius in NUMBER)
AS
  pi      constant NUMBER(9,7) := 3.1415926;
```

```
   area    NUMBER(14,2);
begin
   area := pi*power(radius,2);
   insert into AREAS values (radius, area);
end;
/
```

Removing database link names from procedures allows you to remove the details of the table's physical location from the procedure. If the table changes location, only the synonym will change while the procedure will still be valid.

Debugging Procedures

You can use the SQL*Plus **show errors** command to display all of the errors associated with the most recently created procedural object. The **show errors** command checks the USER_ERRORS data dictionary view for the errors associated with the most recent compilation attempt for that procedural object. **show errors** will display the line and column number for each error, as well as the text of the error message.

To view errors associated with previously created procedural objects, you may query USER_ERRORS directly, as shown in the following listing. Queries against USER_ERRORS are not common, since such a query would imply that you have errors with two or more procedures. The following example queries USER_ERRORS for error messages encountered during the creation of the F_CALCULATE_CIRCLE_AREA function shown earlier in this appendix.

```
select Line,     /*Line number of the error./*
       Position, /*Column number of the error.*/
       Text      /*Text of the error message.*/
  from USER_ERRORS
 where Name = 'F_CALCULATE_CIRCLE_AREA'
 order by Sequence;
```

USING THE DBMS_OUTPUT PACKAGE

In addition to the debugging information provided by the **show errors** command, you may also use the DBMS_OUTPUT package. DBMS_OUTPUT is created when the procedural option is installed in the database.

To use DBMS_OUTPUT, you must issue the

```
set serveroutput on
```

command before executing the procedural object you will be debugging.

DBMS_OUTPUT allows you to use three debugging functions within your package:

PUT	Puts multiple outputs on the same line
PUT_LINE	Puts each output on a separate line
NEW_LINE	Used with PUT; signals the end of the current output line

PUT and PUT_LINE are used to generate the debugging information you wish to display. For example, if you are debugging a procedure that includes a loop, then you may wish to track the changes in a variable with each pass through the loop. To track the variable's value, you may use a command similar to the one shown in the following listing. In this example, the value of the *area* variable is printed, prefixed by the literal string 'Area: '.

```
PUT_LINE('Area: '||area);
```

You may also use PUT and PUT_LINE outside of loops, but such uses may be better accomplished via the use of the **return** command in functions (see the "create function Syntax" section earlier in this appendix).

Creating Your Own Functions

You may use the custom functions you create within your SQL expressions (rather than just calling them via **execute** commands). This allows you to extend the available functionality of SQL, customizing it to your needs. Your functions can be used in the same manner as such ORACLE-provided functions as **SUBSTR** and **TO_CHAR**. The only restriction on their application is that your custom functions cannot be used in CHECK or DEFAULT constraints.

The functions you can call either must be stand-alone functions (created via the **create function** command shown in the previous sections) or must be declared in package specifications (to be covered in the "create package Syntax" section later in this appendix). Procedures are not directly callable from SQL, but may be called by the functions you create.

For example, the query in the following listing executes both the F_CALCULATE_SPHERE_VOLUME and the F_CALCULATE_CIRCLE_AREA functions.

```
select F_CALCULATE_SPHERE_VOLUME(3),
       F_CALCULATE_CIRCLE_AREA(3)
  from DUAL;
```

In order to be used within a query, your functions must follow the same guidelines as ORACLE's functions. Most notably, they must not update the database, and they must contain only IN parameters.

Customizing Error Conditions

You may establish custom error conditions within procedural objects. For each of the error conditions you define, you may select an error message that will appear when the error occurs. You can set the error numbers and messages that are displayed to the user via the RAISE_APPLICATION_ERROR procedure, which may be called from within any procedural object.

You can call RAISE_APPLICATION_ERROR from within procedures, packages, and functions. RAISE_APPLICATION_ERROR requires two inputs: the message number and the message text. You get to assign both the message number and the text that will be displayed to the user. This is a very powerful addition to the standard exceptions that are available in PL/SQL (see Table A-2 earlier in the chapter).

The following example shows the F_CALCULATE_CIRCLE_AREA function shown earlier in this appendix. In this version, however, it has an additional section (shown without boldfacing). Titled EXCEPTION, the additional section tells ORACLE how to handle nonstandard processing. In this example, the VALUE_ERROR exception's standard message is overridden via the RAISE_APPLICATION_ERROR procedure:

```
create function F_CALCULATE_CIRCLE_AREA (Radius IN number)
  RETURN NUMBER
  IS
  pi      constant NUMBER(9,7) := 3.1415926;
  area    NUMBER(14,2);
begin
  area := pi*power(radius,2);
  RETURN(area);
EXCEPTION
    when VALUE_ERROR then
        RAISE_APPLICATION_ERROR (-20100,
          'Error occurred during area calculation.');
end;
/
```

In the preceding example, the VALUE_ERROR exception was used. If you wish to define custom exceptions, you need to name the exception in a Declarations section of the procedure. As shown in the following listing, the Declarations section should include entries for each of the custom exceptions you have defined, listed as type "EXCEPTION."

```
some_custom_error EXCEPTION;
```

PROGRAMMER'S NOTE   *If you are using the exceptions already defined within PL/SQL, then you do not need to list them in the Declarations section of the procedural object. See Table A-2 earlier in the chapter for a list of the predefined exceptions.*

In the **exception** portion of the procedural object's code, you tell the database how to handle the exceptions. It begins with the keyword **exception**, followed by a **when** clause for each of the exceptions. Each exception may call the RAISE_APPLICATION_ERROR procedure.

The RAISE_APPLICATION_ERROR procedure takes two input parameters: the error number of your choosing (which must be between -20001 and -20999) and the error message to be displayed. In the example shown above, only one exception was defined. Multiple exceptions can be defined, as shown in the following listing; you may use the **when others** clause to handle all nonspecified exceptions.

```
EXCEPTION
    when VALUE_ERROR then
        RAISE_APPLICATION_ERROR (-20100,
            'Error occurred during area calculation.');
    when SOME_CUSTOM_ERROR then
        RAISE_APPLICATION_ERROR (-20101,
            'Some custom error message.');
```

The use of the RAISE_APPLICATION_ERROR procedure gives you great flexibility in managing the error conditions that may be encountered within your procedural objects.

create package Syntax

When creating packages, the package specification and the package body are created separately. Thus there are two commands to use: **create package** for the package specification, and **create package body** for the package body. Both of these commands require that you have the CREATE PROCEDURE system privilege. If the package is to be created in a schema other than your own, then you must have the CREATE ANY PROCEDURE system privilege.

The syntax for creating package specifications is

```
create [or replace] package [user.] package
{IS | AS}
PL/SQL package specification;
```

A *package specification* consists of the list of functions, procedures, variables, constants, cursors, and exceptions that will be available to users of the package.

A sample **create package** command is shown in the following listing. In this example, the RADIUS_PACKAGE package is created. The package contains three separate functions:

F_CALCULATE_CIRCLE_AREA	Given a radius value, calculates the area of a circle (*pi*radius*radius*).
F_CALCULATE_SPHERE_VOLUME	Given a radius value, calculates the volume of a sphere (*pi*radius*radius*radius*4/3*).
F_CALCULATE_SPHERE_AREA	Given a radius value, calculates the surface area of a sphere (4**pi*radius*radius*).

```
create or replace package RADIUS_PACKAGE
AS
   function F_CALCULATE_CIRCLE_AREA(Radius IN NUMBER) RETURN NUMBER;
     PRAGMA RESTRICT_REFERENCES(F_CALCULATE_CIRCLE_AREA, WNDS);
   function F_CALCULATE_SPHERE_VOLUME(Radius IN NUMBER) RETURN NUMBER;
     PRAGMA RESTRICT_REFERENCES(F_CALCULATE_SPHERE_VOLUME, WNDS);
   function F_CALCULATE_SPHERE_AREA(Radius IN NUMBER) RETURN NUMBER;
     PRAGMA RESTRICT_REFERENCES(F_CALCULATE_SPHERE_AREA, WNDS);
end RADIUS_PACKAGE;
```

PROGRAMMER'S NOTE *You may append the name of the procedural object to the **end** clause, as shown in the preceding example. This addition may make it easier to coordinate the logic within your code.*

Each of the functions listed in the package specification has a PRAGMA RESTRICT_REFERENCES command associated with it. The PRAGMA RESTRICT_REFERENCES command tells ORACLE what types of operations the functions perform—in this example, the WNDS (Write No Database State) flag is specified. When you define a function using this flag, you guarantee that the function will not update database tables. You must use the WNDS flag for all functions within packages that you will use as part of your queries. Other available restrictions include RNDS (Read No Database State), WNPS (Write No Package State—no values of packaged variables are changed), and RNPS (Read No Package State—no values of packaged variables are referenced). The WNDS flag is the most commonly used PRAGMA RESTRICT_REFERENCES flag.

A *package body* contains the PL/SQL blocks and specifications for all of the public objects listed in the package specification. The package body may include objects that are not listed in the package specification; such objects are said to be *private* and are not available to users of the package. Private objects may only be called by other objects within the same package body. A package body may also include code that is run every time the package is invoked, regardless of the part of the package that is executed—see the next section "Initializing Packages" for an example.

The syntax for creating package bodies is

```
create [or replace] package body [user.] package body
{IS | AS}
PL/SQL package body;
```

The name of the package body should be the same as the name of the package specification. Continuing the RADIUS_PACKAGE example, its package body can be created via the **create package body** command shown in the following example:

```
create package body RADIUS_PACKAGE
AS
function F_CALCULATE_CIRCLE_AREA(Radius IN NUMBER)
  RETURN NUMBER
```

```
  IS
  pi      constant NUMBER(9,7) := 3.1415926;
  area    NUMBER(14,2);
 begin
  area := pi*power(radius,2);
  RETURN(area);
end F_CALCULATE_CIRCLE_AREA;
function F_CALCULATE_SPHERE_VOLUME(Radius IN NUMBER)
 RETURN NUMBER
  IS
  pi      constant NUMBER(9,7) := 3.1415926;
  volume   NUMBER(14,2);
 begin
  volume := (4/3)*pi*power(radius,3);
  RETURN(volume);
end F_CALCULATE_SPHERE_VOLUME;
function F_CALCULATE_SPHERE_AREA(Radius IN NUMBER)
RETURN NUMBER
  IS
  pi      constant NUMBER(9,7) := 3.1415926;
  area    NUMBER(14,2);
 begin
  area := 4*pi*power(radius,2);
  RETURN(area);
end F_CALCULATE_SPHERE_AREA;
end RADIUS_PACKAGE;
/
```

The **create package body** command shown in the preceding example combines the **create function** commands for three separate functions into a single package. The **end** clauses all have the names of their associated objects appended to them (shown without boldfacing in the prior listing). Modifying the **end** clauses in this manner helps to clarify the ending points of the object code.

Additional functions, procedures, exceptions, variables, cursors, and constants may be defined within the package body, but they will not be available to the public unless they have been declared within the package specification (via the **create package** command). If a user has been granted EXECUTE privilege on a package, then that user can access any of the public objects that are declared in the package specification.

Initializing Packages

Package specifications may include code that is to be run the first time a user executes the package. In the following example, the RADIUS_PACKAGE package body is modified to include a SQL statement that records the current user's username and the timestamp for the start of the package execution. Two new variables must also be declared in the package body in order to record these values.

Since the two new variables are declared within the package body, they are not available to the public. Within the package body, they are separated from the procedures and functions. The package initialization code is shown without boldfacing in the following listing:

```
create or replace package body RADIUS_PACKAGE
AS
User_Name VARCHAR2 (32);
Entry_Date DATE;
function F_CALCULATE_CIRCLE_AREA(Radius IN NUMBER)
 RETURN NUMBER
  IS
  pi      constant NUMBER(9,7) := 3.1415926;
  area    NUMBER(14,2);
 begin
  area := pi*power(radius,2);
  RETURN(area);
end F_CALCULATE_CIRCLE_AREA;
function F_CALCULATE_SPHERE_VOLUME(Radius IN NUMBER)
 RETURN NUMBER
  IS
  pi      constant NUMBER(9,7) := 3.1415926;
  volume    NUMBER(14,2);
 begin
  volume := (4/3)*pi*power(radius,3);
  RETURN(volume);
end F_CALCULATE_SPHERE_VOLUME;
function F_CALCULATE_SPHERE_AREA(Radius IN NUMBER)
RETURN NUMBER
  IS
  pi      constant NUMBER(9,7) := 3.1415926;
  area    NUMBER(14,2);
 begin
  area := 4*pi*power(radius,2);
  RETURN(area);
end F_CALCULATE_SPHERE_AREA;
BEGIN
   select User, SysDate
```

```
      into User_Name, Entry_Date
      from DUAL;
end RADIUS_PACKAGE;
/
```

PROGRAMMER'S NOTE *The code that is to be run every time the package is executed is stored in its own PL/SQL block at the bottom of the package body. It does not have its own **end** clause; it uses the package body's **end** clause.*

Every time the RADIUS_PACKAGE package is executed, the *User_Name* and *Entry_ Date* variables will be populated by the query shown in the previous listing. The functions and procedures within the package can access both of the new variables.

To **execute** a procedure or function that is within a package, specify both the package name and the name of the procedure or function in the **execute** command, as shown in the following listing:

```
select RADIUS_PACKAGE.F_CALCULATE_SPHERE_AREA(5)
  from DUAL;


RADIUS_PACKAGE.F_CALCULATE_SPHERE_AREA(5)
-----------------------------------------
                                   314.16
```

To this point, all of the examples of function execution within SQL statements specified a value for the *radius* input variable. Instead of specifying values for the variables, you can use column values instead. For example, the RADIUS_VALS table shown earlier in this appendix has a column named Radius. The following query selects the Radius values from the RADIUS_VALS table and performs a function on them. For this example, the RADIUS_VALS table contains three records, with Radius values of 3, 4, and 10.

```
select RADIUS_PACKAGE.F_CALCULATE_SPHERE_VOLUME(Radius)
 from RADIUS_VALS;
```

The output generated is shown in the following listing.

```
RADIUS_PACKAGE.F_CALCULATE_SPHERE_VOLUME(RADIUS)
------------------------------------------------
                                           113.1
                                          268.08
                                         4188.79
```

As shown by this example, you can use your custom functions anywhere you use the functions provided by ORACLE. If you place your functions within packages, then you must use the PRAGMA RESTRICT_REFERENCES flags as shown in the sample code that creates the RADIUS_PACKAGE package specification.

Viewing Source Code for Existing Procedural Objects

You can query the source code for existing procedures, functions, packages, and package bodies from the following data dictionary views:

USER_SOURCE	For procedural objects owned by the user
ALL_SOURCE	For procedural objects owned by the user or to which the user has been granted access
DBA_SOURCE	For all procedural objects in the database

Select information from the USER_SOURCE view via a query similar to the one shown in the following listing. In this example, the Text column is selected, ordered by the Line number. The Name of the object and the object Type are used to define which object's source code is to be displayed. The following example uses the F_CALCULATE_CIRCLE_AREA procedure shown earlier in this appendix:

```
select Text
  from USER_SOURCE
 where Name = 'F_CALCULATE_CIRCLE_AREA'
   and Type = 'FUNCTION'
 order by Line;


TEXT
----------------------------------------------------
function F_CALCULATE_CIRCLE_AREA (Radius IN number)
  RETURN NUMBER
  IS
  pi      constant NUMBER(9,7) := 3.1415926;
  area    NUMBER(14,2);
begin
  area := pi*power(radius,2);
  RETURN(area);
end;


9 rows selected.
```

As shown in the preceding example, the USER_SOURCE view contains one record for each line of the F_CALCULATE_CIRCLE_AREA procedure. The sequence of the lines is maintained by the Line column values; therefore, the Line column should be used in the **order by** clause, as shown.

Compiling Procedures, Functions, and Packages

ORACLE compiles procedural objects when they are created. However, procedures, functions, and packages may become invalid if the database objects they reference change. The next time the procedural objects are executed, they will be recompiled by the database.

You can avoid this runtime compiling—and the performance degradation it may cause—by explicitly recompiling the procedures, functions, and packages. To recompile a procedure, use the **alter procedure** command, as shown in the following listing. The **compile** clause is the only valid option for this command.

```
alter procedure P_CALCULATE_CIRCLE_AREA compile;
```

In order to use this command, you must either own the procedure or have ALTER ANY PROCEDURE system privilege.

To recompile a function, use the **alter function** command, with the **compile** clause:

```
alter function F_CALCULATE_SPHERE_VOLUME compile;
```

In order to use this command, you must either own the function or have ALTER ANY PROCEDURE system privilege.

When recompiling packages, you may either recompile both the package specification and body or just the package body. By default, both the package specification and the package body will be recompiled. You cannot use the **alter function** or **alter procedure** command to recompile functions and procedures stored within a package.

If the source code for the procedures or functions within the package body has changed but the package specification has not, then you may wish to recompile only the package body. In most cases, it is appropriate to recompile both the specification and the package body.

The syntax for the **alter package** command is

```
alter package [user.] package_name
compile [PACKAGE | BODY];
```

To recompile a package, use the **alter package** command shown above, with the **compile** clause, as shown in the following example:

```
alter package RADIUS_PACKAGE compile;
```

In order to use this command, you must either own the package or have ALTER ANY PROCEDURE system privilege. Since neither PACKAGE nor BODY was specified in the preceding example, the default of PACKAGE was used, resulting in the recompilation of both the package specification and the package body.

Replacing Procedures, Functions, and Packages

Procedures, functions, and packages may be replaced via their respective **create or replace** commands. Using the **or replace** clause keeps in place any existing grants that have been made for those objects. If you choose to drop and recreate procedural objects, then you will have to grant any EXECUTE privileges that had previously been granted.

Dropping Procedures, Functions, and Packages

To drop a procedure, use the **drop procedure** command, as shown in the following listing. In order to drop a procedure, you must either own the procedure or have DROP ANY PROCEDURE system privilege.

```
drop procedure P_CALCULATE_CIRCLE_AREA;
```

To drop a function, use the **drop function** command. In order to drop a function, you must either own the function or have DROP ANY PROCEDURE system privilege.

```
drop function F_CALCULATE_SPHERE_VOLUME;
```

To drop a package, use the **drop package** command, as shown in the following listing. In order to drop a package, you must either own the package or have DROP ANY PROCEDURE system privilege.

```
drop package RADIUS_PACKAGE;
```

To drop a package body, use the **drop package** command with the **body** clause, as shown in the following listing. In order to drop a package body, you must either own the package or have DROP ANY PROCEDURE system privilege.

```
drop package body RADIUS_PACKAGE;
```

Using Dynamic SQL

You can use *dynamic SQL* to create general-purpose procedures and to execute DDL commands within PL/SQL. You can use dynamic SQL to execute SQL commands that are built at runtime rather than at program creation time. You can use dynamic SQL within your stored procedural objects (such as packages) and in anonymous PL/SQL blocks.

Dynamic SQL requires the use of the DBMS_SQL package. In the following sections of this appendix, you will see examples of dynamic SQL, followed by a description of the procedures within the DBMS_SQL package.

The script in the following example creates a procedure called ANYSTRING. The ANYSTRING procedure has a single input variable: a SQL command. When you execute the ANYSTRING procedure, you pass it the SQL command to execute; the SQL command may be either DML commands (such as **select** or **insert**) or DDL commands (such as **create table**).

```
create or replace procedure ANYSTRING(String IN VARCHAR2) AS
    Cursor_Name INTEGER;
    Ret INTEGER;
BEGIN
    Cursor_Name := DBMS_SQL.OPEN_CURSOR;
    DBMS_SQL.PARSE(Cursor_Name, String, dbms_sql.Native);
    Ret := DBMS_SQL.EXECUTE(Cursor_Name);
    DBMS_SQL.CLOSE_CURSOR(Cursor_Name);
END;
/
```

You can execute the ANYSTRING procedure via the **execute** command, as shown in the following examples of DDL and DML commands.

```
execute ANYSTRING('create table CD (Artist VARCHAR2(25),
                   Title VARCHAR2(25)) ');

execute ANYSTRING('insert into CD values(''NEIL FINN'',
                   ''TRY WHISTLING THIS'') ');
```

The first command in the preceding listing executes the following SQL command:

```
create table CD
(Artist VARCHAR2(25),
 Title  VARCHAR2(25));
```

The second command in the listing inserts a record into the CD table:

```
insert into CD values ('NEIL FINN', 'TRY WHISTLING THIS');
```

If the SQL statements passed to ANYSTRING contain quotes, each quote should be replaced with a set of two quotes, as shown in the preceding execution of ANYSTRING for the **insert** command. After each command, you will receive the response:

```
PL/SQL procedure successfully completed.
```

You can verify that the commands succeeded by querying the new table:

```
select * from CD;


ARTIST                     TITLE
------------------------   ------------------------
NEIL FINN                  TRY WHISTLING THIS
```

In the following sections, you will see descriptions of the major functions and procedures used within dynamic SQL statements.

OPEN_CURSOR

The **OPEN_CURSOR** function of the DBMS_SQL package opens a cursor and returns to your program a cursor ID number. Thus, within the ANYSTRING procedure, the *cursor_name* variable is defined as an INTEGER datatype:

```
Cursor_Name INTEGER;
```

Within the Executable Commands section, the *cursor_name* variable is set to the output of the **OPEN_CURSOR** execution:

```
    Cursor_Name := DBMS_SQL.OPEN_CURSOR;
```

PARSE

Parsing a statement checks its syntax and associates the statement with the cursor. To parse a statement, use the **PARSE** procedure of the DBMS_SQL package. For example, in the ANYSTRING procedure, the following command parses the SQL command. **PARSE** takes three parameters: the cursor ID, the command being parsed, and a language flag.

```
DBMS_SQL.PARSE(Cursor_Name, String, dbms_sql.Native);
```

The language flag specifies the behavior for the statement. The "Native" setting shown in this example specifies behavior according to the current version of the database. Other values for the language flag of PARSE include "v6" for ORACLE Version 6 and "v7" for ORACLE7.

PROGRAMMER'S NOTE   *DDL commands (such as **create table**) are executed when they are parsed.*

BIND_VARIABLE and BIND_ARRAY

If your dynamic SQL procedure performs data manipulation, then you will need to use bind variables. Any dynamic SQL command that **insert**s, **update**s, or **delete**s records needs to use either the **BIND_VARIABLE** or **BIND_ARRAY** procedure within DBMS_SQL as part of its processing. You must call one of these procedures to supply the value of a variable in your program to the placeholder. When the SQL statement is then executed, ORACLE uses the data that your program has placed in the output and input, or bind, variables.

For example, the **PARSE** execution in the following listing parses a SQL command in which one of the values is unknown—the value of the bind variable used in the procedure.

```
DBMS_SQL.PARSE(Cursor_Name, 'delete from CD where Artist > :artist',
                  dbms_sql.Native);
```

Following the **PARSE** execution, you must bind the *:artist* bind variable to the *artist_name* variable passed to the procedure. When a user executes the procedure, a value will be specified for the *artist_name* variable. The **BIND_VARIABLE** procedure shown in the following listing will bind the *artist_name* value to the *:artist* bind variable used by the command string being parsed.

```
DBMS_SQL.BIND_VARIABLE(Cursor_Name, ':artist', artist_name);
```

You can use dynamic SQL to execute a DML statement multiple times—each time with a different bind variable. You can use the **BIND_ARRAY** procedure to bind an array of values, each of which will be used as an input variable once per **EXECUTE**.

EXECUTE

To execute your dynamically created SQL statement, use the **EXECUTE** function of the DBMS_SQL package. The following listing, from the ANYSTRING procedure, shows the use of the **EXECUTE** function

```
Ret := DBMS_SQL.EXECUTE(Cursor_Name);
```

When you use the **EXECUTE** function, you pass the cursor ID value (in this example, the *cursor_name* variable) as input. The *ret* variable holds the output of the **EXECUTE** function, which will be the number of rows processed (if the executed statement performs DML).

DEFINE_COLUMN

If your cursor performs a query, then you must execute the **DEFINE_COLUMN** function once for each column being selected. If the column is defined with a LONG datatype, then you must use the **DEFINE_COLUMN_LONG** function in place of **DEFINE_COLUMN**. If you are selecting values into a PL/SQL array, then you must use **DEFINE_ARRAY** in place of **DEFINE_COLUMN**.

For example, consider the query parsed in the following command:

```
DBMS_SQL.PARSE(Cursor_Name,'select Artist, Title from CD',
                  dbms_sql.Native);
```

Prior to executing the cursor, you must define the columns by their position in the query, as shown in the following listing.

```
DBMS_SQL.DEFINE_COLUMN(Cursor_Name, 1, Artist, 25);
DBMS_SQL.DEFINE_COLUMN(Cursor_Name, 2, Title, 25);
```

Once you have defined the columns, you can use the **EXECUTE** function to execute the cursor.

FETCH_ROWS, EXECUTE_AND_FETCH, and COLUMN_VALUE

If your dynamic SQL command performs a query, you can call the **FETCH_ROWS** function to retrieve the query's rows. The **EXECUTE_AND_FETCH** function both executes and fetches rows.

For example, suppose there is a table called CD_COPY, with the same column definitions as the CD table created earlier in this appendix. You can use dynamic SQL to **select** records from the CD table and **insert** them into the CD_COPY table. For this example, the Get_CD_Cursor statement will retrieve rows from the CD table, and the Insert_CD_Copy_Cursor will insert the retrieved values into the CD_COPY table.

In this example, the Get_CD_Cursor cursor has already been parsed. The example code executes the **FETCH_ROWS** function. If the number of rows fetched is greater than 0, then the record will be processed.

```
if DBMS_SQL.FETCH_ROWS(Get_CD_Cursor)>0 then
```

For the fetched record, the **COLUMN_VALUE** procedure is executed once for each column selected:

```
DBMS_SQL.COLUMN_VALUE(Get_CD_Cursor, 1, Artist);
DBMS_SQL.COLUMN_VALUE(Get_CD_Cursor, 2, Title);
```

Now that the queried values have been bound to variables, you can bind those values into the cursor that **insert**s records into the CD_COPY table.

```
DBMS_SQL.BIND_VARIABLE(Insert_CD_Copy_Cursor, 'artist', Artist);
DBMS_SQL.BIND_VARIABLE(Insert_CD_Copy_Cursor, 'title', Title);
```

You can now execute the cursor that **insert**s values into the CD_COPY table.

```
Ret := DBMS_SQL.EXECUTE(Insert_CD_COPY_Cursor);
```

The *ret* variable will hold the number of rows **insert**ed into the CD_COPY table. If you called a procedure from within an anonymous PL/SQL block, execute the **VARIABLE_VALUE** function to retrieve the values assigned to its output variables.

CLOSE_CURSOR

You can close an open cursor by executing the **CLOSE_CURSOR** procedure of the DBMS_SQL package. The example in the following listing, from the ANYSTRING procedure, shows that the **CLOSE_CURSOR** procedure uses the cursor ID value as its sole input parameter.

```
DBMS_SQL.CLOSE_CURSOR(Cursor_Name);
```

Closing a cursor frees the memory used by the cursor and reduces the number of concurrently open cursors in your session.

Table A-3 lists the functions and procedures available in dynamic SQL, along with brief descriptions.

Function or Procedure	Description
BIND_ARRAY	Binds a value to an array.
BIND_VARIABLE	Binds a value to a variable.
CLOSE_CURSOR	Closes a cursor.
COLUMN_VALUE	Returns the value of a cursor element within a cursor's query.
COLUMN_VALUE_LONG	Returns all or a portion of a LONG datatype element within a cursor's query.
DEFINE_ARRAY	Defines an array to be selected from a cursor's query.
DEFINE_COLUMN	Defines a column to be selected from a cursor's query.
DEFINE_COLUMN_LONG	Defines a LONG datatype column to be selected from a cursor's query.
EXECUTE	Executes a cursor.
EXECUTE_AND_FETCH	Executes a cursor and fetches rows from the cursor.
FETCH_ROWS	Fetches a row from a cursor.
IS_OPEN	Checks to see if a cursor is open; possible return values are TRUE and FALSE.
LAST_ERROR_POSITION	Returns the position in the SQL statement where an error occurred.
LAST_ROW_COUNT	Shows the number of rows fetched.
LAST_ROW_ID	Shows the ROWID value of the last row processed.
LAST_SQL_FUNCTION_CODE	Returns the SQL function code for a statement.
OPEN_CURSOR	Opens a cursor and returns the cursor ID value.
PARSE	Parses a statement. If the statement is a DDL command, it is immediately executed.
VARIABLE_VALUE	Returns the value of a variable in a cursor.

TABLE A-3. Procedures and Functions in DBMS_SQL

Index

G

H

M

N

W

About the CD-ROM

The CD-ROM that comes with this book includes the major scripts featured in this book. The scripts are all available as plain ASCII text files so you can easily copy them to the operating platform of your choice. The scripts are available individually and as part of "zipped" files on a chapter-by-chapter basis.

For details on the use of the scripts and interpretation of the output, see the appropriate chapter of this book. The script file names on the CD match the script file names shown in each chapter.

The directories on the CD-ROM are

Directory	Description
ZIPS	Contains the "zipped" files for all of the chapters. The other directories contain the individual files extracted from the "zipped" files. The directories are named after the type of script rather than the chapter number.
ORACLE8	Contains the Oracle8-specific scripts from Chapter 1
PERFORM	Contains the performance management scripts from Chapter 2
TRANSACT	Contains the transaction management scripts from Chapter 3
DATAMGMT	Contains the data management scripts from Chapter 4
OBJECTS	Contains the object management scripts from Chapter 5
SPACE	Contains the space management scripts from Chapter 6
USERS	Contains the user management scripts from Chapter 7
DBMGMT	Contains the database management scripts from Chapter 8
APPENDIX	Contains the scripts from Appendix A. Since the scripts in Appendix A are not named, they are compiled into a single file with remarks indicating the section of the appendix from which they are extracted.